Professional Cookery

The Process Approach

To my wife, Margaret

Professional Cookery

The Process Approach

Daniel R. Stevenson

Senior Lecturer in Food and Beverage Operations,
Department of Catering Management, Oxford Polytechnic

Hutchinson

London   Melbourne   Sydney   Auckland   Johannesburg

HUTCHINSON & Co. (Publishers) Ltd

An imprint of Century Hutchinson Ltd

Brookmount House, 62-65 Chandos Place, London WC2N 4NW

Century Hutchinson Australia (Pty) Ltd
PO Box 496, 16-22 Church Street, Hawthorn, Melbourne,
Victoria 3122, Australia

Century Hutchinson New Zealand Ltd
PO Box 40-086, Glenfield, Auckland 10, New Zealand

Century Hutchinson South Africa (Pty) Ltd
PO Box 337, Bergvlei 2012, South Africa

First published 1985
Reprinted 1986

© Daniel R. Stevenson 1985
Illustrations © Hutchinson & Co. (Publishers) Ltd

Typeset in 10pt Plantin by Oxprint Ltd, Oxford

Printed and bound in Great Britain by
Anchor Brendon Ltd, Tiptree, Essex

British Library Cataloguing in Publication Data
Stevenson, Daniel R.
    Professional cookery.
    1. Quantity cookery   2. Food service
    I. Title
    641.5'7   TX820

ISBN 0 09 158331 4

Hutchinson Catering and Hotel Management Books
Series Editor: John Fuller

Contents

Preface

The most common form of communication in cookery is the *recipe* which has been established for hundreds of years. Three factors have played a vital role in its development:

The time of day, i.e., breakfast, lunch or dinner

The particular course within any meal, e.g. soup, main course or sweet

The commodities to be cooked, e.g. fish, chicken, beef or vegetables

These three factors define a recipe and provide a structure for the arrangement of cookery information. For example, most cookery books are a collection of individual recipes arranged by course (soup, main course, etc.) or commodity (fish, vegetable, etc.). In addition the culinary basics such as mirepoix, roux, stocks and sauces, etc. (which are important when teaching and learning cookery) are viewed as products which are essential to the production of dishes. This is a *product centred approach*. Fundamental to this approach is acquiring cookery knowledge and ability by exposure to individual recipes. Any similarity in production techniques between dishes is indicated by grouping related dishes or recipes. Rarely are different types of dishes related by production. For instance, roux-thickened soups are not related to roux-thickened stews.

Although this is the traditional or conventional approach to presenting cookery information, there are disadvantages when common production techniques are not highlighted and where end products are the fundamental vehicle for learning. For example, because recipes are independently presented, important details which might contribute to the success of a dish are not adequately identified. Students or apprentices thus find it difficult when faced with a collection of recipes to determine what is fundamental cookery knowledge. This often leads to students becoming over dependent on cookery books. A product centred approach does not encourage creativity in cookery. Well-known dishes are frequently used as a medium for teaching cookery and the instruments to demonstrate cookery ability. This can result in the mechanical reproduction of dishes for menus. Dish creation in this case is rare.

To overcome these disadvantages, this book presents a process centred approach to cookery. The aim is to make explicit the techniques and practices of professional cookery. It is designed to illustrate cookery processes as the most fundamental aspect of cookery. Dishes are treated as end products of cookery processes. Unlike a product centred approach featuring individual recipes, most dishes in this book are presented with variations of processes. The format differs from the usual cookery book. The most important information, i.e. the process, is presented first. This is followed by recipe and dish variations.

A clear and concise distinction is made between fundamental cookery knowledge and individual reference knowledge. Distinguishing between fundamental knowlege and reference knowledge facilitates learning and aids teaching and assessing both practical and theoretical studies (not only of cookery but of related subjects which form part of cookery courses).

The structure of the information reveals the relationship between cookery practice and dish creation. When presented with a list of ingredients, students may be asked to match the ingredients to a suitable process or vice versa, presented with a process and asked to select their own individual ingredients. This stimulates dish invention.

The book is designed to be used as a textbook incorporating assessment tests and may be read progressively from beginning to end. It includes aspects of larder, general kitchen and bakery work and contains a wide range of recipes.

This textbook is designed to provide a comprehensive knowledge of the production processes behind the countless dishes which make up all forms of cookery.

DRS
Oxford

Acknowledgements

I wish to thank the following colleagues in the Department of Catering Management, Oxford Polytechnic, for their assistance:

Dr Peter Fellows
Mr Jacques Gianino
Mr Clive Robertson
Dr Patricia Scobie
Mr David Simmons
Mr Stuart Soames
Dr Richard Tomlins
Mr David Walker

I wish to especially thank: Mrs Evelyn J. S. MacGregor, former Head of Department, Motherwell College, who was responsible for my involvement with this type of approach; Dr David Atkinson for his assistance with the French aspects of the text; Mr Alan Frost, Head of Department, Lews Castle College, for his valuable assistance throughout the planning and developing of the manuscript and his contribution to the pastry sections; and Professor John Fuller for his guidance.

How to use the book

This book is designed to be a teaching textbook on food production and includes larder, general kitchen and bakery work. Unlike most cookery books, which contain a collection of individual recipes, *many of the recipes in this book are grouped together by method of production*. Most chapters are divided into sections or processes which contain the following information:

1 A general method for a group of dishes – this is called a *base method*.
2 A general recipe for a group of dishes – this is called a *base recipe*.
3 Important information to 1 and 2 above, e.g. culinary terms, cooking times and hotplate service details etc.
4 A list of the dishes contained in the section with the individual instructions which are applied to the base method and recipe to produce the dishes.
5 Suitable garnishes for the dishes in the section where appropriate.

Presentation of information

The information is divided into two distinct types of reference:

(a) *Basic information* for the preparation of a group of dishes, see 1, 2 and 3 above.
(b) *Specific information* for the preparation of individual dishes, see 4 and 5 above.

The basic information (a), is found at the beginning of each section and may be presented as a part of a page, a full page or two pages. This is the most important information because it mostly consists of fundamental cookery knowledge. Students of cookery, be they apprentices or keen amateurs, should eventually have command of this knowledge without having to refer to the textbook (especially the base methods, related culinary terms and essential information). The specific information (b), which is the separate instructions for each dish in the section, follows the basic information (a).

Use as a textbook

The process sections are designed as *modules of learning* which may be read progressively from beginning to end, concluding with an assessment test.

Use as a recipe book

Procedure

1 Look up the individual recipe which is to be prepared.
2 Follow the instructions, assembling any ingredients which are stated.
3 Turn to the main process section and assemble any ingredients which are also stated.
4 Prepare the dish following the instructions in the base method.

Note: When an instruction in the base method does not apply (e.g. an instruction for an ingredient not used in the dish being cooked) move on to the next instruction.

Important: The intention of a process approach to cookery is to constantly reinforce the fundamental aspects of cookery. Therefore the reader should pay particular attention to the base method and explanatory notes, and should also attempt to reach a level of competence where dishes can be prepared with little or no reference to the base method – step 4 above.

All recipes are for four portions unless otherwise stated.

Referencing/indexing

Chapter 2 has been specially designed as a culinary reference/index. This will enable the reader to locate information on culinary preparations, dishes, commodity preparation and fundamental procedures. It also includes a list of culinary terms.

Chapter 1
Introduction

Throughout history, preparing and cooking food has always been a fundamental aspect of human behaviour. From the earliest times various means of cooking food have been developed: suspending food over open fires, boiling food in clay pots and baking food in simple earth ovens are some of the procedures that have been used to cook food in the past. Today many of these procedures have become more complex due to progress and development within a technological society. Food materials and equipment have changed substantially over the years. However the various cooking procedures may still be classified as 'methods of cooking'. The important methods of cooking are:

grilling   boiling
roasting   poaching
baking   steaming
frying   stewing
             braising

These methods, which are described in detail in the appropriate chapters throughout the book, are usually subdivided into two groups:

1   *Dry methods of cooking*:   grilling, roasting, baking and frying
2   *Moist methods of cooking*:   boiling, poaching, steaming, stewing and braising.

The methods of cooking having been listed, it is important to state why food should be cooked in the first place. The object of cooking food may be to:

(a)   make it tender, digestible and palatable;
(b)   produce a desired flavour, texture and eating quality;
(c)   increase the desire to eat by making the food more attractive and pleasing to the eye (not forgetting the nose);
(d)   destroy harmful bacteria.

At this stage we can summarize by saying there are general methods of cooking foods and obvious reasons why food is cooked.

Let us now consider the way in which cookery information is usually presented, i.e. 'the recipe'. Over the years cooks have created many thousands of dishes. The individual dish is the result of culinary skill and knowledge and as such is the most important link between a cook and consumer. It is therefore easy to understand why most cookery books primarily contain a selection of recipes for individual dishes. The recipes may be grouped together or categorized into the same divisions as a meal, e.g. soup, fish, entrée and sweet dishes etc., or by commodity, e.g. chicken, beef and game dishes etc. In some instances both categories are used to give a comprehensive reference to dishes. These two ways of grouping recipes may contribute a good deal to a sensible arrangement of recipes but there is one fundamental disadvantage to both of these formats. To group recipes as parts of a meal will bring together many dishes which are totally different except for the common element of being part of a meal. For example, split-pea soup, beef consommé and cream of celery soup are all soups, yet, other than this, they have nothing else in common. The same disadvantage is also encountered when grouping recipes by commodity.

As previously stated, cooks have produced thousands, if not millions, of dishes, *but one aspect they all share is the production element*, i.e. they have all been produced by culinary activity. This is the most important aspect common to individual dishes because *the production element can be examined to reveal basic skills and activities fundamental to cookery*. In this book, dishes which are made in a similar manner, i.e. which have the same underlying production element, are grouped together.

Process approach to food production

In what way can the production elements of countless dishes be determined? The answer to this question is to identify the areas of production which are general to all cookery. These can be revealed by examining the work undertaken by the cook when producing food.

Table 1 illustrates the main areas of production with some examples of the activities which would make up these areas. It should be noted that many of the activities listed in the diagram are of a very general and basic nature, e.g. weighing, peeling and stirring etc.

There are several important points to be made when examining food production in this manner. First *the*

Table 1

Areas of production	Description
Selecting food materials	Recognizing and identifying materials. This also includes the quality of the materials.
Measuring food materials	Measuring, weighing and counting of the materials.
Separating or dividing food materials	Techniques applied to materials such as washing, peeling, slicing, dicing, straining, filleting and boning etc.
Combining food materials	Techniques applied to materials such as mixing, stirring, whisking, beating and blending etc.
Applying heat to food materials	The application of heat to food in conjunction with particular equipment. This may be moist or dry heat and include the use of equipment such as stoves, boilers, ovens or grills.
Withdrawing heat from food materials	Removal of heat from food, i.e. cooling, chilling or freezing foods.

Table 2

Dish: Buttered cauliflower   *Yield*: 4 portions

Area of production	Activities/skills
1 *Selecting*:	One good-quality cauliflower.
2 *Measuring*:	Medium size, i.e. 750 g approximately.
3 *Separating*:	Remove the leaves by cutting through the stalk just below the flower head. Make a small hole in the base of the stalk to assist even cooking.
4 *Separating*:	Wash the cauliflower in salt water removing any insects or spots of deterioration.
5 *Heat application*:	Add the water to the cooking utensil, cover with a lid and bring to the boil. Add salt.
6 *Combining and heat application*:	Immerse the prepared vegetable in the boiling water. Simmer until cooked.
7 *Separating*:	Drain the vegetable carefully and thoroughly.
8 *Dividing*:	Cut into four portions and place into a vegetable dish.
9 *Combining*:	Brush over with melted butter and serve.

information is expressed as a set of activities which are cookery skills or techniques. This means the definition of any dish would consist of information about *a selection of materials subjected to a plan of action*, the plan of action being *a sequence of activities which make up the production process*.

In Table 2 the method of preparing and cooking buttered cauliflower is given. There is nothing unusual in this set of instructions (with the possible exception that production areas are included), but there is one extremely interesting aspect to the information. *The method of producing buttered cauliflower is almost identical to that of producing buttered artichokes, asparagus, broccoli, corn on the cob, celeriac and root fennel; even courgettes and marrow may be cooked in this manner.* The only changes are the type of vegetable, vegetable preparation and portioning and the cooking time.

This example may be taken much further than simply the cooking of cauliflower. Those elements of production which are fundamental to all vegetables can be separated and presented as the method common to the production of the vegetables. Individual vegetable preparation would then be matched to a common production element to form a group of dishes.

This approach which *concentrates on the skills and techniques of cookery* and in turn the *patterns of production which lie behind a group of dishes* is known as the *process approach* to food production. In this text a *process* refers to the *essential activities and related knowledge involved in producing a satisfactory product or group of products*.

Within the context of the approach where does one expect to find the methods of cooking which are listed at the beginning of the chapter? Since methods of cooking always reflect a particular type of heat application, e.g. roasting, grilling, frying and boiling etc., they can be used as very general categories of production. This general nature can then be accurately defined by process groupings and associated dishes. Most methods of cooking are dealt with in separate chapters which are subdivided into process sections.

At this stage it is appropriate to distinguish between the terms *cooking* and *cookery*. When we refer to *methods of cooking*, as stated earlier we imply some form of heat application; we do not include aspects of food preparation with no heat application, e.g. salads, fruits and sauces such as mayonnaise etc. On the other hand, the term *cookery* covers all aspects of food preparation and production.

The limitation of being restricted to heat application does not apply to a process approach. For example, a process relating to a group of salads would simply have no area of heat application. There may also be times when part of a process is singled out to be a separate process within a much larger process; e.g. preparing a joint for roasting may be taken as a butchery process. In other words each area of a process may be examined at a much greater depth and become a more specific process in its own right.

Principles of cookery

The description of cookery which has been presented can be said to be in 'operational terms', i.e. areas of production and methods of cooking explained by way of processes. To go one step further would be to try to determine what are the principles of cookery which exist within a process. Referring to the example given in Table 2 with the cooking of cauliflower we see that the steps of production are clearly defined but how much does this information contribute to an understanding of why and how a process operates? The following points may be made to make the information more comprehensive:

(a)   The transfer of heat within the water takes place by convection.
(b)   The cauliflower receives the heat and is cooked through by means of conduction.
(c)   Water is a good medium to use when cooking cauliflower because it assists in the tender cooking of the vegetable. The physical properties of the cauliflower make it unsuitable for most dry methods of cooking, e.g. grilling would result in the cauliflower drying out and becoming hard.

These *fundamental characteristics* (which are discovered and not devised) such as the *type of heat transfer*, *the commodity structure* and the *chemical and physical changes*, which are all concerned with a process or method, *are examples of the 'principles of cookery'. The principles of cookery are the fundamental laws or rules of nature which relate to cookery.*

The first part of this chapter has been concerned with the relationship between dishes and cookery processes. A good deal of attention has been given to the ways in which recipes may be grouped by means of production. There are also some important points to be made regarding recipes as lists of ingredients.

Recipe yield

A recipe is a list of ingredients which should produce a predetermined number of portions or physical quantity of food, e.g. a recipe may be for only one portion or a thousand portions. This yield or output of food for a particular situation may be termed the *scale of operation* and is dictated by consumer requirements or service demands.

Recipe balance

The list of ingredients for a given recipe must be measured in some way (an area of production – see Table 1) to ensure that not only the correct yield will be obtained but also *that the correct ratio between the ingredients is achieved*. This relationship may be seen in bakery products. Bakers usually relate the weight of the ingredients in a recipe to the total flour weight. Puff pastry recipes may be described as 'full puff', 'three-quarter puff' and 'half puff' recipes. This means the fat is equal to the flour in weight, three-quarters the flour in weight and half the flour in weight. When the fat content in the recipe is reduced the height or lift the pastry will achieve in the oven will also be reduced, see page 325. Each time the fat content is changed the balance of the recipe is altered, which in turn affects the finished product. *A balanced recipe, therefore, is one in which the product is of consistent quality.* In the interests of recipe balance, how exact must one be when measuring ingredients? The answer to this statement depends on the ingredients being used.

Non-critical ingredients within a recipe

The quantities of some ingredients within a recipe may be varied considerably at the discretion of the cook preparing the dish. For example, the amount of basic vegetable flavouring which is included in many soups, sauces and stews etc, is not critical (see 'mirepoix' on page 39). The quantity of carrots to be used in tomato sauce or brown beef stew can be varied considerably with little effect on recipe balance. There is of course an upper limit to the quantity which can be used and if this is exceeded the dish takes on the characteristic flavour of the vegetable. In some instances an *ingredient may even be omitted*, e.g. parsley stalks or sprigs of thyme may be left out of a recipe because a cook does not agree with their use or because they are out of season etc. In these instances *the ingredients and their respective amounts can be said to be non-critical to recipe balance*. It is important for the reader to note that the creation of individuality and personal taste come substantially into this category: many ingredients can be manipulated to give one's personal touch to a dish.

This is a move towards the artistic and away from the mechanical use of ingredients.

Many trained cooks often use their experience to judge the required quantity of these types of ingredient, rather than objectively measure them on scales etc. To the layman this type of measurement may look as though guesswork is the rule of thumb rather than experience.

It should be stressed that although the quantities of non-critical ingredients may be altered or omitted from a recipe, *in many instances they are measured exactly so that a specific quality, taste and cost may be maintained.*

Semi-critical ingredients within a recipe

Like non-critical ingredients, the quantities of many of *these ingredients within a recipe are primarily designed to produce a specific quality of product.* For example, the quantity of curry powder or spice in a curry is designed to produce a particular curry, altering the tomato purée in a tomato sauce will increase or decrease the tomato flavour – mild or strong. In addition, thickening agents may also be increased or reduced to produce a thick or thin soup. However, to produce the specific quality which is desired in a product requires these ingredients to be measured exactly. *Unlike non-critical ingredients, semi-critical ingredients cannot be omitted from a recipe.* It may come as a surprise to many people studying cookery to find that many experienced cooks can also measure these ingredients by experience and eye. *Also any changes which take place in the product because of small inaccuracies of measurement are usually able to be corrected by an experienced cook.*

Critical ingredients within a recipe

Up to this point we have given examples of ingredients which can be adjusted substantially or even omitted from a recipe. Also we have considered other ingredients which are subject to much smaller variations of measurement and cannot be omitted from a recipe. But *there is one group of ingredients that plays a vital role in relation to recipe balance.* With these ingredients any *variation in measurement will not only affect a particular quality in the product, but will also have a predominant effect on the total quality.* In bakery work, the making of cakes and yeast doughs have ingredients which must be measured exactly if recipe balance is to be maintained. A cake made with too much baking powder or a yeast dough which has too high a salt content is likely to be unfit for service and may have to be discarded. *When measuring these ingredients, the cook should always use accurate scales and measures and give attention to exact detail.*

Processes – response to technological development

At the beginning of this chapter it was stated that cooking procedures have evolved from the earliest times but that *food materials* and *equipment* have changed substantially over the years. It is appropriate to end this chapter by considering the effects of technological development on cookery processes.

Developments in food processing and new types of equipment often result in existing processes being modified or new processes being introduced which create change in traditional practice.

Food materials

Commodities and their fundamental characteristics set the scene for all production procedures, therefore any changes in the type or nature of the commodities required for a particular cookery process is likely to affect the method element of that process. Food materials can be obtained in many different forms and the reader should consult a commodities textbook for detailed information.

Commodities may be used which are:

(a) fresh;
(b) traditionally preserved or processed: dried, frozen, pickled, salted and smoked;
(c) processed: quick-frozen, quick-chilled, quick-dried, accelerated freeze-dried, canned, vacuum-packed and irradiated.
New methods of processing basic commodities such as sugar, flour and fat etc. are also continually being developed.

When processed commodities or foods are selected for use they may affect traditional cookery processes at two levels.

Ingredient level
Amendments or changes may have to be made when a different type of ingredient is used for a dish. Examples of this can be seen in many of the process sections within this book: when soup powders or frozen or tinned vegetables are used to flavour cream soups (page 169) or when dried or crystallized albumen is used to make meringue (page 402).

In some instances processes are specifically designed for special ingredients – see high-ratio cakes and sponges, page 374.

Product level
When a pre-prepared food or convenience food is used a cookery process may be *altered extensively* (e.g. when using a packet table jelly the procedure is simplified considerably) *or made unnecessary* (e.g. pre-prepared

ice-cream only requires portioning). When using pre-prepared products the cook should always follow the manufacturer's instructions.

Equipment

Progress in design results in equipment which, in contrast to existing equipment:

(a)   is safer to use;
(b)   functions more efficiently;
(c)   makes a more economical use of energy;
(d)   requires less labour, skill or effort to operate;
(e)   takes up less space.

In relation to cookery processes, new types of equipment may also have features which are different from traditional equipment, e.g. *pressure* fryers, *high-speed* steamers and *microwave* cookers etc. In most cases these new types of equipment merely modify traditional methods of cooking, therefore a description of their use is to be found in the appropriate chapter dealing with steaming, deep-frying or grilling etc. However, microwave cooking is not a modification of any traditional method of cooking, and is therefore featured as an additional method of cooking in a separate chapter.

Chapter 2
Complete reference guide to the book

An important function of any textbook is to provide the reader with a comprehensive means of locating information. This aspect is even more important with a teaching textbook where it is desirable that the arrangement of reference information be structured into groupings or classifications which complement the subject concerned.

This chapter has been designed as a reference source and is divided into five sections. The first three sections make reference to all the recipes and items of preparation within the textbook. The remaining two sections deal with important procedures which are fundamental to food production and culinary terms:

Culinary preparations – kitchen, larder and pastry
Reference here is made to the various preparations which form the very basis of cookery. This section is similar to Escoffier's 'fonds de cuisine' (fundamentals of cookery) but is extended and includes pastry preparations.
Commodity preparation
In this section the preparation of commodities is listed under the commodities, which are arranged in alphabetical order. The various cuts or derivative items are also listed.
Menu list of dishes
In addition to the main purpose of being a source of reference for dishes, this section is designed to illustrate the construction of a menu, i.e. the various courses, their contents and an indication of the distinctive features of the dishes: grilled, poached or type of thickening etc. This arrangement is useful when planning menus.
Fundamental procedures
A list of some of the basic techniques and small processes of food production.
Culinary terms

Important: In most instances the preparations and dishes are classified as an aid to learning, e.g. hors-d'oeuvre – hors-d'oeuvre classification; soups – soup classification; sauces – sauce classification.

Culinary preparation – kitchen and larder

Basic preparations

		page
Aspic jellies		83
Beurre manié		121
Bouquet garni		39
Brine		43
Tomates concassées:	raw	39
	cooked	273
Cooking liquors:	blanc and plain	113–14
	court-bouillon with vinegar and with wine	116
Dry pickle		43
Duxelles, au vin		274
Fresh tomato purée and provençale		273
Liaison		390
Marinades:	à la grecque	43
	à la portugaise	43
	for Bismarck herring	43
	instant	43
	plain	43
Matignon		39
Mirepoix, blanc		39
Oignon clouté		39
Panadas:	frangipane	74
Parsley:	branches and chopped	39
	deep-fried	295
Roux, blond, brown, composite and white		165
Sabayon		388
Seasoning, compound and mignonette pepper		43
Spiced vinegar		43
Stocks and glazes:	beef, chicken, ham, lamb, pork and veal	81
	fish	150

	page
Croûtons	89
Fleurons	327

Forcemeats and stuffings
Forcemeats: farce à gratin, godiveau, mousseline and panada types — 73–4
Cooked stuffings: herb, herb and lemon, sage and sage and onion — 75

See also bakery and confectionary items on page 29

Commodity preparation

Fundamental procedures

Bard (barder)   To cover the surface of meat, poultry or *game* with slices of pork or bacon fat to prevent the flesh drying out when cooking (especially roasting).

Baste (arroser)   To coat a joint or bird etc., with the roasting fat during cooking, see page 239.

Bat out (battre)   To flatten out pieces of flesh with a cutlet bat usually between polythene, see page 57.

Beard (ébarber)   To remove the outer fringe or trail from shellfish, especially oysters, see page 72.

Blanch (blanchir)
1   The first cooking of deep-fried potatoes, see page 289.
2   To enable the removal of skin from tomatoes, grapes or peaches etc., see page 39.
3   To enable the removal of superfluous material from sweetbreads prior to cooking, see page 212.
4   To make vegetables limp prior to braising, see page 202.
5   To remove the initial scum when preparing stocks, cooking liquors or soups, see page 86.
6   To retain the colour of vegetables, see page 202.
7   To whiten in colour bones or flesh, see page 183.

Clarify (clarifier)   To make clear, liquids such as stocks, consommés, aspic jellies and table jellies etc., see page 83.
This also applies to butter which has been allowed to clear by remaining melted and allowing the sediment and milk solids to separate out.

Coat or mask (napper)   To cover or coat with sauce.

Coat with breadcrumbs (paner)   To pass through seasoned flour, eggwash and breadcrumbs, see page 292.

Cook out   The cooking of a roux before any recipe liquid is added, see page 166.

Deglaze (déglacer)   To swill out a cooking utensil in which food has been cooked, with stock, wine or sauce etc. This is to retain the flavour of the sediment or soluble extractives, see page 254.

Drain (égoutter)   To drain off liquid from food in a colander or chinois, see page 126. Alternatively to remove the excess fat or oil from deep-fried foods, see page 291.

Draw and gut (vider)   To remove the intestines from feathered game or poultry, see page 67. Also to remove the intestines from hare or rabbit, see page 64.

Enrich with butter (monter au beurre)   To add butter to sauces, soups or stews to add flavour and richness in taste, see page 202.

Ferment   To allow a yeast batter or dough to rest for a certain time at a specific temperature in order for the yeast to develop and multiply, see page 348.

Flame (flamber)   To set a spirit (brandy, liqueur or whisky etc.) on fire within a cooking procedure, see page 149).

Froth   To coat a roast with flour just before cooking is completed to achieve a good colour, see page 240.

Gild (dorer)   To allow a brown colour to develop. To coat with eggwash prior to cooking in order to develop a brown colour, see page 327.

Glaze (glacer)
1   To brown a dish under a salamander, see page 203.
2   To coat a flan or tart with glaze, see page 335.
3   To cook glazed vegetables, see page 97.
4   To cover with fondant, see page 329.
5   To sprinkle with sugar then caramelize under a salamander or in a hot oven, see page 330.

Grate (râper)   To pass food through a grater.

Gratinate (gratiner)   To sprinkle with breadcrumbs or cheese and brown under the salamander or in an oven, see page 203.

Incise (ciseler)   To cut small incisions across the back of fish prior to grilling or shallow frying, see page 71.

Joint (découper)   To cut poultry or feathered game into suitable pieces for sautés, stews or pies etc., see page 68. The term also applies to hare and rabbit, see page 65.

Knife manipulation   See basic knife technique on page 35.
Bone out   (désosser)
Carve   (découper)

Chop – fine   (hacher)
Chop – rough   (concasser)
Cut into pieces   (émincer)
Shred – fine   (ciseler)

Lard (larder)   To insert strips of pork of bacon fat into raw flesh with special needles (larding needles), see page 57.

Liaise (lier)   To complete a sauce, soup or stew with cream or a mixture of egg yolks and cream (liaison), see page 390.

Macerate (macérer)   To soak food in wine or liqueur, often applied to fruits.

Marinate (mariner)   To soak food in a marinade, see page 42.

Mix to a clear dough   To mix a dough until all the ingredients are combined.

Pass (passer)   To pass food through a sieve or strainer.

Pluck (plumer)   To remove the feathers from poultry or game, see page 66.

Prove   The final fermentation of yeast goods after shaping but prior to baking, see page 352.

Purée   To make food into a fine mass or purée by passing through a sieve or liquidizer etc.

Refresh (rafraîchir)   To cool food under cold running water, see page 125.

Reduce (réduire)   To boil down a liquid or sauce.

Reheat (réchauffer)   To reheat food, see vegetables, page 130.

Score   To lightly mark or cut the outer surface of a joint prior to roasting or poêler, see page 63.

Sear (saisir)   To shallow-fry the surface of flesh until brown, see page 191.

Season (assaisonner)   To add salt or salt and pepper to food.

Sieve (passer)   To pass food through a sieve.

Singe   To brown; usually applied to composite roux for brown stews etc., see step 6 for brown stews, curries and goulash, page 185.

Skim (dégraisser/dépouiller)   To remove impurities (fat and scum) from the surface of a liquid.

Strain (passer)   To strain.

Sweat (suer)   To shallow-fry food usually with the use of a lid and avoiding colour development, see page 149.

Test for cooking   To determine if food is cooked. This varies with the food being cooked and may be done by:
1   Taste.
2   Test by thermometer, see pages 241–2
3   Pressure test, see page 306

4   Puncture test, see page 242

Tie   To tie poultry and feathered game with string prior to cooking, see page 68.

Truss (brider)   To use a trussing needle and string to tie poultry and feathered game prior to cooking, see page 67.

Turn (tourner)   To cut vegetables into barrel or olive-shapes, see page 40. Also to cut a spiral design in mushrooms.

Turn (puff pastry)   A method of folding puff pastry, see page 324.

Whisk to ribbon stage   To whisk a mixture (sabayon or sponge etc.) until it is very light and fluffy. The whisk marks should be visible (for a very short period) when the whisk is withdrawn.

Withdraw sinews from poultry and feathered game   To pull out the leg sinews from poultry and feathered game (especially turkeys) prior to cooking, see page 67.

Culinary terms

à la broche   Spit roasted.

appareil   A prepared mixture of food, e.g. appareil à crêpe (pancake batter).

aromates   Aromatic herbs, spices and vegetables.

au four   Baked in an oven.

au naturel   Plainly cooked and served.

bain-marie
1   A piece of equipment containing a water bath which is used to keep foods hot without scorching.
2   A container used for the hot storage of sauces and soups etc.
3   A shallow container of water used as a cooking utensil to prevent foods cooking too quickly or burning, see crème caramel, page 392.

baron   A large joint of meat:
Baron of beef: double sirloin of beef.
Baron of lamb: saddle and two legs.

barquette   A small boat-shaped pastry tartlet.

bouillon   Unclarified stock.

chapelure   Browned breadcrumbs.

charcutière   Products of pork butchery, e.g. commercially prepared sausages.

chemiser   To coat an item of food or line a mould with jelly.

chiffonnade   Finely cut strips of food, e.g. lettuce or sorrel.

chinois   A conical strainer.

contiser   To insert slices of truffle or garlic into meat, poultry, game or fish.

cordon   A ribbon or thread of sauce circling a dish.

coupe   An individual serving bowl.

cru   Raw.

cuit   Cooked.

dariole   Small cork-shaped mould.

estouffade   A rich brown beef-stock or brown beef-stew.

fécule   Starch flour, e.g. arrowroot, cornflour, potato flour or rice flour.

fouet   A whisk.

fouetter   To whisk.

frapper   To chill.

friandises   A name for petits fours.

friture   A frying-kettle.

gaufrette   Wafer biscuit.

gros sel   Coarse salt.

hâtelet   A decorative skewer.

lardons   Bâtons or dice of bacon used as a garnish for dishes.

mandoline   A machine used for slicing potatoes or vegetables.

marmite   A stock pot.

matelote   A type of fish stew.

mie de pain   White breadcrumb.

mignardises   A name for petits fours.

mise en place   Preparation prior to cooking or serving.

mijoter   To simmer slowly.

moulin   A pepper mill.

natives   A menu term for English oysters.

panaché   Mixed (colour).

panure   See chapelure.

physalis   Cape gooseberries.

piquante   Sharp or spicy in flavour.

plat à sauter   A shallow pan with straight sides used for frying.

pluches   Leaves or shreds of herbs, e.g. chervil, thyme.

racines   Root vegetables, e.g. carrots, turnips, parsnips etc.

ravier   A small hors-d'oeuvre dish.

rocher   A scoop of ice-cream.

sauteuse   A shallow pan with sloping sides used for frying and preparing sabayons etc.

sec, sèche   Dry.
smorgasbord   Open sandwiches (Scandinavian).
spatula   A flat wooden spoon.
suer   To shallow-fry without developing colour.

tamis   A fine cloth used for straining sauces and soups etc.
tasse   A cup.
terrine   An earthenware dish with a lid.
timbale   A deep round dish.
tranche   A slice.

vesiga   The dried spinal cord of the sturgeon.
voiler   To cover or veil with spun sugar.

zeste   The rind of citrus fruits, e.g. lemon, orange or lime etc.

Chapter 3

Basic cold preparatory work I

The cook's basic knife set

Cutting equipment plays an important role in cookery operations. Although it is not possible in this text to deal with all the various items of cutting equipment used in the kitchen it is worthwhile to give attention to the basic tools used by the cook. See Table 3.

In addition to these hand tools, many other items of equipment may be used as part of the cook's personal equipment, e.g. carving knives, parisienne spoons (which cut root vegetables and melons etc., into balls of various sizes), couteau à canneler (which cuts strips from citrus fruits and vegetables), trussing needles and piping bags and tubes etc.

Points concerning knives

Type of metal used for knives

Knives may be purchased in carbon steel or stainless steel. Carbon steel knives are quite easy to keep sharp and are not as expensive as equivalent stainless steel knives. The disadvantage with these knives is that they discolour during usage and will rust if left lying in damp conditions (when storing carbon steel knives for prolonged periods a light smear of grease applied on the blades will reduce the risk of rusting). Stainless steel knives do not rust or stain but they are more expensive and also more difficult to sharpen than carbon steel knives.

In some cutting operations a stainless steel knife should

Table 3

Name	Specifications Shape of blade	Length of blade	Uses
Cook's knives (see Figure 1)	Broad blade tapering to a point	Various lengths, e.g. 125 mm to 355 mm Most popular sizes 200 mm and 250 mm	Slicing, dicing, chopping, shredding and peeling turnips etc.
Turning knife	Same shape as the cook's knives above but much smaller	Varies between 75 mm and 100 mm	Peeling onions, scraping vegetables, paring vegetables and turning vegetables etc.
Filleting knife	Narrow blade tapering to a point	Varies between 150 mm and 175 mm	Filleting fish and certain trimming techniques
Peeler	Various shapes	65 mm approximately	Peeling carrots, cucumber, asparagus and potatoes etc.
Palette knives	Straight blunt-edged blade with a round end	Various lengths e.g. 100 mm to 300 mm Most popular sizes 200 mm to 250 mm	Lifting and turning foods during cooking, scraping out bowls and trays etc.
Steel		Various lengths e.g. 225 mm to 400 mm Most popular sizes 300 mm to 350 mm	Keeping a sharp edge on cutting knives.
Cook's fork		Various lengths Most popular size prong length of 175 mm approximately	Turning roasts during cooking and holding foods during carving etc.

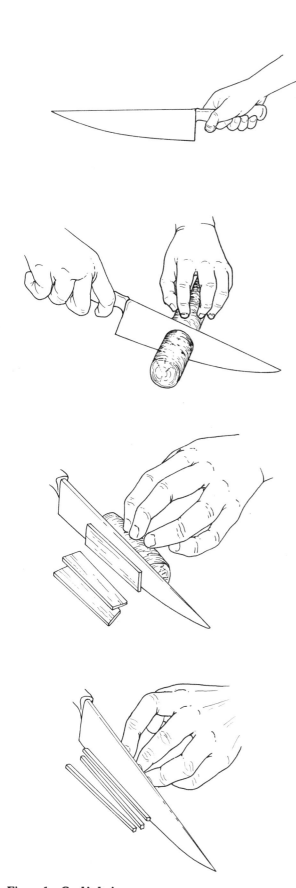

Figure 1 *Cook's knives*

be used to avoid staining or tainting the food, e.g. cutting hard boiled eggs and carving smoked salmon etc. For these reasons it is advisable to have turning knives and carving knives made of stainless steel.

Handle and blade design

Two types of handle design are found in professional cooks' knives:

Pin tang knives: this is where a pin attaches the blade to the handle. The pin runs from the blade through the centre of the handle.
Scale tang knives: in this design the blade is continued as a flange on to which the handle is fitted.

The strongest and most durable design is the full scale tang knife. Here the blade flange is the full depth of the handle. The handle consists of two side pieces attached to the flange of the blade. Although pin tang knives are cheaper than scale tang ones, they can last for many years when used correctly.

Note: Before purchasing knives, seek advice from a good craftsman or consult a reputable knife supplier.

Important points when handling knives

1 Cutting procedures should be carried out on a proper chopping board with sufficient space on the table to execute the operation smoothly and efficiently.
2 Always select the correct knife for the job in hand.
3 Items to be cut should be placed to the left of the cutting board. After cutting the items should be passed to the right and placed into bowls or trays. This work flow should be reversed if the operator is left handed.
4 Knives must be kept sharp at all times. A blunt knife is a dangerous knife because excessive pressure is required to cut the item; this can result in the item suddenly breaking or the knife slipping and going out of control.
5 Correct knife technique and finger manipulation should be practised until a smooth, well co-ordinated cutting motion is achieved.
   Holding the knife: The knife should be held in the right hand between the thumb and the forefinger with the remaining fingers curling under the handle (see Figure 1). The forefinger should not be placed along the top of the blade.
   Holding the item to be cut: With most cutting techniques, *the left hand holding the food should have the fingers turned parallel to the knife blade with the thumb tucked behind* (see Figure 1). The nails of the

fingers should be turned inwards to avoid being cut as the knife moves towards the fingers. When this technique is adopted the blade will stop at the knuckles of the fingers with no injury to the fingers. *Cutting motion*:   The knife should be moved back and forwards in a gliding motion. The blade should move downwards and forwards when cutting then backwards and upwards prior to the next downward cutting stroke. The front edge of the blade should always be on the table during the movement to ensure the knife is fully under control. This motion is sometimes amended to up and down strokes when slicing cucumbers or mushrooms which are very easily cut. The cutting action should never be attempted with the sharp edge of the blade coming towards the fingers or body (except when shaping or turning vegetables where the blade of the turning knife moves towards the thumb in a controlled manner (see Figure 2)).

6   Some knives may inadvertently sit with the sharp edge of the blade upwards when placed on the table or cutting board. When this happens the knife should be placed flat on the table.

7   Never try to catch a knife if it accidentally falls off the table.

8   Avoid carrying knives about the kitchen unless they are in a protective case. When a knife has to be carried keep the point to the floor and the sharp edge of the blade to the back.

9   Never leave knives in a sink, especially in water where they cannot be seen.

10   When using a steel, hold it steady in the left hand with the point facing upwards at an angle of 45°. Run both edges of the blade down the steel in circular sweeps at a slight angle. A good guide is to hold the knife at the same angle as that on the heel of the knife. The sharpening action should be carried out six or seven times in one operation, then the edge of the blade tested for sharpness. Some cooks run the knife in an upward movement on the steel. This technique is to be recommended when sharpening a long knife or using a short steel; this is also advisable when using a poorly designed steel (one with little or no guard).

11   When testing a knife for sharpness, run the fleshy part of the thumb lightly *across* the edge of the blade. When the knife is sharp the blade should scrape the finger with a distinctive rasping sensation (even sound). A dull or blunt edge will not produce the rasping sensation. This test should be made at various points along the blade to ensure that the whole length of the blade is sharp. On no account should the finger be moved along the knife as this is likely to cause injury.

Motorized cutting equipment

Food processors, vertical cutting machines and vegetable cutting/slicing machines

A complete range of machines is available for *chopping*, *slicing*, *shredding* and *cutting* a variety of shapes. The machines vary considerably in size, capacity and functions (some machines also prepare pastry, doughs and sauces) therefore the reader should consult manufacturers' brochures or an equipment textbook.

Important: Motorized cutting equipment can be *dangerous* therefore the operator should be thoroughly versed in their use prior to operating.

Section one
Elementary preparation of vegetables

Root vegetables	*Method*
★Carrots Parsnips Salsifis Spring turnip	Cutting equipment: Hand peeler 1 Wash the vegetables and remove any blemishes or spots of deterioration. 2 Cut off the top and bottom ends of the vegetable with a knife. 3 Peel with the peeler.

Important: Salsifis should be placed in lemon or salt water to prevent discoloration.

Swedes and large turnips	Cutting equipment: Cook's knife Use medium or large size knife depending on the size of the swede. 1 Wash the vegetable. 2 Cut off the top and bottom of the vegetable with the cook's knife. 3 Cut off the skin around the sides. The thickness of the skin can be seen after the first piece of skin is cut from the side of the swede.

Tubers

★Potatoes Jerusalem artichokes	Prepare as root vegetables above, i.e. carrots and spring turnips etc. Omit step 2 as these vegetables have no top or bottom ends.

Bulbous roots

Onions Shallots	Cutting equipment: Turning knife Peel the vegetable by cutting through

★ These are often mechanically peeled.

the top and pulling the skin downwards. Continue this procedure both at the top and bottom of the vegetable until all the skin is removed.

Garlic

Cutting equipment: Cook's knife – medium length.
To separate the cloves: lightly hit the garlic head with the palm of the hand.
To peel the cloves: lightly hit the clove with the flat of the blade of the cook's knife – the skin can then be easily peeled off the clove. Remove root end.
To crush the cloves: flatten each clove with a blow using the flat of the blade of the cook's knife. Sprinkle with a little salt then scrape the garlic to a paste using the knife blade.

Leeks

Cutting equipment: Turning knife or small cook's knife.
1   Wash the leek, remove any discoloured leaves then cut off the root end.
2   Make a lengthwise cut through the leek starting just behind the root end. A further cut may be required for a large leek.
3   Wash well under running water to remove any dirt which may be lodged within the leaves.

Leaves

Lettuce

Plunge the lettuce in and out of cold water then separate the leaves. Re-wash under running cold water.

Spinach

Remove the stems from the leaves then wash in plenty of cold water.

Cabbage and spring greens

Cutting equipment: Cook's knife
1   Wash the vegetable then cut through the bottom stalk and remove any wilted leaves.
2   Quarter the cabbage then cut out the centre stalk. Also cut out any large ribs present in the leaves.

Sprouts

Cutting equipment: Turning knife
1   Trim off any discoloured leaves then cut a small cross in the base

of the stem – 1 mm in thickness approximately.
2   Wash in cold water.

Chicory

Trim the stem then remove any deteriorated leaves. Wash in cold water.

Stems and stalks

Asparagus

Cutting equipment: Turning knife or peeler
1   Lightly scrape the stems from just under the flower downwards to the root. With larger asparagus it may be necessary to remove the tips of the leaves with the back of the turning knife.
2   Wash, then tie into small bundles with the heads level. Cut the bundles evenly across at the root end.

Celery

Cutting equipment: Small cook's knife
1   Wash the celery then trim off the root end. This is done at an angle in the same manner as sharpening a pencil.
2   Trim the celery head and remove any deteriorated stalks. A peeler may be used to remove any blemishes.
3   Re-wash the celery thoroughly in cold running water inspecting the inner stalks for dirt.

Seakale

Cutting equipment: Turning knife
1   Remove any discoloured leaves then trim the roots.
2   Wash, then tie into bundles.

Flowers

Cauliflower

Cutting equipment: Small cook's knife
1   Cut through the stalk at the base of the vegetable just below the flower head and remove the outer leaves.
2   Make a small hole in the base of the stem.
3   Wash in salted water ensuring that any dirt or insects have been removed.

Broccoli

Cutting equipment: Turning knife
Trim the stalks to short lengths
underneath the flower heads. Wash
in cold water.

Globe artichokes

Cutting equipment: Small cook's
knife and scissors
1   Cut across the top leaves of the
    artichoke removing approximately
    one third of its height.
2   Remove the tips of the remaining
    leaves by cutting straight across
    with scissors.
3   Cut off the stalk close to the base
    of the vegetable. Rub over the
    bottom of the artichoke with
    lemon to avoid discoloration.

Globe artichoke
bottoms

Cutting equipment: Cook's knife
and turning knife
1   Cut across the artichoke leaving
    the bottom piece about 20 mm in
    thickness.
2   Cut off the stalk close to the base
    and pull out any large leaves.
3   Carefully pare the bottom of the
    vegetable until all the leaf and
    green material is removed. Rub
    over with lemon immediately the
    base is pared.
4   Scrape out the furry centre of the
    vegetable (the choke) and trim the
    sides if required.
5   Place the prepared artichoke
    immediately into lemon water.
    Leave in the water until required
    for cooking.

Seeds

Peas

Remove peas from the shells and
wash.

French beans

Top and tail the beans then wash.

Note: If necessary, remove the
strings from the beans when topping
and tailing. Break off or cut the top
almost through then pull to the side of
the vegetable – this should pull the
string off. Repeat the procedure with
the bottom of the bean.

Runner beans

Prepare as above then cut the beans
into thin strips.

Fruit vegetables

Cucumber
Marrow
Pumpkin

Cutting equipment: Peeler and
cook's knife
Preparation for cooking:
1   Peel the vegetable with a peeler.
2   Cut in half then scoop out the
    seeds with a spoon.
3   Cut into pieces: vegetable stews
    20 mm dice approximately,
    stuffed vegetables 50 mm shapes
    approximately.

Note: Cucumber may be cut into
small barrel shapes with two-thirds of
the centre removed with a parisienne
spoon.

Aubergines

Preparation for fried aubergine:
Remove alternate strips of the skin
with a peeler then cut across the
aubergine at a slant into 5 mm slices
approximately.
Preparation for stuffed aubergine:
1   Cut the vegetable in half length-
    wise.
2   Cut a criss-cross into the centre of
    the flesh with the point of a
    turning knife.
After this the aubergine is brushed
with oil or butter then cooked in a
moderately hot oven until tender
(8–10 minutes). The pulp is then
scooped out from the centre with a
spoon.

Courgettes

Wash, then remove the skin with a
peeler.
Vegetable stews: Cut into 20 mm
pieces approximately.
Dressed courgettes: Small courgettes
may be peeled then left whole or cut
into pieces as above.

Tomatoes

Sliced tomatoes: Wash, then remove
the eye with the point of a turning
knife. Cut the tomato into neat slices.

Note: Slices are usually cut across
the tomato but in this text the
preference is to slice the tomato
downwards because this does not
produce a slice with a root end and the
tomato sits more securely when
cutting.

Tomato case:
1 Wash, then remove the eye.
2 Cut the top off tomato then scoop out the seeds carefully with a parisienne spoon.

Peppers *Sliced pepper*: Cut the pepper in half lengthwise then remove the seeds and pith. Cut into thin slices.
Stuffed pepper: Cut off the stalk at the top of the pepper then carefully remove the seeds and pith.

Fungi

Mushrooms Pick the mushroom and trim the stalk or remove completely. Wash in cold water and drain well just prior to cooking.

Note: Field mushrooms require peeling but cultivated mushrooms should not be peeled.

Herbs

Fresh herbs are washed then used in small bunches or sprigs.

Fennel In addition to the leaves, root fennel may be cooked as a vegetable. Prepare in the same way as celery.

After basic preparation, vegetables and herbs may be used for a variety of purposes, e.g. sauces, soups, stews, dressed vegetables or garnishes etc.

Basic preparatory terms (mise en place) for vegetables

The terms listed below form part of the everyday language of professional cookery:

Mise en place This is the term for all the preparation which is required before a dish (or group of dishes) is ready for service.

Bouquet garni A faggot or bundle of herbs consisting of bay leaves, parsley stalks and thyme. The herbs are placed inside a leek leaf, celery pieces or muslin then tied with string.
Uses: A basic flavouring agent for many soups, sauces and stews etc.

Mirepoix Roughly cut pieces of onion, carrot, celery (sometimes leek) and bay leaves and thyme.
Uses: The fundamental vegetable flavouring in many soups, sauces and stews etc.

Mirepoix blanc The same as above but using only white vegetables, i.e. omitting the carrot and using the white of leeks.

Matignon This term is often used for the vegetables which are placed in a roasting tray and on which a roast sits during cooking. They prevent the roast from burning on the base of the tray and add flavour to the gravy. The matignon consists of the same vegetables as the mirepoix but the size of cutting the vegetables varies with the cooking time of the joint, i.e. long cooking times require large pieces or whole vegetables to reduce the risk of shrivelling and burning.

Oignon clouté This is an onion which has been studded with cloves and a bay leaf. It is used when making white sauce (Béchamel), certain soups and boiled meat dishes.

Persil haché Chopped parsley.

Persil concassé Roughly-chopped parsley.

Persil en branches Branch or sprig parsley.

Concassé de tomates Roughly-chopped tomato flesh. Blanch, skin and pip the tomatoes as follows:
1 Remove the eyes from the tomatoes then immerse into boiling water for 5 seconds approximately.
2 Remove, then test to see if the skins can be removed. If the skins cannot be easily removed, immerse the tomatoes for a further 2–3 seconds.
3 Immediately plunge the tomatoes into cold water.
4 Peel off the skins then halve the tomatoes across the middle.
5 Remove the pips then chop the flesh into large pieces.

Terms for cuts of vegetables

Bâtons Small stick shapes like small matchsticks, i.e. 2 × 2 × 15 mm. The collective term for vegetables cut into bâtons is jardinière.

Brunoise A *very* small dice – 1 mm sides.

Chiffonnade Thin strands or shreds of leaf vegetables.

Demidoff Crescents of vegetables with serrated sides. The vegetables are shaped into small cylinders then the sides grooved with a demidoff knife or strip cutter (couteau à caneler). The grooved cylinders are halved lengthwise, the centre removed then sliced into crescents.

Julienne Very thin strips of vegetables – ½ mm × ½ mm × 30 mm.

Macédoine A dice of vegetables – 5 mm sides.

Paysanne This term refers to vegetables which are cut into:
1 triangles or squares with 10 mm sides;
2 circles with 10 mm across their diameters.

Légumes tournés This refers to vegetables which have been *turned* with a turning knife. There are two distinct types of turning technique:
1 Shaping root vegetables etc., into small barrel shapes (see Figure 2).
2 Cutting a decorative groove on the surface of mushrooms.

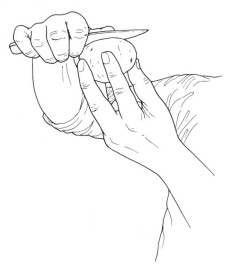

Figure 2 *Finger position – peeling and turning vegetables*

Section two   Elementary preparation of fruits

Hard fruits	*Method*
Apples and pears	*Slices* Peel with a peeler, cut into quarters then remove the core. Cut into neat slices. *Whole fruit* (a) *Preparation of apples for baking*: Wash, then remove the core with an apple corer. Make an incision through the skin around the centre of the apple. (b) *Preparation of apples and pears when baking in pastry*: Wash and peel the fruit then remove the core with an apple corer. (c) *Preparation of pears for poaching*: Peel the pears, leaving on the stalk. Remove the eyes and neatly trim so that the pears will stand upright.

Citrus fruits	
Grapefruit Lemons Limes Oranges	(a) *Removing the skin and pith*: Remove the top and bottom ends of the fruit then cut off the skin around the sides. Trim off any remaining pith. (b) *Cutting the fruit into segments*: Peel the fruit as above then carefully remove the segments from in between the skins.

(c) *Preparation of half grapefruit*: Halve the grapefruit then loosen the segments between the skins with a grapefruit knife or turning knife.

Citrus fruits, especially lemons, are often cut into peeled slices, cannelé-cut slices and wedges.

Stone fruits

Peaches Apricots Nectarines Plums Cherries	These fruits are simply halved and the stones removed. *Note*: Fruits such as peaches may be skinned in exactly the same manner as tomatoes, see tomato concassé, page 39.

Soft fruits

Strawberries Raspberries	Remove the husks and any other foreign matter. Wash and dry when required for use.
Gooseberries	Top and tail then lightly scrape over the surface of the gooseberries. Wash and drain well.

Tropical and other fruits

Grapes	Wash, cut in half lengthwise then remove the seeds. *Note*: In some instances the grapes are skinned. If this proves difficult, blanch and skin like tomatoes, see page 39.
Melons (large)	Cut a small piece from the top and bottom of the melon then cut in half lengthwise. Remove the seeds with a spoon then use as required. Melon flesh may be cut into large wedges (boats), slices, dice or scooped into balls with a parisienne spoon. Small melons are treated the same as above but are usually served in halves instead of wedges (because of their size).
Pineapple	Remove the top and bottom of the pineapple then cut off the skin around the sides. Cut into slices then remove the centre stalk with a pastry cutter.

Terms for the preparation of fruit

Macédoine A dice of fruits – 10 mm sides.
Van-Dyke Cutting lemons, oranges and tomatoes etc. into halves with a decorative serrated design.
Corbeille de fruits A basket of fruits.

Section three Preparation of salad dressings and savoury creams

Vinaigrette

Base method

Step 1   Place the vinegar, mustard, salt and pepper into a mixing bowl then whisk until combined.

Step 2   Whisk in the oil to thoroughly combine all the ingredients.

Information

Vinaigrette is a basic salad dressing. Derivative dressings are prepared with the addition of further ingredients – see below.

Base recipe (yields 1 medium sauceboat)

60 ml salad oil
20 ml vinegar
1 g French mustard (½ tsp approximately.)
Pinch salt and pepper
Note the ratio of three parts oil to one part vinegar.

Derivative dressings

Garlic dressing

Place a well-crushed clove of garlic into the mixing bowl with the vinegar and mustard and complete the dressing as stated. Add a garnish of sieved hard-boiled egg (½ egg approximately).

Sauce gribiche

Add the following ingredients to the basic ingredients: 1 sieved hard-boiled egg yolk, Julienne of hard-boiled egg white, chopped gherkins, capers, chives, parsley and tarragon.

Sauce ravigote

Garnish the vinaigrette with chopped shallots (5 g), chopped capers (5 g) and chopped chives, parsley, chervil and tarragon (5 g).

Roquefort dressing

Place 40 g Roquefort into a mixing bowl then mash with a fork. Slowly add the vinaigrette while constantly mixing with a whisk.

Thousand island dressing

Add the following ingredients to the basic vinaigrette: ½ sieved hard-boiled egg, chopped shallots (5 g), chopped red and green pimento (5 g) and chopped parsley and tarragon (2½ g approximately).

Note: Tabasco sauce, tomato ketchup and cooked lobster coral are also sometimes included in this dressing. This dressing is sometimes prepared with mayonnaise.

See mayonnaise sauce and derivatives on page 387.

Flavoured creams

These dressings are simply made by flavouring whipped cream.
Mustard cream (crème moutarde)
Curry cream (crème kari)
Paprika cream (crème paprika)
Herb cream (crème aux fines herbes)
Horseradish cream (raifort Chantilly)
Horseradish sauce (sauce raifort – this is often made in the same manner as horseradish cream above.)

Procedure: Whisk the cream until stiff then add the appropriate flavouring ingredient. Season to taste.

Note: When preparing horseradish cream the root is grated and added to cream together with a little lemon juice or vinegar to enhance flavour and reduce discoloration.

Section four Preparation of sweet cream mixtures

Flavoured sweet creams

These are made by flavouring sweetened whipped cream. Examples: brandy cream, whisky cream, liqueur cream etc.

Chantilly cream (crème Chantilly)

This is vanilla flavoured whipped cream which is lightly sweetened with caster sugar.

Syllabub

This is a whipped cream which is flavoured with wine and lemon and lightly sweetened with sugar.

Procedure: Whisk ¼ litre cream to a heavy thick mixture then add 50 g caster sugar, 75 ml white wine and the juice and zest of half a lemon. Blend together then serve in goblets. A little white wine may be placed in the base of the goblets before adding the syllabub.

Fruit fools (apple fool, rhubarb fool, strawberry fool etc.)

These are mixtures of fruit purée, whipped cream and stiffly whisked egg whites which are sweetened with caster sugar.

Procedure: Mix together 300 g desired fruit purée, 200 ml whipped cream, 75 g caster sugar (quantity varies with the type of purée used) and 75 ml stiffly whisked egg whites (three egg whites approximately). Place the mixture into goblets or coupes and decorate with rosettes of whipped cream.

Cream-based mousses (strawberry, raspberry, peach etc.)

These are prepared in a similar manner to fruit fools.

Procedure: Blend together 300 ml whipped cream, 150 ml fruit purée, 75 g caster sugar, good squeeze of lemon juice and any colouring if required. Serve in goblets with sponge finger biscuits.

Section five   Preparation of compound butters (beurres composés)

These are flavoured butters which are used as an accompaniment to many grilled meat, poultry and game dishes. Because they melt over the food they serve the same function as a sauce. The alternative name for compound butters is 'hard butter sauces'.

Production details:
1 Cream the butter.
2 *Add the flavouring ingredients.
3 Place on to a sheet of dampened greaseproof paper then roll into a neat cylinder – 20 mm diameter approximately.
4 Place in a cold cabinet and allow to harden.
5 Remove the paper and cut into neat rondels.
6 Serve in a sauceboat in ice water or place on the grilled food when serving.

Anchovy butter (beurre d'anchois)
40 g butter, 10 g anchovy fillets (4–5 fillets), squeeze lemon juice. Add a pinch of cayenne pepper.

Beurre Bercy
40 g butter, 5 g finely chopped blanched shallots[†], 5 g diced blanched bone marrow, pinch of chopped parsley, 1 tspn. meat glaze, squeeze lemon juice and 25 ml white wine[†].

* Items such as chopped onions, shallots and bone marrow etc., must be blanched (part cooked in boiling water then refreshed) before adding to the butter.
[†]Blanch the shallots in the white wine, reducing the liquid.

Garlic butter (beurre d'ail)
40 g butter, 2½ g pounded garlic (two cloves) and pinch of pepper.

Parsley butter (beurre maître-d'hôtel)
40 g butter, squeeze of lemon juice, good pinch of chopped parsley (2½ g) and pinch cayenne pepper. Also optional, 5 g finely chopped shallot or onion.

Snail butter (beurre escargots)
40 g butter, 10 ml brandy (2 teaspoons), 5 g finely chopped shallots, 1 clove crushed garlic, a good pinch of chopped parsley and salt and pepper.

Sweet butters

In addition to savoury butters, butters may also be sweetened and flavoured. These are prepared in the same manner as savoury butters with the butter and sugar being creamed together then the flavouring added.
Uses: Served with crêpes and Christmas pudding etc.

Brandy butter
40 g butter, 40 g icing sugar and one measure of brandy.

Sherry butter
As above, using sherry in place of brandy.

Liqueur butter
The same as brandy butter, adding the appropriate liqueur, in place of brandy.

Buttercreams

One of the simplest ways of producing buttercream is to use the same method as sweet butters above. See also pages 108–405. *Uses*:   Filling for cakes and pastries etc.

Recipe and production details: Cream together an equal quantity of sieved icing sugar and butter then flavour (and colour) as required. *Examples*:   vanilla, coffee, orange and kirsch.

Section six   Preparation of marinades, spiced vinegars, brines and seasonings

Marinades

These are liquors which are used to increase the tenderness of flesh – usually game and butcher's meats. They also add flavour and act as a short-term preservative or pickle.

Procedure: The piece of meat or game is allowed to soak in the marinade prior to cooking. The period of time required for marinading depends on the type of flesh and the size of joint; varying between 2–18 hours. Fish is also sometimes marinaded but this is mostly to add flavour and is therefore carried out for a short period, e.g. 15–45 minutes.

Plain marinade (marinade ordinaire)
Mirepoix of vegetables (i.e. 200 g chopped onion, 150 g chopped carrots, 50 g chopped celery, sprig of thyme, parsley stalks and bay leaf). Also six peppercorns, 100 ml white wine (red is also used), 40 ml vinegar, 25 ml oil. Other flavourings such as garlic, cloves and brandy may also be included in the recipe to alter the basic marinade. *Uses*: Butcher's meats, game and poultry.

Production details: Place all the ingredients into a porcelain or stainless steel bowl. The joint is placed in a bowl and the marinade sprinkled over the top. Cover with a sheet of oiled greaseproof paper and allow to stand until required for cooking. Turn the joint occasionally during marinading and at the same time baste over the liquor.

Instant marinade (marinade instantanée)
25 g finely chopped shallot or onion, good pinch of chopped parsley (2½ g), juice of a half lemon, 100 ml oil and a pinch of salt and pepper. *Uses*: Fish and poultry.

Production details: As for plain marinade – see above.

Marinade for Bismarck herring
25 g chopped onion, 1 bay leaf, 6 peppercorns, 1 clove, squeeze lemon juice, 150 ml white vinegar, 50 ml white wine and a pinch of salt.

Production details: Place the ingredients in a pan and bring to the boil. Pour into a bowl, allow to cool then strain.

Note: The preparation of Bismarck herring is explained on page 48.

Marinade à la grecque
½ bay leaf, 6 peppercorns, 3 coriander seeds, juice of 1 lemon, 250 ml water and 50 ml oil. *Uses*: Hors-d'oeuvre.

Production details: Place the ingredients in a pan and bring to the boil. Add the appropriate vegetable and cook lightly in the marinade.* Allow to cool, then serve.

Note: Button onions, cauliflower and celery etc., may be prepared in this style.

Marinade à la portugaise
40 g finely chopped onion, ½ bay leaf, 3 crushed peppercorns, little crushed garlic (¼ clove), good pinch of chopped parsley, sprig of thyme, 250 g raw tomato concassé, 5 g tomato purée (optional), 40 ml oil and 100 ml water.

Production details: Prepare as cooked tomato concassé on

page 273, adding the additional ingredients. Add the appropriate vegetable and cook lightly in the marinade.*

Note: The same vegetables as à la grecque above may be used.

Spiced vinegar
2½ g peppercorns, 2½ g cloves, 2½ g root ginger, 2½ g cinnamon stick, 2½ g Jamaica pepper, 2½ g mace and 600 ml vinegar. *Uses*: Pickling vegetables.

Production details: Crush the spices and place in a pan with the vinegar. Bring to the boil then allow to cool. Strain the vinegar before use.

Mint sauce
This is basically a flavoured vinegar.
Small bunch of mint (30 g approximately), 5 g caster sugar, 150 ml vinegar. *Uses*: Roast lamb.

Production details: Pick and wash the leaves then dry with a cloth. Chop the leaves with the sugar then place into a bowl. Add the vinegar.

Brine (saumure)
This is used to produce pickled salt meats which are cooked by boiling, see page 90.
5 l water, 25 g saltpetre, 1 kg salt and 150 g brown sugar. *Uses*: Silverside and brisket beef. Also beef tongues.

Production details: Place the ingredients in a pan and boil for 15 minutes, skimming as required. Allow the mixture to become cold before immersing the joint for pickling. Keep the joint covered with the pickle (also cover the container) for 7–10 days. Large joints will require to be syringed with pickle occasionally during soaking.

Dry pickle (saumure au sel)
1 kg salt, 40 g saltpetre and 150 g sugar.
Note: Spices such as Jamaica pepper and ground cloves may also be added.

Production details: Prick the joint with a needle then rub on the saltpetre. Cover with sugar and salt and press down with a lid or board. Turn the meat occasionally. Leave in a very cool place for 6–10 weeks.

Seasonings
The main seasonings are salt and pepper but spices may also be used.

Mignonnette pepper
This is the pepper from peppercorns which have been crushed under a heavy weight or ground in a coarse mill.

Compound seasoning
In addition to just salt and pepper mixed together, some chefs make up their own compound seasoning which consists of salt and pepper and a selection of spices, e.g. ground Jamaica pepper, cloves, ginger and nutmeg.

* Vegetables to be cooked in an à la grecque or portugaise marinade are usually blanched prior to cooking.

Section seven   Preparation of salads

Salads may be divided into two groups:

Simple or single salads: These consist of one main item.
Compound or mixed salads: These consist of several
items.

Simple or single salads

Beetroot salad (salade de betterave)
200 g cooked beetroot, 15 g finely chopped onion, 30 ml
vinaigrette, seasoning and chopped parsley.

Cut the beetroot into slices or dice then add the onion and
bind with the vinaigrette. Dress in a ravier or salad dish
and sprinkle with the chopped parsley.

Potato salad (salade de pommes de terre)
200 g cooked potatoes, 15 g finely chopped onion, 50 ml
mayonnaise, seasoning and chopped parsley.

Allow the potatoes to cool then peel off the skins and cut
into a dice – 10 mm approximately. Add the onion and
seasoning then bind together with the mayonnaise. Dress
in a ravier or salad dish and sprinkle with chopped parsley.

Cucumber salad (salade de concombre)
½ medium sized cucumber, 30 ml vinaigrette, seasoning
and chopped parsley.

Peel and thinly slice the cucumber. Arrange the slices of
cucumber in a ravier then lightly season. Coat with the
vinaigrette and sprinkle over the chopped parsley.

Note: A little vinegar is sometimes used in place of
vinaigrette.

Various bean salads (e.g. French beans, red beans, butter beans)
200 g appropriate cooked beans, 15 g finely chopped
onion, 30 ml vinaigrette, seasoning and chopped parsley.

Mix together the beans and onion then lightly season.
Bind with the vinaigrette then dress in a ravier or salad
dish. Sprinkle with chopped parsley.

Rice salad (salade de riz)
120 g cooked rice (60 g raw rice approximately, see page
125), 50 g raw tomato concassé, see page 39, 30 ml
vinaigrette, seasoning and chopped parsley. Additional
garnish may also include peas, diced pimentos and
sweetcorn etc.

Combine all the ingredients, lightly season then bind
together with the vinaigrette. Dress in a ravier or salad
dish then sprinkle with chopped parsley (optional).

Tomato salad (salade de tomate)
4 medium tomatoes (200 g approximately) 15 g finely
chopped onion, 30 ml vinaigrette, seasoning and chopped
parsley.

Blanch and skin the tomatoes if desired. Cut into thin
slices and arrange in ravier or salad dish. Lightly season
then sprinkle over the onion, vinaigrette and parsley.

Fruit-based simple salads

Apple salad
4 small apples and 50–75 ml mayonnaise.

Peel, core and dice the apples then bind with the
mayonnaise sauce. Dress in a ravier or salad dish.

Grapefruit salad
2 large grapefruits.

Cut the grapefruits into segments then dress in a ravier
with a little of the juice.

Orange salad
4 small oranges.

Cut the oranges into segments then dress in a ravier with a
little of the juice.

Florida salad
Prepare as orange salad above but dress the segments on
lettuce leaves or quarters of lettuce and serve separately a
sauceboat of acidulated cream.

Salade Ninon
Prepare as Florida salad above but replace the acidulated
cream with a vinaigrette made with lemon juice and
orange juice.

Salade Manon
Prepare as grapefruit salad above but dress the segments
on lettuce leaves or quarters and accompany with a
vinaigrette made with lemon juice.

Compound or mixed salads

Coleslaw
175 g white cabbage, 50 g carrot, 25 g onion, seasoning
and 100 ml mayonnaise.
Additional ingredients (optional):   pimento, apple, raisins
and nuts etc.

Wash, peel and finely shred the vegetables. Mix together
then bind with the mayonnaise sauce.

Potato and watercress salad (salade cressonnière)
300 g cooked potatoes, 1 bunch of watercress, 1 hard-
boiled egg, pinch chopped parsley, seasoning and 40 ml
vinaigrette.

Slice the potatoes and pick the watercress then mix
together. Dress in a salad bowl. Sieve the egg and sprinkle
over the potatoes and cress together with the chopped

parsley. Serve the vinaigrette separately. Alternatively bind the potatoes and cress with the vinaigrette.

French salad (salade française)
Lettuce, cucumber, tomato, beetroot, quarters of hard-boiled egg and vinaigrette.

Dress neatly in a salad bowl and accompany with the vinaigrette.

Note: Additional salad vegetables such as cress, chopped chives and tarragon etc., are sometimes included in the recipe.

Mixed salad (salade panachée)
All types of salad vegetables in season, e.g. lettuce, cucumber, tomatoes, radishes, spring onion, chicory and watercress etc.

Dress neatly in a salad bowl and accompany with vinaigrette.

Green salad (salade verte)
This consists of a selection of green salad vegetables in season: lettuce, watercress, curly chicory, chives and spring onions etc.

Dress in a salad bowl and accompany with vinaigrette.

Salade niçoise
150 g cooked potatoes, 150 g cooked French beans, 2 medium tomatoes (100 g approximately), 8 stoned olives, 5 g capers, 8 small anchovy fillets, seasoning and vinaigrette dressing (50 ml approximately).
Additional ingredients (optional): lettuce and pieces of cooked tuna fish.

Skin and remove the seeds from the tomatoes then cut the flesh into medium-sized dice, see page 39. Cut the potatoes into a dice (10 mm approximately) then mix together with the beans and tomato flesh. Add the seasoning and bind with the vinaigrette. Dress the mixture in a salad bowl and decorate with the olives, anchovies and capers.

Russian salad (salade russe)
100 g carrots, 100 g turnips, 50 g French beans, 50 g peas, seasoning and 75 ml mayonnaise.

Wash and peel the carrots and turnips then cut into macédoine, see page 39. Wash beans and cut into small diamond shapes. Cook all the vegetables separately in boiling salted water then refresh and *drain well*. Mix the vegetables together, add seasoning and bind together with the mayonnaise. Dress in a salad dish or ravier.

Fruit-based compound salads

Salade japonaise
This salad consists of a dice of fresh fruit, e.g. apples, oranges, pineapples and tomato flesh bound together with acidulated cream. The mixture is dressed on lettuce or served in an orange.

Salade mimosa
Orange segments, grapes and slices of banana bound together with acidulated cream and served on lettuce leaves or quarters.

Salade Waldorf
Diced apples, celery or celeriac and half walnuts bound together with mayonnaise and dressed on lettuce leaves or quarters. Alternatively the mixture may be served in a scooped-out apple.

Egg, fish, meat and poultry salads

These salads may be served as:

1 Part of an hors-d'oeuvre variés, see page 49.
2 A single or individual hors-d'oeuvre, see page 46.
3 A main course dish.

Most of the salads in this section may be served for each of the above purposes with the portion size being varied accordingly. When a salad is usually only appropriate to one group, an indication is made in brackets.

Egg mayonnaise (oeuf à la mayonnaise)
Served for hors-d'oeuvre variés: Hard-boiled eggs, see page 121, cut into quarters and dressed in a ravier. Coat with mayonnaise and decorate with anchovy fillets and capers.
Served as an individual hors-d'oeuvre: Two halves of hard-boiled egg dressed on a lettuce leaf (on a side or fish plate). Coat with mayonnaise and garnish with a small selection of salad vegetables: tomato, cucumber, cress and spring onion etc.
Served as a main course dish: Prepared the same as above but increasing the portion size to 2–3 eggs and garnishing with a good selection of salad vegetables; potato salad and Russian salad is usually also added. Decorate with anchovy fillets and capers if desired.

Fish salad (salade de poisson) (Hors-d'oeuvre variés and individual hors-d'oeuvre)
One fish course portion
75 g cooked flaked fish, 50 g cucumber (¼ cucumber), 1 hard-boiled egg, ¼ lettuce, 2 stoned olives, 2 anchovy fillets, 6 capers, seasoning, 30 ml vinaigrette and chopped parsley.

Cut the cucumber and egg into dice – 5 mm approximately – then mix together with the flaked fish. Bind the mixture with the vinaigrette. Finely shred the lettuce (chiffonnade) and place into the ravier or dish. Neatly arrange the mixture on top of the lettuce then decorate with the olives, anchovies, capers and chopped parsley.

Shellfish salad (salade de fruits de mer)
One fish course portion
Prepare as fish salad above but replace the fish with a
selection of cooked shellfish, e.g. prawns, scampi,
mussels, scallops and crab etc.
Note: Single shellfish salads such as prawn, scampi and
lobster may be made in exactly the same manner using the
appropriate shellfish as the main item.

Fish Mayonnaise (mayonnaise de poisson)
Prepare the same as fish salad but omit the vinaigrette and
coat the fish mixture with mayonnaise prior to decorating.

**Salmon Mayonnaise (mayonnaise de saumon) (Hors-
d'oeuvre variés and individual hors-d'oeuvre)**
One fish course portion
75 g cooked flaked salmon, 50 g cucumber (¼ cucumber),
1 quarter hard-boiled egg, ¼ lettuce, quarter of tomato, 1
stoned olive, 2 anchovy fillets, 6 capers, chopped parsley,
seasoning and 50 ml mayonnaise approximately.

Finely shred the lettuce and place into the ravier or dish.
Arrange the salmon on top of the lettuce then garnish
round the sides with the egg, tomato and cucumber cut
into thin slices. When ready for service, coat the salmon
with the mayonnaise and decorate the top with the olive,
anchovies, capers and chopped parsley.

**Cold salmon and mayonnaise sauce (saumon froid,
sauce mayonnaise) (Individual hors-d'oeuvre and main
course)**
This consists of suitable sized portions of cooked cold
salmon (suprêmes or darnes etc., see page 72) dressed on
lettuce leaves (or garnished with lettuce quarters) and
garnished with tomato, thinly sliced cucumber, hard-
boiled egg and cress etc. Serve a sauceboat of mayonnaise
separately.

**Dressed crab (crabe froid, sauce mayonnaise)
(Individual hors-d'oeuvre)**
One fish course portion
1 cooked cold crab (500 g approximately, see pages
73–116), 1 hard-boiled egg, chopped parsley, 75 ml
mayonnaise, a little fresh white breadcrumbs and small
French salad to be served separately if desired.

Prepare the crab as stated on page 73, retaining the
cleaned top shell for service. Mix the soft dark meat (and
orange meat) of the crab with a little fresh white
breadcrumbs and mayonnaise to form a paste. Break up
the white flesh and place aside. Place the crab paste into
both ends of the shell and smooth down the surface with a
palette knife. Dress the white meat in the centre then
decorate over the top with lines of sieved egg yolk, sieved
egg white and chopped parsley. Serve chilled
accompanied with a sauceboat of mayonnaise and French
salad if desired.

**Cold lobster and mayonnaise sauce (homard froid,
sauce mayonnaise) (Individual hors-d'oeuvre and main
course)**
One fish course portion
½ cooked cold lobster (500 g lobster), quarter hard-boiled
egg, quarter tomato, ¼ lettuce, 6 capers, 2 anchovy fillets
and sauceboat of mayonnaise.

Prepare the lobster halves as stated on page 72. Line the
front cavity of the lobster with lettuce or shredded
lettuce then place in the flesh from the claws. Dress the
carapace on a dish and garnish with the tomato, egg and
lettuce. Decorate the top of the carapace with the capers
and anchovies and accompany with mayonnaise.

**Meat salad (salade de viande) (Hors-d'oeuvre variés
and individual hors-d'oeuvre)**
One starter portion
75 g cooked meat, 1 small tomato, 10 g finely sliced onion,
20 g cooked French beans, 20 g gherkins, chopped
parsley, seasoning and 30 ml vinaigrette approximately.

Cut the meat and gherkins into thin strips (julienne).
Blanch, skin and remove the seeds from the tomato then
cut into dice. Mix all the ingredients together, season then
bind with the vinaigrette. Dress on a ravier or dish and
sprinkle with chopped parsley.

Note: Other cooked flesh such as chicken and ham etc.
may be used. In addition olives, capers and pieces of
hard-boiled egg are also sometimes included in the recipe.

**Chicken salad, ham salad, roast beef salad, tongue
salad etc. (Main course)**
Many main course salads simply consist of a main item,
e.g. pieces of cooked cold chicken, slices of ham or roast
beef etc., which is garnished with a selection of salad
vegetables. A suitable cold sauce, e.g. vinaigrette,
ravigote, mayonnaise or verte is usually served separately.

Section eight   Preparation of hors-d'oeuvre

Hors-d'oeuvre are traditionally served as a starter course
to luncheon menus with the exception of the finer, non-
vegetable types (such as caviar, smoked salmon, oysters
and cantaloup melon etc.) which are sometimes served on
dinner menus. Hors-d'oeuvre should be light and delicate
and always stimulate the appetite. Presentation should
highlight a clean, fresh appearance with a good colour
balance where appropriate.

Single item hors-d'oeuvre; (a)   Various cocktails

Grapefruit cocktail
Allow one small grapefruit per portion. Cut the grapefruit
into segments (see page 40) then dress in a cocktail glass

with the juice. Serve chilled – top with a cherry if desired. The glass is sometimes rimmed with egg white then dipped in coloured sugar.

Orange cocktail
Prepare as above using oranges in place of grapefruit.

Florida cocktail
This consists of a mixture of grapefruit segments, orange segments and pieces of pineapple. This cocktail may be made without the pineapple.

Miami cocktail
The same as Florida cocktail, adding melon cubes.

Melon cocktail
One Honeydew melon will yield 6–8 portions approximately. Cut the melon into dice or scoop out into balls with a parisienne spoon (see page 40). Dress in a cocktail glass with the juice and serve chilled; top with a cherry if desired.

Pineapple cocktail
One pineapple will yield 6–8 portions approximately. Cut the pineapple into dice (see page 40) and dress in a cocktail glass with the juice. Serve chilled – top with a cherry if desired.

Shellfish cocktails (yield one portion)
Prawn cocktail (cocktail de crevettes roses)
Shrimp cocktail (cocktail de crevettes)
Lobster cocktail (cocktail de homard)
Scampi cocktail (cocktail de scampi/langoustines)
Scallop cocktail (cocktail de coquilles St-Jacques)

Basic recipe for one cocktail:
Main item: 25–40 g prepared shellfish
Sauce: 35–50 ml sauce Marie-Rose (see page 387)
Garnish: shredded lettuce (2–3 leaves), 1 stuffed olive, 1 anchovy fillet

Production details:
1   Wash the lettuce, drain thoroughly then cut into a chiffonnade (finely shred). Place the chiffonnade into the cocktail glass.
2   Bind the prepared shellfish with a little cocktail sauce then place into the cocktail dish on top of the chiffonnade.
3   Decorate with the stuffed olive and anchovy (which is usually wrapped round the olive).

Note: The cocktail may also be decorated with a suitable piece of the appropriate shellfish.

(b) Fruits

Chilled half grapefruit (demi-pamplemousse frappé)
Halve the chilled grapefruit, then loosen the segments between the skins with a grapefruit knife or turning knife.

Decorate the centre with a cherry then serve in a coupe or other suitable dish.

Note: The chilled grapefruit may be flavoured with a spoonful of kirsch, sherry or Madeira before service.

Demi-pamplemousse mexicaine
1 half grapefruit, spoonful of sherry – 10 ml approximately, 5 g brown sugar, 5 g caster sugar and half a small red pimento.

Prepare the grapefruit as half grapefruit above then sprinkle over the sherry and brown sugar. Allow to macerate for 30 minutes approximately. Cut the pimento into thin strips and decorate the top of the grapefruit. Sprinkle with the caster sugar then brown under the salamander. Serve hot.

Chilled melon (Honeydew) (melon frappé)
Allow 4–6 portions from a medium melon. Cut the chilled melon into wedges (see page 40). Decorate with a cherry and serve well chilled. Serve separately a little ground ginger and caster sugar.

Melon vénitienne
Prepare as above but decorate the wedge like a boat using a slice of orange and cherry impaled like a sail on a cocktail stick.

Important: It is not good practice to cut the melon wedges prior to service because the melon bleeds, losing both juice and flavour.

Cantaloup melon
Charentais melon
Ogen melon
Allow half a melon or one whole melon depending on size.

Preparing half a melon: Cut the melon in half then remove the seeds. Serve chilled.
Preparing a whole melon: Cut a slice off the top of the melon to act as a lid. Remove the seeds, replace the lid and serve chilled.

Melon de Charente au porto
Prepare as above but fill the interior of the melon with port and macerate for 20–30 minutes.

Melon with Parma ham (melon au jambon de Parme)
Prepare a wedge of melon then remove the skin. Place on a side place or other suitable dish and decorate with 1 or 2 thin slices of Parma ham.

Avocado pear (avocat à la vinaigrette)
Allow half a pear per portion. Halve the pear and remove the stone. Serve on a bed of lettuce (tomato, cucumber and cress may also be included as a garnish), accompanied with a sauceboat of vinaigrette, see page 41.

Avocat Épicure

Ingredients for two portions: 1 avocado pear, 20 g gherkins, 20 g walnuts, ¼ lettuce, 2 pickled walnuts, seasoning, paprika pepper and 30 ml mayonnaise.

Production details:

1   Halve the pear, remove the stone then carefully scoop out the flesh without damaging the skin.
2   Cut the flesh into dice, the gherkins into a small dice and break the walnuts into small pieces.
3   Bind together the pear flesh, gherkins and walnut pieces with the mayonnaise and add seasoning and paprika.
4   Place the mixture into the pear shells and decorate with the pickled walnuts. Serve on a bed of lettuce.

Avocat Singapour

Ingredients for two portions: 1 avocado pear, 40 g white crab meat, squeeze lemon juice, 20 ml mayonnaise, spoonful whipped cream (15 ml approximately), ¼ lettuce, 2 small lemon wedges, seasoning and pinch of cayenne pepper.

Production details:

1   Halve the pear, remove the stone then carefully scoop out the flesh and cut into dice.
2   Flake the crab meat then mix with the pear dice.
3   Lightly season, adding the pinch of cayenne pepper then add the lemon juice. Bind the mixture with the whipped cream and mayonnaise.
4   Place the mixture in the avocado shells.
5   Serve chilled, garnished with the lettuce and lemon wedges.

(c) Eggs

Egg mayonnaise (oeuf à la mayonnaise)

See page 45.

Poached eggs in aspic (oeufs en gelée)

Ingredients for four portions: 4 trimmed poached eggs, 250–300 ml aspic jelly, see page 83, 4 decorative pieces of pimento etc. (traditionally truffle).

Place each egg in a cocotte dish then add enough aspic to reach a height half way up the egg. Allow to set (this will reduce the risk of small pieces of egg white floating to the top of the finished aspic). Decorate the top of the egg with the pimento or truffle then cover with the remaining aspic. Allow to set then serve chilled in the cocotte dish.

(d) Vegetables

Savoury cucumber

Ingredients for one portion: ¼ small cucumber
Filling consisting of: 50 g cooked meat, fish or poultry, 1 hard-boiled egg cut into dice, 15 g cooked French beans cut into dice, seasoning, chopped parsley and vinaigrette

to bind (25 ml approximately).
Salad vegetable garnish: lettuce, tomato and cress etc.

Production details:

1   Cut the cucumber into four small barrel shapes then remove the centre with a parisienne spoon. Blanch until tender in boiling salted water then allow to cool.
2   Prepare the filling by cutting the meat or poultry into dice (or flake fish) and mixing with the rest of the ingredients.
3   Fill the cucumber cases with the filling and sprinkle with chopped parsley. Dress on a plate or dish garnished with the lettuce, tomato and cress.

Danish cucumber (concombre danoise)

This is prepared the same as savoury cucumber above, but using a filling consisting of flaked salmon, diced marinaded herring (Bismarck) and diced hard-boiled eggs. Sprinkle the filled cases with grated horseradish just prior to service.

Monaco tomatoes (tomates monégasque)

These consist of tomato cases which are lightly seasoned and sprinkled with vinegar then stuffed with a mixture of flaked cooked tuna fish, diced hard-boiled eggs and chopped onions and chives.

(e) Fish

Bismarck herring

Ingredients for two portions:* 2 small herrings, Bismarck marinade (page 43), 40 g sliced onion, 1 bay leaf, a few mustard seeds, 3–4 peppercorns, small piece of shredded chilli pepper and 20 g sliced salt cucumber.

Production details:

1   Bone and clean the herring then soak them in a brine consisting of 500 ml water and 50 g salt for 2 hours.
2   Place the herring in a suitable pickling jar or crock with the vegetables and spices then cover with the marinade.
3   Cover and store in a cool place for 5–6 days.

Rollmops

These are prepared the same as Bismarck herring above but roll up the fillets prior to pickling. The fillets are sometimes wrapped round a piece of salt cucumber.

Soused herring

Ingredients for two portions: 2 small herring.
Pickling liquor: 25 g thin carrot rings, 25 g thin onion rings, ½ bay leaf, 4 peppercorns, sprig of thyme, pinch salt, pinch sugar, 200 ml vinegar and 50 ml water.

Production details:

1   Prepare the pickling liquor by mixing all the

---

* It is usual practice to prepare several portions of these pickled fish at the one time, therefore increase the marinade recipe as required.

ingredients together in a suitable pan and bringing to the boil. Boil for 2–3 minutes then allow to cool. *Do not strain.*

2 Bone and clean the herring then roll up with the skin outwards. Place in an earthenware dish.

3 Pour over the liquor and vegetables, cover with greaseproof paper and cook in a moderate oven for 15 minutes approximately.

4 Allow to cool then serve with the liquor and vegetables.

Note: Because of the singular nature of this hors-d'oeuvre it has not been placed in an appropriate chapter with heat treatment.

Fish salad, Shellfish salad, Fish mayonnaise, Dressed crab, Cold lobster and Mayonnaise sauce
See page 46.

Potted shrimps
These are usually prepared commercially but may be made as required by mixing peeled shrimps with melted butter and seasoning with salt, pepper and nutmeg.

Fill small pots with the shrimps, covering with the butter then allow to cool and set. Serve in the pots or turn out on to a bed of lettuce and garnish with tomato, cucumber and cress.

Oysters (huîtres nature)
Allow 6 oysters per portion, 1 wedge of lemon and brown bread and butter.

Note: The elementary preparation of oysters is stated on page 72.

Serve the oysters in their deep shells on a bed of crushed ice with the lemon (and branch parsley – optional). Accompany with the brown bread and butter.

Huîtres Borchardt
Dress the raw shelled oysters on slices of tomato and surround with a border of caviar. Serve on a side plate or other suitable dish.

Caviar
This is the specially salted roe of various types of female sturgeon, e.g. Beluga (large eggs, dark grey colour), Ocietrova (medium sized eggs, dark green colour), Sevruga (small eggs, dark green or black). These fish produce various qualities of caviar with the name Malossol indicating first quality.
Allow 20–25 g per portion. Serve in the original tin or jar on crushed ice or an ice socle.

(f) *Pâtés and terrines*

Pâté de foie gras
This is a high quality pâté made with goose livers. The pâté which is usually commercially prepared may be purchased in tins or porcelain containers.

Service:
(a) *Tinned foie gras:* Remove the pâté from the tin and trim off any excess fat. Cut into slices (10 mm approximately) and dress on plates or a salver lined with a little aspic. Accompany with warm brioche or hot toast.
(b) *Porcelain containers:* Serve in the container embedded in crushed ice. Accompany as above with warm brioche or hot toast.

Liver pâté (pâté de foie/maison)
The preparation of this pâté is explained on page 75.

Service: Cut into slices (10 mm approximately) and serve on plates or a salver on a bed of lettuce. The pâté may be garnished with tomato, cucumber and cress etc. Accompany with fingers of hot toast.

(g) *Smoked dishes*

Smoked salmon (saumon fumé)
Allow 25–40 g trimmed smoked salmon per portion, i.e. 3–4 thin slices.

Service: Dress the slices on an oval salver or suitable dish and decorate with a wedge of lemon and branch parsley. Serve buttered brown bread separately.

Smoked trout (truite fumée)
Allow 1 small trout per portion.

Service: Remove the skin from both sides of the trout and serve on a salver or suitable dish, garnish with a wedge of lemon (tomato and lettuce etc., may also be added) and cress. Serve separately a sauceboat of horseradish sauce.

Smoked eel (anguille fumée)
Smoked mackerel (maquereau fumé)
These may be thinly sliced and served in the same manner as smoked salmon.

Commercially prepared smoked or cooked sausages (saucisson)
Examples: Salami – German, Danish and Polish etc., liver sausage, Mortadella, Cervelat, and garlic sausage.

Service: The sausages are thinly sliced then dressed on a salver or suitable dish.

Note: Sausages with a soft texture, e.g. garlic sausage and liver sausage, are cut into thicker slices than the firm types.

Variety hors-d'oeuvre (hors-d'oeuvre variés)
This consists of an assortment of hors-d'oeuvre items which are each served in a ravier or hors-d'oeuvre dish.

The hors-d'oeuvre selection is usually brought to the table where the diner makes his or her choice of items. Many of the individual hors-d'oeuvre in the previous section are suitable for a variety hors-d'oeuvre.

Examples

(a)	Various simple salads	Beetroot, cucumber, potato and rice etc.
(b)	Various compound salads	Coleslaw, Russian salad and Waldorf salad etc.
(c)	Egg, fish and meat salads	Egg mayonnaise, fish salad, sardines, shellfish salad and meat salad etc.
(d)	Pickled items	Bismarck herring, rollmops and soused herring etc.
(e)	Smoked items	Salami, Mortadella, garlic sausage etc.
(f)	Vegetable preparations	1 Vegetables prepared *à la grecque*, e.g. cauliflower, celery and button onions. 2 Vegetables prepared *à la portugaise*, e.g. same vegetables as à la grecque above.

Production details: Prepare the vegetables, leaving the onions whole, cutting the cauliflower into florets or celery into short lengths. Cook as stated on page 43.

Cocktail hors-d'oeuvre (canapés à la russe)

This type of hors-d'oeuvre is served at cocktail parties or finger buffet receptions and may consist of hot and cold items.

Examples – cold

(a)	Toast-based items	Small toast shapes, e.g. fingers, triangles or squares etc. garnished with sardines, slices of boiled eggs, tomato, cucumber, cheese, anchovies, sliced cooked meats, smoked salmon, caviar and sliced smoked sausage etc.
(b)	Biscuit/pastry-based items	These are garnished in the same manner as toast shapes above.
(c)	Vegetable-based items	Pieces of celery stalks or cucumber etc. cut into boat shapes, filled with cream cheese, prawns Marie-Rose or pâté etc.

(d)	Choux paste items – Carolines and Duchesses	These are baked choux paste shapes filled with a savoury stuffing, e.g. pâté, ham purée or cheese etc. *Carolines* The paste is piped into 'C' shapes (30 mm length). *Duchesses* The paste is piped into éclair shapes.

(e) Game chips, cheese straws and various nuts served in small bowls or dishes.

(f) Cubes of fruit, cheese, cooked chipolata sausages, gherkins and olives served on cocktail sticks.

(g) Sandwiches and filled bridge rolls.

Examples – hot

(a)	Puff pastry items	Bouchées filled with chicken, prawns, salmon and ham in a suitable sauce, see pages 194–8. Also cheese ramekins, see page 327.
(b)	Savoury short pastry items	Barquettes or tartelettes filled as bouchées above, see pages 194–8. Also miniature quiche lorraine, see page 393.

(c) Miniature sausage rolls

(d) Miniature savouries, e.g. devils on horseback, angels on horseback and canapé Diane etc.

Section nine   Cheese (fromages)

Cheeses are normally presented to the diner on a cheese board or trolley. A good selection should be offered, consisting of cheeses from the categories listed below.

Service details

Most large cheeses are cut into pieces or wedges, although some cheeses such as Stilton and Brie etc. may be served whole or in halves. Cheeses in wooden boxes should be removed from the box and placed on the lid for ease of service. Cheeses should be in a ripe condition and served around room temperature. The cheese board may be attractively garnished with salad vegetables, e.g. cucumber, tomato, lettuce, cress or celery etc.

Accompaniments

Cruet, butter, selection of cheese biscuits, thin pieces of celery stalks in crushed ice and radishes. Caster sugar is also an accompaniment with cream cheeses, e.g. Petit Suisse.

Storage of cheese

Cheeses should be stored in a dark, airy room at a

temperature of between 8–10°C and a moisture percentage of 80–90%. Alternatively the cheeses may be wrapped in polythene or foil and kept in a chill or cold room; temperatures as above.

Various categories of cheese

Hard cheeses: Cheddar, Cheshire, Double Gloucester, Gruyère and Emmental etc.
Semi-hard cheeses: Caerphilly, Derby, Edam, Saint-Nectaire, Saint-Paulin and Tome etc.
Blue-vein cheeses: Danish Blue, Gorgonzola, Roquefort and Stilton etc.
Soft cheeses: Brie, Camembert, Demi-sel, Petit Suisse and Sainte-Maure etc.
Fromage blanc: A low-fat curd cheese which is commercially prepared in France. When not available a similar product may be prepared by thoroughly mixing together or liquidizing equal quantities of low-fat cottage cheese and low-fat natural yoghurt.

Section ten   Sandwiches

Points on sandwich preparation (plain sandwiches)

1 The use of very fresh bread should be avoided as it is likely to tear or become doughy when handled. Bread which is approximately twelve hours old should be used (does not apply to Vienna or crusty bread).
2 Ensure the butter is soft and spreads easily when the sandwiches have to be prepared.
3 Tinned or processed commodities, e.g. corned beef, sardines, tinned tongue and salmon etc., *do not require additional seasoning*. However, freshly cooked commodities, e.g. slices of roast chicken, roast beef, poached fish and boiled eggs etc., may require a little seasoning.
4 A sharp bread knife should be used to cut the sandwiches.
5 When sandwiches are to be used for '*packed meals*' it is advisable to cover the sandwiches with lettuce leaves (or 1 layer of dampened paper) to reduce staling.

Technical term

Round of sandwiches:
This is the term used when referring to a basic quantity of sandwiches. It consists of 2 white bread slices (square sandwich pan) or 4 small brown bread slices which will yield 4 triangles, squares or fingers of completed sandwich.

Production details:
1 Lay the required number of bread slices in rows along the table.

2 Spread with butter.
3 Spread or place the filling on alternate rows of bread along the table, i.e. rows 1, 3 and 5 etc.
4 Place the remaining slices of bread on top of the filled rows, i.e. rows 2, 4 and 6 etc.
5 Trim off the crusts and cut into four diagonally.
6 Place on a salver or plate lined with a dishpaper. Garnish if desired with cress, parsley, tomato or cucumber etc.

Note: When a large selection of sandwiches is required it is usual to prepare the different varieties in batches. The batches are placed on trays and covered with dampened paper or cloth to reduce staling. When the sandwiches are to be trayed, a round is taken from each batch and placed one on top of the other (to a height which is still suitable for cutting, 4–6 rounds high). When the sandwiches are cut this will produce a variety of neat triangles.

Sandwich spreads or fillings

These may be made with finely chopped, grated or puréed commodities, e.g. meat, fish, poultry, cheese and boiled eggs.

Production details: Bind the chopped or puréed ingredients with a little mayonnaise to produce a spreading mixture.

Various types of sandwich

Plain sandwiches
Triangular, square and finger shapes (white and brown bread)
Examples of fillings: tomato, tomato and lettuce, cucumber, cheese, cheese and chutney, boiled egg, roast beef, chicken or turkey, salmon and smoked salmon (brown bread).

Rolled sandwiches (usually brown bread)
Examples: asparagus rolls, salsify rolls and palm heart rolls etc.

Production details: Spread the bread with cream cheese and trim off the crusts. Place the selected vegetable at the bottom of each slice then roll up.

Pinwheel sandwiches (white and brown bread)
Examples: Various fillings e.g. pâté, cheese, chicken, tongue and sardine etc.

Production details:
1 Remove the side crusts and the crust from one end of a long unsliced pan loaf.
2 Cut down the crust at the remaining end to the bottom crust, but do not detach. This will act as a stop for the knife when slicing the bread.
3 Cut a thin, even slice along the loaf.

4 Spread the surface of the slice with butter then the
   filling (various fillings may be used on the same slice to
   give a variety of flavours and colours).
5 Roll up each slice tightly, similar to a swiss roll.
6 Cut into neat slices.

Hot toast sandwiches

These consist of a variety of ingredients, spread or placed
between two or more slices of toasted bread.

Production details
Base recipe: 2 slices toast and butter.
1 Toast the bread then lightly spread with butter. Also
   spread with mayonnaise if stated in the recipe.
2 Add the filling in layers on to one of the toast bases.
   Lightly season if appropriate.
3 Place the remaining slice of toast on top then trim off
   the crusts.
4 Serve the sandwich immediately on a salver or plate
   lined with a dishpaper.

Important: (a) Some sandwiches may have to be heated
through in the oven to ensure the correct temperature for
service, e.g. club sandwich.
(b) When cutting into triangles, cocktail sticks are
inserted into each corner of the sandwich just prior to
cutting. This will hold the sandwich in position when
serving.

Examples

Bookmaker sandwich	*Filling:* Grilled or sautéd *minute steak* spread with mustard.
Broadway sandwich	*Filling:* Mayonnaise, smoked salmon, shredded lettuce and slices of hard-boiled egg.
Club sandwich	*Filling:* Mayonnaise, shredded lettuce, sliced tomato, grilled rashers of streaky bacon, slices of cooked breast of chicken and final layer of shredded lettuce.
Double-decker sandwich Treble-decker sandwich Quadro-decker sandwich	These are multi-layered sandwiches; double-decker: 3 slices of buttered toast; treble: 4 slices, and quadro: 5 slices. Any suitable hot filling may be used. *Example fillings:* 1 layer of grilled streaky bacon, toast, 1 layer of grilled steak, toast, 1 layer of fried egg and top with toast spread with mustard.

Open sandwiches (smorgasbord)

These sandwiches are Scandinavian in origin and consist
of a base of white, brown or rye bread spread with butter
and garnished with any type of delicatessen, meats,
pickled fish, salads and vegetables etc. They are often
decorated with sliced tomato, radishes, cucumber, onion
rings, olives, gherkins, capers, chutney and pickles etc.

Examples
Smoked salmon, mayonnaise and crab meat.
Pickled herring, sieved hard-boiled egg and chopped
gherkins.
Sliced smoked ham, boiled egg, gherkins and onion rings.
Shredded lettuce, sliced hard-boiled egg, tomato, chicken
and mayonnaise.
Minced raw beef, raw egg, chopped horseradish, onion
rings and parsley.
Scrambled egg, sliced radishes, asparagus tips and sliced
gherkins.

Assessment exercise

1 Describe the knife technique to slice a carrot in a safe
   manner.
2 List six important points which are essential to the
   safe use of knives.
3 Describe how to chop an onion finely.
4 Define the following terms: bouquet garni; mirepoix;
   matignon; oignon clouté; concassé de tomates;
   brunoise; chiffonnade; macédoine; paysanne;
   julienne.
5 What is the common ratio of oil to vinegar when
   preparing vinaigrette?
6 What is a compound butter?
7 What is the difference between a simple salad and a
   compound salad?
8 Name four simple salads and four compound salads.
9 Explain how to prepare Bismarck herring and soused
   herring.
10 Describe the following sandwiches: pinwheel
   sandwich; bookmaker sandwich; club sandwich;
   treble-decker sandwich.

Chapter 4
Basic cold preparatory work II

One important aspect of the quality of a dish is the selection and basic preparation of the ingredients to be cooked. This is particularly the case when selecting butcher meats, poultry, game and fish.

Section one   Beef (boeuf)

Points on quality

The Meat and Livestock Commission (MLC) use the following grading system to indicate important points on quality:

Age of animal: The animal is at its best for eating between 1½ and 2 years but many animals are killed just under 1½ years for economic reasons. The symbol 'Y' is used for young animals and 'T' for mature animals.
Sex of animal: Flesh from the steer is considered best ('S'); followed by flesh from the heifer ('H' – young uncalved cow). Older animals produce tougher flesh and usually have higher fat contents. Bull meat ('B') is dark red in colour, while cow meat ('C') usually has oily, yellow fat with poorer conformation than younger animals.
Fat content: The fat should be creamy white in colour with a brittle texture. Joints such as sirloin and wing rib should have flecks of fat through the flesh (marbled). The fat covering of an animal is divided into five grades: 1 being the least fatty and 5 the most fatty. A good grade is 2. Symbol 'P' indicates patchy fat and 'U' excessive cod or udder fat.
Conformation: A well-fleshed animal, yielding a high meat content is most suitable. Again a 1–5 grading is used: 5 being the best grade and 1 the poorest grade.
Texture: The flesh should be firm and springy to the touch. There should not be excessive moisture or drip (fluid coming from the joint(s)) present.
Colour: The flesh should be a good red colour. A bright red colour may indicate a lack of conditioning and young meat. A deep red colour can indicate flesh from a mature animal – bull.
Smell: The flesh and fat should have a healthy smell with no unpleasant odours.

Hanging and conditioning

To ensure maximum flavour and tenderness, the flesh or carcase should be hung in a dry, well-ventilated atmosphere at a temperature of 2–3° C. Suggested times for conditioning: quarters – 10 to 14 days; sirloin – 2 to 3 weeks and rump – 3 to 4 weeks. Well-hung meat usually develops a dark-brown red colour, especially on the outer or cut surfaces.

Suggested order of dissection

A side of beef is divided into two quarters, i.e. forequarter and hindquarter. This is done between the wing ribs and fore ribs – between the tenth and eleventh ribs.

Forequarter
1   Remove the shank.
2   Remove the neck.
3   Remove brisket.
4   Remove flat ribs.
5   Remove fore ribs.
6   Remove middle ribs.
The remaining joint is the chuck.

Hindquarter
1   Remove suet fat and kidney.
2   Divide into two pieces between the rump and the top piece (this is the piece of leg containing the topside, thick flank, silverside and shin).
3   Remove the shin from the top piece.
4   Divide the top piece into thick flank, topside and silverside.
5   Remove the thin flank.
6   Remove the rump from the sirloin and wing rib.
7   Divide wing rib from sirloin.

Joints and cuts – hindquarter

Wing rib
1   Cut down between the eye of the meat and the flat piece of bone to the base of the backbone (A).
2   Remove the backbone along the base of the ribs with a saw or cleaver (B). This is called *to chine the joint*.

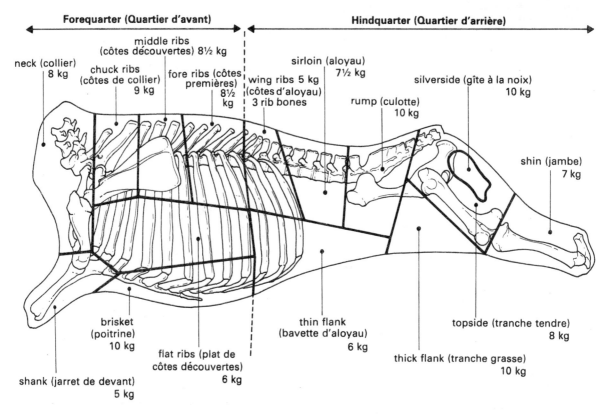

Figure 3 *Beef (boeuf) – 115 kg approximately*

3 If desired trim off the fat from the bottom of the rib to expose the three rib bones (C).
4 Remove the thick part of the sinew under the top layer of fat (D). Season under the fat.
5 Tie the joint securely. The bones which have been chined off should be tied back on to protect the joint when roasting.

Fore rib (prepare as wing rib)

Derivative cut from wing rib
Côte à l'os: This is a large rib steak with the bone attached similar to a lamb cutlet. It is served to two or more customers – weight 750 g and over.

Sirloin
Preparation of sirloin for roasting (whole):
1 Cut down between the eye of meat (A).
2 Cut between the fillet and chine bone (B).
3 Partly detach the contrefilet along the chine bone to allow for sawing or cleavering.
4 Saw or cleaver through the bone taking care not to damage the fillet.
5 Remove the chine bone.
6 Trim off the sinew and nerve as 4 above.

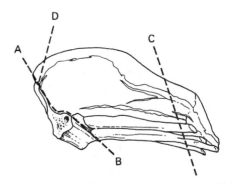

Figure 4 *Joints and cuts – wing rib*

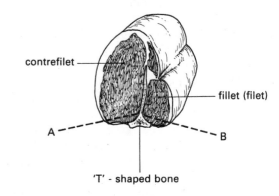

Figure 5 *Preparation of sirloin*

7   Trim off any excess fat.
8   Season under the flap of fat then replace the chine bone.
9   Tie securely with string.

Note: In many instances the fillet is removed prior to roasting because it is likely to overcook.

Boning out the sirloin:
1   Bone out the fillet.
2   Bone out the contrefilet.
3   Trim up the fillet removing the outer covering of sinew.
4   Trim up the contrefilet removing the sinew and nerve at the top layer of fat (same as step 4 D).
5   Trim off the bottom flap along the length of the contrefilet just after the eye of meat. Trim off any remaining sinew or excessive fat.

Derivative cuts from the sirloin:
(a)   *Cuts from the whole sirloin*:

'T'-bone steak:	A steak cut through the whole sirloin and containing a large piece of fillet. Often served to two people – 900 g approximately.
Porterhouse steak:	Same as above but is sometimes cut further up the sirloin and therefore contains a smaller piece of fillet.

(b)   *Cuts from the contrefilet*:

Entrecôte (sirloin steak):	A steak cut from the contrefilet – 250 g approximately (20 mm in thickness approximately).
Entrecôte double:	A large entrecôte steak – 500 g approximately.
Entrecôte minute:	A flattened (batted out) entrecôte.
Carpet bag steak:	A double entrecôte incised and stuffed with oysters (4–6 oysters). The incisions are sewn up with fat.

(c)   *Cuts from the fillet*:

*Chateaubriand:	A large fillet steak cut from the head of the fillet (A). Two or more portions – 500 g and over.
Filet (fillet steak):	Most of the fillet may be used for this steak – (A), (B) and (C). Weight 150 g and over.
Tournedos:	A neat round steak cut from the middle of the fillet (C). Each steak is usually tied with string (also sometimes back fat).

* The head of the fillet is boned out of the rump of beef.

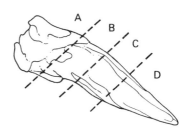

Figure 6   *Cuts from the fillet*

	Traditionally more than one tournedos would be served per portion. Weight – 150 g and over. Alternatively two or three 100 g steaks.
Médaillons and Bâtons:	These are small slices or stick shapes cut from the tail of the fillet (D).
Paillard:	This is a flattened-out fillet steak (escalope).

Rump
1   Carefully bone out from the hip bone.
2   Trim off excess fat and sinews.

Derivative cuts:

Rump steak:	Cut the rump into 20 mm slices approximately – 250 g approximately.
Point steak:	Cut as above but from the triangular piece of rump.

Thick flank
1   Bone out the thick flank from the leg.
2   Trim off excess fat and sinew and use as required.

Braising: Cut into suitably sized pieces and tie with string. Alternatively cut into steaks.

Topside
1   Carefully bone out the aitchbone and separate from the silverside.
2   Trim off excess fat and sinew.

Braising and roasting: Cut into suitably sized pieces and tie with string. May also be cut into steaks for braising.

Silverside
1   Carefully remove the round bone.
2   Trim off excess fat and sinew.

Boiled joints: Tie securely with string.

Shin
1   Remove the bone.
2   Trim off all the sinews and any excess fat.

Methods of cooking suitable for the various joints

Name of joint	Methods of cooking	Example dishes
Forequarter		
Shank	Boiling and stewing	Stock, consommé and stews etc.
Neck	Stewing	Stews and minced beef etc.
Chuck ribs	Stewing, pot roasting and casserole cooking	Stews, braises and pies etc.
Flat ribs	Stewing	Stews and minced beef. Also sausages
Brisket	Boiling and stewing	Boiled brisket (salted and unsalted) stews, minced beef. Also sausages
Middle ribs	Roasting, braising and pot roasting	Roast beef, braised beef and casseroled beef
Fore ribs	Roasting	Roast beef
Hindquarter		
Wing rib	Roasting	Roast beef. Also côte à l'os – see preparation of wing rib
Sirloin	Roasting. Also grilling and frying when boned out	Roast sirloin. Also entrecôtes, 'T'-bone steaks and minute steaks etc. – see preparation of sirloin
Rump	Roasting and braising	Roast and braised rump. Also rump and point steaks
Thin flank	Boiling and stewing	Stews and pies etc. Also sausages
Thick flank	Boiling, stewing and braising	Boiled beef, stews and braised beef
Silverside	Boiling and stewing	Boiled silverside (salted and unsalted) and stews
Topside	Roasting, braising and stewing	Roast beef, braised beef, beef olives and stews etc.
Shin	Boiling and stewing	Stocks, consommés and stews etc.

Preparation of beef offal

See page 65.

Section two   Veal (veau)

Veal is the flesh of the calf which is considered to be at its best when obtained from an animal 3 months old approximately.

Points on quality

Age of animal: Flesh from the very young calf (2–3 weeks = bobby calf) is usually avoided because of its poor yield and tendency to be tough and insipid. A milk-fed calf (fed veal) 2–3 months old produces the finest eating quality.
Fat content: There should be a thin covering of creamy-white fat.
Conformation: The joints should be reasonably well-fleshed although the bones are large in relation to the flesh (big on the bone). The bones should be pinkish white and comparatively soft and porous when broken.
Texture: The flesh should be firm in texture with a fine grain. Cut surfaces should be slightly moist with no sign of stickiness.
Colour: The flesh should be a very pale pink colour. Red coloured flesh indicates that the animal has been fed on solid food or grazed.

Hanging and conditioning

Veal is usually only hung for a very short period after slaughter (4–7 days). It should be hung in a dry, well ventilated atmosphere at 2–3°C.

Suggested order of dissection (side of veal)

1   Remove short forequarter.
2   Remove the shoulder.
3   Remove the breast and divide the remaining piece into neck and low cutlets.

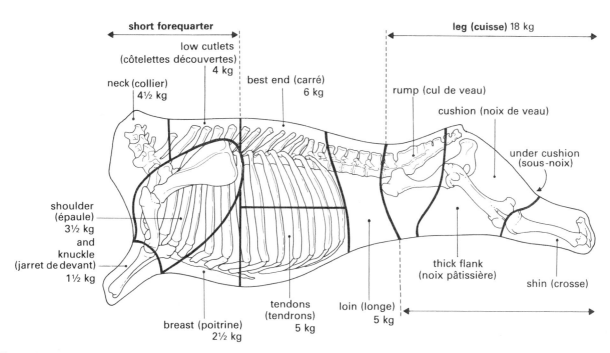

Figure 7 *Veal (veau) – 50 kg approximately*

4 Remove the best end from the hindquarter. Cut off the bottom rib piece or tendons.
Note: The fillet of veal may be boned out before removing the best end.
5 Remove the loin. This leaves the whole leg of veal.

Dissection of leg
1 Remove shin.
2 Remove aitch bone.
3 Trim off outer fat.
4 Bone out the joints following the seams between the joints.

Note: The rump is not removed when boning leg.

Joints and cuts

Leg
When boned out, each of the joints or large muscles is trimmed to remove the sinew and fat, i.e. cushion, under cushion and thick flank. The joints can then be coated with oil and kept covered in a chill. Alternatively they can be frozen.

Derivative cuts from the cushion, under cushion and thick flank
Escalopes: Cut slices across the grain of the muscle then bat out (flatten) with a cutlet bat between polythene. This should produce a large, very thin slice – 150 mm diameter and 2 mm in thickness (100 g approximately).
Grenadins: Cut small thick slices across the muscle i.e. 75–100 mm diameter and 20 mm in thickness 150–200 g

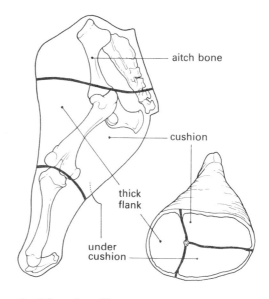

Figure 8 *Dissection of leg*

approximately. The slices are then *larded* (see page 31) with strips of pork fat.
Fricandeau: This is a large grenadin. Cut a thick slice *along* the cushion e.g. 175 mm in length and 20 mm in thickness (250–400 g approximately). Lard the slice with pork fat.
Médaillons: These are small round slices. Cut neat circular slices across the grain of the muscle – 50 mm diameter and 3–4 mm in thickness (30 g approximately).

Piccatas: These are small escalopes. Prepare as escalopes above but half the size, i.e. 75 mm diameter approximately.

Shin

(a) Remove the bone then use flesh as required.
(b) Cut and saw into thick slices (25 mm approximately). This is done when braising the shin – Osso bucco.

Preparation of whole leg of veal for roasting (small leg)

See page 63.

Preparation of loin, best end and shoulder

See page 63.

Calf's head (tête de veau)

1 Cut an incision down the front of the head.
2 Bone out the head from the incision. Follow round the skull and remove the flesh and skin in one piece.
3 Remove the tongue.
4 Carefully cut off the top of the skull with a saw or cleaver. This should expose but not damage the brain. Remove the brain and soak in cold salted water. The membrane round the brain should be removed and the blood washed off. Store the brain in cold salted water.
5 Wash the flesh in cold water then store in water with a little lemon juice added.
6 Prior to cooking the flesh is blanched and refreshed then cut into squares – 30 mm approximately.

Preparation of veal offal

See page 65.

Section three   Lamb and mutton (agneau et mouton)

Points on quality

Age of animal: Lamb is the term used to define an animal which is under 12 months old at the time of slaughter. Various terms are used to describe the type of lamb, e.g. milk lamb (suckling) and grass lamb. After 1 year old the term mutton must be used. Sheep at 1½ years old which have not lambed (or become pregnant) – maiden ewes – and castrated males of the same age (1½–2 years) – hoggets – produce good quality mutton.

Sex of animal: This is not very important in lamb as the animals are slaughtered before sex characteristics are markedly developed. As stated above, maiden ewes and hoggets both produce good quality mutton.

Fat content: The fat should be firm and creamy-white in colour and be evenly distributed across the carcase. Like beef, the MLC grade the fat content in five grades – 1 being the leanest and 5 the fattest. Most meat falls into categories 2, 3 and 4.

Conformation: Like beef a well-fleshed animal is most suitable. However the MLC grading is not the same as for beef; there are only four grades, three of which are indicated by symbols 'Z' very poor, 'C' poor and 'E' very good conformation. Average conformation is not indicated by a symbol.

Texture, colour and smell: The flesh should be firm and of fine texture. Lamb flesh should be a dull red colour and mutton flesh a dull brownish-red. Lamb and mutton flesh should have a pleasant smell with no undesirable odours.

Various joints and suitable methods of cooking

Name of joint	Methods of cooking	Example of dishes/cuts
Short forequarter		
Shoulder	Roasting, braising and stewing	Roast and braised shoulder (often stuffed). Veal stew
Low cutlets	Stewing	Veal stew (ragoût and blanquette)
Neck	Stewing	Veal stew (ragoût and blanquette)
Breast	Stewing and roasting (second class)	Veal stew (ragoût and blanquette)
Hindquarter		
Shin	Boiling, stewing and braising	Stock, jelly, stews and Osso bucco
Cushion	Roasting, frying and braising	Roast cushion, braised cushion, escalopes and grenadins etc.
Under cushion	Same as cushion	Same as cushion
Thick flank	Same as cushion	Same as cushion
Rump	Same as cushion	Same as cushion
Loin	Roasting, frying and braising	Roast loin, braised loin, fried veal chops and noisettes etc.
Best end	Roasting, frying and braising	Roast best end, fried veal cutlets, braised best end

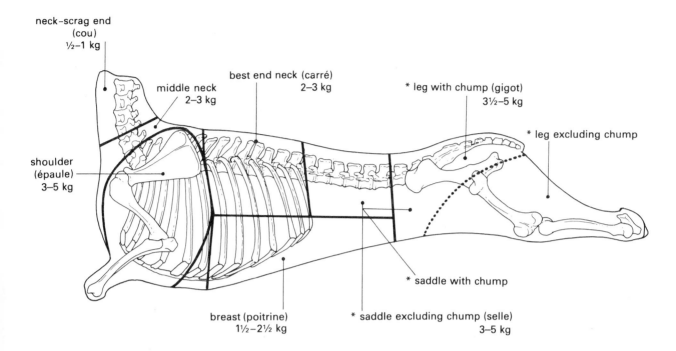

Figure 9 *Lambs and mutton (agneau et mouton) – carcases 15–25 kg*

Hanging and conditioning

The carcase should be hung for a period of 2–7 days depending on temperature (7 days at 2°C). Most carcases are sold to the butcher within 2 days of slaughter.

Suggested order of dissection (carcase of lamb)

1 Remove the short forequarter from the carcase, i.e. scrag end neck, middle neck and shoulder.
2 Remove the shoulders.
3 Divide the remaining piece of forequarter into middle neck and scrag end neck.
4 Remove the breasts.
5 Remove the best ends.
6 Divide the saddle from the legs.

Joints and cuts

Preparation of saddle, leg of lamb for roasting
See page 63.

Preparation of best end and shoulder
See page 63.

Preparation of offal
See page 65.

Various joints and suitable methods of cooking

Name of joint	Methods of cooking	Example dishes/cuts
Leg	Roasting, frying and grilling	Roast leg, grilled gigot chops
Saddle	Roasting, frying and grilling	Roast saddle, grilled loin chops and noisettes etc.
Best end	Roasting, frying and grilling	Roast best end and grilled cutlets etc.
Middle neck	Roasting (second class) and stewing	Roast lamb and navarin (stew)
Shoulder	Roasting and stewing	Roast shoulder and navarin
Scrag end neck	Boiling and stewing	Mutton broth and Irish stew etc.

Section four   Pork (porc)

Points on quality

Age of animal: Pigs are usually slaughtered at a young age, therefore age is not as important as for other animals. A very young pig is called a suckling pig (cochon de lait).

Sex of animal: Like age above, because immature animals are slaughtered, sex is not an important factor.

Fat content: The fat should be reasonably firm and white in colour. The quantity of fat on the carcase is important because excessive fat means a poor lean content. The MLC grade carcases according to a measurement taken on the long loin above the last rib bone. The depth of fat at 65 mm from the backbone (or at 45 mm and 80 mm) is measured in millimetres and stamped on the trotter of the hind leg.

Conformation: Good conformation is indicated as above.

Texture and colour: The flesh should be firm with a fine texture. It should be pale pink in colour without excessive moisture on cut surfaces. The skin should also be smooth. Bones should be small, fairly pliable and pinkish.

Smell: Pleasant with no undesirable odours.

Hanging and conditioning

Pork requires very little hanging. A period of 4–7 days (from slaughter, distribution and sale to catering establishment) is sufficient to condition the meat.

Suggested order of dissection

1   Remove the head then split the carcase into two sides.
2   Remove the legs. Cut off the trotters (hind feet).
3   Remove the shoulders. Cut off the trotters.
4   Separate the belly from the loin.

Joints and cuts

Preparation of leg of pork for roasting
See page 63.

Loin: roasting on the bone: Saw off the botton of the chine bone – see removal of chine bone for wing rib (B), page 54. Trim off excess fat and sinew then score through the skin in strips.

Boned loin: Remove the filet mignon. Bone out then trim off excess fat and sinew. Score through the skin in strips.

Note: The loin may be roasted without the fillet in a flat piece or the fillet placed inside and the joint rolled and tied with string (a rolled joint is sometimes stuffed).

Chops: Trim off excess fat and sinew then remove the skin. Cut into chops (15–20 mm in thickness). Chop off excess bone and neatly trim the fat.

Pork fillet: Remove fat and sinews in the same manner as beef or veal fillets.

Pork escalopes: Best quality escalopes of pork are prepared from pork fillets.

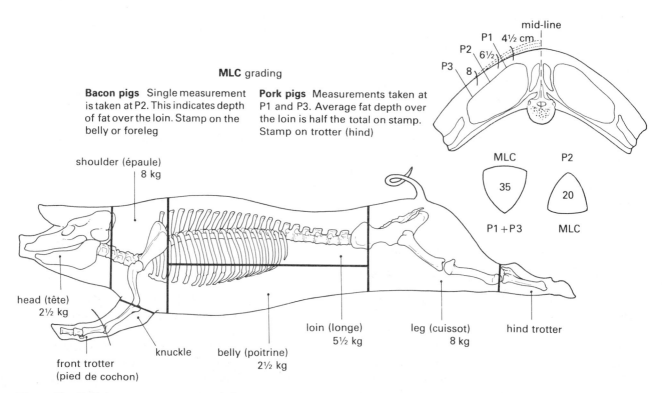

Figure 10   *Pork (porc) – side of pork: 26½ kg*

Cut each trimmed fillet at a slant into two or three pieces depending on size. Flatten into escalopes under polythene with a cutlet bat – see various escalope style cuts on page 57.

Belly: Remove the rib bones. Neatly trim and remove the skin. *Boiling*:   Roll up the joint and tie with string. May be stuffed then rolled.

Shoulder: Bone out the shoulder removing rib bones, back bone, shoulder blade and shoulder bone. Remove excess fat and sinew and score the skin. Add seasoning then roll and tie the joint. May be stuffed then rolled.

Note: This is a large shoulder which may be divided into spare rib and shoulder.

Trotters: Blanch the trotters in boiling water for 5 minutes then refresh in cold water. Remove the hairs by scraping with the back of a knife then rewash in cold water. Split in half lengthwise.

Head: Bone out as for calf's head or split in half and remove the tongue and brain.

Preparation of pork offal
See page 65.

Various joints and suitable methods of cooking

Name of joint	Methods of cooking	Example dishes/cuts
Trotters	Boiling. Sometimes grilled after boiling	Boiled trotters
Leg	Roasting and boiling	Roast leg. Boiled leg
Loin	Roasting, frying and grilling	Roast loin, grilled and sautéd chops
Belly	Boiling	Pies and sausages. Also boiled belly of pork and pease pudding
Shoulder	Roasting and boiling	Roast shoulder, pies and sausages
Head	Boiling	Brawn

Section five   Bacon and ham (lard et jambon)

Bacon is the name given to a side of pork from a 'bacon pig' which has been cured by salting in brine or cured by salting in brine and then smoked.

Gammon and ham

(a)   A gammon is a hind leg cut from a side of bacon. It is usually cut square across the aitch bone.

(b)   A ham is the hind leg cut from a side of pork. Hams may be cured 'dry' in salt and saltpetre or 'wet' in brine. Some hams are 'smoked' to varying degrees and then left to mature. A ham is usually cut with a round end (around the aitch bone).

Types of bacon

Examples of two common cures in bacon are Wiltshire and Ayrshire.

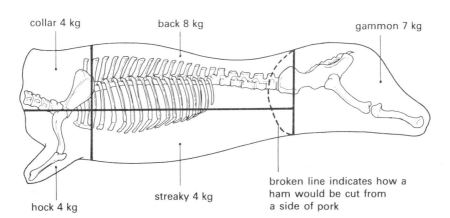

Figure 11   *Side of bacon – 27 kg approximately*

Wiltshire cure: This is the whole side of pig with skin on and bone in. It may be smoked or unsmoked (green).
Ayrshire: This bacon is cured by the joint. The joints are skinned, boned and rolled and tied with string.

Points on quality

Fat content: The fat should be firm and white with a slight tinge of pink. In addition, the rind should be smooth, thin and flexible.
Conformation: There should be a good lean content on the prime joints, e.g. back and leg etc., without an excessive fat content.
Texture: The lean should be firm and dry. There should be very little sign of mould on inside surfaces.
Smell: There should be no unpleasant smell, especially at shoulder pockets or bone joints.

Storage

Bacon and ham should be stored in a cool, dry, well ventilated atmosphere (8°C approximately).

Joints and cuts

Gammon Whole gammon for boiling: Soak the gammon for 12 hours approximately.
Whole boned gammon for boiling: Bone out the aitch bone then remove the leg bone to the shank. (Hollow out with the point of the boning knife. Roll and tie with string.)
Gammon steaks: Cut fairly thick slices across the gammon (15–25 mm approximately). The thickness of the slices will vary depending on the part of the gammon being cut. Very large slices should not be cut across the whole piece unless two or more neatly shaped steaks can be obtained.
Back: Remove the bones and rind then use as required, e.g. cut into rashers.
Streaky: Same as back.
Hock: Remove leg bone. The bottom shank may also be removed. Tie with string. *Note*: The joint may be left unboned.
Collar: Remove the bones, i.e. shoulder blade and neck. Tie with string. *Note*: Remove the rind when the joint has to be sliced into rashers.

Various joints and suitable methods of cooking

Name of joint	Methods of cooking	Example dish/cut
Gammon	Boiling, frying and grilling	Boiled gammon and grilled gammon steaks
Back	Frying and grilling	Grilled bacon rashers
Streaky	Same as back	Same as back
Hock	Boiling and grilling	Boiled bacon and grilled rashers
Collar	Same as hock	Same as hock

Section six General preparation of joints of butcher meats and furred game

Preparation of large fillets for roasting (i.e. beef and veal)

Trim off the sinew but leave on any fat which is not covering sinew – mostly at the bottom and sides of the fillet. The fringe meat or chain running along the side of the fillet may also be removed. Lard with pork fat if desired then tie with string.

Preparation of large fillets for steaks

Prepare as above but leave on a minimum of fat or trim off all the fat. Cut the fillet as required – see cuts from a fillet of beef on page 55.

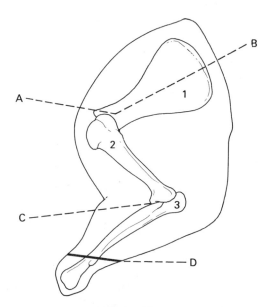

Figure 12 *Preparation of shoulder*

Preparation of shoulder for roasting

Lamb, mutton, veal and venison. See also shoulder of pork – page 61.

1 Feel for the ball and socket joint then make an incision with the tip of the boning knife between the ball and socket, (A).
2 Bend back the shoulder to dislocate the joint.
3 Bone out the shoulder blade (1) as follows: Cut down the centre of the blade bone (B) then cut across each side to expose the bone. Carefully bone out the top of the bone clear of the ball joint and down to the ridge on the inside of the blade bone. If this is done correctly the blade bone should now be able to be pulled out down to the bottom 20 mm. Cut free with a knife.
4 Bone out the top shoulder bone (2).
5 Trim the end of the knuckle to leave a piece of clean bone (30 mm length approximately), (D). Alternatively bone out the knuckle.
6 Remove excess fat and any small blood vessels.
7 Season inside then roll up and tie with string.

Note: The shoulder may be stuffed then rolled.

Preparation of leg for roasting or boiling

Lamb, mutton, veal, pork and venison.

1 Cut down along the aitch bone and through the ball and socket joint, (A).
2 Bone out the aitch bone.
3 Trim the bottom knuckle and bone (bottom 40 mm approximately) then saw off the knuckle leaving a piece of clean bone, (B).
4 Remove any excess fat then season the inside.
5 Tie with string.

Preparation of leg chops (gigot chops)

Cut through the centre of the leg to produce slices or chops with a small piece of centre bone.

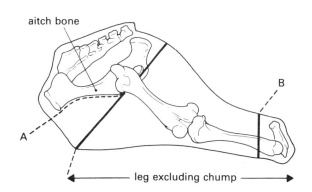

Figure 13 Preparation of leg

Preparation of chump chops

Cut across the chump section of the leg (see above) to produce thick slices with a varied bone content.

Preparation of a saddle for roasting

Lamb, mutton, veal and venison.

1 Pull off the skin.
2 Trim the flaps to neatly fit the underside.
3 Remove the kidneys, excess fat and sinews.
4 Neatly score the top fat in a criss-cross fashion.
5 Season the inside then tie with string.

Note: Saddles of venison may be completely trimmed of all skin, fat and sinew and then larded prior to cooking.
Saddle with chump: When the saddle has the chump attached, proceed as above but split the tail into two halves, roll down each half towards the saddle and secure with a small skewer. Cover with oiled paper or tinfoil for protection when cooking.

Preparation of loins

Lamb, mutton, veal and venison. See also loin of pork, page 60.
Prepare as above then split the saddle down through the backbone with a cleaver into two loins.

Single loin chops: Cut across the loin to produce chops. Single loin chops have little or no filet mignon. Equivalent beef cut is Porterhouse steaks.
Double loin chops: Cut the loin into chops. Double loin chops contain a full piece of filet mignon. Equivalent beef cut is T-bone steaks.
Barnsley chops (crown chops): These chops are cut across an unsplit saddle, i.e. two loin chops attached to the backbone.

Note: Loin chops may be prepared with a piece of kidney inserted back into position and secured with a small skewer or cocktail stick.

Preparation of best ends

Lamb, mutton, veal and venison.

1 Cut down each side of the backbone along the length of the best end, (A).
2 Using a cleaver or saw, cut each side of the chine bone to remove the best ends; cut at an angle and not into the flesh, (B).
3 Pull off the skin. Start at the front end of the breast and pull downwards and across. *Note*: When skinning veal, venison and poorer qualities of lamb and mutton (especially poorly-stored mutton or lamb) use the point of a small knife to loosen the skin.

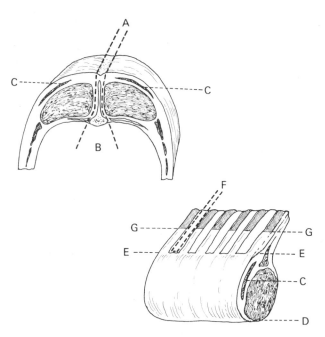

Figure 14   *Preparation of best ends*

4   Remove the tip of the blade bone (if present) with a small knife, (C).
5   Remove the tough sinew (sometimes called the camel's hair) which runs along the top inside of the fat, (D).
6   Cut across the fat into the rib bones parallel to the eye of the meat. Cut a distance of between 25–40 mm above the eye of the meat, (E). Remove the fat.
7   Cut out the fat from between the ribs, (F). Clean the rib bones both at the front and back.
8   Place the ribs of the best end, flat down on a butcher's block and *carefully* shorten with a cleaver to 30 mm approximately, (G).

Preparation of a best end for roasting

Prepare as above then lightly score the fat with the point of a knife in a criss-cross fashion.

Note: For lamb and mutton traditionally a best end is cut to six rib bones, but it is common practice to use eight rib bone best ends. The disadvantage with more than six ribs is that the rib bones narrow inwards changing the shape and the piece of blade bone increases substantially producing a deep flap in the best end.

Preparation of cutlets (côtelettes, lamb and mutton)

Divide evenly between each rib bone then lightly flatten and trim.

Double cutlet   (côtelette double, lamb and mutton):
Cut double the thickness of a single cutlet, i.e. two rib bones.

Butcher's cutlet   (côtelette bouchère, lamb and mutton):
Prepare the best end as stated but do not trim off the fat or clean the ribs, i.e. omit steps (6), (7) and (8). Divide between each rib bone producing untrimmed cutlets.
Note: When a best end has seven or eight ribs, it is usually necessary to cut between the larger spaces of the seventh and eighth ribs producing cutlets with no rib bones; this is a further disadvantage with a long best end – see previous note.

Preparation of noisettes

Lamb, mutton, veal and venison. Bone out a loin or best end of the appropriate commodity (traditionally the loin is used) then trim up the eye of meat leaving a small triangular edge of fat. Cut into slices which are 15–20 mm in thickness.

Preparation of rosettes

Bone out a loin as for noisettes above but leave a well trimmed flap of fat which can surround the eye of meat. Roll the flap of fat round the meat and tie with string – one circle of string per rosette. Cut between each circle of string to form the rosettes (same thickness as noisettes).

Preparation of rabbit or hare

Season of the year: Hares: August to March.
Rabbits: September to March.
Signs of quality: Young animals which are well-fleshed should be selected. Although it is not easy to determine the age, the ears of young animals should tear fairly easily. In addition the bottom jaw of a rabbit should break quite easily, whereas the claws of hares should be short and also break quite easily.
Storage: Hang by the forelegs in a cool place. Hare is usually hung for 7–9 days to develop a gamey flavour.

1   Remove the bottom legs at the first joint, (A).
2   Pinch up the fur and skin at the middle of the leg, (B), and slit with the point of a knife. Insert the fingers and manipulate to remove the flesh from the skin. Pull the leg out of the fur through the slit.
3   Repeat the same procedure with the other leg then cut off the tail between the flesh and skin, (C).
4   Hold the back legs with one hand and pull the skin down off the body to the forelegs.
5   Remove the skin from the forelegs then pull up to the ears.
6   Cut off the ears, (D), then pull the skin over the head.
7   Make an incision in the lower belly up to the start of the rib cage, (E).
8   Remove the intestines into a basin. *Note*:   When drawing a hare *do not puncture* the membrane at the chest cavity.

9　Place a bowl under the chest cavity (especially with hare) and puncture the chest membrane removing the liver, heart and lungs and allowing the blood to run into the bowl. Place aside any intestines to be used.

10　Cut off the head.

Preparation of hare or rabbit for roasting

1　Wipe and clean then neatly trim the bottom of the rib cage and any excessive opening flaps.

2　Remove the membrane and sinew which runs down the back and along part of the underside (this is removed with a small knife in the same manner as trimming a fillet of beef). This applies mostly to hare.

3　Lard with strips of pork fat (if desired) and bard with pork fat across the back. Tie with string to secure the barding fat.

Preparation of hare or rabbit for stews, sautés and pies (cut into joints)

1　Remove the legs from the body; if the front legs are very small, leave them attached to the forequarter.

2　Cut the legs into even-sized pieces, e.g. divide the front legs in two and the rear legs into three or four depending on size.

3　Trim off the rib cage up to the flesh. Trim off the sinew and membrane, see 2 above.

4　Cut off the forequarter and divide into two depending on size.

5　Divide the saddle into 4–6 pieces depending on size.

Section seven　Preparation of offal

Liver　(lamb, mutton, veal and ox)

Remove any tubes and gristle and the thin outer skin. Cut at a slant into thin slices (10 mm in thickness approximately).

Kidneys　(lamb and mutton)

Preparation for grilling

1　Remove the outer skin then cut into the middle and open out.

2　Trim the centre fat if necessary then insert two cocktail sticks or small skewers to keep the kidney open when cooking (if not using a grilling wire).

Preparation for sauté

1　Remove the skin then cut in half. Trim the centre fat if necessary.

2　Cut at a slant into neat pieces, e.g. two or three pieces per half kidney depending on size.

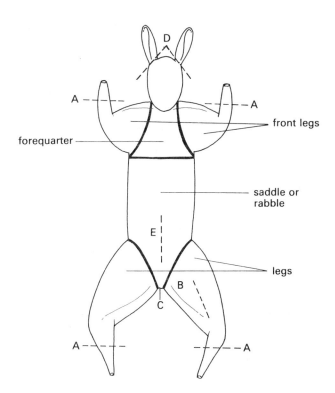

Figure 15　*Preparation of hare*

Kidneys　(beef and veal)

Remove the skin then cut in half lengthwise through the centre fat. Remove the fat and gristle then cut into slices or dice.

Tripe　(beef)

In Britain, tripe is usually purchased trimmed and blanched, i.e. *dressed*. Dressed tripe only requires to be cut into suitable pieces, e.g. 20 mm dice.

Sweetbreads　(lamb, mutton and veal)

Soak the sweetbreads in cold, salty water if they contain excessive blood (2–3 hours). Wash under cold running water.

Blanch and trim prior to cooking, see page 212.

Brains　(lamb, mutton and veal)

Soak the brains in cold salty water to remove any blood then wash under cold running water. Remove the membrane and rewash.

Tongue　(lamb, mutton, veal and ox)

Remove any bone and gristle from the back of the tongue then wash in cold water. Soak pickled tongues in cold water for 4–6 hours prior to cooking.

Section eight   Poultry and feathered game

Poultry   (volaille)

This is the term for all domestic birds reared for eating.

Chicken

Chicken is classified according to size and age as follows:

Single spring chicken   (poussin)
    400 g each approximately
Double spring chicken   (poussin double)
    800 g each approximately
Small chicken   (poulet de grain)
    1¼ kg each approximately
Medium chicken   (poulet à la reine)
    1½ kg each approximately
Large chicken   (poularde)
    2 kg each approximately
Capon   (chapon)
    3½ kg each approximately
Boiling fowl   (poule)
    Various sizes

Note: The French term for chicken is poulet. However the term *volaille* is sometimes used to describe suprêmes of chicken etc., but *never* for the whole chicken.

Quality:
1   Lower tip of the breast bone should be pliable. This is a sign the bird is young and is therefore suitable for dry-heat methods of cookery.
2   Good conformation, i.e. firm plump breast and full fleshy legs.
3   Creamy-white skin which is not dried out or torn.
4   Sweet smell.

See general preparation.

Duck and duckling   (canard and caneton)

Available all year round. Best between March–August. Sizes vary depending on the type of duck and duckling, e.g. 1½–2 kg each.

Quality:
1   The upper beak should be able to be broken between the fingers and the lower beak should be flexible.
2   Good conformation without excessive fat under the skin.
3   Sweet smell.

See general preparation.

Goose   (oie)

Available all year round. *Size*:   5–7 kg.

Quality: See duck above. See general preparation.

Turkey   (dinde, dindon and dindonneau)

Fresh turkey is available from September to March. *Sizes and weights vary considerably*:   3–25 kg. See general preparation.

Guinea fowl   (pintade)

Fresh guinea fowl is available from February to June. *Size*:   1–1½ kg. See general preparation.

Feathered game (gibier de plume)

Although it is traditional practice to serve fresh game birds killed in season, most game birds can be purchased frozen in graded sizes.

Grouse   (coq de bruyère)

Available from 12th August to 9th December. *Size*: 300–450 g each.

Quality: Short spurs which are fairly smooth.
Important: Unlike most game birds, grouse is eaten freshly killed and is not hung prior to cooking. See general preparation.

Partridge   (perdreau)

Available from September to January. *Size*:   250–500 g each.

Quality: Young birds have a fairly weak wish bone and beak and smooth legs.
Hanging time: 3–6 days. See general preparation.

Pheasant   (faisan)

Available from October to February. *Size*:   1–2 kg each.

Quality: Young birds have smooth legs and flexible breast bone.
Hanging time: 5–8 days. See general preparation.

Snipe and woodcock   (bécassine and bécasse)

Size: Snipe   100 g each approximately;
Woodcock   200–300 g each.
Snipe available from September to December.
Woodcock available from September to January.
Hanging time: 3–4 days. See general preparation.

Section nine   General preparation of poultry and feathered game

Plucking

Pluck the feathers out of the skin in the opposite direction to which they lie with a wet thumb and forefinger. Small pens or the bases of feathers which are difficult to grip with the fingers can usually be pulled out with a small knife; grip the pen between the back of the blade and the thumb.

Singeing

Hold the bird at the head and feet and pass over a small gas or spirit flame. Singe off the small fine feathers and hairs but do not burn or blacken the skin.

Removing leg sinews (turkeys – chicken may also have the leg sinews removed)

1 Break the bones of the bottom legs just above the claws; use the back of a cleaver and do not cut through the skin and scales.
2 Twist the claws to detach the bone and wind the sinews like a rope. Untwist and this should expose the sinews.
3 Draw out the sinews as follows:
    (a) Place the claw into a V-shaped mounted bracket and pull downwards on the top of the leg just under the exposed sinews.
    (b) Insert a *blunted* butcher's hook round each sinew and pull out one at a time.

Drawing and gutting (all birds except snipe and woodcock)

1 Cut a slit along the skin at the back of the neck down to the head. Cut off the head.
2 Remove the neck from the slit leaving a broad flap suitable for holding in the stuffing – trim if very long.
3 Detach the windpipe and crop bag.
4 Cut off the neck close to the body.
5 Push the forefinger into the neck opening and loosen the intestines from the breast cavity.
6 Turn the bird round and cut off the vent ring.
7 Insert the forefinger through the vent opening and loosen the intestines from the cavity walls as before.
8 Draw out the intestines. Ensure the fingers are placed right at the back of the intestines; pulling from the middle of the intestines may burst the gall bladder and cause bitterness. Care should be taken not to burst the vent opening when pulling out the intestines.
9 Use the forefinger to remove the lungs which are recessed into the top base of the carcase.
10 Wipe clean with a cloth. Wash in cold water if the intestines have burst when drawing and dry with a cloth.
11 Remove the liver from the intestines then carefully detach the gall bladder – *do not burst*.
12 Remove heart and kidneys.
13 Slit the gizzard and remove any detachable lining and stomach contents. Trim and wash.
14 Thoroughly wash all boards and equipment.

Snipe and woodcock

1 Prepare as above but leave on the head and long beak (to be used for trussing). Remove the eyes and clean up the neck and skull.
2 Remove the gall bladder, large intestine and gizzard but leave in the remaining intestines (traditional practice when roasting).

Trussing and tying (all birds except snipe and woodcock)

Trussing (French one-string method)

Preliminary procedure:
1 Remove the wish bone using a small knife and fingers.
2 Remove wing tips.
3 Cut off all the spurs and toes but leave the middle toes long, i.e. cut off the nails only.
4 If the legs are to be cleaned, dip them in boiling water then rub off the scales with a dry cloth.
5 Season the bird inside.

Trussing with needle and string:
1 Place string through the eye of the needle.
2 Place the bird on its back then push the legs down firmly into shape.
3 Insert the needle into the thigh just under the drumstick.
4 Pass the needle through the inside of the bird and come out through the wing bone.
5 Pull the neck flap over the back of the bird (enclosing any stuffing) then sew down on to and across the carcase and out through the opposite wing bone.
6 Turn the needle round and go back through the carcase and come out through the opposite leg at a similar position to entry in the first leg. This means the string will have crossed over making an X shape within the carcase.
7 Loop over the leg and pierce the needle back into the carcase under the leg and cross through to come out at a point directly above the first position.
8 Remove the needle and loop the string over the leg. This will pull both legs down and into position when the string is tightened.
9 Make a slip knot and tighten.
10 When the knot has been tightened enough to produce a neat shape, lock the knot by twisting the string round the thumb and forefinger to form a loop, pull the string through and tighten.

Trussing for roasting:
Proceed as stated keeping the claws in a straight position or pointing slightly upwards.

Trussing for boiling or poêler:
Bend back the bottom of the legs (and claws) then loop the string over to hold secure.

Two-string method

This is simpler than the one-string to learn but has the disadvantage of requiring two separate strings.

1 Insert the needle through the middle of the left leg and cross over to the same point on the opposite leg (see spot which is indicated on the roasting chicken in Figure 16).
2 Turn over and pierce the wing bone then sew down the neck flap coming out through the opposite wing bone.
3 Make a slip knot and tighten into shape. Lock the slip knot.
4 Draw the legs down into shape by inserting the needle through the base of the carcase and loop over the legs (return back through the carcase). Tie securely.

Tying a bird

1 Proceed as for trussing with the preliminary procedures and step 2 for trussing.
2 Pass the string under the carcase and legs.
3 Pull the string up over the legs and twist round both ends.
4 Bring both ends of the string downwards and round under the claws (with the loop between the claws) then tighten to draw the legs into the carcase).
5 Turn the bird over onto its breast then bring the string along the side of the leg and across the wing bone. Pull the string across the slot betwen the neck stump and carcase (this will hold the neck skin and any stuffing).
6 Bring the second string along the other leg and over the wing bone in the same manner to meet the first string.
7 Make the slip knot and tighten. Lock the slip knot.

Note: This is a very good method of tying a bird as it produces a nice shape with a well-raised breast.

Snipe and woodcock

Pull the head along the side of the bird and secure the legs with the beak.

Barding birds for roasting

The breast of birds (especially game birds) may be covered with strips of bacon or pork fat to prevent excessive drying-out of the flesh when roasting. The fat which is tied on with string is removed prior to service.

Jointing a bird or cutting for sauté (four portions; traditional practice)

1 Carry out the basic preparation, i.e. pluck, singe, gut then remove the wish bone.
2 Remove the legs then cut in half through the joint, (A).
3 Cut off the top knuckle pieces, (B).
4 Cut off the bottom knuckle of the drumsticks, (C),

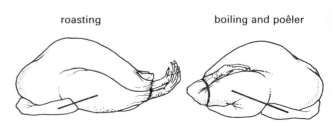

roasting   boiling and poêler

Figure 16 *Trussing for roasting and boiling or poêler*

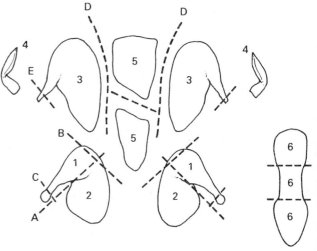

1 Drumstick (pilon de cuisse)
2 Thigh (gras de cuisse)
3 Wing (aile)
4 Winglet (aileron)
5 Breast (blanc)
6 Carcase (carcasse)

Figure 17 *Jointing a bird*

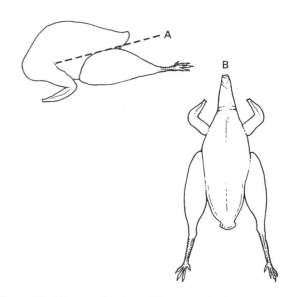

Figure 18 *Preparation for grilling – toad style*

then push down the bone at the top of the drumstick to expose a clean piece of bottom leg bone.

5   Cut off the winglets.
6   Remove the wings by cutting parallel to the breast bone and down through the wing joints close to the carcase, (D) (ensure that the wings and breast will produce four similar-sized portions). Use the top of the cook's knife and carefully separate the back end of the wing from the carcase.
7   Trim the wing bones and chop off the bottom knuckle, (E).
8   Stand the bird with the parson's nose upright then chop down between the carcase and the breast using a large cook's knife. Trim any excess rib cage off the breast section.
9   Cut the breast in half.
10 Cut the carcase into three pieces (when presenting joints on the carcase).

Presentation of cooked joints on the carcase:
1   Place the cooked pieces of carcase on the serving dish with the top two pieces side by side and the parson's nose at the back.
2   Place the two pieces of breast down the middle of the two pieces of carcase then arrange the wings at the sides (in the same manner as the diagram).
3   Place the two thigh pieces each side of the parson's nose then place the two drumsticks on top.

Note: The carcase pieces are not served. In addition the winglets are not normally used but are kept back for some other purpose.

Jointing a cooked bird   (roasted or boiled etc.)

This is done in exactly the same manner as described above.

Preparation of suprêmes

1   Carry out the basic preparation, i.e. pluck, singe and gut then remove the wish bone.
2   Remove the legs.
3   Cut off the winglets then remove the skin from the breast.
4   Cut along and down the breast bone then down through the wing joint close to the carcase.
5   Carefully detach the suprêmes using the top of the cook's knife in a filleting action where necessary.
6   Trim off the flesh from the wing bones and scrape the bones clean. Chop off the knuckles.
7   Trim off the small sinews from the fillets.
8   Cut a pocket along the thick side of each suprême and insert the fillets.
9   Lightly flatten and shape with a cutlet bat.

Preparation for grilling

1   Carry out the basic preparation, i.e. pluck, singe and gut then remove the wish bone.
2   Cut off the claws (and winglets if desired).
3   Split the bird through the back with a large knife – insert the knife through the neck opening and cut towards the parson's nose.
4   Open out the bird and lightly flatten with a cutlet bat.
5   Remove the ribs with a small knife.

Preparation for grilling – toad style (en crapaudine)

1   Carry out the basic preparation as above.
2   Do not detach the winglets or claws but cut the nails off the claws.
3   Push the legs back then cut down through the rib cage from the bottom of the breast to the wing bone, (A).
4   Pull the breast forward into the toad shape, (B).
5   Lightly flatten with a cutlet bat.

Boning a bird for a rolled roast or galantine

1   Carry out the basic preparation, i.e. pluck, singe and gut then remove the wish bone. Also cut off the parson's nose, winglets and claws (above the joints).
2   Turn the bird on its breast then slit the skin down the middle of the back.
3   Using a small knife, start at the slit and cut inwards along the carcase.
4   Detach the legs at the ball and socket joint and fillet down round the rib cage towards the breast bone.
5   Detach the wing joints from the carcase and continue down round the rib cage and breast bone.
6   Carefully fillet round the top of the breast bone without bursting or cutting the skin. Remove the carcase.
7   Very carefully separate the skin from the flesh of the legs then pull each leg through the skin.
8   Remove the wing bones in the same manner.
9   Carefully remove the breast and wing flesh from the skin.

Reconstruction of bird for roasting or boiling

Proceed to step 6 above but leave on the parson's nose. Pack and reshape the bird with an appropriate stuffing or forcemeat and sew up with fine string.

Galantines

Bone out the bird and remove the flesh from the skin as described above (proceed to step 9). Prepare a mousseline forcemeat with the flesh (page 73) and any garnish which is to be included in the galantine, e.g. pistachio nuts, strips of tongue, ham or chicken breast etc. Lay out the chicken skin on a cloth then cover with a layer of the forcemeat. Add the garnish if appropriate and cover with a further layer of forcemeat. Mould into a roll surrounded with the skin and cloth then secure each end with string.

Galantines are poached in stock (made from the bones) until cooked then allowed to cool in the stock (or removed and lightly pressed into an oval shape). They may be decorated or sliced and served in aspic with a suitable garnish.

Section ten   Fish

In catering, fish is often classified according to the dispersion of fat or body oil throughout the fish.

White fish

The flesh of white fish contains very little fat or body oil; most of the fat or oil is stored in the liver. Examples are cod, haddock, halibut, sole, turbot and whiting etc.

Oily fish

The flesh of oily fish contains a substantial proportion of body fat or oil. Examples are herring, mackerel, salmon, trout, pilchard and whitebait.

Points on quality:

Conformation: well-fleshed
Texture: firm
Smell: pleasant fish smell
Eyes: moist, fresh appearance
Gills: bright red
Skin: moist skin and scales

Preparation of fish

General techniques
Washing   Wash the fish under cold running water at each stage of preparation.
Removing scales   Hold the tail of the fish and scrape off the scales from tail to head with the knife held at a slight angle.
Removing fins   *Round fish:*   Cut off the fins with fish scissors.

Flat fish: Place the fish on a board and raise the fins with the stroke of a knife. Cut off the fins with the knife. Alternatively use fish scissors.
Removing gills   Open the gill slits and detach the gills with a small knife or scissors.
Removing intestines   *Round fish:*   Make a small incision along the belly from the vent. Remove the intestines with the back of a spoon or small ladle. Also scrape the backbone with the spoon or ladle to remove

the blood tract. *Note:*   Be careful not to break the ligament between the bottom of the head and the belly.

Flat fish: Cut a slit just under the head into the pocket which holds the intestines. Remove intestines, roe and congealed blood. Use the fingers to squeeze out the remaining roe. *Note:*   This is usually done after removing the head.
Removing skin   *Dover sole:*   Skin from tail to head. Cut across the tail through the skin then scrape to detach enough skin to be gripped with the fingers. Pull off the black skin. If appropriate repeat the same procedure to remove the white skin.

All other sole (also plaice and flounder):   Skin from head to tail.
1   Cut round the head beginning at the gill slits, then insert the knife just under the skin above the side fins.
2   Push the point of the knife along between the side fins and skin.
3   Insert the point of the knife in through the gill slit and push along between the skin and the remaining side fins.
4   Lift up the skin at the top of the head (which has been detached when slitting the side fins) and work with the thumb to loosen from the flesh.
5   Continue this action until the skin is detached along the cut under and across the head.
6   When the skin is detached across the top of the fish, hold the head firmly under the palm of the hand and pull off the black skin.

Fish fillets:
1   Place the fillet with the skin downwards on a cutting board.
2   Hold the tail and cut through the flesh to the skin.
3   Hold the blade at an angle (45° approximately) and move forwards and backwards with a slight pushing action; at the same time lightly pull the skin from the tail end. *Note:*   Do not use any downward pressure.

Whiting:
1   Wash and remove scales, fins and intestines.
2   Rewash then cut a slit through the skin along the length of the back from head to tail.
3   Cut another slit along the belly from head to tail.
4   Loosen the skin from the flesh at the gill slit on one side of the fish then pull carefully from head to tail.
5   Turn over the fish and remove the skin in the same manner.
Filleting   One of the most important aspects of filleting fish is the cutting of the flesh from the bone by drawing the flexible blade of the filleting knife across the surface of the bones.

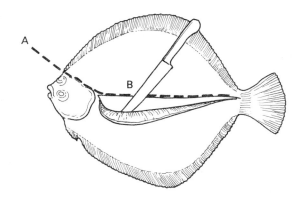

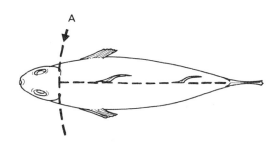

Figure 19 *Filleting fish*

Flat fish (sole, plaice, halibut and turbot etc.):
1 Make an incision down the centre of the fish to the tail (usually indicated by a natural line), (A).
2 Cut off the flesh of the left fillet by carefully drawing the knife down the backbones, (B). The fillet is lifted back by the left hand during cutting.
3 Turn the fish round then detach the opposite fillet in the same manner.
4 Turn the fish over and repeat the operation removing the other two fillets.
5 Cut off the black skin and white if appropriate (or pull off the black skin at the start – various soles and flounders). *Note:* Remove the scales if the skin is to be left on.

Round fish (salmon, trout and cod etc.):
1 Remove scales, fins and intestines then wash.
2 Cut up behind the head to the backbone then turn the knife and cut down the centre of the fish carefully following the backbone, see (A). The palm of the left hand is usually placed flat on the fish to assist filleting.
3 Turn the fish over and repeat the procedure, removing the second fillet. Alternatively cut under the bone without turning the fish over.

Styles of fish for cooking

Whole fish for grilling
1 Carry out elementary preparation, i.e. wash and remove the scales, fins, black skin from flat fish, head and intestines. If the head is to be left on (trout, red mullet and dover sole etc.) remove the eyes and gills.
2 Wash thoroughly then drain.
Note: When preparing round fish for grilling, several small incisions are cut across the back of the fish but *through the skin only*, i.e. 1 mm in depth. This is to reduce the likelihood of the skin bursting when cooking (term: ciseler).

Whole fish for shallow-frying Prepare the fish the same as for grilling above (see page 307).

Whole fish for deep-frying This usually only applies to white fish as oily fish should never be deep-fried (see page 291).

Curled fish (en colère – usually whiting):
1 Carry out the elementary preparation, i.e. wash and remove the scales, fins, intestines and skin (see opposite page).
Note: Do not cut off the tail but trim slightly.
2 Clean the head and remove the eyes and gills.
3 Insert the tail into the mouth then close the mouth to hold the tail. Alternatively the tail may be inserted through the eyes; this is the procedure with fish other than whiting which do not have the teeth structure to hold the tail.

Colbert or Richelieu:
1 Carry out the elementary preparation as for grilling but remove both skins.
2 Make an incision down the middle of the fish as if filleting but start 20 mm approximately under the head and finish 20 mm approximately above the tail.
3 Detach the first 10 mm of both fillets each side of the bone then fold back to form a pocket or recess, see the left-hand side of Figure 19 (B) as an example.
4 Split the backbone with a knife within the pocket in three places – top, middle and bottom of the pocket (this is so that the bone can be removed after cooking). The fish is breaded prior to frying (page 292).

Cuts of fish

Fillet (filet) The strip of flesh removed from the bone from tail to head. A flat fish produces two double or four single fillets (depending on size), and a round fish produces two fillets.

Délice A trimmed folded fillet from a small fish, e.g. sole or plaice. The fillet is lightly tapped with the back of a knife on the underside at one-third and two-thirds its length, then the top and bottom are folded under.

Cravate   A fillet from a small fish folded into a loop. The opening is sometimes supported with a small ball of potato during poaching.

En goujons   Fillets of fish cut at an angle into thin strips: 50 mm × 5 mm approximately.

Paupiette   A fillet from a small fish which is very lightly flattened with a cutlet bat, spread with fish forcemeat then rolled up presentation side outwards (the side removed from the bone).

Suprême   A neat slice cut at a slant from the fillet of a large fish, e.g. halibut, turbot or salmon etc.

Darne   A fish steak cut from a round fish, e.g. salmon or cod etc.

Tronçon   A fish steak cut from a flat fish, e.g. turbot, halibut or brill etc.

Côtelette   A half darne (the shape resembles a cutlet).

Section eleven   Shellfish

Shellfish is usually classified into:

Molluscs: cockles, mussels, oysters, scallops and clams etc.

Crustaceans: shrimps, prawns, scampi, lobster, crawfish and crayfish etc.

Points on quality (fresh shellfish)

All shellfish: The shellfish should be alive and heavy in relation to size. The shells of molluscs should be tightly closed which indicates the fish is alive and with crustaceans there should be obvious signs of activity.

   It is important that fresh shellfish be purchased alive. After death shellfish deteriorate rapidly and lose body fluids (and therefore weight).

Preparation of mussels (or cockles) for cooking

1   Inspect the mussels carefully, removing any dead mussels and mussels filled with sand.
2   Thoroughly wash the mussels in several changes of water to remove grit and sand.
3   Scrape with a knife to remove any barnacles or hairs.
4   Thoroughly rewash the mussels then drain ready for cooking.

Preparation of scallops for cooking

Remove the live scallops from their shells as follows (this is called *shucking*).
1   Wash the scallops.
2   Hold the scallop in the palm of the hand with the flat shell downwards.
3   Insert a thin bladed knife through a small opening between the shells in the right side of the hinge.

4   Cut along the flat shell to sever the muscle from the shell.
5   Turn over the scallop and remove the flat shell.
6   Remove the fish then trim to leave only the white flesh and curved orange roe.
7   Wash and drain.

Preparation of oysters

1   Hold the oyster in a cloth in the palm of the hand with the hinge to the right.
2   Insert an oyster knife into the hinge then push and twist to break the hinge.
3   Push the oyster knife closely along the top shell severing the muscle of the oyster from the shell (if the oyster has a flat shell, cut along this shell).
4   Carefully trim off the beard and remove any small pieces of shell.
5   Carefully detach the oyster from the bottom shell (flat shell oysters) then turn over (this side is more attractive for presentation). Ensure that the fish juices are kept in the shell.

Important: If the oysters are very gritty or have been opened badly and covered with splinters of shell then (and only then) they should be lightly washed in salted cold water and placed back into the shells.

Cutting and jointing a live lobster ready for cooking (américaine and Newburg etc.)

1   Kill the lobster by inserting a cook's knife through the head just under the eyes.
2   Wash the lobster then cut off the legs and claws.
3   Crack the claws with the back of a knife, (A).
4   Cut off the body (carapace) from the tail, (B).
5   Cut the carapace in half lengthwise, (C).
6   Remove the very hard pieces of brain from the carapace then place the intestines and any coral into a bowl (to be mixed with butter, see below).
7   Cut the tail through the shell into thick slices, (D).
8   Remove any dirt trail from the pieces of tail.

Special lobster butter for thickening sauces
This is made by pounding or liquidising the lobster coral and intestines with softened butter. The quantity of butter which is required is 20–25 g butter per lobster.

Cutting a cooked lobster

1   Remove the claws and legs.
2   Pull back the bottom pincer of each claw and break off. This should remove the blade bone from inside each claw.
3   Crack the claws with the back of a knife and withdraw the flesh.

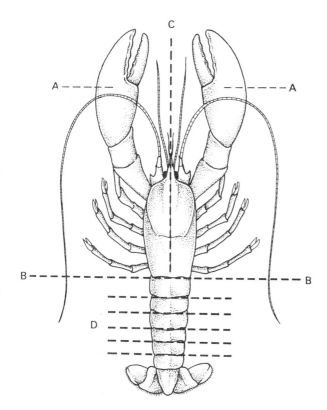

Figure 20 *Cutting and jointing a lobster*

4 Split the lobster in half lengthwise. This is done by inserting the knife through the natural line of the carapace just above the tail then cutting downwards through the tail. Turn the lobster round then completely split in two; take care not to damage the head.
5 Remove the cooked flesh from the tail.
6 Remove and discard all the intestines (except any red coral which can be used as a decoration for shellfish cocktails etc.) then wash both half carapaces.

Note: When preparing cold lobster the tail flesh is cut into neat pieces then reformed back in the shell (see page 46).

Killing a crab prior to cooking

Insert a skewer just above the mouth parts into the crab.
Note: If a crab is not killed prior to cooking it is likely to shed its claws.

Removing the flesh from a cooked crab

1 Remove the claws and legs.
2 Pull back and detach the bottom pincer of each claw then crack the claws and remove the meat. The meat may also be removed from the legs but this is time-consuming.

3 Open the crab by carefully pulling out the soft under-shell (or purse).
4 Remove the gills and discard. Also remove the sac behind the eyes and discard.
5 Split the bony centre of the soft under-shell with a knife and withdraw the white and brown flesh using a fork. *Note*: Keep the white and dark meats separate.
6 Withdraw the soft dark meat and orange meat from the crab shell.
7 If the shell is to be used for presentation, wash thoroughly then break along the natural line to extend the opening. This is done by pressing the outside of the shell along the natural line.

Preparing scampi for cooking

De-vein the shellfish by twisting the middle tail fin from side to side to dislocate then carefully pull outwards removing the dirt tract. After this pull the tail section away from the body. Reserve the head and claws for shellfish stock or sauce.

Trussing small shellfish (crayfish and scampi)

Just prior to cooking lift up the tail of the fish over its head and insert the bottom pincers into the tail. Cook immediately. The fish should sit tail over head on a serving dish.

Section twelve Preparation of forcemeats, stuffings, pâtés and terrines, made-up items and pie and pudding fillings

Forcemeats and stuffings

Forcemeats are mixtures made from meat, game, poultry, offal, fish or shellfish. The ingredients are usually very finely cut, pounded or sieved then bound with eggs, egg whites or a panada (binding agent). Forcemeats are used for mousses, savoury soufflés, galantines, quenelles, meat balls and stuffings etc.

Mousseline forcemeat (high quality)
Base recipe: (yield 500 g approximately)
Main item: 300 g flesh (free from skin and bone etc.), e.g. chicken, veal, pork, game, fish or shellfish.*
Binding agent: 50 ml egg whites (2 egg whites approximately).
Seasoning: Good pinch of salt (1 g approximately) and pinch pepper.
Cream: 250 ml double cream.

* When preparing a shellfish forcemeat such as lobster, whiting is often added together with important flavourings such as lobster coral.
Example: 150 g lobster flesh, 100 g whiting flesh and 50 g coral.

Base method:

1 Mince the main item very fine then add the seasoning.
2 Place into a bowl over ice.
3 Stir well with a spatula and gradually add the egg whites.
4 Gradually add four-fifths of the cream (200 ml) stirring until very smooth.
5 Test the texture of the mixture by gently poaching a very small quantity in a little stock. If the texture is too firm continue to add cream until the correct texture is obtained (soft, smooth eating). *Note*:   In the unlikely event of the texture being too soft, add a little extra egg white until the texture is correct.

Forcemeats incorporating a panada

Base recipe: (yield 500 g approximately)
Main item: 250 g flesh (free from skin and bone etc.), e.g. chicken, veal, pork, game, fish and shellfish.*
Binding agents: 125 g frangipane panada (see below) and 1 egg.
Seasoning: Good pinch of salt (1 g approximately) and pinch pepper.
Cream: 125 ml double cream.

Note: Meat and game forcemeats often include a small proportion of veal flesh and pork fat. Example: 150 g flesh, 50 g veal flesh and 50 g diced pork fat.

Base method:

1 Mince the main item/s very fine then add the seasoning.
2 Place into a bowl over ice then gradually add the panada and egg, stirring well with a spatula.
3 When the mixture is very smooth allow to rest for 20–30 mins.
4 Gradually add four-fifths of the cream (100 ml) stirring until very smooth.
5 Test the texture of the mixture as described for mousseline forcemeats, step 5.

Frangipane panada

250 ml milk, 75 g butter, good pinch of salt, pinch of pepper and nutmeg, 75 g flour and 4 egg yolks.

Method:

1 Heat the milk with the butter and seasoning.
2 Cream together the yolks and flour in a bowl.
3 Slowly pour the milk and butter on to the creamed flour and egg yolks while stirring constantly.
4 Transfer the mixture to a sauteuse then cook until the mixture leaves the sides of the pan and the flour gelatinizes (4 mins. approximately).
5 Spread on to a buttered tray and cover with a piece of buttered paper.
6 Allow to cool before use.

Godiveau (veal and kidney fat forcemeat)

Base recipe: (yield 500 g approximately)
Main items: 200 g lean diced veal (free of fat and sinews etc.), 200 g white beef suet.
Binding agent: 70 ml egg (2 small eggs approximately).
Seasoning: Good pinch of salt and a pinch of pepper.
Ice water: 100–130 ml ice water.

Method:

1 Dice the veal and finely chop the suet (after removing all the skin and sinew).
2 Mix together then mince very finely. Add the seasoning.
3 Place into a bowl over ice then gradually add the egg stirring well with a spatula.
4 Allow to rest on the ice for one hour approximately.
5 Slowly add the ice water whilst stirring constantly. Keep adding the water until a smooth fine paste is obtained. *Note*:   Test the mixture as described for mousseline forcemeat, step 5, after adding two-thirds of the water.

Quenelles

These are *egg-shaped* pieces of fine forcemeat (forcemeat from above recipes – as appropriate). The forcemeat is shaped with two spoons then placed into a buttered pan; the size of the quenelles is dependent on use, e.g. soup, garnish or fish course, and is achieved by using various spoon sizes. When all the quenelles have been shaped and placed in the pan, hot stock is gently added then the quenelles allowed to poach on a low heat.

Note: Alternatively the mixture may be placed in a piping bag and piped into small shapes which are detached with a knife dipped in hot water on to the buttered pan.

Sautéd liver forcemeat (farce à gratin)

The preparation of these forcemeats is described on page 76.

Pasta stuffings (ravioli and cannelloni)

Florentine stuffing

20 g butter, 25 g finely chopped onion, 5 g crushed garlic, 200 g well drained chopped spinach, salt, pepper and nutmeg and 1 egg yolk.
Sweat the onion and garlic in the butter for 2–3 mins. then allow to cool. Mix all the ingredients together.

Italienne stuffing

20 g butter, 25 g finely chopped onion, 5 g crushed garlic, 80 g well drained chopped spinach, 80.g cooked beef (finely minced), 40 g cooked brains (chopped), salt and pepper, 25–50 ml espagnole and 1 egg yolk.
Sweat the onion and garlic in the butter for 2–3 mins. then allow to cool. Mix all the ingredients together using only enough espagnole to produce a thick mixture.

Stuffings

In addition to the forcemeats described previously there is a range of preparations which are primarily made with vegetables and white breadcrumbs; however a small quantity of pork sausagemeat is sometimes added to some stuffings to give body and texture.

Cooked stuffings served with roast meat, game and poultry

These are prepared separately from the roast joint or bird and are served as an accompaniment.

Sage stuffing
Recipe:
40 g lard or dripping (preferably from the roasting tray), 50 g chopped onion, 2 g sage (half a teaspoon), 5 g chopped parsley, 100 g white breadcrumbs and salt and pepper.

Method:
1 Sweat the onions down in the fat without colouring for 3–4 mins.
2 Add the sage and sweat down for a further 2 mins. approximately.
3 Add the breadcrumbs, seasoning and chopped parsley.
4 Combine all the ingredients and check the seasoning.

Sage and onion stuffing
As above increasing the quantity of onions to 100 g.

Herb stuffing
Same as sage stuffing but replace the sage with mixed herbs.

Herb and lemon stuffing
Same as herb stuffing adding the grated zest of one lemon.

Raw stuffings used for stuffed meat, poultry and game
These stuffings are used for stuffing a joint or bird prior to roasting. However they are sometimes rolled in oiled greaseproof paper then cooked separately in a tray with a little stock in the oven (or steamer). Unlike the cooked stuffings above they are usually sliced into neat portions and not spooned out.

English style stuffing
Recipe:
20 g butter, 50 g chopped onions, 50 g chopped suet, 100 g white breadcrumbs, 1 small egg, 5 g chopped parsley, 1 g thyme (third of a teaspoon), grated zest of half a lemon and salt and pepper. *Note*: 40 g of pork sausage meat may be added to this stuffing.
See base method which follows.

Chestnut stuffing
Recipe:
20 g butter, 50 g chopped onions, 30 g chopped suet, 75 g white breadcrumbs, 150 g peeled chopped chestnuts, 75 g pork sausagemeat, 1 small egg, 5 g mixed herbs and salt and pepper.

Sage and onion stuffing
Prepare as English-style stuffing but increase the onions to 100 g, replace the thyme with sage and omit the lemon zest.

Base method for raw stuffings:
1 Sweat the onions down in the butter without colouring for 3–4 mins.
2 Add the dried herbs and sweat down for a further 2 mins. approximately then allow to cool.
3 Place the sweated onions and herbs in a bowl and add the rest of the ingredients except the egg.
4 Mix all the ingredients together then bind with egg.

Pâtés

Pâtés may be grouped into two types of preparation:

1 *Fine forcemeats* (page 73) alternated in layers with strips or small fillets of flesh, strips of pork fat and truffles etc. The filling is placed in a raised pie mould lined with hot-water pastry. The top of the filling is usually lined with strips of pork fat (the pastry shell may also be lined with this fat) then covered with pastry. The pâté is cooked and completed in the same manner as raised pies on page 339.

2 *Fine or coarse purées of liver, pork flesh, pork fat and vegetables etc.*, cooked in a porcelain container or pâté tin lined with pork fat, e.g. pâté de foie gras, pâté de foie and pâté maison etc.

Pâté de foie
Recipe: (yield 6–8 portions)
20 g butter, 50 g lean pork, 50 g fat pork, 200 g liver (pork or lamb), 30 g chopped onion, 1 clove garlic, bay leaf, sprig of thyme, chervil, parsley stalks and salt and pepper. Also 300 g sliced pork fat to be used for lining and covering the pâté.

Method:
See base method for pâtés below.

Pâté maison
Prepare the same as liver pâté but use only chicken livers and replace the fat pork with fat bacon. Also add 30 ml double cream.

Method:
See base method for pâtés below.

Sautéd liver forcemeats (game farce/farce à gratin)
Recipe:
20 g butter, 100 g fat bacon, 200 g livers (usually chicken livers mixed with the livers of the appropriate bird, e.g. pheasant, grouse or duckling), 30 g chopped onion, small piece of garlic, half a bay leaf, sprig of thyme and salt and pepper.

Method:
Follow the base method for pâtés below to step 3.

Base method for liver pâtés:
1   Melt the butter in a plat à sauter then add any fat bacon, fat pork, lean pork, onion, garlic, bay leaves, parsley stalks, thyme and chervil and sweat down without developing colour for 4–5 mins.
2   Add the livers and stiffen in the hot fat.
3   Remove the bay leaf and parsley stalks then pass the mixture through a coarse mincer.
4   Pass the mixture through a fine mincer then through a sieve. Alternatively liquidize the mixture.
5   If there is cream in the recipe, stir into the mixture.
6   Add the seasoning.
7   Line the porcelain terrine or pâté tin with the sliced pork fat. Ensure the end of the slices hang over the container.
8   Add the pâté mixture and draw over the ends of the slices of fat. Neatly cover with further slices of pork fat.
9   If possible cut a piece of wood which neatly fits the inside of the pâté tin then cover with greaseproof paper.
10 Place the papered wood neatly over the pâté then wrap the tin in greaseproof paper and secure with string.
11 Cook the pâté in a moderate oven (175° C) in a tray containing water (bain-marie) for 1–1¼ hours.
12 Allow to cool slightly then place weights on the top of the pâté (to sit on the wood and press the pâté). Leave till cold.
13 Remove the paper, dip the container in tepid water then turn out the pâté.
14 Serve in slices, see page 49.

Terrines

These are prepared in the same manner as pâtés (type 1) but the mixture is cooked in a terrine which is lined with pork fat. After cooking the mixture may have to be lightly pressed as it cools to retain an even shape. When cold the top may be covered with fresh melted pork fat or aspic jelly made from the bones of the flesh which is used. When preparing game terrines, the flesh is usually marinaded in brandy or Madeira wine which is later sprinkled over the mixture as it is layered into the terrine.

Made-up items

Hamburgers or Vienna steaks
Recipe: (yield four 100 g hamburgers)
Main item: 370 g lean minced beef.
Butter: 10 g butter.
Onion: 20 g finely chopped onion.
Breadcrumbs: 15 g fresh white breadcrumbs (optional).
Egg: 20 ml egg (half a medium egg).
Seasoning: Good pinch of salt and a pinch of pepper.

Method:
1   Lightly sweat down the onion in the butter then allow to cool.
2   Mix all the ingredients together thoroughly to a fine paste.
3   Divide the mixture into four pieces then shape into flat cakes.
4   Store on an oiled tray until required for use.

Bitoks
Recipe: (yield four 100 g bitoks)
Main item: 300 g lean minced beef.
Butter: 25 g butter.
Onions: 25 g finely chopped onion.
Breadcrumbs: 50 g white breadcrumbs.
Milk: 100 ml milk.
Seasoning: Good pinch of salt and a pinch of pepper and nutmeg.

Method:
1   Soak the breadcrumbs in the milk then squeeze out to remove the surplus liquid.
2   Lightly sweat down the onions in the butter then allow to cool.
3   Mix all the ingredients thoroughly together to a fine paste.
4   Complete as hamburgers above.

Pojarski cutlets
These are very fine forcemeat cutlets made from veal, pork or salmon etc., which are floured (or panéd) then shallow-fried.

Recipe: (yield four 100 g cutlets)
Main item: 350 g lean minced veal, pork or salmon flesh etc.
Breadcrumbs: 50 g white breadcrumbs.
Milk: 100 ml milk.
Cream: 40 ml cream.
Egg white: 1 egg white.
Seasoning: Good pinch of salt and a pinch of pepper.

Note: When preparing salmon Pojarski the breadcrumbs may have to be increased to bind the mixture.

Method:

1 Soak the breadcrumbs in the milk then squeeze out to remove the surplus liquid.
2 Pound or bowl chop the flesh with the soaked crumbs and egg white.
3 Add the seasoning then blend in the cream.
4 Divide the mixture into four pieces then shape as cutlets.
5 Store on an oiled tray ready for use (flouring or paner then shallow-fried).

Fishcakes

Recipe: (yield four 75 g fishcakes)
Main item: 200 g flaked cooked fish.
Mashed potato: 100 g dry mashed potato.
Butter: 10 g butter
Onion: 15 g finely chopped onion or shallots.
Egg yolk: 1 egg yolk.
Parsley: Good pinch of chopped parsley.
Seasoning: Good pinch of salt and a pinch of pepper.

Method:

1 Sweat down the onions in the butter then allow to cool.
2 Thoroughly mix all the ingredients together.
3 Divide the mixture into four pieces then shape into flat cakes.
4 Pass through flour, eggwash and breadcrumbs.
5 Neatly reshape then mark a criss-cross design on top of each fishcake with the palette knife.

Durham cutlets

These are prepared the same as fishcakes above replacing the fish with cooked minced beef. The yield is four 75 g cutlets.

Savoury pie and pudding fillings (raw fillings cooked in a pie or pudding)

Steak pie and steak pudding

Recipe: (yield four portions)
Main item: 500 g beef (topside, thick flank or rump etc.).
Onion: 100 g chopped onion.
Parsley: Good pinch of chopped parsley.
Flour: 10 g flour.
Worcester sauce: 2–3 drops of sauce.
Seasoning: Good pinch of salt (1 g) and pinch pepper.
Stock: 150 ml brown stock approximately.

Method:

1 Trim any fat or gristle from the beef then cut into small escalopes (25 mm in length approximately).
2 Mix together the beef, onions, parsley, seasoning and flour.

3 Add the Worcester sauce then mix in the cold stock.
4 Allow to stand for at least 1 hour before use.
5 Complete as stated on page 331.

Steak and kidney pie/pudding

The same as steak pie but replace 100 g of the steak with 100 g ox kidney trimmed and diced.

Steak, kidney and mushroom pie/pudding

The same as steak and kidney pie above adding 100 g of washed quartered mushrooms.

Chicken pie

Recipe: (yield four portions)
Main item: 1 × 1½ kg chicken, 8 small slices of streaky bacon.
Garnish: 100 g button onions, 100 g button mushrooms, good pinch of chopped parsley.
Seasoning: Salt and pepper.
Stock: 200 ml chicken stock.

Method:

1 Cut the chicken into joints then lightly season.
2 Wrap each piece of chicken with the bacon then place in the pie dish.
3 Add the garnish then the stock.
4 Complete as stated on page 331.

Game pies

Recipe: (yield four individual pies)
Main item: 250 g trimmed game flesh (venison, hare, grouse or pheasant etc.).
 50 g diced pork fat.
Onion: 15 g finely chopped onion or shallots.
Wine or spirit: 20 ml brandy or port wine.
Stock: 25 ml game stock.
Seasoning: Salt and pepper.

Method:

1 Cut the game flesh into small dice or very small escalopes.
2 Mix with the remaining ingredients and add the seasoning.
3 Complete as stated on page 340.

Pork pies

Recipe: (yield four individual pies)
Main item: 250 g pork flesh.
 50 g diced pork fat.
Onion: 15 g finely chopped onion or shallots.
Stock: 25 ml stock.
Seasoning: Salt and pepper.

Method:

Cut the flesh into small dice or very small escalopes then

mix together with the remaining ingredients. Complete as stated on page 340.

Veal and ham pies

(Yield four individual pies.)
Prepare the same as pork pies but *replace* the pork and pork fat with 200 g lean veal and 100 g fat ham (or bacon).

Veal, ham and egg pie   (large)

These are prepared with the same mixture as veal and ham pies above and hard-boiled eggs, see page 340.

Cornish pasties

Recipe:
150 g coarse-minced beef, 100 g finely diced blanched potato, 50 g chopped onion and salt and pepper.

Method:
Thoroughly mix all the ingredients together. Complete as stated on page 338.

Assessment exercise

1 Describe the factors which are important when purchasing a large joint of beef.
2 Define the following terms: entrecôte; chateaubriand; tournedos; escalope; noisette; paillard; quenelle; galantine.
3 List the joints in a side of beef which are (a) moist-heat cooked, (b) dry-heat cooked and (c) traditionally braised.
4 Describe how to prepare a leg of lamb for roasting.
5 Name the terms for the various sizes of chicken. Also give the approximate weight of each bird.
6 Explain how to cut a bird for sauté.
7 Identify four different styles of preparing a fillet of fish for cooking and serving.
8 Describe how to cut a live lobster for cooking.
9 Describe how to cut a cooked lobster for lobster salad.
10 What is a forcemeat?
11 Explain the difference between a pâté and a terrine.
12 What is a Vienna steak?

Chapter 5
Boiling and poaching

The terms boiling and poaching refer to moist methods of cooking where the food is cooked in a liquid containing water.

Boiling: The food is cooked at boiling point. This may range from a rapid boiling action, e.g. when cooking green leaf vegetables, to a slow simmering movement, e.g. cooking meat and poultry.

Poaching: The food is cooked at temperatures usually between 75–93°C. At the lower temperature there is no liquid movement but as the temperature is increased the liquid begins to simmer (or sparkle) *very slowly*. Examples of poaching in still liquids are poached eggs and poached fish where the texture and appearance of the commodity can be adversely affected by liquid movement. When poaching meat or poultry the liquid is usually brought to a *very slow simmer* but it is important to note that the term poaching is normally associated with commodities requiring delicate cooking where no liquid movement should be the rule.

When boiling or poaching foods there are two fundamental aspects to the many procedures:

1 where the food is placed in cold liquid then brought to the boil and cooked;
2 where the food is placed or immersed into very hot or boiling liquid and cooked.

The first part of this chapter is concerned with processes where the food is placed into cold liquid then brought to the boil and the second part of the chapter with processes where food is immersed into boiling liquid.

Part one Foods placed into cold liquid then brought to the boil and cooked

There are many reasons for starting the cooking of some commodities in cold liquid. Two important reasons are:

a) The *clarity of the cooking liquor* is assisted with the removal of scum or impurities. This must always be removed as it forms or it will be dispersed back through the cooked liquid by the simmering action.
b) It is safe, quick and easy simply to cover with cold liquid and bring to the boil as opposed to adding

commodities to boiling liquid, especially when large quantities of both food and liquid are involved (e.g. large batch of potatoes).

When boiling or poaching foods the liquid content should always be kept to a minimum to reduce flavour dilution in excess liquid; pots and cooking utensils should be of such size and volume as to immerse the commodity with as little liquid as possible being used.

Although, as a general rule, this part of the chapter is concerned with foods where the cooking process is started in a cold liquid, there are some ingredients which are added when the liquid is boiling or simmering.

In many dishes the vegetable content is added after simmering has commenced or as near to the end of the total cooking time as possible to retain nutritional value, colour and texture. This often means adding the vegetables to the simmering liquid in a sequence dictated by their respective cooking times. Adding the vegetables to simmering liquid also reduces the risk of burning by keeping the vegetables moving off the base of the cooking utensil (this movement caused by simmering action is apparent in broths etc.).

Jams, jellies and boiled-sugar products are also included in this section because they follow the basic procedure of combining the main ingredients then applying heat.

Part one (A) in this chapter is concerned with boiling savoury items and Part one (B) is concerned with sweet items.

The scope of boiling and poaching is very wide, therefore specific meanings for these methods of cooking must be directly related to appropriate processes within this chapter. This means that there is no recipe ingredients diagram or essential activities diagram for the chapter.

Part two Foods placed into very hot or boiling liquids and cooked

There are many reasons for placing foods into very hot or boiling liquid, e.g.:

1 to retain as much nutritional value and colour as possible when cooking green vegetables;

2 to set or coagulate protein when poaching eggs;
3 to reduce the risk of burning when preparing starch-thickened mixtures or simply to keep the cooking times of food to a minimum.

In some instances there are exceptions to the rule. For example, when poaching whole fish, the fish should be placed into cold liquid then brought to near boiling-point to avoid distortion and tearing of the flesh (with the exception of blue trout). Also when cooking mussels, the heat is applied to the raw shellfish; here the liquid from the shellfish is brought to a rapid boil producing a cooking medium of liquor and steam.

The Pellicle theory

It is often suggested that placing fish[1]*, meat, poultry or game into very hot or boiling liquid coagulates the outer proteins of the commodity thus helping to *seal* in the juices and therefore retain goodness and reduce shrinkage. This belief, which is also applied to the searing of commodities when stewing[2], braising[2], roasting[3] and grilling appears to be a popular cookery myth. However there is no evidence to support this myth. On the contrary, most sealing techniques are likely to increase shrinkage and weight loss, a fact that has been known for quite some time as the dates of the research indicate, see References.

Thickening

Many mixtures are thickened as an integral part of boiling processes. Methods of thickening may be classified as follows.

Blood thickening Adding blood at the end of a boiling process, see jugged hare on page 193.

Butter thickenings
Butter thickening: Adding butter at the end of a boiling process – monter au beurre. See page 202.
Butter and flour thickening: Adding a mixture of creamed butter and flour (beurre manié) usually at the end of a process. See this chapter, page 120.
Butter and lobster thickening: Adding a mixture of butter and lobster intestines pounded or liquidized together, at the end of a boiling process. See Chapter 7, Section four.

Egg yolk and liaison thickening Adding egg yolks or a mixture of egg yolks and cream (liaison) at the end of a boiling process. See Chapter 8, Section six.

Fécule thickening Adding starch flour, e.g. arrowroot or cornflour. See this chapter, Section twenty.

Flour thickening (flour and water paste) Adding a mixture of flour blended with water (white wash or jayzee). In traditional practice this method of thickening is rare and is frowned upon by many chefs. However it is commonly used to thicken sauces and mixtures which are to be quick frozen; flour and/or special thickening starches are added in this manner.

Fruit thickening Using fruits which cook to a thick pulp or purée. See this chapter, page 104.

Reduction thickening Boiling down a stock containing liquid or sauce to a gelatinous or syrup-like consistency.

Roux thickening Using a roux. This is dealt with in detail in Chapter 8.

Sugar thickening Producing syrups or crystallized syrups or coatings etc. See this chapter, page 105.

Vegetable thickenings
Cereal thickenings: Adding rice, oatmeal or maize etc. See this chapter, Section three.
Pulse thickenings: Adding lentils, split-peas or dried beans etc. See this chapter, page 86.
Root vegetable thickenings: Adding floury root vegetables, e.g. potatoes or Jerusalem artichokes. See Chapter 7, page 88.

Combination of above When preparing some dishes a combination of the above thickenings may be used.

---

* Superior figures refer to the References on page 416.

Part one (A) — Foods placed into cold liquid then brought to the boil and cooked: savoury items

Section one Stocks and glazes

Base method

Step 1	A Assemble ingredients. B Break up bones and remove any fat or marrow. C Wash, peel and prepare the vegetables, i.e. *White stocks*: Peel the vegetables and leave whole. *Brown stocks*: Peel the vegetables and roughly chop.
Step 2	*Brown stocks* Place the bones in a roasting tray and brown in the oven. *White stocks*
Step 3	When light brown, add the vegetables and allow to colour.
Step 4	Place the bones in the stockpot or large saucepan.
Step 5	Remove the vegetables and place into the boiler. Drain off excess fat from the roasting tray, swill with a little cold water then boil for 2–3 mins. Add to the bones.
Step 6	Cover with cold water and bring to the boil.
Step 7	If the water is very cloudy, refresh with cold water then reboil.
Step 8	Add the vegetables.
Step 9	Slowly simmer for 6–8 hours, topping up with additional cold water as required.
Step 10	Clean round the sides of the pan, removing any dried scum and also skim as required.
Step 11	Strain the stock into a clean pan.

Important points

Step 9
Slow simmering: Stock must never be boiled quickly as it is likely to become cloudy.
Step 10
Seasoning: Salt must *not* be added to stocks but a few peppercorns may be added during cooking (unless a glaze is to be produced, see below).

Step 11
Storage: Stocks are usually taken fresh from the stockpot and used as required. When they are to be stored they should be cooled as quickly as possible then kept in a chill.
Note: During cooling, air should be allowed to circulate under the base of the pot (or cold water). *Never* cover with a lid when cooling.

Base recipe   (Yield 5 litres)

Main items:	2 kg raw bones; beef, veal, mutton or chicken etc.
Base vegetables:	200 g onions, 200 g carrots, 50 g celery, 50 g leeks, sprig of thyme, bay leaf and parsley stalks.
Water:	5 litres of water.

White beef stock (fonds blanc/fonds de marmite)

Brown beef stock (fonds brun)

Strong brown beef stock (estouffade)

White veal stock (fonds de veau)

Brown veal stock (fonds brun de veau)

White mutton stock (fonds de mouton)

Brown mutton stock (fonds brun de mouton)

White chicken stock (fonds de volaille)

Brown chicken stock (fonds brun de volaille)

Ham stock (fumet de jambon)

Brown game stock (fonds de gibier)

For fish stock see page 150.

Glazes

These are heavily concentrated stocks.

Meat glaze (glace de viande)

Chicken glaze (glace de volaille)

Veal glaze (glace de veau)

Game glaze (glace de gibier)

Recipe
5 litres of stock will yield 100–150 ml glaze.

Method
1 Boil down the stock in a saucepan.
2 Decant into a smaller saucepan and continue boiling down.
3 When thick and concentrated pour into jars, cool and store chilled.

Uses
Glazes are added to stocks or sauces to improve or increase the strength of flavour. In addition they may be used as a base for certain meat sauces.

Section two Consommés and aspic jellies (Fish, meat, game and poultry)

Base method

Step 1	Mise en place
	A Assemble ingredients.
	B Wash, peel and finely cut or mince the vegetables.
	C *Aspic jellies*: Soak the leaf gelatine in cold water.
Step 2	Prepare the clarification mixture as follows: thoroughly mix together the vegetables, minced flesh, egg whites and any tomato purée.
Step 3	Place the clarification mixture into a pot or boiler with a tap at the bottom⋆, add the cold stock and thoroughly whisk together.
	Aspic jellies: Add the soaked gelatine at this stage.
Step 4	Place on a cool stove and slowly bring to the boil. Stir only at the commencement of heating – *do not stir over 50° C*.
Step 5	Slowly simmer leaving the crust of the clarification undisturbed.
	Simmering time: Beef, poultry and game consommés and aspics: 1½ hours approximately.
	Fish consommés and aspics: 20 mins. approximately.
Step 6	Carefully strain the liquid (out of the tap or if no tap is present at one side of the clarification with as little disturbance as possible) through a double folded muslin or clean fine cloth into a pot or bowl.
Step 7	Correct the colour (if appropriate), check the seasoning and remove any surface grease with a dishpaper.
Step 8	*Consommés*: Serve in a consommé cup and saucer.
	Aspic jellies: Cool and use as required.

⋆ One should use a pot or boiler with a tap but this may only be possible when dealing with large quantities.

Important points

Step 1
Selection of ingredients: Blood, flesh and acid assist the clarification of savoury consommés and aspics and should be incorporated into the recipes where possible. Small quantities of tomato purée not only assist the clarification but add richness in colour and complement flavour.
Step 4
Stirring the mixture: The mixture is stirred initially to prevent burning and allow the gelatine in aspics to dissolve through the mixture but this must only be done up to a temperature prior to egg-white coagulation.
Step 5
Cooking the mixtures: The mixture should only *very slowly simmer* (or tick over); too fast a simmer or boil may break up the crust and no simmering movement is likely to result in the crust sinking down into the mixture. The crust should *never be disturbed*.

Step 6

Straining the liquid: The clarified mixture must be strained slowly, carefully allowing the mixture to trickle through the muslin cloth.

Step 7

Adding colouring and seasoning: This is done at a suitable point where the crust is open due to the simmering action (the opening may be carefully widened if very small).

RECIPES

Poultry, beef and game consommés

Base liquid:	1½ litres of appropriate brown stock
Clarification:	150 g lean minced beef (plus any appropriate trimmings – chicken or appropriate flesh, or game flesh, giblets and necks etc.). 100 g vegetables, i.e. carrot, onion, celery, leek and a sprig of thyme, ½ bay leaf and parsley stalks. 40 ml egg whites (2 egg whites approximately). 10 g tomato purée (optional).
Seasoning:	4 peppercorns added to the clarification and salt sprinkled in near the end of cooking – step 7.

Poultry, beef and game aspics

These are savoury jellies and are made by adding 50 g leaf gelatine to the appropriate consommée recipe. The exact quantity of gelatine will vary depending on how gelatinous the content of the basic stock used. After preparing the aspic it should be tested by placing a small quantity on a plate and allowing to set in a refrigerator. If the aspic is too firm add a little clear stock and retest.

Fish consommés

Base liquid:	1½ litres of good fish stock, 10 ml lemon juice (¼ lemon approximately) and 50 ml white wine.
Clarification:	150 g minced white fish flesh, 100 g chopped onions, sprig of thyme, ½ bay leaf and parsley stalks and 40 ml egg whites (2 eggs approximately).
Seasoning:	4 peppercorns added to the clarification and salt sprinkled in near the end of cooking – step 7.

Fish aspic

Add 50 g leaf gelatine to the above recipe; see poultry, beef and game aspics.

Beef consommés

Carmen   Add 50 g tomato purée and 50 g chopped pimento to the clarification. Garnish with diamonds of tomato flesh, cooked red pimento, boiled rice and a few shreds of blanched chervil.

Célestine   Thicken the strained consommé with a little cooked tapioca and garnish with thin strips of savoury pancake containing freshly chopped herbs (see page 285).

Julienne   Garnish the consommé with a julienne (thin strips) of vegetable, i.e. carrots, turnips, celery, leek, sorrel and chervil and peas; all cooked in a little consommé or salted water.

Petite marmite   Strong consommé of beef and chicken garnished with small turned cooked carrots and turnips, a julienne of celery, leek and cabbage, a dice of cooked boiled beef and chicken and slices of poached bone marrow. Accompany with toasted bread flûtes.

Croûte-au-pot   The same as petite marmite omitting the garnish of beef and chicken. When preparing the flûtes dip them in a little stock fat before drying in the oven.

En gelée   Prepare the consommé adding 30 g soaked leaf gelatine to the cold stock and clarification. When cold and set, lightly whisk to form a fine sparkling jelly before serving. *Note*: The exact quantity of gelatine to be added will vary depending on the strength of the basic stock – see how to test the strength of aspics, on opposite page.

Chicken consommés

Aurore   Add 50 g tomato purée to the clarification and when strained thicken with a little cooked tapioca. Garnish with a julienne of cooked chicken.

Royale   Garnish the consommé with small diamonds or cubes of savoury egg custard (page 393). The royale is carefully cut then stored in a bowl containing a little consommé prior to service in the consommé.

Caroline   The same as royale adding a little boiled rice and thin strips of blanched chervil.

Poule-au-pot   This is a strong chicken consommé made with pieces (or whole) of boiling fowl. Complete and garnish the same as petite marmite adding the dice of cooked fowl.

Clear oxtail soup (consommé aux queues de boeuf)

Prepare the consommé using brown oxtail stock. After clarifying infuse with turtle herbs and garnish with a brunoise (very small dice) of carrots, turnips, celery, leeks and peas cooked in a little consommé or salted water. Add a measure of Madeira wine when serving.

Polish bortsch (bortsch polonaise)

Prepare the consommé using strong duck stock and add to the clarification 50 g root fennel and a good sprig of marjoram. Cook in the consommé a piece of skinned duck and a piece of boiling beef (75 g each approximately). When strained, add the juice from a finely grated fresh beetroot and garnish with a julienne of carrot, leek and beetroot (all cooked) and the duck and beef cut into dice.

Serve separately: sour cream, beetroot juice and small puff pastry patties filled with duck purée.

Game consommé (consommé Diane)

Prepare the consommé using game stock and any available minced game trimmings added to the clarification. Garnish with a julienne of cooked game flesh and add a measure of Madeira wine when serving.

Fish consommé (consommé carmélite)

Prepare a fish consommé then lightly thicken with a little arrowroot diluted in cold water. Garnish with round white fish quenelles (page 74) and plain boiled rice.

Turtle soup (tortue claire)

Nowadays this soup is rarely prepared in the kitchen and is usually only available as a manufactured product. The preparation simply consists of heating the tinned soup (a little beef and chicken consommé is sometimes added) and finishing with a little Madeira wine when serving. Accompany with quarters of lemon and cheese straws (page 327).

In some instances turtle soup is prepared using dried turtle meat as follows:

1   Soak 50 g dried turtle meat in cold water for 24 hours.
2   Remove from the water and simmer in a little chicken consommé until tender.
3   Prepare 1 litre of beef consommé adding some raw chicken trimmings and the turtle cooking liquor.
4   When strained, flavour with turtle herbs and thicken with a little arrowroot diluted in cold water.
5   Dice the cooked turtle meat and add to the soup, check seasoning and finish with a measure of Madeira wine. Serve with the garnish of lemon and cheese straws.

Section three   Broths and plain boiled garnished soups

Base method

Step 1	Mise en place
	A Soak the cereal (or pulse) in cold water for several hours.
	B Assemble ingredients.
	C Wash and peel the vegetables then cut into a small dice 2–3 mm.
	D Trim up any fleshy bones, scrag flesh or fowl.
Step 2	Place the stock or water in a saucepan and add any bones, scrag flesh or boiling fowl.
Step 3	Bring to the boil, skim if required then add any barley or marrow fat peas and simmer for 1 hour approximately. Skim as required.
Step 4	Add the base vegetables *except* the leeks and simmer for 10–15 mins. A bouquet garni is also added at this stage.
Step 5	Add the leeks and any rice then simmer until cooked.
Step 6	Check the seasoning, consistency and temperature. Remove the bouquet garni if used. Remove any flesh from bones and dice and replace in soup. Sprinkle with roughly chopped parsley when serving.

Important points

Step 3
Cloudy liquid: If the liquid is very cloudy when boiling point is reached (because of the bones or flesh used), refresh under cold running water and return to step 2.

Steps 3, 4 and 5
Topping up with additional liquid: The soup should be topped up with additional liquid as and when required.

Steps 3, 4 and 5
Cooking time: This usually varies between 1½–2 hours depending on the type of ingredients used.

Step 5
The use of fresh leguminous vegetables: When fresh or frozen peas or beans are used, they are added near the end of the cooking period and allowed to cook through.

Base recipe   (yield 4 portions)

Base liquid:	1 litre of white stock or water – see each broth below.
	Note: Fleshy bones or pieces of fowl may be used as appropriate: use 100 g scrag flesh or fowl per litre approximately.
Cereal or pulse:	25 g cereal or pulse vegetables.
Vegetable garnish:	50 g onion, 50 g carrot, 50 g turnip, 30 g celery and 30 g leek.
	1 bouquet garni (optional).
Seasoning:	Salt and pepper.
Parsley:	A little roughly chopped parsley.

Scotch broth

Use mutton stock or mutton bones and water. Also use barley as the cereal. *Note*:   A few marrowfat peas or fresh/frozen peas may also be added.

Chicken broth

Use chicken stock and a small piece of boiling fowl or chicken. Also use long grain rice as the cereal.

Pulse broth

Use white stock and a mixture of pulse vegetables (30 g approximately).

Barley broth

Use white stock and a piece of boiling beef. Use barley as the cereal and increase the quantity in the base recipe to 40 g.

88 *Professional Cookery*

Section four   Pulse soups and pulse vegetables

Base method

Step 1	Mise en place
	A Soak the pulse vegetable in cold water for 12 hours approximately. B Assemble ingredients. C Prepare the *base* vegetables: Pulse soups (*except* green-pea) Roughly chop the vegetables. Green-pea soup and green-pea purée. Leave the carrot whole and roughly chop the remaining vegetables. Pulse vegetables and pulse purées. Leave the vegetables whole (where possible).
Step 2	Place two-thirds of the water or stock (1 litre) in a saucepan and add the bones.
Step 3	Drain the water off the soaked pulse and add the pulse to the stock and bones.
Step 4	Bring to the boil, stirring as required to prevent burning.
Step 5	Skim off the scum as it forms on top of the liquid. Also remove any dried scum which forms on the sides of the pan.
Step 6	Add the base vegetables.
Step 7	Slowly simmer. Skim and top up with additional stock as required throughout the cooking period. *Note*: When preparing purées allow the purée to dry out.

Whole pulse vegetables (vegetable course)	*Soups and purées*	
When cooked, remove the base vegetables.	Remove the carrots when preparing *split-pea soups* or *purées*. Pass through a soup machine, sieve or liquidizer. Place into a clean pan and reboil.	

Check consistency, seasoning and temperature.

	Soups	*Purées*
Serve in a vegetable or entrée dish with a little of the cooking liquor.	Serve in soup tureen or plates accompanied with any garnish, e.g. croûtons.	Place in vegetable or entrée dish then neatly shape and mark with a palette knife dipped in hot water.

PULSE SOUPS

Base recipe: (yield 4 portions)

Pulse vegetables:	200 g pulse vegetables, see below.
Base vegetables:	50 g carrot, 50 g onion, 25 g celery, 25 g leek, sprig of thyme, ½ bay leaf and parsley stalks.
Bones:	100 g bacon or ham bones.
Liquid:	1½ litres water or white stock.
Seasoning:	Salt and white pepper.

Lentil soup (purée de lentilles)

Use lentils as pulse vegetable.

Potage Esaü

Lentil soup adding garnish of boiled long grain rice (25 g) and liaising with cream just prior to service.

Potage gentilhomme

Prepare Esaü above but use game stock and add a measure of Madeira wine near the end of the cooking period. Also add a dice of bacon to the garnish.

Split-pea soup (purée de pois cassés)

Use split-peas as the pulse vegetable.

Yellow split-pea soup (purée égyptienne)

Use yellow split peas as the pulse vegetable.

Red bean soup (purée Condé)

Use red beans as the pulse vegetable and 200 ml red wine in the cooking liquid.

Haricot bean soup (purée soissonnaise)

Use haricot beans as the pulse vegetable.

Production: Follow the instructions in the base method.
Cooking time: 1½–2 hours.
Traditional accompaniments: Basic pulse soups (usually ungarnished soups) are often served with *croûtons* i.e. a dice of crisp fried bread. Remove the crusts from a slice of bread then cut into a 5 mm dice. Shallow-fry in a little butter (25 g) until crisp and golden brown.

PULSE VEGETABLES

Base recipe: (yield 4 portions)

The same as for pulse soups above but use half the

quantity of the pulse vegetable (100 g).

Red beans (haricots rouges)   Use red beans in recipe.
Haricot beans (haricots blancs)   Use haricot beans in recipe.
Flageolet beans (haricots flageolets)   Use flageolet beans in recipe.
Butter beans   Use butter beans in recipe.
Marrowfat peas   Use marrowfat peas in recipe.

Derivatives

au beurre   Brush the cooked vegetable with a little melted butter and sprinkle with chopped parsley.

américaine   Drain from the cooking liquor and bind with 200 ml hot tomato sauce.

en purée   Follow instructions in the base method for a purée of vegetables: Purée Esaü – lentil; Purée Conti – lentil; Purée Condé – red bean; Purée Musard – flageolet bean; Pease pudding – yellow split-pea.

Section five   Boiled meat and poultry

Base method

Step 1	Mise en place
	A Assemble ingredients.
	B Tie the joint or bird with string (tongue does not require to be tied).
	C *Salted meats* (pickled ham and tongue): Soak in cold water up to 24 hours then discard the soaking liquid.
	D Wash, peel and prepare the vegetables, i.e. leave small vegetables whole and cut large vegetables into neat pieces.
Step 2	Place the joint or bird in a saucepan, cover with cold water (or stock) then bring to the boil.
Step 3	Wipe the sides of the pan to remove any scum and skim the cooking liquor. Repeat this procedure as required during cooking.
Step 4	Add the bouquet garni and celery and allow to simmer for 40 mins. approximately.
Step 5	Add the carrots and onions and simmer for a further 15 mins. approximately.
Step 6	Add the remaining vegetables and simmer until all the vegetables and meat are cooked – see important points.
Step 7	Remove the joint and allow to cool slightly. *Note*: Remove any rind or fat if preparing ham or tongue.
Step 8	Carve the joint into 4–8 neat slices and place on the serving dish. When preparing poultry cut into joints, see page 69.
Step 9	Cut the whole pieces of vegetables (large turnips, swedes, cabbage and celery etc.) into four neat portions then arrange all the vegetables around the serving dish.
Step 10	Coat the meat or poultry with a little of the very hot cooking liquor. Ensure the dish is hot.
Step 11	Serve the completed dish accompanied with the cooking liquor and any other suitable garnish, see individual recipe.

Important points

Step 1

Selection of ingredients: This method of cooking is suitable for the joints and flesh from mature animals. It is appropriate to older fowl (boiling birds) but not chicken – this is dealt with on page 114.

Step 2

Starting the cooking of pieces of flesh from mature animals in cold water then bringing to the boil helps to remove the blood, fat and undesirable odours associated with poor quality commodities.

Step 2

Size of cooking utensil: The cooking utensil should only be large enough to accommodate the meat and vegetables, thus keeping the amount of water to a minimum.

Step 6

Adding seasoning: Fresh meats may be seasoned during cooking but pickled or salted meats must not have any salt added during cooking. However all dishes should be checked for seasoning on completing the cooking.

Step 6

Cooking times:

Fresh and salted meats (medium-sized joints, 3 kg approximately)   1 hour per kg approximately.

Poultry (boiling fowl):   1¼ hour per kg approximately.

Note: The cooking times of meat and poultry vary considerably and the above times are rough approximations. Therefore the test for cooking must be made at various times during the process.

Vegetables: The addition of the vegetables into the boiling liquid is determined by their respective cooking times. These cooking times vary substantially therefore *occasional inspections* should be made to ascertain whether a particular vegetable has cooked earlier than anticipated and removed if this is found to be the case.

Step 6

Test for cooking: There should be little resistance felt when inserting a small needle or cocktail stick. In addition the flesh should yield under firm pressure without being spongy. Stringing or breaking apart of the cooked flesh is a sign of overcooking.

Step 6

Cooking loss: This ranges from 40–50% depending on the size of the joint and should be taken into account when calculating portion yield (small joints losing a greater percentage of weight than large joints).

Step 11

Hot storage: Boiled meat or poultry dishes may be kept hot for short periods during service, this is done by keeping both the sliced meat and vegetables in the cooking liquor.

Base recipe   (yield 4 portions)

Main item:	See individual dish or commodity below.
Vegetable garnish:	100 g celery, 100 g carrots, 100 g onions (4 small onions), 100 g piece of turnip or swede, 100 g leek, 100 g piece of cabbage and 100 g potatoes (4 small potatoes).
Additional flavouring:	Bouquet garni.
Liquid:	Water or cold white stock to cover.
Parsley:	A little chopped parsley for the top of the vegetables (optional).

Boiled beef – French style (boeuf bouilli à la française)

Use a 600 g piece of beef, i.e. brisket, fresh silverside, or thin flank etc.

Prepare as stated and accompany with coarse salt and pickled gherkins with the cooking liquor.

Boiled leg of mutton with caper sauce

Use a piece of leg mutton – 1 kg approximately (depending on bone content).

Follow the instructions to Step 6 then prepare a caper sauce with the cooking liquor (see page 171). Serve as stated accompanied with the sauce.

Pot-au-feu

This is prepared the same as boiled beef with the addition of pieces of fowl. This dish may be served as a soup; halve the quantities in the base recipe and when cooked, cut the vegetables into paysanne and the meat and poultry into a neat dice.

Boiled silverside and dumplings

Use a 600 g piece of pickled silverside. Prepare as stated; traditionally only the carrots and onions in the base recipe are used.

Prepare 100 g suet pastry (page 342) and mould into

small dumplings. Add to the meat at the end of the cooking period and poach until cooked (15 mins. approximately).

Boiled hen, ham, gammon, tongue or salt port etc.

These are prepared as stated in the base method with the range of vegetables used at the discretion of the cook. When the items are to be boiled only and not served as dishes the base vegetables are omitted or only onion and carrots used.

Section six   Irish stew

Base method

Step 1	Mise en place
	A Assemble ingredients.
	B Trim off excess fat from the mutton or lamb then cut into a neat dice (25 mm approximately). (If using neck cutlets, leave on the bone.)
	C Wash and peel the vegetables.
	D Turn the potatoes into barrel shapes (35–40 mm) reserving the trimmings.
	E Cut into small pieces the potato trimmings, ordinary onions, celery, white leek and cabbage.
Step 2	Blanch and refresh the meat.
Step 3	Drain the mutton flesh and place in a saucepan then cover with the white stock or water. Bring to the boil and skim if required.
Step 4	Add the small pieces of potato, onion, celery, leek and cabbage and simmer for 1 hour approximately (until the meat is almost cooked).
Step 5	Add the button onions and simmer for a further 10 mins. approximately.
Step 6	Add the turned potatoes and complete the cooking.
Step 7	Check seasoning, consistency and temperature.
Step 8	Place in an entrée dish etc., and sprinkle with chopped parsley. Accompany with pickled red cabbage.

Important points

Step 2

Blanching and refreshing: The meat is placed in a saucepan and covered with cold water then brought to the boil. After this it is refreshed under cold running water until all the scum has been removed.

Steps 3, 4, 5 and 6

Cooking time: This will vary with the quality of the meat used but should be between 1½–2 hours.

Base recipe   (yield 4 portions)

Main item:	600 g boneless stewing mutton or lamb (or 800 g neck cutlets).
Base vegetables:	500 g potatoes, 100 g onions, 100 g celery, 100 g white leek and 100 g white cabbage.
Vegetable garnish:	100 g button onions and turned potatoes *from the potatoes above*.
Bouquet garni:	1 bouquet garni (optional).
Liquid:	White stock or water to cover.
Seasoning:	Salt and pepper.
Parsley:	Pinch of chopped parsley.
Garnish:	A small dish of pickled red cabbage.

Section seven   Plain boiled root vegetables (potatoes, carrots and turnips, parsnips, beetroot and Jerusalem artichokes)

Base method

Step 1	Mise en place
	A Assemble ingredients.
	B *Vegetables peeled then cooked* (all vegetables *except* beetroot): Wash, scrub and peel the vegetables. Cut large vegetables into suitable sizes for cooking.
	Vegetables cooked then peeled (beetroot and some potato dishes, see recipe): Wash, scrub and remove any spots or mould from the vegetables.
Step 2	Place the vegetables in a saucepan and cover with water.
Step 3	Place on the stove, add salt and bring to the boil.
Step 4	Simmer slowly until cooked.
Step 5	Carefully drain the vegetables and complete as stated in the individual recipe.
Step 6	*Puréed vegetables* Add any recipe butter to the vegetables and leave at the side of the stove (lid on) to dry.
Step 7	Pass through a sieve, ricer or triturator then check the seasoning adding pepper and salt if necessary.
Step 8	Complete as stated in the individual recipe.

Important points

Step 1

Selection of vegetables: As a general rule good quality, firm root vegetables should always be selected.

There are many varieties of potato, and a variety should be selected which suits the dish to be prepared; some potatoes cook soft and mealy and are therefore suitable for purées while others cook firm and are more suitable for dishes in which the potatoes are left whole or sliced, e.g. sautés and rissolé potatoes. The cook should be aware of the types of potato available on the local market and their cooking quality.

Step 1

Preparation: Carrots, turnips, swedes, parsnips and Jerusalem artichokes are peeled prior to cooking but *beetroot is not peeled* because it would bleed and deteriorate during cooking. In some instances potatoes are left unpeeled (e.g. sautées and potato salad) because the skin reduces the likelihood of the potato breaking up during cooking and also imparts flavour.

Step 2

Covering with water: Covering with cold water should only be the rule when there is a risk of scalding the operator (see page 79). In all other circumstances hot (on tap) or boiling water should be used to keep the cooking time to a minimum.

Step 4

Test for cooking: The cooking times of vegetables vary substantially, therefore the test for cooking should be made regularly while simmering. Potatoes, carrots, turnips, parsnips and Jerusalem artichokes: there should be little resistance when a small knife is inserted. Beetroot are usually cooked when the skin can be removed.

Base recipe

As a general rule allow 500 g root vegetables per four portions.

Dishes using potatoes peeled prior to cooking

Plain boiled potatoes (pommes nature/anglaise)

Cut or turn the potatoes into even-sized pieces then follow the instructions stated in the base recipe and method. Serve plain in a vegetable dish.

Parsley potatoes (pommes persillées)

The same as plain boiled potatoes but brushed with a little melted butter and sprinkled with chopped parsley for service.

Pommes Quelin   Cut the raw potatoes with a parisienne spoon and then prepare the same as parsley potatoes.

Minted potatoes (pommes à la menthe)

Prepare the same as boiled potatoes adding a few mint stalks during cooking and placing a few blanched mint leaves on top of the potatoes for service.

Snow or riced potatoes (pommes en neige)

Cut the potatoes into even-sized pieces then follow the base method and recipe for puréed vegetables. Pass through a potato masher (ricer) directly into the vegetable dish (leaving as it falls and resembling snow) then serve immediately.

Mashed potatoes (pommes en purée)

Cut the potatoes into even-sized pieces then proceed as stated for puréed vegetables adding 25 g butter per 400 g potato. Work in 25 ml hot milk per 400 g potato until light and fluffy. Serve in a vegetable dish shaping with a palette knife and marking with the knife or a spoon dipped in hot water.

Mashed potatoes with cheese (pommes au gratin)

Mashed potatoes brushed with melted butter and sprinkled with grated cheese then gratinated under the grill or salamander until golden brown.

Creamed potatoes (pommes en purée à la crème)

Mashed potatoes coated with a little warm cream for service.

Pommes mousseline   Mashed potatoes with 25–50 ml of double cream beaten in until very light and creamy.

Pommes Biarritz   Mashed potatoes mixing through 25 g diced red pimento and 50 g diced cooked ham sweated in a little butter.

Duchess potatoes (pommes duchesse)

The same mixture as mashed potato but adding 25 ml egg yolk (1 small egg yolk) per 400 g potato in place of the milk (this is used to bind the mixture into a fine pliable mass). Season with salt, pepper and a pinch of nutmeg.

Pipe the potato mixture on to a greased tray resembling a solid spiral (40 mm × 40 mm) and place in a hot oven to heat through. Remove, brush with eggwash and brown under the salamander. Serve in a suitable vegetable dish.

Marquis potatoes (pommes marquise)

Prepare the same as duchesse, piping into the shape of nests and filling with hot tomato concassé (see page 273). Sprinkle with chopped parsley for service.

Brioche potatoes (pommes en brioche)

Prepare the same as duchesse potatoes shaping into two balls, i.e. 1 × 300 mm and 1 × 100 mm. Place the small ball on top of the large ball and press down with a floured finger or implement.

Pommes galette Prepare a duchesse mixture, shape like fishcakes and criss-cross the top. Shallow-fry in a preheated frying pan only polished with fat until golden brown. Serve in a vegetable dish with some branch parsley placed at the side.

Croquette potatoes (pommes croquettes)

Duchesse mixture shaped into cylinders, i.e. 40 mm × 20 mm and passed through flour, eggwash and breadcrumbs. Correct the shape by carefully rolling then fry in hot fat until heated through and golden-brown. Serve on a dishpaper on a salver or vegetable dish, see page 298 on deep-frying of foods.

Almond potatoes (pommes amandines)

Croquette potatoes using nib almonds in place of breadcrumbs.

Pommes Berny Duchesse mixture adding a little chopped truffle and shaping like apricots. Finish the same as croquette potatoes using flaked almonds in place of breadcrumbs. A piece of parsley stalk or leek leaf may be inserted into the completed potato to resemble an apricot.

Pommes Saint-Florentin/royale Duchesse mixture adding ham and shaping into oblongs. Finish the same as croquette potatoes using crushed vermicelli in place of breadcrumbs.

Pommes dauphine Two parts duchesse potato mixed with one part choux paste, e.g. 300 g duchesse potato to 150 g choux paste, see page 344. Shape with two spoons dipped in hot water and place on to oiled paper. Fry in hot oil the same as croquette potatoes.

Pommes Lorette Prepare the same as dauphine (but in cigar shapes) adding 5–10 g parmesan cheese to the basic mixture.

Pommes Bussy Prepare the same as dauphine adding a little chopped truffle and chopped parsley to the basic mixture.

Pommes caronel Prepare the same as dauphine adding thin strips of truffle (julienne) to the basic mixture.

Pommes Elizabeth Prepare the same as dauphine adding 50 g chopped cooked spinach (see page 135) to the basic mixture.

Pommes belle-promenade Prepare the same as dauphine

adding a dice of cooked artichoke and truffle to the basic mixture.

Pommes rissolées These are precooked potatoes (boiled) shallow-fried and tossed in hot fat until golden brown. See page 276.

Dishes using unpeeled potatoes on completion of cooking

Pommes Alphonse Peel and slice the hot cooked potato and toss in melted parsley butter, seasoning with salt and pepper. Place in the serving dish and sprinkle with grated cheese then brown under the salamander (gratinate).

Pommes à la crème Peel and slice the cooked potato and place in a clean cooking utensil. Add 25 g butter and 25 ml milk, bring quickly to the boil and toss occasionally. Add cream to bind and serve in a vegetable dish.
Note: The potato should be cooked a little underdone prior to completing with milk and butter.

Pommes maître-d'hôtel Prepare the same as à la crème adding chopped parsley for service.

Pommes Schneider Prepare the same as à la crème but adding 25 ml stock in place of milk and a little meat glaze instead of cream. Serve in a vegetable dish sprinkled with chopped parsley.

Sweet potatoes (patates)

Follow the instructions given in the base recipe and method completing in the same styles as mashed, creamed, duchesse or croquette potatoes etc.

Jerusalem artichokes (topinambours)

Follow the instructions given in the base recipe and method completing in the same styles as plain boiled or mashed potatoes etc.

Topinambours à la crème Follow the instructions given in the base recipe and method for peeled vegetables. After draining the artichokes roll in 200 ml sauce crème (page 169) or cream, season with salt and pepper and serve in a vegetable dish.

Topinambours hollandaise Prepare the same as à la crème replacing the cream sauce with hollandaise sauce, see page 389.

Topinambours Coligny Prepare the artichokes plainly boiled then after draining roll in 25 g butter, a little lemon juice and meat glaze to bind, see page 82. Serve in a vegetable dish sprinkled with chopped parsley.

Topinambours maître-d'hôtel The same as à la crème sprinkled with fresh chopped herbs for service.

Carrots and turnips (carottes et navets)

The basic preparation for these vegetables, i.e. peeling, cutting and turning is explained in Chapter 3, page 36. Baby carrots and turnips may be cooked and served whole but larger vegetables require to be cut or shaped before cooking.

Buttered carrots (carottes au beurre) Follow the instructions given in the base recipe and method, leaving the vegetables whole or shaping as desired. After draining the vegetable brush with a little melted butter and sprinkle with chopped parsley.

Buttered turnip (navets au beurre) Prepare the same as buttered carrots.

Mashed turnips (purée de navets) Follow the instructions given in the base recipe and method for puréed vegetables. Use 25 g butter, Step 6. The turnip is cut into medium-sized cubes to assist even cooking. Season with salt and pepper and serve in a vegetable dish shaped and marked with a pallet knife or spoon dipped in hot water.
Note: A small quantity of mashed potato is often added to the turnip purée to stabilize the mixture.

Parsnips (panais)

These are prepared the same as carrots and for the various styles of preparation see topinambour.

Mixed vegetables (macédoine de légumes)

Cut 200 g each of prepared carrot and turnip into 5 mm dice and cook as stated. After draining add 50 g each cooked peas and diamonds of green beans. Correct temperature and season and brush with a little butter (alternatively, toss in hot butter).

Beetroot (betterave)

Follow the instructions given in the base recipe and method for vegetables cooked unpeeled. Baby beets are more suitable to be served as a hot vegetable than the larger varieties which are normally sliced for service. After draining the vegetable peel and season with salt and pepper. Serve hot in a vegetable dish. They may be prepared à la crème, au beurre or served with a suitable sauce, e.g. sauce piquante.

Mixed vegetable purées (purées de légumes composées)

Individual vegetable purées may be mixed together to produce a compound or mixed purée. The following mixtures are produced from the single vegetable purées included in this section:

Palestine: Jerusalem artichoke and potato.

Saxone: Turnip, potato and onion.

Technical terms for single vegetable purées

Mashed potatoes: purée Parmentier.
Mashed turnip: purée Freneuse.

Important: This method of preparation is for the cooking of large quantities of these vegetables. Small quantities of these vegetables are usually cooked *glacé*, see page 97.

Section eight Glazed vegetables (légumes glacés)

Base method

Step 1	Mise en place
	A Assemble ingredients.
	B Wash, peel and shape the vegetables (turned, dice or bâtons etc.).
Step 2	A Place the vegetables in a small saucepan.
	B Add the butter and sugar.
	C Add seasoning then cover with water.
Step 3	Bring to the boil and cook steadily allowing the water to evaporate.
	Note: Toss the vegetables frequently when evaporation has reduced the water content.
Step 4	Test for cooking. If still underdone, add a little extra water.
Step 5	Continue cooking (and tossing) until all the water has evaporated and the vegetable is cooked and glazed.

Important points

Steps 3, 4 and 5

Speed of cooking: This is carried out in relation to the cooking time of the vegetable concerned. It may be necessary to alter the speed of cooking, i.e. increase or decrease the boiling speed and therefore the evaporation rate during the cooking of a vegetable. The speed of cooking is usually increased at the end or near the end of the cooking period when the vegetable is almost cooked and remaining liquid has to be evaporated off to form the glaze.

Important;   Different vegetables should never be mixed together (e.g. carrots and turnips etc.) when cooking glacé as the cooking times vary.

Note: Some cooks use a lid at the beginning (or middle) of the cooking period.

Step 5

Glazed appearance: The glazed appearance is produced by the butter and sugar which forms a coating round the vegetables when all the liquid has evaporated. Vegetable dishes incorporating a mineral or spa water are usually cooked in this manner because the goodness and flavour which would be lost with ordinary boiling and drained vegetables is avoided.

Base recipe   (yield 4 portions)

Main item:	500–800 g vegetable depending on the method of shaping, i.e. carrots, turnips, swedes or parsnips.
Butter:	15 g butter or margarine approximately.
Sugar:	15 g caster sugar.
Seasoning:	Pinch salt and pepper.

Dishes

Plain glazed vegetables   Follow the recipe and method above.

A la crème   Cook the vegetables as stated then add cream sauce or cream and bind together.

Carottes Vichy   Thinly slice the carrots then cook glacé.
Note: Although this method of cooking usually denotes a style it may more accurately contain Vichy water.

Cooking glazed chestnuts and glazed button onions

When cooking these vegetables the cooking procedure has to be amended because of their delicate nature. Proceed as stated but remove the vegetables from the liquid when cooked. Reduce the liquor to a glaze, add the vegetables then roll together.

Part one (B) — Foods placed into cold liquid then brought to the boil and cooked: sweet items

Section nine   Fruit jellies (table jellies)

Base method

Step 1	Mise en place
	A Assemble ingredients.
	B Prepare the fruit:
	Citrus fruits (lemon, orange, lime and grapefruit): 1 Remove the zest with a peeler. 2 Cut off the pith and discard then slice up the fruit.
	Raspberries and strawberries: Remove the husks and any deteriorated fruit then wash.
	Stone fruits (plums, cherries and greengages etc.): Wash, remove the stones and cut up the fruit.
	C Soak the leaf gelatine in cold water.
Step 2	Place all the ingredients in a saucepan and whisk thoroughly together.
Step 3	Place on the stove and slowly bring to the boil. Do not stir over 50°C.
Step 4	Slowly simmer for 20 mins. leaving the crust of the clarification undisturbed.
Step 5	Carefully strain through a muslin or jelly bag into a clean bowl.
Step 6	Check the colour, acidity (lemon juice may be added) and sweetness then drop a small quantity on a plate and allow to set in refrigerator. If the jelly is too firm add a little water and retest.
Step 7	When the correct consistency has been achieved cool the jelly as quickly as possible then pour into mould and place into the refrigerator to set.
Step 8	When set, unmould by momentarily dipping in hot water and inverting on to the serving dish.

Important points

See the important points listed for aspic jelly, page 83.

Base recipe   (yield 1 litre)

Base liquid:	1 litre of cold water.
Sugar:	200 g granulated sugar.
Egg whites:	40 ml egg white (2 eggs approximately).
Base flavour:	Small piece of bay leaf, cinnamon stick and 4 coriander seeds.
Fruit content:	*Lemon jelly:* Use 3 lemons. *Orange jelly:* Use 2 oranges and 1 lemon. *Raspberry jelly:* Use 250 g ripe fruit. *Strawberry jelly:* Use 250 g ripe fruit. *Stone fruit jellies:* Use 250 g ripe fruit.
Gelatine:	40 g leaf gelatine.
Colouring:	Appropriate food colouring (if necessary).

Liqueur jellies (gelée à la liqueur)

Prepare the selected fruit jelly and add a good measure of
appropriate liqueur just prior to setting point.

Swedish jelly (gelée suédoise)

Garnish the jelly with a variety of fruits. Set the jelly in
layers in the mould adding the fruit to each layer.

Russian jelly (gelée à la russe)

When the jelly is cold and about to set place in a mixing
machine and whisk until very light and resembling a stiff
foam. Place in the mould and allow to set.

Section ten   Fruit jams, jellies and sauces

Base method

Apricot, barberry, bilberry, blackcurrant, cranberry, gooseberry, greengage, damson, loganberry, melon, mulberry, peach and plum.

Step 1	Mise en place A Assemble ingredients. B Wash the fruit and remove any stalks, seeds, stones, or spots of mould or deterioration. C Cut large fruit into pieces.
Step 2	Place the fruit in a preserving pan and add any acid – see individual recipe and important points
Step 3	*Fruits requiring preliminary stewing*: (Plum, damson, apricot, peach, cranberry, blackcurrant and gooseberry, see important points) Add the recipe water, bring to the boil and simmer until the fruit is tender.
Step 4	Add the sugar and gently heat until the sugar is completely dissolved, stirring occasionally to prevent burning.
Step 5	Bring to the boil and boil continuously until setting point is reached, see important points. *Note*: Remove any scum which forms on the surface of the jam as and when required.
Step 6	Allow the jam to cool slightly and thicken to prevent whole fruit or pieces of fruit floating on the jam surface when put in jars.
Step 7	Pour the jam into sterile jars then immediately cover with waxed paper discs.
Step 8	Seal the jar with the lid which has been previously sterilized then label and store in a cool place.

Important points

Step 2

Addition of acid: The presence of acid is necessary for the formation of a good gel and the inversion of the sugar. Too little acid present may not only result in a poor gel but may also produce a jam which is sugary or granulated. Fruits deficient in acid, e.g. melon and peach, require acid to be added to the recipe but the exact amount varies with the type of fruit. Quantity of acid to be added per 1 kg of fruit: 25 ml lemon juice of 5 g citric acid crystals.

Note: This is only a general guide and may vary considerably with the type of fruit used, therefore test batches should be made to ascertain the exact quantity of acid required for any one type of fruit. Too much acid produces a lumpy jam with a very firm set.

Step 3

Fruits requiring preliminary stewing: Some fruits require a period of cooking to soften the skins. In addition certain fruits set with a very firm gel thus requiring additional water to produce the correct strength of gel.

Step 5

Cooking until setting point is reached: This may be tested in two ways:

1   When some of the boiling jam is dropped from a spoon the last drops to fall should fall very slowly or run together forming a sheet or flake.

2   When a few spots of the boiling jam are dropped on to a cold dry plate, allowed to cool and then pressed with the fingers, they should wrinkle and indicate the strength of the set.

Step 5

Adding colouring: Some fruits contain very little colour pigmentation and therefore require the addition of artificial colour to achieve the correct colour.

Base recipe for jams prepared with an equal quantity of fruit and sugar

Main item:	1 kg fruit, e.g. apricot, barberry, bilberry, cranberry, greengage, melon, plum, mulberry, damson and peach.
Sugar:	1 kg sugar.
Water:	250 ml water (used to stew fruits with tough skins, e.g. plums, damsons, apricots, peaches, greengages and cranberries).
Acid:	25 ml lemon juice or 5 g citric acid (to be used for fruits with a low acid content, i.e. peaches, melon).

Base recipe for fruits prepared with one and a quarter times the sugar weight to fruit weight

Main item:	1 kg fruit, i.e. blackcurrant, gooseberry and loganberry.
Sugar:	1¼ kg sugar.
Water:	500 ml water.

Base method for jams which require pectin to be added

Strawberry, raspberry and cherry.

Step 1	Mise en place
	A Assemble ingredients.
	B Remove any stalks or seeds and inspect the fruit for insects.
	C Lightly wash the fruit then drain carefully and thoroughly.
	D Place the fruit in a preserving pan, add the sugar and lemon juice and leave to stand for 1 hour.

↓

Step 2	Place on the stove and gently heat the fruit until the sugar has dissolved. Stir occasionally to prevent burning.

↓

Step 3	Bring to the boil and boil continuously for 4 mins. stirring to prevent burning. *Note*: A small piece of butter (30 g approximately) may be added to reduce foaming and jam loss.

↓

Step 4	Remove the mixture from the heat, add the liquid pectin and stir well until completely mixed. Cool slightly then put in jars, see previous base method, steps 6, 7 and 8.

Important points

Step 4
Addition of pectin: This carbohydrate is already present in many fruits and is chiefly responsible for the gelling or setting properties of the jam. Some fruits contain very little pectin therefore commercially prepared liquid pectin has to be added. In some instances the manufacturer issues instructions for its use and these should be followed.

Base recipe

Main item:	1 kg fruit, i.e. strawberries, raspberries or cherries.
Sugar:	1¼ kg sugar.
Acid:	40 ml lemon juice (1 large lemon).
Pectin:	250 ml liquid pectin.

Fruit jellies
Redcurrant, blackcurrant and gooseberry

To produce fruit jellies, boil the berries in water to extract a full fruit flavour then strain and press the liquor out of the berries. Add 800 g sugar to each litre of liquor then boil until setting point is reached, see step 5 for fruit jams.

Fruit glazes

Apricot glaze Boil apricot jam with a little water to produce a coating consistency then strain. Use while hot.

Red glaze Boil redcurrant jelly with a little water to produce a coating consistency. Use while hot.

Arrowroot glazes The preparation of these glazes is explained on page 145.

Jam sauces

Hot jam sauces These are prepared by boiling together jam and water then thickening with a little arrowroot – see fécule thickened sauces on page 145.

Cold jam sauces Strawberry sauce (sauce de fraises), Raspberry sauce (sauce Melba), Gooseberry sauce (sauce de groseilles), Cherry sauce (sauce de cerises), Blackcurrant sauce (sauce de cassis)

Production: The economical method of preparing these sauces is as follows:
1 Boil together 200 g of the appropriate fruit jam and 50 ml water.
2 Strain if required then allow to cool.
3 When cold flavour with a little kirsch (optional).
Note: Fresh raspberry and strawberry sauces may be made by simply puréeing the fresh fruit and adding sugar to taste.

Cold buffet sauces based on redcurrant jelly

Cumberland sauce (yield 6–8 portions)
Recipe:
10 g finely chopped shallot or onion, zest and juice from a ½ orange, 200 g redcurrant jelly, 25 ml port wine, a pinch of English mustard, 10 ml lemon juice (½ small lemon) and a little cayenne pepper and ground ginger.

Method:
1 Blanch the shallots in a little boiling water for 10 seconds then drain well and allow to cool.
2 Peel the zest from the orange then cut into very fine strips (julienne). Blanch in boiling water for 1–2 mins approximately, then drain well and allow to cool.
3 Melt the redcurrant jelly in a bowl then whisk in the port wine and the juice from the half orange.
4 Dilute the mustard in the lemon juice and also add to the melted redcurrant jelly.
5 Garnish with the blanched shallots and orange zest then season with the cayenne pepper and ground ginger. Serve cold.

Oxford sauce
The same as Cumberland sauce but grate the zest from both the orange and lemon (instead of cutting into strips) and add directly to the melted redcurrant jelly. Serve cold.

Section eleven   Fruit pulps, purées and sauces

Base method

Apple, cranberry and gooseberry

Step 1	Mise en place

A   Assemble ingredients.
B   Prepare the fruit:

Apples: Peel, core and wash the apples then cut into slices or pieces.

Cranberries: Inspect the cranberries and remove any stalks or foreign bodies. Wash and drain.

Gooseberries: Top and tail the gooseberries then lightly scrape over the surfaces to remove any hairs. Wash and drain.

Note: The preparation of fruits for cooking is explained on page 40.

Step 2	Place the fruit in a tin-lined or stainless steel saucepan then add the sugar, water and any lemon juice.

Step 3	Cook to a soft pulp stirring as required to prevent burning.

Step 4	Pass the pulp through a sieve or liquidizer if required.

Step 5	Check the sugar content, consistency and temperature.

Step 6	Blend through any butter or margarine if stated in the recipe.

Important points

Step 2
Cooking the mixture in a tin-lined or stainless steel saucepan: Some fruits (especially cranberries) should not be cooked in an iron or aluminium pan as they discolour and develop a metallic taste.

Recipes for fruit pulp sauces   (yield 4 portions approximately)

Apple sauce
300 g cooking apples, 20 g sugar, juice of ¼ lemon, 25 ml water (1 tablespoon) and 10 g butter.

Sieve the pulp at step 4 then complete as stated. Serve warm.

Cranberry sauce
150 g cranberries, 40 g sugar and 100 ml water.

This sauce may be left as a pulp or sieved to a smooth purée. It is served warm with hot dishes but may alternatively be served as a cold buffet sauce.

Gooseberry sauce
300 g gooseberries, 50 g sugar, juice of ¼ lemon and 100 ml water.

Like cranberry sauce this sauce may also be served as a pulp or smooth purée and warm or cold.

Fruit pulps
Fruit pulps are often used as fillings for tarts and pies etc. When a firm pulp is required, follow the instructions in the base method but use as little water as possible.

Section twelve   Sugar boiling and boiled-sugar products

Base method

Step 1	Place the sugar and water into the sugar boiling pan.
Step 2	Bring to the boil on a low heat stirring occasionally.
Step 3	Boil for 30 secs. approximately then remove the syrup from the boil and check the clarity; the syrup should be clear with no undissolved crystals.
Step 4	Clean round the sides of the pan with a clean brush dipped in water.
Step 5	Reboil the syrup and boil quickly – *do not stir*.
Step 6	Remove any scum which forms on the surface of the solution and keep the sides of the pan clean, i.e. lightly wash down any splashes of sugar from the sides of the pan. When a sugar thermometer is used the surface above the sugar should also be kept clean.
Step 7	Add any glucose or dissolved cream of tartar at 107°C and allow to boil through the solution.
Step 8	Boil quickly to the stated degree or condition. *Note*: If the syrup is to be coloured, add the colouring just before the required temperature is reached (2 degrees approximately) and allow to boil through the syrup.
Step 9	Remove the sugar solution from the heat and check the temperature by placing the pan into cold water for 3–4 seconds i.e. until the boiling action stops.
Step 10	Complete as stated for the individual product concerned – see individual recipes.

Important points

Step 1

Type of sugar to be used: A very clean sugar should be used for sugar boiling, especially for pulled sugar work and crystallizing syrups. Traditionally loaf or cube sugar is used but this is less suitable nowadays because of a change in the refining process. The best sugar is pure sucrose which may be purchased from most catering suppliers. However, granulated sugar is a suitable alternative because it is much cleaner and purer nowadays than it was in the past.

Step 1

Type of cooking utensil to be used: A stout heavy pan made from untinned copper is most suitable. This is because in addition to being a good conductor of heat, *copper has a smooth surface*. Pans made from aluminium tend to pit and score which produces surfaces likely to trap undissolved sugar crystals – increasing the risk of premature crystallization.

Important: When preparing greased sugar solutions, e.g. toffees/tablets etc., a tin-lined copper pan must be used.

Steps 2 and 3

Dissolving the sugar crystals: Sugar solutions initially consist of sugar crystals dissolved in water. Continued boiling reduces the water content until only melted sugar remains. Solutions which contain a high proportion of sugar to water (usually 70% or more) are called *hot super-saturated solutions*. These liquids *will turn back to crystals very easily* – agitation of the solution or the addition of even one grain of sugar will cause the solution to revert back to crystals. Premature crystallization is called *graining*.

Steps 3–8

Measures to be taken to avoid graining: Ensure there is no undissolved crystals in the syrup prior to rapid boiling.

Do not stir the solution when boiling.

Wash down the sides of the pan and thermometer with a clean brush dipped in water to remove any sugar splashes which may turn to crystals and drop into the boiling sugar. *Note*:   The addition of confectioner's glucose and acid reduces the risk of graining and this is called *cutting the grain*. The addition of fat also reduces the possibility of graining and this is called *greasing the grain*.

Step 7

Adding glucose or acid: Glucose decomposes at a faster rate than cane sugar and is therefore usually added at the last possible moment *to avoid discoloration* of the solution. However, when preparing very small batches of boiled sugar which reach the desired condition quickly, the glucose (or acid) may be added when boiling commences.

Steps 5–8

Speed of cooking: The solution should be boiled quickly to control the amount of inversion (breakdown of the sugar into simpler sugars) – the slower the cooking, the greater the amount of inversion.

Step 8

Degrees of cooking/condition of sugar solution:

Thread degree (107°C):   Lightly touch the boiling sugar with a dry finger. Join the finger and forefinger together and then separate – a thin elastic thread of sugar should form.

Pearl degree (110°C):   As above but the thread should be stronger and thicker forming pearl-like beads at the ends of the thread as it breaks.

Blow degree (113°C):   Dip a small piece of looped wire into the solution and remove. A thin film of sugar should form as a window across the loop which when gently blown will expand a little then break.

Feather degree (115°C):   As above but the sugar film should be able to be blown off into long bubbles.

Soft ball degree (118°C):   Dip the thumb and forefinger into a bowl of cold water then immediately dip into the boiling sugar closing the fingers to catch some of the boiling syrup. Very quickly dip the fingers back into the cold water. The sugar should be able to be *moulded into a soft ball*.

Important: This test may appear to be dangerous but provided the operation is done quickly no burning should result.

Hard ball degree (121°C):   Same as soft ball but a much firmer ball is produced when pressed with the fingers.

Small crack degree (138°C):   Test as above but the sugar can no longer be moulded with the fingers. The sugar sets quickly into irregular shapes with brittle *outer* surfaces – the centre of the sugar still remains sticky. *Note*: this is sometimes tested with the teeth.

Hard crack degree (154°C):   As above but the sugar sets in a completely hard and brittle mass which cracks sharply when pressed with the fingers or crunched with the teeth.

Caramel (155°C+):   When the hard crack degree has been passed the sugar starts to develop colour. Initially the solution develops a pale amber colour which *rapidly* darkens until almost black. Pale caramels are mild in flavour but the flavour increases as the colour deepens.

Important: Care must be taken not to darken the caramel too much as this produces a bitter taste.

Step 10

Pouring sugar solutions: When pouring sugar solutions the last drops in the pan should never be scraped out as this will affect the sugar mass.

Recipes

Crystallizing syrup (106°C)

Prepare the syrup using 400 g sugar and 125 ml water. The density of the sugar should be between 32–36 Baumé (59–67% of sugar); the lower degree for the formation of very fine crystals. See preparation of crystallized fondants on page 108.

Fondant (115°C)

Prepare a sugar solution using 2½ kg sugar, 750 ml water and 400 g glucose (or alternatively 5 g cream of tartar moistened in 25 ml water).

After checking the syrup pour on to a water-splashed marble slab with four steel bars to contain the syrup. Splash the surface of the syrup with water and allow to cool to 38°C.

Remove the bars and work the syrup with a metal spatula until it turns to a hard white mass then cover with a clean moist cloth and leave for 30 mins. approximately. After this, work the fondant to a smooth paste then store in an airtight container – see the various uses for fondant on page 108.

Rock sugar (138°C)

Prepare a solution using 400 g sugar and 125 ml water. After checking the syrup stir in thoroughly 20 g royal icing which contains no acid (see page 408). The solution will bubble and froth fiercely but stir constantly for 20 secs. approximately then pour into a slightly greased bowl or tray and allow to rise and set. Cut or break into pieces and use as desired.

Uses: Decoration of edible models, sweets and petits fours arrangements.

Spun sugar (145°C)

Prepare a solution using 400 g sugar, 125 ml water and 25 g glucose. Colour as appropriate at step 8.

After checking the syrup a fine wire whisk with the ends cut off is dipped into the sugar then withdrawn and shaken vigorously over one or more oiled metal bars. When shaken the sugar flies off into thin strands which resemble thread. These are gathered up and used as a decoration for sweets or gâteaux.

Sugar syrup for dipped or glazed petits fours (154°C)

Prepare a solution using 400 g sugar, 125 ml water and 100 g glucose. After checking the syrup, dip the prepared petits fours, e.g. orange segments, grapes and marzipan fruits into the syrup and place on an oiled marble slab to set.

Caramel (155°C+)

Prepare a solution using 100 g sugar and 40 ml water. Boil to a good golden brown colour then check the solution.

When required for crème caramel (page 393), carefully add 30 ml *hot* water into the caramel after checking. When the water has thoroughly combined with the sugar, pour into four dariole moulds or one charlotte mould and allow to cool.

Important: Adding the water to the hot caramel results in the hot sugar spurting from the pan, therefore the arm should be protected with a cloth and long sleeves.

Butterscotch sauce

Prepare as caramel above but replace the hot water which is added to the caramel with 100 ml double cream. Do not check the caramel but simply whisk in the cream in a thin stream. Use hot or cold.

Praline

Prepare as caramel using 400 g sugar, 125 ml water and 100 g glucose. Do not check the caramel but stir through 150 g warmed nib almonds and 150 g roast hazelnut pieces. When the nuts are completely combined with the caramel, pour on to a lightly oiled marble slab and allow to cool.

Crush with a rolling pin to a powder for ice cream etc. Praline is also used for building centre-pieces where it is cut when warm, allowed to cool then stuck together with hot caramel.

Stock syrup

This is a simple syrup made by boiling together sugar and water until the sugar is dissolved (steps 1 and 2 only).

Recipe: 250 ml water and 100 g sugar.

Uses: poaching fruits.

Flavoured syrups for babas and savarins

250 ml stock syrup, ½ lemon, ½ orange, small piece of cinnamon stick, ½ bay leaf, 2–3 coriander seeds and 2 cloves. Also liqueur as appropriate, e.g. 25 ml rum for rum babas.

1   Prepare the stock syrup (steps 1 and 2 only of the base method).
2   Remove the zest and juice from the orange and lemon and discard the white pith.
3   Place all the ingredients into the stock syrup *except* any liqueur and boil together for 2–3 mins.
4   Allow to cool slightly then add any liqueur.

Syrups for freezing into water-ices and sorbets etc.

Flavoured syrups may be placed into an ice-cream turbine then frozen to produce a wide range of ices, see page 401. Prepare all syrups with a density⋆ of 15–16 Baumé (27–29% of sugar) unless otherwise stated.

Lemon ice

1 litre of water, 400 g granulated sugar, 5 lemons and 1 egg white.

Prepare as flavoured syrups above then strain and allow to cool. When cool whisk through the egg white and then freeze.

Orange ice

Prepare as lemon ice but use 1 lemon and 4 oranges.

Raspberry, strawberry, pineapple and grape ices

Base recipe:

600 ml water, 400 g granulated sugar, 400 g appropriate fruit purée, 1 lemon and 1 egg white.

Prepare a flavoured syrup as indicated using the water, sugar and lemon then strain. Allow to cool then add the fruit purée and whisk through the egg white.

Note: A few drops of appropriate food colouring may be added to achieve the correct appearance.

Derivative ices

Sorbets

Prepare as water ices with a density⋆ of 15–16 Baumé (27–29% sugar). When frozen add a good spoonful (100 ml approximately) of Italian meringue and allow to mix through the water ice.

Marquises

Prepare as sorbets above but replace the meringue with lightly whipped sweetened cream.

Granités

Prepare as water ices but adjust the density⋆ to 10–12

⋆ Density is quickly and easily measured using a hand-held refractometer.

Baumé (18–22% sugar). This produces a granular or coarse-textured water ice.

Caramel colour or blackjack

This is prepared by boiling sugar and water to a black smoking mass. Taking the precautions mentioned when adding water to boiling sugar, a little boiling water is combined with the black mass which is then placed back on the stove and reboiled. This is boiled until smooth then allowed to cool. If the mixture is too thick a little boiling water is added to correct the consistency.

Note: Preparing blackjack leaves a cooking utensil which is difficult and time-consuming to clean.

Preparation of fondant for coating or dipping cakes, fancies or petits fours etc.

Warm the fondant in a bain marie (water bath), stirring occasionally. As the fondant warms through, dilute with a little stock syrup until a temperature around blood heat (38 °C) and a good coating consistency is obtained. This is important as the finished quality of the fondant depends on the correct coating consistency and temperature being maintained; too high a temperature and too thick a consistency result in producing a fondant coating with a dull finish.

Important: Only sufficient quantities of fondant should be prepared at any one time as reheating coating fondants increases the sugar crystal size thus reducing quality, i.e. shine and appearance. Fondant may be coloured and flavoured to taste during the preparation.

Dipping and coating

Arrange the articles to be treated in batches on wires placed on trays. Ensure that no loose crumbs or particles are adhering to the products to be coated. Dip or coat the articles evenly in one operation then allow to dry.

Piping

Fondant for piping should be at a lower temperature than that for coating. The fondant is placed into greaseproof piping bags as and when required. The tip of the paper piping bag is cut off with a pair of scissors to a size suitable for the operation.

Fondant soft centres (for chocolates)

Warm 250 g fondant in a bain marie and 5 g yeast water (this consists of 1 part yeast to three parts water by weight). Slowly stir and heat to a temperature of about 68–70 °C; this will kill the yeast but not destroy its *invertase* which will have a softening effect on the fondant centre within about 3–5 days of moulding the fondant and coating with chocolate. High temperatures must be avoided as this will result in a hard centre and the destruction of the enzyme. Flavour and colour are added to taste.

Moulding procedure
Prepare a tray or shape with sieved (aerated) cornflour to a depth of 35 mm approximately and lightly smooth flat. Make impressions in the cornflour with the appropriate tool or other suitable object then pour the prepared fondant through a funnel using a stop-stick to control the flow (a paper piping bag and small wooden spoon can be used) into the starch impressions. When complete allow to stand undisturbed for 1½–2 hours. After this remove the fondants and brush off all the adhering starch. Arrange all the various shapes and flavours in batches ready for dipping in chocolate. *Note*:   Special flexible trays are now available which are easier to use and less time-consuming for the moulding of fondant centres.

Fondant butter cream

Bring to room temperature 200 g butter and 225 g fondant then combine and beat together ensuring a smooth creamy mass with no lumps.

Crystallized or glazed fondants

Prepare the moulded fondants as described previously then place on a draining wire. Insert the draining wire and fondants into a tray of medium depth then very slowly and carefully pour over the cold crystallized syrup. Allow to sit completely undisturbed for 6–12 hours until the fondants form a coating of fine crystals (the lower the density the finer the crystals but the longer the period of immersion). Remove the fondants and drain on a sieve then allow to dry.

Important: Strict sugar boiling practice, using the finest quality of sugar and absolute cleanliness must be the rule when preparing these goods. A temperature of 21–22 °C should be maintained during the period of immersion and drying.

Liqueur chocolates

Prepare a syrup using 400 g sugar and 125 ml water. Boil to 110 °C, and check only momentarily in cold water. Add 30 ml of selected liqueur and cover immediately with a damp cloth and lid and allow to stand for 3 minutes. Pass the syrup through a clean muslin then pour into slightly warmed starch moulds, see moulding fondants.

Note: The cornflour should be compressed until firm before making the shape so that a very smooth impression is formed (using aerated cornflour tends to produce a rough skin and blisters on the crystallized shell of the syrup). Sprinkle a good layer of cornflour over the moulded syrup shapes and leave in a warm dry place to set. Remove the syrup shells very carefully and with great care lightly dust off the cornflour. Dip and coat with chocolate; this may require the couverture to be heated to a slightly higher temperature in turn reducing the gloss, but this is not of any great importance as the chocolates are usually wrapped in silver paper when completed.

Important: It is essential that the instructions in the base method are followed to the last detail and that absolute cleanliness is the rule. This is important as the centres may crystallize all the way through and be ruined. When a batch of syrup fails to crystallize sufficiently (too fragile a shell) reduce the liqueur content, e.g. 5 ml approximately.

Coconut icing

Prepare a solution as stated in the base method using 400 g sugar and 125 ml water. Boil to 114°C, remove from the heat then place a 20 g piece of fondant into the syrup and allow to warm for 30 seconds. Stir the warmed fondant thoroughly through the syrup then add 30 g glucose and continue stirring until the syrup just begins to turn opaque. Mix 100 g desiccated coconut quickly into the mixture and pour immediately into trays lined with greaseproof paper and allow to cool.

American icing

Prepare a solution as stated in the base method using 400 g sugar, 125 ml water and 25 g glucose – boiling to 118°C. Beat 50 ml egg white (2 egg whites approximately) to a stiff snow then slowly pour on the hot syrup while continuously beating. Add any essence and continue beating to a smooth white mixture almost on setting point. Coat the gâteaux or pastry etc., and allow to set.

Nougat Montélimart

Prepare a solution as stated in the base method using 350 g sugar and 100 ml water. Add 100 g glucose and 100 g honey at the same time as the glucose and boil to 135°C. When preparing the solution beat 50 ml egg white (2 egg whites approximately) to a stiff snow then remove the whisk from the machine and fit the cake beater. Pour the hot syrup into the whisked egg whites while beating and continue beating until the mixture is firm in consistency. Warm 50 g nib almonds, 25 g roasted broken hazelnuts, 50 g chopped pistachio nuts and 50 g glacé cherries (cut into pieces) then add to the mixture at slow speed. Pour the nougat into a tray or frame lined with wafer paper and also cover the top of the nougat with paper. Place a tray on top and add weights to press the nougat whilst cooling. Leave overnight then cut with a moist hot knife. Present with the cut side showing.

Turkish delight

Place 20 g gelatine into a bowl then add 100 ml water and allow to soak until soft and pliable. Add flavour and colour to taste at this stage – usually a dash of lemon and orange flavour although a little spirit, such as rum, may be used. Prepare the syrup using 325 g sugar and 100 ml water. Boil to 107°C, then add 40 g honey and proceed to boil quickly to 118°C. Pour the syrup on to the water, gelatine and flavour and stir until thoroughly combined then pour the mixture into trays splashed with water and allow to set. Remove the jelly from the trays and place onto a board dusted with icing sugar, then cut to shape, dusting each piece with a little more icing sugar. After 2–3 hours brush off the sugar and coat with chocolate or store with the icing sugar in an airtight container.

Greased sugar produce

Butterscotch

Prepare a solution as stated in the base method using 400 g sugar, 125 ml water and 75 g glucose. Boil to 126°C, then add 100 g butter in small pieces and while stirring heat to 138°C, then pour into a greased tray or oiled marble slab. When sufficiently cool mark the squares then when cold break into pieces and store in an airtight tin or container.

*Fudge

Place 400 g sugar, 100 g glucose, 125 ml cream and 100 g butter in the cooking utensil and heat while stirring to 116°C. Add 50 g fondant and stir thoroughly into the mixture. Pour into an oiled tray and allow to cool then cut into pieces. Store in an airtight container.

Vanilla fudge: Add 2–3 drops vanilla essence to the above mixture.
Chocolate fudge: Add 100 g block chocolate to the basic fudge ingredients.
Coffee fudge: Add enough coffee essence to the basic fudge ingredients to produce a full coffee flavour – this depends on the essence used.

*Rich toffee caramels

Place 280 g sugar, 100 g glucose and 200 ml cream in the cooking utensil and heat whilst stirring to 121°C. Add 40 g butter in small pieces and while stirring heat to 128°C. Complete the same as butterscotch.

*Treacle toffee

Melt 300 g butter in the cooking utensil then add 300 g brown sugar, 100 g golden syrup and 200 g treacle. Heat

---

* These products contain milk fat and milk solids which will burn or scorch unless the mixture is stirred while cooking. Unlike plain sugar solutions, the grease or fat prevents graining therefore the instructions stated in the base method for sugar solutions do not apply.
Note: The *test for cooking* is easier and more accurate with the cold water or physical test.

while stirring to 126–138°C (the lower temperature for chewy-type toffee, the higher temperature for hard-type toffee). Complete the same as butterscotch.

*Chocolate toffee caramels

Place 400 g sugar, 75 g glucose and 250 ml cream in the cooking utensil and heat while stirring to 121°C. Melt 100 g butter and 75 g unsweetened block cocoa then add to the boiling mixture. Continue heating while stirring to 148°C. Complete the same as butterscotch.

Pulled sugar work

Decorative pieces of pulled sugar work are extremely attractive but their production demands considerable skill and patience on the part of the operator. The enthusiastic apprentice or student will have to spend many hours practising the various skills or techniques (not to mention suffering the odd finger blister) required to be mastered and a sound knowledge of sugar boiling is essential.

Note: One useful tip for learners is to practise with a solution which is boiled to 138°C instead of 150°C. This will produce a mixture which is fairly easy to pull and shape (but will deteriorate more rapidly) while the operator becomes accustomed to handling the hot sugar; the temperature should be gradually increased until the sugar can be handled after boiling to the stated degree.

Method:

1   Follow the base method for sugar boiling using 400 g sugar, 125 ml water and 125 g glucose. Boil sugar to 150°C, then check the syrup. Alternatively a pinch of cream of tartar diluted in a little water may be used in place of the glucose. Colour should be added at 148°C, see base method.

2   Pour the sugar on to a lightly oiled marble slab and as the sugar spreads flip over the outside edges into the centre with a broad palette knife. Continue this operation ensuring that the whole mass cools evenly and no hard areas are allowed to form.

3   Lift the sugar mass when cool enough to handle and commence pulling the sugar. This is done by holding the sugar at each end and lightly pulling outwards. As the centre of the sugar drops, bring both ends together in one hand then quickly catch the dropping centre. Twist and repeat this operation until a smooth, very silky sheen is obtained.

4   Place the conditioned sugar into a heat resistant bowl (plastic type etc., to reduce heat loss) and place under a heat lamp or at the mouth of an oven and use as required.

Making flowers, stems and leaves

Flower petals

Pull a thin piece of sugar from the conditioned mass with the thumb and forefinger in a twisting motion to produce a very thin round shape with a fine edge. Indent like a petal with the fingers and allow to cool.

Flower stems

Take some thin wire of a suitable length and cover with green pulled sugar, smoothing down to form the shape of a thin stem.

Flower leaves

Pull the sugar to the desired leaf shape and mark with the back of a knife to resemble leaf veins. Alternatively use a special leaf mould.

Various flowers

Unless the operator is familiar with the shape of the various flowers and their petals etc., it is recommended that a gardening book illustrating the various flowers by means of coloured photographs be used. Many different shapes can be made by pulling with the fingers and using implements such as scissors and needles etc.

Once the petals, leaves and stems have been made they are carefully stuck together (by means of a hot wire or spirit flame the edges which are to be joined are lightly melted) to form the desired flower shape.

Pulled sugar baskets

To weave baskets certain pieces of specialized equipment are required, e.g. a wooden or metal peg board with an uneven number of holes and fitting dowels, a directional heat lamp, spirit flame, marble slab, scissors and broad-bladed pallet knife.

Method:

1   Pull the sugar and condition as stated for pulled sugar work.

2   Lightly oil the peg board, dowels and scissors.

3   Remove a piece of the conditioned sugar and pull the end outwards into a thin strip – do not have the strip too thick as it tends to sag when woven.

4   Weave the strip round the dowels carefully and quickly, ensuring that the strip is woven level and that successive layers contain just enough heat to stick together; this is attained with practice.
    Note: When the sugar becomes difficult to weave, cut with the scissors and continue after joining the fresh strip to the cut end (for neatness this should be done on the inside).

5   Continue to a suitable height up the peg board.

6   Pull out the pegs slowly and carefully – keep the pegs straight and avoid touching the sugar.

7   Prepare a basket top by twisting or plaiting a thick strand or rope of pulled sugar then carefully place on top of the woven sugar. Touching the sugar with a piece of hot metal or spirit flame will ensure it sticks securely. Very carefully turn the basket upside down.

8   Prepare pulled sugar dowels of the appropriate length then insert into the openings left by the weaving dowels.

9   Prepare a basket bottom the same as the top and fit in place then carefully turn the basket back to the original position – top uppermost.

10 Bend a thin piece of wire to handle shape – the breadth of the inside of the basket. Twist pulled sugar round the wire to completely cover.

11 Carefully attach the handle to the basket using the same method as previously described.
    Note: Many different handle shapes may be made using three or more wire sections.

12 Decorate as required and present filled with petits fours etc.

Pulled sugar ribbons and bows

Plain ribbons

Take a fairly thick, even strip of conditioned sugar and pull lengthwise until a uniform thickness of ribbon is achieved then quickly place into position, e.g. wind round the handle of the basket. Trim off the ends before hardening.

Multi-coloured ribbons

Prepared as above placing one or more coloured pieces of conditioned sugar side by side on a wooden board. Press together then flatten to an even thickness with a wooden rolling pin. If required trim the edges with a warm knife. Pull out the sugar to the required length, see plain ribbon.
Note: If more strips are desired, quickly fold the ribbon after the initial pulling, carefully lining up the strips by order of colour then complete the pulling; this will double the number of strips.
Important: During the procedure the conditioned sugar may be kept warm with the heat lamp or worked near a heat source, e.g. oven or hotplate; this should be done applying the minimum amount of heat as the quality of the end product will be affected with overheating.

Bows

Prepare strips as above but cut into short pieces. Bend five of the pieces into loops (this depends on the type of bow) and leave two or more plain with the ends cut to a point – a slight twist to these strips can increase effect.

Form the bow by taking one loop as the central loop and attaching the other four – two at each side. Warm the ends with the spirit flame to stick together. The trailing strands of the bow are made with the remaining pointed strips which are decoratively inserted behind the loops and attached as described.

Poured sugar produce

Various centre pieces and shapes can be produced in poured sugar which may range from very complex designs consisting of many different coloured sections to simple yet effective figures produced in three or four colours.

Method:

1   Draw a design on the marble slab and make reference to the various colours which are to be poured into each individual shape, e.g.
    1 red;   2 green;   3 blue,   etc.

2   Take some plasticine and shape into thin strips.

3   Lay these strips along the design, pressing lightly to secure to the marble slab.
    Note: Ensure that the edges of the plasticine are the correct shape and very smooth as this will be the outer lines and figural detail of the model.

4   Lightly oil the areas of the design including the plasticine edges with a small brush. This must be done very gently avoiding moving the plasticine.

5   Prepare the sugar following the instructions in the base method using 400 g sugar, 125 ml water and 25 g glucose. Boil the solution to 154°C, colouring as appropriate.

6   Pour the sugar carefully into a metal funnel and with the aid of a drop-stick run the coloured sugar into the appropriate sections of the model.
    Note: This can be done with a paper piping bag held inside a thick cloth. Traditionally this paper piping bag containing the hot sugar solution would be used to form the sectional areas of the model in place of plasticine.
    Important: This method of making the outline, i.e. piping hot sugar from a paper bag is the most efficient (with practice) but it is also the most dangerous; severe burns may result.

7   Allow to set, then repeat the operation with a different
    colour as dictated by the diagram. The plasticine
    border is removed at various stages and the next batch
    of sugar run in to complete the model in sections.

8   When almost cold *very carefully* detach the model from
    the marble slab by applying gentle pressure to the sides
    until the model moves.

9   Use as a decorative piece or sweet garnish.

Part two — Foods placed into very hot or boiling liquid and then cooked

Section one Commodities cooked in a white cooking liquor (blanc)

Many deep-poached or boiled foods are cooked in liquors which enhance and complement their flavours. The next three sections (Sections one, two and three) are concerned with the development of cooking liquors and respective dishes.

Base method

Step 1	Mise en place
	A Assemble ingredients.
	B Prepare the item/s to be cooked in the blanc, see individual recipe.
Step 2	Place the cold water in a saucepan and whisk in the flour. Add the salt and lemon juice.
Step 3	Bring to the boil stirring frequently to avoid lumps. Strain if necessary.
Step 4	Add the prepared main item/s into the blanc and simmer until cooked.
Step 5	Remove from the blanc and drain carefully.
Step 6	Complete as stated for each individual recipe.

Important points

A blanc is a special cooking liquor used for certain vegetables and meats. It is used for vegetables which discolour easily (helping to retain their white colour) and meats and offal which are to be cooked as white as possible.

Base recipe   (yield 1 litre)

Main item:	See each individual recipe.
Blanc:	1 litre of water, 25 ml lemon juice (1 lemon), 10 g salt and 20 g flour.

Vegetables cooked in a blanc

Artichoke bottoms (fonds d'artichauts)
Allow 3–4 medium-sized bottoms per portion.
   Prepare the artichoke bottoms as explained on page 38, then cook immediately as stated.
Cooking time: 10–15 mins.

Serving: See general style of service for Section thirteen vegetables, i.e. au beurre, à la crème and aux fines herbes etc.
Note: It is usual to cut the artichoke bottoms into quarters when serving ungarnished.

Salsify (salsifis)
Allow 500 g salsify per four portions.
   Wash, peel and rewash the salsify then place in acidulated water to avoid discolouration until required for cooking. Cut into 40 mm lengths then cook as stated.
Service: See general styles of service for Section thirteen vegetables, i.e. au beurre, à la crème and aux fines herbes etc.

Cardoons (cardons)
Allow 500 g cardoons per four portions.
   Wash the vegetables then cut off the outer green stalks and discard. Cut the white stalks into 40 mm lengths then place into acidulated water. Remove the fibrous part of the heart then cut the heart the same as the stalks. Also remove any excessive fibrous strings if present. Cook as stated.

Cooking time: 1–2 hours.
Service: See Section thirteen, i.e. au beurre and à la crème etc.

Strawberry spinach stalks (côtes de blettes)
Allow 500 g stalks per four portions.

Prepare the same as cardoon stalks and cook as stated.

Service: See Section thirteen, i.e. au beurre and à la crème etc.

Note: The leaves of the plant are cooked in the same manner as ordinary spinach, see page 133.

Meats cooked in a blanc

Calf's head (tête de veau)
One calf's head will yield 6–8 portions.

Prepare the calf's head as stated on page 58, removing the brains and tongue and cutting the flesh into 30 mm squares approximately.

Complete as follows:

1   Add the pieces of head to the boiling blanc and simmer until cooked (a studded onion, carrot, sprig of thyme, bay leaf and a few parsley stalks are also sometimes added).
2   Boil the tongue separately in salted water and when cooked remove the skin then cut into thick slices.
3   Poach the brain separately in a vinegar court-bouillon (page 116) for 15 mins. approximately then cut into thick slices.

Service: Dish the pieces of head in an entrée dish and garnish with the slices of tongue and brain. Coat with a little of the cooking liquor.

Calf's head English-style (tête de veau à l'anglaise)
Prepare as above adding slices of boiled bacon (page 90) and accompany with a sauceboat of parsley sauce (page 169).

Calf's head and vinaigrette sauce (tête de veau vinaigrette)
Prepare the calf's head as stated and accompany with vinaigrette sauce (page 41).

Cock's combs and kidneys are also cooked in a blanc.

Section two   Commodities cooked in a plain cooking liquor (chicken and pork)

Base method

Step 1	Mise en place
	A Assemble ingredients.
	B Prepare the main item/s, see each individual recipe.
	C Wash and peel the vegetables and leave whole.
Step 2	Place all the ingredients for the cooking liquor into a saucepan, bring to the boil and simmer for 20 mins. approximately.
Step 3	Add the prepared main item/s and simmer slowly.
Step 4	Remove the main item/s when cooked and drain carefully.
Step 5	Complete as stated in each individual recipe.

Important information

Deep-poached or boiled foods should be cooked in liquors which enhance and complement their flavours. A plain cooking liquor, as the name suggests consists of water, vegetables and seasoning. In some instances stock may be used in place of water especially when the liquor is to form the base of a sauce.

Step 1
Cooking chickens which have been frozen: These must always be completely defrosted prior to cooking to avoid uneven cooking and possible food poisoning.

Step 2
Amount of cooking liquor to be used: The amount of cooking liquor used should only be sufficient to cover the main item/s. This requires the use of a suitably sized pot which will keep the cooking liquor to a minimum.

Step 3
Adding the poultry or meat into a simmering liquid: White meats such as chicken and pork can be placed into boiling liquids when commencing cooking. These meats do not require to be placed into cold liquids and brought to the boil because of the relatively small amounts of scum produced during cooking. However, poorer quality meats, such as boiling fowls, should be started in cold liquid, see page 90.

Step 3
Cooking times: Chicken: medium size, e.g. 1½ kg 30–40 mins.
Pork trotters: 2–3 hours.

Step 4
Test for cooking:
Chicken: The juices from inside the cooked bird (especially when piercing the leg with a needle) should show no sign of blood.
Internal temperature: 70°C approximately.
Pork: The flesh should yield under pressure with no sign of sponginess.

Step 5
Hot storage: Chickens and trotters may be kept hot for short periods during service but the flesh should be covered with a little stock and a lid to avoid deterioration. Any sauce should be added when serving.

Base recipe (yield 1 litre)

Main item:	See each individual recipe.
Cooking liquor:	1 litre of water (or stock), 50 g onion, 50 g carrot, 25 g celery, 25 g leek, sprig of thyme, ½ bay leaf and a few parsley stalks, 10 g salt and 5 peppercorns.

Poultry dishes

Plain poached chicken (poulet poché)
Allow 1 × 1½ kg chicken per four portions.
Clean and truss the chicken as stated on page 67. When cooked and drained allow to cool slightly then *remove the skin* and cut into joints.

Poached chicken with braised rice and suprême sauce (poulet poché au riz, sauce suprême)
Proceed as for poached chicken then:
1 Prepare a suprême sauce with 500 ml of the cooking liquor, see page 171.
2 Prepare a riz pilaff with 100 g rice and the cooking liquor as the stock, see page 224.
Service: Dress the rice in an entrée dish, arrange the chicken pieces on top then coat with the suprême sauce. Do not use the base vegetables from the cooking liquor.

Vichy style chicken (poulet poché Vichy)
Prepare the same as above but replace the braised rice with 200 g Vichy carrots (page 98).

Metropole style chicken (poulet poché Métropole)
Proceed as for poached chicken then:
1 Prepare a suprême sauce with 500 ml of the cooking liquor, see page 171.
2 Prepare a garnish of 200 g button onions and eight plain or turned mushrooms cooked separately in a little cooking liquor.
3 Cook four small artichoke bottoms in a blanc (page 113).
Service: Serve the chicken in an entrée dish coated with the sauce and garnished with the button onions, mushrooms and artichoke bottoms. Also add four heart-shaped croûtons fried golden brown in a little butter and with the ends dipped in parsley.

English style chicken (Poulet poché à l'anglaise)
Proceed as stated for poached chicken but *double* the vegetables in the cooking liquor and add a 100 g piece of turnip. Also add 100 g of shelled peas when the chicken is poaching and complete the cooking. Prepare a suprême sauce with 500 ml of the cooking liquor.
Service: Serve the chicken pieces coated with the sauce and garnished with the vegetables and slices of hot tongue.

Pork trotters (pieds de porc)

Allow 1 trotter per portion.
Scald the trotters by boiling in water for a few minutes then scrape off any hairs with the back of a knife. Wash the trotters in cold water then split down the middle. Cook as stated, cool slightly then carefully remove the bones.
Service: Serve in an entrée dish with a little of the cooking liquor. Accompany with a suitable sauce, e.g. vinaigrette or parsley sauce etc.

Section three   Commodities cooked in court-bouillons (fish, shellfish and brains)

Base method

Step 1	Mise en place
	A Assemble ingredients.
	B Prepare the main item/s, see each individual recipe.
	C Wash, peel and thinly slice the vegetables.

↓

Step 2	Place all the ingredients for the court-bouillon into a saucepan, bring to the boil and simmer.
	Vinegar court-bouillon: 15–20 mins.
	White court-bouillon and wine court-bouillons: 2–3 mins.

↓

Step 3	Strain into the fish-poaching pan.

↓

Step 4	*Whole fish*	*Cuts of fish, shellfish and brains*
	Allow the court-bouillon to cool.	

↓

Step 5	Place the whole fish in the court-bouillon.
	Note: The fish should be completely covered with liquid.

↓   ↓

Step 6	Bring the court-bouillon to a temperature just short of boiling point (except for lobster, see important points).

↓   ↓

Step 7	Add the prepared main item/s.

↓   ↓

Step 8	Allow to cook at a temperature just short of boiling point (except for lobster and crabs which are boiled, see important points).

↓

Step 9	Remove the item/s when cooked and drain carefully.
	Note: Large fish and sometimes shellfish are left to cool in the court-bouillon when they are to be served cold or stored in a chill, see important points.

↓

Step 10	Complete as stated in each individual recipe.

Court-bouillons are cooking liquors which contain vinegar, lemon juice or wine and also certain vegetables and seasoning. They are used when deep-poaching fish, shellfish and animal brains.

There are three main types of court-bouillon (not including the blanc in Section one which is sometimes called a special court-bouillon).

Vinegar court-bouillon (court-bouillon ordinaire)

This is commonly used to cook oily fish and shellfish because the vegetables in conjunction with the acid in the vinegar complement the flavour of the fish. In addition, acid has a tenderizing effect on the shellfish flesh.

Unlike plain cooking liquors (and wine court-bouillons) the vinegar court-bouillon is never used as a base for accompanying sauces but is usually only added to the serving dish on which the main item is served.
Uses: Poached salmon, trout, skate, shellfish and brains etc.

Recipe   (yield 1 litre)
1 litre of water, 50 g onion, 50 g carrot, 25 g celery, 25 g leek, sprig of thyme, ½ bay leaf, a few parsley stalks, 10 g salt, 5 peppercorns and 50 ml white vinegar.

White court-bouillon (court-bouillon blanc)

This is used for poached white fish, e.g. cod, halibut and turbot etc.

Recipe   (yield 1 litre)
1 litre of water, 100 g onion, sprig of thyme, ½ bay leaf, a few parsley stalks, 10 g salt, 5 peppercorns and 30 ml lemon juice (1 large lemon).

Wine court-bouillons

These may be made with red or white wine:

White wine court-bouillon (court-bouillon au vin blanc)
This is used for white fish and fresh water fish.

Red wine court-bouillon (court-bouillon au vin rouge)
This is used for fresh water fish.

Recipe   (1 litre approximately)
1 litre of fish stock, ¼ litre of wine (white or red), 50 g onion, sprig of thyme, ½ bay leaf, a few parsley stalks, 10 g salt, 5 peppercorns and a good squeeze of lemon juice (¼ lemon approximately).

Important points

Step 3
Straining the court-bouillon: Although it is traditional practice to strain the court-bouillon prior to use, many cooks leave the liquor unstrained.

Step 4
Cooking whole fish: These are placed in cold court-bouillon and then brought to poaching temperature. This *reduces the distortion* brought about when applying heat to whole fish or large pieces of fish.
Using frozen fish: Large fish should always be defrosted prior to cooking to avoid uneven cooking and possible food poisoning. However, small cuts of fish and small shellfish, e.g. scampi tails, may be cooked from a frozen state at step 7.

Step 7
Cooking all other items: All other items are placed into the simmering court-bouillon and then cooked.

Step 8
Speed of cooking: Most of the commodities are cooked in a very slow simmering liquid but it is desirable to cook very delicate items such as whole fish which may very easily overcook in very hot liquid with *no simmering movement*.
Large shellfish e.g. lobsters and crabs etc. These are the exception to the slow cooking rule. When cooking these shellfish the liquid should be kept *boiling* so that the cooking time can be exactly controlled.[5] This is particularly important with ripe female lobsters because if the water is not kept boiling there is a possibility that the ovary of the lobster will remain black – at 70°C approximately the female ovary may take as long as 30 mins. to turn red and at lower temperatures may remain black regardless of cooking time.

Step 9
Cooking times:
Fish: This varies with the type and size of fish but usually only takes minutes, e.g. a 200 g trout takes about 5–6 mins. to cook whereas a 5 kg salmon will require about 25–35 mins. cooking.
Large shellfish e.g. lobster and crabs etc.
Medium size (¾ kg approximately) = 20–25 mins.
Large (1¼ kg approximately)   = 35–40 mins.
Small shellfish
Very small fish (shrimps etc.)   = 3 mins approximately.
Scampi and jumbo prawns   = 5–6 mins.
Important: See first-instance cooking and carry-over cooking below.

Step 5
First-instance cooking: The time taken for the commodities to reach cooking temperature will have a considerable effect on the stated cooking times and must therefore be taken into account. The liquid and commodities should be brought up to cooking temperature as fast as possible.

Step 9
Carry-over cooking: Deep-poached fish prepared for cold service is usually allowed to cool in the cooking liquor to avoid damage and drying out while cooling. During the

initial stages of cooling the fish is still cooking therefore this carry-over cooking must be taken into account and the cooking times which are stated amended accordingly. The fish should be cooled as quickly as possible.

Step 9

Test for cooking:

Fish: The flesh should yield under pressure with no sign of sponginess. In addition the cooked flesh should leave the bone quite easily. Internal temperature 65°C.

Small shellfish: The flesh should be firm with no sign of sponginess and part under pressure. Tough and shrunken flesh is a sign of overcooking.

Large shellfish: The cooking time is the most important factor with large whole shellfish where the flesh is enclosed in bone.

Step 9

Storage of deep-poached fish: Although large shellfish may be drained and stored in a chill on trays, deep-poached fish is usually stored in a chill in the cooking liquor.

Deep-poached oily fish: salmon trout, sea trout and grayling etc.

Main item:	Fish steaks:	Allow 200 g each per portion.
	Whole fish:	This varies depending on the size of the fish, e.g. 1 trout per portion or 1 sea trout per 2 portions etc.
Cooking liquor:	Vinegar court-bouillon to cover.	
Garnish (hot service):	Branch parsley, 1 piece of lemon per portion, 1 plain boiled potato per portion and a little cooking liquor.	
Production:	Prepare the fish for cooking (see page 70) then cook as stated.	
	After draining, scrape off the skin with a palette knife and remove the centre bone of fish steaks with the point of a turning knife.	
	Hot service: Place the cooked fish on a suitable serving dish with a little of the cooking liquor and neatly decorate with the garnish. Accompany with a suitable sauce, e.g. hollandaise or mousseline etc. For cold service see page 46.	

Deep-poached white fish, cod, halibut and turbot etc.

This is the very same procedure as for oily fish but with the white court-bouillon being used. The basic garnish and accompanying sauces are the same.

General styles for deep-poached fish

Au beurre blanc

Prepare the same as au court-bouillon but accompany with beurre blanc in place of hollandaise or mousseline sauce.

Beurre blanc: 160 g butter cut into small pieces, 30 ml white wine vinegar, 50 ml dry white wine, 30 ml cream, 20 g finely chopped shallots, salt and pepper.

1   Place the vinegar, wine and shallots into a sauteuse and reduce by two-thirds.
2   Add the cream and bring to the boil.
3   Reduce the heat and whisk in the butter until combined.
4   Add seasoning then strain or leave unstrained.

Au court-bouillon

Prepare the court-bouillon with the vegetables cut into neat shapes, e.g. paysanne or demidoff etc. (page 39). Poach the fish and serve with the basic garnish, i.e. parsley, plain boiled potato and lemon and the shaped court-bouillon vegetables. Accompany with a suitable sauce, e.g. hollandaise or mousseline.

Hollandaise

This is the poached fish served with the basic garnish and accompanied with hollandaise sauce.

Individual styles for deep-poached fish

Blue trout (truite au bleu)

This dish must be prepared using live trout.

1   Hold the trout firmly and kill with a blow delivered with a heavy piece of wood to the back of the head.
2   Gut and remove the gills and eyes but *do not remove the scales or scrape the skin.*
3   Pass the trout through vinegar and leave for 5 mins. approximately.
4   Cook and serve the trout as stated but place into a simmering *vinegar court-bouillon* (this is the *exception to the rule* of placing whole fish in cold liquor then cooking).
5   Garnish and serve as au court-bouillon above.

Note: Trout prepared in this fashion becomes distorted and misshaped with the skin turning blue.

Skate with black butter (raie au beurre noir)
Allow 500—600 g skate wings per four portions.

Remove the skin from the wings and cut into four neat portions. Poach in a *vinegar court-bouillon. Cooking time*: 10 mins. approximately.

Service: Place the cooked drained fish on a serving dish. Heat 75 g butter in a preheated iron pan and cook (while shaking the pan) till dark brown then add 10 ml vinegar (1 dessertspoon) and 40 g capers. Coat the fish with the prepared butter then sprinkle with chopped parsley.

Deep-poached shellfish: lobster, crabs, scampi, prawns and scallops etc.

Main item:	Lobster: Allow 1 × ¾–1 kg lobster per two portions.
	Crab: Allow 1 crab per portion.
	Scampi: Allow 500 g tails per four portions (1¼ kg live scampi)
	Prawns: *Allow 600 g whole prawns per four portions.
	Scallops: Allow 2–3 scallops per portion.
Cooking liquor:	*Vinegar court-bouillon* to cover.
Production:	All shellfish except scallops: wash the shellfish then cook as stated. All the shellfish are placed into the court-bouillon alive (or fresh frozen) with the exception of crabs, see page 73. Lobsters may also be killed and then cooked.
	Scallops: Remove from the shells and trim (see page 72) then cook as stated for 8–10 mins.
	Important: Many shellfish dishes are prepared using cooked shellfish. This is because shellfish deteriorate rapidly after death and are difficult to store alive. For various dishes see pages 46 and 181.

Deep-poaching brains: calf and lamb brains

Main item:	Allow 1–2 brains per portion.
Cooking liquid:	*Vinegar court-bouillon* to cover.
Production:	Prepare the brains for cooking (page 65) then cook as stated simmering very slowly. *Cooking time*: 15 mins. approximately.
	Service: Brains served hot are usually bound with a suitable sauce, e.g. allemande and poulette, then dressed in a timbale or serving dish.

* Portion sizes are for fish course or small main course portions with the exception of prawns which are for an hors-d'oeuvre course.

Brains with black butter (cervelle au beurre noir)
Allow the poached brains to cool then cut into thick slices. Pass through flour then shallow fry in butter until golden brown. Dress in a service dish then complete the same as skate with black butter.

Section four   Mussels

Base method

Step 1	Mise en place
	A Assemble ingredients.
	B Prepare the mussels for cooking: wash and remove any sand, scrape off any barnacles then rewash. Check that the shells are tightly closed as this is a sign of freshness. Drain the mussels in a colander ready for cooking.
	C Finely chop the shallots.
	↓
Step 2	Place the mussels in a saucepan with the shallots, lemon juice and wine. Do not add any seasoning.
	↓
Step 3	Cover with a tight-fitting lid then place on a very hot stove.
	↓
Step 4	Cook very quickly under cover until the shells open – 5 mins approximately.
	↓
Step 5	Drain the cooking liquor into a clean pan, allow to stand for a few minutes then decant to remove any sand or shell etc. Taste the liquor to determine the salt content.
	↓
Step 6	Inspect the mussels and remove the beards.
	↓
Step 7	*Mussels served in a sauce*
	Halve the shells then replace the mussels into the largest shells, dress in a deep serving dish and keep hot.
	↓
Step 8	Bring the cooking liquor to the boil then whisk in the beurre manié.
	↓
Step 9	Bring the liquor back to the boil, check the seasoning and consistency then pour over the mussels. Sprinkle with a little chopped parsley and serve.

Important points

Step 5

Testing the mussel cooking liquor for salt content: The shellfish liquor contains natural salt therefore it must be tasted to determine the exact salt content; this varies with different mussels. When the liquor is very salty, only a proportion of it should be used and the difference made up with fish stock.

When the mussels are not finished with a sauce but plainly cooked the liquor is reserved for fish sauces etc.

Base recipe (yield 4 portions)

Main item:	1 kg mussels.
Base vegetables:	25 g shallots or onion.
Liquid:	50 ml white wine and 5 ml lemon juice (¼ lemon approximately).
Beurre manié (thickening butter):	30 g butter and 20 g flour creamed together.
Seasoning:	Salt (if required), pepper and cayenne pepper.

Moules marinière
This is the name for the basic dish stated in the base recipe and method. *Note*: Some cooks add a little cream (25–50 ml) to the cooking liquor prior to thickening.

Moules à la crème
Prepare the same as marinière but add a good measure of cream to the cooking liquor (100 ml approximately) at step 8 then reduce down to remove excess liquid before thickening with the beurre manié.

Moules bonne-femme
Prepare as marinière but add 100 g sliced mushrooms and 50 g celery cut into thin strips when cooking the mussels. Do not strain off the garnish when draining the cooking liquor – step 5.

Moules rochelaise
The cooking liquor is not used for this dish.
 Stuff the shells with parsley butter flavoured with chopped fresh thyme. Place a cooked mussel in each shell then spread a little more of the butter on top. Heat through in a moderate oven then serve.

Section five   Boiled eggs

Base method

Step 1	Mise en place
	A Assemble ingredients.
	B Place a saucepan of water on the stove and bring to the boil.

Step 2	Place the eggs into a wire basket and submerge into the boiling water.

Step 3	Bring back to the boil as quickly as possible then simmer until cooked, see important points.

Step 4	*Soft-boiled eggs*	*Soft-boiled shelled eggs and hard-boiled eggs*
	Serve the cooked eggs in egg cups.	Cool the eggs quickly under cold running water then shell carefully.

Step 5		*Boiled eggs served hot*: Reheat in very hot salty water for 3–4 mins. then use as required, see each individual recipe.

Important points

Step 3
First instance cooking: The time taken for the eggs to reach boiling point has a considerable effect on the cooking time, therefore the eggs should be placed into as large a quantity of boiling water as possible then brought back to the boil as quickly as possible.

Step 3
Cooking times: (grades 2 and 3)
Soft-boiled eggs = 2–4 mins.
Soft-boiled shelled eggs = 4–5 mins.
Hard-boiled eggs = 8 mins.
Important: Hard-boiled eggs must be cooked for the correct period of time and cooled as quickly as possible after cooking to prevent the formation of *ferrous sulphide* on the outside of the coagulated egg yolk. This is the dark green deposit which is formed from the union of iron found chiefly in the yolk with hydrogen sulphide (formed from sulphur in the egg white).

Step 4
Shelling eggs: Tap the egg on each end then roll gently under the hand on a flat surface. This separates the shell from the egg which is then removed with the fingers. Great care must be taken with soft-boiled shelled eggs to avoid bursting the yolk.

Step 5
Storage: Store in cold water in a refrigerator.

Soft-boiled eggs (oeufs à la coque)
As stated in the base method this is a soft-boiled egg served in an egg cup (usually at breakfast time).

Soft-boiled shelled eggs (oeufs mollets)
The various styles for poached eggs apply to oeufs mollets, see next section.

Hard-boiled eggs (oeufs durs)
(Yield 4 portions)   Allow 1 egg per portion.

Chimay eggs (oeufs Chimay)
These are prepared as follows:
1   Prepare 250 ml Mornay sauce (page 169).
2   Boil and cool the eggs as stated then halve lengthwise, remove the yolks and pass through a sieve.
3   Prepare a duxelles of mushrooms using 50 g mushrooms approximately (page 274), then add the sieved yolks and mix together.
4   Pipe the yolk mixture into the whites then place on to the serving dish (the bottom of which should be coated with a little of the Mornay sauce).
5   Coat the eggs with the Mornay sauce, sprinkle with a little grated parmesan cheese then heat through in a moderate oven allowing a good colour to develop.

Aurore eggs (oeufs Aurore)
Prepare the same as Chimay but coat with sauce consisting of 150 ml Béchamel and 100 ml tomato sauce mixed together.

Curried eggs (oeufs au kari)
Halve the hot eggs and place on a bed of plain boiled rice then coat with curry sauce which has been strained (page 178).

Tripe eggs (oeufs à la tripe)
Slice the eggs and place on a serving dish which has been buttered. Coat with Soubise sauce (page 169) and sprinkle with chopped parsley.

Scotch eggs
Allow 1 hard-boiled egg and 100 g sausagemeat (usually pork) per portion. Flour, eggwash and breadcrumbs.
1   Lightly flour the egg then cover with the sausagemeat.
2   Pass through the flour, eggwash and breadcrumb.
3   Deep fry, see page 293.

Section six   Poached eggs

Base method

Step 1	Mise en place Assemble ingredients.
Step 2	Place the water and vinegar in a low-sided cooking utensil (50–60 mm in depth) and bring to the boil.
Step 3	Reduce the heat to allow the liquid to leave the boil then carefully break in the egg with the white enveloping the yolk.
Step 4	Cook in the very hot water until the white is set but the yolk still liquid (2½–4 mins. depending on temperature).
Step 5	Very carefully remove the egg with a perforated spoon and place into a bowl of ice water. Trim the egg if necessary.
Step 6	When required for service reheat the egg by placing it in very hot salty water for 1 min. approximately.
Step 7	Carefully drain on a cloth then complete as stated in each individual recipe.

Important points

Step 1
Use of acid and salt: These both aid coagulation of the egg white during cooking. However it is desirable to use vinegar only because the addition of salt produces a less shiny opaque egg.

Step 1
Quantity of vinegar used: Vinegar is added to aid coagulation of the egg white at the initial stages of cooking. The quantity of vinegar which should be used varies with the condition of the eggs; fresh eggs hold together well during cooking therefore the amount of vinegar which is required is very small and may even be omitted. The older the eggs, the thinner the egg whites and in turn the greater the quantity of vinegar required to reduce the spread of the whites during cooking.

Step 5
Storage of poached eggs: Poached eggs are kept in cold water in a chill or refrigerator and may be prepared well in advance of service.

Poached eggs on toast
Place the hot well-drained eggs on shapes of buttered toast with the crusts removed.

Argenteuil
Place the hot well-drained eggs on tartlet cases which have been garnished with asparagus tips. Coat the eggs with cream sauce which has been flavoured and coloured with a purée of green asparagus.

Bénédictine
Place the hot drained eggs on muffins or circles of buttered toast which have been garnished with slices of hot tongue. Coat the eggs with hollandaise sauce and decorate with slices of truffle.

Bombay
Place the hot drained eggs on a bed of plain boiled rice and coat with curry sauce which has been strained.

Mornay/au gratin

Place the hot drained eggs on tartlet cases or shapes of buttered toast with the crusts removed. Coat with Mornay sauce and sprinkle with grated parmesan then gratinate until golden brown under the salamander.

Florentine

Place the hot drained eggs on a bed of cooked spinach arranged neatly on the serving dish and complete the same as Mornay above.

Cendrillon

Prepare the same as Mornay but place each hot poached egg in a scooped baked potato. After gratinating, garnish each egg with a slice of truffle. The potato pulp is usually mashed and piped neatly around the top of the potato.

Section seven   Cocotte eggs

Base method

Step 1	Mise en place
	Assemble ingredients.
Step 2	Butter and season the cocotte dishes.
Step 3	Break the eggs carefully into the dishes.
Step 4	Place the cocottes into a sauté pan or deep-sided tray containing a little boiling water (15 mm in depth approximately) and cover with a tight-fitting lid.
Step 5	Boil quickly for 2–3 mins. until the eggs are lightly set with the yolks remaining liquid.
Step 6	Remove from the water and dry the dishes then serve on a salver lined with a dishpaper.

Important points

Step 4

Quantity of water used: The water should only reach half the height of the cocotte dishes to avoid soaking the eggs during cooking.

Note: Some cooks place a sheet of cardboard or thick paper on the bottom of the cooking pan on to which the eggs are placed. This reduces the amount of direct heat applied to the base of the cocottes and avoids overcooking the bottom of the eggs.

A la crème/miroir

Coat each egg with a little hot cream when serving.

Au jus

Coat each egg with a little hot jus lié (page 160) when serving.

A la reine

Garnish the bottom of each cocotte dish with a mixture consisting of minced cooked chicken bound with a little velouté sauce and cream. Break in the eggs and proceed as stated. Coat each egg with a little hot cream when serving.

Aux tomates

Garnish the bottom of each cocotte dish with a little tomato concassé then break in the eggs and cook as stated. Coat each egg with a little hot tomato sauce when serving.

Soubise

Garnish the bottom of each cocotte dish with a little Soubise purée (page 225). Coat with melted meat glaze (page 82) when serving.

Section eight Plain boiled rice

Base method

Step 1	Mise en place
	Assemble ingredients.
Step 2	Place the water and salt into a saucepan and bring to the boil.
Step 3	Sprinkle the rice into the boiling water and stir frequently until the water reboils.
Step 4	Simmer slowly until the rice is cooked (12–16 mins.) stirring occasionally to avoid burning and the rice grains sticking together.
Step 5	When cooked drain in a colander and test for excessive surface starch, i.e. if the rice is sticky and is required for immediate service then wash or rinse with very hot water and repeat draining procedure.
Step 6	*Storage and reheating of rice for hot service*: Place the rice under cold running water and refresh until the water is clear.
Step 7	Store in a chill or refrigerator *in cold water* until required for service.
Step 8	Drain the cold rice then heat in very hot salted water.
Step 9	Drain the hot rice thoroughly then place on a tray or colander, cover with a clean cloth then dry out in a cool oven or hotplate. The rice should be dry with each grain separate.

Important points

Step 1

Type of rice used: A good quality hard, cooking rice should be used, e.g. patna or basmati.

Step 1

Washing rice prior to cooking: Rice should only be washed if necessary. Clean bulk rice should be sprinkled directly into the boiling water; washing the rice increases the likelihood of the rice grains sticking together.

Step 2

Quantity of water used: Rice should be cooked in a large quantity of boiling water to avoid excessive starch in the water; especially when the rice is required for immediate service. *Ratio*:   Allow 1 litre of water per 100 g rice approximately.

Step 4

Test for cooking: Apply pressure to the cooked grains by lightly squeezing between the fingers; the grains should be tender but firm and still retain their shape.

Recipe   (4 portions)

160–200 g long grain rice, sufficient water to cover, i.e. 2 litres approximately and 20 g salt (10 g per litre approximately).

Riz indienne/riz nature

Both these terms refer to plain boiled rice.

Section nine   Pastas

Base method

Step 1	Mise en place
	Assemble ingredients

Step 2	Place the water and salt into a saucepan and bring to the boil.

Step 3	Add the pasta into the boiling water and stir to keep separate.

Step 4	Cook the pasta on a rolling boil, stirring occasionally to keep separate and prevent burning.

Step 5	When cooked drain in a colander and test for excessive surface starch, i.e. if the pasta is sticky and is required for immediate service then wash or rinse with very hot water and repeat draining procedure.

Note:	The storage and reheating of pastas is the same as that for plain boiled rice (steps 6, 7 and 8) with the exception of step 9. The pasta is simply drained and not covered with a cloth or placed in an oven.

Important points

Step 1

Alimentary pastes (pâtes alimentaires):   This is the name for the pasta products originally from Italy which are made from durum wheat flour. They are shaped and dried doughs which are obtainable in a large variety of shapes. These pastas are sometimes referred to as macaroni products but this term may be misleading.

Step 1

Fresh pastas: Some pastas (not only Italian) may be prepared fresh, e.g. nouilles, ravioli, cannelloni and lasagne etc. The preparation of fresh pasta dough is explained on page 322.

Step 2

Adding oil to the cooking water: Some cooks add a little oil to the water when cooking the pasta. This helps to keep the pasta from sticking together and prevents the boiling water from splashing out of the pan.

Ratio: 10 ml oil per litre of water approximately.

Step 5

Cooking times:

Macaroni, spaghetti, lasagne (dry) and rigatoni etc. = 12–15 mins.

Fresh pastas, e.g. nouilles, ravioli and lasagne . = 6–8 mins.

Step 5

Test for cooking: The pasta should be firm but without the original raw hardness. It should break or split when pressed with the fingers.

Pastas are often cooked 'al dente' or firm to the teeth; here the cooking is terminated when there is still a slight bone or hardness in the pasta.

Step 5

Hot storage of pasta: Pastas should be prepared when required for service with as little hot storage as possible to prevent deterioration.

Base recipe (4 main course portions)

Main item:	Dried pastas:	macaroni, spaghetti, nouilles, lasagne, tuchetti (small elbow shapes), rigatoni (large elbow shapes), shells and ribbon-shaped pasta etc.	= 160–200 g pasta.
	Fresh pasta: (see page 323)	Nouilles, lasagne and ravioli etc.	= 400 g pasta approximately.
Water:	2 litres approximately.		
Salt:	20 g salt approximately.		

Dishes using spaghetti, nouilles, macaroni, rigatoni, shells and ribbon-shaped pastas

Italienne

Toss the hot drained pasta in hot butter (25–50 g) and at the same time add 50 g grated parmesan cheese. Season with salt and mill pepper then place in the serving dish. Accompany with grated parmesan cheese.

Au gratin

Prepare the same as italienne but add only half the quantity of cheese then bind with Mornay sauce (300 ml approximately). Place in the serving dish, sprinkle with the remaining cheese then gratinate under a salamander.

Napolitaine

Prepare the same as italienne but add 100 g tomato concassé with the cheese then bind with tomato sauce (300 ml approximately).

Niçoise

Prepare the same as napolitaine but replace the butter with oil into which 100 g chopped onion and a clove of crushed garlic have been added and sweated (prior to adding the pasta).

Milanaise

Prepare the same as napolitaine adding thin strips (julienne) of ham, tongue, truffle and cooked mushrooms (50 g each approximately – except truffle).

Bolonaise (usually spaghetti)

Toss the pasta in hot butter (25–50 g), season with salt and mill pepper then place in the serving dish. Accompany with bolonaise sauce (page 195) and grated parmesan.

Alternatively place the sauce into the middle of the seasoned and buttered spaghetti and sprinkle over the cheese.

Dishes using fresh pasta – ravioli, cannelloni and lasagne

Ravioli

Italienne

Prepare the pasta with italienne stuffing, page 74. Cook as stated.

Toss the hot drained pasta in hot butter (25 g approximately) then bind with tomato sauce and place in the serving dish. Sprinkle over the top with grated parmesan cheese then gratinate under a hot salamander. *Important*:   This term is also used with spaghetti and nouilles etc, but does not include the tomato sauce.

Florentine

Prepare the pasta with florentine stuffing, page 74. Cook as stated then toss the hot drained pasta in foaming butter. Bind with Mornay sauce (250 ml approximately) and place in the serving dish. Sprinkle over the top with grated parmesan cheese then gratinate under a hot salamander.

Napolitaine

Prepare the same as italienne above adding 100 g tomato concassé to the pasta prior to binding with the tomato sauce.

Cannelloni

Cannelloni consists of squares of pasta paste (50–70 mm) which have been poached, cooled then spread with stuffing and rolled. When required for service, the stuffed pasta is placed in a buttered or sauced earthenware dish then coated with sauce and cheese and reheated and gratinated in a hot oven. See italienne and florentine above.

Lasagne verdi al forno

Butter an earthenware dish then place alternate layers of the following items:
1 A layer of cooked drained lasagne.
2 Coat with a layer of bolonaise sauce (page 195).
3 Place a second layer of lasagne on top of the bolonaise sauce.
4 Coat with a layer of cream sauce lightly flavoured with nutmeg (page 169).
Repeat steps 1–4 until the dish has been filled; finish with a layer of lasagne topped with the cream sauce, i.e. step 4. Sprinkle with grated parmesan cheese then bake until brown (and thoroughly heated through) in a hot oven. *Note*:   Parmesan cheese may be sprinkled liberally on each layer of sauce during the preparation.

Section ten   Potato gnocchi

Base method

Step 1	Mise en place
	A Assemble ingredients.
	B Prepare the tomato sauce (page 178).
	C Prepare the gnocchi as follows:
	1 Boil or bake the potatoes, remove the skins then mash into a bowl.
	2 Mix through the flour, egg yolk, butter and seasoning.
	3 Mould the mixture into small balls (20 mm diameter, approximately) and slightly flatten with a fork.
Step 2	Place the balls into simmering salted water and allow to poach until cooked (5–8 mins. approximately). Remove the gnocchi and drain.
Step 3	Melt butter in a sauteuse or plat à sauter, add the gnocchi then roll in the butter.
Step 4	Add the tomato sauce and blend together.
Step 5	Place in a serving dish, sprinkle with parmesan cheese then gratinate until golden brown under a hot salamander.

Important points

Gnocchi are small savoury dumplings often served on lunch menus and in speciality restaurants. They vary considerably in content and style.

Step 2

Speed of cooking: The gnocchi should be cooked in very hot water with no simmering movement to avoid distortion or breaking up.

Step 2

Test for cooking: When raw, gnocchi have a soft plastic-like texture but when cooked they should become reasonably firm through to the centre. There should be a slight springiness when lightly squeezed with the fingers.

Step 2

Storage of gnocchi prior to service: Gnocchi break up very easily and are therefore very difficult to store hot except for very short periods. Because of this, gnocchi are cooked then *placed into cold water* and reheated for service.

Recipes

Italian gnocchi (gnocchi italienne)   (yield 4 portions)

Main item:	200 g washed potatoes.
Binding:	1 egg yolk, 20 g butter and 50 g flour.
Seasoning:	Salt, pepper and nutmeg.
Butter:	25 g butter.
Sauce:	250 ml tomato sauce.
Cheese:	20 g parmesan cheese.

Piedmont gnocchi (gnocchi piémontaise)

Prepare the same as above but add 50 g cooked minced chicken into the gnocchi mixture.

Section eleven Choux paste gnocchi (gnocchi parisienne) and spatzelli

Base method

Step 1	Mise en place
	A Assemble ingredients.
	B Prepare the basic mixture:
	Gnocchi parisienne: Prepare 300 g choux paste (see page 344).
	Spatzelli: Prepare a thick paste with the flour, egg, milk, salt and nutmeg, i.e. sieve together the flour, salt and nutmeg, add the egg and milk and mix to a smooth paste. Do not overmix.
Step 2	Place the mixture into a piping bag with a plain tube (5–8 mm diameter) or special press (spatzelli press) then pipe or press the mixture into a pan of very hot salty water.
Step 3	Allow to cook in the very hot water for 8–10 mins.
Step 4	Complete as gnocchi italienne from step 3 using Mornay sauce.
	Note: Spatzelli are usually only rolled in melted butter or are left plain and used as a garnish for dishes, e.g. Hungarian goulash.

Important points

See important points for gnocchi in Section 10.

Recipes (yield 4 portions)

Choux paste gnocchi (gnocchi parisienne)

Main item:	300 g choux paste.
Butter:	25 g butter.
Sauce:	250 ml thin Mornay sauce.
Cheese:	10 g grated parmesan.

Spatzelli
200 g plain flour, 5 g salt, pinch nutmeg, 1 egg and 150 ml milk.

See also gnocchi romaine on page 140.

Section twelve Suet pastry dumplings

These are made from suet pastry (page 341) which is shaped into small balls – 30 mm diameter approximately – then poached in very hot salty water or stock. They are usually served as a garnish to boiled silverside and meat stews.

Section thirteen   Plain boiled vegetables: flower, stem and fruit vegetables

Base method

Step 1	Mise en place
	A Assemble ingredients.
	B Wash and prepare the vegetables.

Step 2   Place the water into a saucepan and add the salt. Cover with a lid and bring to the boil.

Step 3   Submerge the prepared vegetable in the boiling liquid.

Step 4   Slowly simmer until cooked – see cooking times for each individual vegetable.
Important: Test for cooking regularly throughout the cooking time.

Step 5	*Vegetables served when cooked*	*Vegetables which are to be refreshed and reheated* Cool quickly under cold running water then drain thoroughly. Place on a suitable dish, cover and store in a chill until required for service.
Step 6		Reheat the vegetable by placing in a basket then submerging into very hot salted water. (The pot of water and basket is called a '*Chauffin*'.) This will take about 1–2 mins. depending on the thickness of the vegetable and quantity of water.

Step 7   Drain the vegetable carefully and thoroughly. Correct seasoning if required.

Step 8   Dress the vegetable neatly in a vegetable or entrée dish – see individual recipes.

Important points

Steps 2, 3 and 4
Covering the cooking utensil: The use of a lid on the saucepan brings the mixture through the boil more quickly and thus saves on fuel. However leaving a lid on during cooking requires the cook to inspect the vegetables from time to time to ascertain the speed of cooking.
Step 4
Test for cooking: The vegetable should be tender but firm. Test the vegetable by applying slight pressure from the fingers or insert a small knife and test for firmness.

Note: Globe artichokes are tested at the base of the vegetable.
Step 5
Vegetables reheated for service: Although vegetables should be freshly cooked for service, there are times when this is not practicable, e.g. large quantities of vegetables required for à la carte service. The procedure which is then adopted is described in the base method. See also the use of the high-speed steamer on page 146 and the use of the microwave on page 414.

Step 8

Hot storage: Vegetables deteriorate rapidly when overcooked or stored hot for prolonged periods, therefore they should be served as soon as cooked or reheated.

Note: *Cooking frozen vegetables*: Follow the instructions in the base method plunging the *frozen* vegetable into the boiling liquid. Frozen vegetables usually require less cooking than fresh vegetables, therefore test for cooking at frequent periods.

Base recipe

Water: A quantity of water sufficient to submerge the vegetable.

Salt: 10 g per litre approximately.

Production: Follow the instructions in the base method.

Cooking times: See each individual vegetable below.

Asparagus (asperges)

Allow 6–8 medium stalks per portion.

Production: Wash, scrape down the stalks and tie into bundles, see page 37.

Follow the instructions stated in the base method.

Cooking time: 10–15 mins.

Service: Remove the string and dress neatly in a vegetable dish, alternatively serve on a napkin on a silver flat dish. Accompany with a suitable sauce, e.g. hollandaise, maltaise or melted butter. *Cold service*: Serve accompanied with mayonnaise or vinaigrette.

Cauliflower (chou-fleur)

1 medium cauliflower per 4–6 portions.

Production: Wash, trim and re-wash the cauliflower, see page 37.

Follow the instructions in the base method.

Cooking time: 15 mins. approximately.

Service: Dress neatly in a vegetable dish, see 'Styles of service', page 132.

Broccoli (brocoli)

Allow 80–100 g brocolli per portion (without excessive stalks).

Production: Wash, then trim the stalks to within 30 mm of the flower heads.

Follow the instructions in the base method.

Cooking time: 15 mins. approximately.

Service: Dress neatly in a vegetable dish, see 'Styles of service', page 132.

Corn on the cob (maïs nature)

Allow 1 medium cob per portion.

Production: Remove any outer fibrous leaves then trim the stem.

Follow the instructions in the base method.

Cooking time: 6 mins. approximately. *Do not overcook*.

Service: Insert corn skewers into the stem at each end then serve on a napkin accompanied with a sauceboat of melted butter.

Celeriac (céleri-rave)

Allow 100 g celeriac per portion.

Production: Wash and peel the vegetable then cut into dice or large bâtons; alternatively turn into barrel shapes.

Follow the instructions in the base method.

Cooking time: 20 mins. approximately.

Service: Dress neatly in a vegetable dish, see 'Styles of service', page 132.

Cucumber, marrow and courgettes (concombre, courge et courgettes)

Allow 400 g vegetable per 4 portions.

Production: Courgettes: Wash then peel the vegetables. Leave whole or cut into neat pieces, see page 38.

Cucumber and marrow: Wash then peel the vegetable. Cut in half and remove the seeds. Cut into neat pieces 30–40 mm in length.

Follow the instructions in the base method.

Cooking times: 8–10 mins. approximately.

Service: Dress neatly in a vegetable dish, see 'Styles of service', page 132.

Artichokes (artichauts)

Allow 1 artichoke per portion.

Production: Wash, trim and prepare the vegetable as stated on page 38, then follow the instructions in the base method.

Cooking time: 15–20 mins.

Complete as follows:

1 Cool the vegetable in cold running water or blast chiller.

2 Remove the centre of the vegetable, i.e. the heart and choke, clean out the fibrous area.

3 Reheat or serve cold with the centre (the leaves of the choke) turned upside down and replaced in the middle of the artichoke.

Service: Serve on a napkin or serviette with a suitable sauce, e.g. hollandaise, mousseline or vinaigrette (cold service).

Styles of service for all vegetables (except corn on the cob and globe artichokes)

Au beurre (buttered)
Brush the hot vegetable with melted butter (25 g approximately) when serving.

A la crème
Coat the hot vegetable with cream sauce (250 ml approximately) or serve the sauce separately in a sauceboat.

Aux fines herbes
Brush the hot vegetables with melted butter then sprinkle with freshly chopped herbs (parsley, chives and chervil etc.).

Hollandaise
Serve the hot vegetable accompanied with a sauceboat of hollandaise sauce.

Italienne
Coat the vegetable with sauce italienne then sprinkle over the top with grated parmesan cheese. Place under a hot salamander and gratinate to a good brown colour.

Milanaise
Sprinkle over the top of the vegetable with grated parmesan cheese then place under a hot salamander and gratinate to a good brown colour. Coat with a little nut-brown butter (25 g) when serving.

Mousseline
Serve the hot vegetable accompanied with a sauceboat of mousseline sauce.

Mornay and au gratin
Coat the vegetable with Mornay sauce then sprinkle over the top with grated parmesan cheese. Place under a hot salamander and gratinate to a good brown colour.

Polonaise
Coat the vegetable with the following mixture:
1 Melt 50 g butter and add 25 g white breadcrumbs. Cook slowly until golden brown.
2 Add 1 sieved hard-boiled egg and heat through thoroughly. Sprinkle with chopped parsley when serving.

Styles of service for specific vegetables

Stuffed marrow or cucumber (courge/concombre farcie)
Peel and cut the vegetables as explained on page 38, then cook as stated. Fill the centre of the cooked drained vegetable with a duxelles of mushroom (page 274).

Brush with melted butter and sprinkle with grated parmesan then gratinate under a hot salamander.

Succotash
Toss together 250 g hot corn kernels and 200 g hot lima beans in 25 g foaming butter then season with salt and mill pepper.
Note: The succotash may be lightly bound with a little veal velouté.

Section fourteen **Plain boiled vegetables: green leaf and fresh leguminous vegetables – cabbage, Brussels sprouts, spinach, peas, French beans, broad beans and lima beans**

Base method

Step 1	Mise en place
	A Assemble ingredients.
	B Wash and prepare the vegetable.
Step 2	Place a *small* quantity of water in a saucepan, add a little salt and bring to the boil.
Step 3	Add the prepared vegetable, cover with a lid and quickly reboil.
	Note: *Frozen vegetables*: Add the vegetable in its frozen state.
Step 4	Cook the vegetable *quickly*.
	Important: During cooking *remove* the lid occasionally and toss or turn the vegetable. Also check the water content and do not allow to boil dry.
Step 5	When cooked, drain the vegetable and check the seasoning.
	Note: When the vegetables are to be refreshed and reheated for service follow steps 5 and 6 in the previous base method (except spinach, see page 135).

The cooking of green vegetables is a controversial subject because many cooks differ in the opinion as to what is the best method. Some cooks use large quantities of boiling water and do not cover the cooking utensil (traditional practice), while others use a little boiling water cooking the vegetables quickly with the aid of a lid.

In this text the above base method is considered to be the most suitable method of cooking green vegetables because it is quick and therefore retains much of the flavour and nutritional value of the vegetables.

Important points

Step 1

Mise en place: The preparation of the vegetable prior to cooking is an important factor in the retention of colour, flavour and nutritional value in the cooked vegetable. Vegetables should never be allowed to soak in water.

Step 1

Quantities of vegetables to be cooked: Small batches of vegetables prepared and cooked when required for service (and during service) ensure that the vegetable retains the maximum flavour, colour, texture and nutritional value as well as keeping the development of off-flavours to a minimum.

Step 2

Quantity of water to be used: The use of small quantities of water is desirable as less goodness is lost during cooking. Excessive water extracts more nutritional value and flavour than a little water because some of the acids, sugars and minerals contained in the vegetable cells are water-soluble.

Step 3

Placing the vegetable into boiling water: This reduces cooking time, an important factor in quality, and minimizes vitamin loss brought about by oxidative enzymes.

Step 3

The use of a lid during cooking: The use of a lid during cooking reduces cooking time and allows much of the cooking of the vegetable to take place in water vapour or steam.[6] However it has been indicated by research that *volatile acids can accelerate the decomposition of sulphur compounds* (and in turn the development of off-flavours) and the green pigment chlorophyll and that the *constant* use of a lid during cooking does not allow these acids to escape. Removal of the lid during cooking to turn or toss the vegetable and inspect the water content allows most of these acids to escape. The quantity of water used should be sufficient to cook the vegetable without scorching.

Step 4

Speed of cooking: This should be fast to result in the shortest possible cooking time.

Steps 3, 4 and 5

Cooking times:

Peas, French beans and cabbage:	6–10 mins.
Broad beans, lima beans and sprouts:	10–15 mins.
Spinach:	3–5 mins.

Step 5

Test for cooking: The vegetable should be firm but tender; a slight crispness is also considered desirable. Softness in texture, loss of colour and strong odours are signs of overcooking.

Important: The above times are only approximate and may vary substantially therefore the test for cooking should be made regularly.

Steps 3, 4 and 5

Cooking frozen vegetables: Frozen vegetables are treated in the same manner as fresh vegetables, but because of processing prior to freezing, usually require very little cooking.

Note: Batch sizes of frozen vegetables to be cooked is an important factor in relation to first instance cooking, i.e. cooking takes place while the water is returning to boiling point.

Step 5

Service: Vegetables should be cooked when required for service with the minimum amount of hot storage time.

Step 5

Use of a chauffin: As indicated in step 5 the vegetable may be refreshed under cold running water, drained, then stored on a tray which is kept in a chill or refrigerator. When required for service the vegetable is placed in a basket and dipped into a pan of very hot salted water (called a chauffin) to be reheated then completed as desired. This is often done for à la carte and function service where a large selection of vegetables may be requested in a very short space of time.

One way of avoiding the use of a chauffin is to use a high-speed steamer. The vegetable may be taken straight from the freezer to the steamer and then to the customer; using this type of equipment will eliminate the procedure of blanching, refreshing and then reheating the vegetables – see page 146.

Step 2

Use of soda when cooking green vegetables: This enhances the green colour of the vegetables by changing the chlorophyll to chlorophyllin but its use is rarely recommended as the nutritional value, flavour and texture may be adversely affected.[7] However some research has indicated that *extremely small quantities* of baking soda do not significantly affect the vitamin C content possibly due to the reduced cooking time brought about when using soda.

Recipes

Peas (petits pois)

Allow 1 kg of fresh peas per 4 portions.

Prepare for cooking as stated on page 38 then follow the instructions in the base method.

Buttered peas (petits pois au beurre)

Toss the peas in a little foaming butter (20 g approximately) after cooking and draining. Alternatively brush over the tops of the peas with melted butter.

Minted peas (petits pois à la menthe)

Add a few mint stalks to the water when cooking. When cooked and drained, toss the peas in a little melted butter (20 g approximately) and when seasoning add a good pinch of caster sugar. Serve garnished with blanched fresh mint leaves.

Edible pod or sugar peas (petits pois mange-tout)

Allow ½ kg sugar-peas per 4 portions.

Prepare the peas for cooking in the same manner as French beans on page 38, then follow the instructions in the base method.

Serve buttered or minted as described above.

French beans (haricots verts)

Allow ½ kg French beans per 4 portions.

Prepare for cooking as stated on page 38, then follow the instructions in the base method.

Buttered French beans (haricots verts au beurre)

Toss the French beans in a little foaming butter (20 g approximately) after cooking and draining. Alternatively brush over the tops of the beans with melted butter.

Panachés

Toss together, equal quantities of French beans and flageolet beans in a little foaming butter (20 g approximately).

Tourangelle

Bind the cooked drained French beans with 100 ml Béchamel sauce flavoured with garlic. Sprinkle with chopped parsley when serving.

Broad beans (fèves)

Allow 1 kg beans per 4 portions.

Shell the beans then cook as stated.

Note: If the skins of the beans are tough then remove the inside by lightly slitting the skins then gently pressing.

Buttered broad beans (fèves au beurre)

Lightly toss the cooked drained beans in a little foaming butter (20 g approximately).

à la crème

Prepare as buttered broad beans above then bind the beans with a little cream. Check seasoning and temperature then serve.

Lima beans (fèves de Lima)
Treat the same as broad beans above.

Cabbage (chou), Green cabbage (chou vert), Spring greens (choux de printemps) and Curly kale
Allow ½ kg of vegetable per 4 portions.

Prepare all the vegetables for cooking like cabbage (see page 37) then follow the instructions in the base method.
Important: The leaves are usually quite finely shredded to keep the cooking time to a minimum.

English-style cabbage (chou à l'anglaise)
Press the drained seasoned cabbage between two plates to compress and shape the cabbage then cut into wedges.
Note: Cooked whole leaves may be placed at the bottom and top of the cabbage prior to pressing and shaping.

Buttered cabbage or spring greens
Lightly toss the cooked drained cabbage or greens in a little foaming butter (20 g approximately).

Brussels sprouts (choux de Bruxelles)
Allow ½ kg of Brussels sprouts per 4 portions.

Prepare the sprouts for cooking as stated on page 37, then follow the instructions in the base method.

Buttered Brussels sprouts (choux de Bruxelles au beurre)
Toss the cooked drained sprouts in a little foaming butter (20 g approximately).
A la crème
Prepare as buttered sprouts above then bind with a little cream (or cream sauce). Check seasoning and temperature.
Au gratin
Prepare as buttered sprouts then bind with Mornay sauce, sprinkle with grated parmesan then gratinate until golden brown under a salamander.
Milanaise
Complete the sprouts the same as vegetables milanaise (page 132).
Polonaise
Complete the sprouts the same as vegetables polonaise (page 132).
Limousine
Prepare as buttered sprouts adding pieces of cooked chestnuts.

Spinach (épinards), Strawberry spinach (blettes), and curly endive (chicorée frisée)
Allow 1 kg of vegetable per 4 portions.

Prepare all the vegetables for cooking like spinach (see page 37) then follow the instructions in the base method.

Drain the cooked leaves thoroughly by placing in a strainer or sieve then press to expel the water and produce a dry mass.
Important: The leaves are reheated as follows:

Place the pressed leaves in a pan with hot butter and loosen with a fork. Sweat off the leaves in the butter until hot enough for service. Check seasoning and add milled pepper. Alternatively the leaves may be refreshed under cold water then squeezed dry into balls which are reheated as above when required for service.

Spinach recipes
Although the following recipes are for spinach, strawberry spinach and curly endives may also be used.

Buttered spinach (épinards au beurre)
Prepare and cook as stated in the base method and reheat or correct the temperature in butter as described above.

Spinach purée (épinards en purée)
Pass the cooked drained spinach through a sieve or liquidizer then reheat in a little foaming butter (15 g approximately). Check seasoning then add milled pepper.

Place the hot purée in the serving dish then spread and mark with a palette knife dipped in hot water.
A la crème
Prepare as spinach purée but bind with a little hot cream after reheating in the butter. Coat with a little hot cream when serving.
Subrics
Mix together 200 g cold, *very dry* spinach purée, *50 g very thick* Béchamel sauce and 2 eggs then season with salt, pepper and nutmeg. Spoon the mixture (like dropped scones) on to the base of a hot frying pan containing a little foaming butter and fry on each side until set. Arrange neatly on a serving dish and accompany with cream sauce.
Viroflay
Cook the spinach in two operations:
1 Half the quantity of raw spinach consisting of the largest leaves. Lightly cook as stated then refresh under cold water and drain well.
2 Cook the remaining spinach then make into a purée.
3 Prepare a rice Soubise (page 225) with 100 g rice then mix with the spinach purée.
4 Divide the mixture into 8 balls then wrap with the spinach leaves.
5 Place the balls on a buttered tray, coat with Mornay sauce then sprinkle with grated parmesan. Heat through and gratinate in a hot oven.

Section fifteen   French-style peas

Base method

Step 1	Mise en place
	A Assemble ingredients.
	B Prepare the vegetables:
	Peas: Remove from their shells and wash.
	Onions: Peel and wash.
	Lettuce: Wash, drain well then finely shred.
	C Prepare the beurre manié, i.e. cream together the butter (20 g) and flour (10 g) and place aside (not in a refrigerator).
Step 2	Place the peas, onions, shredded lettuce, seasoning, sugar and cooking butter into a saucepan.
Step 3	Barely cover with white stock or water.
Step 4	Cover with a lid then cook until all the ingredients are tender.
Step 5	Slowly blend the beurre manié through the mixture while shaking the pan until it thickens.
Step 6	Check the seasoning then serve.

Important information

Using frozen peas: When using frozen peas, which cook much quicker than fresh peas, proceed as follows: omit the peas at step 2 and add at step 4 when the other vegetables are almost cooked (especially the onions).

Note: French-style peas may be cooked as a casserole vegetable, see étuvée, page 223.

Base recipe   (yield 4 portions)

Main item:	1 kg fresh peas (320 g frozen peas approximately).
Vegetable garnish:	12 button onions (40 g approximately) ½ lettuce.
Caster sugar:	Good pinch (2 g approximately)
	Note: Not usually required when using good quality *frozen* peas.
Seasoning:	Salt and pepper.
Cooking butter:	10 g butter.
Beurre manié:	20 g butter and 10 g flour.

Derivatives

Petits pois bonne-femme

Add a dice of bacon (60 g approximately) which has been blanched until half cooked then refreshed in cold water to the peas at step 2.

Petits pois paysanne

Add a slightly cooked paysanne of vegetables (page 39), to the peas at step 2.

Note: The paysanne should include carrots and turnips and in addition slices of celery and leek.

Section sixteen   Poaching fruits

Base method

Step 1	Mise en place

A Prepare the poaching syrup, i.e. basic stock syrup consisting of 500 ml water and 200 g granulated sugar brought to the boil. Also add the juice of half a lemon.
Note: The preparation of syrups and sugar solutions is explained in detail in Part A, Section 12 of this chapter (see page 105).

B Prepare the fruit:
Hard fruits (apples and pears etc):
1   *Poached quarters of fruit*:
Peel, cut into quarters then remove core.
2   *Poached whole fruit* (pears):
This is explained on page 40.

Stone fruits (cherries and plums etc.):
Wash the fruit and remove any stalks and blemishes.
Note: Peaches are blanched and skinned prior to poaching (like tomatoes, see page 39).

Gooseberries:
This is explained on page 40.

Blackcurrants and redcurrants:
Remove the stalks then wash.

Rhubarb:
Remove the leaves then trim off the heels at the base of the stalks. Wash and cut into 40 mm lengths. *Note*:   Green rhubarb must be peeled prior to cooking.
Important: See important points regarding rhubarb.

Dried fruits (prunes and figs):
Wash the fruit and remove any unwanted material, e.g. stalks or pieces of twig etc. Soak in cold water for several hours prior to cooking.
Note: The soaking water may be used adding the appropriate quantity of sugar. Also flavourings such as cinnamon stick and vanilla essence may be added to the syrup.

Step 2	*All fruits except very soft fruits:* Add the prepared fruit into the boiling syrup and allow to *very slowly simmer* until cooked. *Note*: See cooking of rhubarb below.	*Very soft fruits, e.g. raspberries and strawberries:* Place the prepared fruit into a bowl then pour over the hot syrup.

Step 3	Leave the fruit to cool in the syrup when required for cold service.

Important points

Step 1
Quantity of sugar used in the syrup: Certain fruits may require additional sugar, e.g. rhubarb, plums and gooseberries etc. When the fruit is very sour *double* the sugar content.

Step 1
Quantity of syrup required to poach the fruit: There should be enough syrup to cover the fruit when poaching. Also, if any fruit floats on top of the syrup when cooking, *cover with a piece of greaseproof paper* to maintain even cooking.

Step 1

Preparation of fruit: The fruit should be prepared just prior to cooking. Fruits which discolour when peeled should be placed in water containing a little lemon juice (or pinch of salt) until ready for cooking.

Step 1

Soaking dried fruits: Traditionally dried fruits are soaked overnight but prolonged soaking does not improve the quality of the poached fruit. Soaking in water at a temperature of 80° C approximately reduces the soaking time to 2 hours and produces a product with a superior texture and flavour.

Step 2

Cooking rhubarb: Although rhubarb may be cooked as stated in the above base method it is more suitable to poach it in a cool oven covered with greaseproof paper. A little red colouring should be added.

Step 2

Cooking times: The cooking times of fruits vary considerably with the type of fruit, variety and degree of ripeness of the fruit. Soft fruits only have to be covered with the hot syrup whereas some hard fruits may take several minutes poaching.

Important: Apples cook very quickly then deteriorate rapidly therefore it is usual practice to add the fruit, bring back to simmering point then allow to cool.

Step 2

Test for cooking: The texture of the fruit should be firm but tender with fruit still retaining a good shape. Excessive softness and loss of shape are signs of overcooking.

Important: Because fruits are left to cool in their cooking liquor, carry-over cooking is an important element of the cooking time and must be allowed for when removing the fruit from the heat.

Step 3

Storage of poached fruits: Store in the cooking liquor in a chill or refrigerator.

Base recipe   (yield 4 portions)

Main item:	Fresh fruits:	Allow 350–400 g fruit per 4 portions.
	Dried fruits:	Allow 175–200 g fruit per 4 portions.
Syrup:	Stock syrup with lemon to cover (see base method, step 1 A).	

Dishes using poached fruits

Compotes

This is the poached fruit served with the cooking liquor in a glass, porcelain or silver bowl.

Examples: Compote of cherries (compote de cerises), Compote of peaches (compote de pêches), Compote of pears (compote de poires).

Jubilee cherries (cerises jubilé)

Drain the hot poached cherries then place into a serving dish and keep warm. Reduce the cooking liquor to a quantity only sufficient to cover the cherries then thicken slightly with arrowroot diluted in cold water. Pour the thickened liquor over the cherries and flame with a little kirsch heated in a ladle.

Pears in red wine (poires au vin rouge)

Add 200 ml red wine and a small piece of cinnamon stick to the stock syrup when poaching the pears (a little red colour may also be added to deepen the colour).

Serve warm with the cooking liquor and accompany with ratafia biscuits (page 408).

Dishes using poached or fresh fruits

In many instances ripe fruits do not have to be cooked but simply placed directly into the cold syrup after initial preparation, e.g. fruit salad. Also some fruits are used fresh without having to be stored in a cold syrup, e.g. strawberries and raspberries.

Although these fruits are not poached but served raw, they are included in this chapter for ease of reference.

Styles for various fruits

Cardinal

Dress the fruit on strawberry ice-cream then coat with Melba sauce (page 103). Decorate with whipped cream and toasted sliced almonds.

Carmen

Dress the fruit on vanilla ice-cream then coat with butterscotch sauce (page 107) mixed with whipped cream. Decorate with whipped cream and grated chocolate.

Condé

Dress the fruit on a bed of cold rice pudding (page 142) mixed with a little whipped cream then coat with apricot glaze (page 103) flavoured with kirsch. Decorate with whipped cream, glacé cherries and diamonds of angelica.

Hélène (usually pears)

Dress the fruit on vanilla ice-cream and decorate with whipped cream. Serve separately hot chocolate sauce.

Melba (usually peaches)

Dress the fruit on vanilla ice-cream then coat with Melba sauce. Decorate with whipped cream.

Fresh fruit salad (salade de fruits)

Allow 500 g of fresh fruit per 4 portions, e.g. 1 apple, 1 orange, 1 pear, 25 g green grapes, 25 g black grapes, 25 g cherries and ½ banana.

Prepare stock syrup using quarter of the recipe given in the base method then allow to cool.

Cut large fruits into slices and small fruits such as grapes and cherries into halves and remove the seeds (see page 40).

Place the fruits into the cold syrup as soon as prepared.
Note: Bananas are added to the fruit salad just prior to service.

Coupes

These consist of fruit, ice-cream and sauce or cream etc., served in a coupe dish.

Alexandra
Place fruit salad flavoured with kirsch into the coupe, add a ball of strawberry ice-cream and decorate with whipped cream.

Andalouse
Place orange segments flavoured with maraschino in the coupe, add a ball of lemon water-ice and decorate with whipped cream.

Edna-May
Place a ball of vanilla ice-cream in the coupe and cover with ripe cherries or poached cherries. Coat with Melba sauce (page 103) and decorate with whipped cream.

Jacques
Place fruit salad in the coupe and flavour with kirsch. Add a ball of ice-cream consisting of half lemon water-ice and half strawberry ice-cream. Decorate with a rosette of whipped cream and a black grape.

Jamaïque
Place pineapple slices which have been macerated in rum in the coupe, add a ball of coffee ice-cream and decorate with whipped cream and crystallized violets.

Vénus
Place a half-peach, flat side up in the coupe and sit on top a ball of vanilla ice-cream. Decorate with a large fresh strawberry and surround with whipped cream.

Individual fruit dishes

Pineapple créole (ananas créole)
Prepare rice for moulding (page 397) then dress in the shape of a half-pineapple on a serving dish and allow to set. Arrange slices of pineapple over the top of the rice to resemble a half-pineapple then coat with apricot glaze. The fruit may be decorated with strips of angelica and currants for additional effect. Place the leaves from the pineapple at the end of the rice.

Romanoff strawberries (fraises Romanoff)
Macerate the strawberries with a little stock syrup flavoured with curaçao. Place in the serving dish and decorate with whipped cream.

Section seventeen   Savoury starch mixtures – gnocchi romaine, polenta, porridge and bread sauce

Base method

Step 1	Mise en place
	Assemble ingredients.
	↓
Step 2	Place the liquid in a saucepan and bring to the boil. When preparing bread sauce, add the studded onion at this stage, cover with a lid and allow to infuse for 10–15 mins.
	↓
Step 3	Sprinkle in the main item stirring constantly to avoid forming lumps.
	↓
Step 4	Slowly simmer until cooked, stirring frequently.
	Cooking times: Gnocchi romaine, polenta and porridge = 15–20 mins.
	Bread sauce = 2–3 mins.

Step 5	*Gnocchi romaine and polenta* Add the seasoning, remove from the boil then mix in the egg yolk and butter.	*Porridge* Add the seasoning and check the consistency.	*Bread sauce* Remove the studded onion, add the seasoning and blend in the butter.
Step 6	Turn out on to a greased tray and allow to cool.		
Step 7	Remove from the tray and cut into wedges, circles or crescents etc.		
Step 8	Heat butter in a sauteuse or plat à sauter, add the shapes and sauté lightly.		
Step 9	Place into a serving dish, sprinkle with cheese then gratinate until brown.		
Step 10	Serve	Serve	Serve

Important points

Gnocchi romaine
A type of small savoury dumpling based on semolina. See also Sections 10 and 11.

Polenta
A thick mixture of maize or buckwheat flour which is cooled and shaped then completed similar to gnocchi romaine or used as a garnish to meat and poultry dishes.

Porridge
The traditional oatmeal mixture served at breakfast time. The oatmeal may be added at various stages of cooking to produce a porridge with a range of textures.

Steps 3 and 4
Stirring starch mixtures: Starch mixtures should be stirred frequently during cooking to accelerate gelatinization of the starch, produce a mixture with a uniform texture and reduce the likelihood of burning.
Step 5
Adding fat to starch mixtures: This is added on removal from the boil to avoid separation and surface fat.
Step 9
Adding cheese to starch mixtures (gnocchi romaine):   In some recipes this is added into the mixture just prior to cooling and shaping but because this has a softening effect on the starch mixture when hot it is added as a finishing ingredient.

Recipes   (yield 4 portions)

Gnocchi romaine

Main item:	100 g semolina.
Liquid:	500 ml milk.
Seasoning:	Salt, pepper and nutmeg.
Binding agent:	1 egg yolk.
Butter:	25 g butter.
Butter:	50 g butter
Cheese:	25 g grated parmesan.

Polenta
The same as gnocchi romaine using buckwheat or maize flour.

Porridge

Main item:	75 g oatmeal.
Liquid:	1 litre of water.
Seasoning:	Salt (10 g approximately).

Bread sauce (sauce pain)   (4–6 portions)

Main item:	30 g white breadcrumbs.
Liquid:	250 ml milk.
Seasoning:	Salt and pepper.
Studded onion:	1 small studded onion (page 39).
Butter:	10 g butter.

Section eighteen   Sweet starch mixtures – rice, semolina, tapioca and sago

Base method for sweet puddings

Step 1	Mise en place
	Assemble ingredients.
Step 2	Place the milk in a saucepan and bring to the boil.
Step 3	Sprinkle in the main item, stirring constantly to avoid forming lumps.
Step 4	Slowly simmer until cooked stirring frequently.
	Cooking times: Semolina, tapioca and sago = 15–20 mins.
	Rice = 45 mins. approximately.
Step 5	Add the sugar and vanilla essence and stir until the sugar is dissolved.
Step 6	Remove from the boil and blend through any egg yolk and butter.
Step 7	Pour into a pie dish, earthernware dish or any other suitable serving dish.
	Note: For rice pudding sprinkle the surface with a little grated nutmeg.
Step 8	*Optional*: Brown the surface of the pudding under a hot salamander then serve.

Base method for starch moulds

These are prepared as above following steps 1–6 and omitting the butter. The cooked mixtures are poured into moulds which have been rinsed with cold water. When cold and set, turn out on to a serving dish and accompany with a suitable sauce, e.g. jam sauce.

Important points

Step 1
Type of rice to be used: A good quality round grain soft cooking rice should be used to achieve the correct consistency of mixture, e.g. Carolina and pearl type rices.

Step 2
Preparing the cooking utensil: Prior to adding the milk to the cooking utensil, some cooks rinse the utensil with cold water; this is said to reduce the likelihood of burning or scorching the base of the pan during the heating of the milk.

Step 4
Stirring the mixtures: See Section 17.

Step 5
Adding sugar to starch mixtures: This is added on completing the cooking of the mixture to reduce the likelihood of burning and to keep to a minimum[8] the thinning effect produced by sugar in starch mixtures.

Base recipe   (yield 4 portions)

Main item:	Rice pudding: 50 g round grain rice.
	Semolina pudding: 40 g semolina.
	Tapioca pudding: 40 g tapioca.
	Sago pudding: 40 g sago.
	Rice mould: 80 g round grain rice.
	All other moulds: 60 g semolina, tapioca or sago.
Other ingredients:	500 ml milk, 50 g sugar, 2–3 drops of vanilla essence, 1 egg yolk, 10 g butter (except moulds) and pinch of nutmeg (rice puddings only).

Section nineteen   Sauces and starch mixtures thickened with cornflour – custard sauce, almond sauce, spirit sauces, chocolate sauce and blancmange

Base method

Step 1	Mise en place
	A Assemble ingredients.
	B *Chocolate sauce using block chocolate*: Grate the chocolate and place aside.
Step 2	Place a little of the cold milk (50 ml approximately) into a bowl, add the cornflour and mix together.
	Note: *Chocolate sauce using cocoa powder*: Add the cocoa powder to the milk and cornflour and mix through until smooth.
Step 3	Place the remaining milk into a saucepan and bring to the boil.
	Note: *Chocolate sauce using block chocolate*: Add the grated chocolate to the milk when heating.
Step 4	Stir in the diluted cornflour mixture into the hot milk. Stir constantly until a smooth mixture is obtained.
Step 5	Reboil and simmer for 2–3 mins. stirring occasionally to avoid burning.
Step 6	Remove from the boil and mix in the recipe sugar and any essence, spirit, wine or butter.
Step 7	*Cornflour mould* (blancmange) Pour the mixture into the mould or four small moulds which have been rinsed in cold water. Allow to cool and set.
Step 8	Turn out on to a serving dish, decorate as required and serve with a cold jam sauce.

Important points

See Section 20, sauces and starch mixtures thickened with arrowroot.

Recipes   (yield 4 portions)

Custard sauce
250 ml milk, 10 g custard powder and 25 g sugar.

Almond sauce
250 ml milk, 10 g cornflour, 25 g sugar and 2–3 drops of almond essence.

Brandy sauce, whisky sauce and sherry sauce
250 ml milk, 10 g cornflour, 25 g sugar and a good measure of appropriate spirit or fortified wine (30 ml approximately).

Chocolate sauce
250 ml milk, 10 g cornflour, 50 g sugar, 50 g block chocolate (or 15 g cocoa powder) and 5 g butter.

Blancmange
500 ml milk, 50 g cornflour, 50 g sugar, 2–3 drops vanilla essence and 10 g butter. Decorate to taste: whipped cream, glacé cherries and pieces of angelica.

Section twenty   Sauces and starch mixtures thickened with arrowroot – jam sauce, syrup sauce, citrus fruit sauces, lemon or orange curds and plain fruit glaze

Base method

Step 1	Mise en place
	A Assemble ingredients.
	B *Citrus fruit sauces*: Thinly peel off the zest and cut into very thin strips. Blanch in a little boiling water then refresh and drain and place aside. Halve the fruit and squeeze out the juice then place aside.
	C *Lemon and orange curd*: Grate the zest from the fruit and place aside. Halve the fruit and squeeze out the juice then place aside.
Step 2	Place the recipe liquid and any jam, syrup or sugar into a saucepan and bring to the boil.
	Important: When preparing lemon and orange curds and citrus sauces *do not add the fresh fruit* juice at this stage but at step 6 below.
Step 3	Dilute the arrowroot in a little cold water.
Step 4	Stir in the diluted arrowroot mixture in to the hot liquid. Stir constantly until a smooth mixture is obtained.
Step 5	Reboil and simmer for 2–3 mins. Strain if required.
Step 6	*Citrus fruit sauces*: Add the juice and blanched zest then check temperature, consistency and colour.
	Lemon and orange curds: Remove from the heat and mix in the butter, fruit juice and zest then bind with egg yolk.

Important points

Steps 1 and 3

Using starch thickenings: Cornflour or arrowroot must be mixed with cold liquid to disperse the starch particles through the hot liquid. Constant stirring while adding the diluted starch is also an important factor in obtaining a smooth preparation.

Step 2

Using sugar in starch-thickened liquids: When sugar is used in relatively large concentrations it reduces the thickness of the starch mixture[8], possibly because it competes with the starch for water; if not enough water is available the starch granules cannot swell sufficiently to produce complete gelatinization of all the starch in the recipe.

Step 5

Boiling mixtures until clear: The mixture should be simmered until fairly clear. Arrowroot produces a mixture with a good clarity and should be used in preference to cornflour when a clear mixture is required.

Step 6

Adding acid to starch-thickened mixtures: Acid decreases the viscosity of starch mixtures but small amounts do not appear to have any great effect.

Note: A better natural fruit flavour is retained when citrus fruit juice is added at the end of the cooking period.

Important: Starch mixtures are a good medium for bacterial growth and therefore must be handled hygienically.

Recipes (yield 4 portions)

Jam sauce (apricot, raspberry and strawberry etc.)

Main item:	200 g selected jam.
Water:	100 ml water.
Arrowroot:	10 g arrowroot.
Note:	A little kirsch may be added to jam sauces just prior to service.

Syrup sauce

Main item:	150 g golden syrup.
Water:	200 ml water.
Lemon juice:	Juice from 1 small lemon.
Arrowroot:	10 g arrowroot.

Citrus fruit sauces (lemon, orange and lime etc.)

Main item:	50 ml juice, i.e. juice from 1 large fruit or 2 small fruits approximately.
Water:	250 ml water.
Sugar:	50 g sugar.
Arrowroot:	10 g arrowroot.

Lemon or orange curd

Main item:	50 ml juice, i.e. juice from 1 large fruit or 2 small fruits approximately.
Water:	200 ml water.
Sugar:	*Lemon curd*: 100 g sugar.
	Orange curd: 50 g sugar.
Arrowroot:	25 g arrowroot.
Butter:	25 g butter.
Egg yolk:	1–2 egg yolks.

Plain fruit glaze

Main item:	200 ml fruit juice.
Lemon juice:	5 ml lemon juice (¼ lemon approximately).
Sugar:	Add sugar to taste.
Arrowroot:	10 g arrowroot.

Assessment exercise

1. Define the difference between the terms boiling and poaching.
2. Why are some foods placed into cold liquid then brought to the boil and cooked whereas others are placed into boiling liquid and cooked? Give six examples of each.
3. What is a meat glaze?
4. Describe how to prepare duchesse potatoes.
5. Name six derivatives of duchesse potato mixture.
6. Explain how to prepare glazed vegetables.
7. What is Irish stew and how is it thickened?
8. Describe how to clarify consommés, aspic jellies and fruit jellies.
9. What is pectin?
10. Describe how to make strawberry jam and explain why pectin must be added.
11. What is stock syrup?
12. Explain how to make caramel.
13. What are the important precautions one must take to avoid premature crystallization when preparing a sugar solution?
14. What is fondant?
15. Explain how to cook green leaf vegetables.
16. What is a court-bouillon?
17. Name three types of court-bouillon.
18. Name two types of soft-boiled eggs.
19. What are gnocchi?
20. Name three types of gnocchi.
21. Describe how to cook mussels.
22. What type of rice should be used when cooking a rice pudding?
23. Explain how to make plain fruit glaze.
24. What effect does sugar have on starch-thickened liquids?

Chapter 6
Steaming

Steaming foods involves surrounding the food with steam which transfers its heat to the food by means of conduction.

Steaming food may be carried out in a closed pan with a little boiling water, a steaming cabinet (conventional steamer) or a specially designed steamer which operates at high pressures.

The pressure at which food is steamed is important because high-pressure steaming means more heat and higher temperatures present in the cooking chamber than low-pressure steaming. This results in the food cooking more quickly in a high-pressure steamer than in a low-pressure steamer.

Various types of steaming equipment

Steaming equipment may be grouped according to the pressure at which they operate:

Atmospheric and low-pressure steamers

These pieces of equipment use *low-pressure moist steam* with an operating pressure usually between 0–17 kN/m^2 (atmospheric pressure to 2½ lbs per square inch). They are suitable for all types of steaming and are the most common steamers to be found in traditional kitchens. Cooking may take place with steam produced within the equipment or alternatively steam produced in a separate boiler and fed into the steaming cabinet as and when required.

It is important to note that cooking is carried out in *moist steam* with a considerable amount of water vapour present in the cooking chamber. This water vapour in turn *produces considerable amounts of surface water which necessitates the use of perforated containers* for most foods and coverings on steam puddings etc.

Low-pressure steaming may be used to produce a variety of plainly cooked foods but many chefs restrict their use to such items as hard-boiled eggs, potatoes, turnips, beetroot, certain shellfish and steam puddings. This is because steaming does not produce any cooking liquors which can be used for the basis of vehicle sauces.

Cooking temperatures with this type of steaming varies from boiling point to 103°C approximately.

High-pressure steaming

These pieces of equipment are specially designed to operate at pressures usually between 70–105 kN/m^2 (10–15 lbs per square inch) using steam free of water vapour. This means that the chamber does not build up quantities of surface water, an important aspect in the retention of nutrients when steaming food. In addition the steam is usually free of air which is an important factor in the retention of vitamins.

High-pressure steaming is fast and is ideally suitable for most commodities, especially vegetables.

One range of foods which is unsuitable for high-pressure steaming are puddings and steam sponges aerated with baking powder; the pressures used do not allow the mixture to aerate and become light. To overcome this difficulty many high-speed steamers also operate at low pressures.

An important feature of these steamers is the number of portions or servings of certain foods the machine is capable of cooking in a very short period; one machine is capable of cooking 5 kg of frozen peas in 2 minutes. A high-speed steamer may be used for the cooking of frozen vegetables for à la carte service which *will eliminate the procedure of blanching, refreshing and then reheating the vegetables*. This means a considerable saving in fuel, time, labour and wastage because the vegetables are taken straight from the freezer to the steamer and then to the customer; this can be done with all vegetables which are *free flowing* (IQF foods – individually quick frozen).

One frozen vegetable which is less suitable for this type of steaming is broccoli – this remains hard for quite long periods.

The steam in a high-speed steamer may be produced in a separate steam generator and fed directly into the steaming cabinet or alternatively produced within the steamer itself. In some steamers the *steam is sprayed on to the food* in 'jet steams' at a high velocity (300 km per hour approximately) with a view to penetrating the food and reducing cooking times even further than with an ordinary high-speed steamer.

Important points when using steamers

Low-pressure steamers

1 Steaming cabinets must always be pre-heated before use unless the steam is supplied from an external boiler or steam generator.
2 Care must be taken when opening the door after use, ensuring that any steam supplied from an external source is switched off. The *operator should stand behind the door* using the door as a shield from escaping water vapour.
3 Most food must be placed in perforated containers or trays to allow condensation and surface water to drain off the food.
4 Puddings must be covered to prevent condensation and surface water soaking into the mixture.

High-pressure steamers

1 These are safe and easy to operate. The door is designed so that it cannot be opened during cooking. However the operator should still stand back when opening the door after the pressure has dropped (and let go of the handle if it opens inwards).
2 The operator must pay important attention to cooking times as the food will quickly overcook if the timer is not switched to the exact cooking time.

Technical terms

Steam: Water in the form of gas/vapour.
Pressure: Force per unit area. This is measured in thousand Newtons per square metre, kN/m^2.

Base method for steaming foods

Steaming is a simple way of applying heat to food as the food is only placed in the steamer and the steam applied. For the preparation of sweet and savoury puddings see Chapter 16, pages 342–70.

Step 1	Mise en place A Assemble ingredients. B Prepare the food ready for steaming.
Step 2	Place the food into the cooking containers or on to the steamer trays.
Step 3	Open the steamer door, place the food inside then close the door securely.
Step 4	Turn on the steam if using steam from an external source and set the timer if appropriate.
Step 5	Cook the food for the required period of time.
Step 6	Turn off the steam if using steam from an external source and wait until the pressure drops.
Step 7	Open the door and test the food for cooking. Open the door as instructed above (low-pressure steaming point 2 and high-pressure steaming point 1).
Step 8	Remove the food.
Step 9	Leave the steamer door open when the steamer is not in use to allow a circulation of air within the chamber.

Note: The units stated are above atmospheric pressure, i.e. gauge pressure. This means a reading of zero at atmospheric pressure.

Newton: Approximately one tenth of the force required to hold 1 kg against gravity.

Cooking temperatures when using high-speed steamers

Pressure and temperature equivalents are as follows:

kN/m^2		*Temperature* (approximate)
17	(2½ lbs psi)	103.5°C
35	(5 lbs psi)	108 °C
70	(10 lbs psi)	115 °C
105	(15 lbs psi)	122 °C

Cooking times

Low-pressure steaming (Atmospheric)

Potatoes	(small/large quarters)	14–20 mins.
Beetroot	(whole)	1–4 hours.
Turnips	(20 mm cubes)	½–1 hours.
Eggs	(hard cooked)	7–8 mins.
Puddings (4 portion): steamed fruit pudding, steamed jam/currant roll, and steamed sponge pudding		1–1½ hours.
Christmas pudding		5 hours.
Steak and kidney pudding		3–3½ hours.

High-pressure steaming (100 kN/m² approximately – 14 lbs psi)

The following times are approximations only. Consult the manufacturer's instructions.

Asparagus tips (fresh and frozen)	1½–2 mins.
French beans (fresh and frozen)	1½–2 mins.
Lima beans (fresh and frozen)	2–2½ mins.
Beetroot (young/whole)	8–10 mins.
Beetroot (mature/whole)	10–14 mins.
Brussels sprouts (fresh and frozen)	2½–3 mins.
Cabbage (shredded)	1–1½ mins.
Corn on cob (medium – fresh and frozen)	5–6 mins.
Peas (fresh and frozen)	1–2 mins.
Potatoes (quarters covered with hot water)	4–5 mins.
Turnips (20 mm cubes)	6–8 mins.
Chicken quarters (individual cooking)	3–5 mins.
Chicken quarters (multiple cooking)	7–8 mins.

Other foods –see manufacturer's instructions.

Assessment exercise

1 Describe steaming as a method of cooking.
2 Define the metric term for measuring pressure.
3 What are the most common working pressures for steamers and high-speed steamers?
4 What are the advantages of high-pressure steaming compared with low-pressure steaming?
5 Name one group of foods unsuitable for high-pressure steaming.
6 Why do many cooks prefer to poach or boil fish, meat or poultry rather than cook them in a steamer?
7 What are the important safety precautions one would take when using a steamer?
8 List four vegetables and give the approximate cooking times for low-pressure steaming and high-pressure steaming.

Chapter 7
Preliminary shallow-frying and sweating

There are many dishes where an important part of the cooking operation consists of shallow-frying many of the ingredients in the recipes, especially vegetables. This is done as a preliminary procedure to the main cooking operation, which in this chapter is boiling, and is divided into:

(a) Sweating: *Slow frying in shallow fat using a lid and without any development of colour.* This form of shallow-frying has a pronounced effect on a completed dish. For example when the vegetable content of a soup is sweated in butter, a distinctive flavour with a richness in taste is noticeable in the completed soup.

(b) Shallow-frying: This is plain shallow-frying which develops colour and flavour.

Sweating vegetables in soups

Many cooks believe that the procedure of sweating vegetables is one of the secrets of producing a good soup. Thus, in keeping with this line of thought, the time allowed for sweating the vegetables may be quite long, varying between 3–20 mins. However, although long sweating periods are desirable, the time period should never be such that the vegetables in the cooked soup lose their texture and appearance; an important point when a soup has a long cooking time, e.g. soups containing a cereal or pulse vegetable.

Vegetables in a soup which are not sweated

There may be several vegetables in the recipe which are not sweated. This is because certain vegetables develop off-flavours, lose or change colour, become very soft or mushy and in general deteriorate. Examples are fresh peas and beans, tomato concassé as a garnish and potatoes. These vegetables are usually added to the simmering soup.

Spiced dishes

It is common practice to sweat the spices in order to produce a characteristic flavour and aroma.

Using dehydrated vegetables

Many of the vegetables used in this chapter may be replaced with dehydrated or freeze-dried vegetables but they would not normally be sweated. Follow the manufacturer's instructions detailed on the bag.

Using frozen vegetables

Frozen vegetables, such as peas and beans etc., are placed into the simmering soup. They should be placed into the soup without defrosting unless they have to be cut or treated to some form of preparation.

Shallow-frying ingredients for sauces, soups and thickened gravy

This is carried out to develop colour and produce the same characteristics as sweating.

Important: Shallow-frying as a cookery process (prime cooking) is dealt with in detail in Chapter 11. This also includes sweated vegetable dishes and garnishes.

Important process procedures

To flame with spirit (flamber)

Bisques and lobster dishes
Spirit, often brandy, is added to these dishes after sweating.
Procedure: Open the stove so that the pan is sitting on a naked flame. Add the spirit and tilt the pan towards the flame. The spirit will immediately vaporize and ignite.
Reason: Promotes flavour.

To sear flesh

Meat and game pie mixtures
The shallow-frying and browning of flesh in hot fat (usually the recipe fat).
Reason: Promotes colour and flavour.

Section one   Fish stock (fumet de poisson)

Base method

Step 1	Mise en place
	A Assemble ingredients.
	B Wash the bones.
	C Peel and slice onions.
Step 2	Melt the butter or margarine in a large saucepan then add the fish bones, sliced onions, bay leaves and parsley stalks.
Step 3	Cover with a piece of greaseproof paper and lid then sweat down for 6–8 mins.
Step 4	Remove the paper and add the lemon juice, water and peppercorns then bring to the boil.
Step 5	Slowly simmer for 20 mins., skimming as required then strain.

Base recipe   (yield 5 litres)

Main item:	2 kg white fish bones, e.g. sole, turbot, or whiting .
Frying medium:	50 g butter of margarine.
Base vegetables:	250 g onions, 2 bay leaves and parsley stalks.
Liquid:	5 litres of cold water and 50 ml lemon juice (1 lemon approximately).
Seasoning:	5 peppercorns – *no salt* is added.

Fish glaze (glace de poisson)
Reduce the stock to a glaze, see page 82.

Section two   Unpassed vegetable soups

Base method

Step 1	Mise en place
	A Assemble ingredients.
	B Wash and peel the vegetables then cut into the desired shapes:
	Leek and potato soup = Dice 5 mm
	Welsh leek broth (also bacon) = Dice 20 mm
	Clam chowder = Dice 3–5 mm
	Cock-a-leekie and brown onion soup = Thin strips or shreds
	Minestrone and potage paysanne = Paysanne

Step 2	Melt the butter, margarine or fat in a saucepan.

Step 3	*Brown onion soup* Add the onions and shallow-fry until golden brown – 30 mins. approximately.	*All other soups* Add any diced pork or bacon and any onions, carrots, celery, leeks, turnip or crushed garlic and slowly sweat down for 10–15 mins.

Step 4	Add any flour stated in the recipe and mix together. Cook out for 2–3 mins.

Step 5	Blend in the recipe liquid, bring to the boil and add a bouquet garni if desired.

Step 6	Add any potatoes, rice, pasta, tomato purée, fresh peas or French beans, cabbage or pork fat pellets.

Step 7	Allow to simmer for 10–15 mins. then add any frozen peas or French beans.

Step 8	Skim and top up with additional liquid if required.

Step 9	When cooked remove bouquet garni if used and add any tomato concassé. *Note*: The vegetables should still hold their shape and not be overcooked.

Step 10	Blend through any milk, cream or enriching butter.

Step 11	Check consistency, seasoning and temperature.

Step 12	Sprinkle with chopped parsley or any other stated fresh herbs.

Step 13	Ladle into serving dish and serve separately any stated accompaniments.

Recipes

All recipes are for four portions.

Leek and potato soup

25 g butter, 50 g onion, 300 g leeks, 250 g potatoes and 800 ml chicken stock.
Cooking time: 15 mins. approximately.

Potage bonne-femme

The same as leek and potato soup above adding 25–50 ml cream and 25 g butter blended through the soup just prior to serving.

Leek broth (Welsh)

25 g butter, 200 g salt bacon, 75 g carrots, 75 g cabbage, 50 g potatoes, 300 g leeks, 1 litre white stock and 25 g oatmeal.

Follow the instructions sprinkling the oatmeal to the simmering soup at step 6.
Cooking time: 1 hour approximately.
Note: The vegetables are sometimes strained out of broth prior to adding the oatmeal; the broth is served as the first course which is later followed by the vegetables.

Cock-a-Leekie

25 g butter, 50 g onion, 300 g leeks, 25 g long grain rice and 1 litre chicken stock.
Garnish: 100 g cooked chicken cut into thin strips and 50 g lightly cooked prunes (optional) cut into strips and added immediately before service.
Cooking time: 30 mins. approximately.

Minestrone

25 g butter or pork fat, 50 g onion, 50 g carrot, 50 g turnip, 50 g celery, 50 g leeks, 10 g long grain rice, 20 g short lengths of spaghetti, 20 g tomato purée, 20 g peas, 20 g diamonds of French beans, 50 g raw tomato concassé, 50 g pork fat pellets and 1 litre of white stock.
Pork fat pellets: Finely chop together into a paste and roll into small balls the following ingredients: 50 g pork fat or fat bacon, 1 clove of garlic and a few sprigs of parsley.
Cooking time: 45 mins–1 hour.
Service: Serve accompanied with toasted bread flûtes and grated parmesan.

Potage paysanne

25 g butter, 50 g onion, 50 g carrots, 50 g turnips, 50 g celery, 50 g leeks, 25 g peas, 25 g diamonds of French beans, 50 g potatoes and 1 litre white stock.
Cooking time: 45 mins.–1 hour.
Service: Sprinkle with chopped chervil and parsley.

Clam chowder

25 g butter, 8–16 clams (depending on type and size) poached in 1 litre of fish stock, 150 g onions, 200 g white leeks, 200 g potatoes, 50 g pickled salt pork cut into small dice, 50 ml cream and 4 cracker biscuits.

Dice the clams and place aside. Follow the instructions then add the clams as garnish. Break the biscuits into pieces, stir through the soup and sprinkle with mixed herbs.
Cooking time: 45 mins. approximately.

Brown onion soup (soupe à l'oignon)

25 g butter, 500 g onions, 10 g flour and 1 litre brown stock. Follow the instructions seasoning with salt and milled pepper.
Cooking time: 15 mins. approximately (simmering time)
Service: Float toasted bread flûtes on top of the soup, sprinkle with grated parmesan and brown under salamander.

Section three   Fresh vegetable purée soups

Base method

Step 1	Mise en place
	A Assemble ingredients.
	B Wash, peel and prepare the vegetables:
	Onions, celery and leeks: roughly chop.
	Garlic: crush.
	Turnips: roughly chop (small pieces).
	Carrots: thinly slice.
	Potatoes: slice.
	C Prepare any garnish or accompaniments.
Step 2	Melt the butter, margarine or oil in a saucepan.
Step 3	Add any onion, shallot, garlic, celery, leek, carrot, turnip, swede, thyme and bay leaf.
Step 4	Slowly sweat down for 8–10 minutes.
Step 5	Stir in the stock and any hot milk if stated in the recipe and bring to the boil.
Step 6	Add any potatoes, round grain rice, tomato purée and tomato concassé.
Step 7	Slowly simmer, stirring occasionally to reduce the risk of burning.
Step 8	Skim as required during cooking and top up with additional stock if necessary.
Step 9	When cooked, remove the bay leaf then pass through a soup machine or liquidizer.
Step 10	Add any garnish then blend through cream if stated in the recipe – hot soups only.
Step 11	Check consistency, seasoning and temperature.
Step 12	Complete as stated in the individual recipe, see service and serve with any accompaniments.

Recipes

Most of the soups in this section may be referred to as 'cream soups' when the recipe liquid contains milk and chicken stock and the soup is liaised with cream when serving (50 ml approximately). All recipes are for four portions.

Carrot and rice soup (purée Crécy)

25 g butter, 75 g onion, 25 g celery, 25 g white leek, 400 g carrots, sprig of thyme, ½ bay leaf, 50 g round grain rice, 1 litre white chicken stock and seasoning.

Cooking time: 1–1¼ hours.

Garnish: Garnish with boiled long grain rice (20 g approximately).

Potato soup (purée Parmentier)

25 g butter, 75 g onion, 25 g celery, 25 g white leek, 450 g potatoes, sprig of thyme, ½ bay leaf, 1 litre of white chicken stock and seasoning.

Cooking time: 45 mins. approximately.

Service: Sprinkle with chopped parsley and accompany with croûtons.

Potato and watercress soup (purée cressonnière)

Prepare the same as potato soup adding a small bunch of washed picked watercress with the potatoes, step 6.

Garnish: Garnish with 12–16 small leaves of watercress blanched in boiling water. These are removed from the bunch prior to adding to the soup.

Vichysoisse (hot or chilled)

10 g butter, 75 g onion, 200 g white leeks, 300 g potatoes, sprig of thyme, ½ bay leaf, 1 litre of white chicken stock and seasoning.

Cooking time: 30–40 mins.

Hot service: Blend 100 ml cream into the hot soup, step 10, then sprinkle with chopped chives and chopped parsley.

Chilled service: Chill the soup after puréeing, step 9. When serving lightly whip 100 ml cream and fold through the soup. Sprinkle with chopped chives and chopped parsley.

Important: Skim the soup and remove surface fat.

Vegetable soup (purée de légumes)

25 g butter, 75 g onion, 50 g celery, 50 g leek, 50 g carrot, 50 g turnip, 150 g potatoes, sprig of thyme, ½ bay leaf, 1 litre white chicken stock and seasoning.

Cooking time: 45 mins. approximately.

Service: Sprinkle with chopped parsley and accompany with croûtons.

Fresh tomato soup with pounded basil (hot or chilled – cuisine minceur)

10 ml olive oil, 50 g shallots, 75 g leeks, 50 g carrot, 1 clove garlic, sprig of thyme, ½ bay leaf, 30 g tomato purée, 400 g raw tomato concassé, 800 ml chicken stock and seasoning.

Cooking time: 20 mins. approximately.

Service: Pound to a paste, sprigs of fresh basil (5 g approximately) and a little olive oil (5 ml – 1 tsp) then blend through the hot or chilled soup when serving. Decorate with a blanched sprig of fresh basil.

Section four   Bisques and lobster dishes

Base method

Step 1	Mise en place A Assemble ingredients. B Prepare the shellfish: Fresh lobster and lobster butter for enriching sauce, see page 72. Fresh crayfish and shrimps, see page 73. Scampi, see page 73. C Wash, peel and prepare the vegetables: Cut all vegetables into a fine dice except garlic, which is crushed. D Prepare any accompaniments stated in the individual recipe.
Step 2	Heat the oil and butter in a sauté pan then add the shellfish and quickly sauté on all sides.
Step 3	Pour off the excess fat then add the base vegetables and sweat down for 2–3 mins. approximately.
Step 4	Flame with the brandy then add the lemon juice, wine and fish stock.
Step 5	Add any rice, tomato purée and tomato concassé.
Step 6	Lightly season then cover with a lid and slowly simmer.

	Bisques	*Lobster dishes*
Step 7	When cooked, remove the shellfish and separate the fish from the shells.	When cooked, remove the pieces of lobster and separate the meat from the shells.
Step 8	Cut the flesh into dice and keep hot for garnish.	Place the meat into a timbale or entrée dish then cover and keep hot.
Step 9	Pass the mixture through a sieve, soup machine or liquidizer.	Reduce the cooking liquor to 250–300 ml.
Step 10	Pass the mixture through a fine strainer or tammy cloth to ensure there are no small pieces of shell present.	Blend in the lobster butter, stirring continuously until the mixture thickens then remove from the heat.
Step 11	Add the garnish then blend in the cream (and enriching butter).	Check the seasoning then pass the sauce through a coarse strainer on to the pieces of hot lobster.
Step 12	Check seasoning, consistency and temperature.	Sprinkle with a little chopped parsley and decorate with the shells. Accompany with the riz pilaff if applicable.

Bisques

Bisques are shellfish soups made with crustaceans. In this section the soups are rice-thickened but see also page 178.

Base recipe   (yield 4 portions)

Main item:	*Lobster* (Bisque de homard)
	Scampi (Bisque de langoustines)
	Crayfish (Bisque d'écrevisses)
	Shrimps (Bisque de crevettes)
	Use 150–200 g fresh shellfish or shellfish trimmings, e.g. claws, legs or pieces of carapace
	or
	300–400 g cooked shellfish trimmings (economical recipe).
Frying medium:	10 ml oil and 10 g butter.
Base vegetables:	50 g onion, 50 g carrot, 25 g celery and 25 g leek.
Liquid:	25 ml brandy, squeeze of lemon juice, 100 ml white wine and 1 litre fish stock.
Tomato purée:	25 g tomato purée.
Thickening:	75 g round grain rice.
Cream:	50 ml cream.
Seasoning:	Salt, pepper and cayenne pepper.
Enriching butter (*optional*):	20 g butter.

Follow the instructions in the base method using hot stock.
Cooking time: 45 mins. approximately.

Lobster dishes   (yield 4 portions, small)

Lobster American (homard américaine)

Main item:	2 live lobsters (1–1¼ kg).
Frying medium:	50 ml oil and 25 g butter.
Base vegetables:	50 g shallots and 1 clove crushed garlic.
Liquid:	25–50 ml brandy, squeeze lemon juice, 100 ml dry white wine and 250 ml fish stock.
Tomato purée (*optional*):	20 g tomato purée.
Tomato concassé:	200 g raw tomato concassé.
Seasoning:	Salt, pepper and cayenne pepper.
Enriching butter (*to be pounded with intestines*):	50 g butter.

Follow the instructions in the base method using hot stock.
Cooking time: 20 mins. approximately.
Service: Sprinkle with chopped parsley and accompany with braised rice (use 200 g rice).

Lobster Newburg

Prepare the same as American but *omit* the tomato concassé and tomato purée and replace white wine with 50 ml Marsala. Also add 100 ml cream when reducing the cooking liquor – step 9.

Note: This dish is often prepared with cooked lobster, see page 181.

Section five   Heavy fish soups and stews

Base method

Step 1	Mise en place
	A Assemble ingredients.
	B Cut the large fish and shellfish into pieces – small darnes, tronçons and rondels etc., and leave the small fish whole.
	C Finely dice the onions and leeks and crush the garlic.
	D Prepare the slices of toasted French bread which are served as an accompaniment.
Step 2	Heat the oil in a wide saucepan then add the shellfish and quickly sauté on all sides.
Step 3	Add the base vegetables and sweat for 3–4 mins.
Step 4	Add the fish and sweat down under cover for a further 2–3 mins. Turn carefully when sweating to avoid breaking the fish.
Step 5	Add the tomato concassé, wine and fish stock and bring to the boil.
Step 6	Lightly season then add the saffron.
Step 7	Quickly boil until cooked (this amalgamates the stock and oil). Lightly season.
Step 8	Serve in a large soup tureen with slices of toasted French bread. Alternatively separate the fish from the cooking liquor and serve on a large plate like a pyramid. Accompany with the liquor in a soup tureen and slices of toasted French bread.

Bouillabaisse marseillaise	(yield 10–12 portions)
Main items:	Selection of fish and shellfish comprising: 100 g conger eel, 100 g rascasses, 100 g red mullet, 200 g John Dory, 200 g rock fish, 200 g gurnet, 200 g angler fish, 200 g crawfish and 200 g lobster – any other suitable fish.
Frying medium:	100 ml olive oil.
Base vegetables:	300 g onion, 300 g white of leek, 2 cloves of crushed garlic, sprig of thyme and fennel and 1 bay leaf.
Liquid:	150 ml white wine and enough fish stock to cover the fish.
Tomato concassée:	400 g tomato concassé.
Saffron:	Good pinch of powdered saffron or a few strands of saffron.
Seasoning:	Salt, mill pepper and cayenne pepper.

Bouillabaisse parisienne
Prepare the same as Marseillaise adding 200 g raw scampi
tails, step 2, and 100 g cooked mussels (and cooking
liquor) at step 7. Lightly thicken the completed soup with
a little beurre manié. Also rub the slices of French bread
with garlic prior to toasting.

Bouillabaisse calaisienne or Ocean
Prepare the same as Marseillaise above but use fish
commonly found in the North Sea, e.g. turbot, whiting,
hake, angler fish, conger eel, lobster and mussels etc.

Section six   Pie mixtures

This is an economical method of preparing pie mixtures because the flesh used is stewing quality. Pies prepared with
raw fillings are dealt with on page 77.

Base method

Step 1	Mise en place
	A Assemble ingredients.
	B Prepare the meat, game or poultry: Trim and dice the meat or furred game. Joint any poultry or feathered game.
	C Peel and finely chop the onions.
	D Prepare any stated garnish.
Step 2	Melt the fat in a saucepan, add the flesh and sear.
Step 3	Add the onion and any garlic and sweat for 6–8 mins.
Step 4	Add the stock and bring to the boil then simmer until almost cooked. Skim and top up with additional stock as required.
Step 5	Add any flavouring, e.g. Worcester sauce, redcurrant jelly, fruit juice or mustard etc.
Step 6	Dilute the arrowroot in cold water and pour into the mixture stirring continuously until the mixture reboils.
Step 7	Add any garnish, e.g. button onions, mushrooms, chopped parsley or fruit then check seasoning and consistency.
Step 8	Cool quickly then remove any solidified fat.
Step 9	Mix through any spirit or liqueur then place the mixture in the pie dish ready to be covered with pastry and baked, see page 331.

Base recipe for all pie mixtures   (yield 4 portions)

Main item:	This produces the appropriate pie mixture, see below.
Frying medium:	20 g lard or dripping.
Base vegetables:	100 g onion.
Liquid:	500 ml brown stock.
Thickening:	10 g arrowroot and 25 ml water.

Steak pie
Use 500 g stewing steak and a good dash of Worcester
sauce (5 ml). Also add chopped parsley.

Steak and kidney pie
Same as steak pie but replace 100 g of the steak with ox
kidney.

Steak, kidney and mushroom pie
Same as steak and kidney pie adding 100 g washed,
quartered mushrooms.

Duck pie
Use a 1½–2 kg duck. Part of the brown stock may be
replaced with red wine and a measure of port added when
the mixture is cold. Fruit such as cherries or oranges may
also be added.

Game pie
Use 500 g game, e.g. hare, pheasant, partridge and
venison etc. Part of the brown stock may be replaced with
red wine and a measure of port or brandy added if desired.
A little redcurrant jelly is often added to this type of pie. A
suitable garnish is button onions and mushrooms (60 g
each approximately).

Section seven   Thickened gravy (jus lié)

Method

Step 1	Mise en place
	A Assemble ingredients.
	B Chop the bones into small pieces.
	C Wash, peel and roughly chop the vegetables.
Step 2	Melt the dripping in a saucepan, add the bones and fry until golden-brown.
Step 3	Add the base vegetables and continue frying until the vegetables are lightly coloured.
Step 4	Drain off excess fat then add the stock, tomato purée and peppercorns.
Step 5	Simmer for 2½–3 hours skimming as required and topping up with additional stock.
Step 6	Dilute the arrowroot in the cold water and pour into the stock stirring continuously until the mixture reboils. Simmer for 2–3 minutes.
Step 7	Strain into a clean pan and check consistency and seasoning.

Base recipe   (yield 1 litre)

Main item:	250 g small veal bones.
Frying medium:	20 g dripping.
Base vegetables:	100 g onion, 100 g carrot, 50 g celery, 50 g leek, sprig of thyme, ½ bay leaf and parsley stalks.
Liquid:	1 litre brown stock (veal).
Tomato purée:	20 g tomato purée.
Seasoning:	5 peppercorns.
Thickening:	20 g arrowroot and 50 ml cold water.

Section eight   Spiced dishes

Shallow-frying and sweating is an important feature with many spiced dishes (known as 'curry dishes' in European countries). The following dishes which have been chosen from three countries illustrate this aspect.

Base method – shellfish, chicken and butcher meats

Step 1	Mise en place
	A Assemble ingredients.
	B Prepare the main item:
	Shellfish (shrimps, prawns and scampi etc.): Remove from the shells.
	Chicken: Cut into joints then remove the skin.
	Butcher meats (beef, mutton and pork): Trim off excess fat then cut into cubes (25 mm approximately).
	C Prepare the spice paste: liquidize the ingredients or pound using a mortar and pestle.
	D Prepare any accompanying garnish stated in the individual recipe.
Step 2	Heat the oil in a saucepan.
Step 3	*Chicken dishes* *Shellfish and butcher meats*
	Add the chicken and fry on all sides until lightly coloured. Remove from the pan and place aside.
Step 4	Add any chopped onions and fry until golden brown.
Step 5	Add the spice paste and sweat for 4–5 mins.
Step 6	Add the main item and shallow-fry:
	Shellfish: 2–3 mins.
	Butcher meats: 10–15 mins.
Step 7	Add any tomatoes, tomato concentrate or fresh coriander.
Step 8	Blend in the recipe liquid, e.g. water, stock, coconut milk, soy sauce, vinegar, lemon juice or yoghurt etc.
Step 9	Bring to the boil then simmer until cooked:
	Chicken: 15–20 mins; *shellfish*: 2–3 mins; *Butcher meats*: 1–1½ hours.
Step 10	Check the seasoning.

Important points

Step 1

Using spices: In some recipes, spices are added direct without a spice paste being made (though not in this section).

Step 5

Frying the spice paste: Ensure the spices do not burn, especially when they are frying on their own. A few drops of water may be added to prevent burning.

Step 9

Cooking: The mixtures are usually simmered to a reduced sauce which coats the meat and poultry.

RECIPES   (yield 4 main course portions)

Murgh kari – chicken curry (India)

Main item:	1½ kg chicken.
Onion:	150 g finely chopped onions.
Spice paste:	10 g garlic, 10 g root ginger, 7½ g ground coriander (1 teaspoon), 2 g ground fennel (¼ teaspoon), 7½ g turmeric, 7½ g ground cumin, 5–10 g cayenne pepper, 7½ g garam marsala, 5 g lemon zest (½ teaspoon), 15 ml water (1 tablespoon) and 15 ml vegetable oil
Frying oil:	50 ml vegetable oil.
Tomatoes:	100 g tomato concassé.
Fresh coriander:	30 g finely chopped fresh coriander.
Liquid:	100 ml water *or* chicken stock and 150 g yoghurt.
Seasoning:	2½ g salt.
Finishing:	15 ml lemon juice (½ lemon). *Do not add* the lemon with the cooking liquid.
Procedure:	Follow the instructions. Dish the chicken and coat with the sauce then sprinkle with the lemon juice.

Gulĕ kambing – lamb curry (Indonesia)

Main item:	600 g boneless stewing mutton.
Onion:	150 g finely chopped onions.
Spice paste:	10 g garlic, 10 g root ginger, 10 g turmeric, 10–20 g chopped chilli peppers, 5 g lemon zest, 30 g ground almonds, 2½ g salt, 30 ml water (enough water to make a paste) and 15 ml oil.
Frying oil:	40 ml vegetable oil.
Tomatoes:	100 g tomato concassé.
Liquid:	200 ml coconut milk and 100 ml water or mutton stock.
Finishing:	100 g sliced onions, 5 g crushed cloves, 10 g crushed coriander seeds and 2½ g crushed cumin seeds (½ teaspoon) and 20 ml oil.
Procedure:	Follow the instructions. Shallow-fry the finishing ingredients above until golden brown then add to the stew just before completion of cooking – 10 mins. approximately.

Kari bongkong trasak – curried shrimps and marrow (or cucumber) (Cambodia)

Main item:	800 g–1 kg shrimps (unshelled weight).
Spice paste:	30 g spring onion, 10 g garlic, 10 g root ginger, 15 g ground coriander (2 teaspoons), 7½ g ground fennel (1 teaspoon), 3½ g turmeric (½ teaspoon), 10–15 g hot chilli powder, 10 g lemon zest, 15 ml water (1 tablespoon) and 15 ml peanut oil.
Frying oil:	40 ml peanut oil.
Liquid:	300 ml coconut milk, 30 ml lemon juice (1 lemon) and 25 ml fish sauce (if not available, pound 10 g anchovy fillets and mix with 15 ml soy sauce).
Sugar:	5 g caster sugar.
Garnish:	Small vegetable marrow (½ cucumber) (peel, cut in half and remove seeds. Cut into thick slices, 15 mm approximately).
Procedure:	Follow the instructions. Add the marrow (cucumber) and sugar at step 9 then complete the cooking.

Table 4 Recipe ingredients

	Vegetable soups	Spiced dishes	Bisques	Lobster dishes	Fish soups/stews	Pie fillings
Main item	Vegetables	Shellfish, butcher meats and chicken	Crustaceans	Lobster	Fish and shellfish	Beef, duck and game
Frying medium	Butter, margarine or oil	Oil or ghee	Butter and oil	Butter and oil	Oil	Dripping or lard etc.
Base vegetables	—	Usually: onions, garlic, root ginger and spices	Mirepoix	Shallots, or onions and garlic	Onions, garlic, thyme, fennel and bay leaves	Onions and garlic
Liquid	White stock	Water, stock, coconut milk, soy sauce or yoghurt etc.	Brandy, white wine, fish stock and lemon juice	Brandy, white wine, fish stock and lemon juice	White wine and fish stock	Brown stock, wine or spirits
Thickening	Vegetables, rice and oatmeal etc.	Reduced vegetables	Rice	Lobster butter	—	Arrowroot
Additional flavourings	Cream, tomato purée, herbs and salt pork etc.	Tomatoes and flavouring sauces	Tomato purée and cream	Tomatoes, tomato purée and cream	Saffron	Worcester sauce, herbs, fruit and red-currant jelly

Assessment exercise

1 Define the term 'to sweat'.
2 What are the characteristic qualities imparted to a mixture when the vegetables in the recipe are sweated?
3 List six ways, described in this chapter, in which liquids or mixtures may be thickened.

4 Give seven examples when preparing a mixture where sweating is the general method of cooking and 20 examples where it is part of a larger process.
5 What is the French term for 'to sweat'?

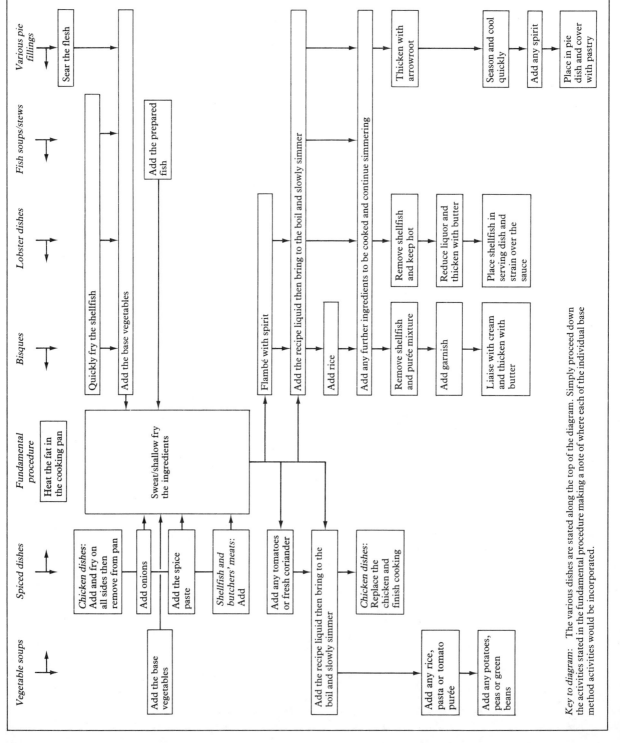

Key to diagram: The various dishes are stated along the top of the diagram. Simply proceed down the activities stated in the fundamental procedure making a note of where each of the individual base method activities would be incorporated.

Figure 21 *Essential activities for dishes requiring preliminary shallow frying*

Chapter 8
Roux thickening

Dishes and parts of dishes consisting of thickened liquids may vary considerably in content, method of processing and thickening agent. The classification on page 80 identifies the various methods of thickening sauces, soups and stews etc., and most of these methods have already been dealt with in Chapters 5 and 7. This chapter is concerned with the processes that include roux thickening and which produce a wide range of products.

Roux

A roux is a mixture of fat and flour in approximately equal quantities.

Types of roux

White roux (roux blanc) and blond roux (roux blond)

The fat, which is usually butter or margarine, is melted in a saucepan then the flour added and stirred in to produce a mixture with a consistency similar to damp clinging sand. Both roux are cooked for a short period over a low heat *without any colour development*: this cooking period is called 'cooking out'.

Note: Traditionally a distinction is made between a white and blond roux in relation to cooking out time – blond roux requiring a longer period of cooking out than white roux. However, it would appear that a roux improves with *slow* cooking out up to a point just short of colour development.

Brown roux (roux brun)

The roux is cooked until it is a medium brown colour. This should be carried out slowly and carefully as the mixture reaches an exceedingly high temperature. The cooking may be done on top of the stove or in an oven, but regardless of method, the roux must *always be stirred often* to acquire an even brown colour. Insufficient stirring results in the roux becoming burnt and speckled. It is also important not to allow the roux to become too dark as this produces a burnt or bitter taste.

Important: A brown roux should be *allowed to cool* to a temperature which allows the cook to blend in the liquid without the risk of severe burning or scalding.

Composite roux

This is a roux which is prepared containing meat and/or vegetables etc. The fat is used to sear the meat or sweat vegetables prior to adding the flour.

Proportion of roux to liquid

Sauces (1 litre)		*Soups and stews* (1 litre)		*Panadas* (1 litre)	
Fat:	100 g	*Fat*:	50 g	*Fat*:	200 g
Flour:	100 g	*Flour*:	50 g	*Flour*:	200 g
Total:	200 g	*Total*:	100 g	*Total*:	400 g

Important points when preparing roux-thickened preparations

Mise en place

The preparation of the dishes may be staggered to fit into a scheduled work plan, e.g. plain roux can be cooked before required – this may be done in a hotplate therefore reducing the need for attention; meats and vegetables can be prepared in advance.

Blending the roux and liquid together

When blending the roux and liquid together it is advisable to use a hot liquid but not a very hot roux, as this reduces the risk of burning or scalding the operator. The liquid should be added to the roux in stages with each addition being blended in to produce a smooth mixture before further liquid is added – this is very important in the initial stages of blending.

Wooden spatulas should be used where possible to prevent discoloration caused by metal striking metal, especially with aluminium saucepans; a whisk may be used if required but the operator should avoid striking the saucepan – this is not important if using tin-lined copper pans.

Cooking the mixtures

Mixtures should simmer slowly or deterioration is likely to occur, e.g. deterioration of colour, flavour and appearance – recipe fat may separate out from the mixture and float on top as surface grease.

Traditional cooking times are less appropriate today

because of modern methods of refining flour; this refers to plain mixtures such as Béchamel and velouté sauces where the suggested times of 20 mins. and 1 hour may be reduced by as much as 60% with little or no difference in quality. Furthermore, it is advisable to substantially reduce the cooking times if the sauce is to be stored hot prior to service, e.g. simmer Béchamel for 2–3 mins. to complete the gelatinization of the starch then place in the bain-marie.

Mixtures containing vegetables and meats, e.g. soups and sauces, must be simmered until the vegetable or meat is cooked. The cooking of most mixtures may be carried out in a cool oven, provided the saucepan or cooking utensil is covered with a lid.

Control procedures

Roux-thickened mixtures must be stirred frequently to prevent sticking and burning on the base of the saucepan. The spatula is a good guide as to whether the mixture is cooking satisfactorily or has started to burn on the base of the saucepan.

The spatula can be drawn over the base of the pan, revealing by touch any mixture adhering to the bottom of the pan. If burning is suspected transfer the mixture into a clean pan.

Covering a saucepan with a lid when cooking on top of a stove will bring the mixture more quickly to the boil but the cook will not see the mixture. Therefore if a lid is to be used the mixture should be inspected regularly to determine the 'speed of cooking'.

The consistency of a mixture can only be determined after the mixture reaches boiling point. This is an important point when determining whether or not all the recipe liquid is required. It may be advisable in some instances, e.g. when cooking stews and braisings, not to use too much liquid at the initial stages of cooking. This may result in the meat being cooked before the sauce attains the required consistency. To avoid this problem the mixture may be 'topped up' with liquid as and when required.

Hot storage

Most roux-thickened preparations may be kept hot for short periods during service. Sauces, soups and stews should be kept covered with a piece of buttered paper or the surface covered over with a small quantity of liquid (appropriate liquid in recipe – stock or milk etc.) to reduce the likelihood of a skin forming over the surface.

It is advisable to store the mixtures in a 'bain-marie' (temperature 90–95°C), to reduce the risk of burning. Occasional stirring may also be required to even out temperature differences which may result during storage, e.g. soups should be stirred from the bottom when ladling out of a storage container.

Prolonged heated storage is undesirable as this may cause general deterioration in the finished product, e.g. discoloration, undesirable odours and flavours and consistency changes.

Important process procedures

To add a liaison

Velouté sauces, blanquettes and fricassées.
A liaison is a mixture of egg yolks and cream which is blended into certain white sauces and stews on completion of cooking.
Procedures: Mix together the egg yolks and cream. Remove the sauce or stew from the boil then blend in the liaison. Do not reboil.

To blanch

Blanchir.
This procedure varies with the main commodity which is to be blanched.
Meat for blanquettes and ox kidneys for braising.
To place the meat or kidneys in a pan, cover with cold water then bring to the boil. When the water boils the pan is placed under cold running water and the meat refreshed.
Reason: Blood, fat and impurities which would have a detrimental effect on the sauce of the dish are removed. Blanching is only required with poor quality meats.

To cook out

All roux.
The cooking of a roux before any recipe liquid is added. When preparing white mixtures, care must be taken to avoid developing any colour but with brown mixtures this helps to promote colour.
Reason: Cooks the flour producing a mellow taste.

To sear flesh

Brown stews and braisings.
The shallow-frying and browning of flesh in hot fat (usually the recipe fat).
Reason: Promotes colour and flavour. Does not seal in meat juices as is often suggested.

To sweat

Vegetables.
The slow-frying of vegetables in butter, margarine or fat usually with a lid on the cooking utensil.
Reason: Promotes flavour. See Chapter 7.

To deglaze

Salmis.
To swill a cooking utensil with water, wine, stock or sauce after dry-heat cooking meat, game or poultry.
Reason: Promotes flavour by using the soluble extracts lost from the flesh during cooking.

Section one   White sauces and soups

Base method

Step 1	Mise en place
	A Assemble ingredients.
	B *Soups*: Wash and prepare the vegetables.
	Base vegetables: Roughly chop.
	Main vegetable: Artichokes, cauliflower and celery: roughly chop.
	Asparagus: use trimmings.
	Mushrooms: slice.
Step 2	Melt the butter or margarine in a saucepan.

	Sauces	*Soups*
Step 3		Add the vegetables, i.e. base and main vegetables.
		Note: This does not apply to mushrooms which are the only exception. These are added into the simmering soup, step 8.
Step 4		Slowly sweat down for 8–10 mins.
Step 5	Add the flour and mix together.	
Step 6	Cook out the mixture on a low heat for 4–5 mins. Do not allow to brown.	
Step 7	Slowly blend in the hot recipe liquid, stirring smooth with each addition of liquid.	
Step 8	Bring to the boil then slowly simmer. Add any mushrooms.	
Step 9	Skim off surface fat and impurities as required. Also adjust the consistency as required.	
Step 10	When cooked strain the sauce if required.	Remove the piece of vegetable (or mushrooms) which is to be used as garnish then pass the soup through a soup machine or liquidizer.
Step 11		Cut the vegetable which is to be the garnish for the soup into small neat pieces. Add to the soup.
Step 12		Blend the cream through the soup.
Step 13	Check the consistency, seasoning and temperature.	

Béchamel sauce   (yield ½ litre; 10 portions approximately)

White roux:	50 g butter or margarine. 50 g flour.
Liquid:	500 ml milk.
Studded onion:	½ onion, 1 bay leaf and 1 clove.
Seasoning:	Salt and white pepper.

Follow the instructions in the base method, heating the milk in a saucepan with the studded onion. Also add the onion to the sauce when cooking, step 8.
Traditional cooking time: 15–20 mins.

Velouté sauce   (yield ½ litre; 10 portions approximately)

Blond roux:	50 g butter or margarine. 50 g flour.
Liquid:	500 ml white stock (chicken, veal or fish etc.).
Seasoning:	Salt and white pepper.

Follow the instructions in the base method using hot stock.
Traditional cooking time: 1 hour approximately.

Cream soups (vegetable)   (yield 1 litre; 4 portions)

White roux (composite):	50 g butter or margarine. 50 g flour.
Main vegetable:	This determines the flavour of the soup, see below.
Base vegetables:	75 g onion, 25 g celery, 25 g white leek, sprig of thyme and piece of bay leaf. (*Note*: When a base vegetable is also the main vegetable it is not required, e.g. cream of onion soup, omit the base onion).
Liquid:	1 litre white chicken stock.
Seasoning:	Salt and white pepper.
Cream:	25–50 ml cream.

Cream of artichoke (crème d'artichauts)	200 g roughly chopped artichokes.
Cream of cauliflower (crème Du Barry)	200 g roughly chopped cauliflower.
Cream of celery (crème de céleri)	200 g roughly chopped celery.
Cream of asparagus (crème d'asperges)	400 g asparagus trimmings.
Cream of mushroom (crème de champignons)	100 g sliced white mushrooms.

Follow the instructions in the base method using hot liquid. Keep a small quantity of the main vegetable in one piece (or whole if mushrooms) and remove prior to passing through the soup machine. Add in small pieces as garnish at step 11.

Cooking time: 45 mins.–1 hour, until vegetables are tender.

Note: Very tough or stringy vegetables, e.g. mature celery, should be blanched or parboiled prior to sweating down, step 4.

Using a convenience food as the main ingredient in cream soups

Although the ingredients in the base recipe consist of fresh vegetables, these may be replaced with selected convenience foods, especially when a vegetable is out of season or extremely expensive in its raw state.

Frozen vegetables

Cauliflower and asparagus etc. Add the quantity of frozen vegetable stated in the base recipe to the simmering soup, step 8, and simmer until tender. The vegetable should be added to the soup in its frozen state.

Dehydrated vegetables

Onions, carrots and mushrooms etc. These may be incorporated into the simmering soup following the manufacturer's instructions on usage and yield.

Tinned vegetables

Celery and asparagus etc. Replace part of the base liquid with the strained vegetable liquor. Remove a small quantity of the vegetable and cut into dice or strips for garnish. Purée the remaining vegetables, and add to the simmering soup 10 minutes before completion of cooking. The amount of vegetables required will vary with the vegetable used but the quantity added should be sufficient to produce a soup with a decided flavour.

Powdered soup mixes

A combination of fresh thin chicken soup (crème reine), see page 173, and powdered soup mix is sometimes used, especially when the vegetable concerned is extremely expensive, e.g. asparagus.

Production: Reduce the base recipe roux quantities by half. When almost cooked blend in a sufficient quantity of soup mix diluted with water, milk or cold stock and complete the cooking, refer to the time stated on the packed to cook the mix. The amount of mix used should be sufficient to produce a decided taste and consistency.

Derivatives of Béchamel   (quantities for ½ litre of sauce; 10 portions approximately)

Mornay

Add 50 g of grated cheese into the boiling Béchamel on completion of cooking, step 10 (or during hot storage) and stir until melted through the sauce. Traditionally half Gruyère and half parmesan would be the cheese used.

Cream (sauce crème)

Add 100 ml cream approximately, to the sauce and adjust the consistency to that of pouring double cream.

Anchovy (sauce aux anchois)

Add anchovy essence to taste, 5 ml approximately.

Parsley (sauce au persil)

Add chopped parsley until generously dispersed through sauce.

Egg (sauce aux oeufs)

Add a small dice of hard-boiled eggs, 2 eggs approximately.

Mustard (sauce moutarde)

Add diluted English mustard to taste.

Onion (sauce aux oignons)

Add 100 g of diced onions, sweat without colour in 20 g butter, to the sauce on completion of cooking and straining.

Sauce Soubise

The same as onion sauce but strain the onions out of the sauce after allowing flavour to develop.

Base method for preparing derivatives of velouté sauces,
i.e. garnished sauces

Step 1	Melt the butter in a saucepan then add the finely chopped shallot or onion.
Step 2	Sweat the shallot or onion for 2 mins. approximately.
Step 3	Add mushrooms if stated in the recipe and sweat for a further 3–4 mins.
Step 4	Add tomato concassé if stated in the recipe. *Note*: Half the quantity of tomatoes may be added at this stage and the remaining half at step 11, if a sauce with tomatoes as a good visible garnish is required.
Step 5	Add any herbs or parsley stated in the recipe.
Step 6	Add any wine, vinegar or lemon juice and boil down until quite thick and concentrated.
Step 7	Add any cream and reduce further to a coating consistency.
Step 8	Add the velouté sauce and simmer for 2–3 minutes. Also skim if required.
Step 9	Add enriching butter: remove the sauce from the boil and blend through the butter. Do not reboil.
Step 10	*Plain sauces*	*Glazed sauces* Fold the sabayon through the sauce.
Step 11	Check the consistency, seasoning and temperature.	

Derivatives of velouté sauces (quantities for ½ litre of sauce; 10 portions approximately)

To produce the derivatives of velouté sauces, assemble the ingredients stated in the appropriate recipe then follow the instructions in the base recipe above.

Derivatives of fish velouté

Bercy
25 g butter, 50 g finely chopped shallot or onion, chopped parsley, 100 ml white wine, squeeze lemon juice, 50 ml cream and 2–3 good spoonfuls of sabayon (50 ml approximately).
Optional: Enriching butter: 20 g approximately.

Bonne-femme
Same as Bercy, adding 200 g sliced button mushrooms.

Bréval
Same as bonne-femme, adding 200 g tomato concassé.

Dugléré
Same as Bercy without the sabayon and adding 300 g tomato concassé.

Vin blanc
When preparing the fish velouté, replace 100 ml of the fish stock with white wine and add a good squeeze of lemon juice. When cooked and strained, liaise with 50 ml cream and enrich with 20 g butter. Complete the seasoning with a

little cayenne pepper. If the sauce is to be glazed, add 2–3 good spoonfuls of sabayon.

Derivatives of chicken velouté

Bonnefoy
25 g butter, 100 g finely chopped shallot or onion, a good pinch of chopped taragon, 100 ml white wine and enrich with 20 g butter.

Smitaine
25 g butter, 100 g finely chopped onion or shallot, juice of 1 lemon and 200 ml sour cream. Also flavour to taste with a little mushroom ketchup, 10 ml approximately.

Aurore
25 g butter, 100 g finely chopped onion or shallot, 300 g tomato concassé, 50 ml cream and enrich with 20 g butter approximately.

Suprême
Add 50 g of white mushroom trimmings and a few drops of lemon juice (¼ lemon approximately) to the basic chicken velouté when cooking. When the velouté has been strained, thicken with a liaison of 1 egg yolk and 50 ml cream just prior to service.

Ivoire or Albuféra
Add meat glaze to the basic velouté when cooked to produce a decided flavour and ivory colour.

Hongroise
25 g butter, 100 g finely chopped shallot or onion, 10 g paprika added after sweating down the onion, step 2, 100 ml white wine, 50 ml cream and 20 g enriching butter.
Note: This sauce is sometimes prepared including tomato concassé (200 g approximately).

Derivatives of veal velouté

Allemande
Prepare the same as sauce suprême using veal velouté in place of chicken velouté.

Poulette
Same as allemande garnished with chopped parsley.

Derivatives of mutton velouté

Caper sauce (sauces aux câpres)
Garnish the basic velouté when strained with 40 g whole capers then liaise with 50 ml cream. *Optional*:   20 g enriching butter.

Section two   Chicken soups and various vegetable soups

Base method

Step 1	Mise en place
	A Assemble ingredients.
	B Wash and prepare the vegetables:
	Base vegetables, i.e. onion, celery and leek: roughly chop.
	Additional vegetables, i.e. turnips: roughly chop; carrots: usually sliced;
	potatoes: usually sliced.
Step 2	Melt the butter or margarine in a saucepan.
Step 3	Add the base vegetables.
Step 4	Slowly sweat for 8–10 mins.
Step 5	Add the flour and mix together.
Step 6	Cook out the mixture on a low heat for 4–5 mins. Do not allow to brown.
Step 7	Slowly blend in the hot chicken stock (or milk), stirring smooth with each addition of liquid.
Step 8	Bring to the boil.
Step 9	Slowly simmer, stirring occasionally to reduce the risk of burning.
Step 10	Skim as required during cooking. Top up with additional stock if required.
Step 11	*Fresh purée soups* Stir in the vegetable purée, e.g. pea or bean etc. just prior to completion of cooking, i.e. 5 minutes approximately.
Step 12	When cooked pass the soup through a soup machine or liquidizer.
Step 13	Add any garnish then blend the cream through the soup.
Step 14	Check the consistency, seasoning and temperature.

Base recipe   (yield 1 litre; 4–6 portions depending on quantity of total vegetables used)

Roux:	50 g butter or margarine and 50 g flour.
Base vegetables:	75 g onion, 25 g celery, 25 g white leek, sprig of thyme and piece of bay leaf.
Liquid:	1 litre white chicken stock.
Seasoning:	Salt and white pepper.
Cream:	25–50 ml.

Chicken soup (*crème reine*)

Follow the instructions using a good strong chicken stock and garnish with a small dice of cooked chicken, 25 g approximately.

Crème Agnès-Sorel

Follow the instructions adding 50 g white mushroom trimmings to the soup at step 9. Garnish the soup with thin strips of cooked chicken, mushroom and tongue (30 g each approximately).

Crème Doria

Follow the instructions adding 200 g diced cucumber into the simmering soup at step 9. Garnish with 60 g diced cucumber removed before puréeing the soup and boiled long grain rice (20 g approximately).

Crème Jeannette

Follow the instructions adding 200 g sliced salsify to the base vegetables, step 3. Garnish with boiled long grain rice and a small dice of cooked chicken (20 g each approximately).

Fresh green-pea soup (*crème St-Germain*)

Follow the instructions adding a fresh green-pea purée, made with 200 g shelled peas, at step 11 (see page 134). Garnish the soup with 25 g cooked peas and thin strands of lettuce blanched in boiling water. *Note*:   Traditionally milk instead of chicken stock is used in this recipe.

Fresh French bean soup (*crème favorite*)

Prepare the same as above but use a purée of French beans and garnish with small pieces of French beans.

Fresh fennel soup (*English*)

Follow the instructions adding 1 small fennel which has been roughly chopped to the base vegetables at step 3. Add 50 g sliced potato to the simmering soup at step 9.

Fresh spinach soup (*Scottish*)

Follow the instructions adding a fresh spinach purée made with 200 g spinach at step 11 (see page 135). When serving the soup sprinkle with a little chopped chives and mint leaves.

Crème florentine

This is the French version of fresh spinach soup and is made the same as above but omit the chives and mint leaves. Garnish with short thin strands of spinach which have been blanched in a little boiling water.

Sweetcorn soup (*crème de maïs*)

Follow the instructions adding 200 g sweetcorn kernels into the simmering soup at step 9. Garnish with sweetcorn kernels (25 g approximately).

Section three   Brown sauces and soups

Base method

Step 1	Mise en place
	A Assemble ingredients.
	B Wash and prepare the base vegetables, i.e. roughly chop.
	C Soups: Trim the flesh then cut into pieces.

Step 2	Melt the fat in a saucepan, add the flour and cook to a golden-brown colour stirring frequently. Allow the mixture to cool, see notes on page 165.

Step 3	Stir in the tomato purée.

Step 4	Slowly blend in three-quarters of the brown stock (1¼ litres approximately), stirring smooth with each addition. Bring to the boil.

Step 5	*Brown sauce* Fry the base vegetables in a little hot fat in a frying pan until lightly browned.	*Brown soups* Fry the flesh in a little hot fat in a frying pan, add the base vegetables and continue frying until lightly browned.

Step 6	Add the coloured base vegetables and flesh if appropriate into the simmering mixture and continue cooking. During cooking, skim as required and top up with additional stock as the mixture reduces.	

Step 7	When cooked, strain the sauce.	When cooked, strain the soup and cut the cooked flesh to be used as the garnish into a small dice.

Step 8	*Demi-glace* Add an equal quantity of rich brown stock (1 litre) and reduce down by half, i.e. 1 litre of sauce.	Blend through any sherry or cream and check the consistency, seasoning and temperature.

Brown sauce (sauce espagnole)   (yield 1 litre)

Roux:	80 g dripping and 120 g flour.
Base vegetables:	100 g onion, 100 g carrot, 50 g celery and 50 g leek, sprig of thyme, ½ bay leaf and parsley stalks.
Tomato purée:	50 g tomato purée.
Liquid:	1½–2 litres brown stock.
	Follow the instructions in the base method. *Cooking time:* 4 hours approximately.

Basic brown soup recipe   (yield 1 litre)

Roux:	40 g dripping and 60 g flour.
Base vegetables:	100 g onion, 100 g carrots, 50 g celery, 50 g leek, sprig of thyme, ½ bay leaf and parsley stalks.
Tomato purée:	50 g tomato purée.
Liquid:	1½–2 litres brown stock.
Main item:	This determines the flavour of the soup – see each individual recipe below.
	Follow the instructions in the base method. *Cooking time:* 4 hours approximately.

Brown soups   (quantities for 1 litre, 4 portions)

Kidney soup   (soupe aux rognons)
Use 200 g ox kidney cut into pieces. Garnish with a little of the diced cooked kidney.

Oxtail soup
Use 200 g oxtail cut into pieces. Garnish the soup with a small dice of the cooked oxtail.

Thick brown game soup   (venison, pheasant and hare etc.)
Use 200 g diced game flesh and brown game stock. Garnish with a little of the cooked game flesh and add a measure of sherry when serving. *Note:*   10 g of redcurrant jelly may be added during cooking, step 6.

Base method for preparing the derivatives of brown sauces

	Group C sauces	Group B sauces	Group A sauces
Step 1	Melt the butter or margarine in a saucepan.		Place in a saucepan any onion, shallot, bay leaf, thyme, parsley stalks and mignonette pepper.
Step 2	Add the shallot or onion and shallow-fry for 3 mins. approximately.	Add the onion, shallot, carrot, celery, leek, bay leaf, thyme, parsley stalks and mignonette pepper.	
Step 3	Add any mushrooms and cook for a further 4–5 mins.	Shallow-fry for 8–10 mins.	
Step 4	Add any vinegar or wine and boil down until quite concentrated – three-quarter reduction approximately.		
Step 5	Add any tomato concassé.		
Step 6	Add the brown sauce or demi-glace (½ litre) and simmer: Group C sauces 3–4 mins. Group A and B sauces 20–30 mins. Exceptions au madère, au porto and au xérès; simmer for 1 min. only.		
Step 7	Add any chopped herbs or parsley and also any cooked ham.	Add any diluted mustard, redcurrant jelly or honey in the recipe and reboil.	
Step 8		Pass the sauce through a fine strainer then add any garnish stated in the individual recipe.	
Step 9	Check the consistency, seasoning and temperature.		

Derivatives of brown sauce (quantities for ½ litre sauce; 10 portions approximately)

Bordelaise (Group A)
50 g chopped shallots, sprig of thyme, bay leaf, pinch mignonette pepper and 200 ml red wine.

Diable (Group A)
50 g chopped shallots, good pinch mignonette pepper (2½ g approximately), 50 ml vinegar, 50 ml white wine and pinch of cayenne pepper.

Piquante (Group A)
Prepare sauce diable above and when strained garnish with 80 g chopped gherkins, 40 g chopped capers and 10 g mixed herbs.

Madère, au porto and au xérès (Group A)
Reduce down 100 ml of the appropriate wine, start at step 4. Enrich with 20 g butter. Should not require straining, step 8.

Robert (Group B)
20 g butter, 50 g chopped shallots, 50 ml vinegar, 50 ml white wine, pinch mignonette pepper and 1 teaspoon English mustard (5 g approximately) diluted in a little water.

Charcutière (Group B)
Same as sauce Robert adding a garnish of 50 g gherkins cut into thin strips.

Reform (Group B)
20 g butter, 50 g each chopped onion and carrot, 20 g each chopped celery and leek, bay leaf, sprig of thyme and parsley stalks, 50 ml vinegar, good pinch of mignonette pepper and 40 g redcurrant jelly. Garnish the strained sauce with 50 g each cooked egg white, mushrooms, beetroot, tongue, gherkin and truffle all cut into thin strips.

Aux champignons (Group C)
40 g butter, 50 g finely chopped shallot, 200 g sliced mushrooms, 100 ml white wine and chopped parsley.

Chasseur (Group C)
As above adding 200 g tomato concassé and pinch of chopped tarragon.

Italienne (Group C)
20 g butter, 50 g finely chopped shallot, 100 g chopped mushrooms, 100 g tomato concassé, 50 g chopped cooked ham and a good pinch of fines herbes.

Lyonnaise (Group C)
40 g butter, 400 g sliced onions, 50 ml each vinegar and white wine.

Section four   Tomato, curry and shellfish sauces and soups

Base method

Step 1	Mise en place
	
	A Assemble ingredients.
	B Wash and prepare the vegetables:
	Tomato sauce and soup, i.e. onions, carrots, celery and leeks: roughly chop.
	   Garlic: crush. Bacon: cut into pieces.
	Curry sauce and soup Onion: finely chop. Garlic: crush.
	Shellfish sauces and soups Onions, carrots, celery and leeks: roughly chop (small).
	   Garlic: crush.

Step 2	Melt the butter/oil in a saucepan.
Step 3	*Shellfish sauces and soups* Add the shellfish and quickly fry for 3–4 minutes. *Tomato sauce and soup* Add the bacon and fry for 2–3 minutes. *Curry sauce and soup*
Step 4	Add the base vegetables and sweat for 5 mins. approximately.
Step 5	Add the brandy and flame. Mix in the curry powder and sweat for a further 2 mins.
Step 6	Add the flour and mix together. Cook out the mixture over a low heat for 4–5 mins. approximately.
Step 7	Add the tomato purée and mix together.
Step 8	Slowly blend in the hot liquid, stirring smooth with each addition of liquid.
Step 9	Bring the mixture to the boil and simmer slowly. Stir occasionally.
Step 10	Add the fruit base and continue cooking.
Step 11	Skim as required during cooking. Also top up with additional stock if required.
Step 12	Pass the sauce or soup through a sieve or strainer. *Optional*: Pass the sauce or soup through a strainer if a smooth mixture is required.
Step 13	Add any garnish then blend through any recipe cream.
Step 14	Check the consistency, seasoning and temperature.

Tomato sauce (sauce tomate)   (½ litre)

Roux: 50 g butter and 50 g flour.

Base vegetables: 50 g onion, 50 g carrots, 25 g celery, 25 g leek, ½ clove garlic, sprig of thyme, ½ bay leaf and parsley stalks.

Bacon: 25 g bacon scraps.

Tomato purée: 50 g tomato purée.

Liquid: ½ litre stock.

Seasoning: Salt and white pepper.

Tomato soup (crème de tomate)   (1 litre)

Roux: 50 g butter and 50 g flour.

Base vegetables: 100 g onion, 100 g carrots, 50 g celery, 50 g leeks, 1 clove garlic, sprig of thyme, ½ bay leaf and parsley stalks.

Bacon: 50 g bacon scraps.

Tomato purée: 100 g tomato purée.

Liquid: 1 litre stock.

Seasoning: Salt and white pepper.

Optional: 50 ml cream.

Follow the instructions in the base method. *Cooking time:* 1 hour approximately.

Curry sauce (sauce kari)   (½ litre)

Roux: 50 g butter and 50 g flour.

Base vegetables: 100 g onion and ½ clove garlic.

Curry powder: 15 g curry powder.

Tomato purée: 10 g tomato purée.

Liquid: ½ litre brown stock.

Fruit base: 10 g desiccated coconut, 10 g sultanas (chopped), 30 g mango chutney, 50 g cooking apples (chopped).

Curry soup (mulligatawny)   (1 litre)

Roux: 50 g butter and 50 g flour.

Base vegetables: 200 g onion and 1 clove garlic.

Curry powder: 30 g curry powder.

Tomato purée: 20 g tomato purée.

Liquid: 1 litre brown stock.

Fruit base: 10 g desiccated coconut, 10 g sultanas (chopped), 30 g mango chutney, 50 g cooking apples (chopped).

Garnish: 20 g cooked long grain rice.

Optional: 50 ml cream.

Follow the instructions in the base method. *Cooking time:* ¾–1 hour.

Shellfish sauce (crustaceans)   (½ litre)

Roux: 25 ml oil, 25 g butter and 50 g flour.

Shellfish: 250 g lobster, scampi or prawn shells or legs etc.

Brandy: 20 ml brandy approximately.

Base vegetables: 50 g onion, 50 g carrots, 25 g celery, 25 g leeks, ¼ clove garlic, sprig of thyme, ½ bay leaf and parsley stalks.

Tomato purée: 25 g tomato purée.

Liquid: ½ litre fish stock, 50 ml white wine, squeeze lemon juice.

Cream: 25 ml cream.

Shellfish soup (crustaceans)   (1 litre)

Roux: 25 ml oil, 25 g butter and 50 g flour.

Shellfish: 500 g lobster, scampi or prawn shells or legs etc.

Brandy: 40 ml brandy approximately.

Base vegetables: 100 g onion, 100 g carrots, 50 g celery, 50 g leeks, ½ clove garlic, sprig of thyme, ½ bay leaf and parsley stalks.

Tomato purée: 50 g tomato purée.

Liquid: 1 litre fish stock, 50 ml white wine, squeeze lemon juice.

Cream: 50 ml cream.

Follow the instructions in the base method. *Cooking time:* 30 mins. approximately.

Section five   Shellfish dishes using cooked shellfish

Base method

Step 1	Mise en place
	A Assemble ingredients.
	B Prepare the cooked shellfish:
	Lobster: Remove from the shells and cut the tail into neat collops. Leave the shelled claws whole unless very large.
	Scallops: Slice into neat médaillons.
	Scampi and prawns: Leave whole.
	C Prepare any sauce, garnish or accompaniments stated in the individual recipe.
Step 2	Melt the butter in a sauteuse, add the shellfish then *very* slowly sauté for 1–2 mins. Remove from the pan and keep hot.
Step 3	Add any chopped shallot, onion or crushed garlic to the sauteuse and sweat for 1–2 mins.
Step 4	Add any spirit, e.g. brandy or whisky etc. and flame.
Step 5	Add any mushrooms and sweat for 2–3 mins.
Step 6	Add any wine, lemon juice and/or fish stock and reduce down by two-thirds.
Step 7	Add any tomato concassé. Add at step 11 if a neat visible garnish is desired.
Step 8	Add any cream and further reduce down by half.
Step 9	Add the stated sauce, e.g. Béchamel, velouté, shellfish or demi-glace and simmer for 1–2 mins. Add any mustard at this stage.
Step 10	Add any chopped herbs, e.g. parsley, tarragon or chervil etc. and any cheese.
Step 11	Check consistency and seasoning then add the shellfish and correct the temperature.
Step 12	Fold through any sabayon if stated in the recipe.
Step 13	Thicken with a liaison or enrich with butter if stated in the recipe.
Step 14	Place the mixture into a serving dish or heated carapaces as appropriate.

	Plain dishes	*Glazed dishes*	*Gratinated dishes*
Step 15		Brown under a hot salamander.	Sprinkle with the cheese then brown under a hot salamander.

Step 16	Serve with any stated accompaniments.

Base recipe   (yield 4 portions)

Main items:	The following shellfish may be used with the dishes in this section: *Lobster:* 2 × 750 g cooked lobsters *Scampi and prawns:* 500 g cooked fish approximately. *Scallops:* 8 cooked scallops.
Frying medium:	10 g butter.
Seasoning:	Salt, pepper and cayenne pepper.
Additional ingredients:	See each individual recipe below.

Dishes

Américaine
20 g finely chopped onion or shallot, 25 ml brandy, 50 ml white wine, 100 g raw tomato concassé, 250 ml shellfish sauce (see page 178) and 10 g enriching butter. Sprinkle with chopped parsley and accompany with riz pilaff. See also fresh lobster américaine.

Indienne
25 g finely chopped shallot or onion, ¼ clove crushed garlic, 25 ml white wine or coconut milk, 25 ml cream and 250 ml curry sauce. Serve in a suitable dish (the carapace may be used for large shellfish) accompanied with plain boiled rice and accompaniments for curry.

Eveline
10 g finely chopped onion, 25 ml brandy, 50 g sliced button mushrooms, 25 ml white wine, 50 ml cream, 200 ml white wine sauce and 50 ml sabayon (2 tablespoons approximately). Place the mixture into four large baked potatoes which have had the pulp removed and prepared en purée' with the addition of a fine dice of leeks sweat in butter (the purée is lined round the inside of the potato). Glaze under a hot salamander.

Dumas
10 g finely chopped shallot or onion, 50 ml white wine, 100 g tomato concassé, 250 ml demi-glace or jus lié and 10 g butter for enriching. Serve in a timbale with fleurons.

Mornay
30 ml cream (start at step 8 after sautéing the fish), 250 ml Béchamel and 50 g grated cheese. Place the mixture into the heated carapace or shells (unless using small fish), sprinkle with grated parmesan (20 g approximately) and gratinate under a hot salamander.

Thermidor (usually lobster)
25 g finely chopped shallot or onion, 30 ml white wine, 25 ml fish stock, chopped parsley, 250 ml Béchamel, ½ g English mustard (¼ teaspoon) diluted in a little water and 30 g grated cheese. Put the mixture into the heated carapaces, sprinkle with grated parmesan (20 g approximately) and gratinate under a hot salamander.

Dishes not using a roux-thickened sauce but applicable to the base method

Newburg
10 g finely chopped shallot, 25 ml Madeira and 100 ml cream. Complete the mixture, step 8, with a liaison of 2 egg yolks and 100 ml cream. Accompany with riz pilaff.

Provençale
50 g finely chopped onion or shallot, 1 clove of crushed garlic and 300–400 g raw tomato concassé. Allow the concassé to cook to a sauce consistency. Accompany with riz pilaff.

Section six   The fricassée and blanquette

These are two white stews which differ according to whether the main commodity is cooked in a thickened liquid or unthickened liquid.

Fricassée

In a fricassée the flesh is cooked in a white sauce, therefore to avoid discoloration the total cooking time should not exceed 1 hour approximately. Flesh which requires a longer period than this to cook tender should be cooked as a blanquette.

Base method

Step 1	Mise en place
	A Assemble ingredients.
	B Prepare the main commodity:
	Butcher meats – trim and cut into 20 mm cubes.
	Rabbit – cut into joints.
	Chicken – cut into joints.
	C Prepare any garnish.
Step 2	Melt the butter in a sauté pan and add the main commodity.
Step 3	Slowly sweat without colouring using a lid for 6–8 mins. Turn as required.
Step 4	Mix in the recipe flour and cook out without colouring.
Step 5	Blend in the stock, stirring smooth with each addition.
Step 6	Bring to the boil and simmer slowly. Skim as required.
Step 7	When almost cooked remove the main commodity and place into a clean pan.
Step 8	Strain the sauce over the meat and add the garnish which is to be cooked. Complete the cooking.
Step 9	When cooked, remove from the boil and blend in the liaison.
Step 10	Check the seasoning, consistency and temperature.
Step 11	Dress in an entrée dish and sprinkle with a little chopped parsley.

Base recipe   (yield 4 portions)

Meat fricassées:	500g flesh, e.g. veal, lamb, pork or 1 small rabbit.
Poultry fricassée:	1½ kg chicken.
Roux:	50 g butter and 40 g flour.
Liquid:	½ litre appropriate white stock.
Liaison:	1 egg yolk and 100 ml cream.
Seasoning:	Salt and white pepper.
Garnishes:	See under 'blanquettes'.
	Follow the instructions in the base method. *Cooking times*: Veal, lamb, pork and rabbit = 1 hour approximately. Chicken = 40 mins approximately.

Blanquette

This type of stew is ideal for cooking poor-quality flesh. This is because the flesh is cooked in an unthickened liquid, i.e. stock, and is therefore less subject to discoloration with prolonged cooking than the fricassée. This process is also suitable for the cooking of tripe, although when this is done it is not usually called a blanquette.

Base method

Step 1	Mise en place
	A Assemble ingredients. B Prepare the main commodity, see fricassée. C Prepare any stated garnish.
Step 2	Blanch and refresh the main commodity then place in a saucepan.
Step 3	Add the base vegetables, cover with the stock and bring to the boil.
Step 4	Simmer slowly until almost cooked. Top up with stock and skim as required.
Step 5	Drain off the cooking liquor and prepare a velouté sauce using the liquor.
Step 6	Strain over the meat and complete the cooking.
Step 7	Add any garnish then remove from the boil. Blend in the liaison.
Step 8	Check the consistency, seasoning and temperature.
Step 9	Dress in an entrée dish and sprinkle with a little chopped parsley.

Base recipe   (yield 4 portions)

Meat blanquettes:	500 g flesh, e.g. veal, lamb, pork or 1 small rabbit.
Poultry blanquettes:	1½ kg chicken or hen.
Roux:	25 g butter or margarine and 25 g flour.
Base vegetables:	50 g whole carrots, 1 studded onion (50 g approximately), bouquet garni.
Liquid:	½ litre appropriate stock.
Liaison:	1 egg yolk and 100 ml cream.
Seasoning:	Salt and white pepper.
Garnish:	See below.

Follow the instructions in the base method.
Cooking time: 1–3 hours, depending on quality.

Ancient style (à l'ancienne)
Garnish with 100 g button onions and 100 g button
mushrooms. Add to a fricassée at step 8 (onions first
followed by mushrooms 10 mins. later approximately).
For a blanquette, cook separately in a little butter and
stock and add as garnish at step 7.

Carel
Add 50 g pimento cut into thin strips and sweat down in a
little butter. Also add 50 g peanuts.

Tripe and onions (blanquette process)
Use 500 g blanched tripe cut into 20 mm cubes. Replace
half the stock with milk and the base vegetables with 250 g
sliced onions. Do not strain out the onions and liaise with
cream only.

Section seven   Brown stews, curries and goulash

Base method

Step 1	Mise en place

A   Assemble ingredients.
B   Prepare the main commodity:
Beef, veal, lamb and mutton – trim off any excess fat and sinew then cut into 20 mm
   dice.
Oxtails – cut through the joints into pieces.
Chicken – cut into joints.
Rabbit – cut into joints.
C   Wash, peel and prepare the base vegetables, i.e.
Brown stews – roughly chop the base vegetables.
Curries and goulash – finely chop the onion and crush the garlic.

Step 2	Place the recipe fat in a saucepan and heat on the stove.		
Step 3	Add the main commodity and sear the flesh until brown.		
Step 4	Add the base vegetables and fry for 8–10 mins.		
Step 5	Add any spice stated in the recipe, sweat for 2–3 mins then mix in the recipe flour.		
Step 6	Cook out the mixture on a low heat for 4–5 mins.		
Step 7	Mix in the tomato purée.		
Step 8	Slowly blend in the hot brown stock, stirring smooth with each addition of liquid. Bring to the boil then *slowly simmer*.		
Step 9	Skim as required.		
Step 10	Top up with stock if required.		
Step 11	*Brown stews*	*Curries* Chop together the fruit base and stir into the mixture – this is usually done after 20 mins. cooking approximately.	*Goulash*
Step 12	When cooked, remove the meat or main item and place into a clean pan.		When almost cooked add the potatoes and complete the cooking.
Step 13	Strain the sauce over the cooked meat.	When cooked check the temperature, seasoning and consistency.	
Step 14	Check consistency, seasoning and temperature and serve in an entrée dish.	Place in entrée dish and serve with the accompaniments.	Place in entrée dish and sprinkle with the heated spatzelli or gnocchi.

Base brown stew recipe   (yield 4 portions)

All the recipes for brown stews have the same basic ingredients.
This is for all stews *except* oxtails. When preparing oxtails *double the quantity* of *all* ingredients.

Main item:	This produces the appropriate stew, see below.
Roux:	25 g fat or lard and 25 g flour.
Base vegetables:	50 g onion, 50 g carrot, 25 g celery, 25 g leek, sprig of thyme, ½ bay leaf and parsley stalks.
Tomato purée:	25 g tomato purée.
Liquid:	½ litre brown stock.
Brown beef stew (ragoût de boeuf)	Use 500 g stewing beef.
Brown veal stew (ragoût de veau)	Use 500 g stewing veal.
Brown lamb stew (navarin d'agneau)	Use 600 g boneless stewing lamb.
Brown mutton stew (navarin de mouton)	Use 600 g boneless stewing mutton.
Stewed oxtails (ragoût de queue de boeuf)	Use 1 kg oxtails.
Brown rabbit stew (ragoût de lapin)	Use 1 small rabbit.
	Follow the instructions in the base method using hot stock. *Cooking times:* All stews except oxtail 1½–2 hours. Oxtails 2–3 hours.

Basic curry recipe (traditional European curries, see also page 161)   (yield 4 portions)

Main item:	Use the same commodities and quantities as brown stews above, e.g. beef curry – kari de boeuf. Chicken curry: 1½ kg chicken.
Roux:	25 g fat or lard and 25 g flour.
Base vegetables:	150 g onions and 1 clove garlic.
Curry powder:	15 g curry powder.
Tomato purée:	10 g tomato purée.
Liquid:	½ litre brown stock.
Fruit base (all chopped):	50 g cooking apples, 50 g mango chutney, 10 g sultanas and 10 g desiccated coconut.
	Follow the instructions in the base method using hot stock. *Cooking times:* All curries *except* chicken 1½–2 hours. Chicken 45 mins.–1 hour.
Accompaniments:	Plain boiled rice using 200 g long grain rice. This is served on a separate dish or as a border/base to the curry. Also poppadoms, Bombay duck, chapatis, chopped fruits and onions etc.

Basic goulash recipe   (yield 4 portions)

Main item:	500 g stewing veal or beef.
Roux:	25 g fat or lard and 25 g flour.
Base vegetables:	100 g onions and ½ clove garlic.
Paprika:	25 g paprika.
Tomato purée:	10 g tomato purée.
Liquid:	½ litre brown stock.
Garnish:	200 g raw shaped potatoes, e.g. balls, 50 g plain spatzelli or gnocchi parisienne, see page 129.

Follow the instructions in the base method using hot stock.
Cooking time: 1½–2 hours.

Further dishes and garnishes are given on page 192.

Section eight   Mutton bean stew and chilli con carne

Base method

Step 1	Mise en place
	A Cook the beans using brown stock keeping a little underdone, see page 88.
	B Assemble ingredients.
	C Trim and cut the meat:
	Mutton bean stew: 20 mm dice.
	Chilli con carne: 10 mm dice (sometimes minced).
	D Crush the garlic. Remove the seeds from fresh chillis and finely shred.
	E Prepare the garnish.
Step 2	Melt the fat in a saucepan then sear the meat.
Step 3	Add the crushed garlic, cook for 3–4 mins then mix in the flour.
	Chilli con carne: add chilli powder at this stage prior to flour.
Step 4	Cook out the mixture on a low heat for 4–5 mins then mix in the tomato purée.
Step 5	Slowly blend in the hot stock, stirring smooth with each addition.
Step 6	Bring to the boil and simmer for 45 mins. Skim and top up with additional liquor as required.
Step 7	Add the beans and continue cooking.
	Chilli con carne: Add the shredded chillis with the beans.
Step 8	*Mutton bean stew* *Chilli con carne*
	Fry the button onions and dice of bacon in a little hot fat until lightly browned and add to the stew.
Step 9	When cooked check the consistency, seasoning and temperature.
Step 10	Place in an entrée dish and sprinkle with a little chopped parsley. Place in an entrée dish and serve accompanied with the garnish.

Mutton bean stew (haricot de mouton) (yield 4 portions)

Main item:	600 g boneless stewing mutton.
Roux:	25 g fat and 25 g flour.
Base vegetable:	1 clove garlic.
Tomato purée:	10 g tomato purée.
Liquid:	½ litre bean cooking liquid.
Beans:	100 g haricot beans.
Garnish:	100 g button onions, 50 g blanched dice of bacon.

Chilli con carne (yield 4 portions)

Main item:	500 g stewing beef.
Roux:	25 g fat and 25 g flour.
Base vegetable:	1 clove garlic.
Tomato purée:	10 g tomato purée.
Liquid:	½ litre bean cooking liquid.
Beans:	100 g red beans.
Chilli powder:	25 g fresh chillis or 15 g chilli powder.
Garnish (served separately):	raw onion rings and hot tomato concassé.

Follow the instructions in the base method using hot stock, i.e. bean cooking liquor.
Cooking time (*not* including prior cooking of beans): 1½–2 hours.

Section nine   Brown game stews (feathered game only)

This stew may be made with raw or cooked game. When using cooked game it is a reheated or réchauffé dish therefore it is important that correct hygienic practices are strictly followed. The term for this type of stew is 'salmis'.

Base method

Step 1	Mise en place A Assemble ingredients. B Draw, clean and truss the bird/s. C Wash, peel and roughly chop the vegetables.
Step 2	Roast the bird/s keeping underdone then allow to cool slightly.
Step 3	Cut into joints and place in a sauté pan or plat à sauter with the brandy and a little demi-glace. Cover with a lid and keep hot.
Step 4	Melt the butter in a saucepan and add the base vegetables. Chop the carcase and also add to the vegetables. Fry until lightly coloured.
Step 5	Decant off excess fat then déglacer with the red wine.
Step 6	Add the demi-glace, bring to the boil and simmer for 20–30 mins. Skim and adjust the consistency with a little stock if required.
Step 7	Strain the sauce on to the jointed bird/s and complete the cooking. Add and cook the mushrooms at the end of the cooking period.
Step 8	Check consistency, seasoning and temperature then arrange neatly on an entrée dish etc. Garnish with the heart-shaped croûtons. Sprinkle with a little chopped parsley.

Base recipe   (4 portions)

Main item:	Pheasant (faisan): 1 bird. Duck (canard): 1 bird. Grouse (coq de bruyère): 2 birds. Guinea fowl (pintade): 2 birds. Partridge (perdreau): 2 birds.
Frying butter:	25 g butter.
Base vegetables:	50 g onion, 50 g carrots, 25 g celery, 25 g leeks, sprig of thyme, ½ bay leaf and parsley stalks.
Liquid:	25 ml brandy and 50 ml red wine.
Sauce:	½ litre demi-glace.
Garnish:	100 g small mushrooms, 4 fried heart-shaped croûtons.
	Follow the instructions in the base method. *Cooking time*: This varies considerably depending on quality.

Section ten   Braised red meats, furred game, poultry and offal

When braising a commodity, a brown sauce or thickened gravy may be used (traditional practice) or alternatively the sauce may be prepared as part of the process.

Base method

Step 1	Mise en place
	A Assemble ingredients.
	B Prepare the main commodity:
	Whole pieces of flesh: Trim then tie with string.
	Steaks and chops: Trim off excess fat.
	Poultry: Truss the drawn and cleaned bird with string.
	Liver: Remove any skin or tubes then cut into slices.
	Tongue: Leave whole.
	C Wash, peel and roughly chop the base vegetables.

Step 2	Place the fat into a small braising pan or saucepan, heat on the stove then *sear* the main commodity.

Step 3	Add the base vegetables then fry for 8–10 mins.

Step 4	*Using brown sauce*	*Preparing the sauce* Mix in the recipe flour then cook out for 8–10 mins.

Step 5	Decant off excess fat then add the thin brown sauce or thickened gravy.	Mix in the tomato purée then slowly blend in the stock.

Step 6	Bring to the boil and skim then cover with a lid and cook in the oven at 175°C approximately. During cooking baste large pieces with the sauce and top up with stock if required. *Note:* The sauce should reach two-thirds the height of large pieces or barely cover small cuts – steaks, chops and slices of liver.

Step 7	When cooked, remove the main commodity and strain the sauce into a clean pan. Skim off the grease from the sauce then check the consistency, seasoning and temperature.

Step 8	*Joints*: remove the string then cut into neat slices across the grain.
	Poultry: remove the string then cut into joints.

Step 9	Dress the slices or pieces in an entrée dish then coat with some of the sauce. Garnish as desired then serve the remaining sauce in a sauceboat.

Base recipe:	All methods	(yield 4 portions)
Main item:		See individual recipes.
Base vegetables:		50 g onions, 50 g carrot, 25 g celery, 25 g leek, sprig of thyme, ½ bay leaf and parsley stalks.
		Optional: ½ clove of crushed garlic.

Method using brown sauce

Searing fat:	20 g fat (lard or dripping etc.)
Sauce:	500 ml thin brown sauce or thickened gravy (e.g. ½ brown sauce and ½ brown stock approximately).

Method preparing the sauce

Roux:	25 g fat (lard or dripping) and 25 g flour.
Tomato purée:	25 g tomato purée.
Liquid:	500 ml brown stock.

Braised beef (boeuf braisé)
Allow 600 g piece of topside or rump beef per four portions.
 Follow the instructions in the base method.
Cooking time: 2–3 hours.

Braised venison (venaison braisée)
Allow 600 g piece topside or rump venison per four portions.
 Follow the instructions in the base method.
Cooking time: 2–3 hours.

Braised steaks
Allow 1 × 150 g slice of rump or good stewing steak per portion.

Braised chops
Allow 1 × 150 g chump or gigot mutton chop per portion.
 Follow the instructions in the base method.
Cooking time: 2 hours approximately.

Beef olives (paupiettes de boeuf)
Allow 400 g piece of topside or rump beef (veal, venison and turkey etc. may also be used).
Stuffing: 100 g minced beef or sausagemeat, 5 g butter, 25 g chopped onions, 5 g chopped parsley (2 teaspoons), pinch mixed herbs (¼ teaspoon), ½ egg and seasoning.
Basic preparation:
1 Trim the beef then cut into four slices across the grain.
2 Flatten out with a cutlet bat.
3 Trim the slices to 150 mm × 100 mm then mince the trimmings and add to the stuffing.
4 Place the stuffing down the centre of each slice then neatly roll up.
5 Secure with string or small skewers.

Stuffing: Sweat down the onions and allow to cool. Mix all the ingredients together.
 Follow the instructions in the base method.
Cooking time: 1½–2 hours.

Braised duck (canard braisé)
Allow 1 × 2 kg duck (approximately) per four portions (pigeon, grouse and pheasant etc. may also be used).
Proceed as stated but *double the quantities of all ingredient in the base recipe.*
Cooking time: 1½–2 hours depending on quality.

Braised ox liver (foie de boeuf braisé)
Allow 500 g ox liver per four portions.
 Follow the instructions in the base method.
Cooking time: 1½–2 hours.
Important: Ox liver and kidneys are likely to produce impurities which will be difficult to remove from the finished sauce. To avoid this problem, blanch the liver or kidneys in cold water prior to braising.

Braised tongue (langue de boeuf braisée)
Allow 1 small fresh ox tongue per 4–6 portions.
 Follow the instructions in the base method.
Cooking time: 2–3 hours.

Further dishes and garnishes are given on page 193.

Further dishes and garnishes for brown stews and braisings

The following stews are derived from the base recipe and method for brown stews.

Exeter stew
Prepare beef stew as stated but strain out the base vegetables before fully cooked. Add small suet pastry dumplings well flavoured with parsley and a little mixed herbs and complete the cooking.

Glasgow stew
Prepare the same as above but flavour the dumplings with chopped raisins.

Beef in ale (English)
Use the basic recipe and method for brown beef stew but cut the base vegetables into thin strips. Add 50 g lean bacon cut into strips to the beef, step 3, and replace half the stock with beer – ¼ litre of ale. Also add a measure of port when cooking. Do not strain.

Jugged hare (civet de lièvre)
Assemble the base recipe ingredients using a small hare as the main item and add a clove of garlic to the vegetables.

Cut the hare into joints and collect the blood from the chest. After this, marinade the pieces of hare with the base vegetables and ¼ litre of red wine for 4–6 hours. Remove the hare and vegetables from the marinade and wipe off excess liquid.

Proceed as stated in the base method adding the base vegetables as indicated at step 4 and the red wine from the marinade with the brown stock, step 8.

Just prior to straining the sauce over the cooked hare, step 13, slowly mix in the blood to the boiling sauce and allow to thicken. Do not reboil.

For suitable garnish see bourguignonne.

The following dishes are derived from the base recipe and method for braised meats, game, poultry and offal.

Braised duckling with orange (caneton à l'orange)
Assemble the recipe ingredients for braised duck/duckling and add 3 oranges and 1 lemon.

Remove the zest from 1 orange and the lemon and cut into thin strips. Blanch in a little boiling water. Remove the segments from 2 oranges and the juice from the remaining orange and lemon.

Proceed as stated in the base method adding the orange and lemon juice to the strained and skimmed sauce at step 7. Check the consistency, temperature and seasoning then add the blanched strips of zest.

Garnish the duckling with the orange segments (heated) and coat with the sauce.

Braised pigeon (pigeon en compote)
Allow ½ pigeon per portion.

Follow the instructions using the basic recipe ingredients and add 50 ml white wine with the brown sauce, step 5. Garnish the pigeon for service with glazed button onions and cubes of blanched bacon fried in a little butter.

Braised beef or venison in red wine sauce
Assemble the ingredients for braised beef or venison. Lard the flesh with strips of pork fat if desired then marinade with the base vegetables and ¼ litre of red wine for 6 hours approximately.

Proceed as stated in the base method adding the base vegetables as indicated at step 3 and the red wine from the marinade with the sauce, step 5.

Braised ox liver and onions (foie de boeuf lyonnaise)
Assemble the ingredients in the basic recipe *but replace* all the base vegetables with 200 g sliced onions.

Follow the instructions in the base method but *do not* strain out the onions at step 7.

Garnishes for brown stews and braisings
Garnishes may be neatly arranged around the serving dish or alternatively with stews blended through the sauce and meat. Some items of garnish such as balls of cauliflower or cabbage and braised lettuce etc. should be placed neatly around the serving dish.

Alsacienne
100–200 g braised sauerkraut and 4–8 slices of heated continental sausage.

Aux primeurs
Turned and glazed carrots and turnips (40 g each approximately), glazed button onions (40 g), cooked peas and diamonds of cooked French beans (15 g each) and small turned plain boiled potatoes.

Bourgeoise
Large turned and glazed carrots and turnips (60 g each) and blanched cubes of bacon fried in a little butter.

Bourguignonne
Glazed button onions (100 g approximately), blanched cubes of bacon fried in a little butter (60 g), button mushrooms (60 g) fried with the dice of bacon and four heart-shaped croûtons also fried in a little butter.

Jardinière
Carrots and turnips cut into bâtons and cooked glazed (60 g each approximately). Mixed with cooked peas and diamonds of cooked French beans (30 g each).

Nivernaise
Turned glazed carrots and turnips and glazed button onions (60 g each approximately). Also four turned boiled potatoes and four small braised lettuce.

Printanière
Turned glazed carrots and turnips and glazed button onions (60 g each approximately). Also cooked peas and diamonds of cooked French beans (30 g each approximately).

Section eleven   Savoury mixtures or salpicons and garnished sauces

Savoury fillings are used for barquettes, bouchées , crêpes, tartlets and vol-au-vents.

Base method

Step 1	Mise en place
	A Assemble ingredients.
	B Prepare any sauces stated in the individual recipe.

Step 2	Melt the recipe fat or butter in a sauteuse or saucepan.

Step 3	Add any onion or crushed garlic and sweat for 2–3 mins.

Step 4	*Raw meat, poultry or game*	*Cooked meat, poultry or game*
	Add the meat, game or poultry and shallow-fry to stiffen the flesh.	
	Note: Allow the flesh to colour when preparing brown mixtures. Do not allow to colour when preparing white mixtures.	

Step 5	Add any mushrooms or peppers and sweat for a further 2–3 mins.

Step 6	Add any spirit or brandy and flame.

Step 7	Add any wine then add the recipe sauce.	Add any wine and reduce down by three-quarters approximately.

Step 8	Simmer until cooked. Skim and top up with stock as required.	Add the various cooked items and heat gently *but thoroughly*. Do not add very delicate items at this stage, e.g. quenelles Add after the sauce, at step 9.

Step 9		Add the recipe sauce and carefully blend with the rest of the ingredients.

Step 10	Liaise with cream if stated in the recipe.

Step 11	Check consistency, seasoning and temperature.

Mixtures or garnished sauces using espagnole or demi-lace   (yield 4 portions)

Bolonaise sauce*

10 g butter, 50 g finely chopped onion, 1 small clove of garlic, 125 g finely chopped or minced beef and 125 ml espagnole or jus lié.

Note: This sauce is often prepared with a tomato flavour – add half espagnole and half tomato sauce if this is desired.

Minced beef*

25 g dripping, 100 g chopped onion, 400 g lean minced beef and 250 ml espagnole or demi-glace. *Cooking time*:   45 mins. approximately.

Game filling

10 g butter, 25 g finely chopped onion, 200 g cooked game flesh cut into a small dice, 25 ml port and 125 ml espagnole or brown game sauce. *Note*:   A little redcurrant jelly and vinegar may also be added, step 7.

Game purée (purée St-Hubert)

20 g butter, 10 g finely chopped onion, 200 g finely chopped or minced cooked game and only enough espagnole to bind the mixture to a purée (50 ml approximately).

Mixtures using chicken velouté   (yield 4 portions)

Chicken filling

20 g butter, 200 g small dice of cooked chicken, 125 ml chicken velouté and 25 ml cream.

Chicken and mushroom filling

Prepare as chicken above but add 50 g diced button mushrooms as stated, step 5.

Princesse

Prepare the chicken and mushroom filling then add 4–8 asparagus tips cut into short lengths, step 9.

Mixtures using fish velouté   (yield 4 portions)

Seafood filling (fruits de mer)

10 g butter, 10 g finely chopped onion, 25 ml white wine, 200 g cooked shellfish and firm seafish, e.g. mussels, shrimps, diced scampi, lobster or scallops, monkfish, turbot, 125 ml fish velouté and 25 ml cream.

Marinière

10 g butter 10 g finely chopped onion, 25 ml white wine, 100 g cooked mussels, 100 g cooked shrimps, 125 ml fish velouté and 25 ml cream.

Mixtures using curry sauce

Indienne

30 g finely chopped onion, ½ clove of crushed garlic, 200 g diced cooked meat, e.g. mutton, beef or chicken, 125 ml curry sauce and 25 ml cream (optional).

---

* Both bolonaise sauce and minced beef may be prepared with the sauce being made in the process instead of using ready-made brown sauce. When this procedure is to be adopted use the base method for brown stews and amend the above recipes as follows:
Bolonaise sauce: Add 5 g flour and 5 g tomato purée. Also replace the sauce with brown stock.
Minced beef: Add 15 g flour and 10 g tomato purée. Also replace the sauce with brown stock.

Section twelve   Reheated dishes

Some dishes are prepared with cooked meat, poultry or game etc., which involves the reheating of the cooked commodity. The mixtures for these dishes must be thoroughly reheated to avoid the risk of food poisoning and the dishes served when made, with any unused portions being discarded.

The base preparation for many reheated dishes falls into two categories.

Base method for category 1 dishes

Step 1	Mise en place Assemble ingredients.
Step 2	Melt butter in a saucepan then add the onion and any crushed garlic and cook for 2–3 mins. Do not allow to colour when a white mixture is being made.
Step 3	Add any mushrooms or peppers if stated in the recipe and sweat for a further 2–3 mins.
Step 4	Add any spirit, wine or vinegar and reduce down by three-quarters.
Step 5	Add the cooked flesh.
Step 6	Add any tomato purée stated in the recipe.
Step 7	Mix in the sauce then heat thoroughly, stirring as required. Skim if required.
Step 8	Liaise with cream if stated in the recipe.
Step 9	Check consistency and seasoning.
Step 10	Complete as stated in the individual recipe opposite.

Category 1

Shepherd's pie

25 g butter or margarine, 100 g finely chopped onion, 400 g minced cooked mutton and 100–150 ml espagnole.

Place the mixture in an entrée or pie dish and pipe over with 400 g duchesse potatoes. Brush with eggwash and place in a moderate oven until golden brown.

Cottage pie

As above using minced cooked beef in place of mutton. For the preparation of potatoes, see page 94.

Creamed chicken (émince de volaille à la crème)

25 g butter or margarine, 25 g finely chopped onion, 25 ml sherry, 400 g cooked boiled chicken cut into small slices, 150 ml chicken velouté and 25 ml cream.

Serve the mixture in an entrée dish accompanied with braised rice.

Chicken à la king (émincé de volaille à la king)

As above adding 100 g button mushrooms and 50 g diced pimento.

Base method for category 2 dishes

Step 1	Mise en place
	Assemble ingredients.
↓	
Step 2	Melt the fat or butter in a saucepan then add the flour and cook out.
↓	
Step 3	Blend in the hot stock stirring smooth with each addition.
↓	
Step 4	Bring to the boil.
↓	
Step 5	Add the chopped or minced meat and any mushrooms etc., then cook for 4–5 mins. Stir frequently to avoid burning.
↓	
Step 6	Add the egg yolk and mix into the hot mixture.
↓	
Step 7	Spread the mixture on to a greased tray and allow to cool.
↓	
Step 8	Complete as stated in the individual recipe across the page.

Miroton de boeuf (category 1 dish)
25 g butter or margarine, 100 g shredded onion, 50 ml white wine, 10–25 ml vinegar, 400 g sliced cooked beef and 250 ml espagnole.

Serve the mixture in an entrée dish sprinkled with chopped parsley.

Moussaka (category 1 dish)
25 g butter or margarine, 50 g finely chopped onion, 1/2 clove crushed garlic, 400 g diced cooked mutton, 25 g tomato purée and 125 ml espagnole.

Place the mixture in an earthenware dish then neatly cover with:
A 200 g sliced skinned tomatoes.
B 200 g sliced peeled aubergines (5 mm slices) passed through flour then fried on each side in hot oil.
Lightly season with mill pepper then sprinkle with breadcrumbs, grated parmesan and a little melted butter. Gratinate in a hot oven until golden brown then sprinkle with chopped parsley.

Category 2

Croquettes of beef, game or chicken etc.
20 g butter or margarine, 20 g flour, 100 ml stock, 200 g minced cooked flesh and 1 egg yolk.

Divide the mixture into 4–8 even-sized pieces then shape like corks and coat with flour, eggwash and breadcrumbs. Deep-fry in hot fat and serve accompanied with a suitable sauce, e.g. diable, piquante or tomato, see page 293.

Cutlets (côtelettes)
Prepare as croquettes above but in cutlet shapes.

Rissoles
Prepare the same mixture as for croquettes but enclose between 8 rounds of puff pastry and seal well. Deep-fry and serve with a suitable sauce, see page 293.

Cromesquis à la russe
20 g butter, 20 g flour, 100 ml stock, 150 g cooked chicken, 40 g tongue, 20 g cooked mushrooms (all cut into small dice) and 1 egg yolk.

Divide the mixture into 4–8 even-sized pieces and wrap each in a slice of bacon. Pass through flour and batter and deep-fry.

Serve accompanied with a suitable sauce, see page 293.

Section thirteen   Savouries and cocktail hors-d'oeuvre

Base method

Step 1	Mise en place

A   Assemble ingredients.
B   Prepare the toast, i.e. spread with the butter then remove the crusts and cut into four neat rectangles, squares or circles.

Step 2	Prepare the mixture as stated in the base method for salpicons, section 11, except Welsh rarebit, see below.

Summary of Section 11

Raw items (kidneys and herring roe)
2   Melt the butter in a sauteuse.
4   Add raw items and lightly shallow fry to stiffen the flesh.
7   Add the recipe sauce.
8   Simmer until cooked.
11   Correct consistency, seasoning and temperature.

Pre-cooked items
2   Melt the butter in a sauteuse.
8   Add the cooked main item/s and heat gently but thoroughly.
9   Add the recipe sauce and blend together to a stiff mixture.
11   Correct consistency, seasoning and temperature.

Step 3	Dress the mixture on the toast shapes then add any garnish stated in the individual recipe. Serve on a salver lined with a dishpaper decorated with the parsley or radishes placed to the side of the savoury.

Base recipe   (yield 4 small savouries)

Main item:	See each individual savoury below.
Seasoning:	Salt, pepper and cayenne pepper.
Savoury base:	2 slices of toasted bread spread with butter, 20 g approximately.
Decoration (optional):	Sprig parsley or radishes.

Savouries prepared with a mixture using Béchamel

Croûte Derby

Mixture: 5 g butter, 100 g chopped cooked ham and 50 ml Béchamel approximately.
Decorate each savoury with half a pickled walnut.

Croûte yorkaise

As above but decorate each savoury with diamonds of ham.

Croûte Windsor

As Derby above but decorate each savoury with a large grilled mushroom.

Welsh rarebit

Mixture:

A Prepare a thick Mornay sauce using 10 g butter, 10 g flour, 100 ml milk and 100 g cheddar cheese, see page 167.
B Reduce to a glaze 50 ml beer, 2–3 drops Worcester sauce and a pinch of English mustard.
C Add to the Mornay sauce and bind with 1 egg yolk then correct seasoning.
D Allow to cool then spread the mixture on to the toast and glaze under a hot salamander.

Buck rarebit

Welsh rarebit with a hot poached egg on each savoury.

See also canapé Ivanhoë and canapé Ritchie on page 208.

Savouries prepared with a mixture using devil sauce

Devilled kidneys on toast

Mixture: 10 g butter, 4 raw lambs' kidneys cut into slices and 100 ml devil sauce approximately.

Devilled chicken on toast

Mixture: 10 g butter, 100 g small dice of cooked chicken and 100 ml devil sauce approximately.

Canapé Méphisto

Mixture: 10 g butter, 12–16 raw herring roes and 100 ml devil sauce.

Savouries prepared with a mixture using curry sauce

Croûte radjah

Mixture: 5 g butter, 100 g cooked chopped ham and 50 ml curry sauce approximately.
Decorate each savoury with a small spoonful of heated mango chutney.

Croûte indienne

Mixture: 5 g butter, 150 g shrimps or prawns and 100 ml curry sauce.
Decorate each savoury with a small spoonful of heated mango chutney.

Croûte Charlemagne

Prepare as indienne above but omit the chutney.

Table 5 *Recipe ingredients for roux-thickened preparations*

	Béchamel	Veloutés	White soups	Brown sauce	Brown soups	Brown stews and braisings	Fricassées	Blanquettes
Type of roux	White	Blond	White/composite	Brown	Brown	Composite	White	White
Main commodity	—	—	Specific vegetable	—	Ox kidney or game etc.	Beef, mutton, veal or game etc.	Chicken, veal or pork etc.	Chicken, veal or pork etc.
Base vegetables	Studded onion	—	Onion, celery and leek	Mirepoix	Mirepoix	Mirepoix	—	Carrot and onion
Liquid	Milk	White stock	White stock	Brown stock	Brown stock	Brown stock	White stock	White stock
Additional flavouring	—	—	Cream	Tomato purée	Tomato purée	Tomato purée	Cream and egg yolk	Cream and egg yolk

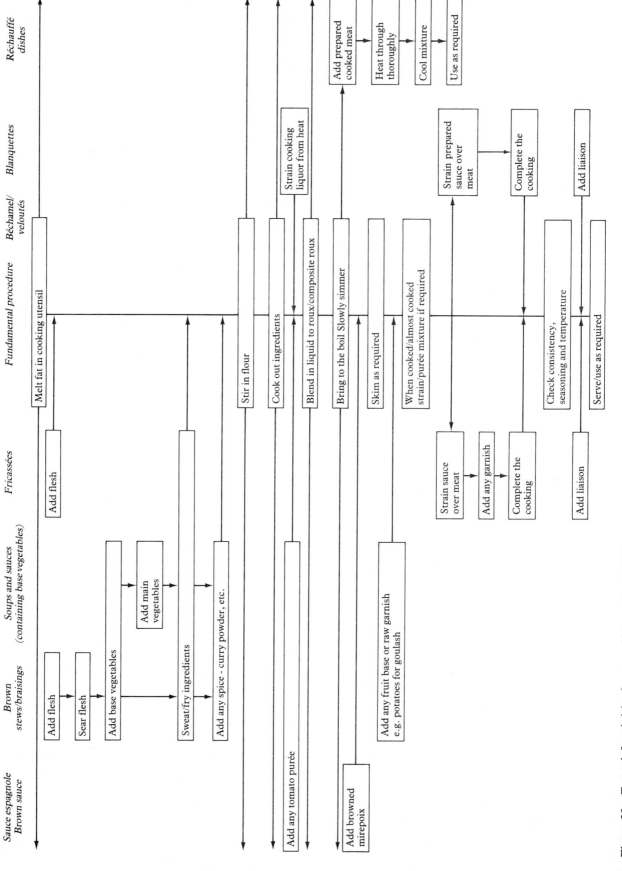

Figure 22   *Essential activities for roux-thickened preparations*

Assessment exercise

1 What is a *roux*?
2 Name the different types of roux.
3 Describe the various sections that would be found in the recipes for roux-thickened preparations.
4 Name two types of basic white sauce and describe their differences.
5 Name and describe *four derivative sauces* for each of the basic white sauces in Question 4.
6 Explain in detail, the meaning of the following *culinary terms* and *activities*:

Mise en place	To sear
Mirepoix	To sweat
Liaison	To cook out
Chinois	To simmer
Jus lié	To reduce
Oignon clouté	To reduce to a glaze
Glaze	To purée
Bouquet garni	Monter au beurre
Demi-glace	Dégraisser
Salmis	Déglacer

7 Name and describe the basic steps of production (essential activities) that are common to *all* roux-thickened dishes.
8 What are the differences between the two white stews fricassee and blanquette?
9 Describe the important points to be considered when storing roux-thickened preparations during service.
10 Give a general description for the term 'stewing' with reference to white and brown stews.
11 Braising and stewing have many common elements; state any differences.
12 Briefly describe the test to determine when meat is cooked in a stew.
13 Explain what care should be taken when blending hot liquid into the various types of roux.
14 State the approximate cooking times for white sauces, cream and velouté soups and brown sauces.
15 Name two stews in which a spice is a predominant ingredient.
16 The following list of ingredients would be used when preparing brown veal stew:

Pepper	Parsley stalks	Bay leaves
Onions	Fat	Tomato purée
Flour	Thyme	Brown stock
Celery	Stewing veal	Carrots
		Salt

(a) Arrange the ingredients into appropriate recipe sections, and describe the function of each ingredient.
(b) Indicate the ingredients which would be either *semi-critical* or *non-critical* to recipe balance (Revision Chapter 1).
(c) List the essential activities of preparation in order of production.
(d) State any alterations which would be required to change the recipe to brown mutton stew.
(e) Name and describe an appropriate garnish that would give the stew further definition and individuality.

17 Turn to page 170 and note the instructions on how to prepare derivative sauces from various basic velouté sauces.

List ingredients of your own choice, i.e. type of velouté, herbs, vegetables, etc., that would be appropriate to these instructions, thus creating your own unique sauce.

Chapter 9
Oven cooking

This chapter is divided into three parts which deal with many of the processes involving oven cooking. However it does not include oven roasting or the baking of pastries, flour products or egg preparations which are dealt with in Chapters 10, 14 and 15.

Part one – Special applications of shallow-poaching and braising

Many different dishes consist of fish, meat or vegetables which are cooked in a small quantity of liquid under cover in an oven. The main commodity is placed on a vegetable base and a cooking liquid added to approximately two-thirds the height of the commodity. When the commodity is cooked it is removed from the cooking utensil and the resulting cooking liquor boiled down until thick and concentrated. This reduced liquor is called a 'glaze' and it is used to produce a sauce which tastes of or carries the flavour of the main commodity; this is known as a 'vehicle sauce'. Although the main commodities may range from fish to vegetables and the cooking times from minutes to hours, the basic steps to the preparation of these dishes follow this similar or common theme.

Important process procedures

To blanch (blanchir)

This procedure varies with the main commodity which is to be blanched:

Vegetables
To immerse the cleaned vegetable in boiling, salted water and simmer for a specific period. After this the vegetable is cooled and refreshed under cold running water.
Reasons:
1 Crisp vegetables become limp, reduced in volume and easy to shape.
2 Helps to retain colour.
3 Reduces the bitterness present in some vegetables, e.g. mature celery.

Pickled meats and sweetbreads
To cover with cold water, bring to the boil and simmer for a specific period. After this the commodity is refreshed under cold running water.
Reasons:
1 Reduces the salt content of pickled meats.
2 Aids in the removal of impurities.
3 Facilitates the removal of undesirable tissue, skin or membranes.

To enrich sauces with butter

Monter au beurre. This is done as follows: remove the sauce from the heat so that it does *not* boil. Add the butter in pieces and shake into or stir through the sauce. Do not allow to reboil or the butter will separate out of the sauce

To reduce a cooking liquid to a glaze

Réduire à glace. To boil down a cooking liquor until thick and concentrated.
Important: When this is done with cream present (e.g. step 8, shallow-poached fish) the reduction must not be taken too far or the fat content of the cream will separate out of the liquid.
   To ensure that the liquid reduces down evenly the pan i shaken in a circular motion occasionally while reducing.
Reason: To evaporate off excess water from a cooking liquid.

To sear flesh

To shallow-fry and brown the surface of flesh in hot fat.
Reasons: Promotes colour and flavour.

Section one   Shallow-poached fish dishes

Base method

Step 1	Mise en place
	A Assemble ingredients.
	B Prepare the fish. See preparation of whole fish and cuts of fish, pages 70–2.
	C Finely chop the shallots and prepare any stated garnish.
	D *Glazed fish dishes*: Prepare the sabayon (when the fish is cooking or the cooking liquor reducing).
Step 2	Butter the base of a fish-cooking dish then add the shallots and any garnish to be cooked with the fish, e.g. chopped parsley, sliced mushrooms or tomatoes etc.
Step 3	Place the fish on top of the shallots and garnish – presentation side upwards.
Step 4	Add the cooking liquid up to two-thirds the height of the fish approximately.
Step 5	Cover with a piece of buttered paper and lid then place on top of the stove and bring almost to boiling point. Place in the oven and cook at 175°C approximately.
Step 6	When cooked, remove the fish and drain then keep warm covered with the cooking paper.
Step 7	Reduce the cooking liquor to a glaze.
Step 8	Add the cream and reduce further to a coating consistency.
Step 9	Add the recipe sauce and bring to the boil.
Step 10	Optional: Enrich with butter.
Step 11	*Glazed dishes* *Plain dishes* *Gratinated dishes*
	Mix through the sabayon.
Step 12	Check the seasoning, consistency and temperature of the sauce then coat the base of the serving dish with a little of the sauce.
Step 13	Place the fish on the serving dish and coat with the remaining sauce.
Step 14	Place under a hot salamander and allow to brown. Sprinkle over the cheese, and brown under salamander.
Step 15	Garnish with the fleurons etc. and serve.

Shallow-poached fish dishes

Fish dishes which contain a wide variety of flavoured sauces, e.g. wine, vegetable, herb or spice sauces, are usually prepared in this manner. The flavour and important characteristics of all the ingredients are contained within the sauce because the cooking liquor becomes the foundation of the sauce and is not discarded.

This method of cooking is suitable for all fish and cuts of fish and shellfish such as scallops, clams and oysters.

Important points when shallow-poaching fish

Step 1

Mise en place: The preparation of the fish is usually staggered to fit into a scheduled work plan especially for banquet or function service. For example, the fish may be trayed up and covered with the cooking paper without any recipe liquid and kept in a chill until required for service. Sauces such as fish velouté, Béchamel and lobster would be ready prepared prior to cooking the fish; this would also apply to vegetables such as tomato concassé and grated cheese etc.

Step 3

Presentation side of fish: The fish is cooked and presented for service with the presentation side upwards, i.e.
Whole flat fish: White skin side.
Fillets: Underside removed from the bone.
Small round fish and fish steaks: Either side.

Step 6

Test to determine if the fish is cooked: The fish is cooked when the bone and flesh can be easily separated with a small knife or the fingers. The flesh should also yield under pressure from the fingers with no sign of sponginess. Internal temperature for most fish: 67°C.

Step 6

Draining the fish: The fish must be thoroughly drained after cooking to prevent any excess cooking liquor spoiling the sauced fish.

Step 6

Removing the skin from the fish: Shallow-poached fish is never presented for service with any skin present (traditional practice for sauced dishes) because of the skin's undesirable texture and appearance when cooked in moisture. Although the skin on many fish can be removed prior to cooking, this is difficult on some fish and it is easier to remove after cooking, e.g. on salmon and trout and the white skin of lemon sole and plaice etc.
Procedure: Lightly scrape off the skin with the back of a knife or palette knife. When removing the skin from fish steaks, use a knife as before or catch and roll off the skin with a fork.

Step 6

Removing the centre bone from a fish steak: Insert the point of an office knife into the centre of the bone until firmly lodged then carefully pull outwards removing the bone.

Step 6

Removing the side bones from a whole flat fish: Place the drained cooked fish on a tray and with a palette knife, press down and pull outwards simultaneously the side bones at the edge of the flesh. This does not apply when the fish has been trimmed up to the flesh leaving no side fins (continental practice).

Steps 7 and 8

Reducing down the cooking liquor and cream: This is usually done rapidly to keep the preparation time to a minimum therefore the cook must ensure that the reduction is not allowed to proceed too far as the fat will separate out of the cream or burning will result. During the reducing down the pan is shaken or the mixture stirred occasionally to facilitate an even reduction of the liquid.

Step 10

Adding the enriching butter: The mixture must never be allowed to boil after the butter has been added or the butter may separate out from the sauce and the fat float on top.

Step 13

Dishing the fish: To prevent the cooked fish from sticking to the service dish, a little sauce should be placed on the base of the dish before placing on the fish. The presentation side of the fish should also be placed upwards.

Step 15

Service: Chopped parsley is suitable for most fish dishes which are *not* glazed or gratinated but branch parsley is unsuitable because of its appearance and taste in relation to the fish sauce.

Step 15

Holding time for service: The fish should be served immediately, but if hot storage for service for a short period cannot be avoided, then keep the fish and sauce separate and complete the dish when required.

Step 15

Function service: When preparing the fish for function service, the fish and sauce would normally be prepared separately but the cooking liquor should still be reduced to a glaze and added to the sauce. The preparation of the various sauces separate from the fish is explained on page 170.

Most shallow-poached fish dishes can be prepared from the following base recipe.

Base shallow-poached fish recipe   (yield 4 main course portions)

Butter for the base of the cooking dish:	5 g butter approximately.
Base vegetables:	25 g finely chopped shallot or onion.
Cooking liquid:	50 ml white wine, 150 ml fish stock and 5 ml lemon juice (¼ lemon approximately).
Sauce (Béchamel, fish velouté or lobster sauce):	300 ml sauce approximately, see each individual recipe.
Cream:	50 ml cream.
Enriching butter (optional):	10 g butter.
Glazed dishes (see each individual recipe):	50 ml sabayon (2 large spoonfuls).
Garnish:	8 fleurons (puff pastry crescents).

Main commodity (The preparation of fish and cuts of fish is explained on pages 70–2.)

Fish fillets:	Dover sole, lemon sole and plaice etc. 8 × 75 g fillets approximately.
Whole flat fish:	Dover sole, lemon sole and plaice etc. 4 × 400 g fish.
Small round fish:	Trout, haddock and whiting etc. 4 × 200 g fish.
Fish steaks:	Salmon, halibut and turbot etc. 4 × 200 g fish steaks.
Production:	Follow the instructions in the base method after making reference to the individual dish to be prepared, see below. *Cooking time:* 5–10 mins approximately, for most small fish and cuts of fish.

Dishes using Béchamel sauce

A la crème (plain)
Base recipe increasing the cream to 100 ml.

Mornay (gratinated)
Base recipe adding 50 g grated cheese after step 11. Remove the sauce from the heat and stir until the cheese has melted. Sprinkle with 20 g Parmesan when gratinating.

Florentine (gratinated)
Prepare as Mornay above but place the poached fish on a bed of cooked spinach (200 g approximately), arranged neatly on the serving dish.

Cubat (gratinated)
Prepare as Mornay but place the poached fish on a bed of dry duxelles (200 g approximately) arranged on the serving dish.

Dishes using fish velouté

Bercy (glazed)
Base recipe adding a generous sprinkling of chopped parsley to the onion on the cooking dish, step 3.

Bonne-femme (glazed)
Base recipe adding chopped parsley and 100 g slices white mushrooms at step 3. Use slices of boiled potatoes or a border of duchesse potato in place of fleurons.

Dugléré (plain)
Base recipe adding chopped parsley and 200 g tomato concassé at step 3.

Véronique (glazed)
Base recipe but garnish the top of the poached fish with skinned seeded grapes before coating with the sauce (50 g grapes approximately). Some cooks add the grapes as a garnish after glazing the fish.

Dishes using lobster sauce

Américaine (plain)

Base recipe and method garnishing each piece of cooked fish with one or two slices of cooked lobster tail sautéd in a little butter, step 13, prior to coating with sauce.

Nantua (plain)

Base recipe and method adding 100 g tomato concassé to the onion on the base of the fish-cooking dish, step 3. Also add 25 ml brandy with the cooking liquid, step 4. Use a little cayenne pepper when seasoning.

Shallow-poached shellfish dishes – molluscs

In this section, scallops have been selected as the shallow-poached mollusc. However, oysters and many different types of clam may be cooked in this manner.

Scallops (coquilles St-Jacques)   (allow 2–3 scallops per portion)

Production: Remove the fish from their shells with an oyster knife then trim off the inedible fringe leaving only the white flesh and orange roe. Also clean off any pieces of broken shell.

Prepare as stated in the base method for shallow-poached fish.

Cooking time: 5–8 mins.

When the scallops are cooked they are often sliced into neat rondels prior to dishing and coating with sauce.

Coquilles St-Jacques indienne (plain)

Prepare as stated using curry sauce in the base recipe. Place the cooked scallops on a bed of plain boiled long grain rice prior to coating with sauce. Alternatively, serve the rice in a separate dish.

Coquilles St-Jacques parisienne (glazed)

Base recipe for shallow-poached fish increasing the white wine to 100 ml and using fish velouté as the recipe sauce. Also add a little chopped truffle to the sauce, step 11.

Braised fish dishes

Fish may be braised whole or in large pieces. The fish which are traditionally associated with braising are salmon, trout, halibut, turbot and sturgeon etc.

Production: Shallow-poached fish and braised fish are very similar in production, therefore the same base recipe and method can be used but with the following amendments:

A   The flesh of the fish is sometimes *larded* with strips of bacon or pork fat, gherkin and carrot etc.

B   The fish is often covered with thin strips of bacon or pork fat prior to cooking.

C   A finely diced mirepoix is used as the base vegetables.

These vegetables are strained out of the cooking liquor after cooking the fish, on completing step 8.

D   The quantities of cooking liquid and sauce may have to be *increased* depending on the size of the fish used.

Braised fish dishes are usually elaborate in content and extensively garnished. The following example is typical of a braised fish dish.

Saumon Victoria

Bard the salmon with pork fat prior to cooking. Proceed as stated in the base recipe and method using red wine in the cooking liquid and lobster sauce. Garnish round the dish with anchovy tartlets and slices of cooked lobster tail sautéd in butter.

Section two   Savouries and cocktail hors-d'oeuvre using shallow-poached fish

Smoked fish, especially smoked haddock, is often used for these dishes. However, different types of fish may be used to produce a variety of these savouries.

Base method

This is a simplified version of the base method in Section 1.

Step 1	Mise en place
	A Assemble ingredients.
	B Trim the fish fillets removing any backbone or fins etc.
	C Prepare the toast, i.e. spread with the butter then remove the crusts and cut into four neat rectangles, squares or circles etc.

↓

Step 2	Lightly butter a shallow pan or fish-cooking dish then place the fish into the dish.

↓

Step 3	Barely cover with the fish stock or milk then cover with a piece of buttered paper and lid.

↓

Step 4	Place on top of the stove and bring almost to the boil. Cook slowly at the side of the stove or in an oven at 175° C.

↓

Step 5	When cooked, take the fish out of the pan and remove any skin or bones.

↓

Step 6	Flake the fish into small pieces and place into a clean pan.

↓   ↓

Step 7	*Plain fish mixture*	*Sauced fish mixture* Add enough Béchamel to bind the fish.

↓   ↓

Step 8	Add the seasoning and check the temperature.

↓

Step 9	Dress the mixture on top of the toast shapes then add any garnish stated in the individual recipe, see below. Serve on a salver lined with a dishpaper then decorate with the parsley or radishes placed to the side of the savouries.

Base recipe   (yield 4 small savouries)

Main item:	200 g trimmed smoked haddock fillets.
Cooking liquid:	200 ml fish stock or milk.
Seasoning:	Salt, pepper and cayenne pepper.
Savoury base:	2 slices of toasted bread spread with butter – 20 g approximately.
Decoration (optional):	Sprig parsley or radishes.

Smoked haddock on toast (canapé hollandaise)

Proceed as stated for plain fish mixture, garnishing each savoury with 2 slices of hard-boiled egg sprinkled with a little cayenne pepper.

Canapé Ivanhoë

Proceed as stated binding the fish mixture with a little Béchamel sauce, 40 ml approximately. Garnish each savoury with a cooked mushroom head.

Canapé Ritchie

Proceed as stated binding the fish mixture with a little Béchamel sauce, 40 ml approximately. Sprinkle each savoury with grated parmesan cheese and gratinate under a salamander until golden-brown.

Section three Braised ham, tongue and veal

Base method

Step 1	Mise en place A Assemble ingredients. B Prepare the main item ready for braising, see the individual recipe. C Wash and peel the vegetables then roughly chop.

	Veal	*Ham or tongue*
Step 2	Heat the fat in a small braising pan, add the veal and fry until the surface is brown in colour. Decant off any excess fat.	Place the piece of ham or tongue in a saucepan and cover with cold water. Bring to the boil and slowly simmer for the time stated in the individual recipe under 'blanching'. Refresh in cold water. For ham see the individual recipe.
Step 3	Place the base vegetables in the braising pan and sit the piece of veal on top.	Place the base vegetables in a small braising pan and sit the piece of ham or tongue on top.

Step 4	Add the brown stock until two-thirds the height of the joint.
Step 5	Cover with a lid, bring almost to the boil on top of the stove then place in an oven at 175°C approximately.
Step 6	During cooking, frequently baste the joint with the cooking liquor. Also skim as required.
Step 7	Remove the joint when cooked and keep hot in a hotplate.
Step 8	Boil down the cooking liquor until quite thick and concentrated then add the jus lié or demi-glace. Simmer for 5 mins. approximately then strain into a clean pan. Remove the fat from the top of the cooking liquor when it forms. Check the seasoning, consistency and temperature of the sauce.
Step 9	Remove any string from the joint then carve into neat slices. Alternatively the joint may be served whole – in this case it may be *glazed* to produce an attractive appearance (see important points).
Step 10	Place the slices of meat on a suitable serving dish, e.g. entrée dish, then arrange the garnish neatly around the sides. Coat the slices with the hot sauce then serve. When serving a whole joint pour a ribbon of sauce around the joint then serve. Accompany with the remaining sauce in a sauceboat.

Braised ham, tongue and veal dishes

The method of cooking these meats is very similar to a traditional method of cooking known as 'white meat braising'. This method of cooking was used to braise *white meats* which are lamb, veal, turkey, chicken, young pork and in addition the sweetbreads of lamb and veal.

The process given for the meats is exactly the same as white meat braising but with one important difference at step 2. In white meat braising the main commodity is surrounded with very strong stock which is boiled down until it produces a glaze coating on the surfaces of the commodity. This was done because it was believed that the gelatinous coating sealed in the meat juices during the cooking of the commodity. Research does not confirm this belief, see page 80. This procedure has been omitted from the base method.

All white meats may be cooked by the method given, although veal is the only example used. Braised ham and tongue are also included in the section (even though they are not white meats) because the braising process is the same. Red meat braising has been dealt with in Chapter 8, page 191. The basic preparation of butcher meats is explained on pages 53–65.

Important points when braising ham, tongue and veal

Step 1
Mise en place: The preparation of the dish may be staggered to fit into a scheduled work plan.
Step 1
Soaking pickled meats: It is extremely important that the salt content of pickled meats be *substantially reduced* prior to cooking. If this is not done the cooking liquor will be too salty for use in the recipe sauce. When meat is very salty it should be soaked in several changes of cold water over a 12–24 hour period. It is also wise to taste the cooking liquor when reducing down, step 8, to ensure there is no excessive salt present. If the liquor is salty then only use a small quantity in the recipe sauce.
Step 7
Test to determine if the meat is cooked:
White meats: Insert a cocktail stick or needle into the thickest part of the meat then withdraw, allowing the juices to escape. The joint is cooked when there is no trace of blood. *Internal temperatures*:   75°C approximately, except pork which is 80°C approximately.

The temperature test may be used because white meats are good quality meats (dry heat quality).
Ham and tongue: No resistance should be felt when inserting a thin needle or cocktail stick. There should also be no sign of sponginess under pressure. When testing a whole ham or gammon, the small bone next to the shank bone should be able to be pulled out when the ham is cooked.
Step 9
Carving the joint: Joints should be left for a short period of time in the hotplate (15–20 mins. approximately) after cooking to lose their very high temperature and facilitate carving. Carve the pieces of cooked meat into neat slices across the grain of the meat.
Step 9
Glazing a whole joint: This is done to produce an attractive shiny appearance on the surface of the joint.
Procedure: At the latter part of cooking remove the lid from the cooking utensil and coat the joint occasionally with the cooking liquor and allow to dry. The procedure may be continued after cooking in front of a cool oven until the desired result is obtained. See also the preparation of sugar glazed ham.

Base recipe   (yield 4 portions)

Main item:	See individual recipes.
Searing fat (veal only):	20 g lard or dripping.
Base vegetables:	50 g carrot, 50 g onion, 25 g celery, 25 g leek, sprig of thyme, bay leaf and parsley stalks.
Cooking liquid:	200–500 ml brown stock, see base method, step 4.
Sauce:	300 ml jus lié or demi-glace.
Garnish:	Garnishes for various dishes are given on the opposite page.

Braised ham (jambon braisé)

Allow 600 g piece of ham (boneless) per 4 portions.

Soak the ham for several hours in cold water. Blanch for 20 mins. approximately. Remove the rind and any excess fat then stud with cloves (3 cloves).

Note: The removal of the rind may not apply to small joints which are usually boned and rolled with the rind removed.

Follow the instructions in the base recipe and method.

Cooking time: 1½–2 hours.

Braised ham with pineapple (jambon braisé à l'ananas)

Follow the instructions using the base recipe and method replacing 50 ml of the brown stock with pineapple juice, step 4.

Garnish with slices of pineapple, sprinkled with brown sugar and glazed under the salamander, step 10.

Sugar glazed ham

Follow the instructions using the base recipe and method. When the ham is cooked, remove from the braising pan, place on a cooking tray and sprinkle over the top with a mixture of brown sugar and a little cinnamon. Place in a hot oven and allow the sugar coating to caramelize. Serve whole or in slices.

Braised tongue (langue de boeuf/d'agneau braisée)

Allow 1 small pickled, ox tongue* per 4–6 portions.
Allow 2 pickled sheep's tongues* per portion.

Soak the tongue/s for several hours in cold water. Blanch for 20 mins. approximately.

Follow the instructions using the base recipe and method.

Cooking time: 2–3 hours.

When cooked, remove the skin, any gristle and small bones.

Braised cushion of veal

Allow 1 piece nut of veal (500 g approximately) per 4 portions.

Tie the veal with string. The piece may also be larded with strips of bacon or pork fat before tying with string.

Follow the instructions using the base recipe and method.

Cooking time: 1–1½ hours.

* When braising a fresh tongue follow the base recipe and method on page 191.

Garnishes for braised ham, tongue and veal

Madeira, port or sherry sauce (madère, porto or xérès)

Follow the instructions adding 25–50 ml Madeira, port or sherry wine to the cooking liquor when reducing to a glaze at step 8.

Bourgeoise

Follow the instructions using the base recipe and method. Garnish with glazed carrots (100 g approximately), brown glazed button onions (100 g approximately) and bacon lardons (100 g approximately).

Briarde

Follow the instructions using the base recipe and method. Garnish with turned carrots cooked à la crème (100 g approximately) and four small braised lettuce.

Florentine

Follow the instructions using the base recipe and method. Dish the slices of meat on a bed of cooked leaf spinach (200 g approximately) placed neatly on the serving dish, step 10.

Section four   Braised sweetbreads

Base method

Step 1	Mise en place
	A Assemble ingredients.
	B Wash the sweetbreads in cold running water. If the sweetbreads contain excessive blood, soak in salted cold water.
	C Wash, peel and roughly chop the base vegetables.

↓

Step 2	Place the sweetbreads in a saucepan and cover with cold water. Bring to the boil and slowly simmer for 10–15 mins. Refresh in cold running water. Trim off any membrane or tough tissue surrounding the sweetbreads with a small knife.

↓

Step 3	Arrange the base vegetables in a small braising pan or plat à sauter then place the sweetbreads on top.

↓

Step 4	Barely cover the sweetbreads with the hot stock.

↓

Step 5	Cover with a piece of buttered greaseproof paper and lid, bring almost to the boil on top of the stove then place in an oven at 175°C.

↓

Step 6	Skim occasionally during cooking and top up with additional stock if required.

↓ ↓ ↓

	Cooking brown	*Cooking white*	*Cooking à la crème*
Step 7	Remove the sweetbreads when cooked and place into a clean pan.	Remove the sweetbreads when almost cooked and keep hot covered with the cooking paper.	
	↓	↓	↓
Step 8	Boil down the cooking liquor until quite thick and concentrated, then add the jus lié or demi-glace. Simmer for 2–3 mins.	Strain the cooking liquor and measure to 250 ml, topping up with additional stock if required.	
	↓	↓	↓
Step 9	Strain over the sweetbreads.	Place the liquor in a clean pan, bring to the boil and thicken with the arrowroot mixed with the cold water.	Prepare a velouté sauce using the liquor and roux stated in the base recipe.
		↓	↓
Step 10		Add the sweetbreads and simmer until cooked. Skim as required.	
	↓	↓	↓

| Step 11 | | | Add the cream and stir through the mixture. |

| Step 12 | Check the consistency, seasoning and temperature of the mixture. |

| Step 13 | Ladle the mixture into an entrée dish and add any garnish if appropriate. |

The base recipe and method in this section is suitable for lamb or veal sweetbreads. Since sweetbreads may be braised brown or white and also completed à la crème, the base recipe contains the information for all three styles of cooking.

Base recipe (all styles) (yield 4 portions)

Main item:	500 g sweetbreads.
Base vegetables:	50 g carrots, 50 g onion, 25 g celery, 25 g leek, sprig of thyme, bay leaf and parsley stalks.

Cooking brown
Cooking liquid:	400 ml brown stock approximately.
Sauce:	250 ml jus lié or demi-glace.

Cooking white
Cooking liquid:	400 ml white stock approximately.
Thickening (fécule):	10 g arrowroot and 50 ml cold water (approximately).

Cooking à la crème
Cooking liquid:	400 ml white stock approximately.
Thickening (roux):	25 g butter or margarine, 25 g flour.
Cream:	25–50 ml cream.

Braised sweetbreads

The process of braising sweetbreads is an extension to the one given for white meat braising and covers the cooking of the sweetbreads 'white' and 'à la crème'.

Important points when braising sweetbreads

Step 7
Test to determine if the sweetbreads are cooked: The flesh of the sweetbreads should yield under pressure without being spongy or elastic. Sweetbreads which are overcooked break up very easily.

Step 13
Holding time for service: Sweetbreads may be kept hot for a short period during service in a bain-marie at 90°C approximately.

Braised sweetbreads brown (ris de veau/agneau braisé)

Follow the instructions in the base recipe and method.
Cooking time: 1 hour approximately.

Madeira, port or sherry sauce (brown)(madère, porto or xérès)
Add 25–50 ml of the appropriate wine to the cooking liquid after reducing down, step 8.
Note: Marsala wine may also be used with sweetbreads.

Champagne, Sauternes or Moselle wine (white)
Replace 150–200 ml of the white stock with the appropriate wine, step 4. Add the wine first, then add the stock to barely cover the sweetbreads.

Comtesse (white)
Stuff the sweetbreads with truffle after blanching and trimming, step 2.
Garnish with braised lettuce and cooked chicken quenelles, step 13.

A la crème
Follow the instructions in the base recipe and method for à la crème.

Poulette (à la crème)
Follow the instructions in the base recipe and method adding 30g white mushroom stalks or trimmings to the sweetbreads when cooking, step 3. Add a squeeze of lemon juice to the sweatbreads when completing the cooking, step 10.

Prepare a liaison with the cream by adding 1–2 egg yolks. Do not reboil after adding the liaison, step 11. Sprinkle with chopped parsley.

Section five   Braised vegetables

Base method

Step 1	Mise en place
	A Assemble ingredients.
	B Wash, peel and prepare the vegetables:
	Main vegetable: See each individual vegetable on the following pages.
	Base vegetables: Roughly chop.
Step 2	Place the main vegetable into a saucepan of boiling salted water and slowly simmer for the period stated in the individual recipe under 'blanching'.
	Refresh in cold water. *Note*: Vegetables which do not require shaping before cooking e.g. fennel and onions, do not have to be refreshed.
Step 3	Arrange the base vegetables on the bottom of a small braising pan or casserole then place the drained blanched vegetable on top. Cover with the slices of fat bacon.
Step 4	Add the brown stock up to two-thirds the height of the main vegetable approximately.
Step 5	Cover with a piece of buttered paper and lid. Bring almost to the boil on top of the stove then cook in the oven at 175° C approximately.
Step 6	When cooked, remove the main vegetable and drain. Cut into portions if appropriate, see celery, leeks and lettuce. Cover with the cooking paper and keep hot.
Step 7	Boil down the cooking liquor until quite thick and concentrated then add the jus lié or demi-glace.
Step 8	Simmer for 2–3 mins., then strain into a clean pan. Skim off any fat.
Step 9	Check the seasoning, consistency and temperature of the sauce.
	Note: The sauce should be kept thin.
Step 10	Neatly arrange the vegetable on a vegetable or entrée dish etc., then coat with the sauce. A little chopped parsley is often sprinkled over the root vegetables and onions.

Base recipe (yield 4 portions)

All vegetables *except* chicory, see page 216.

Main vegetable:	See individual recipes.
Base vegetables: (when a base vegetable is also the main vegetable it is not needed, e.g. braised celery – omit the base celery).	50 g carrot, 50 g onion, 25 g celery, 25 g leek, sprig of thyme, ½ bay leaf and parsley stalks.
Fat bacon:	4 thin slices.
Liquid:	300 ml brown stock.
Sauce:	100 ml jus lié or demi-glace.

Derivative styles of braised vegetables are given on page 216.

Braised vegetables

This method of cooking produces a variety of vegetable dishes which include an accompanying vehicle sauce. A wide range of vegetables are suitable for this style of cooking, e.g.

Bulbous roots: onions and leeks.
Stems: celery and root fennel.
Leaves: cabbage and lettuce.
Flowers: globe artichokes.
Fruit vegetables: red and green pimentos.

The basic preparation of vegetables is explained on pages 36–9.

Important points when braising vegetables

Step 1
The preparation of the vegetables may be staggered to fit into a scheduled work plan.

Step 3
Use of bacon or pork fat: This helps to keep the vegetable moist during cooking and in many instances improves the flavour and adds richness to the vegetable. However this use of fat is optional therefore it may be omitted from the recipe. *Note:*   Bacon rind is often used as a cheaper alternative.

Step 6
Test to determine if the vegetable is cooked: The vegetable should yield under slight pressure from the fingers. In addition, when testing celery and fennel etc. no resistance should be felt when inserting a very small knife or cocktail stick.

Step 10
Holding time for service: Braised vegetables may be kept hot for a limited period during service but this should be done keeping the vegetable and sauce separate. The vegetable is coated with sauce when required for service.

Braised artichokes (artichauts braisés)
Allow 1 artichoke per portion.
    Wash and trim the artichokes ready for braising, see page 38. Blanch for 10 mins. and, when refreshed, remove the hearts and chokes then cut into quarters.
    Follow the instructions in the base method.
Cooking time: 40 mins. approximately.

Braised cabbage (chou braisé)
Allow 600 g cabbage per four portions.
    Wash the cabbage and remove any wilted leaves. Cut into wedge-shaped portions *leaving on* the centre stalk. Blanch until the cabbage ribs are limp – 20 mins. approximately. When refreshed, remove the centre stalks.
    Roll up the pieces and squeeze one at a time in a clean cloth to form neat balls.
    Follow the instructions in the base method.
Cooking time: 1½ hours approximately.

Braised celery (céleri braisé)
Allow one head (500 g approximately) per four portions.
    Wash and trim the head of celery removing any deteriorated leaves, see page 37. Cut the head to 100 mm in length approximately. Blanch for 20 mins. then proceed as stated in the base method.
Cooking time: 2½ hours approximately.
When cooked, cut lengthwise into four neat portions.

Braised fennel (fenouil braisé)
Allow two heads (500 g) per four portions.
    Prepare as celery above.

Braised leeks (poireaux braisés)
Allow 500 g small leeks per four portions.
    Wash and trim the leeks then tie together into a bundle. Blanch for 5 mins. then proceed as stated.
Cooking time: 40 mins. approximately.
    When cooked, drain the leeks then press out excess liquid with the back of a knife. Neatly fold each leek.

Braised lettuce (laitue braisée)

Allow two large lettuce per four portions.

Wash the lettuce and blanch for 2–3 mins. When refreshed, squeeze out excess liquid keeping the outer leaves surrounding the lettuce.

Follow the instructions in the base method.

Cooking time: 1 hour approximately.

When cooked, press out excess liquid with the back of a knife and divide each lettuce in half. Fold into neat portions. Traditionally served with fried heart-shaped croûtons.

Braised onions (oignons braisés)

Allow one onion per portion (100–120 g each).

Wash and peel the onion leaving on a short section of stem. Blanch for 10 mins. then proceed as stated in the base method.

Cooking time: 1½ hours approximately.

Braised peppers (poivrons braisés)

Allow one small pepper (70 g approximately) per portion.

Cut the tops off the peppers and remove the seeds.

Note: The pepper may be skinned before cooking by rubbing over with oil then placing under a hot salamander.

Fill each pepper with braised rice (use 150 g raw rice approximately per four portions) then replace the tops.

Follow the instructions in the base method but *do not blanch*.

Cooking time: 1 hour approximately.

Braised chicory (endive braisée)

Allow one chicory per portion.

Production: Wash, trim and remove any wilted leaves.

Place in a buttered pan, lightly season and add a squeeze of lemon juice. Cover with a tight-fitting lid and cook in an oven at 175°C.

Cooking time: 45 mins.–1 hour.

Proceed from step 6 for braised vegetables using jus lié or demi-glace as the sauce.

Any of the general styles for braised vegetables may be used, see below.

Derivative braised vegetable dishes

Artichauts Lucullus

Proceed as for braised artichokes replacing 50 ml of the brown stock with Madeira wine. Use jus lié as the sauce.

Artichauts barigoule

Proceed as stated for braised artichokes but leave whole. After removing the heart and choke, stuff each artichoke with dry duxelles (30 g approximately) then wrap with a slice of the fat bacon and tie with string.

Stuffed braised cabbage (chou farci braisé)

Proceed as stated for braised cabbage enclosing in each ball of cabbage 25 g sausagemeat.

Stuffed braised lettuce (laitue farcie braisée)

Proceed as stated for braised lettuce enclosing 50 g sausagemeat within each lettuce after blanching and refreshing.

Stuffed braised onions (oignons farcis braisés)

Proceed as stated for braised onions but after blanching, cut the tops off each onion and scoop out the centre. Finely chop the centres of the onions and mix with dry duxelles (50 g approximately). Place the mixture into each onion and cover with a slice of the fat bacon.

Piments – indienne, grecque and égyptienne

Proceed as stated for braised pepper stuffing with the appropriate derivative of braised rice.

General styles for all braised vegetables

A la crème

Use white stock as the recipe liquid and cream sauce in place of jus lié or demi-glace.

Milanaise

Sprinkle each cooked, drained vegetable, step 6, with grated parmesan cheese and gratinate under a salamander until golden-brown. When serving, pour the sauce around the gratinated vegetable in a thin stream.

Au madère, porto and xérès

Add 25 ml madeira, port or sherry to the reduced cooking liquor at step 7 then add the jus lié or demi-glace.

Recipe ingredients

The following table shows the pattern of the key ingredients in the base recipe for each process section.

Table 6 *Recipe ingredients*

	Shallow-poached fish	Braised vegetables	Braised white meats	Braised sweetbreads
Main item	Fish and shellfish: cod, haddock, halibut, salmon, sole, trout, turbot and whiting etc. Scallops, clams and oysters etc.	Cabbage, celery, fennel, leeks, globe artichokes, lettuce, onions, pimentos etc.	Veal, lamb, pork, chicken, turkey Also ham and tongue although not white meats	Veal and lamb sweetbreads
Base vegetables	Finely chopped onion or shallot	Mirepoix	Mirepoix	Mirepoix
Cooking liquor	Fish stock, lemon and white wine	Brown stock	Brown stock	Brown stock or white stock
Sauce	Béchamel, velouté or lobster sauce etc.	Jus lié or demi-glace	Jus lié or demi-glace	Jus lié, demi-glace, cooking liquor and arrowroot, cooking liquor and roux

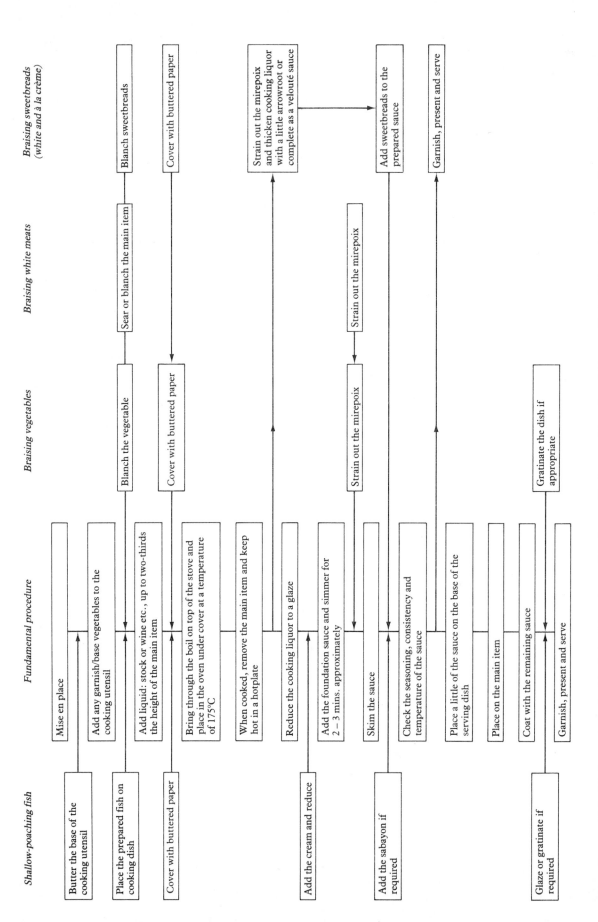

Key to diagram: Each of the base methods of cooking is stated along the top of the diagram. Simply proceed down the activities stated in the fundamental procedure making a note of where each of the individual base method activities would be incorporated.

Part two – Casseroles, hotpots, daubes and riz pilaffs

There are many dishes cooked in the oven where the cooking utensil fulfils a distinctive part of the cooking operation. The cooking utensil may be used to produce the following.

Slowly stewed casserole dishes of meat, game, poultry or vegetables

In this type of cooking the main items are cooked in a casserole (or special casserole cooker) in the presence of a water-containing liquid, e.g. wine, stock, water or milk. It may mean slow cooking in a tightly closed container using steam trapped within the container as an aid to cooking or alternatively using an uncovered container with a view to developing colour on the surface of the food. When preparing some dishes the lid may only be used for part of the cooking operation then removed and the surface of the food allowed to develop colour. This is usually the procedure with hotpots which contain a top covering of sliced potatoes. Many of these dishes are served in the cooking utensil.

Important points

Quantity of liquid used in the casserole or cooking dish: The quantity of liquid used when cooking hotpots or casserole-style vegetables is important – too little liquid may result in the contents drying out and burning, too much liquid will result in the hotpots or vegetables becoming waterlogged and soggy. When preparing hotpots the liquid is usually added until it is just below the top of the main items and with vegetables the same rule applies; less liquid is added to watery vegetables which do not have a long cooking time. The rule with vegetables is to use only sufficient liquid to allow the vegetables to cook without drying out and burning.

Service in the cooking utensil: When the dish is to be served in the cooking utensil, e.g. casserole or earthenware dish, it is important to remove any splashes of liquid on the surface of the casserole or dish prior to cooking. This will reduce the amount of cleaning required to make the casserole suitable for service.

The term 'étuver' is often applied to vegetables cooked in this manner. This is defined as the slow cooking of foods in their juices under cover in an oven.

Braised rice dishes

Braised rice is cooked in a covered container allowing the rice to cook in a minimum amount of liquid without the surface drying out and browning. Risotto is also included in this chapter because of its similarity in production with braised rice although it is not often oven cooked.

Important points

The difference between a riz pilaf and risotto is often defined in operational terms therefore the reader should pay attention to the base recipe and method. This is especially important when estimating the quantity of liquid used for each measurement of rice and liquid. The method used by many cooks to measure the quantity of rice and stock is by volume rather than weight, e.g. one ladle of rice and two ladles of stock for riz pilaffs.

Important process procedures

To sear flesh

Hotpots and casseroles
The shallow-frying and browning of flesh in hot fat.
Reason: Promotes colour and flavour.

To sweat

Vegetables
The slow frying of vegetables in butter, margarine or lard etc., usually with a lid on the cooking utensil.
Reason: Promotes flavour.

Section one   Hotpots and casserole-style meat dishes using potatoes

Base method

Step 1	Mise en place
	A Assemble ingredients.
	B Prepare the main items:
	Lamb and mutton: Trim off excess fat.
	Grouse and rabbit: Cut into joints.
	C Prepare the vegetables:
	Onions, celery and cabbage: Cut into slices. Does not apply to button onions.
	Potatoes: Peel and thinly slice (2 mm thickness approximately).
Step 2	Heat the fat in a frying pan then sear the recipe flesh – meat and game etc. Reserve the fat for coating the potatoes.
Step 3	Line the base of a casserole with a layer of the sliced potatoes and a layer of sliced onions (for Highland hotpot – button onions) then lightly season.
Step 4	Place the meat or game and any bacon rashers on top then add any vegetable garnish – mushrooms, celery or cabbage etc. Season liberally then add the liquid to just below the top of the main item/s.
Step 5	Place the remaining onions on top then cover with the rest of the potatoes neatly overlapping in rows. Brush over the top with melted fat.
Step 6	Place in the oven at 190–200°C and cook until lightly coloured. Reduce the temperature to 175°C approximately and cook slowly, occasionally pressing down with a fish slice. Use the lid for prolonged cooking times (over 1½ hours).
Step 7	When cooked, clean round the sides of the casserole, brush over the top of the potatoes with a little more melted fat and sprinkle with parsley.

Note: A variety of hotpots may be made using the above method, e.g. chicken, beef, veal and pork hotpots.
Procedures: Cut the meat into cubes or joint the chicken. Step 2 may be omitted, leaving the meat plain. Garnish to taste with suitable vegetables at step 4, e.g. onions, carrots, celery and leeks.

Lancashire hotpot
25 g lard or dripping, 500 g neck cutlets of lamb or mutton, 100 g sliced kidneys, 200 g onions, 400 g potatoes, ¾ litre of white stock, seasoning and chopped parsley.
   Follow the instructions.
Cooking time: 2–2½ hours.
Service: Serve with pickled red cabbage.

Bolton hotpot
Prepare as above adding 100 g button mushrooms as the vegetable garnish. Also carefully lift the crust and add 8–12 oysters when almost cooked. Replace potatoes and complete the cooking.

Highland hotpot
25 g lard, 1 grouse, 1 small rabbit, 8 half rashers of streaky bacon, 100 g celery, 100 g white cabbage, 100 button onions, 300 g potatoes, 100 ml red wine, 600 m brown stock, salt, pepper and a good pinch of allspice.
   Follow the instructions.
Cooking time: 2–2½ hours.

Loin chop Champvallon
25 g lard or dripping, 8 loin chops, 200 g onions, 400 g potatoes, ¾ litre of brown stock and seasoning.
   Follow the instructions using a shallow casserole or earthenware dish. *Cooking time*:   1½–2 hours.

Section two   Carbonnade of beef and farmhouse casseroles

Base method

Step 1	Mise en place
	a Assemble ingredients.
	B Prepare the meat:
	Beef for carbonnade: Trim then cut into thin slices.
	Neck cutlets of lamb: Trim off excess fat.
	Stewing lamb: Trim off excess fat then cut into cubes – 20 mm.
	C Prepare the vegetables:
	Onions: Peel and cut into slices.
	Carrots: Peel and cut into thick slices.
Step 2	Pass the meat through the flour then fry in half the fat until lightly browned.
Step 3	Fry the onions and any garlic and carrots in the remaining fat until lightly browned.
Step 4	Place the meat and vegetables in layers in a casserole, lightly season and add any sugar.
	Carbonnades: Complete the top with a layer of the fried onions.
Step 5	Add the recipe liquid (together with any flavourings, e.g. Worcester sauce) until just barely covering the meat.
Step 6	Cover with a tight-fitting lid then cook in the oven at 190° C approximately.
Step 7	When cooked, remove excess surface fat and clean round the sides of the casserole. Sprinkle with chopped parsley if desired.

Recipes   (yield 4 portions)

Carbonnade of beef (carbonnade de boeuf)

600 g topside or thick flank of beef, 50 g flour, 40 g lard or dripping, 250 g onions, 300 ml beer, 300 ml brown stock approximately, 10 g caster sugar, seasoning and chopped parsley.

Follow the instructions.

Cooking time: 2 hours approximately.

Lamb and cider casserole

600 g neck cutlets of lamb, 50 g flour, 40 g lard or dripping, 150 g onions, 1 clove of crushed garlic, 300 ml cider, 300 ml brown stock approximately, good dash of Worcester sauce and seasoning.

Follow the instructions.

Cooking time: 1½–2 hours.

Lamb and mint casserole

600 g boneless stewing lamb, 50 g flour, 40 g lard or dripping, 100 g onions, 200 g shelled peas, 25 g chopped fresh mint, 600 ml brown stock and seasoning.

Follow the instructions adding the peas and chopped mint 30 mins. before cooking is completed, step 6.

Cooking time: 1½–2 hours.

Poor man's goose

600 g boneless stewing lamb, 50 g flour, 40 g lard or dripping, 150 g onions, 150 g carrots, 600 ml brown stock and seasoning.

Follow the instructions.

Cooking time: 1½–2 hours.

Section three   Daubes

These are casserole-style meat dishes cooked in an oven cooking pot called a 'daubière'.

Beef daube (daube provençale)

Recipe   (yield 4 portions)

Main item:	500 g beef, i.e. topside or thick flank etc., 75 g blanched salt belly of pork, 40 g blanched pork rind.
Larding fat:	100 g pork fat.
Vegetables:	50 g chopped onions, 50 g sliced carrots, 50 g diced mushrooms, 200 g raw tomato concassé, 1 clove crushed garlic, 16 stoned black olives and a bouquet garni containing the zest from ½ orange.
Marinade:	300 ml white wine, 30 ml brandy, good squeeze lemon juice and 20 ml olive oil.
Sauce:	300 ml jus lié.
Seasoning:	Salt and pepper.
Hot water paste:	100 g flour and 70–80 ml water, i.e. enough water to produce a soft dough.
Method:	1 Cut the beef into large cubes (30 mm) and the salt belly and pork rind into cubes or squares (15 mm).
	2 Cut the larding fat into strips for larding then flavour with the garlic, i.e. crush the garlic with a little salt then mix together with the larding strips.
	3 Lard the cubes of beef then place into a bowl with the marinade and allow to stand for 4–5 hours.
	4 Transfer the beef and marinade to the cooking utensil then add the pork and pork rind, vegetables, bouquet garni and seasoning.
	5 Add the jus lié until the contents are barely covered then seal down the casserole lid with the water paste.
	6 Cook for 2 hours in a moderate oven then carefully remove the lid and withdraw the bouquet garni.
	7 Skim off excess fat, check the seasoning then replace the lid and serve.

Mutton daube (daube avignonnaise)

Prepare the same way as beef daube but use mutton in place of beef and red wine in the marinade. Also omit the pork rind and use fat bacon instead of salt belly of pork. Cover the mixture with slices of bacon before sealing down the lid.

ection four   Vegetables cooked in a casserole

ase method

tep 1	Mise en place
	A Assemble ingredients.
	B Prepare the vegetables:
	Cabbage: 1 Wash and trim the cabbage then remove the centre stalk.
	2 Shred the cabbage then rewash.
	Sauerkraut: Wash the sauerkraut in cold water if very salty.
	Peas: Pod the peas then wash and drain.
	C Prepare any other vegetables or garnish stated in the individual recipe.

tep 2	Place the vegetable in a casserole then season and add any butter, onions, carrots, bacon, herbs, spices or sugar.

tep 3	Add any wine, vinegar and/or stock to a level just under the top of the vegetables. Cover with a piece of buttered greaseproof paper and lid then place in the oven at 175°C.

tep 4	Allow to cook then add any apple or Frankfurt sausage just prior to completion of cooking. Continue cooking until the vegetables are tender.

tep 5	Remove any onions, carrots, bacon or bouquet garni which are used as basic flavouring (not the onions in casseroled peas) then check the seasoning.
	Clean round the sides of the container before serving or alternatively serve in a vegetable dish. Serve sauerkraut as stated in the recipe below.

abbage dishes   (yield 4 portions)

abbage in a casserole (chou étuvé)

)0 g firm cabbage, 30 g butter, 50 g whole carrot, 50 g udded onion, 50 g piece of fat bacon, bouquet garni ptional) and ½ litre white stock approximately.

Follow the instructions.
ooking time: 1½–2 hours.

raised red cabbage (chou flamande)

)0 g red cabbage, 50 g butter, 200 ml vinegar, 150 g diced ooking apple and 10 g caster sugar.

Follow the instructions.
ooking time: 1½–2 hours.

hou Valenciennes

repare as above but add 50 g sliced Frankfurt sausage at te same time as the apples.

ressed sauerkraut (choucroute garnie)

)0 g sauerkraut, 100 g whole carrots, 100 g button nions, 350 g piece of fat bacon, bouquet garni with the addition of 2½ g juniper berries and 4 peppercorns. 600 ml white stock approximately and 8 small Frankfurt sausages.

Follow the instructions.
Cooking time: 2½–3½ hours.
Service: Remove the carrot, onions, bacon, sausages, and bouquet garni. Discard the bouquet garni. Slice the carrot, bacon and sausages. Neatly garnish the sauerkraut with the slices of bacon, sausage and vegetables.

Peas in a casserole (petits pois étuvés)

1 kg fresh peas, 25 g butter, 12–16 button onions, 2–3 lettuce leaves cut into fine strands, pinch sugar and 300–400 ml white stock.

Follow the instructions. *Note*:   The peas may be thickened with a little beurre manié when cooked but this is optional.
Cooking time: 20 mins.–¾ hour depending on type of peas.
Important: See French style peas and derivatives, page 136.

Section five   Riz pilaffs and risottos

Base method

Step 1	Mise en place A Assemble ingredients. B Finely chop the shallots or onions. C Prepare any additional garnish or sauces required in the recipe.
Step 2	Melt half the butter in a sauteuse.
Step 3	Add the chopped shallot or onion and sweat for 2–3 mins. Also at this stage add any garlic, raw meat, poultry, pimentos or mushrooms and sweat with the onions.
Step 4	Add the rice and sweat for a further 2–3 mins. stirring frequently.

	Riz pilaffs	*Risottos*
Step 5	Add the recipe liquid and lightly season.	Add half the quantity of stock and lightly season.
Step 6	Add any fresh podded peas, fresh French beans or powdered saffron.	
Step 7	Cover with a piece of buttered greaseproof paper and lid then cook in the oven at 220°C approximately.	Bring to the boil then cook slowly at the side of the stove or over a low heat covered with a piece of buttered greaseproof paper and lid.
Step 8		Stir frequently adding more stock as required. Use a fork near the end of the cooking period to avoid breaking the rice.
Step 9	When cooked the stock should have evaporated leaving the rice grains quite dry and easily separable.	When cooked the stock should have evaporated leaving the rice grains slightly pasty with an attractive moist eating quality.
Step 10	Add any *cooked* meat, shellfish, peas, French beans, sweetcorn, tomato concassé, truffle and grated cheese and lightly stir through with a fork.	
Step 11	Fork through the remaining butter and check the seasoning and temperature.	

Base recipe   (yield 4 small portions)

Main item:	100 g rice (long grain – Arborio, Piedmont or Basmati etc.).
Frying medium:	50 g butter.
Base vegetables:	50 g shallots or onion.
Liquid:	*Riz pilaffs*: 180 ml chicken stock (2 stock to 1 rice by volume).
	Risottos: 250 ml chicken stock (3 stock to 1 rice by volume).
Seasoning:	Salt and milled pepper.

Follow the instructions.
Cooking time: 15 mins. approximately.

Riz pilaff/risotto with cheese italienne
Add 50 g grated cheese as indicated.

Riz pilaff/risotto with mushrooms
Add 50–100 g sliced mushrooms as indicated.

Riz créole (riz pilaff)
Add 50 g sliced mushrooms, 30 g diced pimentos and 50 g raw tomato concassé.

Riz égyptienne (riz pilaff)
Add 50 g sliced mushrooms, 50 g small dice of cooked ham and 100 g sliced chicken livers stiffened in a little hot butter, step 10.

Riz à la grecque (riz pilaff)
Add 30 g diced red pimentos, 100 g sausagemeat rolled into small balls, after step 6, and 25 g cooked peas.

Risotto milanaise
Add 50 g sliced mushrooms, a good pinch of powdered saffron, 100 g raw tomato concassé and 50 g grated cheese.

Risotto piémontaise
Add 50 g sliced mushrooms, 30 g diced pimentos and 15 g diced truffle.

Risi e bisi
Add 25 g small dice of raw ham, 100 g fresh podded peas and 30 g grated parmesan
Note: Cook in slightly more liquid than an ordinary risotto and serve grated parmesan separately.

Paella
Add ½ clove crushed garlic, 25 g diced raw lean pork, 25 g diced raw chicken, 25 g sliced mushrooms, 25 g diced red pimentos, good pinch of powdered saffron, 50 g cooked scampi, 50 g cooked prawns, 12 cooked mussels, 10 g cooked peas, 10 g diamonds of cooked French beans and 50 g raw tomato concassé. Alternatively, use raw shellfish (added at step 3).

Fish kedgeree (cadgéry de poisson)
Prepare the basic riz pilaff recipe then add 200 g cooked flaked fish and 2 hard-boiled eggs cut into dice. Serve a sauceboat of curry sauce separately.
Note: This dish may be presented in various forms, e.g. the fish, rice and eggs may be placed in layers in the serving dish or the fish and eggs mixed with the curry sauce and served in the centre of the riz pilaff. The fish used often names the dish, e.g. salmon kedgeree.

Purée Soubise
This is a rice thickened onion purée. Prepare a rice mixture in the same way as risotto but use a soft cooking rice, i.e. round grain pudding rice and increase the onion in the base recipe to 200 g. Continue cooking and adding stock until the rice is well cooked. Pound to a purée.

Table 7   *Recipe ingredients*

	Hotpots	*Farmhouse casseroles and carbonnades*	*Casseroled vegetables*	*Rice dishes*
Main item	Beef, mutton, chicken and game	Beef, mutton, chicken and game	Cabbage, red cabbage, sauerkraut and peas	Rice
Recipe fat	Lard or dripping	Lard or dripping	Butter, margarine or fat bacon	Butter or margarine
Vegetables and fruits	Onions, potatoes, mushrooms, carrots and herbs etc.	Onions, carrots, peas and herbs etc.	Onions, carrots, lettuce, herbs and apples etc.	Onions, mushrooms, tomatoes, pimentos, peas and beans etc.
Liquid	Stock or wine	Stock, cider or beer	Stock or vinegar	Stock
Other ingredients	—	Worcester sauce	Sugar, Frankfurt sausages and fat bacon	Ham, chicken livers, fish, shellfish, eggs and cheese etc.

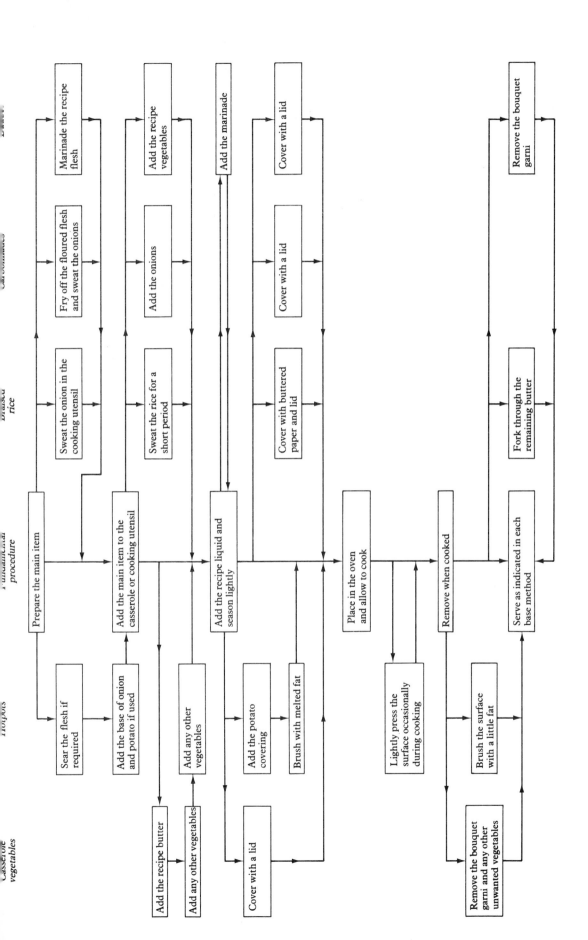

Figure 24   Essential activities for casseroles, hot-pots, daubes and braised rice

Part three — Individual applications

This final part of oven cooking deals with processes which are less related to one another than the two previous parts of oven cooking, therefore there is no recipe analysis diagram or essential activities diagram.

Section one   Oeufs sur le plat

Base method

Step 1	Mise en place A Assemble ingredients. B Prepare any garnish or sauces.
Step 2	Butter the base of the sur le plat dishes then add a little seasoning.
Step 3	Garnish the base of the dishes with any cooked bacon, ham or cooked onions etc.
Step 4	Break an egg into each dish then lightly season.
Step 5	Coat each egg yolk with a little melted butter.
Step 6	Place the dishes at the side of the stove over a gentle heat and allow the whites of each egg to set lightly at the base of the dish.
Step 7	Place the dishes in a moderate oven and complete the cooking. The white should be set but the yolk still soft.
Step 8	Add any stated garnish or sauce and serve immediately.

Base recipe   (yield 4 small portions)

Main item:	4 eggs.
Preparation of dishes:	10 g butter.
Seasoning:	Salt and pepper.
Coating butter (optional):	15 g butter (melted).

Américaine
Garnish the bottom of each dish with two half rashers of grilled bacon. Surround the cooked egg with a ribbon of tomato sauce when serving.

A la crème
Coat the cooked eggs with a little warmed cream when serving.

Bercy
Garnish each cooked egg with a grilled chipolata sausage then surround with a ribbon of tomato sauce.

Au lard
Prepare the same as américaine but omit the tomato sauce.

Lyonnaise

Garnish the bottom of each dish with thinly sliced onions (25 g each) sautéd until brown in a little butter. Complete the cooked eggs with a ribbon of lyonnaise sauce when serving.

Miroir

Prepare as à la crème but coat the eggs with the cream prior to cooking (in place of the butter, step 5).

Omer pasha

Garnish the bottom of each dish with finely chopped onions which have been sweated down in a little butter. After adding the eggs and coating with the butter sprinkle over the tops with grated parmesan cheese. Place under the salamander when cooked (if necessary) to lightly colour.

Parmentier (non-derivative dish)

Bake two potatoes then halve lengthwise. Scoop out the centres and prepare a purée with the pulp. Line each half potato with the purée in the form of a serving dish. Break an egg into each potato then coat with a little cream. Cook in a moderate oven then serve.

Section two   Heating snails in the oven

This section applies to pre-prepared snails, i.e. tinned or snails in jars etc. and not fresh snails.

Snails served in a garlic and brandy butter (escargots bourguignonne)

Procedure: (1 portion = 6 snails)

1   Prepare 90 g of snail butter, beurre escargots, see page 42.
2   Place a little butter in each snail shell, insert the snail then cover with more butter.
3   Allow to heat thoroughly in an oven at 180°C for 4 to 5 mins. approximately. Ensure that the shells have the open end facing upwards therefore retaining the butter.
4   Serve in a snail dish when very hot.

Important: To produce a range of snail dishes the snail butter may be replaced with:

A   any suitable compound butter;
B   a suitable sauce, e.g. herb-, cream- or wine-flavoured sauce etc.

Examples:
Chablisienne: White wine and shallot reduction cohered with meat glaze.
Dijonnaise: White wine and shallot reduction with diced bone marrow, garlic and chopped truffles.

Section three   Paper-bag cookery

Base method

Step 1	Mise en place

A   Assemble ingredients.

B   Prepare the main items:
   Fish: Remove scales, eyes, intestines and fins then wash. *Note*:   Traditionally red mullet is cooked with the intestines.
   Chicken: Prepare suprêmes.
   Cutlets: Prepare cutlets.

C   Trim the ham to the shape of the main items and prepare any sauce.

D   Prepare the paper (some cooks use tinfoil):
   1   Cut the greaseproof paper to a size 1½ times the length and 3 times the breadth of each main item.
   2   Fold the paper in half then cut to the shape of the main item but much larger. This should be a half heart-shape for suprêmes and cutlets and a long half moon shape for small round fish. Opened out the paper will be the shape of a large heart or long oval.
   3   Oil the paper on both sides.

Step 2

Fish

Cutlets and suprêmes
Shallow-fry on both sides in the butter and oil until almost cooked.

Step 3   Place a slice of cooked ham on one side of each papillotte and coat with a little of the recipe sauce (not required for herrings). Place the main item on top, coat with some more sauce then cover with a slice of ham.

Step 4   Enclose within the paper-bags. Seal the edges well with a series of small folds which are individually crimped and bent over tightly.

Step 5   Place the papillottes on an oiled tray and cook in a hot oven at 230°C. The papillottes will puff up and brown provided the paper is sealed correctly. Serve immediately.

Herring in a paper-bag (hareng calaisienne)
4 small herring, 50 g chopped onion or shallots, 100 g sliced mushrooms and 100 g parsley butter. Mix together the shallots, mushrooms and parsley butter and stuff into the centre of each herring together with the roes if available.
   Follow the instructions.
Cooking time in bag: 15 mins.

Red mullet in a paper-bag (rouget en papillotte)
4 red mullets, 8 slices of cooked ham (optional) and ¼ litre of sauce italienne.
   Follow the instructions.
Cooking time in bag: 15 mins.

Wing and breast of chicken in a paper-bag (suprême d volaille en papillotte)
4 suprêmes of chicken, 10 g oil, 20 g butter, 8 slices of ham and ¼ litre sauce italienne (or other suitable sauce).
   Follow the instructions.
Cooking time in bag: 20 mins.

Veal cutlet or pork cutlet in a paper-bag (côte de veau/porc en papillotte)
4 veal or pork cutlets, 10 g oil, 20 g butter, 8 slices of ham and ¼ litre sauce italienne (or other suitable sauce).
   Follow the instructions.
Cooking time in bag: 20–25 mins.

Section four   Oven cooked tomatoes

Base method

Step 1	Mise en place
	A Assemble ingredients.
	B Prepare the filling given in the individual recipe.
	C Neatly remove the eyes of the tomatoes then cut off the ends – at the opposite sides to the eyes.
	D Scoop out the seeds leaving a tomato case then season inside with the salt and pepper.

↓

Step 2	Fill the tomatoes with the stuffing then place on to a lightly oiled cooking tray.

↓

Step 3	Complete the tomatoes as follows:

Tomatoes served with a tomato lid:
Replace the tomato lid, brush with a little oil then place in an oven at 200°C for 4 mins. approximately. Serve in a vegetable dish garnished with branch parsley.

Tomatoes served gratinated:
1   Brush over the tomatoes with a little melted butter or margarine.
2   Sprinkle over breadcrumbs or grated cheese (see recipe), then place in an oven at 200°C for 4 mins. approximately★.
3   Gratinate the tomatoes under a hot salamander to a good colour (if required) then serve in a vegetable dish as above. Note the tomato lid may be inserted in an open fashion between the stuffing and the tomato.

★ The tomatoes must be thoroughly heated but must not be allowed to overcook as they will burst and collapse.

Base recipe

Main item:	4 medium tomatoes (100 g each approximately).
Seasoning:	Salt and pepper.
Stuffing/filling:	See individual recipe.
Other ingredients:	See individual recipe.

Dishes

Stuffed tomatoes (tomates farcies)
Fill the tomatoes with a duxelles – 100 g approximately, see page 274 – and complete as stated replacing the lid.

Tomates farcies au gratin
Prepare as stuffed tomatoes above but do not use the lid and complete as gratinated tomatoes using a little melted butter, 5 g approximately, and white breadcrumbs, 5 g approximately.
Note: These tomatoes sometimes contain a dice of cooked veal and freshly chopped herbs.

Tomates farcies italienne
Prepare as stuffed gratinated tomatoes using a stuffing consisting of risotto italienne, 100 g approximately, and grated parmesan cheese, 5 g approximately.

Tomates farcies portugaise
Fill the tomatoes with a mixture of riz pilaff and tomato concassé and complete as stated replacing the lid.

Section five   Oven cooked potatoes

Sliced and cubed potatoes

Base method

Step 1	Mise en place
	A Assemble ingredients.
	B Wash, peel and thinly slice the potatoes (1–1½ mm thickness).
	C Prepare any other garnish stated in the individual recipe.

Step 2	*Savoury potatoes* Peel and thinly slice the onions then sweat in half the butter.	*dauphinoise and savoyarde* Mix together half the butter and the garlic.
Step 3	Lightly butter a shallow earthenware dish.	Butter a shallow earthenware dish with the garlic butter.
Step 4	Place the sliced potatoes into the dish in layers with any onions, cheese, seasoning and spices. Leave the best slices aside to complete the top.	
Step 5	Add the recipe liquid until almost at the top of the potatoes then add the remaining potatoes in overlapping rows across the top.	
Step 6	Brush over the surface with melted butter or margarine.	Sprinkle with grated cheese.
Step 7	Cook in an oven at 200°C approximately without a lid. Occasionally press down the potatoes with a fish slice to produce a firm texture.	
Step 8	Clean round the sides of the container.	

Dishes using sliced potatoes   (yield 4 portions)

Savoury potatoes (pommes boulangère)
500 g potatoes, 40 g butter or margarine, 100 g onions, 250–300 ml white stock, seasoning and chopped parsley.
   Follow the instructions completing with chopped parsley.
Cooking time: 1½–2 hours.

Pommes dauphinoise (gratin dauphinois)
500 g potatoes, 30 g butter, ½ clove of crushed garlic, 300–400 ml milk, 40 g grated Gruyère cheese, 20 g grated parmesan, salt, pepper and nutmeg.

   Follow the instructions.
Cooking time: 1½ hours approximately.

Pommes savoyarde
Prepare as dauphinoise above replacing the milk with white stock.

Dishes using cubed potatoes (non-derivative dish)

Delmonico potatoes (pommes Delmonico)
500 g potatoes, 350–400 ml milk, 20 g butter, seasoning and 20 g white breadcrumbs. *Note*:   Cream is often used in this recipe; replace 50 ml of the milk with cream.

Production:
1 Assemble the recipe ingredients.
2 Wash, peel then cut the potatoes into cubes – 10 mm approximately.
3 Place the potatoes into a dish or shallow casserole, lightly season then barely cover with the milk.

4 Cover with a lid then cook in an oven at 180°C.
5 When almost cooked, remove the lid and sprinkle with the breadcrumbs and melted butter.
6 Continue cooking until crisp and golden brown.
Cooking time: 1–1¼ hours.

Turned potatoes

Base method

Step 1	Mise en place
	A Assemble ingredients.
	B Prepare the potatoes: Wash, peel and turn the potatoes:
	fondantes: 50 mm in length.
	berrichonne and Champignol: 40 mm in length.
	C Prepare any garnish stated in the individual recipe.
Step 2	Butter the base of a plat à sauter or shallow earthenware container then add any garnish, e.g. onion or lardons etc. *Note*: The onions and lardons may be sweated down in a little of the recipe butter.
Step 3	Place in the potatoes then add the recipe liquid up to half the height of the potatoes approximately. Lightly season.
Step 4	Brush over the tops of the potatoes with melted butter then cook in an oven at 220°C. During cooking occasionally brush over the tops of the potatoes with melted butter.
Step 5	Continue cooking until the potatoes are golden-brown in colour and the stock has evaporated and been absorbed by the potatoes. Brush over the tops of the potatoes with butter when serving.

Dishes using turned potatoes

Fondant potatoes (pommes fondantes)
600 g potatoes, 30 g butter, 250–300 ml white stock and seasoning.
Follow the instructions.
Cooking time: 1½ hours approximately.

Pommes berrichonne
600 g potatoes, 30 g butter, 75 g diced onions, 80 g lardons of bacon, 250–300 ml white stock and seasoning.

Follow the instructions.
Cooking time: 1½ hours approximately.

Pommes Champignol
600 g potatoes, 30 g butter 250–300 ml white stock, 20 g parmesan cheese and seasoning.
Follow the instructions. Sprinkle the cooked potatoes with the parmesan cheese then gratinate under a salamander.
Cooking time: 1½ hours approximately.

Layered potatoes

Anna-style potatoes (pommes Anna)
700 g potatoes, 40 g butter, 10 ml oil and seasoning.
Production:
1 Wash, peel then trim the potatoes into cylinders (20 mm).
2 Slice the potato cylinders into thin slices (2 mm), then dry in a cloth.
3 Place the oil in an Anna Mould or small iron frying pan then heat gently.
4 Lay the potatoes in circles round the base of the pan overlapping each slice.
5 Continue to add the potatoes in layers and as each layer is completed season lightly and coat with a little melted butter.

6 When complete, place the potatoes in a hot oven (230°C) and cook for 45 mins. approximately. Durin cooking occasionally press the potatoes lightly into a firm shape.
7 Turn out of the mould and cut into portions or leave whole.

Derivatives

Pommes Annette/Darphin
Prepare as Anna but cut the potatoes into thin strips (u 500 g potatoes).

Pommes Voisin
Prepare as Anna but sprinkle each layer with parmesa

Section six   Baked potatoes

Base method

Step 1	Mise en place
	A Assemble ingredients.
	B Wash the potatoes and remove any spots or blemishes.
	C Dry thoroughly then pierce over the surface of each potato using a fork or skewer.
	D Lightly coat the surface of each potato with the oil.
Step 2	Place a layer of salt on a flat cooking tray then sit the potatoes on top.
Step 3	Place in the oven and cook at 200°C until tender – 1¼ hours approximately.
Step 4	Remove the potatoes from the tray and brush off any adhering salts.
Step 5	Use as required.

Important points

Step 1
Piercing the potatoes: This allows the steam to escape from the potatoes and avoids badly damaging the skins. Avoid cutting an incision around the potato.
Step 1
Oiling the potato skins: A little oil rubbed into the potato skins helps to keep the skins moist and supple during cooking. In addition, a little oil rubbed on to the skins after cooking gives an attractive shiny appearance.

Step 3
Using salt when cooking: This acts as an insulator between the tray and the potatoes, preventing the skins being scorched. However, placing the potatoes on to the *open* oven shelves does very little harm to the skins.
Step 3
Test for cooking: Test with a cocktail stick in the same manner as boiled potatoes. Alternatively, press the potatoes with the finger to determine tenderness.

Base recipe

Main item:	4 potatoes (200–300 g each).
Oil:	10 ml oil.
Seasoning:	Coarse salt.

Baked potatoes (pommes au four)

Additional ingredients: 20 g butter or margarine.
1   Prepare the potatoes as stated, and when cooked, dress on the serving dish on top of a dishpaper or in a serviette.
2   Cut a cross-wise incision on the top of each potato then press the sides to neatly open the potato. Place a small piece of butter in the cavity of each potato and serve.

Gratin potatoes (pommes gratinées)

Additional ingredients: 40 g butter or margarine, a little hot milk or cream, 25 ml approximately, 20 g parmesan cheese and salt and pepper.
1   Halve the cooked potatoes lengthwise and remove the pulp with a spoon into a bowl.
2   Mash the pulp and mix in three-quarters of the butter, the milk or cream and then check the seasoning.
3   Put the purée back into the potato shells then brush with the remaining butter (melted) and sprinkle with the cheese.
4   Place in a hot oven, 220°C, and allow to heat through thoroughly and develop a brown crust. Note: The crust colour may develop under a hot salamander. Serve as above.

Macaire potatoes (pommes Macaire)

Additional ingredients: 20 g butter or margarine and salt and pepper.
1   Halve the cooked potatoes and remove the pulp as described above.
2   Lightly mash the potatoes then add the butter and seasoning. Mix to a stiff purée.
3   Mould into a roll on a floured table then divide into fishcake shapes (galettes).
4   Fry in a pan which has been very lightly oiled (like a griddle plate) until golden-brown on both sides.
5   Serve in a vegetable dish (do not use a dishpaper or serviette).

Byron potatoes (pommes Byron)

Prepare as Macaire potatoes above then sprinkle each fried galette with a little grated cheese and add a little cream. Gratinate under a salamander then serve.

Section seven   Baked apples

Base method

Step 1	Mise en place
	A Assemble ingredients.
	B Wash and core the apples.
	C Make an incision round the centre of each apple; this should be done cutting to a depth which is *just under the skin and no more.*
Step 2	Place the apples in a deep-sided dish then fill the centres with the sugar. Add a clove to the sugar in each apple.
Step 3	Place a small piece of butter, 5 g, on top of each apple then add the water to the dish.
Step 4	Cook in oven at 200°C until tender – 30 mins. approximately. *Note:* Occasionally baste the apples with the cooking liquor during cooking.
Step 5	Use as required.

Important points

Step 1
Coring the apples: Remove the cores using an apple corer.
Step 1
Cutting an incision round the apple: An incision should be made completely round the apple to avoid the apple bursting during cooking.
Step 4
Cooking the apples: The apples should be cooked until tender but overcooking must be avoided because apples deteriorate rapidly when overheated. The test for cooking may be carried out by inserting a cocktail stick or lightly pressing with the fingers – the apples should be firm but tender with no hardness.

Dishes

Baked apples (pommes bonne-femme)
Prepare and cook as stated in the recipe and method. Place in the service dish with a little of the cooking liquor and accompany with a sauceboat of custard sauce.

Stuffed baked apples
As above but fill the centre with washed sultanas mixed with the recipe sugar prior to cooking.

Châtelaine apples (pommes châtelaine)
Prepare and cook the apples then remove from the cooking liquor. Place on a tray then fill the centre of each apple with a mixture of diced cherries bound with apricot purée. Coat each apple with a thin frangipane, see page 399, then sprinkle with crushed macaroon biscuits, see page 408, and gratinate until golden-brown.

Base recipe   (yield 4 portions)

Main item:	4 medium cooking apples (125 g each approximately).
Sugar:	50 g sugar.
Spices:	4 cloves.
Butter:	20 g butter.
Liquid	100 ml water.

Assessment exercise

1 Give a general explanation of the term 'braising'.
2 List the steps common to the base methods for all braised vegetable, white meat and shallow-poached fish dishes.
3 Define the following culinary terms in relation to braising and shallow-poaching fish: blanchir; dégraisser, dégorger, glace (a glaze); glacer; cartouche; sabayon.
4 What is the approximate oven temperature for cooking all braised dishes?
5 Both the terms to glaze and gratinate mean to brown under the salamander. State the differences between the two terms.
6 State the difference between white meat braising and red meat braising.
7 Define the terms: tronçon; darne; fricandeau; délice; grenadin; médaillon; paupiette; cravate.
8 Briefly explain the following garnishes with reference to braised dishes: milanaise; polonaise; au jus; florentine.
9 The procedure for casserole-style cooking varies with the commodities being cooked. Describe six types of casserole cooking.
10 Define the term 'étuver'.
11 What is a hotpot?
12 What is the difference between a riz pilaff and a risotto?
  Name two types of rice suitable for each.
13 Describe what is meant by cooking 'en papillotte'. Name twelve commodities suitable for this method of cooking.
14 What is sauerkraut? Name two menu terms which indicate that sauerkraut is present in a dish.

Chapter 10

Roasting and pot roasting

Roasting is cooking food in dry heat with the presence of fat or oil, either in an oven or on a spit. Foods suitable for roasting are good-quality joints of butcher meats, poultry, furred and feathered game and certain vegetables, especially potatoes.

Oven roasting

The main form of heat application in oven roasting is convected heat, although radiated heat given out from the sides of the oven and conducted heat produced from a metal cooking tray are also present. In different operations the balance between the various forms of heat application may differ depending on the food being cooked. For example, when roasting a fillet of beef it is advisable to reduce the amount of conducted heat as much as possible to prevent the joint frying on the base of the tray; this may result in a dry hard surface being formed on the area of the fillet touching the tray. In contrast to the above example, when roasting potatoes the intention is to expose the surface of the potatoes to a substantial amount of conducted heat to produce the crisp golden-brown finish.

Spit roasting

This is the original form of roasting going back long before the development of the first ovens and involves the mounting of the joints in front of a carefully controlled fire. During cooking the joint is turned slowly and cooked by direct radiated heat although convected heat may be present depending on how the joint is situated over the fire.

Several advantages and disadvantages are encountered with each type of roasting but because of the many disadvantages associated with spit roasting it is rarely practised, with the possible exception of special parties.

The advantages of oven roasting compared to spit roasting are primarily:

(a) oven temperatures can be easily maintained or altered at the discretion of the cook;
(b) less energy or fuel is required because the heat is contained in the oven;
(c) there is less risk of fire;
(d) the use of a cooking tray results in an excellent vehicle liquor, i.e. gravy being obtained;
(e) the roasting procedure in an oven is less complicated.

The main disadvantage with oven roasting compared with spit roasting is that the oven traps much of the steam given off by the food during cooking and this has an undesirable effect on the texture, colour and flavour of the roast. Roasts produced on a spit can have a quality unrivalled by oven roasting.

Important points when spit roasting foods

Since spit roasting is not common in catering establishments there is no method attributed to it in this chapter but the following points are given to allow the reader some understanding of the operation.

1 The joint is mounted on a spit bar and rack and is slowly rotated over an open fire.
2 During cooking the joint is basted with fat.
3 The speed of cooking is controlled by:
   (a) rotating speed of joint;
   (b) moving the joint nearer to or further away from the heat source;
   (c) controlling the fuel source to produce a low heat or intense heat;
   (d) moving the burning chars to increase or decrease the amount of radiated heat at any one point of the joint;
   (e) using shields to eliminate radiated heat to any one part of the joint or carcase, e.g. an iron shield held in front of the belly part of an animal to avoid overcooking – a pig iron.
4 Some commodities (usually game) are heavily barded or covered with oiled paper or water paste to prevent drying out or scorching. This usually applies to the small parts of a commodity, e.g. the ears of suckling pigs and the thin ends of legs of a whole animal.
5 Large joints or whole carcases are often carved at certain points during roasting for maximum flavour, serving the correct degree of cooking and providing a service which offers the novelty of a speciality function.

Poêler (pot roasting)

This form of cooking, unlike oven roasting and spit roasting, incorporates the use of a cooking utensil with a lid. This is therefore *not true roasting* because part of the cooking involves exposing the food to *moist heat* i.e. steam trapped within the cooking utensil. The commodity is cooked with vegetables known as a matignon and butter is the only type of fat which should be used. To allow the joint or bird to colour, the lid is removed before the correct degree of cooking is achieved; this lets the steam escape and enables the dry heat to colour the commodity. After cooking the juices left within the container are used to form the basis of the accompanying sauce.

The use of fat or oil when roasting

This is very important to the roasting process. It acts as a cooking medium and fulfils various functions e.g. prevents the joint from drying out and becoming hard and is essential to the development of the characteristic taste, texture and appearance of roast products. Many foods contain a high proportion of fat and therefore require very little additional fat to aid the cooking process.

The use of salt when roasting

Traditionally most commodities to be roasted are seasoned prior to cooking. However there are occasions when this will retard the development of colour on the surface of the joint. Since salt attracts meat juices to the surface of the commodity it tends to delay browning, especially in convected heat, i.e. oven roasting. This is particularly important with joints containing large areas of lean flesh where the intention is to develop a good colour. To avoid this problem, the joint can be coloured in a hot oven and then seasoned. Alternatively the joint may be cooked at the appropriate temperature and seasoned when colour has been developed. Many studies indicate that the penentration of salt into a joint when roasting is not as considerable as one would think – the penetration is 5–6 mm in depth approximately.

Speed of cooking

In recent years it has been suggested that roasting should be conducted at lower temperatures than has been the tradition.[9,10,11]. Most experiments point to the conclusion that low-temperature roasting causes less shrinkage and produces a more juicy joint than high-temperature roasting.[12] One experiment revealed that when two identical joints were roasted at different temperatures, the shrinkage and weight loss were very different. One joint was roasted at 148°C resulting in a weight loss of 22% of the original weight of the joint, whereas the second joint, roasted at 232°C, had a weight loss of 36% of the original weight of the joint. The procedure adopted in this chapter is to cook the joint at a speed sufficient to complete the cooking and develop colour simultaneously (with the exception of lean flesh which is lightly coloured prior to seasoning – see the use of salt).

Note: The traditional practice of initial high-temperature roasting to keep in meat juices cannot be substantiated by research but on the contrary may increase the loss of soluble extractives and in turn weight loss, see page 80.

Slow-cooking ovens

A recent development is an oven which is designed to cook (and hold in hot storage) food at low temperatures, e.g. temperatures of 70°C+ being maintained for 1–24 hours. This type of slow cooking[13] renders most qualities of joints tender and therefore has economic advantages, especially for low-cost markets. However, commodities cooked in this manner do not appear to produce the quality associated with a true roast and tend to have steamed-like characteristics without a full roast flavour.

Covering a roast during cooking

In some instances commodities are enveloped in tin foil or water paste (a soft dough made from water and flour) prior to oven cooking. Covering the commodities in this way is usually practised when dubious quality is being used because the covering traps steam which is an aid to tender cooking of poor-quality roasts. This of course is not true roasting but like pot roasting is a form of covered oven roasting which is unnecessary when cooking good-quality commodities. Covering a joint also increases the weight loss.[14]

Roaster bags are also sometimes used to cover joints. These bags, which are designed to allow the meat to colour and at the same time the steam to escape, help to keep the oven clean but add to the cost of producing the roast and do not appear to have much application in the industry.[15] Roaster bags also increase weight loss.

Cooking times

The cooking time of roasts may vary considerably depending on many different factors:

(a) type of oven – ordinary oven or convection oven;
(b) capacity and heat output of the oven;

(c) where the joint or bird is placed in the oven;
(d) type of joint – boned, boned and rolled or on the
     bone;
(e) oven temperature;
(f) quantity of food cooked at any one time and size,
     weight and thickness of roast.

The operator should treat suggested cooking times as
rough guides only and determine degree of cooking with a
temperature probe. The internal temperature for each
commodity is stated in the individual recipe.

Carry-over cooking

When a roast is removed from the oven, cooking will
continue for a further period as the roast is cooling down.
The length of time carry-over cooking continues is
determined by the size, thickness and surface area of the
roast and cooking temperature. The rise of internal
temperature brought about by carry-over cooking should
be allowed for when determining the degree of cooking as
the joint will sit for a resting period before carving and
service. As a rough guide the allowance made for carry-
over cooking varies from 2–4°C, for small joints and may
be as much as 15–20°C for very large joints.

Technical terms

To bard (barder)   To cover the surface of the meat,
   poultry or *game* with slices of pork or bacon fat to
   prevent the flesh drying out when cooking.
To lard (larder)   To insert strips of pork or bacon fat into
   raw flesh by means of special needles. This adds
   moistness to the eating quality of the joint.
To froth   This is the coating of roasts with flour just
   before cooking is completed. This technique (which is
   rarely seen these days) is applied to joints which have
   been roasted in a waterpaste covering (spit roasted
   venison) to develop a coloured surface.
En casserole   To pot roast in a casserole. This term was
   traditionally used to indicate that the dish *was not
   garnished*.
En cocotte   This is the same as en casserole but was
   traditionally used to indicate the dish *was garnished*.
Matignon   The term for the basic vegetables used in pot
   roasting, see the base recipe.
   Note: Matignon also has an old-fashioned definition
   which should not be confused with the above definition.
To baste (arroser)   To coat a joint or bird etc. with the
   roasting fat during cooking. Basting with fat helps to
   keep the joint moist and facilitates carving.
Trivet   An implement placed into the roasting tray to
   raise the item being cooked off the base of the tray and
   out of the fat and drippings.

Section one   Roast butcher meats and furred game

Base method

Step 1	Mise en place
	A Assemble ingredients.
	B Prepare the joint for roasting.
	C Prepare any vegetables or bones required as a base for the roast. The roasting tray should be lined with vegetables or bones when the joint has no bones to raise it out of the drippings when cooking.
	D Prepare any garnish and accompanying sauces.

↓

Step 2	Place the joint in the roasting tray and coat with the fat or oil.

↓

Step 3	Place the joint in a hot oven at 225°C and allow to brown slightly.

↓

Step 4	Add the seasoning and reduce the oven temperature to 150–175°C.

↓

Step 5	Allow to cook slowly, basting as required until the correct degree of cooking is obtained:

Summary:

Underdone (saignant)	Beef★, mutton★, venison★ and hare★	=	55–60°C
Just done (à point)	Beef, mutton, venison and lamb★	=	66–71°C
Well done (bien cuit)	Beef, veal★ and rabbit★	=	75–77°C
	Lamb and pork★	=	78–80°C

★ This indicates the most appropriate degree of cooking.

↓

Step 6	Remove the joint from the oven and place into a hotplate or store in a warm place for 15–20 mins. (more appropriate to large joints, see important points).

↓

Step 7	Carve the joint into neat slices across the grain and place on to the serving dish.

↓

Step 8	Coat with a little of the hot gravy.

↓

Step 9	Decorate with the watercress and any other stated garnish. Serve accompanied with the roast gravy and any other stated sauces or garnish.

Important points when roasting butcher meats and furred game

Step 1C

Preparation of roasting tray: Joints should never be placed directly on to a roasting tray unless they have a bone content which raises them off the base of the pan.

They should be placed on a trivet, bones, matignon (see technical terms on page 39) or halves of potato.

This reduces the amount of *conducted heat* to the base of the joint and prevents it frying and becoming hard on the underside. This is especially important with joints containing areas of lean flesh, e.g. fillet of beef and the inner side of best ends of lamb.

Step 2

Placing the joint into the roasting tray: Joints should be placed into the roasting tray with the fat top uppermost. This allows the joint to be basted with its own fat during cooking.

Step 3

Placing the joint into a hot oven: The joint is placed into a hot oven to colour but after this the temperature is reduced to allow the joint to cook slowly with the minimum shrinkage and weight loss, see page 239. This is less important where the joints have a good natural fat covering, e.g. rib of beef; here the joint can be cooked at the same temperature throughout (unless corrective measures are required) coinciding cooking and colour development. See adding salt below.

Step 4

Adding seasoning: When seasoning joints which have a considerable amount of surface lean flesh, it is advisable to add the seasoning after colour has been developed. This is because salt retards colour development (especially when oven roasting).

Step 5

Various degrees of cooking: The internal temperature of the various degrees of cooking are stated in the base method. The stating of one individual temperature for a degree of cooking has been avoided as this does not take into account carry-over cooking, individual preferences for slight differences of internal colour and whether the beef was ripe or unripe prior to cooking; unripe beef usually requires a higher internal temperature to lose the red pigmentation than ripe beef.

Step 5

Test for cooking: To test to determine the degree of cooking may be made as follows:

Test by thermometer: This is the most accurate means of testing the degree of cooking. A temperature probe is inserted into the joint and the internal temperature read from a digital display. *Note*:   Mechanical thermometers are inserted into the thickest part of the joint prior to roasting and the temperature inspected during cooking.

Degrees of cooking (see base method):

Underdone: 55–60°C

Just done: 66–71°C

Well done: 75–78°C

Pressure test: The joint is squeezed with the fingers or roasting tongs with a view to determining the resistance or sponginess of the flesh, e.g. sponginess indicates that the joint is underdone, whereas the absence of sponginess with the meat yielding under pressure indicates that the joint is cooked through (see also page 306).

Puncture test: Insert a small needle or cocktail stick, then withdraw and press the joint forcing the juices to escape. The amount of blood present in the meat juices indicates the degree of cooking, e.g. a considerable amount of blood present indicates the joint is very underdone, traces of blood indicate underdone up to just done and no trace of blood indicates cooked through.

Step 6

Hot storage of joint prior to carving: The joint should be allowed to rest or settle for a short period to facilitate carving and reduce the likelihood of the operator being burned.

Base method for roast gravy

Step 1	Allow the sediment to settle on the bottom of the roasting tray then carefully decant off the fat.
Step 2	Place the roasting tray on the top of the stove and sprinkle the bottom with a little salt. Heat until the sediment adheres to the bottom of the tray and develops a light brown colour.
Step 3	Decant a second time removing the remaining fat then add the brown stock and simmer for 2–3 mins.
Step 4	Check the seasoning and strain into a container ready for service. Skim off surface fat as necessary.

Base recipe (yield 4 portions)

Main item*:	*Joints on the bone*: 1 kg joint approximately (subject to bone content).
	Boned joints: 700 g flesh approximately.
Fat:	25 g fat or 25 ml oil.
Seasoning:	Salt.
Gravy:	400 ml brown stock.
Garnish:	See each individual recipe below.

* Joints of beef on the bone, e.g. rib and sirloin, are likely to be an unsuitable shape for roasting when cut to 1 kg joints.

Beef (sirloin, contrefilet, fillet, wing rib and fore rib)

Prepare the joint ready for roasting (pages 53–62) then cook as stated in the base method, keeping underdone.
Cooking time: 30 mins. per kg plus 30 mins. per joint.
Internal temperature: 55–60°C.
Garnish: Garnish with a small bunch of watercress and four portions of Yorkshire pudding (page 383). Serve separately a sauceboat of gravy and a sauceboat of horseradish sauce.

Lamb and mutton (leg, saddle, shoulder, best end and middle neck)

Prepare the joint ready for roasting (pages 59–64) then cook as stated. Traditionally mutton is cooked a little underdone and lamb cooked through.
Cooking time: 40 mins. per kg plus 40 mins. per joint.
Internal temperature: Mutton = 50–62°C
Lamb = 66–71°C
Garnish: Garnish with a small bunch of watercress.
Lamb: Accompany with gravy and mint sauce.
Mutton: Accompany with gravy, onion sauce and redcurrant jelly.

Veal (cushion, thick flank, under cushion, leg, rump, loin, saddle, and best end)

Prepare the joint ready for roasting (pages 56–63) then cook as stated. It is traditionally cooked through.
Cooking time: 50 mins per kg plus 50 mins. per joint.
Internal temperature: 75–77°C.
Garnish: Garnish with a small bunch of watercress and stuffing (page 75). Accompany with gravy or thickened gravy and redcurrant jelly.

Pork (leg, loin, spare rib and shoulder)

Prepare the joint ready for roasting (page 60) then cook as stated. Pork should be cooked through.
Cooking time: 50 mins. per kg plus 50 mins. per joint.
Internal temperature: 78–80°C.
Remove the crackling prior to carving.
Garnish: Garnish with a small bunch of watercress, pieces of crackling and sage and onion stuffing (page 75). Accompany with gravy and apple sauce.

Venison (leg, haunch, loin, saddle, best end and shoulder)

Prepare the joint ready for roasting (page 63) then cook as stated keeping underdone.
Cooking time: 30 mins. per kg plus 30 mins. over per joint.
Internal temperature: 55–60°C.
Garnish: Garnish with a small bunch of watercress and accompany with gravy and redcurrant jelly. Sauce Oxford or Cambridge is also sometimes served.

Garnished roasts and derivative dishes

Many roast dishes are prepared using a variety of garnishes and accompanying sauces. The joint is prepared following the instructions in the base method but instead of preparing roast gravy, a sauce such as a *demi-glace* or *jus lié derivative is swilled into the cooking utensil* after decanting off the fat. The sauce is served as an accompaniment to the roast joint which is often decorated with a garnish. When a garnished sauce, e.g. chasseur, is to accompany a joint it cannot be strained after swilling into the cooking utensil therefore an appropriate wine or stock is added, reduced almost to a glaze then strained into the sauce.

Note: Many joints are presented for service uncarved or carved and re-assembled, e.g. fillet of beef and saddle of lamb etc. If this is the case the joint may be glazed, i.e. brushed with a little meat glaze to produce an attractive shine and appearance.

Dishes

Boulangère (lamb and mutton)

When the joint is roasting prepare a dish of boulangère potatoes (page 232) ensuring that both cooking times will end at the same time. When the potatoes are quite firm, remove the joint from the roasting tray, place on top of the potatoes and complete the cooking. Serve the joint whole or carved on top of the potatoes garnished with watercress. Accompany with a sauceboat of roast gravy.

Bouquetière

Garnish the joint with bouquets of glazed turnips, glazed carrots, buttered peas, buttered French beans cut into diamonds, small balls of cauliflower coated with hollandaise sauce and château potatoes. Accompany with madeira sauce.

Chasseur

Garnish the joint with château potatoes and accompany with chasseur sauce.

Du Barry

Garnish the joint with small balls of cauliflower Mornay and château potatoes. Accompany with jus lié or plain gravy.

Minted pears (lamb)

Garnish the joint with half pears which have been lightly poached in mint sauce. Accompany with roast gravy.

Persillé (best end of lamb)

Remove the joint from the oven just before cooking is completed (20 mins. approximately) and coat with the following mixture: 50 g white breadcrumbs, 40 g butter, good pinch of chopped parsley and a clove of crushed garlic all mixed thoroughly together. Replace the joint in the oven and complete the cooking, allowing the coating to lightly brown. Serve the same as plain roast lamb with gravy and mint sauce.

Wellington (fillet of beef)

Fillet preparation: Slit the fillet lengthwise and stuff with pâté (foie gras if available). Bard with pork fat then string. Colour the fillet in the oven but keep very underdone then allow to cool. Remove the string (and barding if desired).

Prepare 250 g very dry duxelles and 250 g veal forcemeat (page 73) and thoroughly mix together (when the duxelles is cold).

Roll out 500 g puff pastry and spread the base where the fillet will sit with one-third of the forcemeat. Lay the fillet on top and cover with the remaining forcemeat. Enclose within the pastry. Decorate with strips of pastry if desired, then eggwash and bake at 210–220°C (30–40 mins.).

Leave the fillet whole or carve and re-assemble and garnish with braised lettuce, cooked blanched tomatoes and château potatoes. Accompany with Madeira sauce.

Section two   Roast poultry and feathered game

Base method

Step 1	Mise en place
	A Assemble ingredients.
	B Prepare the bird/s ready for roasting.
	C Prepare any vegetables or bones required as a base for the bird/s (optional).
	D Prepare the garnish and accompanying sauces.
Step 2	Season the bird/s inside and out with salt then place on the roasting tray. The bird/s should be placed *on their sides*.
Step 3	Coat with the fat or oil.

Step 4

Place in to the oven at a temperature suitable for the size of bird:

Birds up to ½ kg in weight: quail, snipe, woodcock, grouse, spring chicken and partridge	=	240–225° C
Birds ½–1 kg in weight: partridge, teal, double spring chicken, pheasant and wild duck	=	225–200° C
Birds 1½–2 kg in weight: medium chicken, pheasant and duckling	=	200–180° C
Birds 2½–5 kg in weight: large chicken, capons and small turkey etc.	=	175–150° C
Birds 7–10 kg in weight: turkey	=	150–125° C
Birds over 10 kg in weight: turkey	=	125–100° C

Step 5

Allow to cook until a light colour is developed then turn over onto the other side. The time this takes obviously varies with the item being roasted.

Step 6

Continue cooking until both sides of the bird/s have developed a light colour then turn breast up.

Step 7

Cook to the required degree allowing a good colour to develop across the surface of the bird/s.

Summary: All birds are cooked through with the possible exception of game which is sometimes kept a little underdone.

Internal temperatures: Cooked through: 75° C
                                        Slightly underdone: 60–65° C

Step 8

Remove from the tray then sit the bird/s vent up to allow steam to escape.

Step 9

Prepare the gravy as stated in Section 1.

Step 10

Service:

Chicken, duckling and game birds: Leave the birds whole or cut into portions. When portioning two-portion birds, e.g. double poussin, grouse and partridge, cut the birds in halves. Birds yielding three or more portions are usually jointed (page 69).

Dress the bird or portions on the serving dish (game on top of fried croûtons spread with farce) then neatly decorate with the garnish. Serve gravy and accompanying sauces (or garnish) separately.

Turkey and large goose: Carve the bird then place the slices of leg meat along the centre of the serving dish. Neatly arrange the white meat on top then coat with a little hot gravy.

Decorate with the garnish and serve the sauces separately.

Important points when roasting poultry and feathered game

Step 1C

Preparation of roasting tray: Vegetables such as onions, carrots and celery (see matignon) may be added to the roasting tray together with any winglets or neck pieces etc., to improve the flavour of the gravy. Unlike joints of butcher meat and furred game, it is not essential to keep poultry and feathered game raised off the base of the roasting tray. The *skinned* flesh of poultry and game (which is barded) develops a crisp golden-brown texture when cooked in contact with the roasting tray (provided correct practices are followed).

Step 2

Seasoning before cooking: Poultry and game can be seasoned prior to cooking (traditional practice) as the skin develops colour easily, regardless of the tendency for salt to retard colour development.

Step 2

Placing the bird into the roasting tray: Place the bird on its side with the breast downwards. When cooking several birds on the same tray ensure they are all facing the same way to facilitate turning.

Step 5

Turning the birds during cooking: Poultry and game should be turned during cooking to ensure that all parts of the bird are roasted evenly. The breasts of the birds are kept downwards for most of the cooking period for protection against excessive heat exposure, overcooking and loss of juiciness. Also the layer of fat on the back of the bird melts during cooking and runs down the bird, aiding basting.

Steps 5, 6 and 7

Speed of cooking: See speed of cooking of butcher meats and furred game. In the base method, the intention is to cook the bird and develop colour simultaneously, therefore the size of the bird is one of the most important factors in relation to the cooking temperature.

Cooking fatty poultry and game: Duck and goose etc. It is accepted practice to roast fatty birds at a high temperature for a short period (220–225° C) then reduce the oven temperature and cook slowly. The reason for this is to remove excess fat and crisp the skin.

Step 7

Cooking times:

Quail, woodcock and snipe   10–30 mins.
Grouse, spring chicken and partridge   25–40 mins.
Chicken, pheasant and duckling   50 mins–1¼ hours.
Turkey   30–40 mins. per kilogramme.

Step 7

Test for cooking: See section 1.

Important: When serving poultry or game underdone there is a risk of food poisoning.

Step 8

Hot storage of birds prior to portioning: See butcher meats and furred game in Section 1.

Note: When removing the bird/s from the roasting tray (and when turning during cooking) the roasting fork should be inserted into a part of the carcase where no damage is done to the flesh (the back of the carcase). The bird should be held over the roasting tray and the juice contained within the carcase carefully emptied out. The bird should then be placed vent up to allow steam to escape. This technique allows the bird to cool quickly and therefore reduces the risk of food poisoning.

Base recipe

Main item:	See each individual bird below.
Roasting fat:	Melted fat or oil.
Seasoning:	Salt.
Gravy:	Brown stock (300–400 ml per four portions)
Garnish and accompanying sauces:	See each individual bird below.

Roast chicken

Single spring chicken   (poussin)   Allow 1 × 400 g poussin per portion.

Double spring chicken   (poussin double)   Allow 1 × 800 g poussin per 2 portions.

Small chicken   (poulet de grain)   Allow 1 × 1¼ kg chicken per 4 portions (small).

Medium chicken   (poulet reine)   Allow 1 × 1½ kg chicken per 4 portions.

Large chicken   (poularde)   Allow 1 × 2 kg chicken per 4–6 portions.

Capon   (chapon)   Allow 1 × 3½ kg chicken per 6–8 portions.

Prepare the chicken for roasting (page 66) then cook as stated in the base method cooking through.

Cooking times: These vary depending on the size of the bird:

Spring chicken   25–40 mins.
Medium chicken   1–1½ hours.

Internal temperature: 75° C approximately.

Garnish: Garnish the chicken with watercress and game chips. Serve separately roast gravy and bread sauce.

Roast turkey (dindon rôti)

Allow 350 g raw weight of turkey per portion.

Prepare the turkey for roasting (including stuffing, see

page 66) then cook as stated in the base method, cooking through.
Cooking time: 30–40 mins. per kilogramme.
Internal temperature: 75°C approximately.
Garnish: Garnish with watercress, slices of stuffing, cooked chipolata sausages and braised chestnuts (optional). Accompany with gravy, bread sauce and cranberry sauce.

Roast duckling (caneton rôti)

Allow 1 × 2 kg duckling per four portions.
   Prepare the duckling for roasting (including stuffing, page 66) then cook as stated in the base method, cooking through.
Cooking time: 1–1½ hours.
Internal temperature: 70°C.
Garnish: Garnish with watercress and game chips. Accompany with gravy, stuffing (in sauceboat) and apple sauce.

Roast goose (oie rôtie)

Allow 350 g raw weight of goose per portion.
   Prepare the goose for roasting then cook as stated (page 66) in the base method cooking through.
Cooking time: 1¼–2 hours depending on size.
Internal temperature: 70°C.
Garnish: The same as duckling.

Roast feathered game

Roast grouse   (coq de bruyère rôti)   Allow 1–2 portions per bird.
Roast pheasant   (faisan rôti)   Allow 3–4 portions per bird.
Roast partridge   (perdreau rôti)   Allow 1–2 portions per bird.

   Prepare the bird/s for roasting (which usually includes barding, see pages 66–8) then cook as stated, keeping slightly underdone.
Cooking time: ½–1 hour depending on size.
Internal temperature: 60–65°C.
Garnish: garnish with watercress and game chips. Also dress on fried croûtons spread with game farce (page 76). Accompany with bread sauce, gravy and breadcrumbs browned in butter.

Garnished roasts and derivative dishes

Roast chicken and bacon (poulet rôti au lard)
Prepare as roast chicken adding 4–8 rashers of cooked streaky bacon. Place the bacon neatly across the top of the dished chicken.

Roast stuffed chicken (poulet rôti à l'anglaise)
Stuff the chicken prior to roasting (page 75). Prepare as roast chicken and neatly garnish with slices of the cooked stuffing when serving.

Roast duckling and orange salad (caneton rôti salade d'orange)
Prepare the same as roast duckling. Accompany with a dish of orange salad and a sauceboat of acidulated cream.

Cantonese roast duckling (non-derivative dish)
Preparation of duckling:
Draw and clean a fresh duckling taking great care not to damage the neck end. Tie the skin at the neck end so that the duckling can be filled with liquid.
   Wipe over the skin with a damp cloth then hang up and allow to dry for 2 hours approximately.
Preparation of liquid filling:
30 ml oil, 50 g chopped onion, 5 g crushed garlic, 50 g spring onions cut into 25 mm pieces, 10 g chopped parsley, 5 g star anise, 4 peppercorns, 50 ml soy sauce, 50 ml sweet sherry, 300 ml brown stock and 20 g sugar.
   Heat the oil in a saucepan then sweat down the onion, garlic, spring onion, parsley, peppercorns and star anise for 2–3 mins. Add the stock and allow to simmer for 5 mins. approximately then add the remaining ingredients.
Roasting the duckling:
Fill the duckling with the mixture then sew up with string. Hang the duckling, vent upwards, in a moderate oven (210°C) and cook for 15 mins. then baste with a mixture consisting of 100 g honey, 30 ml vinegar and 100 ml stock. Reduce the oven temperature to 175°C and allow to cook, occasionally basting with the honey mixture. *Cooking time*:   1 hour approximately.
   Carefully remove the duckling from the oven and pour out the liquor filling into a saucepan. Lightly thicken the liquor with 10 g cornflour diluted in cold water (30 ml) then skim and add 1 g monosodium glutamate powder (½ teaspoon). Carve or joint the duckling, place on a serving dish and accompany with the liquor sauce.

Grouse Rob Roy (Scottish)
Place the cleaned and drawn grouse in a raw marinade flavoured with whisky (page 42) for 12 hours approximately. Truss the grouse then cook as stated using the drained marinade vegetables as a base. When preparing the gravy flambé with whisky then add the marinade liquor and brown stock. Garnish and serve as roast feathered game.

Roast pheasant with oysters (faisan rôti aux huîtres)
Prepare the pheasant for roasting but stuff with a mixture of game farce (page 76), chopped bacon, chopped raw oysters, pinch nutmeg, sweet basil and thyme. Garnish with watercress and halves of lemon. Accompany with the roast gravy.

Section three   Pot roasted (poêler) butcher meats, poultry and game

Base method

Step 1	Mise en place
	A Assemble ingredients.
	B Prepare the joint or bird ready for cooking.
	C Prepare the base vegetables: wash, peel then slice the carrot, onion and celery.
	Note: The longer the cooking time, the larger the vegetables should be cut.
	D Prepare any garnish and accompanying sauces.
	E Melt or soften the recipe butter.

↓

Step 2	Place the base vegetables in a suitable pan, e.g. braising pan or casserole, then put the joint or bird on top.
	Note: It is advisable to colour (shallow-fry) beef fillets before cooking so that the correct degree of cooking and colour are easily achieved. This is an *alternative procedure* to removing the lid and colouring at step 5. This application may be extended to all commodities.

↓

Step 3	Coat with the butter. Cover with a lid and place into a hot oven – 220° C approximately.

↓

Step 4	During cooking, remove the lid and baste with the hot fat.

↓

Step 5	Remove the lid 20 mins. prior to completion of cooking approximately, and allow the joint or bird to colour (unless the joint has been seared prior to cooking). Add the seasoning as soon as colour is developed (see page 239).

↓

Step 6	When the correct degree of cooking is attained remove the joint or bird and keep hot.

↓

Step 7	*Sauce preparation*
	Decant off the fat from the cooking utensil then add the brown stock and simmer for 2–3 mins. Any marinade liquor should be added at this stage and reduced down almost to a glaze prior to adding the stock.

↓

Step 8	Depending on recipe requirements the cooking liquor may be used in three ways:
	(a) Strain into a clean pan and skim then *serve as an unthickened liquor*.
	(b) Strain and skim as above then lightly *thicken with a little arrowroot* diluted in cold water.
	(c) Reduce down the cooking liquor almost to a glaze (skimming as required) then *strain into the sauce which is to accompany the dish*, e.g. Madeira sauce.

tep 9

Service:

Butcher meats and furred game: Remove the string from the joint then place on to the serving dish. Brush with a little meat glaze to produce an attractive appearance. If the joint is to be carved, cut into neat slices across the grain.
Neatly decorate with any garnish and accompany with the sauce.

Poultry and feathered game:

Casserole service: Remove the string from the bird then cut into joints or leave whole. Place into a clean casserole then add any garnish and sprinkle with a little chopped parsley. Replace into the oven and correct the temperature. Accompany with the sauce when serving.

Flat dish (e.g. duckling bigarade):
Place the whole or portioned bird on to the dish, decorate with any garnish then coat with a little of the sauce. Accompany with the remaining sauce in a sauceboat.

mportant points when pot roasting commodities oêler)

tep 5

chieving the correct degree of cooking and colour: It is nportant that the lid be removed at the correct moment f the commodity has not been seared prior to cooking) to chieve both the correct degree of cooking and a good olour. Colour development on a commodity being pot oasted takes longer than an ordinary roast because of the effects of steam on the surface of the food and in addition the sides of the container shield the joint of bird (especially with a casserole) from radiated heat emitted from the baffle plates within the oven.

Important: The process of cooking 'en casserole' is likely to be modified for large-scale operations. The poultry or game is roasted with the vegetables in an ordinary roasting tray then the sauce prepared as stated. In many operations the term refers to this modified practice *with service en casserole*.

---

ase recipe   (yield 4 portions)

Main item:	See each individual item below.
ase vegetables:	50 g carrot, 50 g onion, 25 g celery, sprig of thyme, ½ bay leaf and parsley stalks.
at:	30 g butter.
easoning:	Salt and pepper.
willing stock:	300 ml brown stock (usually veal).
ther ingredients:	See each individual recipe.

---

eef

**illet of beef (filet de boeuf poêlé)
(example)**

llow 600–800 g piece of fillet per four portions.
   Prepare the fillet for cooking (page 62) then cook as tated, keeping underdone.
ooking time: 45 mins. approximately.
nternal temperature: 55–60° C.
   Use the cooking liquor thickened with a little arrowroot s the accompanying sauce or reduce and add jus lié.
ishes: See bouquetière, chasseur and Du Barry, age 244.

Veal

**Cushion of veal (noix de veau poêlée)
(example)**

Allow 600–800 g piece of muscle per four portions.
   Prepare the muscle for cooking (page 57) then cook as stated, cooking through.
Cooking time: 1½ hours approximately.
Internal temperature: 75–77° C.
   Use the cooking liquor thickened with a little arrowroot as the accompanying sauce or reduce and add to jus lié.
Dishes: See beef above.

Venison

Saddle of venison (selle de venaison poêlée)
Allow 1½ kg piece of saddle per four portions.

Prepare the saddle for cooking (page 63) then cook as stated, keeping a little underdone.
Cooking time: 1 hour approximately.
Internal temperature: 58–60°C.

Use the cooking liquor thickened with a little arrowroot as the accompanying sauce or reduce and add jus lié.

Baden-Baden
(example dish)
Place the well-trimmed saddle in a raw marinade with white wine for 12 hours approximately. Remove and wipe dry then cook as stated using the marinade vegetables as a base when cooking (the base vegetables are included in the marinade).

Use the marinade liquor to swill the pan in place of the stock and when reduced add 300 ml of game jus lié.

Garnish the joint with quarter pears which have been poached in water and lemon with a cinnamon stick added. Coat with the sauce and accompany with redcurrant jelly.

Poultry and game

Chicken (poulet poêlé)
Allow a 1½ kg chicken per four portions.

Prepare the chicken for cooking (page 66) then cook as stated, cooking through.
Cooking time: 1¼ hours approximately.
Internal temperature: 75°C.

Use the cooking liquor thickened with arrowroot as the accompanying sauce or reduce and add to jus lié or demi-glace.

Pot-roasted poultry and feathered game dishes

The following dishes are suitable for all poultry and game (except very large birds) unless otherwise indicated.

En casserole
Prepare as stated then lightly thicken the swilling stock with arrowroot, step 8 (b). Leave ungarnished.

Bonne-femme
Prepare as stated then lightly thicken the swilling stock with arrowroot or reduce and add to jus lié or demi-glace, step 8 (b) or (c). Garnish with brown glazed button onions, lardons and cocotte potatoes.

Champeaux
Prepare as bonne-femme but add 50 ml white wine with the brown stock when preparing the sauce.

Demidoff
Prepare as stated then lightly thicken the swilling stock with arrowroot or reduce and add to jus lié, step

8 (b) or (c). Garnish with a cooked vegetable Demidoff (page 39) tossed in a little butter.

Fermière
Prepare as Demidoff but add a cooked vegetable paysann with the addition of peas and diamonds of French beans a the garnish.

Grand-mère
Prepare as stated then lightly thicken the swilling stock with arrowroot or reduce and add to jus lié. Garnish with a dice of cooked mushrooms and bread croûtons frie to a crisp golden-brown in butter.

Polonaise
Stuff the bird prior to cooking with game farce (page 76 Prepare as stated then lightly thicken the swilling stock with arrowroot. When the bird has been transferred to a clean casserole and the temperature corrected, cover the top with polonaise garnish, coat with nut-brown butter and sprinkle with chopped parsley. Serve immediately.
Polonaise garnish:
1   Melt 50 g butter then add 30 g white breadcrumbs.
2   Cook slowly until golden brown.
3   Add one sieved hard-boiled egg and heat through thoroughly.

Bigarade (duckling)
Basic preparation:
1   Prepare and cook as stated.
2   Meanwhile, remove the zest from 2 oranges and 1 lemon and cut into fine strips. Blanch the strips for 2– mins. in boiling water. Also squeeze the juice from th fruit.
3   Cut an additional 2–3 oranges into segments and pla aside.
4   When adding the swilling stock, step 7, also add the fruit juice, 20 ml vinegar (1 tablespoon) and 3–4 cube of sugar. Use arrowroot diluted in cold water to thicken the liquor, step 8 (b).
5   Cut the duckling into joints or use only the breast carved lengthwise into thin slices.
6   Dress neatly on the serving dish then garnish with th orange segments and strips of zest (both heated). Coa with the sauce.

Duckling with cherries (caneton aux cerises)
Prepare and cook the duckling as stated.

When adding the swilling stock, also add 30 ml Madeir wine, a squeeze of lemon juice and 50 ml cherry juice if available. Reduce the liquor then add to a ¼ litre of jus lié or demi-glace.

Cut the duckling into joints then garnish with 100 g stoned cherries which have been heated with 10 ml port wine, the juice of half and orange, a pinch of mixed spic and a little redcurrant jelly. Coat with the sauce and serve

ection four   Roast potatoes

ase method

tep 1	Mise en place
	A Assemble ingredients.
	B Wash, peel and shape the potatoes.
	C Cover the potatoes with water until required for cooking.
	↓
tep 2	Drain the potatoes in a colander.
	↓
tep 3	Heat the fat or oil in the roasting tray then add the potatoes.
	↓
tep 4	Shallow-fry the potatoes in the hot fat for 3–4 mins., occasionally turning with a fish slice.
	↓
tep 5	Lightly season the potatoes with the salt then place in a hot oven – 230°C approximately.
	↓
tep 6	Turn the potatoes during cooking when the surfaces develop colour. Repeat this procedure until the potatoes are cooked, crisp and golden brown.
	↓
tep 7	Remove from the oven and drain thoroughly.
	Optional: Sprinkle with chopped parsley when serving.

mportant points when roasting potatoes

tep 4

hallow-frying the potatoes in the roasting tray: This educes the surface water on the potatoes and makes them ess likely to stick to the cooking utensil.

Note: Potatoes which are to be roasted are sometimes blanched prior to cooking, i.e. boiled for a short period. The reason for blanching potatoes may be to shorten the cooking time or reduce the likelihood of the potatoes sticking to certain types of roasting tray (this is not essential with heavy iron trays).

ase recipe   (yield 4 portions)

Main item:	500–600 g potatoes.
Fat:	25 g fat or oil.
Seasoning:	Salt.

*Olivette potatoes (pommes olivettes)

Cut the potatoes into the shape of small olives using an olive-shaped parisienne spoon. Alternatively turn the potatoes into small olives (20 mm in length approximately).

After draining the potatoes, toss in a little foaming butter.

*Cocotte potatoes (pommes cocotte)

Turn the potatoes into large olive shapes, i.e. 30 mm in length approximately. Cook as stated.

Roast potatoes (pommes rôties)

Turn the potatoes into barrel shapes 40–45 mm in length. Cook as stated.

Château potatoes (pommes château)

Turn the potatoes into large barrel shapes 55–60 mm in length. Cook as stated. *Note*:   Sometimes blanched prior to cooking.

*Noisette potatoes (pommes noisette)

Cut the potatoes with a noisette spoon then cook as stated.
Optional: Toss the potatoes in a little foaming butter just prior to service.

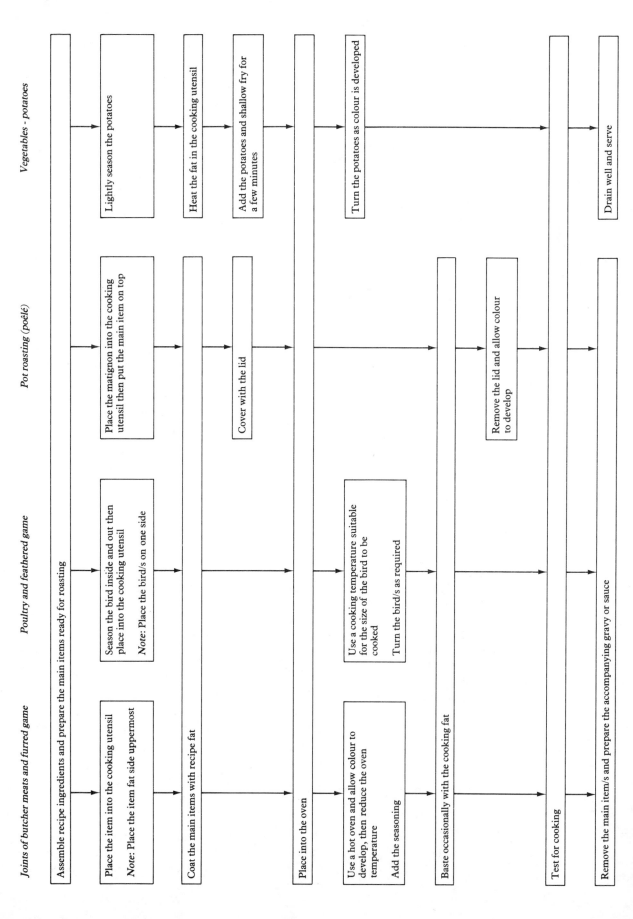

Joints of butcher meats and furred game   *Poultry and feathered game*   *Pot roasting (poêlé)*   *Vegetables - potatoes*

Assemble recipe ingredients and prepare the main items ready for roasting

Place the item into the cooking utensil

Note: Place the item fat side uppermost

Season the bird inside and out then place into the cooking utensil

Note: Place the bird/s on one side

Place the matignon into the cooking utensil then put the main item on top

Lightly season the potatoes

Coat the main items with recipe fat

Cover with the lid

Heat the fat in the cooking utensil

Add the potatoes and shallow fry for a few minutes

Place into the oven

Use a hot oven and allow colour to develop, then reduce the oven temperature

Add the seasoning

Use a cooking temperature suitable for the size of the bird to be cooked

Turn the bird/s as required

Turn the potatoes as colour is developed

Baste occasionally with the cooking fat

Remove the lid and allow colour to develop

Test for cooking

Remove the main item/s and prepare the accompanying gravy or sauce

Drain well and serve

Figure 25   Essential activities of pot roasting and to roast

Parisienne potatoes (pommes parisienne)
Cut the potatoes with a parisienne spoon then cook as
stated. After draining roll in a little meat glaze then
sprinkle with chopped parsley.

Parmentier potatoes (pommes Parmentier)
Cut the potatoes into 10 mm cubes then cook as stated.

Pavée potatoes (pommes pavées)
Cut the potatoes into 20 mm cubes then cook as stated.

Sablée potatoes (pommes sablées)
Prepare as Parmentier but sprinkle with 30 g white
breadcrumbs just before completing the cooking. Mix
through the potatoes and cook until the breadcrumbs are
crisp and brown.

These potatoes may also be cooked by shallow-frying.

assessment exercise

Compare and contrast roasting and pot roasting
(poêler) as methods of cooking.
What are the advantages of oven roasting compared
with spit roasting?
Give two examples where the balance between
convected heat and conducted heat would be
substantially different when oven roasting.
List the approximate temperatures for a joint of beef
cooked underdone, just done and well done.
Describe three ways of testing a roast for the degree of
cooking.
Identify six factors which affect the cooking time of a
joint when roasting.
Define the following terms: matignon; baste; bard;
lard and froth.
Describe three ways in which the liquid used to rinse a
roasting tray or casserole may be completed for
service.

Chapter 11
Shallow-frying

Shallow-frying is a *dry heat* method of cooking whereby food is cooked in a pan or on a solid surface such as a metal plate with a small quantity of hot fat or oil. The food being fried is in direct contact with the cooking utensil therefore the surface of the cooking utensil and the frying medium *conduct* the heat to the food making frying a fast method of cooking.

The term to 'shallow-fry' is a very wide description for many different procedures which are detailed in each process section through the chapter.

Important terms for shallow-frying operations

Meunière   (Miller's wife style)

This term refers to the shallow-frying of fish, shellfish and frog's legs. The fish is floured, shallow-fried, garnished with lemon slices and chopped parsley then coated with nut-brown butter.

Sauter

There are three important meanings to this term:
(a)   The term is often used simply as an alternative to shallow-fry, especially when cooking various small cuts of butcher meats or poultry.
(b)   The term may imply a 'tossing action' during the shallow-frying procedure. Commodities such as mushrooms and sliced potatoes are tossed in the pan (sauter literally means to jump) when frying as opposed to turning with a palette knife or fish slice; the tossing action is much faster.
(c)   The third meaning is more complex than the first two meanings because it refers to a high-quality meat, poultry or game dish prepared with a sauce. The preparation of these sautés consists of a two-stage operation:
  1   The first stage is to shallow-fry the main commodity. It is important to note that the main commodity must be able to be cooked tender by the frying procedure therefore only *good-quality* cuts or items can be used.
  2   When cooked, the commodity is removed and the cooking utensil rinsed with wine, stock or sauce in order to capture the flavour of the soluble extractives lost during frying – the

technical term for this rinsing or swilling of the pan is 'déglacer'. These extractives are deposited on the base of the cooking utensil and play a vital role in adding the flavour of the commodity to the sauce for the dish; the sauce becomes enhanced with the aroma and flavour of the commodity and is called a 'vehicle sauce'. When the sauce has been prepared the commodity and sauce are brought together and the temperature corrected for service. The cooked commodity should possess the quality of a dry heat cut and should *not resemble a stew in taste or texture*. To ensure that this dry heat quality is achieved it is important that the main item and sauce are combined as near to service as possible. In some cookery books the term sauter is also used to denote a stew, especially a veal stew. This use of the term causes confusion and should be avoided.

Sweat (suer)

This is shallow-frying, usually with the aid of a lid and without colour development. In most cases, sweating is a preliminary procedure to boiling (see Chapter 7) but in some instances it is also the method of cooking certain vegetable dishes and garnishes, see Section 6.
Note: Although sweating normally includes the use of a lid, one exception is duxelles, see page 274.

Griddle

This is cooking on a thick-bottomed metal plate (a griddle plate also called a hotplate by many bakers). The plate may or may not be oiled depending on the food to be cooked. A type of griddle plate which is ridged is used for the cooking of steaks, chops and cutlets etc. Bakery produce cooked on a griddle plate is dealt with on pages 361–2.

To flare

This term which has several meanings is commonly used by cooks to refer to a steak or cutlet etc., cooked directly on a cleaned and slightly oiled section of a hot gas stove. During cooking, small quantities of fat spurt from the item being cooked and occasionally burst into flame, especially when turning or moving.

Heat application and temperature control when shallow-frying

The control of temperature when shallow-frying is of considerable importance because the food is cooked by direct contact with a hot surface; this hot surface may reach extremely high temperatures when an open-top stove is used.

In most cases the speed of cooking is controlled by the cook (by means of experience) as few items of small equipment are thermostatically controlled; electric frying pans, electric griddle plates and bratt pans are pieces of equipment with thermostats. Control of cooking in most cases consists of regulating a naked flame or moving the cooking utensil across a solid-top stove to a hotter or cooler section depending on the temperature required.

When using hob units which transfer heat by *induction*, thermostatic control is used with all cooking containers. These hobs operate by producing a magnetic field which creates an intense heat *directly* transferred to the magnetic-based containers (iron, cast, steel or containers designed for induction heating) placed on the cooking surface – only the cooking container is heated.

One common mistake is to fry at too high a temperature resulting in:

Inconsistencies of cooking, e.g. burnt appearance, overcooking and drying out of the commodity.
Fat breakdown.
Development of 'off-flavours'.

The speed of cooking varies with the items being cooked and the approximate frying temperatures for different foods are indicated as follows:

Low-temperature frying:
90–95° C   =   Scrambled eggs and fried eggs.
125–150° C =   Thick cuts of meat, e.g. steaks, veal
                 cutlets and chops etc.

Moderate-frying temperature:
150–175° C =   Cuts of meat, e.g. steaks, chops and
                 cutlets. Fish steaks and small whole fish
                 etc.

Hot-frying temperatures:
175–195° C =   Thin cuts of meat, e.g. thin steaks and
                 liver. Fish fillets, sauté potatoes and
                 crêpes etc.

General information and important points

The cooking utensil is always pre-heated prior to adding the food to be fried because less fat is absorbed into the food, the risk of the food sticking to the pan is reduced (avoiding damage to any coating which may be used) and development of colour is aided.

2   The presentation side of a commodity is fried first.
3   As a general rule the thicker the food the lower the frying temperature.
4   When frying various items in the same pan to be served at the same time, the foods should be placed into the pan in relation to cooking time, i.e. foods requiring the longest cooking times placed in the pan first, e.g. chicken joints, the legs are placed into the pan first then fried for a short period before adding the pieces of breast and wings.
5   The pan is moved across the heat and turned during frying to maintain an even speed of cooking.
6   The food should never be pierced but handled with tongs or a palette knife.
7   Traditionally red meats are turned when small drops of blood appear on the surface of the meat.
8   When shallow-frying large items such as veal cutlets and large pork chops etc., the cooking may be completed in an oven. *Note*: This is less suitable for breaded items as the coating tends to harden.

Types of food suitable for shallow-frying

Tender foods such as good-quality cuts of butcher meat, game, poultry, fish, eggs, vegetables, fruits, pre-cooked items and batters. Also included in this chapter is the preparation of omelettes, scrambled eggs and sur le plat eggs which are all examples of a tender food mostly cooked by conducted heat on a solid surface.

The frying medium

This may be oil, butter, margarine, special frying fats or animal fats such as dripping or lard.

Butter

This provides flavour but burns at a low temperature, therefore it is less suitable for foods requiring high-temperature frying, especially over a prolonged period. The butter may be clarified to remove the milk solids and water, in turn producing a better frying medium than ordinary butter but this purified butter still has a low smoke point.

Animal fats

Lard and dripping are suitable for shallow-frying but have a slight taste and odour of the animal used and because of this many cooks prefer to use oil or specially prepared frying fats.

Oils and special frying fats

Good quality oils and special frying fats are odourless, neutral in taste and have the highest smoke points. The use of these frying mediums is to be recommended when cooking items which require high temperatures for prolonged periods of cooking.

Butter and oil mixture

This is often used by cooks to produce a balance between flavour and temperature, i.e. butter for flavour and oil for temperature. This is suitable for most shallow frying with the exception of prolonged high-temperature frying.

The frying medium fulfils many functions, e.g. *acts as a lubricant*, *conducts heat*, *promotes flavour* and *adds richness of taste*.

Important process procedures

To coat with breadcrumbs (paner)

To pass meat, poultry, fish or game etc., first through seasoned flour then into eggwash and finally into breadcrumbs.

To sear flesh (saisir)

The shallow-frying and browning of flesh in hot fat.

To sweat (faire suer)

The slow-frying of vegetables with a lid on the cooking utensil.

ection one   Shallow-fried fish (à la meunière)

ase method

tep 1	Mise en place A Assemble ingredients. B Prepare the fish. C Prepare the seasoned flour, lemon slices and chopped parsley. D Prepare any garnish stated in the individual recipe. ↓
tep 2	Heat the butter and oil in a frying pan or fish frying pan. ↓
tep 3	Pass the fish through the seasoned flour then shake off all surplus flour. ↓
tep 4	Place the fish into the pan, presentation side downwards, and fry steadily. ↓
tep 5	Turn over when a good colour has developed. Continue frying until cooked. ↓
tep 6	When cooked, remove from the pan and drain to remove surface fat. ↓
tep 7	Place on to the serving dish presentation side upwards and decorate with the garnish. Also sprinkle with the chopped parsley. ↓
tep 8	Prepare the nut-brown butter: 1 Pre-heat a small iron frying pan or omelette pan until hot. 2 Add the butter and keep shaking until an even brown colour is developed. 3 Add a good squeeze of lemon juice and shake through the butter. ↓
tep 9	Coat over the fish with the hot butter when required for service. ↓
tep 10	Serve immediately.

mportant points when shallow-frying fish

tep 1
Mise en place: The preparation of fish is usually taggered to fit into a scheduled work plan especially for anquet or function service.

tep 3
Flouring the fish: The fish should be floured then placed immediately into the pan. Leaving the floured fish sitting n a tray prior to frying is likely to result in the coating ecoming moist and the fish sticking together.

Step 4
Presentation side of fish: The fish should be placed into the pan with the presentation side down and served presentation side up.
Whole flat fish: White skin side. Many cooks leave on the white skin because it develops a good colour and crispness in texture.
Fish fillets: The underside removed from the bone.
Whole round fish and fish steaks: Either side.

Steps 4 and 5
Speed of cooking: The speed of cooking should be such

that raw items cook and develop colour simultaneously. Small items which tend to break up easily, e.g. goujons or strips of fish, are fried very quickly.

Step 6

Test for cooking: The flesh should yield under pressure with no sign of sponginess. In addition, any visible bone

and flesh should be easily separated when easing apart with a small knife or fingers.

Step 10

Service: The fish should be prepared as near to service time as possible and coated with the butter when required for service.

Most shallow-fried fish dishes can be prepared from the following recipe:

Base recipe   (yield 4 main course portions)

Frying medium:	20 g butter and 10 ml oil.
Flour:	50 g seasoned flour.
Cooked butter coating:	50–80 g nut-brown butter.
Garnish:	8–12 thin lemon slices and chopped parsley.

Main commodity   (the preparation of fish and cuts of fish is explained on pages 70–2)

Fish fillets:	Dover sole, lemon sole and plaice etc. = 8 × 75 g fillets approximately.
Whole flat fish:	Dover sole, lemon sole and plaice etc. = 4 × 400 g fish approximately.
Small round fish:	Trout, haddock and whiting etc. = 4 × 200 g fish approximately.
Fish steaks:	Salmon, halibut and turbot etc. = 4 × 200 g steaks approximately.
Production:	Follow the instructions after making reference to the individual dish to be prepared, see below.
	Cooking times: These vary considerably with the thickness of the fish being cooked, e.g. fish fillets 3–4 mins., small whole fish and fish steaks 6–10 mins.

Dishes

Meunière

This is the basic shallow-fried fish stated in the base recipe and method.

Belle-Meunière

Prepare as stated, adding to the garnish small cooked mushrooms, slices of skinned tomato and shallow-fried soft herring roes.

Cléopâtre

Prepare as stated, adding to the garnish cooked shrimps and capers heated in butter and shallow-fried soft herring roes.

Doria

Prepare as stated adding to the garnish small turned shapes of cucumber sweated in butter.

Grenobloise

Prepare as stated adding capers to the nut-brown butter before coating the fish and use lemon segments in place of slices.

Louisiane

Prepare as stated, adding to the garnish rondels of banana and a dice of red pepper fried in butter. Also add a small dice of tomato flesh to the nut-brown butter before coating the fish.

Murat (fish fillets)

Cut the fish 'gudgeon style' (en goujons) and cook the fish as stated. *Note*:   Cook the fish quickly and toss carefully as colour is developed. Add a small dice of cooked artichoke and cooked potato (5 mm approximately) and toss through the fish. Season, squeeze over lemon juice and sprinkle with chopped parsley when serving – *omit the nut-brown butter*.

Clara-Wart

Prepare as Murat replacing the potato with celeriac.

ection two   Shallow-fried butcher meats, offal and made-up items

1se method

Step 1	Mise en place
	A Assemble ingredients.
	B Prepare the main item/s.
	C Prepare any stated garnish or accompanying sauce.

Step 2	Heat the oil in the cooking utensil:
	Frying pan: Add only enough oil to produce a thin film on the base of the pan.
	Griddle pan: Rub the base with an oiled cloth to skin the surface.

Step 3	*All items except liver and hamburgers* Season the item/s.	*Liver* Pass the slices of liver through seasoned flour.

Step 4	Place on to the hot surface of the pan or plate and fry steadily.	Place on to the hot surface of the pan or plate and fry quickly.

Step 5	Turn over with a palette knife or tongs when approximately half cooked and when a good colour has been developed. Continue cooking.
	Note: Thick items such as fillet steaks may also be turned on to their sides and fried. Regulate the speed of cooking to suit the thickness of the item, e.g. reduce the temperature for thick items.

Step 6	Cook to the required degree of cooking, see individual commodity.

Step 7	Remove from the pan and drain well to remove surface fat.

Step 8	Place on to the heated serving dish and neatly decorate with any garnish.

Step 9	Serve and accompany with any stated sauce.

Important points when frying butcher meats, offal and made-up items

Step 1

Mise en place: The preparation of these items is usually staggered to fit into a scheduled work plan. The items are usually prepared ready for cooking in advance as part of a order work programme.

Steps 4 and 5

Speed of cooking: This varies with the type of food being cooked. Most commodities should be fried steadily allowing colour development and cooking to be achieved simultaneously. Thin items and items to be cooked underdone usually have to be fried quickly while large items have to be cooked more slowly. One common *mistake is to fry foods too quickly*, resulting in excess shrinkage and loss of flavour and texture. Although it may be desirable to cook some items quickly at first then reduce the heat and cook more slowly, high-temperature searing should be used with extreme care as this increases the likelihood of burning and general deterioration. Searing (sealing) the flesh does not retain meat juices as formerly thought but may increase the loss of juices and produce excessive shrinkage.

Steps 4 and 5

Control of frying temperature: When using equipment with no thermostat controls the cook regulates the cooking speed by increasing or decreasing the heat or moving the pan nearer to or further away from the heat source. *Visual and audible signs* are used to note the speed of cooking, e.g. loud crackling, sparkling type noises are an indication that the cooking is very fast and corrective action may have to be taken.

Griddle plates and bratt pans incorporating a thermostat control can be set at the appropriate temperature although modification may have to be made depending on the 'recovery time' of the equipment. Some manufacturers print the appropriate settings on the equipment and these should be followed.

Step 9

Shallow-fried foods should be presented for service when cooked. Prolonged hot storage during service time will result in general deterioration, e.g. loss of flavour, dryness in texture and change in the degree of cooking brought about by 'carry-over cooking'.

The following items are often grilled as an alternative method of cooking.

Beef

Entrecôte steaks (entrecôtes)

Allow 200 g trimmed steak per portion, seasoning and oil.

Follow the instructions cooking to the desired degree.
Other suitable cuts: tournedos, fillets and rump steaks etc.

Lamb

Chops and cutlets (chops and côtelettes)

Allow 2–3 trimmed chops or cutlets per portion (100–150 g each), seasoning and oil.

Follow the instructions. Lamb cuts are usually cooked through with mutton being kept slightly underdone.
Other suitable cuts: noisettes and filets mignons etc.

Veal and pork

Chops and cutlets (chops and côtelettes)

Allow 200 g+ trimmed chop or cutlet per portion, seasoning and oil.

Follow the instructions, cooking the chops or cutlets through, especially pork cuts.
Other suitable cuts: escalopes and fillets.

Offal

Lamb/veal liver (foie d'agneau/de veau)

Allow 100 g+ trimmed sliced liver per portion, seasoning and oil.

Follow the instructions keeping the liver slightly underdone.

Lamb's kidneys (rognons d'agneau)

Allow 2 skinned and halved kidneys per portion, seasoning and oil.

Follow the instructions keeping the kidneys slightly underdone.

Made-up items

Hamburgers and bitokes

Allow 100 g+ hamburger or bitokes per portion, seasoning and oil.

Follow the instructions cooking the items through.

Dishes

Sauté (beef and lamb)

Prepare as stated in the base recipe and method garnishing to taste. Accompany with a suitable sauce, e.g. hollandaise.

Bohémienne (beef and lamb)

Place the cooked item on a bed of risotto and decorate the top with a little hot tomato concassé. Surround with a border of French fried onions.

Castillane (beef and lamb)

Dress the cooked items on fried bread croûtons and garnish with tartlets filled with hot tomato concassé. Surround with French fried onions.

Bonne-femme (veal)

Garnish the cooked chop or cutlet with lardons fried in butter, glazed button onions and cocotte potatoes. Sprinkle with chopped parsley.

Charcutière (pork)

Dress the chops on a bed of mashed potato and accompany with a sauceboat of sauce charcutière. Alternatively coat the chops with the sauce.

Fried liver and bacon (foie d'agneau/de veau au lard)

Garnish the cooked liver with slices of grilled or fried streaky bacon. Surround with a ribbon of jus lié and serve a sauceboat of jus lié separately.

ried kidneys and bacon (**rognons d'agneau/de veau au ard**)
Complete the cooked kidneys as above.

Hamburgers
Garnish with French fried onions and accompany with a uitable sauce, e.g. piquante, diable or lyonnaise.

Note: A fried egg is sometimes placed on each hamburger.

Bitokes à la russe
Coat the bitokes with sauce smitaine when serving. Serve a sauceboat of sauce smitaine separately.

Section three   Shallow-fried breaded items (paner)

Base method

Step 1	Mise en place A Assemble ingredients. B Pass the main item/s through the seasoned flour, eggwash and breadcrumbs. C Prepare any stated garnish or accompanying sauces.
Step 2	Heat the butter and oil in a frying pan or plat à sauter.
Step 3	Place the main item/s into the pan presentation side down and fry steadily.
Step 4	Turn over when approximately half cooked and when a good colour has been developed. Continue frying. *Note*: Regulate the speed of cooking to suit the thickness of the item, e.g. reduce the temperature for thick items – cutlets and suprêmes etc.
Step 5	When cooked, remove from the pan and drain well to remove surface fat.
Step 6	Place on the serving dish presentation side upwards.
Step 7	Neatly decorate the serving dish with any stated garnish. Also decorate the top of the main item if applicable, e.g. escalopes with lemon etc.
Step 8	Coat with a nut-brown butter when serving and accompany with any stated sauces.

Important points when shallow-frying breaded items

Step 1
Presentation side of breaded items: One side of the breaded item is usually marked with the back of a knife in a criss-cross fashion – this is the presentation side. Items like chicken suprêmes and joints of chicken have a presentation side – the outside surface.

Steps 3 and 4
Speed of cooking: See 'points when frying butcher meats'.
Note: The speed of cooking should never be so slow that the coating absorbs excessive grease and becomes soggy.
Step 5
Degree of cooking: Most items which are breaded are cooked through.

Step 5

Test for cooking: The pressure test to determine the absence of sponginess is possible with panéd items but this must be done carefully to avoid damaging the coating. Alternatively insert a cocktail stick or small skewer into the thickest part of the item on the underside – no resistance should be felt when inserting the stick. Alternatively, use a temperature probe.

Step 8

Service: Panéd items may be stored hot for *short period* during service but should not be covered with a tigh fitting lid.

Accompanying sauces: These should be served separate and *not coated over* the items as this softens the crisp coating.

Base recipe

Main item: See below.

Coating: Seasoned flour, eggwash and breadcrumbs.

Frying medium: Oil and butter.

Finishing butter: Nut-brown butter – optional.

Escalopes (pork, veal and turkey)
Allow 1–2 escalopes per portion (100 g flesh approximately).
   Follow the instructions.
Cooking time: 2½–3 mins. on each side.

Cutlets (côtelettes) (lamb and mutton)
Allow 2 cutlets per portion (100–150 g each).
   Follow the instructions.
Cooking time: 6–8 mins. on each side.

Suprême of chicken (suprême de volaille)
Allow 1 suprême per portion.
   Follow the instructions.
Cooking time: 6 mins. on each side approximately.

Veal sweetbreads (ris de veau)
Allow 2 medium sweetbreads per portion. Cook the sweetbreads as stated on page 212. When cooked, lightly press under a tray and allow to cool. If the sweetbreads are thick slice through the centre.
   Follow the instructions.
Cooking time: 2½–3 mins. on each side.

Dishes

Escalope de veau/porc

Cordon-bleu
Prepare 1 large escalope per portion and prior to coating place a slice of ham (Parma) and cheese (Gruyère) in the centre and fold inside.
Service: Garnish the escalope with 1–2 thin lemon slices and coat with the nut-brown butter. Also the dish is sometimes garnished with noisette potatoes and broccoli sprigs.

Holstein
Garnish the escalope with a fried egg, 2 criss-crossed anchovy fillets and 1–2 thin lemon slices. Coat with the nut-brown butter.

Milanaise
Neatly garnish the service dish with a small portion of spaghetti milanaise. Garnish the escalope with 1–2 thin lemon slices and coat with the nut-brown butter.

Napolitaine
Prepare the same as milanaise but using spaghetti napolitaine.

Viennoise
Garnish the serving dish with capers, sieved hard-boiled egg yolks, sieved hard-boiled egg whites, thin strips of anchovy fillets and chopped parsley – all arranged like a chevron (V-shaped strips). Decorate the escalope with 1–2 thin lemon slices and criss-crossed anchovy fillets. Coat with the nut-brown butter when serving.

Cutlets

Côtelettes d'agneau Reform
Add a little chopped ham to the breadcrumbs when coating the cutlets.
Service: Place the cutlets on a service dish surrounded with Reform garnish tossed in a little butter. Accompany with a sauceboat of Reform sauce (see page 177).
Reform garnish (3–4 portions):   25 g cooked ham, 25 g

ooked tongue, 25 g cooked egg white, 25 g gherkins, 25 g
ooked mushrooms, 25 g beetroot and 10 g truffle. All cut
nto thin strips.

suprême de volaille

Kiev

Cut a pocket in the suprême and stuff with butter prior to
coating with the breadcrumbs. Secure the pocket with
skewers or cocktail sticks.

Service: Dress the suprêmes on fried bread croûtons and
coat with nut-brown butter. A garnish of vegetable
macédoine tossed in butter and straw potatoes is also
sometimes used.

Maryland

Garnish the service dish with sweetcorn pancake (see page
262), grilled tomato, grilled rasher of streaky bacon, a
fried banana half (see page 269), deep-fried parsley and a
small croquette potato or straw potatoes. Coat the
suprême with nut-brown butter and accompany with
horseradish sauce.

Section four   Sautés of butcher meats, poultry, game and offal with a vehicle sauce

Base method for shallow-frying

The following instructions repeat the procedure given in Section two.

Step 1   Assemble ingredients and prepare the main item/s and any garnish or sauce.
Step 2   Heat the fat in a sauteuse or plat à sauter (1–2 mm in depth approximately).
Step 3   Season the main item/s and place into the pan. *Note:*   Pass escalopes, chicken pieces or suprêmes through flour before frying.
Step 4   Fry steadily until approximately half-way to the desired degree of cooking.
  Important: Cooking white – fry slowly avoiding any colour development. See recipe.
    Cooking brown – fry steadily developing colour. All beef, lamb and mutton dishes.
Step 5   Turn over and complete the cooking. *Note:*   Very small cuts are usually tossed.
Step 6   Remove from the pan and keep hot.

Base method for preparing the vehicle sauce

Step 1	Drain off excess fat from the cooking utensil.	
Step 2	*Preparing garnished sauces* Add any chopped shallots, onions, crushed garlic or pimentoes and sweat for 1 min. approximately.	*Finishing off ready-made sauces* Swill the pan with any wine or stock and reduce down by two-thirds.
Step 3	Add any spirit and flamber.	Add the prepared sauce and simmer for 2–3 mins.
Step 4	Add any mushrooms and sweat for 1 min. approximately.	
Step 5	Déglacer with any wine, lemon juice, fruit juice or vinegar and reduce down by two-thirds.	
Step 6	Add any tomato concassé. *Note:* Add at step 9 if a neat visible garnish is desired.	
Step 7	Add any cream and further reduce down by half. *Note:* If the sauce is to be based on cream, i.e. straight reduction sauce, see important points.	

Step 8	Add any jus lié, demi-glace or velouté and simmer for 1 min. approximately.
Step 9	Add any chopped herbs, e.g. parsley, chives or tarragon etc.
	Note: Add dried herbs at step 4.
Step 10	Check consistency, seasoning and temperature then blend through any enriching butter. Do not add butter to very small cuts at this stage, see below.
Step 11	*Service of individual items*: steaks, cutlets, escalopes and suprêmes etc. Place the main item on the serving dish and neatly decorate with any garnish. Coat with sauce and accompany with remaining sauce in a sauceboat. *Service of very small cuts*: bâtons and collops etc. Place the cooked items into the sauce and mix together. Correct the temperature then add any enriching butter. Place in an entrée dish and serve with any accompaniments, e.g. riz pilaff.

Important points when preparing the sauce for sauté dishes

Step 7

Straight reduction sauces: These are sauces which are prepared without any demi-glace, jus lié or velouté sauces being added. Cream is usually the base for these sauces and it must be reduced with great care until the correct consistency is attained — too little reducing will result in the sauce being thin with poor coating properties, too much reducing will produce a heavy greasy sauce with a clotted appearance.

Step 11

Function/call order service: When a large number of items are required at one time or alternatively various portions requested during a service period, the sauce may be made in advance and déglacéd into the cooking utensil as and when required.

Bringing together the cooked flesh and sauce: As indicated in the base method, the cooked flesh and the sauce are combined for service by either *coating with sauce*, e.g. tournedos, entrecôtes and noisettes, or *blending with sauce*, e.g. bâtons, small collops and sometimes chicken joints. When combining with the sauce it is important that the dish only receives enough heat treatment to correct the temperature for service. Prolonged heating of the cooked food in contact with the sauce may change the degree of cooking, toughen the flesh or produce a texture and taste similar to a stew and not a sauté. It is also important that 'carry-over cooking' be taken into account when frying and storing during sauce preparation; especially when items are ordered saignant, i.e. underdone.

Note: Some cooks complete the cooking of chicken in the sauce because it must be cooked through. When this is done the previous point on texture of the cooked flesh must be considered.

Base recipe

Main item:	See below.
Frying medium:	Oil, clarified butter or a mixture of butter and oil.
Sauce and garnish:	See the individual recipes below.

Entrecôte steaks (entrecôte)

Allow 200 g+ trimmed steak per portion.

Follow the instructions, cooking to the desired degree, and complete the sauce as stated.

Other suitable cuts: fillet steaks, rump steaks and médaillons etc.

Tournedos steaks (tournedos)

Allow 200 g+ trimmed and tied tournedos per portions (or 2 small tournedos)

Follow the instructions cooking to the desired degree and complete the sauce as stated.

Noisettes (lamb, veal and venison)

Allow 2–3 noisettes per portion (200 g flesh approximately).

Follow the instructions and complete the sauce as stated.

Note: Lamb cutlets are usually cooked through with mutton being kept slightly underdone.

Escalopes (veal, pork, turkey and venison)

Allow 1–2 escalopes per portion (100 g flesh approximately)

Note: Turkey and venison escalopes may be smaller – up to 3 per portion.

Follow the instructions cooking through veal, pork and turkey. Venison may be cooked slightly underdone. Complete the sauce as stated.

Cooking time: 1½–3 mins. on each side.

Chicken joints (cut for sauté, see page 68)

Allow 1 medium chicken (1½ kg approximately) per 4 portions. Follow the instructions cooking through the chicken and completing the sauce as stated.

Cooking time: 15–20 mins.

Suprême of chicken (suprême de volaille)

Allow 1 suprême per portion.

Follow the instructions cooking through the chicken and completing the sauce as stated.

Cooking time: 15–20 mins.

Lamb's kidneys (rognons d'agneau)

Allow 2 skinned and halved kidneys per portion.

Follow the instructions keeping the kidneys slightly underdone and completing the sauce as stated.

Cooking time: 5–8 mins.

Dishes for entrecôtes, fillet steaks, tournedos and noisettes etc   (4 portions)

Follow the instructions for *finishing off ready-made sauces and garnished sauces* where stated.

Beaugency (ready-made sauce)

Little oil for frying, 50 ml Madeira and 250 ml demi-glace. Place the items on fried bread croûtons and garnish the dish with 4 artichoke bottoms filled with tomato concassé and topped with slices of poached beef marrow.

Bordelaise (entrecôtes) (ready-made sauce)

Little oil for frying, 50 ml red wine and 250 ml bordelaise sauce (see page 177). Decorate the tops of the streaks with slices of poached beef marrow then coat with the sauce and sprinkle with chopped parsley.

Clermont (ready-made sauce)

Little oil for frying, 50 ml Madeira and 250 ml demi-glace. Garnish the dish with 4 small stuffed braised onions and 4 artichoke bottoms.

Niçoise (noisettes) (ready-made sauce)

Little oil for frying, 50 ml Madeira and 250 ml demi-glace. Place the noisettes on fried bread croûtons and garnish round the dish with 4 small cooked tomatoes, 4 château potatoes and buttered French beans (200 g approximately).

Rossini (tournedos) (ready-made sauce)

Little oil for frying, 50 ml Madeira, 250 ml demi-glace and 10 g butter for enriching.

Place the tournedos on fried croûtons then top with slices of foie gras which have been gently heated. Coat with the sauce and decorate each tournedos with a slice of truffle.

Boeuf Stroganoff (bâtons of fillets)

Follow the instructions for *garnished sauces*.

400–500 g beef fillet cut into bâtons, 40 g butter for frying, 25 g finely chopped shallots or onions, ½ clove of crushed garlic, 25 ml brandy, 10 ml lemon juice (¼ lemon), 350 ml cream, good pinch of chopped fresh tarragon (optional), chopped parsley and 10 g butter for enriching.

Prepare as a straight reduction sauce, see step 7, and serve as stated, for small cuts accompanied with riz pilaff.

Note: 50 ml veal or chicken velouté may be added at step 8 instead of preparing as a straight reduction sauce.

Balmoral (entrecôte)

Follow the instructions for *garnished sauces*.

Little oil for frying, 20 g finely chopped shallot or onion, 25 ml whisky, 350 ml cream and 10 g enriching butter.

Prepare as a straight reduction sauce.

Spread a duxelles on top of the steaks then decorate with turned mushrooms. Garnish round the dish with skinned tomato cases filled with asparagus spruce. Coat the steak with the sauce, sprinkle with a little grated Dunlop cheese and gratinate.

Dishes for escalopes, médaillons and piccatas

Follow the instructions for *garnished sauces* for all dishes.

A la crème (white)

40 g butter for frying, 20 g finely chopped shallot or onion, 25 ml sherry, 350 ml cream and 10 g butter for enriching.

Also add a pinch of cayenne pepper when seasoning. Prepare as a straight reduction sauce, see step 7.
Note: 50 ml veal or chicken velouté may be added at step 8 instead of preparing as a straight reduction sauce.

Hongroise (white)
40 g butter for frying, 50 g finely chopped shallot or onion, 5 g paprika (added after step 2), 50 ml white wine, 50 ml cream, 350 ml chicken or veal velouté and 10 g enriching butter.
Note: Tomato concassé is sometimes added (add 100 g approximately).

Valentino
40 g butter for frying, 20 g finely chopped shallots or onions, 50 g sliced mushrooms, 50 ml cream and 350 ml tomato sauce.
After coating with sauce sprinkle with 50 g grated Gruyère and gratinate under a salamander. Decorate the top of each escalope with 2–3 hot asparagus tips.

Au madère, porto and xérès
40 g butter for frying, 20 g finely chopped shallots or onion, 50 ml Madeira, port or sherry, 350 ml jus lié and 10 g enriching butter.

Marsala
As above using Marsala wine.

Dishes for chicken sauté, chicken suprêmes and turkey escalopes

Follow the instructions for *garnished sauces* for all dishes.

A la crème (white)
See escalope à la crème.

Bagatelle (white)
Prepare as à la crème and garnish the serving dish with glazed carrots (200 g approximately) and hot asparagus tips.

Hongroise (white)
See escalopes hongroise.

Sarah Claire (white) (Scottish)
Cut a pocket in four chicken suprêmes and stuff with raw peeled banana. Secure with cocktail sticks or small skewers. Complete as à la crème then dress the suprêmes on a bed of riz pilaff.

Aux champignons
20 g butter and 20 ml oil for frying, 25 g finely chopped shallots or onion, 50 ml white wine, 100 g sliced mushrooms, 350 ml demi-glace and a good pinch of chopped parsley.

Chasseur
Prepare the same as aux champignons above but add 100 g

of raw tomato concassé and a little chopped tarragon and chervil with the chopped parsley.
Note: Some recipes include brandy (25 ml). Heart-shaped croûtons fried in butter and with the ends dipped in chopped parsley are also sometimes used as a garnish.

Cacciatore
Prepare the same as chasseur replacing the white wine with Chianti.

Romaine
20 g butter and 20 ml oil for frying, 25 g finely chopped shallot or onion, 100 ml Asti wine and 350 ml demi-glace. Dress on a bed of buttered leaf spinach arranged neatly on the service dish.

Dishes for lamb's kidneys

Follow the instructions for *garnished sauces* for all dishes.

Rognons d'agneau sautés
20 g butter and 20 ml oil for frying, 20 g finely chopped shallot or onion, 25 ml sherry, 300 ml demi-glace and a little cayenne pepper to be added with the seasoning. Serve as stated for small cuts or items.

Rognons d'agneau Turbigo
Prepare as above but replace the sherry with 50 ml white wine and add 100 g quartered mushrooms. Also add 8 small cooked chipolata sausages at step 11. Garnish round the dish with heart-shaped croûtons fried in butter.

Section five Shallow-fried vegetables and fruits

Base method

Step 1	Mise en place
	A Assemble ingredients.
	B Prepare the main item:
	Mushrooms: Remove or trim the stalks and wash to remove any dirt. Cut any large mushrooms into suitable pieces.
	Cèpes and morilles: Treat as mushrooms above taking care to remove any grit from the honeycomb section of morilles.
	Onions: Peel and wash the onions. Cut into halves from top to bottom then trim off the root and top ends. Cut lengthwise into thin slices.
	Tomatoes: Wash the tomatoes and remove the eyes. Cut into halves or leave whole if small.
	Apples: Wash, peel and core the apples. Cut into neat rings 10 mm in thickness approximately.
	Bananas: Peel and trim the ends of the banana. Remove any strings and divide into half, cutting at a slant.
	Peaches: Blanch and skin then cut into half and remove the stone.
	Pineapple: Remove the skin then cut into neat rings (10 mm in thickness approximately). Cut out the centre stalk from each ring.
	C Prepare any other ingredients stated in the individual recipe.

Step 2	Heat the butter in a frying pan or plat à sauter.

Step 3	*Vegetables*	*Fruits* (except tomatoes) Pass the fruit through flour.

Step 4	Place into the hot butter and fry steadily allowing colour to develop.

Step 5	Turn over and complete the cooking.
	Note: Mushrooms and onions are usually tossed in the pan during frying (or onions sometimes stirred) whereas fruits, including tomatoes, are carefully turned with a palette knife.

Step 6	Add seasoning.

Step 7	Remove from the pan and place on to the serving dish.

Base recipe

Main item:	See individual recipes below.
Frying medium:	30 g butter or margarine or oil and butter.

Mushrooms

Allow 50–75 g mushrooms per portion.
   Follow the instructions.
Cooking time: 4–6 mins.
Also applicable to cèpes and morilles.

Fried mushrooms (champignons sautés)

Cook as stated and sprinkle with chopped parsley when serving.

Champignons bordelaise

Add 25 g finely chopped shallots to the pan prior to adding the mushrooms. Add a squeeze of lemon juice on completion of cooking and sprinkle with chopped parsley.

Champignons provençale

Same as bordelaise adding a little crushed garlic with the onions.

Stuffed mushrooms (champignons farcis)

Select 4–5 of the largest mushrooms and remove the centre stalks. Cook the mushrooms as stated keeping a little underdone then place on a tray underside uppermost. Meanwhile prepare a duxelles with the stalks and remaining mushrooms (see page 274) then use as a stuffing for the cooked mushrooms. Sprinkle with a little melted butter and a few breadcrumbs then heat through and gratinate in a hot oven.

A la crème

Prepare as sautés reducing the butter to 20 g and *avoiding any colour development*. When almost cooked add 30–50 ml cream and reduce to a coating consistency. Sprinkle with chopped parsley.

Onions

Allow 150–200 g onions per portion.
   Follow the instructions.
Cooking time: 6–8 mins.

Oignons sautés

Prepare as stated sprinkling with chopped parsley when serving.

Tomatoes

Allow 1–2 medium tomatoes per portion.
   Follow the instructions.
Cooking time: 2–4 mins.

Tomates sautées

Prepare as stated. Sprinkle with chopped parsley.

Apples (savoury dish garnish)

Allow 1–2 slices (10 mm approximately) per portion of main item.
   Follow the instructions.
Cooking time: 2–3 mins.

Bananas (savoury dish garnish)

Allow half a banana per portion of main item.
   Follow the instructions.
Cooking time: 2–3 mins.

Peaches (savoury dish garnish)

Allow half a peach per portion of main item.
   Follow the instructions.
Cooking time: 2–3 mins.

Pineapple (savoury dish garnish)

Allow 1–2 pineapple rings per portion of main dish.
   Follow the instructions.
Cooking time: 2–3 mins.

Section six Sweated vegetables and vegetable stews

Base method for cooking a single vegetable

Step 1	Mise en place

      A Assemble ingredients.
      B Prepare the vegetable:
         Aubergines: Peel* and cut into slices (5 mm approximately). Halve very thick aubergines prior to slicing.
         Courgettes: Peel* then cut into regular-sized shapes. Small courgettes may be left whole.
         Cucumber: Peel*, cut into regular-sized pieces (50 mm length) then halve and remove seeds. May be turned into barrel shapes.
         Peppers (capsicums): Cut the peppers in half, remove stalk then withdraw the seeds. Cut into thick strips or squares.
      C Prepare any other stated vegetable or accompaniment in the individual recipe.

Step 2	Melt the butter, margarine or oil in a saucepan then add the prepared vegetable.
Step 3	Slowly sweat occasionally stirring or tossing the vegetable.
Step 4	When cooked lightly season with salt and pepper.

* Nowadays the skins are often left on the vegetable to supply roughage in the diet.

Base method for cooking a combination of vegetables

Step 1	Mise en place

      A Assemble ingredients.
      B Prepare the vegetables, see above.
      C Prepare any accompaniment stated in the individual recipe.

Step 2	Melt the butter, margarine or oil in a saucepan then add any onion or crushed garlic and sweat for 2–3 mins.
Step 3	Add pimentos if stated and sweat for a further 2–3 mins.
Step 4	Add any aubergines, courgettes and cucumber and continue sweating for 6–8 mins. Complete the cooking if there are no tomatoes to be added.
Step 5	Add any tomato concassé and complete the cooking. Check the seasoning.
Step 6	Place in serving dish and sprinkle with chopped parsley.

Important points when sweating vegetables

Steps 2, 3 and 4

The speed of sweating a vegetable or combination of vegetables is related to the types of vegetable involved in the process. Thick pieces of vegetable or turned vegetables must be *sweated very slowly* or they are likely to burn. The lid of the cooking utensil is an aid to cooking because it traps steam. Also liquids such as cream may be added near the end of the cooking process, this acting as a further aid to cooking.

Important: This method of cooking is ideal for small quantities of vegetables but is less suitable for large quantities, especially when there are no high water-containing vegetables in the recipe, e.g. tomatoes. Vegetables such as cucumbers and courgettes are sometimes blanched before sweating to reduce the cooking time and risk of burning. A suitable method for cooking large quantities of these vegetables is given on page 130.

Vegetable stews (e.g. ratatouille): An alternative method for producing these stews is to sweat the vegetables *separately* until cooked then combine them. If tomatoes are in the recipe they are added and cooking completed. Many cooks state this procedure produces the finest vegetable dishes but it is not practicable in most situations.

Dishes (4 portions)

Buttered aubergines (aubergines sautées au beurre)
40 g butter, 2 small aubergines and salt and pepper.
　Follow the instructions, sprinkling with a little chopped parsley when cooked.
Cooking time: 15 mins. approximately.

Aubergines with cream (aubergines à la crème)
Prepare as buttered aubergines but reduce the butter to 25 g and add 50 ml cream just prior to completing the cooking.

Buttered courgettes (courgettes sautées au beurre)
40 g butter, 400 g courgettes and salt and pepper.
　Follow the instructions sprinkling with a little chopped parsley when cooked.
Cooking time: 15–20 mins.

Courgettes à la crème
Prepare as buttered courgettes but reduce the butter to 25 g and add 50 ml cream just prior to completing the cooking.

Courgettes provençale
25 g butter, 50 g chopped onion, ½ clove crushed garlic, 400 g courgettes, 250 g raw tomato concassé, salt and pepper and chopped parsley.

Follow the instructions for cooking a combination of vegetables.
Cooking time: 15–20 mins.

Cucumbers sautéd in butter (concombres sautés au beurre)
40 g butter, 500 g cucumber and salt and pepper.
　Follow the instructions sprinkling with a little chopped parsley when cooked.
Cooking time: 8–10 mins.

Concombres à la crème
Prepare as buttered cucumber but reduce the butter to 25 g and add 50 ml cream just prior to completing cooking.

Concombres provençale
Prepare as courgettes provençale above.

Peppers sautéd in butter (Poivrons sautés au beurre)
40 g butter, 4 medium peppers (75–100 g each) and salt and pepper.
　Follow the instructions sprinkling with a little chopped parsley when cooked.
Cooking time: 8 mins approximately.

Poivrons provençale
Prepare as courgettes provençale above.

Ratatouille
50 ml oil, 100 g sliced onions, ½ clove crushed garlic, 50 g diced pimento, 200 g sliced courgettes, 150 g sliced aubergines and 200 g raw tomato concassé.
　Follow the instructions for cooking a combination of vegetables.
Cooking time: 20–25 mins.

Peperonata (Italian)
20 g butter, 20 ml oil, 100 g sliced onions, ½ clove crushed garlic, 4 medium peppers (50–75 g each) and 200 g raw tomato concassé. Season with salt, pepper and mill pepper.
　Follow the instructions for cooking a combination of vegetables.
Cooking time: 20 mins. approximately.

Brinjal bartha (Indian)
40 g ghee or oil, 150 g roughly chopped onions, 5 g grated root ginger (1½ teaspoons), 5 g garam marsala (1½ teaspoons), 2½ g red chilli powder (½ teaspoon), 5 g turmeric, 2 small aubergines, 100 g raw tomato concassé and salt and pepper.
　Follow the instructions adding the spices after step 2. Cook out to a purée.
Cooking time: 45 mins. approximately.
Served with chapatis and nan bread.

Stuffed aubergines (aubergines farcies)

Base method

Step 1	Mise en place
	A Assemble ingredients.
	B Prepare the aubergines:
	1 Cut off the stalk at the end, then halve.
	2 Criss-cross the flesh with incisions using the point of a knife.
	3 Brush with melted butter or oil then cook in a moderate oven until the flesh softens.
	4 Carefully scoop out the flesh leaving the skin as a shell.
Step 2	Finely chop the flesh then mix together with the duxelles, tomato concassé, chopped parsley and seasoning.
Step 3	Fill the skins with the mixture, sprinkle with the breadcrumbs and a little melted butter. Place in an oven to heat through.
Step 4	Gratinate under the salamander and serve on a salver, vegetable dish or entrée dish. *Optional*: Serve a ribbon of jus lié or demi-glace around the aubergines.

Base recipe   (yield 4 portions)

Main item:	2 small aubergines.
Duxelles:	100 g dry duxelles.
Tomato concassé:	100 g raw tomato concassé.
Seasoning:	Salt and pepper.
Chopped parsley:	A little chopped parsley.
Gratinating:	10 g butter and 40 g breadcrumbs.

Aubergines provençale
Prepare as above but add a small clove of crushed garlic to the duxelles when frying the onion. Also pour a ribbon of tomato sauce around the aubergines.

Aubergines italienne
Prepare as stated but add 40 g finely chopped cooked ham to the filling. Pour a ribbon of sauce italienne around the aubergines.

Aubergines turque
Prepare as stated adding 40 g diced cooked mutton and 20 g cooked rice to the filling. Pour a ribbon of tomato sauce around the aubergines.

Skirlie

This is an oatmeal stuffing which may be served with roast game, minced beef, stews or as a stuffing for vegetables.

Method

Step 1	Melt the fat in a saucepan then add the onion and fry until golden brown.
Step 2	Add the oatmeal which should absorb the fat and sweat, stirring occasionally, for 10 mins. approximately. Season with salt and pepper.

Base recipe (yield 250 g)

Main item:	100 g finely chopped onion.
Frying medium:	50 g suet or dripping.
Oatmeal:	100 g oatmeal.

Tomato concassé and fresh tomato purée

Tomato concassé (tomates concassées)

Base method (yield 200 g)

Step 1	Mise en place
	
	A Assemble ingredients.
	B Prepare *raw tomato concassé*:
	  1 Remove the eyes from the tomatoes, place into a basket and immerse in boiling water.
	  2 Test after 5 seconds to remove skin, if not, replace and test 3–4 seconds later.
	  3 Plunge into cold water and allow to cool.
	  4 Peel off the skins, halve the tomatoes and remove the seeds.
	  5 Roughly chop into large pieces (10–15 mm pieces).

Step 2	Heat the butter or oil in a sauteuse then add the shallot and sweat for 2–3 mins.
Step 3	Add the raw concassé, lightly season then toss in the hot fat and shallots until heated.

Base recipe (yield 200 g approximately)

Main item:	400 g tomatoes.
Frying medium:	25 g buter or oil.
Base vegetable:	25 g finely chopped shallot or onion.
Seasoning:	Salt and pepper.

Provençale

This is a fondue of tomatoes highly flavoured with garlic. Prepare as tomato concassé but add a crushed clove of garlic when sweating the shallots and cook the mixture until surface liquid has evaporated.

Fresh tomato purée

Prepare as tomato concassé but continue the cooking until a fine mass or purée is obtained.

Duxelles   (also known as dry duxelles)

Base method

Step 1	Mise en place
	A Assemble ingredients.
	B Wash the mushrooms, squeeze out excess liquid then finely chop. Squeeze the mushrooms a second time to remove any further liquid.

↓

Step 2	Melt the butter in a sauteuse and add the shallot or onions then sweat for 2–3 mins.

↓

Step 3	Add the mushrooms, lightly season then sweat until cooked, stirring as required, 3–4 mins. Cook until a fairly dry mass is obtained.

Base recipe   (yield 100 g)

Main item:	100 g mushrooms.
Frying medium:	10 g butter.
Base vegetable:	25 g finely chopped shallot or onion.
Seasoning:	Salt and pepper.

Duxelles au vin

Add a ½ clove of garlic to the onions when sweating, then add 50 ml white wine and reduce down prior to adding the mushrooms. Finish off the duxelles with 50 ml demi-glace and 50 g white breadcrumbs and continue cooking until a smooth purée is obtained.

ection seven   Sauté potatoes

ase method

tep 1	Mise en place
	A Assemble ingredients.
	B Prepare the potatoes:
	1 Wash and scrub the potatoes.
	2 Boil until just cooked.
	3 Drain and allow to cool and peel off skins while still warm if possible.
	4 Cut into *slices*, 3–5 mm in thickness.
	C Prepare any garnish or additional ingredients required in the individual recipe.
tep 2	Heat the fat until quite hot in a frying pan.
tep 3	Add the potatoes and fry quickly to develop colour. Avoid tossing or turning until the potato surfaces are set crisp and colour developed.
tep 4	Toss the potatoes occasionally allowing colour to develop on all sides.
tep 5	Add any garnish and toss through the potatoes.
tep 6	Add seasoning, place on serving dish and sprinkle with chopped parsley.

ase recipe   (yield 4 portions)

lain item:	500 g potatoes (firm cooking variety).
rying medium:	30 g lard or dripping.
easoning:	Salt and pepper.
arsley:	Chopped parsley.

Sauté potatoes (pommes sautées)
Prepare and cook as stated in the base recipe and method.

Sauté potatoes with onions (pommes lyonnaise)
Peel and slice 250 g onions then sauté in butter (20 g approximately). Toss through the potatoes at step 5.
Note: This will yield 4–6 portions. The onion weight usually varies between one-third to one-half the weight of the potatoes.

Pommes allemande
Add 25–50 g butter to the frying pan after browning the potatoes. Allow the butter to heat and foam in a space at the top centre of the pan then toss the butter and potatoes together.
Note: These potatoes are usually cut a little thicker than plain sauté potatoes, i.e. 7 mm approximately.

Pommes O'Brien
Add 25–50 g diced cooked pimentos at step 5.

Pommes provençale
Add 15 g butter to the frying pan after browning the potatoes and when foaming add 1 clove of crushed garlic. Toss the foaming garlic butter through the potatoes.

Section eight   Rissolé potatoes (pommes rissolées)

These are cooked potatoes which are shallow-fried in hot fat until crisp and golden brown. Prior to frying the potatoes are turned (30 mm approximately) then plain boiled. This term is also applied to roast potatoes of the same size.

Section nine   Savouries using shallow-fried items

Mushrooms on toast

Champignons sur croûte.

Soft roes on toast

Laitances sur croûte.

Canapé Quo-Vadis
Fried mushrooms and fried soft roes on toast.

Canapé Nina
Fried mushrooms and slices of fried tomato dressed on toast and topped with pickled walnuts.

Section ten   Fried eggs

There are two main types of fried egg:
1   Plain fried eggs (oeufs frits):   This is the plain fried egg which is very popular at breakfast time.
2   French fried eggs (oeufs frits à la française):   This egg is less common than the plain fried egg although many traditional cookery books when referring to fried eggs mean this egg and not the plain fried egg. Strictly speaking, the French fried egg is not shallow-fried but it is included in this section because it is usually pan-fried.

Plain fried eggs
Base method

Step 1	Mise en place Assemble ingredients.
Step 2	Place the butter or oil in the pan and heat gently.
Step 3	Break the egg/s into the pan carefully and fry slowly until the white is set but the yolk is still soft (unless otherwise requested).
Step 4	Carefully remove from the pan with a fish slice and drain well to remove surface fat.

French fried eggs
Base method

Step 1	Mise en place Assemble ingredients.
Step 2	Pour oil into a small frying pan to a depth of 20 mm approximately and heat until quite hot.
Step 3	Break an egg on to a plate then lightly season.
Step 4	Slide the egg off the plate into the hot oil and as the egg spurts quickly flip the white around the yolk with two wooden spoons until the white completely surrounds the yolk. *Note*: The egg is ready when it is smooth and oval in shape and light golden-brown in colour (with a soft yolk).
Step 5	Remove from the pan and drain carefully.

Base recipe

Main item:	1–2 eggs per portion.
Seasoning:	Salt and pepper.
Frying medium:	Butter, clarified butter or oil.

Section eleven   Pan cooking: omelettes

The various omelettes may be grouped as follows:

Folded omelettes: Plain omelette and omelettes with a garnish mixed through the eggs.
Folded omelettes: Omelettes which are stuffed with garnish – omelettes fourrées.
Flat omelettes
Sweet omelettes
Soufflé omelettes

Base method for flat and folded omelettes

Step 1	Mise en place
	A Assemble ingredients.
	B Prepare any garnish.
	C Prepare the pan, i.e. ensure the pan is clean – wipe with a clean dry cloth if required.
	D Prepare the serving dish, i.e. lightly butter the base and keep warm.
Step 2	Break the eggs into a small bowl, add the seasoning (or sugar) and beat well with a fork until the yolks and whites are thoroughly combined – no streaks of white should be present.
Step 3	Heat the omelette pan then proceed as follows:
	Using butter: Add the butter to the pan and continue heating until the butter foams. Shake the pan to disperse the butter over the base of the pan but do not allow the butter to colour.
	Using clarified butter or oil: Add enough clarified butter or oil to barely cover the base of the pan and continue heating for a short period. Pour off surplus butter or oil. *Do not allow to become very hot* and smoke as this will increase the likelihood of sticking.
Step 4	Pour the eggs into the pan then shake the pan while stirring the eggs with a fork until a smooth, very lightly set mixture is obtained.
Step 5	Remove from the heat and loosen the outer edges of the egg by running the fork round between the egg and the pan.

Step 6	*Folded omelettes*	*Flat omelettes*
	Tilt the pan and fold one end of the egg (end at the handle) to the centre.	Brush round the edges of the pan down to the egg with a little melted butter or oil.
Step 7	Tap the handle or bottom of the pan to move the mixture to the edge of the pan then fold over the other end to resemble a cigar shape.	Tap the pan and shake with a circular motion until the mixture slides freely.

| Step 8 | Turn out on to the serving dish and neaten the shape if required. | Bring the mixture to the bottom of the pan opposite the handle then toss over on to the other side. Lightly cook then slide carefully on to the serving dish. |
| Step 9 | Brush òver the surface of the omelette with a little melted butter to produce a light shine and attractive appearance. | |

Base method for soufflé omelettes

Step 1	Mise en place
	See ordinary omelettes across the page.
Step 2	Separate the yolks from the whites.
Step 3	Place the yolks into a small bowl and beat through any seasoning.
Step 4	Place the whites into a scalded mixing bowl, add any sugar (sweet omelettes) and whisk to a stiff snow.
Step 5	Fold the yolks through the whites until completely combined.
Step 6	Add the mixture into the prepared pan (see ordinary omelettes) and place into a moderate oven or under a salamander to cook. *Do not stir.*
Step 7	Allow to cook until very lightly set then carefully fold and serve immediately.
	Note: The omelette must not be allowed to cook through as it will tear or split when folding.

Important points when preparing omelettes

Step 1

Using an omelette pan: An omelette pan is made of heavy iron with a very smooth frying surface which must be treated with great care. It must never be used for any purpose other than that of making omelettes (with the exception of frying eggs). Also an omelette pan *must never be washed* but should be wiped clean with a dry cloth immediately after use.

Skinning or seasoning an omelette pan: At frequent intervals the surface of the pan should be treated as follows:

(a) Place a good layer of salt into the pan and heat gently.
(b) Rub the salt across the base of the pan with a dry cloth to remove any burnt particles or carbon.
(c) Discard the salt and wipe clean.
(d) Pour clean oil into the pan and leave at the side of the stove on a gentle heat for 10–15 mins.
(e) Pour off the oil and use when required.

Step 4

Speed of cooking: The temperature of the pan into which the eggs are added is a crucial factor when preparing omelettes; a pan which is too hot or too cool is likely to cause the egg to stick to the base of the pan. The foaming point of butter and the temperature just short of the smoke point of most oils is a good guide as to when to add the eggs. Experience of time and temperature together with the noise made when the egg enters the pan (audible sizzle but not too pronounced) are all guides to the cooking of a good omelette.

Stirring and shaking the mixture: The mixture must be shaken and stirred quickly and evenly across the base of the pan, especially where the eggs can be seen to be setting. A smooth, slightly congealed mass should be formed as the mixture is stirred. When to stop stirring is extremely important – *stirring must stop immediately the egg is on setting point but not set*. Stirring after setting point will cause wrinkles and blemishes on the skin of the omelette. Some cooks make very little use of a fork but shake the pan quickly. This procedure takes more practice than the fork method but is suitable for the preparation of large numbers of omelettes; once mastered, up to four omelettes at a time can be produced by this method.

Degree of cooking: Omelettes are served with the egg very lightly set unless otherwise requested. Sometimes omelettes are ordered underdone with a slightly runny centre. The term for an underdone omelette is 'baveuse'.

Steps 6 and 7

Shaping the omelette: Traditionally folded omelettes are prepared 'cigar shaped' although some cooks, when preparing large numbers of omelettes, fold the omelettes half-moon shape (this is not considered correct practice by many cooks).

Step 8

Tossing flat omelettes: This requires practice and confidence. As indicated in the base method the sides of the pan should be oiled to allow the omelette to move freely during the tossing action. The omelette is flipped over with a forward and then backward movement.

A simpler way of completing a flat omelette is to cook the top surface *under a salamander* rather than toss it over.

Step 9

Service: Omelettes should be prepared when required for service.

Note: An omelette can be prepared in advance and reheated in a microwave oven provided it is initially cooked slightly underdone.

A good omelette should be lightly set with a completely smooth surface. Some cooks prefer no colour on the surface of the omelette.

Soufflé omelettes: Many of the above points on production do not apply to soufflé omelettes. These omelettes are cooked without stirring to a light golden colour. Like ordinary omelettes they may be sweet or savoury.

Base recipe for all omelettes

Main item:	2–3 eggs.
Frying medium:	10 g butter, clarified butter or oil.
Savoury omelette:	Pinch salt and pepper.
Sweet omelette:	Good pinch of sugar (5 g approximately) and a small pinch of salt.

Folded omelettes   (yield 1 portion)

Plain omelette (omelette nature)
Prepare as stated.

Bacon omelette (omelette au lard)
Mix through the beaten eggs a small dice of cooked bacon (30 g approximately) and proceed as stated.
Optional: Garnish the omelette with a grilled bacon rasher.

Cheese omelette (omelette au fromage)
Mix 20 g grated parmesan (1 dessertspoon) through the beaten eggs and proceed as stated.
Note: When softer cheeses, e.g. cheddar or cheshire etc., are used it is advisable to add the grated cheese just prior to folding the omelette. This is because the fat content will result in a less desirable finish when the cheese is beaten through the egg.

Ham omelette (omelette au jambon)
Mix through the beaten eggs a small dice of cooked ham (30–50 g) and proceed as stated.

Mushroom omelette (omelette aux champignons)
Mix through the beaten eggs sliced mushrooms which have been sautéd in a little butter (30–50 g mushrooms), then proceed as stated.
Note: The mushrooms may be sautéd in the omelette pan prior to adding the eggs.

Onion omelette (omelette aux oignons)
Mix through the beaten eggs sliced onions which have been sautéed in a little butter (40–50 g onions) then proceed as stated.

Potato omelette (omelette Parmentier)
Mix through the beaten eggs a small dice of cooked potato (50 g potato approximately, fried until brown in a little fat) then proceed as stated.

Savoury omelette (omelette aux fines herbes)
Add a good pinch of chopped parsley, chives and chervil to the beaten eggs and proceed as stated.

Omelette bonne-femme
Add to the beaten eggs, sliced sautéed onions, mushrooms and a small dice of fried bacon then proceed as stated.

Omelette grand-mère
Add to the beaten eggs a good pinch of chopped parsley and a small dice of bread (25 g approximately) fried crisp in a little butter then proceed as stated.

Folded omelettes incorporating a stuffed garnish

Omelettes are stuffed with garnish in two ways:

A   The garnish is placed on the centre of the omelette (after step 5) then folded neatly inside as the omelette is shaped.

Examples
Chicken omelette (omelette à la reine)
Stuff the omelette with a cream chicken mixture using 40 g cooked minced chicken heated and bound with a little chicken velouté.

Omelette Agnès-Sorel
Prepare as chicken omelette adding 10 g cooked sliced mushrooms to the chicken mixture. Decorate the top of the omelette with slices of hot tongue and surround with a ribbon of jus lié.

B   The omelette is prepared as a plain omelette then split along the top after placing on the serving dish. The split is then filled with the garnish.

Examples
Kidney omelette (omelette aux rognons)
Cut half a lamb's kidney into small dice then sauté in a little butter until almost cooked. Bind the kidney with a spoonful (50 ml approximately) of demi-glace or jus lié and correct the seasoning. Fill the cavity of the omelette with the garnish and sprinkle with chopped parsley.

Seafood omelette
Prawn, scampi, crab or lobster etc. Prepare the stuffing using 30–40 g cooked, shelled, shellfish. Leave small shellfish whole but cut large shellfish into a neat dice. Heat in a little butter then bind with a spoonful of tomato sauce and a teaspoon of cream (5 ml). Correct the temperature and seasoning adding a pinch of cayenne pepper. Fill the cavity of the omelette.

Tomato omelette (omelette aux tomates)
Stuff the omelette with hot tomato concassé (50 g approximately, see page 273) then sprinkle with chopped parsley. A sauceboat of tomato sauce may be served separately.

Flat omelettes

Examples
Spanish omelette (omelette espagnole)
Add to the beaten eggs, 50 g finely sliced onions and 25 g diced pimento both cooked in a little butter, 40 g raw tomato concassé and a good pinch of chopped parsley.

Omelette fermière
Add to the beaten eggs, 50 g cooked ham cut into a fine dice and a good pinch of chopped parsley.

Omelette paysanne
Add to the beaten eggs a small dice of cooked lean bacon (30 g), a small dice of cooked potato (30 g, see potato omelette), finely sliced onions (30 g) cooked in a little butter and a good pinch of chervil. *Note:*   A small quantity of sorrel which has been cut into fine shreds and sweated in a little butter should also be added if available.

Sweet omelettes

Jam omelette (omelette à la confiture)
This is a folded omelette. Prepare the omelette adding a good spoonful of warmed raspberry jam to the centre of the egg (after step 5) then fold carefully inside. Sprinkle over the top of the omelette with caster sugar then brand a criss-cross pattern on the surface with a hot poker.

Soufflé omelettes (omelettes soufflés)
Most of the garnishes for ordinary omelettes are suitable for soufflé omelettes. However, these omelettes should not be split along the top. When preparing a sweet soufflé omelette, the sugar content may be increased to 20 g approximately.

Section twelve   Pan cooking: scrambled eggs

Base method

Step 1	Mise en place A Assemble ingredients. B Prepare any garnish or sauce.	
Step 2	Break the eggs into a bowl, add the seasoning then whisk together to combine the whites and yolks.	
Step 3	*English-style scrambled eggs* Add the milk and whisk to combine with the eggs.	*French-style scrambled eggs*
Step 4	Heat the butter in a saucepan then add the eggs or eggs and milk.	
Step 5	Place the saucepan in a bain-marie or over a low heat and stir occasionally until the mixture becomes a smooth lightly set mass.	Stir the eggs *continuously* over a moderate heat until a fine mass is obtained.
Step 6	Remove from the heat and stir through the remaining butter.	
Step 7	Check the seasoning then blend through the cream.	

Important points when preparing scrambled eggs

Step 5
Stirring the mixture: The mixture must be stirred
sufficiently to produce a fine mass. Insufficient stirring
will result in the eggs being coarse, lumpy and tough
(particularly for French scrambled eggs).
Step 5
Degree of cooking: The eggs must be removed from the
heat as soon as lightly set. The eggs will coagulate slowly at
first until the overall temperature reaches a stage where
total coagulation results – after this point the consistency
and texture change rapidly. If the eggs are overcooked
they become tough and may show sign of surface water. In
addition iron and sulphur compounds will cause
discoloration.
Step 7
Service: French scrambled eggs must be prepared,
cooked and served as requested. English scrambled eggs
may be stored hot for short periods in a bain-marie.

French-style scrambled eggs (oeufs brouillés)

Base recipe (4 portions)

Main item:	400 ml eggs (8 eggs approximately).
Butter:	40 g butter or margarine.
Seasoning:	Salt and pepper.
Cream (optional):	20 ml cream.

English-style scrambled eggs

Base recipe (4 portions)

As above but using 200 ml egg (4 eggs) and 200 ml milk as the main items.

Scrambled eggs with herbs (oeufs brouillés aux fines herbes)

Add freshly chopped herbs, e.g. parsley, chervil, chives and tarragon at step 6.

Scrambled eggs with mushrooms (oeufs brouillés aux champignons)

Sweat 150–200 g washed, sliced mushrooms in 10 g butter then add enough demi-glace or jus lié to bind the mushrooms. Correct seasoning and consistency then dress the mushrooms along the top of the eggs when serving.

Scrambled eggs with tomatoes

Dress hot tomato concassé (250 g approximately, see page 273) neatly along the top of the eggs when serving and sprinkle with chopped parsley.

Piperade

When preparing the eggs sweat 50 g finely chopped onions and 200 g pimento in the recipe butter, step 4. When the eggs are almost cooked add 200 g raw tomato concassé. Sprinkle with chopped parsley when serving.

Scotch woodcock (savoury)

Prepare the scrambled eggs using half the recipe quantities and 4 rectangles of toast spread with butter. Spread the eggs on to the toast shapes then neatly decorate each shape with 2 criss-crossed anchovy fillets and 4 capers. Serve on a dishpaper.

Section thirteen   Pan cooking: crêpes and pancakes

Base method

Step 1	Mise en place
	A Assemble ingredients.
	B Prepare the batter – the preparation of batters is explained in detail on page 321.
	1 Sieve together the flour and pinch of salt.
	2 Add the egg and half the quantity of milk and mix to a smooth paste.
	3 Add most of the remaining milk and mix to a smooth thin batter.
	4 Correct the consistency to produce a thin batter (similar to single cream).
	5 Melt the butter and whisk into the batter until completely combined.
	C Prepare any garnish or sauce.
Step 2	Heat the pan adding a little of the oil. When hot pour off the surplus oil.
Step 3	Add only enough batter to form a thin coating on the base of the pan.
Step 4	Tilt the pan to spread the batter evenly across the base of the pan. If there is a small quantity of surplus batter allow it to coat the sides of the pan.
Step 5	Cook until golden-brown (1 min. approximately). To determine the degree of cooking, ease one edge of the crêpe away from the pan with a palette knife and inspect the cooked side.
Step 6	Turn the crêpe over and cook the other side. *Note*: Traditionally pancakes are tossed on to the other side but the use of a palette knife is quicker and more efficient.
Step 7	Turn the crêpe out of the pan on to a large plate. This is done by turning the crêpe out on to the palm of the hand then quickly placing on to the plate. Cover with a second plate and keep hot.
Step 8	Repeat the operation until the required number of crêpes is obtained.
	Note: A well-skinned pan should not require oiling every time a crêpe is made, especially with the high-quality batter.
	Place the crêpes one on top of the other and store between plates.

Step 9	*Sweet crêpes* Sprinkle the crêpes with caster sugar then fold in half then half again.	*Stuffed sweet crêpes* Spread the centre of each crêpe with the hot filling then roll up.	*Stuffed savoury crêpes* Add the filling to the centre of each crêpe then roll up.
Step 10	Dress the crêpes on the serving dish then sprinkle with caster sugar.	Trim the ends if required, place on the serving dish and sprinkle with caster sugar.	Trim the ends if required and place on the serving dish.

Important points when preparing crêpes or pancakes

The term crêpe and pannequet are used to define the same item although the word pannequet is rarely used. However some chefs prefer to use the term pannequet when a savoury stuffing is used.

Step 2
Using a crêpe pan: The pan should be wiped clean with a dry cloth immediately after use. See the 'care of omelette pans' on page 279.

Step 2
Oiling the pan: Very little oil or fat should be used when frying crêpes as free surface fat will be absorbed into the crêpes. Oil should only be added to the pan as required – when the crêpes do not leave the pan easily add a little oil before making the next crêpe.

Step 5
Speed of cooking: Crêpes should be cooked in a hot pan. Adding the mixture to a very hot pan or alternatively a very cool pan increases the likelihood of sticking.

Base recipe   (yield 4 portions)

High-quality batter:	200 ml milk, 75 g flour, 50 g butter, 50 ml egg (1 large egg), pinch of salt.
Frying medium:	Little oil to coat the pan, 20 ml approximately.
Sweet crêpes:	40 g caster sugar (to cover the cooked crêpes).
Standard-quality batter:	200 ml milk, 80 g flour, 15 g butter, 50 ml egg (1 large egg), pinch of salt.

Sweet crêpes

Pancakes with lemon (crêpes au citron)
Garnish the dished crêpes with lemon segments. A good squeeze of lemon juice may also be added to the crêpes prior to folding.

Pancakes with orange (crêpes à l'orange)
Garnish the dished crêpes with orange segments. A good squeeze of orange juice may also be added to the crêpes prior to folding.

Stuffed sweet crêpes

Pancakes with apples (crêpes normande)
Prepare an apple pulp using 400 g cooking apples, see page 104. Spread the apples on the centre of the crêpes prior to rolling up, step 9.

Pancakes with pears (crêpes couvent)
Spread the centre of the crêpes with a small dice of poached pears prior to rolling up.

Pancakes with jam (crêpes à la confiture)
Spread the centre of the crêpes with warmed raspberry jam prior to rolling up.

Crêpes parisienne
Spread the centre of the crêpes with a mixture of whipped cream (25 ml approximately) and crushed macaroon biscuits (50 g approximately).

Crêpes à la russe
Prepare the same as parisienne, flavouring the cream and biscuits with kummel and brandy.

Crêpes Gil-Blas
Spread the centre of the crêpes with the following mixture: cream together 50 g caster sugar and 50 g unsalted butter then add 25 g ground hazelnuts and a little lemon juice. Roll up the crêpes, sprinkle with caster sugar as indicated then glaze under a hot salamander.

Crêpes Jeannette
Prepare the same as Gil-Blas but flavour the butter and sugar with maraschino liqueur in place of the hazelnuts.

Crêpes suisse
Prepare the same as crêpes with apples but coat the crêpes with meringue then glaze under the salamander.

Savoury crêpes or pannequets

Chicken pancakes (crêpes à la reine)
Stuff the crêpes with a hot chicken salpicon (see page 195). Serve plain or coat with suprême sauce and sprinkle with chopped parsley.

Princess crêpes
As above stuffing with a princess salpicon, see page 195.

Seafood pancakes (crêpes aux fruits de mer)
Stuff the crêpes with a hot seafood salpicon (see page 195). Serve plain or coat with white wine sauce and sprinkle with chopped parsley.

Game pancakes
Stuff the pancakes with a hot game salpicon (see page 195). Serve plain or surround with a ribbon or brown port sauce.

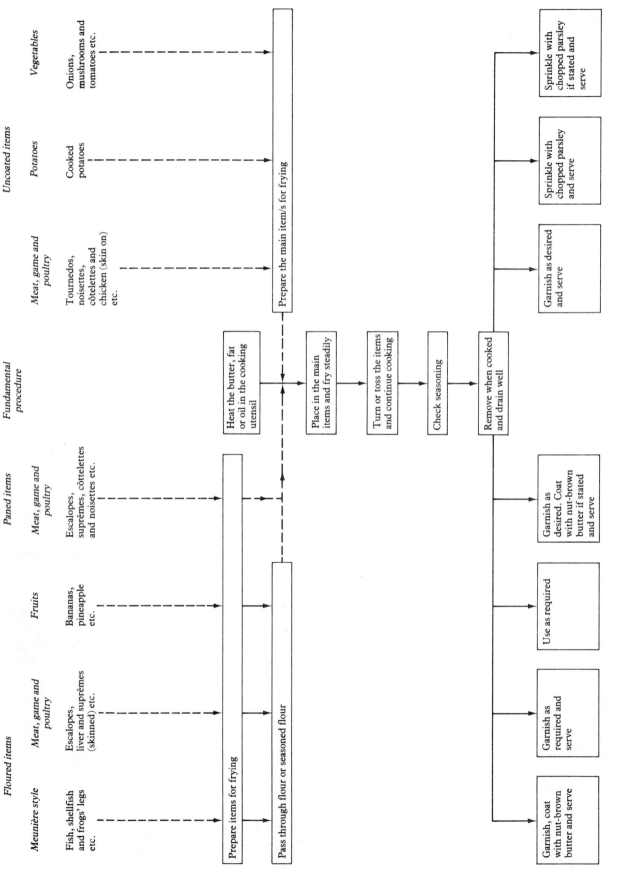

Figure 26 Essential activities for shallow-frying

ssessment exercise

Define the terms sauter and meunière.

Name six pieces of equipment which are used to shallow-fry food.

What is the chief means of heat transfer when shallow-frying food?

Describe three ways in which the cook controls the speed of cooking when shallow-frying foods.

Name three items which are fried slowly and three items which are fried quickly.

Explain the important differences between braised beef with Madeira sauce and sautéd beef with Madeira sauce.

What is a flared steak?

Why is it undesirable to complete the cooking of a sauté containing butcher meats or game in the recipe sauce?

Chapter 12
Deep-frying

Deep-frying is the cooking of food by immersing it in hot fat or oil. The fat heats up by means of convection whereas the surfaces of the food touching the fat receive heat by conduction. Frying is a dry method of cooking which is fast because all the surfaces of the food being fried are exposed to heat at the same time with temperatures as high as 195° C being used.

The frying medium

The frying medium is a crucial factor to the quality of deep-fried foods. The fat or oil used not only contributes to the taste, texture and flavour of the food but in addition must be robust enough to withstand the constant heating and cooling and exposure to impurities without breaking down and deteriorating too quickly.

A good-quality frying medium should be odourless, untainted in taste, have a low melting point and a high smoke point. Traditionally, dripping made from beef fat trimmed from the various joints prepared within the establishment would be used. Lard is also suitable but mutton fat is unsuitable because of its undesirable flavour and high melting point. Good quality oils, e.g. cotton seed and corn oil with smoke points exceeding 200° C make good frying oils but the very best frying mediums are those specifically designed for deep-frying: these have high smoke points and contain additives such as stabilizers and antioxidants which prolong frying life.

Care of frying medium

The following points indicate the care which should be taken in order to get the longest possible working life from a frying medium:

1   *Avoid overheating* the frying medium. Exposing fat to excessive temperatures causes rapid deterioration. When melting solid fat, allow to melt and become liquid slowly (95° C approximately) before increasing the temperature to a degree used for frying – this is to avoid scorching the fat.

    Never exceed a maximum frying temperature of 195° C, even though a frying medium's smoke point may be much higher.

2   *Avoid excessive heating and cooling* of the frying medium. The fryer should be used as required and set to a standby temperature of 120° C approximately when not in use (for short periods). When the fryer is *switched off, keep the fat covered* with as little contact with air as possible.

3   *Season foods away from the fryer to avoid salt being added to the frying medium.* Salt added to the frying medium increases fat deterioration and breakdown. In addition, metals such as copper and iron also increase fat breakdown, therefore the correct frying utensils and equipment should be used.

4   *Never overload the frying medium with high water-containing foods.* A suitable ratio of fat to food should always be maintained when frying, e.g. 6 × 1 for fast recovery equipment or 8 × 1 for less efficient equipment.

5   *Dry wet foods thoroughly before frying.* This is also an important safety precaution.

6   *Check the accuracy of the thermostat at regular intervals.*

7   *Strain the fat to remove food particles each day.* This may have to be done more than once a day when the fryer is used excessively.

8   *Rinse the fryer thoroughly after cleaning to remove any cleaning materials*, e.g. detergent or alkali etc.

9   *Avoid deep-frying fatty foods such as oily fish and gammon* etc.

10 *Coat foods properly to reduce to a minimum the transfer of fats from the foods being fried into the frying medium.*

The frying medium should be changed when it smokes at normal frying temperatures, foams and becomes thin in viscosity.

Important points when deep-frying foods

The operator must be well-trained in the use of the deep fryer and be aware of the potential danger when frying foods. The risk of serious burns and fire may be avoided when correct procedures are used therefore the following points should be read carefully:

1   *A well-designed fryer with a thermostat should be used.* The old fashioned friture which is placed on top of a stove has caused more fires than possibly any other

piece of equipment, and the use of a thermostatically controlled fryer cannot be too strongly recommended.

Much of the development in fryer design has been in the high-volume section of the industry. Fryers are now available with digital temperature dials, push-button filtering, automatic electric controls which control the frying cycle and computer control where the frying operation is continually monitored to aid correct cooking; the computer monitors the rate of oil temperature change for a specific load and type of food and adjusts the cooking time accordingly – the computer is programmed to fry a wide range of food.
The correct level of frying medium should be used. This is sometimes indicated on the side of the fryer and is approximately a half to two-thirds the volume of the frying reservoir.
Always use the correct frying temperature.
Drain wet foods thoroughly before frying.
Do not add too much food into the fryer at any one time. This is especially important when frying thin foods with a high water content where the large proportion of surface areas *results in the formation of considerable quantities of steam* in the frying medium. This causes the fat to rise rapidly in volume – this rapid expansion of the frying medium must be kept under control, see deep-frying thinly-sliced potatoes on page 296.
A spare empty container, e.g. a frying basket or large colander and drainer should always be placed beside the fryer as an emergency precaution. This can be used when the food has to be removed quickly from the fryer to avoid an overspill of hot fat.
Study each base method and be totally conversant with the procedure to be carried out.

Speed of cooking and cooking times of fried foods

The speed of cooking and cooking time is influenced by the following factors.

Size, shape and density of the food.
Ratio of frying medium to food being fried.
Recovery time of fryer: This is the time taken for the fat to return to the desired frying temperature after the cold food is added.
Note: The operator has some control over the recovery period of a fryer by selecting slightly higher temperatures than recommended when using fryers with a long recovery time.
Water content of the food being fried: The higher the water content of the food (when size, shape and quantity remain constant) the longer the frying time.
Initial temperature of the food being fried: The lower the temperature of the food to be fried the longer the cooking time. As a very rough guide the frying time of a

particular item is increased by 25% when fried from a frozen state, e.g. a breaded fish fillet compared with a frozen, breaded fish fillet.
Pressure at which food is fried: Fryers have been developed which fry foods under pressure. The fryers have tight-fitting lids which trap the steam given off by the food. The steam is allowed to build up to 105 kN/m^2(15 psi) where a pressure vent ensures that the safe working pressure is not exceeded. When the cooking cycle is completed, a buzzer sounds and the pressure is automatically decreased. A locking system on the lid prevents the lid being opened until the pressure is released.

Pressure frying produces high-quality fried items quickly, safely and economically. Items such as chops, steaks and chicken pieces can be fried from a raw state with much less likelihood of burning than in a conventional fryer. This is because moisture is trapped inside the food being fried, keeping in juices and acting as a barrier against absorption of the frying medium. Also the frying medium is kept in maximum contact with the food together with good circulation around the food. In conventional frying, a steam barrier tends to develop around the food, causing a layer of cooler fat to surround it.

Foods suitable for deep-frying

As previously stated, frying is a fast method of cooking. This makes it suitable for cuts of food which cook tender when exposed to dry heat. Large cuts and joints of butcher meats and poultry are unsuitable for deep-frying and therefore must be divided into suitable sizes.

Fatty foods such as bacon, mackerel, herring and fatty mutton should never be deep-fried as the natural fat content present in these foods will accelerate the breakdown of the frying medium.

Important process procedures

To blanch (blanchir)

Potatoes
To deep-fry raw potatoes and cook until tender without developing colour.
Reason: Deep-fried potatoes such as frites and Pont-Neuf can be served quickly and in excellent condition. The blanched potatoes are stored on trays then fried as and when required for service.

Deep-frying thinly-sliced raw potatoes

This is the *most dangerous operation* in deep-frying. The water in the potatoes rapidly turns to steam (with the expansion factor of 1700 × 1) making the hot fat react violently and *substantially increase in volume*.

Key instructions:

1   *Dry* the potatoes thoroughly.
2   Add only a *few potatoes at a time*, stir the fat with the spider to remove steam and check expansion of fat before adding more potatoes.
3   Always have a colander and draining tray available in case the potatoes have to be removed quickly from the fat.
4   Keep batch sizes small.
5   Use the correct frying temperature.

Technical terms

Cool zone   The area or channel underneath the heat source in a modern fryer which is designed to trap loose food particles. Since the temperature in this channel is considerably cooler than the frying medium above the heat source, fat breakdown by means of impurities is kept to a minimum.

Smoke point   This is the temperature at which smoke comes continuously from the surface of the frying medium.

Flash point   This is the lowest point at which the vapour from the frying medium ignites when a small flame is applied.

ection one   Deep-fried fish

ase method (this base method applies to all breaded, battered and floured (française) items, see Sections 2, 3, 5, 6 nd 7)

tep 1	Mise en place A Assemble ingredients. B Prepare the fish, see Chapter 4, pages 70–2. C Prepare the coating. D Prepare the accompanying garnish and sauce. E Set the fryers to the correct frying temperature: *Conventional fryers*: Small whole fish = 175–180°C. Fish fillets, en goujons, shellfish and frogs' legs etc. = 185–187°C. Whitebait = 190–195°C.

tep 2	Coat the fish: 1 Breaded: The fish may be breaded in advance of frying.
	                 2 Floured: The fish should be coated immediately prior to frying.
	                 3 Batter: The fish is coated immediately prior to frying.

tep 3	*Breaded and floured* Place into a frying basket after shaking off any loose particles and immerse in the hot fat. | *Battered* Remove from the batter drawing off surplus batter on the sides of the batter bowl then carefully place into the hot fat. *Important*: All items placed directly into the fat should be allowed to slip smoothly into the fat without producing splashes of hot fat.
tep 4	During frying ensure that the items are not sticking together: *Small breaded items*: These may be very lightly shaken apart but care must be taken not to break the coating. *Individual items*: These are kept apart with the use of a metal spider during frying.
tep 5	Turn any whole fish or fillets which float halfway through co king and allow to cook through and develop colour.
tep 6	Remove from the fryer when cooked and drain well to remove surface fat.
tep 7	Place on the serving dish *lined with a dishpaper* and neatly decorate with the garnish. Accompany with any sauce stated in the individual recipe. *Important*: Do not cover with a lid.

Basic recipe for small whole fish and fish fillets   (4 main course portions)

Main item:	*Fish fillets*: Dover sole, lemon sole and plaice = 8 × 75 g fillets.
	Whole flat fish: Dover sole, lemon sole and plaice = 4 × 400 g fish.
	Small round fish: Haddock and whiting etc. = 4 × 300 g fish.
Coating:	There are three basic coatings:
	1 Breaded (paner – English style: à l'anglaise): Pass the fish through seasoned flour, eggwash and breadcrumbs.
	2 Battered: Pass the fish through seasoned flour then batter, see page 321.
	3 Floured (French style: à la française): Pass the fish through milk then coat with seasoned flour.
Garnish:	4 lemon wedges and branch parsley (deep-fried branch parsley is more suitable).
Production:	Follow the instructions in the base method.
	Cooking times: These vary with the thickness of the fish, e.g. fish fillets 1–2 mins, small whole fish 2–3 mins.

Dishes

Fried sole (sole frite), Fried plaice (plie frite), Fried
flounder (flet frit), Fried whiting (merlan frit), fried
haddock (aiglefin frit).
The style of frying may be added to the basic description:
Fried sole French-style (sole frite à la française).

Fried fillets of fish

The description is the same as above with the addition of
the word fillet: Fried fillets of plaice English style (filets de
plie frits à l'anglaise).

Curled whiting (merlan en colère)
Prepare the whole whiting as stated on page 71, with the
tail inserted firmly in the mouth of the fish. Coat the fish
with breadcrumbs and proceed as stated in the base
method. Decorate with the basic garnish and accompany
with a suitable sauce.

Fish Colbert
(Sole, plaice and flounder). Prepare the fish as stated on
page 71, then coat with breadcrumbs. Cook as stated then
carefully remove the cut backbone and insert parsley
butter into the recess. Serve with the basic garnish.

En goujons
(Fish fillets). Cut the fillets into thin strips (see page 72)
then coat with breadcrumbs. Cook as stated and serve
with the basic garnish. Accompany with a suitable sauce,
e.g. tartare.

Orly
(Fish fillets). Marinade the fillets for 20 mins. in an instant
marinade (see page 43). Coat with batter then cook as
stated. Decorate with the basic garnish and accompany
with tomato sauce.

Fried shellfish

Fried mussels (moules frites). Allow 12 cooked mussels
per portion approximately.
Fried scallops (coquilles St-Jacques frites). Allow 2–3
cooked fish per portion.
Fried scampi (scampi frits). Allow 100 g cooked shelled
scampi per portion.
Coat the fish with breadcrumbs and cook as stated in the
base method. Decorate with the basic garnish and
accompany with a suitable sauce. *Note*:   Mussels are
sometimes marinaded in an instant marinade then coated
with batter.

Fried whitebait (blanchailles frites)

Allow 100 g whitebait per portion.
    Inspect the fish removing any unwanted matter then
wash and drain well. Treat à la française and cook as
stated. Decorate with the basic garnish.

Section two   Deep-fried white meats and made-up items

Base method

Follow the instructions in Section One.
Frying temperatures:
White meats (chicken, turkey and veal) and Scotch eggs
165–170° C.
Made-up items 175–180° C.

Chicken (poulet/volaille)

Allow 1½ kg cooked chicken per 4 portions.
Note: Cooked chicken is usually used unless frying in a
pressure fryer.
   Cut the chicken into quarters then remove the skin.
Coat with breadcrumbs or batter then follow the
instructions in the base method (Section 1).
Cooking time: 3–4 mins. (internal temperature 70° C
approximately) (reheating).

Turkey and veal (dinde and veau)

Allow 400 g boned flesh per 4 portions approximately.
   Prepare the flesh into 4 or 8 escalopes. Coat with
breadcrumbs then follow the instructions in the base
method (Section 1).
Cooking time: 2–3 mins.

Dishes

In basket

Prepare as stated then serve in a basket lined with a napkin
or dishpaper. Garnish as desired, e.g. lemon wedges,
branch parsley, French-fried potatoes or baked potato etc.

Orly

Prepare the same as fish Orly.

Tempura (Japanese)

Prepare the chicken or meat in batter as stated in the base
method. Accompany with Tentsuyu, lemon and salt, soy
sauce, grated root ginger and daikon (or small white
turnips).
Tentsuyu: 200 ml dashi (or stock), 50 ml soy sauce, 50 ml
mirin (or sweet sherry), 50 ml daikon and 5 g grated root
ginger.

Viennoise

The term is sometimes used for escalopes which are
breaded, deep-fried as stated then garnished with lemon
segments and deep-fried branch parsley. See also page
262.

Made-up items

Savoury croquettes, e.g. beef, game and chicken etc.
(Croquettes de boeuf, gibier and volaille) (see page 197).

Savoury cutlets, examples as above (see page 197).
Rissoles, examples as above (see page 197).
Cromesquis à la russe (see page 197).
Durham cutlets (see page 77).
Fishcakes (see page 77).
   Cook as stated in section 1 (175–180°C), ensuring that
when colour and crispness are achieved the items are
thoroughly reheated, i.e. internal temperature: 70° C+.
Cooking time: 3–4 mins.
   Serve garnished with deep-fried parsley and accompany
with a suitable sauce, e.g. tomato, lyonnaise, diable or
piquante.

Scotch eggs

Allow 1 egg per portion (see page 122).
   Cook as stated in section 1 (165–170°C), allowing
sufficient time to cook the sausagemeat and reheat the egg.
Cooking time: 5–7 mins.
Hot service: Serve as made-up items above.
Cold service: Garnish with salad vegetables and
accompany with vinaigrette etc. Note: The eggs are
often cut in halves for service.

Section three   Deep-frying pre-prepared frozen items

Examples

Fishfingers, fishcakes, breaded fish, battered fish, breaded meat cutlets, rissoles, croquette potatoes and chipped potatoes etc.

These are bought ready-prepared and are placed into the hot frying medium *without* defrosting. The fryer is usually set at a temperature around 180–185° C but the manufacturer's instructions should be consulted for the exact frying temperature.

Note: Prior to frying thick items, e.g. croquette potatoes, it is advisable to remove the items from the freezer and tray up ready for frying. This is to avoid placing in the fryer with an internal temperature of −18° C; this often results in uneven frying.

Important: This does not mean defrosting but frying at −10° C approximately. Items which have been trayed up for frying should not be refrozen.

Section four   Composite deep-fried dishes

Some dishes consist of various deep-fried commodities served together. They may include a selection of meat, poultry, offal, vegetable and fruit items which are coated and deep-fried then attractively presented for service with an appropriate sauce or garnish.

Fritto misto   (4 portions)

This dish varies in content but the following commodities are given as an example:
4 trimmed lamb cutlets, 4 slices fillet steak, 4 slices of lamb's liver, 4 slices of cooked calf's head or brain, 4 beef or chicken croquettes, 4 cooked artichoke bottoms, 4 spriglets of cooked cauliflower, 2 cooked sliced potatoes and 2 cooked sliced Jerusalem artichokes.
Production: Coat the items as appropriate then deep-fry.
Service: Neatly arrange the fried items in bunches of the same commodity for ease of identification when serving. Garnish with trimmed lemon segments and deep-fried parsley and accompany with a sauceboat of tomato sauce.

Fritto misto di pesce   (4 portions)

This is the same as above but using fish and shellfish in place of meat, poultry and offal, e.g. small fish: smelts and gudgeons etc; fish fillets and cuts of fish; shellfish: prawns; scampi; scallops and mussels etc.

Section five   Deep-fried vegetables

Deep-fried vegetables may be divided into two sections:
1   Vegetables fried from a *raw* state.
2   Vegetables fried from a *cooked* state.

Vegetables fried from a raw state

Fried aubergines (aubergines frites)

Allow 1 large or 2 medium aubergines (400 g approximately) for 4 portions.

Wash, peel and slice the vegetables into 5 mm slices approximately. *Note*:   The slices may be sprinkled with salt and left for 30 mins. then wiped dry to remove excess moisture.

Pass the slices through seasoned flour then shake off the loose flour. Deep fry at 185–187°C until crisp and brown – follow the instructions in the Section 1 base method placing the slices carefully into the fat, steps 4, 5 and 6. Serve immediately.

Fried courgettes (courgettes frites)

Prepare as aubergines above.

French fried onions (oignons frits à la française)

Allow 400 g onions per 4 portions.

Peel then cut the onions into thin slices (3 mm) and separate into rings. Follow the instructions in the base method for section 1 treating à la française.
Frying temperature: 185–187°C.

Deep-fried parsley (persil frit)

This is used as a garnish for many dishes.

Wash and pick into branches then dry thoroughly. Deep-fry at 185–187°C. Fry until the sizzling stops. *Note*:   Avoid overcooking as this results in a loss of colour, i.e. the parsley is kept green.

Tempura vegetables (Japanese)

These are deep-fried in batter and served with the accompaniments stated for chicken tempura in Section 2.
Aubergines: Cut into thick slices.
Broccoli: Divide into flowerettes.
Cauliflower: Divide into flowerettes.
Green peppers: Remove seeds and quarter.
Mushrooms: Leave whole.
Nuts: Use whole almonds, hazelnuts or walnuts etc.
Spring onions: Cut into short lengths.
etc.

Vegetables fried from a cooked state

Most vegetables can be deep-fried after cooking. They are initially cooked a little underdone then passed through flour and batter and deep-fried. An instant marinade (see page 43) may also be used to complement flavour. Information regarding portion size, elementary preparation and initial cooking is to be found on the pages indicated within the brackets.

Examples
Fried artichoke bottoms   Fonds d'artichauts frits   (page 113).
Fried asparagus tips   Pointes d'asperges frites   (page 131).
Fried cauliflower   Chou-fleur frit   (page 131).
Fried cucumber   Concombre frit   (page 131).
Fried celery hearts   Coeurs de céleri frits   (page 215).
Fried root fennel   Fenouil frit   (page 215).
Fried salsify   Salsifis frits   (page 113).
Frying temperature: 185–187°C.

En fritot

This is the term used to indicate the above deep-fried vegetables accompanied with tomato sauce.

Section six   Deep-fried potatoes

Deep-fried potatoes may be divided into two categories:
1   Potatoes fried from a *raw* state.
2   Potatoes fried from a *cooked* state.

Base method for deep-fried raw potatoes

Step 1

Mise en place

A   Assemble ingredients.
B   Wash, peel and cut the potatoes into the desired shape, see individual recipe.
C   Wash the potatoes under cold running water to remove excess starch.
D   Set the fryer to the correct temperature:
Sliced potatoes and small cuts of potato, e.g. crisps, straw, allumettes and mignonettes etc. = 180–185°C.
Medium and large cut potatoes, e.g. frites and Pont Neuf = 165–170°C.
E   Drain the potatoes thoroughly removing all surface water.

Important: Thinly cut and thinly sliced potatoes should be *thoroughly dried for very important safety reasons*, see pages 288–90.

Step 2

Dice and stick-shaped potatoes
Place the potatoes into a frying basket and lower into the fat.

Thinly cut and sliced potatoes
Carefully sprinkle the potatoes into the hot fat *a few at a time*. Use a metal spider to disperse the potatoes through the fat and allow the steam to escape *before adding any more potatoes*, see page 289.

This procedure is quite *dangerous*, especially when using an old-fashioned friture or chip pan.

Step 3

Cook steadily shaking the frying basket occasionally to aid the removal of steam from the fat and to ensure the potatoes are not sticking together.

Fry steadily, occasionally turning the potatoes with a metal spider.

Step 4

Test the potatoes for tenderness.

Step 5

Blanched potatoes
Remove the potatoes when tender but before developing colour and allow to drain well to remove surface fat.

Step 6	Place the potatoes on a tray lined with kitchen paper until required for service.
Step 7	Place into a basket as required and fry at 185–187°C.
Step 8	When the potatoes are crisp and golden-brown in colour, remove from the fat and drain well. Thinly cut and sliced potatoes are usually removed from the fat with a metal spider into a colander which is placed on top of a metal basin to collect the surplus fat.
Step 9	Place the potatoes on the serving dish lined with a dishpaper when serving as a vegetable course (and not as a garnish or plated vegetable).
	Important: Do not cover with a lid.

Potatoes fried from a raw state

Potatoes shaped into dice and stick shapes

Base recipe   Allow 650–750 g potatoes per 4 portions approximately (depending on size of potato and accuracy of shape cut).

Matchstick potatoes (pommes allumettes)
Square the potatoes by removing the round edges then cut into slices which are 40 mm × 2 mm approximately. Cut the slices into sticks like matchsticks, i.e. 2 mm thick approximately.

Mignonette potatoes (pommes mignonnettes)
Prepare the same as matchsticks but double the thickness, i.e. 40 mm × 5mm × 5 mm.

Chipped potatoes (pommes frites)
Prepare the same as matchstick and mignonettes but increase the thickness to 40 mm × 10 mm × 10 mm.

Pont-Neuf potatoes (pommes Pont-Neuf)
This is the largest of the stick variety and is prepared as above but with a thickness of 40 mm × 20 mm × 20 mm.

Battle potatoes (pommes bataille)
Square the potatoes then cut into slices 15 mm in thickness. Cut the slices into strips the same thickness then cut into cubes with 15 mm sides.

Thinly cut and sliced potatoes

Base recipe   Allow 150 g potatoes as a garnish for 4 main course dishes.

Crisps (pommes chips)
Slice the potatoes thinly, i.e. 1 mm approximately.

Collerette potatoes (pommes collerette)
Cut the potatoes into cylinders then groove the sides with a canneler cutter. Slice the cylinders like crisps.

Spiral potatoes (pommes bénédictine)
Cut the potatoes with a spiral vegetable cutter.

Straw potatoes (pommes pailles)
Cut the potatoes into fine strips, i.e. 1 mm in thickness.

Wafer potatoes (pommes gaufrettes)
Cut the potatoes into slices on the mandolin using the corrugated blade and giving a half turn between each slice. This will produce a wafer or trellis pattern; the blade of the mandolin must be set to the correct thickness to cut these potatoes: 2–3 mm.

Woodchip potatoes (pommes copeaux)
Slice the potatoes like crisps but keep as long as possible. Cut the slices into strips varying in width between 5–10 mm to resemble woodchips.

Soufflé potatoes (pommes soufflées)
This type of potato is *not a derivative* of the base method in this section but is completed in hot fat.

Trim the potatoes square, cut into 3 mm slices then dry thoroughly. Place a pan quarter full of oil on to the stove but keep the oil very cool, i.e. 135–140° C. Add 6–8 slices of potato and constantly shake while very slowly frying – the oil should constantly lap over the slices. Inspect the surface of the slices for small *bubbles or blisters* – these should be at various points on the surface of each slice. Remove the slices and place into a hot fryer (195°C) where they should immediately puff out or soufflé. Fry until crisp and golden-brown.

Potatoes fried from a cooked state

Deep-fried potato dishes using cooked potatoes may be divided into (a) deep-fried boiled potatoes which are whole or sliced, and (b) deep-fried duchesse-type potatoes.

(a)   Potatoes which have been plainly boiled can be deep-fried whole (or in large pieces) or cut into slices and deep-fried. These two styles of potato are often *inaccurately described* as roast or sauté potatoes.

> **Potato fritters**
> Cut plain boiled potatoes into thin slices (3–5 mm) then pass through seasoned flour and batter and deep-fry as stated in Section 1.

(b)   Various potato dishes are made with a duchesse mixture which is coated with breadcrumbs, nuts or small pieces of pasta. In addition duchesse potato and choux paste may be combined and then shaped and deep-fried to produce a further group of dishes.

>   The preparation of duchesse potato mixture and the various derivatives which are deep-fried are explained in Chapter 5, page 95.

Duchesse potato derivatives

Almond potatoes (pommes amandines), Croquette potatoes (pommes croquettes), Berny potatoes (pommes Berny), Royal potatoes (pommes royales/St-Florentin)

Production: Deep-fry the potatoes following the instructions in Section 1. Cook until crisp, golden-brown and thoroughly reheated.
Frying temperature and reheating time: 185–187°C for 3 mins. approximately.

Duchesse and choux paste derivatives

Dauphine potatoes (pommes dauphine), Elizabeth potatoes (pommes Elisabeth), Lorette potatoes (pommes Lorette)

Production: The preparation of these potatoes ready for frying including shaping and placing on oiled greaseproof paper is explained on page 95.

  Carefully lower the oiled greaseproof paper containing the potatoes into the hot fat (185–187°C) and allow the potatoes to slip off the paper. Cook until crisp and golden brown (3 mins. approximately) then serve on a salver or entrée dish lined with a dishpaper. Garnish with deep-fried branch parsley (optional).

Deep-fried sweet potatoes

These are prepared as a duchesse mixture in the same manner as ordinary potatoes. All the derivatives for duchesse above may be used for sweet potatoes (French: patates/patates douces).

Section seven   Novelty potatoes

The following styles of potato, while being attractive, are severely limited in their application because of their demand on production time. However they are examples of how cooks attain individuality and novelty with their products and in turn create a meal experience of interest and excitement for guests or customers.

Potato chains (pommes en chaînes)

1   Peel and cut the potato into rectangular shaped slices 3 mm in thickness.
2   Cut slits in each slice to within 2 mm of the top and bottom edges.
3   Weave the knife through the slits then cut horizontally through the 3 mm edge.
4   Turn the potato round and repeat the operation inserting the knife in the opposite weave – this will form two interlocking units.
5   Carefully divide each cross-section of the two units and open out into a chain. Trim the inside end of each link and store in cold water until required for frying.
6   Deep-fry like crisps.

Potato stars (pommes étoile)

1   Peel the potato and cut into cubes.
2   Cut each cube as follows:
    Cut from one of the points to the centre of the cube. Repeat the procedure at the opposite end and remove the wedge of potato. Cut all the points of the potato in the same fashion until a star is obtained.
3   The potato may be deep-fried at this stage or cut still further to produce a star framework with a ball inside.

Section eight Deep-fried fruits (fritters)

Most deep-fried fruits are usually prepared with a batter coating although breadcrumbs are sometimes used. Fresh fruit to be deep-fried should be of good quality and reasonably ripe but not over-ripe. The elementary preparation for each fruit refers to fresh fruit but tinned fruits may be used as appropriate, e.g. apricots, peaches and pineapple etc.

Base method for all deep-fried fruits

Pass the prepared fruit through flour and batter then cook as stated in Section 1 for battered foods. Fry until crisp and golden-brown.

Frying temperature and cooking time: 180°C for 3–4 mins.

Fritters served as a sweet course: When cooked, arrange the fritters on a tray and dust over the tops with caster sugar. Place under a hot salamander until the sugar melts and forms a crisp glaze.

Note: Fruits for fritters are sometimes coated with hot frangipane cream (page 399) which is allowed to cool and set before passing through the flour and batter.

Service of sweet fritters: Serve on a salver lined with a dishpaper and accompany with a sauceboat of apricot sauce and/or crème Chantilly.

Various fritters   (yield 4 portions)

Apple fritters (beignets de pommes)
Allow 300 g cooking apples (2 large apples).
    Wash, peel, core and slice the apples into rings (5 mm).

Apricot fritters (beignets d'abricots)
Allow 300 g apricots (8 medium apricots).
    Wash then cut the apricots into halves and remove the stones.

Banana fritters (beignets de bananes)
Allow 4 medium bananas.
    Peel then trim the ends of each banana. Cut each banana into 2 or 4 neat pieces. This is done by cutting each banana from top to bottom at a slant.

Peach fritters (beignets de pêches)
Allow 4 medium peaches.
    Blanch the peaches (like tomatoes) and remove the skins. Cut into halves and remove the stones.

Pineapple fritters (beignets d'ananas)
Allow 4–8 pineapple rings.
    Remove the skin from the pineapple then cut into rings (10 mm thick approximately). Remove the centre stalks.

Composite fruit fritters

Croquettes
Dice 100 g prepared fruit (peaches, pears, pineapples or mixed fruit) and add to 75 g boiling frangipane cream (page 399). Reduce to a thick consistency then turn out onto an oiled tray and allow to cool. When cold, shape as desired then pass through flour, eggwash and breadcrumbs. Deep fry for 3–4 mins. at 185°C.

En cocon
Individual fruits or a variety of sliced fruits.
    Prepare 4 large crêpes then place the prepared fruit on the centre of each crêpe. Spread a little lemon butter (page 42) over the fruit then neatly envelope inside each crêpe to resemble a cocoon. Pass through flour and batter then deep-fry at 180°C for 3 mins. approximately. Accompany with a sauceboat of thick, slightly-sweetened cream.

Section nine   Deep-fried doughs and pastries

Base method

Step 1	Mise en place

A   Assemble ingredients.
B   Prepare the dough:
Choux paste fritters: Pipe the size of walnuts on to small rectangles of oiled greaseproof paper.
Brioche fritters: Mould the dough into small balls and place on small rectangles of oiled greaseproof paper.
Prove in very little steam until the dough is double in size approximately (30 mins. approximately at 29°C).
Doughnuts: *Powder aerated dough*:   Roll out the dough to 100 mm in thickness approximately.
Cut with a doughnut cutter (or shape into fingers or balls: 40 g weight) and tray up ready for frying.
Yeast bun dough: Shape the dough as described above then place on a well-oiled tray.
Prove in very little steam until the doughnuts are about double in size (30 mins. approximately at 29°C).
C   Set the fryers to the correct temperature:
Choux paste fritters: 170°C approximately.
Doughnuts and brioche fritters: 175°C approximately.
D   Prepare any sauce or garnish.

Step 2	*Choux paste fritters* Place the fritters into the hot fat: carefully lower the paper and fritters into the hot fat and allow to slip off the paper.	*Brioche fritters*	*Doughnuts* Lift off the tray carefully with a palette knife dipped in hot oil on to the fingers and place into the hot fat.
Step 3	Fry the fritters until they have expanded considerably and are very light, crisp and golden-brown – 8 mins. approximately. *Note*: Turn the fritters occasionally during frying.	Allow to fry steadily until one side is cooked then turn over and cook the other side – 6 mins. approximately.	
Step 4	Remove from the fryer and drain thoroughly.		
Step 5	Roll in caster sugar and place on serving dish lined with a dishpaper.		

Choux paste dishes   (yield 4 portions)

Base recipe

Main item:	250 g choux paste (page 344).
Sugar coating:	Caster sugar (small pinch of cinnamon mixed through the sugar is optional).

Dishes

Souffléd fritters (beignets soufflés)
These are the basic fritters stated in the base recipe and method. Accompany with a sauceboat of hot apricot sauce.

Beignets soufflés en surprise
Prepare as above but stuff the fritters after frying with hot pastry cream.

Beignets soufflés dauphine
Prepare as surprise above but flavour the pastry cream with almond essence.

French doughnuts
Pipe the choux paste in rings on the oiled greaseproof paper then cook as stated. When cooked, drain and allow to cool then slit with a knife and fill the interior with crème Chantilly (page 41). Coat the tops with fondant.
Note: Various flavoured creams and fondants may be used.

Cheese fritters (beignets au fromage)
Add 50 g grated cheese to the basic choux paste and season with salt, pepper and cayenne pepper. After frying roll in grated parmesan in place of sugar.

Doughnuts

Base recipe

Main item:	These may be prepared from two basic doughs: 1 Powdered aerated dough (page 362). Yield 8 doughnuts approximately. 2 Yeast bun dough (page 354). Yield 16 doughnuts approximately.

Doughnuts
See base method.

Jam doughnuts
Mould the dough into balls (40 g each) then pierce each ball in the centre and fill with a little raspberry jam. Seal each ball carefully then proceed as stated.

Cream doughnuts
Prepare doughnuts as stated and when cold slit through the centre and fill with whipped cream.
Note: These doughnuts are often made in finger shapes.

Brioche paste fritters

Base recipe

Main item:	Brioche dough (page 358). Yield 10–12 portions.

Beignets viennoise
See base method. Accompany with a sauceboat of hot apricot sauce.
Note: These fritters are sometimes filled with redcurrant jelly in the same manner as jam doughnuts.

Rissoles, see also page 197.

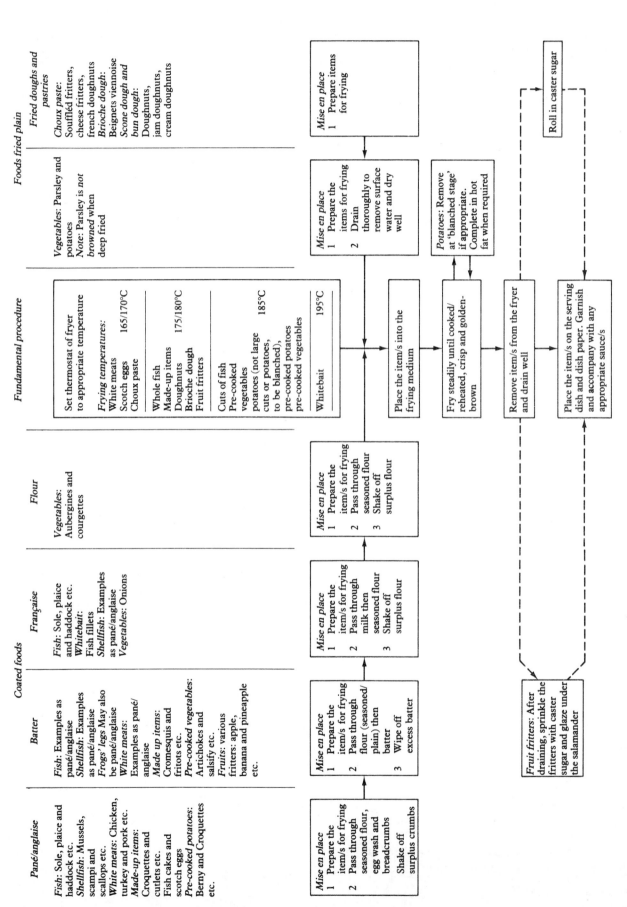

Figure 27 Essential activities for deep frying

Assessment exercise

1 Describe deep-frying as a method of cooking.
2 Define the following terms: cool zone; flash point; smoke point; recovery time.
3 Name four different coatings used when frying foods.
4 What is the desired ratio of frying medium to food when deep-frying?
5 Describe the safety procedures which should be taken when deep-frying crisps or straw potatoes.
6 Define the term 'blanch' in relation to deep-fried foods.
7 What steps can the cook take to ensure maximum life from the frying medium?
8 Why should deep-fried foods never be covered with a lid?

Chapter 13
Grilling

Grilling is cooking by means of dry heat which consists largely of *radiated* heat in the form of '*Infra-red waves*' although some cooking occurs by way of convection from hot air currents and conduction when hot grill bars come in direct contact with the food. Infra-red waves vary in length and this is important in determining the most efficient means of grilling foods. Wavelengths between 1.4–5 millionth of a metre are the most effective for cooking, whereas other wavelengths may not be absorbed well by water and some may not pass through the water vapours formed around foods with a high water content when heated. *High temperatures produce the most suitable infra-red waves* for cooking but the heat exposure should *never be such that the food burns* while cooking.

Cooking by radiated heat can produce a very fast speed of cooking because the food can be moved very close to the heat source and exposed to an extremely high temperature. Also the energy is passed from the heat source to the food almost instantly without having to be carried in water, air or oil etc., and in addition the infra-red waves slightly penetrate the food up to a few millimetres during cooking. Speed of cooking is controlled by either increasing or decreasing the heat source or moving the article further away or nearer to the heat source; it should be noted that the speed of cooking varies *geometrically* to the distance from the heat source, e.g. halving the distance of an article from the heat source increases the speed of cooking four times (inverse square law).

Foods suitable for this method of cooking include fish and *tender* cuts of meat, poultry and game. Veal is unsuitable for grilling due to its very low fat content and, in turn, dry texture when cooked, with the possible exception of loin chops which are fatty. Unless small in size, the various commodities for grilling are prepared into '*cuts*' which allow *even cooking* by keeping all parts of the commodity exposed to the heat the *same distance* from the heat source; using cuts of meat also keeps the cooking time to a suitable limit. Joints of meat are unsuitable for grilling because of their size, therefore an alternative method of cooking such as roasting should be used.

Note: Spit roasting is similar to grilling and involves the cooking of large joints and even whole carcases of meat over radiated heat. Unlike grilling the item is mounted on a special securing rod which is rotated at a controlled speed over a carefully prepared fire or heat source, see page 238.

Most vegetables are unsuitable for cooking by grilling because the vegetables, when exposed to the very dry heat, rapidly dry out and shrivel, forming a hard brittle skin or surface. However, some vegetables may be grilled. Tomatoes are suitable for grilling and so too are mushrooms *provided their surfaces are brushed or coated with oil*; mushrooms deteriorate rapidly and become inedible without an oil coating over their surfaces when cooked by radiant heat.

Various factors determining the temperature/speed of cooking and cooking time when grilling foods

Many different factors determine whether a piece of food should be grilled quickly at a high temperature or slowly at a low temperature in conjunction with the time taken to cook to the required degree of cooking.

1 *Type of commodity*: fish, meat, poultry, game or vegetables.
2 *Physical properties of the food*: degree of tenderness, denseness of food, fat content and degree of hardness or maturity of vegetables etc.
3 *Thickness and size of food*: this is one of the most important factors for all foods.
4 *Degree of cooking*: this varies with the commodity being cooked and ranges from very undercooked to well cooked.
5 *Initial temperature of food*: foods cooked from a chilled or frozen state take longer than foods started at room temperature. Some foods may be grilled from a frozen state – here a proportion of the energy is required to change the ice to water, e.g. to change 1 kg of ice (0°C) to water requires 334 kilojoules of energy; this is without any increase in temperature. See frozen meats on following page.
6 *Colour of food*: The amount of heat absorbed by food when exposed to infra-red waves depends on the colour or reflectivity of the surface of the food; the darker the colour of the surface of the food the faster the rate of energy absorbtion.

Various types of equipment

As mentioned earlier, the type of heat source is an important factor when grilling food but in addition to the most suitable size of wave which should be emitted, the quantity of waves emitted is also important. Some grills are very efficient cookers of food emitting a high proportion of infra-red energy: one specific piece of equipment produces almost 100% infra-red radiation which substantially reduces the cooking time in comparison to a conventional type grill.

The various types of equipment for grilling are usually grouped and classified according to the direction of the heat source:

a) *Over-heat grills*: The food is cooked on greased grill bars over the heat source which may be fired by gas, electricity or charcoal etc. This type of equipment is suitable for fish, meat and poultry grills.

b) *Under-heat grills*: The food is cooked on greased grill bars, grill rack or trays under the heat source which is usually heated by gas or electricity. This type of equipment is suitable for fish, meat and poultry. Items such as sausages, bacon rashers, fruit and meat puddings, mushrooms and tomatoes etc., are usually cooked on trays in this type of equipment.
Note: The trade term for this type of grill is *salamander*.

c) *Between-heat grills*: In this type of grill the food is cooked between electrically heated grill bars. This type of equipment is usually used for meat grills but its limitations of operation make it less versatile than (a) and (b) above.

Gas and electricity are used as fuels for all types of grills but charcoal and solid fuels are restricted to category (a) types. One disadvantage with solid fuels such as charcoal, coke and wood etc. is the preparation of the heat source and the variation in temperature due to the amount of coals or fuel present and degree of combustion, but many people prefer the flavour imparted by specific types of solid fuel, e.g. hickory, oak or applewood charcoals etc. The use of solid fuels for cooking is also dealt with in Chapter 10.

Source temperatures

These may be as low as 232° C and as high as 982° C, depending on the usage and type of equipment but the 'surface temperature' of the food should rarely exceed 260°C to avoid burning. Although as previously stated the cooking speed varies depending on several factors, most foods are grilled at a surface temperature between 149–204° C.

Important information

Grilled foods are usually cooked so that the appropriate degree of cooking and development of colour is achieved simultaneously. Therefore it follows in most cases that the smaller and thinner the item to be cooked the faster the speed of cooking. Also, when cooking meat to the underdone degree the cooking must be fast to develop colour without cooking too far into the flesh.

One general guideline which can be followed with fresh meats, i.e. steaks and chops, is to cook quickly up to a thickness of 15–20 mm and thereafter slow the cooking down correspondingly as thickness increases. This does not apply to made-up items such as sausages or puddings etc.

The *sealing* of meat which is the rapid browning of the outer surface *does not, as was previously thought, seal in soluble extracts and reduce shrinkage*. On the contrary, exposing the surface of the meat to high temperatures *increases shrinkage* rather than reducing it, see page 80. However, an item may be cooked by initially developing colour then reducing the speed of cooking and continuing slowly until the required degree of cooking is attained. Care must be taken *not to overcook the surface* of any flesh as this will *reduce the heat transfer* through the flesh and produce a dry, burnt unsightly product.

Important: Some research articles indicate that moderately low grilling temperatures 150–180°C produce a better end product (superior tenderness, more moist or juicy and less shrunken product) than high grilling temperatures.

Grilling frozen flesh

Fairly thin steaks may be grilled from a frozen state. They are placed over a cool heat until defrosted then the heat increased to normal grilling temperature. As a general guide double the cooking time compared to a similar fresh product.

Important: Although there appears to be a move towards grilling frozen cuts of meat, it should be noted that this *practice presents a possible hygiene hazard* with all meats. Commodities such as chicken and pork must never be cooked from a frozen state because of the risk of food poisoining.

Degree of cooking

Chicken, pork, fish and made-up items, e.g. sausages etc. *must be cooked all the way through the flesh* and are *never served underdone*. This is because there is a risk of *food poisoning* and furthermore many people are *nauseated* after eating these foods undercooked. Beef may be cooked to any degree of cooking although many people prefer steak underdone. Lamb and mutton is usually cooked 'just done – à point', but mutton, lamb's kidneys and lamb's liver are also served underdone.

Note: There is a risk of food poisoning with any meat or flesh served underdone although with beef the risk is minimal.

Test for cooking

This is described in each of the base recipes and methods for the various commodities with the exception of the physical test for cooking meats.

Physical test for determining the degree of cooking of meats

The test requires considerable practice to master but a recommended approach to learning the procedure is as follows:
1   Take a thick raw steak, cutlet or chop etc., and squeeze with the fingers or grilling tongs. Note the texture when pressed from all sides; the raw flesh is very *flabby* with a *characteristic sponginess* identifiable with raw meat. Continued pressure also ruptures or bursts the flesh.
2   Grill very quickly on each side (this must be done to develop colour only), remove from the grill and press to determine texture; although the flesh has coloured and stiffened the feel of *raw meat as described above is easily identifiable.* This degree of cooking is *rare* or *blue – bleu –* and applies only to steaks or cuts of beef.
3   Place the item back on the grill and continue to cook slowly. At about intervals of 1 minute press the item, noting the change in texture; after a short period of grilling on each side the commodity becomes *more resilient in texture* with a *tighter spring* to the flesh than the rare degree. A *firm sponginess* can also be detected as pressure of touch is increased. Meat juices coming to the surface of the item will be *blood red* as the commodity is still *raw at the very centre.* This degree of cooking is *underdone* or saignant.
4   With further cooking the item becomes *firm* in texture but when pressed a slight *sponginess is barely detectable* with surface juices revealing slight *traces of blood*; this is because the commodity is still a little *pink at the centre.* This degree of cooking is *medium* or à point.
5   When cooking beyond medium a stage is reached where there is *no sign of sponginess* and the cooked flesh yields with consistent pressure. *No trace of blood* is apparent in any surface juices as the commodity has cooked through completely.

Summary

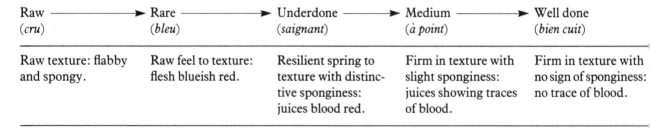

Raw (*cru*)	Rare (*bleu*)	Underdone (*saignant*)	Medium (*à point*)	Well done (*bien cuit*)
Raw texture: flabby and spongy.	Raw feel to texture: flesh blueish red.	Resilient spring to texture with distinctive sponginess: juices blood red.	Firm in texture with slight sponginess: juices showing traces of blood.	Firm in texture with no sign of sponginess: no trace of blood.

Note: The test for cooking is important when grilling all meats such as pork, lamb, mutton and especially beef where the cooking can be terminated at any of the various degress of cooking. See also the test for cooking of chicken and fish, pages 308–13.

Associated culinary terms

The term grilling almost always refers to a *method of cooking* (an activities definition of a method of cooking is given on page 13), but grilling equipment, especially salamanders, are also used for toasting, glazing and gratinating etc.

Section one Grilled fish

Base method

Step 1	Mise en place A Assemble ingredients. B Prepare the fish for cooking, see page 71. C Prepare the seasoned flour and melted butter. D Prepare the garnish and any accompanying sauces. ↓
Step 2	Place the melted butter or oil into a shallow dish. ↓
Step 3	Pass the fish through the seasoned flour, shake off any surplus flour then coat with the melted butter or oil. ↓
Step 4	Place the fish on a cooking tray presentation side downwards. *Note*: When delicate fish fillets are being cooked which cannot be turned, place on to the tray presentation side upwards, see important points. ↓
Step 5	Grill the fish on both sides. *Note*: Cook fillets of fish at a higher temperature than whole fish or fish steaks. ↓
Step 6	When the fish is cooked and golden-brown in colour, remove from the tray or grilling wires and place onto the serving dish, presentation side upwards. ↓
Step 7	Arrange the garnish neatly around the fish. ↓
Step 8	Accompany with any appropriate sauces and/or slices of compound butter stated in the individual recipe. *Note*: The compound butter may be placed on top of the fish when serving.

Important points when grilling fish

Step 1
Mise en place: All types of fish are suitable for grilling. Small fish may be grilled whole or filleted whereas large fish are cut into steaks or smaller pieces to assist cooking. Shellfish such as lobster may be grilled from raw but it is advisable to part cook them in salted water or court-bouillon prior to grilling. This stiffens the flesh and reduces the likelihood of dryness in texture which may result when grilling a lobster from a raw state.
Step 2
Use of fat: This prevents drying out and hardening of the fish surface or skin during cooking. It also adds a richness of taste and in many instances a distinct characteristic flavour to the fish, e.g. butter. Spiced or flavoured butters or oils may be used; these are prepared by sweating different herbs and spices in oil and adding the zest and juice of lemons or limes etc.
Step 3
Coating the fish with flour or cereal: Fish develops very little colour when grilling and therefore should be coated with flour or some other cereal prior to cooking. The flour forms a coating which develops colour easily. Other

cereals may be used to achieve individuality, e.g. breadcrumbs, oatmeal, barley and rice flours or even crushed breakfast cereals.

Step 4

Presentation side of fish:

Whole flat fish: This is the white skin side. Although the *black skin should always be removed*, the removal of the white skin is subject to opinion. In this text it is considered appropriate to leave on the white skin as it develops an attractive colour and appearance.

Whole round fish: This may be either side. However it is good practice to place all the fish with the same side down on the cooking utensil, thus achieving a balanced appearance when dishing and serving.

The skin from white fish, e.g. haddock and whiting, is always removed prior to cooking but when grilling oily fish the skin is left on, e.g. trout, herring and mackerel.

Fish steaks: As above.

Fish fillets: This is the underside removed from the bone and not the side from which the skin was removed.

Step 5

Turning during cooking: When using grilling wires, turning the fish is not a problem, but when the fish is cooked on a tray under a salamander, turning them over may be a delicate operation. When cooking delicate fish which break easily, it is advisable to grill them presentation side upwards until the correct colour is achieved then place the tray on top of the salamander allowing the underside of the fish to cook through with bottom heat.

Step 6

Speed of cooking: The cooking should be done at such a speed that browning and cooking occur simultaneously. Thin items such as fillets require a higher temperature than fish steaks or whole fish.

Step 6

Test for cooking: The flesh should yield under pressure with no sponginess. In addition the bone and flesh can be easily separated when easing apart.

Internal temperature: 65–68°C.

Step 6

Removal of centre bone from fish steaks: This is removed by inserting the point of a turning knife into the middle of the bone and locating firmly then pulling outwards.

Step 8

Service: Grilled fish should be served when cooked with hot storage kept to an absolute minimum. Grilled fish should never be reheated.

Base recipe   (yield 4 portions)

Main item:	*Flat fish*: Sole, plaice and flounder etc. = 4 × 400 g fish.
	Round fish: Haddock, whiting and trout etc. = 4 × 300 g fish.
	Fish steaks: Salmon, cod and turbot etc. = 4 × 200 g steaks.
	Fish fillets: Sole, plaice, haddock and whiting = 8 × 75 g fillets.
Coating:	Seasoned flour, i.e. 50 g flour, pinch salt (5 g approximately) and pinch of pepper.
Fat:	50 g melted butter or oil.
Garnish (basic):	4 pieces of lemon, e.g. wedges, halves or slices, branch parsley and 4–8 slices of a suitable compound butter, e.g. parsley butter.
Production:	Follow the instructions in the base method.
	Cooking times: These vary with the thickness of the fish and intensity of heat source, i.e.
	Fish fillets: 2–3 mins. on each side.
	Small whole fish: 4–5 mins. on each side.
	Fish steaks (15 mm approximately): 4–5 mins. on each side.

Dishes   (Using the above fish as examples)

Grilled sole (sole grillée), Grilled salmon steak (darne de saumon grillée), Grilled trout (truite grillée), Grilled turbot steak (tronçon de turbot grillé).

Note: Grilled salmon steaks are usually accompanied with thin slices of cucumber which are lightly seasoned and sprinkled with a little vinegar.

Grilled herring and mustard sauce

Cook and garnish as stated but omit the compound butter and accompany with a sauceboat of mustard sauce.

Grilled herring with oatmeal

Prepare as stated but omit the flour and pass the fish through the melted butter or oil then coat with fine oatmeal. Include the basic garnish *except* the compound butter.

Grilled mackerel and gooseberry sauce
Cook and garnish as stated but omit the compound butter
and accompany with a sauceboat of gooseberry sauce.

Garnishes for grilled fish

Francillon
Dress the cooked fish on fried bread croûtons then
surround with straw potatoes. Place slices of anchovy
butter on top of the fish and serve tomato sauce separately.

Niçoise
Dress the cooked fish with tomato concassé, anchovy
fillets and black olives. Garnish with lemon segments or
slices.

St-Germain
Pass the fish through breadcrumbs after coating with the
butter or oil. Neatly flatten and mark a criss-cross pattern
with the back of a knife then cook as stated. Garnish with
noisette potatoes and accompany with sauce béarnaise.

Caprice
Coat the fish with white breadcrumbs as in St-Germain
above. Dress the fish with halves of fried banana and
garnish with wedges or slices of lemon and branch parsley.
Accompany with Robert sauce.

Sorrento
Prepare the same as Caprice adding a small pineapple ring,
a piece of peach and tomato flesh (all lightly fried) to
resemble a flower on top of the fish.

Grilled lobster (homard grillé) non-derivative dish

Allow 1 medium lobster (700 g approximately) per 2
portions.
　　Part cook the live lobster in simmering salted water or
court-bouillon (page 116) for 6 mins. then drain. Split the
lobster in half lengthwise then season with salt, pepper
and cayenne pepper. Brush all over with melted butter
then grill to complete the cooking.
　　Serve with the basic garnish for grilled fish omitting the
compound butter. Accompany with melted butter and
devil sauce.

Section two   Grilled butcher meats, offal and made-up items

Base method

Step 1	Mise en place
	A Assemble ingredients.
	B Prepare the items ready for grilling, see pages 54–65.
	C Prepare the garnish and any accompanying sauces.
Step 2	Season the item/s and brush with oil.
	Important: Do not season gammon steaks, bacon rashers or made-up items, e.g. hamburgers or sausages. It is also not advisable to season items which are to be cooked under a salamander until colour has been developed, see important points.
	Bacon rashers do not require an oil coating.
Step 3	*Under-heat grilling* (Salamander-type grills): Place the items on a grilling tray and put under the pre-heated grill. *Over-heat grilling* (charcoal/barbecue-type grills): Place the items on the hot greased grill bars or cooking rack.
Step 4	Turn over when approximately half-cooked and when a good colour has been developed.
Step 5	Baste the items with more oil if required.
Step 6	Grill to the appropriate degree of cooking, allowing a good colour to develop.
Step 7	Place onto the serving dish and decorate with the garnish.
	Note: Remember to remove the skewers or cocktail sticks after grilling kidneys.
Step 8	Accompany with any appropriate sauces and/or slices of compound butter stated in the individual recipe.
	Note: The compound butter may be placed on top of the item/s when serving.

Important points when grilling butcher meats, offal and made-up items

Step 2
Seasoning the foods: The traditional practice of seasoning foods prior to grilling is acceptable for over-heat-type grills where conducted heat from the grill bars easily develops colour. However, it is not advisable to season foods prior to cooking in an under-heat-type grill, i.e. salamander, because the salt draws moisture to the surface of the food and retards colour development. In this case the food is seasoned after colour has been developed.

Step 2
Use of fat: This prevents sticking to the cooking utensil or equipment, keeps the item moist, aids cooking and browning and gives a nice sheen to the cooked end product. As in the case of grilled fish, the oil may be

flavoured to produce a distinct end product.
Important: Butter is unsuitable because of its low smoke point.
Step 4
Turning during cooking: This should always be done with tongs and never any piece of sharp equipment which will puncture the meat and result in a loss of meat juices.

When grilling small items it is usual to cook first on one side allowing colour to develop, then turn over and complete the cooking. Larger items may require turning several times, this may include turning the item on its ends to cook (a thick steak) as well as its sides.
Step 4
Speed of cooking: Colour development and degree of cooking should occur simultaneously. This means fairly slow cooking of thick cuts to be cooked through or fast cooking of thin items and cuts to be cooked rare or underdone.
Note: Prolonged high temperature searing and cooking is undesirable as it causes increased shrinkage and weight loss.
Step 6
Various degrees of cooking: Meats may be cooked to different degrees of cooking. Beef may be cooked to all the stated degrees of cooking whereas lamb and mutton are usually cooked to just done (although some consumers prefer mutton a little underdone). Offal such as liver and kidneys are often served a little underdone, but pork, veal and made-up items should be served cooked through.

Note: The visual signs stated in the following descriptions for degrees of cooking are applicable to red meats, e.g. beef and mutton.
Rare/blue (bleu): This is very underdone, i.e. raw at the centre. The flesh is quickly grilled to achieve colour and only the surfaces are cooked.
Underdone (saignant): The cut flesh is brown on the outside then proceeds to grey, followed by pink which in turn is followed by a good red centre.
Just done (à point): The cut flesh is brown on the outside, proceeding to a grey area then pink in the centre.
Important: This term is sometimes used to describe the most appropriate degree of cooking for a particular commodity, e.g. *poultry just cooked through* and no more. This definition of the term is not used in this book.
Well done (bien cuit): The cut flesh shows no signs of blood, i.e. grey brown in colour all the way through the cooked flesh.
Internal temperatures: These are stated in the section dealing with roasted meats (page 241).
Step 6
Test for cooking: The physical test for identifying the degrees of cooking is explained at the beginning of the chapter.
Step 8
Service: Grilled meats should be served when ready or carry-over cooking may affect the degree of cooking requested by the consumer, e.g. just done becoming well done.

Base recipe

Main item:	See each individual commodity below.
Coating:	Oil.
Seasoning:	Salt and pepper or mill pepper.
Basic garnish:	Watercress, straw potatoes and slices of compound butter (usually parsley butter).

Beef
Entrecôte steaks (entrecôtes)
Allow 200 g+ trimmed steaks per portion.
Follow the instructions, cooking to the desired degree.
Other suitable cuts: Tournedos, fillets and rump steaks etc.

Lamb
Chops and cutlets (chops and côtelettes)
Allow 2–3 trimmed chops or cutlets per portion (100–150 g each).
Follow the instructions. Traditionally lamb is usually cooked through and mutton kept slightly underdone.
Other suitable cuts: Noisettes and filets mignons etc.

Veal and pork
Chops and cutlets (chops and côtelettes)
Allow 200 g+ trimmed chop or cutlet per portion.
Follow the instructions, cooking the chops through, especially pork cuts.

Offal
Lamb/veal liver (foie d'agneau/de veau)
Allow 100 g+ trimmed sliced liver per portion.

Follow the instructions keeping the liver slightly underdone.

Note: When cooking the liver under a salamander, pass through seasoned flour prior to coating with the oil.

Lamb's kidneys (rognons d'agneau)

Allow 2 skinned and halved kidneys per portion.

Follow the instructions keeping the kidneys a little underdone.

Made-up items

Hamburgers and sausages

Allow 100 g+ hamburgers or sausages per portion.

Follow the instructions cooking through both hamburgers and sausages.

Garnishes for grilled meats

Garni

Add the basic garnish above, 4 small grilled tomatoes, 4–8 grilled mushrooms and French fried onions.

Béarnaise

Garnish with the basic garnish but omit the compound butter. Accompany with the sauce béarnaise.

Henri-IV

Basic garnish but replace the straw potatoes with Pont-Neuf potatoes.

Vert-pré

Basic garnish with a good helping of watercress.

Individual dishes

Barbecued spare ribs

Allow 500–750 g ribs per portion.

Prepare the ribs for grilling then place in a barbecue marinade for 4–6 hours. Cook as stated coating several times with the marinade.

Marinade: Sweat 30 g chopped onion and a half clove garlic in 50 ml oil. Add 50 ml vinegar, 50 g tomato purée, 50 g honey, 5 ml Worcester sauce, 20 ml soy sauce, 5 g sugar, 5 g French mustard, a little red colouring and a good pinch of ground basil, salt and pepper. Bring to the boil then allow to cool. Pass through a liquidizer before use.

Mixed grill

A mixed grill may consist of many different items, e.g. sausage, lamb cutlet, kidney, piece of steak and 1–2 bacon rashers. Cook as stated and add the basic garnish.

Tournedos aux poivres verts (cuisine minceur)

Prepare the green pepper sauce then cook the steaks as stated to the required degree.

Plate service: Coat the hot joint plates with the sauce then place the steaks on top.

Sauce aux poivres verts

50 ml armagnac, 100 ml white wine, 250 ml white beef stock, 20 g milk powder, 40 g button mushrooms, 40 ml fromage blanc (page 51), 40 g green peppercorns and 40 finely diced red peppers.

1 Place the armagnac and white wine in a sauteuse and reduce down by two-thirds.
2 Add the stock and whisk in the milk powder.
3 Wash the mushrooms, then poach in the stock mixture.
4 Place in a liquidizer, add the fromage blanc and liquidize.
5 Place back in the sauteuse, add the green peppercorn and pimentos then correct the temperature and seasoning.

Section three   Grilled poultry and feathered game

Base method

Step 1	Mise en place A Assemble ingredients. B Prepare the bird ready for grilling, see page 69. C Prepare the accompanying garnish and any sauces stated in the recipe.
Step 2	Season the bird/s with salt and milled pepper then brush with oil.
Step 3	Place on the pre-heated grill bars or on a tray under a salamander – underside upwards, i.e. rib-cage side.
Step 4	Allow to grill slowly. Small birds 10 mins. approximately, medium birds 20 mins. approximately. Baste with oil occasionally.
Step 5	Turn over, brush with oil and continue grilling until cooked and golden brown. This will take a further 10–20 mins.
Step 6	Brush the presentation side of the bird with melted butter then sprinkle over the surface with breadcrumbs.
Step 7	Place the bird/s under a salamander and grill until the bread coating becomes a crisp golden brown.
Step 8	Place on to the serving dish and decorate with the garnish. Accompany with the appropriate sauce/s.

Important points

Step 3
Cooking the birds: Grilled poultry and feathered game are sometimes part-cooked in the oven then completed by grilling – especially when cooking for large numbers of people. In addition some dishes are accompanied with a vehicle sauce, see Katoff.

Step 5
Test for cooking:
Physical test: Pierce the thickest part of the leg with a small skewer or cocktail stick then withdraw, allowing the juices to escape. The juice should be clear with no traces of blood.
Internal temperature: 75° C approximately.

Step 5
Removal of rib cage: Many chefs remove the rib cage from the bird when cooked to reduce the bone content served to the customer. Alternatively, the rib cage may be removed when the bird is being prepared for cooking.

Base recipe

Main item:	Spring chicken (poussin), Double spring chicken (poussin double), Partridge (perdreau) and Grouse (coq de bruyère) etc.
	Very small birds: Allow 1 bird per portion (350–500 g each).
	Medium birds: Allow 1 bird per 2 portions (800 g–1 kg).
Seasoning:	Salt and milled pepper.
Oil:	Little oil (25 ml approximately).
Coating:	20 g melted butter and white breadcrumbs (25 g approximately).
Basic garnish:	Watercress and straw potatoes. Accompany with a suitable sauce, e.g. diable or piquante. See each individual recipe.

Dishes

Plain grilled (grillé)

Basic recipe and garnish. *Note*:   The breadcrumb coating is commonly used for most poultry and feathered game.

Devilled (diable)

Basic recipe and garnish but coat the bird with a mustard paste during the latter stages of cooking, i.e. the last 3–5 mins. of cooking. Complete with the butter and breadcrumb coating as stated. Accompany with sauce diable.

Mustard paste: 5 g English mustard, good dash of Worcester sauce, 25 ml vinegar, 25 ml water and a pinch of cayenne pepper. Mix the ingredients to a paste.

American-style (américaine)

Prepare the same as devilled chicken but add small grilled tomato/es, mushrooms and streaky bacon to the basic garnish.

Casanova

Prepare the same as devilled chicken but add 20 g chopped cooked ham, chopped parsley and a half clove of crushed garlic to the breadcrumbs and mix together. Dress the cooked birds on a base of Anna potatoes and accompany with Chateaubriand sauce.

Toad-style (en crapaudine)

Cut the bird 'toad shape' prior to cooking (page 69). Cook as stated using the basic recipe and garnish.

Katoff

Roast the split chicken/s in the oven but keep underdone. Complete the cooking by grilling. Dress the bird/s on a base of galette potatoes and acompany with jus lié which has been deglazed in the roasting tray.

Spatchcock

The same as plain grilled adding fan gherkins to the basic garnish. Accompany with sauce diable or piquante.

Note: Many chefs split the chicken toad-style for this dish.

Tandoori chicken (non-derivative)   (4 portions)

Preparation of chicken:

1   Cut a small chicken into halves or a large chicken into joints.
2   Remove the skin and rib cage then cut slits across the flesh.
3   Season the chicken with salt and pepper then sprinkle with paprika and garam marsala.
4   Brush over all the surfaces of the chicken with lemon juice (1 lemon approximately), coloured with a little red and orange colouring.
5   Marinade for 8–12 hours.

Marinade:

100 g yoghurt, 25 ml oil, 5 g garam marsala, 5–10 g small hot peppers, 5 g salt, pinch pepper, 10 g peeled root ginger, 40 g peeled onion, 1 peeled clove of garlic (5 g approximately) and the zest from half a lemon. Liquidize the ingredients to a smooth paste.

Cooking chicken:

Remove the chicken from the marinade and cook under hot grill*. Turn when half-cooked and complete the cooking.

Service:

Serve the chicken with lemon wedges and a salad garnish consisting of strips of onion, lettuce, cucumber and tomato. Accompany with hot nan bread (page 356) and a yoghurt chutney made with yoghurt, freshly chopped coriander leaves and chilli peppers.

---

* This is when no tandoor oven is available.

Section four   Skewers, brochettes and kebabs

Base method

Step 1	Mise en place
	A Assemble ingredients.
	B Prepare the main item/s:
	Lean flesh, e.g. beef, pork, lamb, veal, turkey or chicken etc.: Cut into pieces, squares or rondels 30 mm × 10 mm approximately.
	Kidneys: Remove skin and cut into halves or neat rondels.
	Shellfish: Leave small shellfish whole and cut large shellfish into neat pieces or sections (all shellfish removed from shells).
	Note: The shellfish is often blanched or part cooked before grilling, see page 116.
	C Wash any mushrooms and remove or cut the stalks short.
	D Blanch bay leaves or any other dried leaves if brittle in order to place on the skewer.
	E Prepare aromatic oil if using in the recipe, i.e. liquidize the ingredients stated in the recipe. Place the main items into the oil:
	Fish and shellfish: Marinate for 20 mins. approximately
	Meat and poultry: Marinate for 2 hours approximately.
	F Prepare the braised rice and any garnish or sauce stated in the recipe.

Step 2	Neatly arrange all the items on the skewer and lightly season.

Step 3	*Meat skewers*	*Shellfish skewers*
	Brush with oil or aromatic oil if used and place on the grill bars or on a tray under the salamander.	Brush with melted butter or aromatic oil if used then coat with breadcrumbs.

Step 4	Grill gently until cooked, turning and brushing with oil as required.	Grill until all the items are cooked and crisp golden brown. Sprinkle with extra butter or oil during cooking if required.

Step 5	Remove from the grill and place onto the serving dish on the bed of braised rice. Accompany with any sauces or compound butter stated in the individual recipe.

Base recipe   (yield 4 portions)

Skewer ingredients:	See each individual recipe below.
Seasoning:	Salt and milled pepper.
Oil:	25 ml oil or 50 ml aromatic oil (50 ml oil, 50 g chopped onion and zest and juice of a half lemon).
Garnish:	Riz pilaff using 100 g rice (page 224).

Seafood skewers (brochettes aux fruits de mer)
16 blanched scampi tails, 4 blanched scallops, 8–16 cooked mussels, 4 slices of cooked lobster tail, 8–12 mushrooms, 4 bay leaves, 30 g melted butter or aromatic oil and white breadcrumbs (30 g approximately). Garnish the skewers and riz pilaff with lemon pieces or wedges.

Kebabs orientale
200 g lean mutton, 200 g lean pork, 4 quarters of lamb's kidney, 4 mushrooms, 8 bay leaves and aromatic oil with the addition of 20 g honey. Sprinkle with white breadcrumbs mixed with chopped parsley and thyme during cooking.

Section five   Grilled vegetables

Grilled mushrooms (champignons grillés)   (yield 4 portions)

Main item:	250 g mushrooms.
Fat:	25 g melted butter or oil.
Seasoning:	Salt and pepper.

1 Remove the stalks and wash the mushrooms. *Note*:   Do not peel cultivated mushrooms – peel only if field mushrooms.
2 Wipe off any excess water from the mushrooms.
3 Place on a grilling tray, lightly season then brush all parts of the mushrooms with the butter or oil.
4 Place under the grill and cook quickly for 2–3 mins on each side. *Note*:   Excessive shrinkage and dryness are signs of overcooking.

Grilled tomatoes (tomates grillées)   (yield 4 portions)

Main item:	4–8 tomatoes (400 g approximately).
Fat:	25 g melted butter or oil.
Seasoning:	Salt and pepper.

1 Wash the tomatoes then remove the eyes with the point of a turning knife.
2 Cut a cross shaped incision on top of each tomato.
3 Place the tomatoes on a lightly greased grilling tray then brush over the tops with the melted butter or oil.
4 Lightly season then place under the grill and cook gently.

Section six   Grilled savouries and cocktail hors-d'oeuvre

Base method

Step 1	Mise en place
	A Assemble ingredients.
	B Prepare and cook the savoury garnish, see each individual recipe.
	C Prepare the toast, i.e. spread with butter then remove the crusts and cut into four neat rectangles, squares or circles etc.
Step 2	Neatly arrange the savoury garnish on top of each toast shape and sprinkle with a little cayenne pepper.
Step 3	Place on a salver lined with a dishpaper and garnish with the parsley or radishes.

Base recipe   (yield 4 small savouries)

Savoury garnish:	See each individual savoury.
Toast base:	2 slices of bread and 20 g butter.
Seasoning:	Salt, pepper and cayenne pepper. Do not use salt when garnishing with salt-containing foods.
Garnish:	Branch parsley or radishes.

Dishes

Anchovies on toast (canapé aux anchois)
Garnish the toast with anchovy fillets (80–100 g) which have been heated under the grill on a tray.

Angels on horseback (anges à cheval)
Wrap 12 oysters, each in a half-slice of streaky bacon then place on a skewer. Grill gently for 2–3 mins. on each side until cooked. Remove from the skewer and garnish each toast shape with 3 wrapped oysters.

Croûte baron
Garnish the toast shapes with 8 grilled rashers of streaky bacon, 8 grilled mushrooms and 4 slices of bone marrow which has been poached in a little stock or salted water.

Devils on horseback (diables à cheval)
Carefully remove the stones from 12 soaked or lightly poached prunes then stuff with mango chutney. Wrap each prune in a half rasher of streaky bacon then place on a skewer. Grill gently for 2–3 mins. on each side. Remove from the skewer and garnish each toast shape with 3 wrapped prunes.

Canapé Diane
Wrap 12 chicken livers, each in a half slice of streaky bacon then place on a skewer. Grill gently for 2–3 mins. on each side. Remove from the skewer and garnish each toast shape with 3 wrapped chicken livers.

Canapé Fédora
Garnish the toast shapes with 8 slices of grilled bacon, 8 grilled mushrooms and decorate with 4 stoned olives.

Smoked fish on toast (haddock, bloater or kipper etc.)
Trim and cut 200 g fish fillets into suitable shapes to fit the toast. Place on a lightly oiled tray, brush with melted butter then place under the grill and cook gently for 2–3 mins. on each side. Garnish each toast shape with the grilled smoked fish.

Canapé Yarmouth
As above using kippers.

Canapé Nina
Garnish the toast shapes with 16 grilled mushrooms,

8 slices of tomato (blanched and skinned) and 4 pickled walnuts.

Mushrooms on toast (canapé aux champignons)
Garnish the toast shapes with grilled mushrooms (200 g approximately).

Sardines or sprats on toast (canapé aux sardines/harenguets)
Place the sardines or sprats on a tray then lightly heat under a grill. Garnish each toast shape with the fish.
Note: Leave very small fish whole but cut large fish into halves lengthwise. Remove the bones from large fish.

Table 8 _Recipe ingredients_

	Fish dishes	Meat dishes	Poultry and game dishes	Skewers	Vegetables	Savouries
Main item	Fish or cuts of fish	Cuts of meat	Chicken or feathered game	Slices of meat, poultry, offal, vegetables and herbs	Tomatoes and mushrooms	Pieces of fish, meat, offal, poultry etc., toasted bread
Seasoning	Salt, pepper and cayenne pepper	Salt and milled pepper	Salt and milled pepper	Salt, pepper and milled pepper	Salt and pepper	Salt, pepper and cayenne pepper
Fat	Butter or oil	Oil	Oil	Oil or aromatic oil	Butter or oil	Butter or oil
Starch coating	Flour, breadcrumbs, oatmeal, or ground nuts etc.	—	Breadcrumbs	Breadcrumbs	—	—
Basic garnish/ accompaniment	Lemon, parsley and parsley butter	Watercress, straw potatoes and parsley butter	Watercress, straw potatoes and sauce diable or piquante	Riz pilaff	—	Parsley or radishes

Assessment exercise

1 Describe grilling as a method of cooking.
2 Identify six factors which determine the speed of cooking and cooking time.
3 Name the French terms for: rare; underdone; just done; well done.
4 Describe the various functions fat or oil provides when grilling foods.
5 Name two foods which are coated with flour before grilling. Give one reason why flour is used.
6 Define the following cuts: chateaubriand; Barnsley chop; côte à l'os; carpet bag steak; poussin en crapaudine.
7 What is the French term for 'skewer'?
8 Describe how to make a basic aromatic oil for grilled kebabs. Name two other ingredients which may be added to extend the flavour.
9 Define the following grilled savouries: angels on horseback; devils on horseback; canapé Diane; canapé Yarmouth.

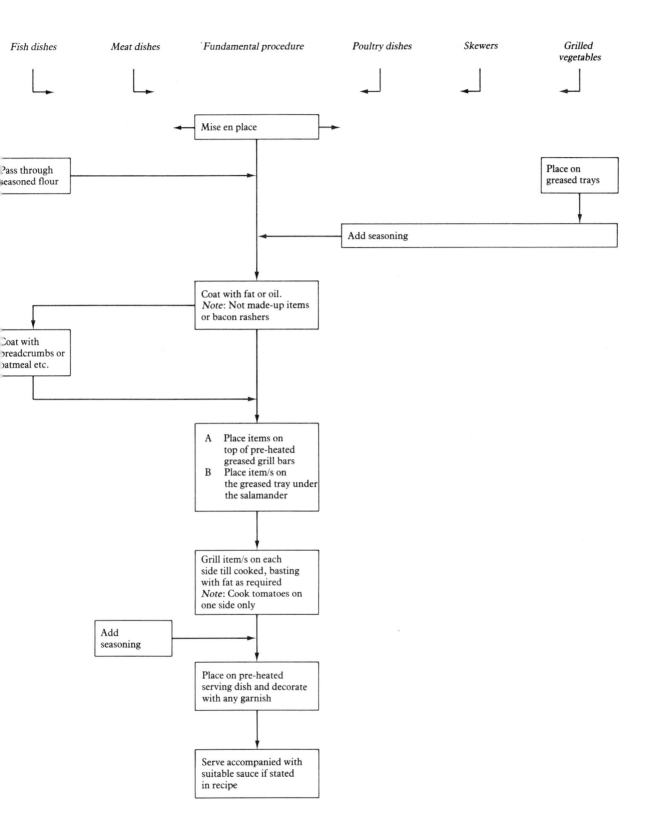

Fish dishes   Meat dishes   *Fundamental procedure*   Poultry dishes   Skewers   Grilled vegetables

Mise en place

Pass through seasoned flour

Place on greased trays

Add seasoning

Coat with fat or oil.
Note: Not made-up items or bacon rashers

Coat with breadcrumbs or oatmeal etc.

A   Place items on top of pre-heated greased grill bars
B   Place item/s on the greased tray under the salamander

Grill item/s on each side till cooked, basting with fat as required
Note: Cook tomatoes on one side only

Add seasoning

Place on pre-heated serving dish and decorate with any garnish

Serve accompanied with suitable sauce if stated in recipe

Key to diagram: The various types of grilled dishes are stated along the top of the diagram together with the fundamental procedure for all grilled dishes. Simply proceed down the activities stated in the fundamental procedure making a note of where each of the individual base method activities should be incorporated.

Figure 28 *Essential activities for grilling*

Chapter 14
Flour products

The term 'flour products' covers a wide range of goods and dishes which are based on *batters*, *doughs*, *pastries* and *sponges*. This chapter is divided into sections which deal with these flour preparations and derivatives. Each section contains the relevant process information for the products with some sections also including a recipe ingredients diagram and an essential activities diagram.

Most of the products in this chapter are *baked* although there are some which are boiled, steamed, shallow-fried or deep-fried. Further details regarding these methods of cooking are to be found in the appropriate chapters.

Baking as a method of cooking

One definition which often causes confusion or ambiguity is that of baking. A general definition of this method of cooking may be phrased as follows: 'The cooking of food in an oven in dry heat. The dry heat is usually modified with steam which has developed within the oven from the food being cooked'.

In Chapter 9, which is concerned with oven cooking, the term baking is used with such items as apples and potatoes where the products are simply being cooked tender. However, with flour products the term often refers to more complex operations. Once again, by adopting a *process approach* (as described in Tables 1 and 2, page 13) operational definitions may be produced and used as a qualification to a general definition or description. For example, compare the two processes of baking potatoes, page 234, and baking cakes, page 364. When baking potatoes the entire operation consists of a fairly simple process but it is a very different matter with cakes; selecting and measuring materials together with careful handling are all very important aspects of the production process – also the heat application in the oven should result in conditions which produce not only the correct temperature, but in addition the correct atmosphere, i.e. sufficient steam produced from the cakes to prevent premature crust formation and therefore low volume. *Note*:   See also the term baking with reference to microwave cooking, page 414.

Correctly designed baking ovens should be used when baking flour products. Traditional general purpose ovens or stove ovens which have large deep cooking compartments often produce very dry atmospheres and considerable temperature differences within the ovens, increasing the likelihood of a poorly baked product.

Recipe balance

This topic, which refers to the relationship between ingredients and quality (see Chapter 1, page 14), is of particular importance to this chapter. Many of the ingredients used in the recipes are *critical to recipe balance* and therefore should be accurately weighed or measured. Measures and scales should be capable of handling small quantities of materials (e.g. 5 ml and 5 g) as the recipes are designed for small-scale production.

Equipment

Weighing materials

Top loading digital scales are available which accurately measure from 0.1 g to 2 kg. These machines, which are suitable for kitchen use, have no scale pan, therefore any suitable container or bowl may be placed on the scale, the scale set to zero (tare weight) then the food added and weighed.

Measuring liquids

Measuring cylinders and syringes are available for the accurate measurement of small quantities of liquid, e.g. 1 ml to 100 ml.

Measuring temperature

Digital thermometers are available which quickly and very accurately measure temperature.

Measuring density

The density of sugar solutions can be quickly measured with a hand-held refractometer. This is much simpler than using hydrometers where a certain temperature must be used when measuring the density of the solution.

The golden rule for the production of flour products is an *attention to detail* when following the instructions in each of the process sections.

Section one   Preparation of batters

Base method

Step 1	Mise en place A Assemble ingredients. B Accurately weigh and measure ingredients.
Step 2	Sieve together the dry ingredients and place in a mixing bowl.
Step 3	Add any eggs and half the recipe liquid then whisk together until smooth.
Step 4	Add the remaining liquid in stages, whisking between each addition until a smooth batter of the correct consistency is obtained.

Step 5	*Frying batter* Add any colouring or oil. Whisk any egg whites to a stiff snow then fold through the batter. Use as stated on page 291.	*Crêpe batter* Melt the butter then whisk through the batter. Cover and allow to rest for 1 hour approximately. Use as stated on page 284.	*Yorkshire pudding batter* Cover and allow to rest for 1 hour approximately. Use as stated on page 383.

Important points

Step 3
Mixing the ingredients to a smooth batter: When commencing to mix a batter only half the recipe liquid approximately is used. This produces a very thick batter which becomes smooth and free from lumps when beaten.
   When the mixture contains lumps it should be strained.

Step 4
Consistency of batters:
Frying batter: This should be thick and cling to the food with a minimum of dripping.
Crêpe and Yorkshire pudding batter: These should be *thin* with a consistency similar to thin pouring cream.

Step 5
Allowing batters to rest: Most batters improve when allowing to rest for short periods (15–90 mins.). The resting period reduces the likelihood of shrinkage and toughness in the finished products. *Note*: Powder-aerated frying batter should be used while the powder can still aerate the batter. See page 359.

Recipes

Note: In all recipes milk may be used in place of milk powder and water.

Frying batters   (to coat 6–8 portions)
1   *Powder-aerated batter*:
    200 g plain flour, 10 g baking powder, 5 g salt, 5 g milk powder and 250 ml water* (yellow colouring is optional).
2   *Traditional batter*:
    200 g plain flour, 5 g salt, 5 g milk powder, 250 ml water*, 20 ml oil and 40 ml egg whites (2 eggs).

Crêpe batter   (yield 6 portions)
1   *High-quality*:
    75 g plain flour, pinch salt, 25 g milk powder, 50 ml egg (1 large egg), 200 ml water and 50 g butter.
2   *Good-quality*:
    80 g plain flour, pinch salt, 25 g milk powder, 40 ml egg (1 medium egg), 200 ml water and 15 g butter.

Yorkshire pudding batter   (yield 6–8 portions)
100 g strong (or plain) flour, 5 g salt and pinch pepper, 40 ml egg (1 medium egg) and 250 ml milk approximately.

*A small quantity of beer is sometimes used in traditional frying batters.

Section two   Preparation of fresh pasta and strudel dough

Many pastas basically consist of a mixture containing strong flour, eggs, oil and water. The recipe and method stated in this section produce excellent results for the following items: noodles (nouilles), ravioli, cannelloni, lasagne, strudel dough and other pastas.

Base method

Step 1	Mise en place
	A Assemble ingredients.
	B Accurately measure and weigh the ingredients.

↓

Step 2	Sieve together the flour and salt.

↓

Step 3	Add the egg, oil and water then mix to a *clear* dough.
	Note: For lasagne verdi add the cold spinach purée when mixing together.

↓

Step 4	Cover and allow to rest for 1–2 hours.
	Use as required:
	Nouilles, ravioli and lasagne etc., see below. Also see pages 126–7.
	Apple strudel, see page 383.

Important points

Step 3

Mixing to a clear dough: The paste is mixed until it is smooth and pliable. The cook should note that strong flour gives the paste strength to withstand the amount of handling and stretching the paste will receive during shaping.

Step 4

Resting the paste: It is important that the paste be allowed to rest and become more extensible. Insufficient resting after doughing up will result in the paste being difficult to shape with a tendency to shrink back when stretching.

Base recipe   (yield 4 portions)

Flour:	200 g strong flour.
Seasoning:	Pinch salt (2½ g approximately).
Egg:	50 ml egg (1 egg).
Oil:	50 ml oil.
Liquid:	50 ml water.

Lasagne verdi

1   Reduce base recipe water to 30 ml★.
2   Include 75 g cooked *well-drained* spinach purée.

★The exact quantity of water to be used is subject to the water content of the spinach.

Preparation of fresh pasta

Noodles (nouilles)

Roll out the paste into one or two very thin rectangles –
take to a thickness of 1 mm and a breadth of 250 mm.
Cut into 5 mm strips, i.e. 250 mm × 5 mm × 1 mm.
Dust lightly with flour to avoid the noodles sticking
together.

Lasagne

Roll out as above but cut the paste into rectangular-
shaped pieces similar to postcard-shapes, i.e. 150 mm
× 75 mm × 1 mm.
Dust lightly with flour to avoid the pieces sticking
together.

Ravioli

Roll out the pastry into two very thin square-shapes
then lightly eggwash; roll out as thin as noodles above.
Pipe out the ravioli stuffing (see page 74) in small
pieces (which should be approximately 10 mm in
diameter) on to one half of the paste. This should be
done in neat rows, piping each piece of stuffing 30 mm
apart.
Note: A pastry cutter (adjustable blades) may be
used to lightly mark the pastry indicating where to
pipe each piece of stuffing.
Cover with the remaining paste taking care to avoid the
formation of air bubbles then press down between
each piece of stuffing to seal the pastry together.
Cut between each line of filling with a serrated wheel
cutter to produce individual ravioli.
Dust lightly with flour to prevent the pieces sticking
together.

Strudel paste

Roll out the paste until very thin (like noodles above)
then place onto a floured cloth.
Carefully pull the paste by easing apart with the back
of the hands until very thin and almost transparent. It
is said a love letter should be able to be read through
the paste.
Complete as stated for apple strudel on page 383.

Note: The oil content in the base recipe may be reduced
to 20 ml and the water content increased to 70 ml if a drier
and less tender paste is desired.

Section three   Puff pastry (pâte feuilletée)

Base method: English-style (see notes)

Step 1	Mise en place
	A Assemble ingredients.
	B Accurately measure and weigh the ingredients.
	↓
Step 2	Sieve together the dry ingredients, i.e. flour, cream powder and salt.
	↓
Step 3	Rub in the cake margarine or butter.
	↓
Step 4	Add the recipe water and mix to a smooth dough.
	↓
Step 5	Cover and allow to rest for 30 mins. approximately.
	Meanwhile condition the pastry margarine to be a similar texture or consistency as the dough – see notes.
	↓
Step 6	Roll out the dough into a rectangle (10 mm in thickness) then place on the prepared pastry margarine in small pieces across two-thirds of the area of the dough.
	Note: Ensure that the pieces of margarine are evenly spaced out across the dough.
	↓
Step 7	Fold over the uncovered piece of dough on top of the centre section then fold again to completely enclose the margarine.
	↓
Step 8	Roll out the dough into a rectangle until 10 mm in thickness approximately then brush off excess flour. Roll out the pastry towards the open ends.
	Fold one end of the rectangle two-thirds of the way along the length of the rectangle then brush off excess flour and fold the other end on top.
	Note: This produces a piece of pastry in three layers and is called a *single turn*, see notes.
	↓
Step 9	Repeat the above operation, i.e. give one further single turn then cover and allow to rest for 1 hour, see notes.
	↓
Step 10	Give two more single turns then cover and allow to rest for a further 1 hour.
	↓
Step 11	Finally give two more single turns (six turns in total, see notes) then cover and allow to rest for 30 mins. before rolling out and shaping into various products.
	↓
Step 12	Roll out and shape as required. Eggwash prior to baking.
	↓
Step 13	Allow to rest for a short period after shaping, i.e. 20–30 mins., then bake until cooked. See baking temperatures in recipe notes.

Important points

Puff pastry: A pastry which is specially prepared to form *laminated dough* which consists of hundreds of very thin layers of dough separated by hundreds of very thin layers of fat. When the pastry is baked it rises considerably because steam produced in the paste is trapped between the layers of dough which are kept apart by the layers of melting fat causing the pastry to rise.

Step 1

Selection of ingredients:

Type of flour to be used: Puff pastry receives considerable handling or working during its preparation, therefore a strong flour should be used.

Type of fat to be used: Fat is used in puff pastry for several reasons but the most important reason is that fat forms an essential constituent of the laminated structure of the pastry. Fats which produce a good laminated structure are as follows:

Pastry margarine: This is a tough elastic-type fat with a high melting point which is specially designed for the preparation of puff paste. It comes under a variety of brand names and in various qualities but it should be noted that the name pastry margarine is misleading because it is not suitable for general pastry work.

Tough butter: This tends to be quite difficult to obtain but produces excellent puff pastry when the excess water is squeezed out. When ordinary butter is used great care must be taken both in regard to handling and temperature control.

Pastry margarine and butter mixtures: Pastry margarine and butter may be thoroughly mixed together to produce an excellent fat both in texture and flavour.

Fat also imparts tenderness to a dough, therefore it is advisable to *rub a small quantity of butter or margarine through the flour* before doughing up, see base recipe and method.

Use of acid: It would appear that acid added to the recipe ingredients assists the stretching capabilities of the flour. As an alternative to cream of tartar a *squeeze of lemon juice may be used*.

Important: Acid must be added in small quantities as an excess will have a detrimental effect by reducing lift instead of increasing it.

Step 5

Conditioning the pastry margarine: It is important that the fat which is to be folded into the dough be the same texture as the dough or uneven stretching between fat and dough will result, producing a poor laminated structure. To condition the fat mix or rub down thoroughly until the correct texture or consistency is achieved.

Steps 8, 9, 10 and 11

Type and number of turns for puff pastry: Folding the pastry as stated in the base method increases the number of layers in the paste. The ideal number of layers to produce the best lift is between 729–1024 .

To achieve the correct number of layers, 6 single turns (also called half turns) or 5 book turns may be used; a book turn is made by folding both ends of the rectangle to the centre then folding together.

Steps 9, 10 and 11

Allowing the pastry to rest: The pastry must be allowed to rest after working or it will be difficult to roll out and will suffer shrinkage.

Steps 8, 9, 10, 11, 12 and 13

Rolling out the pastry: It is *extremely important* that the pastry be rolled out evenly with no banging or thumping as the laminated structure is easily damaged, resulting in a loss of volume.

Steps 9, 10, 11, 12 and 13

Covering the pastry: The pastry must be covered both top and bottom when resting to prevent it forming a skin; a polythene bag is an ideal cover.

Use of scraps: When scraps of puff pastry are to be used they should be pressed together before rolling out instead of being chaffed into a ball. These scraps are sometimes placed under fresh paste but may result in uneven lift.

Note: Paste containing no trimmings is called *virgin paste*.

Step 13

Baking temperatures: Most puff pastry items are baked at 215–220°C.

Storage of puff pastry: Store in a deep freeze unless required for immediate use; a tight wrapping is essential.

French, Scotch and Swiss puff pastry: See following.

Base recipes (approximate yield 500 g pastry)

Important: Puff pastry recipes differ in relation to the total fat content in the recipe and this is indicated by the title for each pastry.

Full puff pastry

This paste is made with *equal quantities of fat and flour*. It is the best quality pastry giving a full lift in the oven and therefore maximum volume in puff paste goods.

200 g strong flour.
Pinch cream of tartar – ½ g (2½ g per 1 kg flour).
Pinch of salt – 1 g.
25 g cake margarine or butter.
125 ml cold water.
175 g pastry margarine.

Three-quarter puff pastry

This paste is made with the fat content being equal to three-quarters the weight of the flour. It produces a good lift in the oven and although less full than the above pastry it is suitable for all puff pastry recipes.

220 g strong flour.

Pinch cream of tartar – ½ g.

Pinch of salt – ½ g.

15 g cake margarine or butter.

135 ml cold water.

150 g pastry margarine.

Half puff pastry

This paste is made with the fat content only being equal to half the flour weight. It produces a low-volume pastry unsuitable for all goods which require a good lift and is therefore rarely made. Examples of use are cheese straws and low-volume currant cake and Eccles cakes etc.

250 g strong flour.

Pinch of cream of tartar – ½ g.

Pinch of salt – 1 g.

15 g cake margarine or butter.

150 ml cold water.

110 g pastry margarine.

French-style puff pastry

This is prepared in the same manner as English-style pastry but with the following alterations:

1 Roll out the basic dough (stage 6) into a square, then roll out the corners leaving a thick centre; the shape should slightly resemble a four-cornered star with a thick centre.

2 When the pastry margarine has been conditioned, shape into a square which will neatly fit into the centre of the star.

3 Place the pastry margarine into the centre of the star-shape then fold over each of the four corners to completely enclose the margarine. Proceed from step 8 in base method.

Scotch-style puff pastry   (rough puff)

This differs from English-style pastry in that the doughing up of the ingredients includes the pastry margarine.

1 Proceed to step 3 in the base method, but after rubbing in the cake margarine add the pastry margarine cut into small cubes (12–15 mm) and mix together. The cubes of margarine are not squeezed into the flour but only mixed through so that they become coated with flour and stay separate.

2 Add the recipe water and dough up then proceed as stated in the base method from step 8 onwards, i.e. allow to rest then commence with the single turns.

Swiss-style puff pastry

This type of pastry is similar to French-style puff pastry where an amount of dough and an amount of pastry margarine are encased together but with the exception that the dough is enveloped inside the margarine.

1 Use the recipe for full puff pastry but reduce the water content to 90 ml.

2 Mix 60 g of the recipe flour into the pastry margarine until completely combined.

3 Proceed with the instructions in the base method with the remaining ingredients to stage 5.

4 Enclose the dough inside the prepared pastry margarine then proceed as stated in the base method from step 8 onwards, i.e. allow to rest then commence with the single turns.

Note: One advantage of preparing Swiss-style puff pastry is that it does not form a skin or crust when allowed to rest or when stored prior to use. It is therefore sometimes called non-crusting puff paste.

Faults in puff paste

Low volume or insufficient lift

Poor laminated structure caused by:

A Use of fats which are too soft for purpose.

B Too much or too little fat used in recipe.

C Poor rolling technique – rolling out the pastry to thicknesses less than 2 mm is likely to break down the laminated structure.

D Too few or too many turns given.

E Baking temperature too low.

Uneven rise

A Fat not evenly distributed throughout the dough.

B Poor rolling-out technique and incorrect folding.

C Insufficient resting time.

D Large temperature variations in the oven when baking.

Excessive fat loss when baking

Note: Some fat will always be lost when baking.

A Too much fat used in recipe.

B Baking temperature too low.

C Insufficient turns or pastry rolled out too thick when giving turns.

Hard pastry

A Too much flour or not enough fat in recipe.

B Flour not brushed off when rolling out and giving turns.

C Over handling.

Puff pastry varieties

Bouchées: Small puff pastry cases   (yield 12 cases approximately)

Ingredients: 200 g puff pastry and eggwash.

Production details:

1 Roll out the pastry until 4 mm in thickness approximately.

Cut out shapes with a round fluted cutter – 40 mm diameter – then place onto a lightly greased baking sheet. Brush over the surfaces with eggwash.

Cut deep into the centre of each shape with a plain cutter of a smaller diameter – 30 mm – leaving a neat rim around the outer edge of each shape.

Allow to rest then bake in a hot oven at 220°C for 20 minutes approximately.

When baked allow to cool then carefully cut out the centre of each cooked pastry case; this will be used as the lid.

Carefully cut out the centre pastry from each shape leaving neat shells.

Alternative method: Proceed as above but roll out more thinly (2½ mm) and cut out two fluted shapes per bouchée. Cut out the centre portion of half the shapes with a plain round cutter – 30 mm diameter – producing neat circular rims 5 mm in diameter and small circle shapes, 30 mm in diameter; these will be the lids of the bouchées. Lightly brush with water the remaining pastry shapes then neatly place the pastry rims on top. Place each bouchée and lid onto a lightly greased baking sheet and allow to rest. Brush with eggwash then bake at 220° C for 20 minutes approximately.

Uses: Bouchées are usually filled with savoury fillings and served as a component of cocktail hors-d'oeuvre. They may also be filled with fruit, whipped cream, jam or lemon curd etc., and served as a sweet pastry.

Vol-au-vent: Puff pastry cases (yield 4 × 100 mm diameter cases approximately)
These are prepared in exactly the same way as bouchées above but are larger in size; they may be prepared as 1-portion, 2-portion or multi-portion cases.

Important: Recommended procedure is to adopt the alternative method given for bouchées above when preparing large pastry cases.

Pastry horns (yield 16 horns approximately)
Ingredients: 200 g puff pastry – trimmings are suitable – egg white and caster sugar.
Production details:
1 Roll out the pastry into a thin sheet, 1½ mm in thickness and 400 mm in length.
2 Cut into strips 20 mm wide then dampen one side of each strip with water.
3 Wind each strip round a horn mould, starting at the point of the mould; the mould should be rotated so that the strip winds on to the mould overlapping itself by half its width (and on to the dampened edge). At the end of the mould, the last part of the strip should be made to fully overlap to produce a straight edge.
4 Brush the top of each horn with eggwhite then dip into caster sugar.

5 Place on to a lightly greased baking sheet and allow to rest.
6 Bake at 210°C for 20 minutes approximately. Remove the moulds while the horns are still warm then allow to cool.

Cream horns (cornets à la crème)
Place a little jam into the bottom of each horn then fill with Chantilly cream, see page 41 and decorate with a glacé cherry.

Fleurons (yield 20 fleurons approximately)
Ingredients: 100 g puff pastry – trimmings are suitable – eggwash.
Production details:
1 Roll out the pastry into a thin sheet 2½ mm in thickness then brush over with eggwash.
2 Cut out crescent shapes with a fluted round cutter, 50 mm in diameter then place on to a lightly greased baking sheet. Allow to rest.
3 Bake at 220°C for 15 minutes approximately.

Uses: Fleurons are the traditional garnish for shallow poached fish dishes, see pages 203–5.

Cheese straws (paillettes d'or/paillettes au fromage) (yield 20 straws approximately)
Ingredients: 100 g puff pastry trimmings, eggwhite and seasoned cheese mixture, i.e. 40 g Parmesan cheese, pinch salt (1 g), pinch paprika (1 g), pinch cayenne pepper (½ g).
Production details:
1 Roll out the pastry into a thin rectangular sheet 1½ mm in thickness.
2 Brush over the surface with eggwhite to lightly dampen then sprinkle on the cheese mixture. Press the mixture into the dampened pastry.
3 Give one single turn, see base method, then roll out to a rectangle 1½ mm thick and 100 mm wide.
4 Brush over with eggwash then cut into thin strips 7 mm wide and 100 mm long.
5 Twist each strip between the fingers (to form spiralled strips) and place on to a greased baking sheet.
6 Allow to rest then bake in a hot oven at 225°C for 10 minutes approximately, until they are a light golden-brown.
7 Serve on a salver lined with a dishpaper.

Uses: Served as an accompaniment to certain clear soups, e.g. turtle soup, and as an appetizer in cocktail bars.

Cheese ramekins (ramequins au fromage) (yield 18 ramekins)
Ingredients: 200 g puff pastry trimmings, 360 g cheese flavoured choux paste, see page 346, 18 small pieces of Gruyère cheese and eggwash.

Production details:

1 Roll out the pastry into a thin sheet 1½ mm in thickness.
2 Cut out shapes that are suitable for lining small pastry patty tins and prick over with a docker or fork.
3 Very lightly grease 18 small patty tins then line with the pastry and allow to rest.
4 Prepare the cheese flavoured choux paste then pipe out as a filling on to the lined patty tins.
5 Lightly brush over with eggwash then place a piece of gruyère cheese on each ramekin.
6 Bake at 200°C for 15 minutes approximately.

Sausage rolls   (yield 8 sausage rolls)

Ingredients: 200 g puff pastry – trimmings are suitable – 280 g sausagemeat and eggwash.

Production details:

1 Roll out the puff pastry into a strip 2 mm thick and 80 mm wide.
2 Shape the sausage meat into a long rope 20 mm in thickness then place along the centre of the pastry strip.
3 Moisten the edges of the pastry with a little water then fold over the sausage meat and seal the edges.
4 Brush over with eggwash then cut into small sausage rolls 50 mm in length approximately.
5 Place the sausage rolls on to a lightly greased baking sheet and allow to rest.
6 Bake at 225°C for 20 minutes approximately.

Note: A much quicker method of shaping the sausage-meat is to soften the meat with cold stock then pipe out along the pastry using a piping bag and very broad plain tube. In addition, the sausage rolls may be marked with a knife or pricked with a fork.

Mince pies   (yield 12 pies)

Ingredients: 200 g puff pastry, 180 g mincemeat, eggwash and icing sugar.

Production details:

1 Roll out the pastry into a thin sheet 2½ mm in thickness.
2 Cut half the pastry into shapes with a round fluted cutter, 50 mm diameter approximately, then place on to a lightly greased baking sheet.
3 Moisten round the edges of each shape with a little water then place a small quantity of mincemeat in the centre, 15 g each.
4 Cut the remaining half of the pastry into shapes with a larger round fluted cutter, 65 mm diameter approximately, then cover the mincemeat and seal down the edges; the back of a small cutter, 35 mm diameter, may be used to press down the pastry around the mincemeat producing a neat rim.
5 Make several cuts across the top of the pies then brush over with eggwash.

6 Allow to rest then bake at 220°C for 20 minutes approximately.
7 When baked, dust over the surfaces of each pie with icing sugar and serve on a round flat etc., lined with a doily.

Palmiers (Pig's ears)   (yield 8 palmiers)

Ingredients: 250 g puff pastry trimmings, caster sugar and suitable sweet filling, e.g. 80 g jam and 250 ml whipped cream.

Production details:

1 Roll out the pastry into a rectangle 400 mm in length, 160 mm in width and 3 mm in thickness.
2 Lightly dampen the surface of the pastry with water then sprinkle over with caster sugar.
3 Fold into three, starting from each end, so as to meet in the middle, then fold in two to form a strip which is approximately 50 mm in width and 160 mm in length.
4 Cut the strip into 16 slices, 10 mm in thickness, then dip each side in caster sugar and place onto a lightly greased baking sheet – place each piece 75 mm apart.
5 Allow to rest then bake at 225°C for 10 minutes (approximately) until light brown then turn over and complete the cooking, developing a good brown caramelized surface.
6 When cold, sandwich pairs of palmiers together with the jam and cream.

Eccles cakes   (yield 6 cakes)

Ingredients: 200 g puff pastry – trimmings are suitable – eggwhite, caster sugar and Eccles cake filling: 25 g butter, 25 g soft brown sugar, 100 g currants and a good pinch of mixed spice, all mixed well together.

Production details:

1 Roll out the pastry to 1½ mm in thickness then cut out round shapes with a cutter, 100 mm diameter.
2 Lightly dampen the edges of the pastry shapes with water then place a spoonful of mixture in the centre of each piece.
3 Fold the edges of the pastry to the centre, seal in the mixture then turn over.
4 Roll out the shapes to 75 mm diameter then brush the tops with eggwhite and dip in caster sugar.
5 Make three slits in the top of each shape then place onto a lightly greased baking sheet and allow to rest.
6 Bake at 215°C for 20 minutes approximately until crisp and golden brown.

Banburys

Prepare as Eccles cakes above but make into boat shapes instead of rounds.

Jam turnovers (chaussons à la confiture)   (yield 4 turnovers)

Ingredients: 200 g puff pastry, 80 g raspberry jam, eggwhite and caster sugar.

Production details:

Roll out the pastry into a square with 240 mm sides and 2½ mm in thickness.

Cut into 4 smaller squares with 120 mm sides then lightly dampen the edges with a little water.

Place a little jam, 20 g approximately, onto the centre of each square then neatly fold over to form a triangle and press down to achieve a good seal – *ensure that the jam is not squeezed towards the edges of the pastry.*

Brush the tops of the turnovers with eggwhite then dip into caster sugar and place onto a lightly greased baking tray.

Allow to rest then bake at 215°C for 20 minutes approximately.

Note: A round or oval cutter is often used to cut out the shapes for turnovers. This requires additional pastry as more wastage is produced when cutting out these shapes.

Apple turnovers (chaussons aux pommes)

Prepare as above but replace the jam with a dry sweetened apple purée, see page 104.

Vanilla turnovers (chaussons à la vanille)

Prepare as jam turnovers but replace the jam with a well-flavoured vanilla pastry cream, see page 399.

Cream puffs (yield 6 puffs approximately)

Ingredients: 200 g puff pastry, eggwhite, caster sugar, 50 g jam and 250 ml whipped cream.

Production details:

Roll out the pastry into a sheet 3 mm in thickness then prick over with a fork or docker.

Cut out shapes with a fluted cutter, 75 mm diameter, or cut into squares with 75 mm sides.

Brush over the surfaces with eggwhite then dip into caster sugar and place onto a lightly greased baking sheet.

Allow to rest then bake at 215°C for 20 minutes approximately.

When cold, split lengthwise then fill with the jam and whipped cream.

Almond slice (dartois aux amandes) (yield 1 × 6 portion slice)

Ingredients: 250 g puff pastry, 40 g apricot jam, 120 g frangipane, see page 372, eggwash and icing sugar.

Production details:

Roll out the pastry into a square, 2½ mm in thickness and with 200 mm sides.

Cut the square into two lengths, one wider than the other, i.e. 1 × 80 mm wide and 1 × 120 mm wide.

Place the narrow strip onto a lightly greased baking sheet and dampen the edges with a little water.

Spread along the centre of the strip a layer of apricot jam then a layer of frangipane.

5 Fold the larger strip in two lengthwise then cut strips across the folded edge 5 mm apart and coming to within 15 mm of the outer edges.

6 Open the strip of pastry and place over the pastry and frangipane then press down along the edges to seal in the filling.

7 Neaten the edges of the pastry and mark with the fingers then brush over with eggwash.

8 Allow to rest then bake at 210°C for 30 minutes approximately. Just prior to removing from the oven, sprinkle over the surface with icing sugar and allow to glaze.

Note: One simple method of achieving an excellent glaze on puff pastry goods is to brush over the surface of the item with golden syrup when withdrawing from the oven.

Gâteau mille-feuilles (thousand leaf gâteau) (yield 1 × 6 portion gâteau)

Note: This gâteau is often called a cream slice but unless it contains *fresh cream* the title must not be used.

Ingredients: 200 g puff pastry, 100 g apricot jam, 250 ml pastry cream, see page 399, 200 g fondant, chocolate flavour and colour and lemon flavour and colour.

Production details:

1 Roll out the pastry into a square 1 mm in thickness and with 300 mm sides approximately.

2 Place onto a lightly greased baking sheet then prick all over with a fork or docker.

3 Cut the pastry into four rectangles then allow to rest.

4 Bake at 225°C for 10 minutes then turn over and complete the cooking – a further 10 minutes approximately.

5 Allow to cool then straighten up the edges of each rectangle with a knife.

6 Reserve the piece of pastry with the flattest and smoothest surface for the top of the gâteau.

7 Spread a layer of pastry cream on one piece of pastry then place a second piece on top.

8 Spread the second piece with apricot jam then place the third piece on top.

9 Spread with pastry cream then place on the piece of pastry reserved for the top of the gâteau.

10 Prepare a white fondant icing for coating and in addition two small quantities of coloured and flavoured fondant for piping, e.g. chocolate and lemon, and place into piping bags, see page 108 for the preparation and use of fondant for coating.

11 Pour and spread the white icing over the surface of the gâteau to form an even coating and immediately pipe on one of the coloured fondants lengthwise in fine lines 10 mm apart.

12 Pipe on the second colour between each line of the first to form alternate, neat, coloured lines.

13 Using the back of a knife and wiping between each

stroke, draw the knife through the lines of fondant in strokes 20 mm apart.

14 Turn the cake around then repeat the strokes with the knife (which will now be going in the opposite direction) in between each of the first strokes.

15 Allow to set then neaten the edges.

16 Serve on a round salver lined with a doily; it is advisable to place this gâteau on a silver cake board, then place the cake board on to a doily and salver (for ease of service).

Note: The icing and marking technique for the above gâteau is termed *marbling*.

Fruit slice (bande aux fruits/tranche aux fruits)   (yield 1 × 6 portion slice)

Ingredients: 250 g puff pastry, 200–350 g fruit (quantity required varies depending on type of fruit used), sugar to sweeten and 40 g apricot glaze (or any other suitable glaze).

Production details:

1 Roll out two-thirds of the pastry into a strip 2 mm thick, 100 mm wide and 200 mm long.

2 Dampen the edges with water then place onto a lightly greased baking sheet.

3 Roll out the remaining pastry until 2 mm in thickness then cut a thin strip 10 mm wide and long enough to be used as a border around the pastry base.

4 Place the strip around the outer edges of the pastry base, press down to seal onto the pastry then mark with the fingers or the back of a knife.

5 Prick over the bottom of the base then brush over the outer edges with eggwash.

6 Depending on the type of fruit used either:

   A *Hard fruits etc.*   Wash, peel and slice the fruit, mix together with the sugar to sweeten then neatly arrange in the pastry case. Bake at 210°C for 30–40 minutes. Coat with the apricot glaze then serve.

   B *Soft ripe fruits.*   Bake the pastry case blind then allow to cool. Spread a layer of pastry cream in the bottom then place the washed, well-drained fruit on top of the pastry cream. Coat with the apricot glaze then serve.

Jalousie   (yield 1 × 6 portion jalousie)

Jam jalousie (jalousie à la confiture), apple jalousie (jalousie aux pommes), frangipane jalousie (jalousie frangipane), mincemeat jalousie.

Ingredients: 250 g puff pastry, eggwash and icing sugar.

Fillings: A   Jam – 150 g jam.

   B   Apple – 400 g cooking apples, peeled, cored and sliced then lightly cooked in butter with a little sugar and cinnamon.

   C   Frangipane – 150 g frangipane, see page 372.

   D   Mincemeat – 200 g mincemeat.

Production details:
Prepare in the same manner as almond slice using the desired filling.

Gâteau Pithiviers   (yield 1 × 6 portion gâteau)

Ingredients: 250 g puff pastry, 150 g frangipane, see page 372, 30 g apricot jam, eggwash and icing sugar.

Production details:

1 Roll out the pastry into two rounds: one round 150 mm in diameter and one 200 mm diameter with both rounds being 2½ mm in thickness.

2 Place the smaller round onto a lightly greased baking sheet then dampen the edges with water.

3 Spread the centre of the small round with the jam leaving a 20 mm clear edge.

4 Prepare the frangipane, then spread in a thick layer on top of the jam leaving the same clear border.

5 Neatly cover the smaller round of pastry and the frangipane with the larger piece of pastry and seal down the edges: *ensure that the mixture is not pressed towards the edges.*

6 Using the point of a knife, make curved slits across the top of the gâteau; each slit is cut from the centre of the gâteau outwards, stopping 15 mm from the edge.

7 Decorate or mark the edge of the gâteau with the fingers then brush with eggwash and allow to rest.

8 Bake at 220°C for 30 minutes approximately. Just prior to removing from the oven, sprinkle over the surface with icing sugar and allow to glaze – see also *golden syrup glaze* under almond slice.

Meat, poultry and game pies

The various meat and game pies which are prepared with puff pastry fall into two categories:

1 Pies in which a *cooked filling* is used.

2 Pies in which a *raw filling* is used.

General information

The preparation of the pastry and covering of the pies with the pastry is identical for both categories of pie but the duration of the baking period may be substantially different. When baking a pie with a pre-cooked filling it is only necessary to bake the pastry and thoroughly reheat (or complete cooking) the filling but when baking a pie with a raw filling the baking time must be sufficient to cook the interior of the pie. Pies which include a raw meat, poultry or game filling necessitate the use of raw commodities of a reasonable quality to avoid excessively long cooking times and possible overcooking and drying out of the pastry.

Various pies

Pies in which a cooked filling is used

Steak pie, steak and kidney pie, steak, kidney and mushroom pie, venison pie, duck pie and game pie.

Preparation of filling: The base recipe and method for four portions of each of the above pie is described in detail on page 158.

Pastry to cover: 200 g puff pastry.

Additional item: eggwash.

Production details: See below.

Pies in which a raw filling is used

Steak pie, steak and kidney pie, steak, kidney and mushroom pie and chicken pie.

Preparation of filling: The method of preparing four portions of each of the above fillings is described in detail on page 77.

Pastry to cover: 200 g puff pastry.

Additional item: eggwash.

Production details for all pies:

1 Roll out the pastry to a size suitable for covering the pie dish and 4 mm in thickness approximately.

2 Neatly trim the pastry to the shape of the pie dish using a similar pie dish as a guide; this should be done cutting the paste slightly larger than the top of the pie dish to allow for the recess between the rim of the dish and the pie filling.

3 Prepare a strip of paste to fit the rim of the pie dish.

4 Place the cold pie filling into the pie dish.

5 Lightly dampen the rim of the pie dish with water then line with the strip of pastry.

6 Dampen the strip of pastry then place on the pastry cover and press down lightly to seal together.

7 Cut a small hole in the top of the pastry to allow the steam to escape and notch the sides for decoration. The back of a knife may be used to mark the cut edge of the paste to increase the flaky appearance.

8 Decorate the pastry if desired and brush over with eggwash.

9 Allow the pie to rest for 30 minutes approximately then bake as follows:

   A *Pies containing a cooked filling*: Bake at 200°C for 40 minutes approximately, until the pastry is cooked and the filling thoroughly reheated.

   B *Pies containing a raw filling*: Bake at 200°C for 20 minutes until the pastry has risen then reduce the oven temperature to 175°C. Bake for a further 30 minutes approximately, then reduce the oven temperature to 140°C. Cover the pie with dampened greaseproof paper to reduce excessive colouring of the paste and continue cooking very slowly until the filling is cooked. During the latter part of the cooking the filling should be inspected to ensure that there is sufficient moisture to continue the cooking and to determine the degree of cooking; this is done by inserting a cocktail stick through the small hole in the pastry and testing for the absence of resistance in the flesh of the filling.

10 Clean round the sides of the pie dish then place on a salver lined with a dishpaper. Surround the pie dish with a pie collar and serve.

Section four   Short pastry and short pastry products

Savoury short pastry (pâte à foncer)

Base method

Step 1	Mise en place A Assemble ingredients. B Accurately measure and weigh the ingredients. C Sieve the flour.
Step 2	Place half the flour and all the fat (recipe ingredients A) into a mixing bowl.
Step 3	Cream together until light and soft, scraping down as required.
Step 4	Dissolve the salt in the water (recipe ingredients B) and add to the creamed fat and flour.
Step 5	Mix in until completely combined, scraping down as required.
Step 6	Add the remaining flour (recipe ingredients C) and mix to a smooth dough.

Important points

Short pastry: This is a pastry made with a mixture of plain soft flour, fat and water or eggs. It may be made savoury with the addition of salt, or sweet with the addition of sugar. When baked the pastry should have a *short eating quality*, i.e. *a crisp tender texture, free from toughness or hardness; this eating quality is achieved by the amount of fat or shortening present* in the recipe and in addition *the method of combining the ingredients*.

Step 1   (selection of ingredients)

Type of flour used: A soft flour (plain) with a weak protein content should be used to reduce the likelihood of toughness in the pastry.

Type of fat or shortening used: This may be butter, margarine or a mixture of butter or margarine and specially prepared shortening. Lard should be avoided when using the 'creaming method' of preparing short pastry with the quantities of ingredients in the base recipes because too short or crumbly a pastry will result, see below. The fat content of the pastry is extremely important because it fulfils the following functions:

A   The crisp, tender eating qualities of good short pastry is mainly brought about by the fat or shortening present in the mixture. This is because the fat coats the flour particles and restricts the formation of the gluten network, see page 347. It is extremely important to note that allowing the gluten network to overdevelop produces toughness and hardness in the pastry.

B   Fat adds flavour to the pastry, especially when butter or margarine is used.

C   Fat enriches the pastry.

Step 1

Quantity of fat used: The fat content of short pastry varies between 40–70% of the flour weight with 50% fat to flour weight often being used.

Step 1

Condition of the fat used: The fat should be left in an area where it becomes soft and pliable without becoming oily. This allows the fat to mix easily with the other ingredients.

Step 4   (savoury short pastry)

Use of water: Water is one of the ingredients in short pastry which must be used with great care because it takes part in the formation of the gluten in the flour which may cause tough pastry. Originally short pastes were made with a fairly high water content and demanded very careful and skilful handling and long resting periods; nowadays much less water is used resulting in pastry being able to take substantial mixing in a machine without toughening and requiring little or no resting time prior to baking, see 'creaming method' below.

Step 5   (sweet pastry)

Addition of sugar to the pastry: Sugar added to short pastry has the following effects on the pastry:

A   Sweetens the pastry.

B   Aids colour development.

C   Increases shortness because it interferes with gluten

development; this is an important point because pastry made with a very high sugar concentration may easily become too short to shape and handle – this is unlikely with quantities of sugar up to 10% of the flour weight.

Production details: *The creaming method:* There are several methods of producing short pastry but the method selected in this section is the creaming method where a proportion of the flour is creamed together with the total fat in the recipe then the remaining ingredients added (see method) and the mixture doughed up.

The reasons for selecting the creaming method are as follows:

The method is designed for large-scale operation using machinery, although it may easily be made by hand*. The pastry can be worked heavily in a machine without becoming tough and hard.

2 The pastry requires little or no resting and the trimmings may be used many times.

Important: The operator must ensure that the instructions in the base method are followed as stated, especially at the creaming stage and incorporating the water.

Storage: Short pastry may be covered and kept in a chill for several days or deep-frozen and kept for prolonged periods.

* Care must be taken when hand-creaming small quantities of fat and flour, not to turn the fat to an oily consistency.

Base recipe (yield 300 g pastry)

Ingredients A: 100 g plain flour and 100 g butter or margarine.

Ingredients B: 40 ml water and pinch of salt (1 g)

Ingredients C: 100 g plain flour.

Medium-quality sweet short pastry

Prepare as savoury pastry but replace the salt with 50 g caster sugar.

High-quality sweet short pastry (pâte sucrée)

Base method

Step 1	Mise en place
	A Assemble ingredients.
	B Accurately measure and weigh ingredients.
	C Sieve the flour.
Step 2	Place the small quantity of flour and all the fat (recipe ingredients A) into a mixing bowl.
Step 3	Cream together until light and soft, scraping down as required.
Step 4	Add the remaining flour and lightly mix into the creamed fat and flour until combined. *Do not overmix.*
Step 5	Mix together the egg, sugar and lemon zest (recipe ingredients C) then add to the mixture.
Step 6	Mix to a smooth dough.

Base recipe   (yield 400 g pastry, approximately)

Ingredients A: 40 g plain flour and 125 g butter or margarine.

Ingredients B: 160 g plain flour.

Ingredients C: 70 g caster sugar, 20 ml egg (½ egg) and a pinch of finely grated lemon zest (1 g).

Faults in short pastry

Toughness and hardness:
Recipe faults
1   Insufficient fat used in recipe.
2   Too much water used in recipe.
3   Incorrect type of flour used.
Method faults
1   Insufficient creaming of (A) ingredients.
2   Not combining the water sufficiently with the creamed fat and flour before adding the final flour content.
Pastry difficult to handle, i.e. too short:
Recipe faults
1   Insufficient water present in recipe.
2   Too high a sugar content.
Crumbly or too short a texture when cooked:
Recipe faults
1   Insufficient water used in recipe.
2   Too much fat used in the recipe, especially lard.

Preparation of flans

Approximate yield of pastry including trimmings:
A   2–4   portions = 150 g pastry and 125 mm diameter flan ring.
B   4–6   portions = 200 g pastry and 150 mm diameter flan ring.
C   6–8   portions = 250 g pastry and 200 mm diameter flan ring.
D   8–10 portions = 350 g pastry and 250 mm diameter flan ring.

Note: As a general guide some cooks allow 25 g of recipe flour per portion but this will vary depending on personal taste, portion size and degree of skill when rolling out the pastry.

Lining a flan ring

1   Take the required quantity of pastry to line a flan ring and mould into a ball.
2   Roll out the ball into a round shape which is 3–4 mm in thickness and 30 mm larger than the flan ring.
    Note: The pastry is turned a few degrees each time it is rolled to keep it a neat round shape; the pastry should also be neatly trimmed to the correct shape if it is rolled out too large.
3   Place the flan ring on to a clean baking tray.

4   Carefully lift up the pastry by rolling it round the rolling pin, then unroll it loosely over the flan ring.
5   Shape the pastry into the flan ring ensuring that the sides are well lined.
6   Trim off the excess pastry by rolling the pin across the top of the ring.
7   Lightly press up the top edge of the pastry with the fingers so that it is even in thickness and just higher than the ring.
8   Decorate the top of the pastry by marking or crimping with the fingers.
9   Use as required.

Baking empty flan cases – baking flan cases blind

1   Pierce over the bottom of the flan ring with a docker or fork.
2   Bake at 200°C for 30 minutes approximately.
    Important: The flan must be inspected at intervals during the baking (especially in the first 15 mins.) to see if the bottom has risen or the sides moved away from the ring. When any movement of the pastry has occurred, press the pastry back into shape with the hand covered with an oven cloth; this must be done before the pastry dries out and sets.
    Remove the ring when the pastry has set and allow the flan to colour evenly.
3   Allow the flans to cool slightly then remove to a cooling wire. Wipe the flan rings with a clean dry cloth.

Note: The flans prior to baking are sometimes lined with a circle of greaseproof paper then filled with dried beans or peas etc., which are removed after the pastry has set and there is no risk of movement; this is done about three-quarters of the way through the baking period then the flan is returned to the oven and allowed to bake until cooked. This procedure is time-consuming and should not be necessary when the pastry is prepared by the creaming method.

Savoury flans   (yield 4 portions)

Cheese and egg flan, cheese and ham flan, quiche lorraine and quiche alsacienne.
Production details: Line a flan ring with savoury pastry then complete as stated for each individual flan, see page 393.

Sweet items

Fruit flans   (yield 4 portions)

Flans incorporating a raw fruit which is cooked in the flan

Apricot flan (flan aux abricots), cherry flan (flan aux cerises), gooseberry flan (flan aux groseilles; groseilles à maquereau), rhubarb flan (flan à la rhubarbe) and plum flan (flan aux prunes).

Ingredients: 200 g sweet short pastry, 250 g fruit approximately, 75 g caster sugar*, 40 ml apricot glaze or red glaze depending on fruit used, see page 103.

Production details:

1   Wash and prepare the fruit, i.e. top and tail gooseberries and stone the cherries and plums etc. – the preparation of various fruits is described in detail on pages 40–137.
2   Line the flan ring with the pastry and pierce the bottom.
3   Sprinkle a layer of the sugar over the base of the flan then neatly arrange the fruit on top.
4   Sprinkle over the remaining sugar then bake at 200°C for 30–40 minutes until the pastry is baked and the fruit cooked. *Note*:   The flan ring should be removed when the pastry is set, i.e. 20–25 minutes from the start of cooking, to allow the sides to develop a good colour.
5   When baked remove from the oven and thinly mask over the top of the fruit with the hot glaze.
6   Serve on a silver cake board placed on a round salver lined with a doily.

Flans incorporating cooked fruits or ripe soft fruits

Flans made with tinned fruits: apricot flan (flan aux abricots), cherry flan (flan aux cerises), peach flan (flan aux pêches), pear flan (flan aux poires), pineapple flan (flan aux ananas) etc.

Flans made with ripe soft fruits: banana flan (flan aux bananes), raspberry flan (flan aux framboises) and strawberry flan (flan aux fraises).

Ingredients: 200 g sweet short pastry, 200 g fruit approximately, a general guideline is to allow 50 g ripe soft fruit or drained tinned fruit per portion, 125 ml pastry cream, see page 399, and 40 ml glaze made with the drained fruit juice when using tinned fruits, see page 144.

Production details:

1   Line the flan ring with the pastry and bake 'blind' then allow to cool.
2   *Prepare the fruit*:
   A   *Tinned fruits*:   Drain the fruit, and, if required, cut or slice into suitable pieces.
   B   *Soft ripe fruits*:   Prepare the fruit ready for filling the flan, see pages 40–137. When using bananas, cut into neat slices then place in a little lemon water to avoid discoloration.
3   Spread the pastry cream over the base of the flan then neatly arrange the fruit on top.
4   Prepare the glaze adding colour if appropriate then thinly mask over the top of the fruit. *Note*:   Although 40 ml glaze should be sufficient to mask a four-portion flan it is difficult to make such a small amount, see recipe and method on page 144.
5   Serve on a silver cake board placed on a round salver lined with a doily.

Apple flan (flan aux pommes)   (yield 4 portions)

Ingredients: 200 g sweet short pastry, 500 g cooking apples, 50 g caster sugar, 10 g butter, pinch of ground cloves and 30 ml apricot glaze.

Production details:

1   Line the flan ring with the pastry and pierce over the base.
2   Place aside 1–2 of the best shaped apples, i.e. 200 g approximately, then prepare an apple purée with the remaining apples, most of the sugar, butter and pinch of cloves, see page 104.
3   Peel and core the selected apples then cut into thin, neat slices. Place into lemon water to avoid discoloration.
4   Bake the flan blind until half cooked, i.e. until the pastry is set, then remove from the oven. Remove the flan ring and wipe clean.
5   Fill the flan with the apple purée then decorate the top with the sliced apples. This is usually done in alternate circles across the surface of the apple purée.
6   Sprinkle the remaining sugar over the sliced apples then replace the flan into the oven and bake until cooked.
7   Thinly mask over the sliced apple with the hot apricot glaze.
8   Serve the same as fruit flan.

Apple meringue flan/pie (flan aux pommes meringué)   (yield 4 portions)

Ingredients: *Flan*:   200 g sweet flan pastry.
Filling: 350 g cooking apples, 25 g caster sugar, 10 g butter and a pinch of cloves. *Meringue*:   50 ml egg white (2 egg whites) and 100 g caster sugar.

Production details:

1   Line the flan ring with the pastry and bake blind.
2   Prepare an apple pulp with the ingredients listed for the filling, see page 104, then place the purée into the baked flan case.
3   Prepare a meringue with the egg white and caster sugar, see page 402, then pipe neatly across the top of the flan.

* This quantity will vary depending on the sweetness of the fruit.

4   Place the flan back in the oven and bake until the meringue is a good colour.
5   Serve the same as fruit flan.

Lemon meringue flan/pie (flan au citron meringué) (yield 4 portions)

Ingredients: *Flan*:   200 g sweet short pastry.
Filling: 170 ml water, 100 g sugar, 30 g arrowroot, 1–2 lemons, 25 g butter and 1 egg yolk. *Meringue*:   50 ml egg white (2 whites) and 100 g caster sugar.
Production details:
1   Line the flan ring with the pastry and bake blind.
2   Prepare the filling following the instructions for arrowroot-thickened mixtures on page 144. Place the filling into the flan case.
3   Prepare a meringue with the egg white and caster sugar, see page 402, then pipe neatly across the top of the flan.
4   Place the flan back in the oven and bake until the meringue is a good colour.
5   Serve the same as fruit flan.

Jam tart   (yield 4 portions)

Ingredients: *Pastry case*:   150 g short pastry, unsweetened, and 100 g jam.
Production details:
1   Roll out the pastry into a round shape which is 3 mm in thickness and large enough to line a 150 mm diameter tart plate.
2   Lightly grease the plate then line with the pastry.
3   Trim off the surplus pastry around the plate, notch and decorate the edges then prick over the base with a docker or fork.
4   Spread the jam over the base of the pastry.
5   Roll out the trimmings of pastry then cut into thin strips 5 mm wide.
6   Decorate the top of the tart with the pastry strips forming a criss-cross lattice.
7   Bake at 220° C for 20 minutes approximately.

Curd tart (lemon, orange or pineapple)

Prepare as jam tart above but use the appropriate curd in place of jam.

Syrup tart   (yield 4 portions)

Ingredients: The same as jam tart but with the following filling: 100 g golden syrup, squeeze of lemon juice (10 ml), 20 ml water and 20 g white breadcrumbs.
Production details: Prepare the filling by warming the syrup and mixing in the remaining ingredients. Complete the same as jam tart.

Treacle tart

Prepare the same as syrup tart but replace half the golden syrup with treacle.

Fruit tarts   (yield 4 portions)

Apple tart (tarte aux pommes), blackcurrant tart (tarte aux cassis), blackberry tart (tarte aux mûres), cherry tart (tarte aux cerises), gooseberry tart (tarte aux groseilles (à maquereau)) and rhubarb tart (tarte à la rhubarbe) etc.
Ingredients: 250 g short pastry, 250 g fruit, 75 g caster sugar – this quantity will vary depending on the sweetness of the fruit, and a very small quantity of water, 10 ml approximately and eggwash.
Production details:
1   Wash and prepare the fruit – the preparation of various fruits is explained on pages 40–137.
2   Place the fruit into a saucepan and add the sugar and water. *Note*:   A little ground cloves may be added when using apples.
3   Lightly stew the fruit, keeping it underdone, then allow to cool. *Note*:   A little pre-gelatinized starch may be blended with a small quantity of water and mixed into the fruit to achieve a good consistency.
4   Line a flan ring or lightly greased tart plate with two-thirds of the pastry, ensuring that the edge of the ring or plate is overlapped with pastry.
5   Place the fruit mixture into the pastry case then lightly dampen around the edge of the pastry with water.
6   Roll out the remaining pastry to a round shape and cover over the top.
7   Press down to seal then trim off the surplus pastry. Decorate around the edge of the pastry by marking or notching with the fingers then cut a neat hole on top of the pastry to allow the steam to escape.
8   Eggwash over the top of the pastry, sprinkle over with caster sugar then bake at 200° C for 30 minutes approximately.
9   Allow to cool slightly then carefully detach from the ring or plate. Serve hot or cold on a silver cake board placed on a round salver lined with a doily.

Fruit pies   (yield 4 portions)

Examples: See fruit tarts above.
Ingredients: 200 g short pastry, 400 g fruit, 100 g sugar, a small quantity of water, 25 ml approximately and eggwash.
Production details:
1   Wash and prepare the fruit, see pages 40–137, then place into a bowl and mix together with the water and sugar.
2   Place the fruit mixture into a suitable pie dish; the fruit mixture should fill the pie dish.
3   Roll out the pastry until it is 4–5 mm thick and approximately the size of the pie dish. Cut the pastry to a size slightly larger than the pie dish using a similar dish as a guide.
4   Prepare a strip of pastry which will surround the top of the pie dish.

Dampen the rim of the dish and line with the strip of pastry.

Dampen the pastry rim then place on the pastry cover and press down the edges to seal.

Notch or mark the edges of the pastry and cut a small hole in the centre.

Brush with eggwash, sprinkle with caster sugar then place on a baking tray and bake at 200° C for 40 minutes approximately.

Clean round the dish and serve on a salver lined with a doily. Accompany with a suitable sauce, e.g. custard or fresh cream.

Fruit barquettes and tartlets

These items are prepared by lining tartlet moulds or barquette moulds (boat-shaped moulds) with pastry and completing in the same manner as the various fruit flans. They may also be prepared with jam, curd, syrup or treacle in the same way as tarts.

Baked apple dumpling (pommes en cage/rabotte/douillon)

Ingredients: 250 g sweet short pastry, 4 small cooking apples (500 g approximately), 60 g caster sugar, pinch of ground cloves and eggwash.

Production details:

1 Peel, core and wash the apples then place into lemon water (or water containing a pinch of salt) to avoid discoloration.

2 Roll out the pastry into a square which is 2½ mm in thickness and cut into four small squares each large enough to cover an apple, i.e. small squares with 100–120 mm sides approximately.

3 Dampen the sides of each square with water then place an apple in the centre of each.

4 Fill the centre of each apple with the sugar and a little ground cloves.

5 Draw up the corners of the pastry to envelope the apples then seal the edges.

6 Roll out the pastry trimmings and cut four small round shapes with a serrated cutter, 30 mm diameter approximately, and place one on top of each apple.

7 Place on to a lightly greased baking tray then brush over with the eggwash.

8 Bake at 200° C for 30 minutes approximately, then serve on a round salver accompanied with custard sauce etc.

Baked pear dumpling (poire en cage/rabotte/douillon)

Prepare the same as baked apple dumpling using medium ripe pears in place of apples and omitting the ground cloves.

Fruit slice (bande aux fruits/tranche aux fruits) (yield 4 portions)

Ingredients: Same ingredients as fruit tart; the filling may be a single fruit which will describe the slice, e.g. apple slice or gooseberry slice etc., or a composite filling consisting of a variety of fruits.

Production details:

1 Prepare and lightly cook the fruit the same as for fruit tart.

2 Roll out the pastry into a square 2½ mm in thickness and with 200 mm sides.

3 Cut the square into two lengths, one wider than the other, i.e. 1 × 80 mm wide and 1 × 120 mm wide.

4 Place the narrow strip onto a lightly greased baking tray and dampen the edges with a little cold water.

5 Place the cooled fruit mixture along the centre of the strip then cover with the larger strip and seal down the edges. Mark along the edges with the fingers.

6 Cut slits across the top of the slice, brush over with eggwash then sprinkle with caster sugar.

7 Bake at 200° C for 30 minutes.

8 Cut into four portions and serve on a round flat lined with a doily.

Bakewell tart (yield 4 portions)

Ingredients: *Pastry case*: 250 sweet short pastry.
Filling: 25 g raspberry jam and 200 g frangipane, see page 372, 30 g apricot glaze and 20 g icing sugar.

Production details:

1 Line a 150 mm diameter flan ring with three-quarters of the pastry then pierce over the bottom with a fork or docker.

2 Spread the base of the flan with the jam and fill with the frangipane then lightly smooth down the surface.

3 Roll out the remaining pastry and any trimmings and cut into thin strips.

4 Place the strips neatly across the top to form a lattice design.

5 Bake at 200° C for 35 minutes approximately.

6 When baked, brush over with the hot apricot glaze, allow to cool slightly then brush over with thin water icing.

Empire biscuits (yield 8 biscuits)

Ingredients: 200 g sweet short pastry, 40 g raspberry jam, 30 g icing sugar and four half glacé cherries.

Production details:

1 Roll out the pastry until it is 3 mm thick and cut into eight rounds with a serrated cutter, 50 mm in diameter approximately.

2 Bake at 200° C for 20 minutes approximately, then allow to cool.

3 Spread the biscuits with the jam and sandwich together.

4 Prepare a water icing by mixing a very small quantity of hot water with the icing sugar and coat the tops of the biscuits.

5 Decorate with the glacé cherries.

Shortbread   (yield 8 portions)
Ingredients:
A *Ingredients*:   150 g butter and 80 g caster sugar.
B *Ingredients*:   100 g soft flour and 10 g rice flour.
C *Ingredients*:   100 g soft flour and 10 g rice flour.
Production details:
1 Cream together the (A) ingredients.
2 Sieve together the (B) ingredients, add to the (A) ingredients and lightly beat together, scraping down as required.
3 Sieve together the (C) ingredients, add to the mixture and mix to a smooth dough.
4 Roll out the dough to a round shape 200 mm in diameter and 10–12 mm in thickness approximately.
5 Lightly dust a 200 mm diameter shortbread mould with rice flour then neatly press in the shortbread dough.
6 Reverse the mould over a lightly greased baking sheet and tap the sides of the mould to remove the shortbread onto the tray. Pierce over the smooth surface with a fork or docker.
7 Bake at 200° C for 30–40 minutes approximately. Dredge with caster sugar on removing from the oven.
Note: The shortbread dough may be rolled out, pierced over with a docker or fork to avoid blisters then cut into small fingers or squares instead of moulding round.

Cornish pasties   (yield 4 pasties)
Savoury pasty made with savoury short pastry (pâte à foncer)
Ingredients: 300 g short pastry, 300 g Cornish pie filling, see page 78, and eggwash.
Production details:
1 Roll out the pastry to a thickness of 3–4 mm then cut into four rounds with a 160 mm diameter plain round cutter.
2 Place the filling onto the pastry rounds then lightly dampen around the edges with water.
3 Fold the pastry in half bringing the edges upwards over the filling, then seal together.
4 Notch the tops neatly then place on a lightly greased and floured baking sheet.
5 Brush over the surfaces with eggwash then bake at 200° C for 40 minutes approximately. *Important*:   The baking time must be sufficient to cook the filling and this will be dependent on the quality of the meat used in the filling or whether the filling has been partly cooked.
6 Serve on a salver lined with a dishpaper accompanied with a suitable sauce, e.g. jus lié, demi-glace or tomato etc.
Note: These pasties may be made with hot-water paste or cold-water paste instead of savoury short pastry, see page 339.

Section five   Hot-water paste and cold-water paste

Base method

Step 1	Mise en place
	A Assemble ingredients.
	B Accurately measure and weigh the ingredients.
	C Sieve the flour.
Step 2	Rub the fat into the flour until a sandy texture is achieved then make a bay.
Step 3	Bring the water and salt to the boil then pour into the bay.
Step 4	Using a spatula, draw the flour into the water and *partially* mix together. Allow the mixture to cool to a temperature at which it can be handled.
Step 5	Lightly mix together until the ingredients are completely combined then allow to cool. *Do not overmix.*
Step 6	Use as required.
Step 7	*Cold-water paste:* Prepare as above but use cold water.

Important points

Hot-water paste: A savoury short pastry used when preparing 'raised pies' – see Various pies below.

Step 3

Use of hot water: The addition of boiling water to the lard and flour appears to produce a firm, plastic-type pastry suitable for raised pies. However cold-water paste is also suitable.

Step 5

Shaping pastry: The pastry is *shaped when cold*. This is unlike some hot-water paste recipes where the pastry is shaped when hot. *Note:*   Pastes which are shaped when they are hot require very skilful handling.

Base recipe   (yield 360 g paste)

Flour:	200 g soft flour.
Fat:	100 g lard.
Liquid:	60 ml water.
Seasoning:	Pinch of salt, 1 g approximately.

Shaping pies

Hand-raised pies   (yield 4 pies prepared with the quantity of paste in the base recipe)

1   Divide off two-thirds of the pastry, i.e. 240 g, and cut into four pieces, each 60 g weight.

2   Shape each piece into a ball then press down the sides of each ball with the heel of the hand to form a shape similar to a steel helmet, known as 'tin hats'.

3   Reverse each pastry shape then press into the centre a lightly floured pie block (or tin or jar etc.) 50 mm in diameter. This should turn the edges upwards producing a shape similar to half raised pie.

4   Lightly press the paste upwards while rotating the block to produce a shape 50–55 mm in height; the shape should be slightly tapered with the bottom a little thicker than the top.

5   Remove the block and place the pastry shape onto a tray dusted with a little flour.

6   Repeat the procedure with the rest of the shapes.

7   Roll out the rest of the pastry until 3 mm thick approximately and cut out the lids with a round cutter 55 mm diameter approximately.

Large pies

These may be prepared in the same manner as above or alternatively the pastry may be rolled out and lined into a lightly greased raised pie mould.

Filling and baking the pies

1 Place the appropriate quantity of filling into the pies and lightly smooth down to a level surface.
2 Dampen around the top edges then cover with the lids and press down to seal.
3 Make a small hole in the lid of each pie to allow the steam to escape then notch around the edges for decoration.
4 Place the pies onto a lightly greased baking tray then brush over the surfaces with eggwash.
5 Bake at 220° C for 30 minutes then reduce the temperature to 175° C and continue baking until the filling is cooked. Test the filling by inserting a small skewer or cocktail stick through the hole of the pie, there should be no resistance when the skewer is inserted into the filling.

Adding aspic jelly to the pies

1 Prepare as 'aspic jelly' by dissolving 5 g gelatine (softened with a little water then squeezed out) in 100 ml strong stock – appropriate to the type of filling. *Note*: The preparation of aspic jellies is dealt with in detail on page 83.
2 Fill the pies with the aspic jelly while they are hot then allow to cool. The pies may require topping up several times as the jelly is absorbed into the pies.
3 When cold and set, serve the pies on a suitable dish garnished with salad vegetables.

Note: Large decorative raised pies may be sliced or partly sliced and served on a salver lined with aspic jelly then suitably garnished.

Various pies

Individual pies

Game pies

Single commodity pies:
Grouse pies, partridge pies, pheasant pies and wild duck pies etc.
1 Prepare the filling as stated on page 77, using 250 g appropriate game flesh.
2 Complete the pies as stated using an aspic jelly prepared with stock made from the game bones and trimmings.

Note: A suitable wine, spirit or liqueur may be used when making the filling or aspic jelly, e.g. Madeira wine or brandy etc.

Composite pies:
Game pies.
These are made as above using several types of game as the filling.

Pork pies

Prepare the filling as stated on page 77, using 250 g pork flesh. Make the pies following the instructions in the base recipe, method and recipe notes.

Veal and ham pies

Prepare as pork pies above using 200 g veal and 100 g fat ham in place of the pork in the filling, see page 78.

Large pies

These may be made in a variety of sizes using the same fillings as above.

Veal, ham and egg pie

1 Line a lightly greased raised pie mould with a suitable quantity of paste.
2 Prepare the filling as stated on page 78, using two thirds veal and one-third ham.
3 Hard-boil enough eggs to place along the centre of the mould when lined.
4 Place a layer of filling into the lined mould (one-third the height) then sit the hard-boiled eggs along the centre.
5 Place the filling around the eggs then continue to the top of the mould. Smooth down to a level surface.
6 Dampen around the edges of the pastry then cover with the lid and press down to seal. Cut a neat hole in the lid.
7 Decorate the pie as desired with pastry leaves etc., then brush over with eggwash.
8 Bake as stated until cooked. *Note*: The pastry may have to be covered with dampened greaseproof paper to avoid excessive colouring if the cooking time is considerable.
9 Complete as stated in the base recipe notes.

Section six   Preparation of suet paste

Suet paste consists of a mixture of flour, baking powder, chopped beef suet, salt and water which is cooked by steaming. During cooking the suet melts into the paste producing a characteristic richness and body with a soft eating texture. In addition the action of the baking powder aerates the paste opening the texture (the suet also has an opening effect on the texture) and provides a quite light eating quality. Suet paste and suet paste mixtures form the basis of various sweet and savoury puddings.

Base method

Step 1	Mise en place	
	A Assemble ingredients. B Accurately measure and weigh the ingredients.	
Step 2	*Basic suet paste* Sieve together the flour, baking powder and salt.	*Sweet mixtures* Add any of the following ingredients if stated in the recipe and sieve together with the flour and baking powder: *Sugar*: caster and soft brown. *Spices*: mixed spice, ginger or cinnamon etc.
Step 3		Add any white breadcrumbs or ground almonds and mix through the dry ingredients.
Step 4	Add the suet and mix through the flour and dry ingredients.	
Step 5		Add any fruit, e.g. currants, sultanas, raisins or mixed peel etc.
Step 6	Add the recipe water.	Make a bay in the dry ingredients then add any eggs, milk, wine, beer or spirits. *Note*: Dissolve any treacle or golden syrup stated in the recipe in the milk before adding to the dry ingredients.
Step 7	Lightly mix together until a fairly stiff paste is formed.	Lightly mix together until all the ingredients are completely combined.
Step 8	Use as required.	

Base recipe   (yield 400 g paste approximately)

Flour:	200 g plain flour.
Baking powder:	5 g baking powder*.
Seasoning:	Good pinch of salt (1 g approximately).
Suet:	100 g chopped beef suet.
Liquid:	120 ml cold water.

* The quantity of baking powder may be increased to 10 g when a light paste is desired.

Faults in suet paste

Tough paste:
1 Too much handling or overworking the paste.
2 Insufficient suet.
3 Excessive cooking.
Soggy and heavy paste:
1 Insufficient cooking or cooking temperature too low.

Savoury items

Steak and kidney pudding   (yield 4 portions)
Ingredients:
Suet paste: quantity in base recipe.
Filling: 400 g stewing steak, 100 g kidney, 75 g onions, 10 g flour, 200 ml cold brown stock, good dash of Worcester sauce (5 ml), chopped parsley and seasoning. The preparation of this filling is described in detail on page 77.
Production details:
1 Lightly grease a suitable pudding basin (800 ml capacity approximately) then line with three-quarters of the pastry.
2 Prepare the filling as stated on page 77 then place into the lined basin leaving a 10 mm gap from the filling to the top of the lined basin.
3 Dampen around the edges of the paste with water then roll out the remaining paste and cover the top. Seal around the edges then neatly trim if required.
4 Cover with a circle of greased greaseproof paper and a pudding cloth which is secured with string and with the ends tied together.
5 Steam for 3½–4 hours, see page 146.
6 When cooked, remove the cloth and paper and clean the sides of the basin.
7 Place on a salver lined with a dishpaper then surround the basin with a serviette.

Steak pudding, steak, kidney and mushroom pudding and steak, kidney and oyster pudding
These are prepared in the same manner as steak and kidney pudding above with the appropriate filling added, see page 77.

Savoury suet dumplings   (yield 16–20 dumplings)
Prepare the quantity of suet paste stated in the recipe then roll into small balls, each 20–25 g in weight. These are used as a garnish for boiled beef or beef stews etc., and are usually poached with the boiled beef or stew at the end of the cooking period – alternatively they may be poached separately in hot stock then added to the dish as a garnish.

Sweet items

Steamed fruit pudding
Apple, blackberry, gooseberry or rhubarb etc.
These are prepared in exactly the same manner as the savoury puddings above replacing the savoury filling with one of the fruit fillings given for fruit pies. Cook for 1½–2 hours approximately and accompany with a sauceboat of custard sauce when serving.

Basic steamed suet pudding   (yield 6–8 portions)
Ingredients: 100 g soft flour, 5 g baking powder, 75 g caster sugar, 100 g white breadcrumbs, 100 g chopped suet, 25 ml egg (½ egg approximately), 120–150 ml milk approximately.
Production details:
Prepare as stated in the base method producing a mixture with a soft dropping consistency – the milk content will vary depending on the dryness of the breadcrumbs. Place the mixture into a greased pudding basin (or pudding sleeve), cover with a greased circle of greaseproof paper and pudding cloth then steam for 2 hours approximately. Serve on a suitable dish accompanied with custard, jam or vanilla sauce.

Various steamed suet puddings
Cherry, date, fig, currant, sultana and raisin.
Prepare the basic steamed suet pudding mixture adding 75–100 g of the appropriate cleaned, dried fruit.

Golden syrup, treacle, jam and marmalade.
Prepare and complete as for basic steamed suet pudding but place the appropriate filling (100 g approximately) into the greased pudding basin before adding the pudding mixture. *Note*:   Do not use a pudding sleeve for these puddings.

Steamed suet rolls   (yield 4–6 portions)
Currant, sultana, raisin, date etc.
Ingredients: 200 g soft flour, 10 g baking powder, 50 g caster sugar, 100 g chopped suet, 75 g appropriate cleaned dried fruit and 120 ml milk approximately.
Production details:
Prepare as stated in the base method producing a fairly firm mixture. Place the mixture into greased greaseproof paper then shape into a roll. Cover with a pudding cloth

hen tie both ends and steam for 2 hours. When cooked, remove the paper and cloth and serve on a suitable dish with a sauceboat of custard sauce.

Golden syrup, treacle, jam, marmalade, mincemeat etc.
Ingredients: Basic suet paste using 10 g baking powder and 100 g of the appropriate filling.
Production details:
1 Prepare the paste as stated then roll out into a rectangle 200 mm × 125 mm approximately.
2 Spread with the filling leaving a border on all sides (15 mm approximately).
3 Dampen around the border with water then fold over the two outside edges to seal in the filling.
4 Roll up the paste starting at the top then wrap in greased greaseproof paper and tie in a pudding cloth.
5 Steam for 2 hours then serve as fruit roll above.

Christmas pudding   (yield 1 kg pudding, i.e. 10–12 portions)
Ingredients:
75 g plain flour
Pinch salt (1 g)
5 g mixed spice
Pinch nutmeg (1 g)
Pinch ginger (1 g)
100 g soft brown sugar
75 g white breadcrumbs
20 g ground almonds
100 g chopped suet
120 g currants
100 g raisins
80 g sultanas
50 mixed peel
25 g chopped cooking apples ⎫ added at the same time
20 g grated carrot ⎭ as the fruit
Recipe liquid: Zest and juice of a half lemon, zest and juice of a half orange, 25 ml sherry, 25 ml brandy, 50 ml stout or ale, 100 ml eggs (2 eggs approximately).
Production details:
1 Prepare the mixture as stated in the base method – this is sometimes allowed to stand 24 hours.
2 Fill a pudding basin with the mixture.
   Important: The basin must be filled to the rim to avoid deterioration during storage.
3 Cover with a circle of greased greaseproof paper and a pudding cloth which is secured with string and with the ends tied together.
4 Steam for 5–6 hours.
5 Serve on a round salver with the top of the pudding garnished with a sprig of holly and dusted with icing sugar. The pudding may also be flamed with brandy.

Note: Traditionally the puddings are prepared 2–3 months in advance (or longer) and stored in a clean dry

atmosphere; this is sometimes done in a specially cut brandy barrel. When required for service the puddings are steamed for 2½ hours approximately.

Prior to storing, the puddings, after cooking, should have the pudding cloth knots untied and the cloths allowed to dry as the pudding is cooling – this is to avoid moisture being retained in the cloth and mould developing. Alternatively, cover with clean cloths.

Scotch clootie dumpling   (yield 16 portions approximately)
Ingredients: 400 g plain flour, 20 g baking powder, 25 g cinnamon, 10 g mixed spice, pinch of ground ginger (1 g), 150 g sultanas, 150 g currants, 150 g caster sugar, 150 g chopped suet, 300 ml milk and 50 g treacle.
Production details:
1 Prepare the mixture as stated in the base method.
2 Take a cloth large enough to hold the mixture and prepare as follows:
   (a) Dip the cloth into boiling water (into the pan which will cook the dumpling).
   (b) Spread the cloth on a table and coat evenly with flour.
   (c) Place the mixture into the middle of the treated cloth then enclose and tie the cloth securely at the top. This is an important step in the operation as the texture of the dumpling largely depends on how tight the cloth is tied. As a general rule the cloth should be tied approximately 20 mm above the height of the mixture hanging in the cloth.
3 Place the dumpling into a large pan of boiling water containing a plate, cover with a lid and allow to boil for 4 hours. *Important*:   The water which must cover the dumpling, must be topped up with boiling water as and when required.
4 When cooked carefully remove the cloth from the base of the dumpling and cover with a plate. Turn the dumpling over to sit on the plate and remove the cloth from the top.
5 Place before an open oven (or in front of a fire) to develop a good skin.
6 Serve in slices.

Section seven   Preparation of choux paste (pâte à choux)

Base method

Step 1	Mise en place
	A Assemble ingredients.
	B Accurately weigh and measure the ingredients.
	C Sieve the flour.

↓

Step 2	Place the water and the fat into a pot and bring to the boil.

↓

Step 3	Add all the flour at one time and mix over a low heat for 1 minute approximately. The mixture should leave the sides of the pot cleanly.

↓

Step 4	Allow to cool, see notes.

↓

Step 5	Add the eggs a little at a time while beating the paste, see notes. Scrape down the bowl occasionally when adding the eggs.

↓

Step 6	Test the paste for consistency, see notes.

↓

Step 7	Use as required.

Important points

Choux paste (pâte à choux):   A very soft paste consisting of gelatinized flour, fat and eggs. When the paste is baked it increases in volume considerably because expanding air and steam produced within the mixture are retained within a network of coagulated gluten and egg albumen; the expansion of the paste continues until the protein network can no longer hold any gas. Also during baking the outer surface of the paste loses moisture and dries out, producing a fine crisp shell.

Step 1

Selection of ingredients.

Type of flour used: A strong flour should be used. This is because the exact quantity of eggs to be used in the paste is partly dependent on the strength of the flour; the stronger the flour, the more eggs are used. It is important to note that the gluten in the flour is coagulated during the initial cooking of the paste, losing its extensibility, therefore it is the egg protein which is the major contributor to the extensibility of the paste.

Step 4

Allowing the mixture to cool: The mixture should be allowed to cool to a *temperature which will not cause any of the egg to coagulate* and become useless. It may be left to cool naturally or placed into a machine and beaten.

Step 5

Adding the eggs: The eggs should be thoroughly beaten into the mixture; it is good practice to add the eggs over a period of 10 minutes while beating at medium speed on a mixing machine.

Step 6

Correct consistency of paste: The paste should be soft with the ability to hold its shape (*just and no more*) when piped.

Step 7

Baking the paste: Bake at 220°C until dry and crisp with a good colour. Insufficient cooking will result in the paste collapsing when removed from the heat.

Storage: The dried paste shells may be stored in an airtight container for short periods or in a deep-freeze cabinet for prolonged periods.

Base recipe

Liquid:	100 ml water.
Fat:	40 g fat, e.g. butter, margarine, lard or a mixture of fats.
Flour:	60 g strong flour.
Egg:	70–100 ml egg (1½–2 eggs).

Faults in choux paste goods

Poor volume:
   Not enough eggs used in mixture.
   Mixture too hot when adding eggs.
   Oven temperature too low.
   Badly mixing the eggs into the paste.

Poor volume with a doughy egg centre: Too many eggs added to the mixture.

Greasy pastry:
   Insufficient recipe water, e.g. water and fat left boiling on the stove causing evaporation of liquid.
   Overcooking the basic mixture.

Collapsed pastry:
   Insufficient baking.
   Paste too soft which necessitates prolonged cooking times.

Choux paste products

Sweet items

Chocolate éclairs (éclairs au chocolat)   (yield 6 éclairs)
Ingredients: 300 g choux paste – base recipe, 60 g fondant, 30 g block chocolate and 150 ml whipped cream.
Production details:
   Place the choux paste into a piping bag with a 15 mm diameter plain tube.
   Pipe out the paste into lengths 100 mm approximately onto a lightly greased baking sheet.
   Bake at 220°C for 25 minutes approximately until very crisp and golden-brown.
   Allow to cool then slit along one side of each éclair.
   Fill each éclair with the whipped cream using a piping bag and star tube.
   Prepare fondant for dipping, see page 108, then add the chocolate which should be melted and mix well together. Add stock syrup (or water) to correct consistency. (Add a little chocolate colour if required.)
   Dip the tops of the éclairs in the fondant, then remove any surplus by lightly running a palette knife across the top.
   Serve on a round salver lined with a doily.

Various éclairs
Many different types of éclairs may be produced by altering the filling and the flavour of the topping, e.g. lemon cream éclairs – lemon flavoured cream and lemon flavoured fondant – coffee cream éclairs etc.

Cream buns (choux à la crème)   (yield 6 cream buns)
Ingredients: 300 g choux paste, 150 ml whipped cream and icing sugar.
Production details: Prepare the same as éclairs above but pipe out the paste into small bulbs 15 mm in diameter approximately. When baked, allow to cool and fill with the whipped cream. Dust the surface with icing sugar and serve on a round salver lined with a doily.
Note: Traditional bakery practice is to cover the buns when baking so that the steam trapped under the cover allows the buns to swell to the fullest possible volume. When the buns are fully risen, the cover is removed and the buns allowed to develop a crisp, coloured surface. In addition a small quantity of vol (ammonia) is added to the paste, i.e. 10 g vol per 1 kg flour.

Léopolds
Prepare the same as éclairs but sprinkle with sugar nibs prior to baking. Fill with raspberry-flavoured cream and serve the same as éclairs.

Rognons
Pipe out the paste in 'kidney shapes' and bake as stated for éclairs. When cold split and fill with whipped cream then coat with coffee-flavoured fondant. Dip into roasted flaked almonds and serve in the same manner as éclairs.

Profiteroles
These are small choux paste buns which can be made in several sizes.

Profiteroles with chocolate sauce (profiteroles au chocolat)
Prepare the same as cream buns but pipe out half the size, i.e 7½ mm diameter. When filled with cream and dusted with icing sugar, dress neatly in a pyramid shape on a suitable service dish and accompany with a sauceboat of cold chocolate sauce.

Swans (cygnes)
These are choux paste buns, piped to resemble swans. The body is piped with a plain 15 mm diameter tube to resemble two adjoining question marks (♀) and the necks are piped very thin using a paper piping bag (𝟸). The necks and the bodies must be piped onto separate trays as they require different cooking times. When baked and cooled the bodies are split and filled with whipped cream, the necks are inserted and the swans dusted over with icing sugar. Serve the same as cream buns.

Souffléd fritters (beignets soufflés)   (yield 4 portions)
Ingredients: 300 g choux paste, caster sugar and 150 ml apricot sauce.
Production details: The preparation, cooking and service of these fritters is explained in detail on page 300.

Savoury items

Cheese fritters (beignets au fromage) (yield 4 portions)
Ingredients: 300 g choux paste, 50 g parmesan cheese and seasoning consisting of salt, pepper and cayenne pepper.
Production details: The preparation, cooking and service of these fritters is explained in detail on page 300.

Carolines and duchesses

These are savoury choux buns which are filled with a variety of fillings, e.g. chicken, ham and salmon , and served as an hors-d'oeuvre or garnish to a dish. Carolines usually tend to be produced *éclair-shaped* and are covered with a *chaudfroid* coating and aspic glaze, whereas duchesses are normally *bun-shaped* and only receive an aspic coating.

Cheese ramekins (ramequins au fromage)   (yield 18 ramekins)

These are tartelettes made with puff paste and choux paste cheese mixture, see cheese fritters above. Increasing the cheese content in the choux paste to 60 g parmesan should produce 360 g mixture, i.e. 18 tartlets with 20 g mixture per tartlet. The method of preparing cheese ramekins is explained in detail on page 327.
Note: Ramekins are sometimes made without the puff paste bases.

Profiteroles

These are small choux paste buns which are usually piped out in the following sizes:
Very small = 2½ mm diameter: These very small buns which are often piped out with a paper piping bag should be pea-size when baked. They are usually used as a garnish for clear soups, see page 84, and may be plain or stuffed with a cooked meat, purée etc.
Small = 5–7½ mm diameter: These are small choux paste buns which are stuffed with a savoury filling and used as a garnish to a dish or part of a cocktail hors-d'oeuvre.
Important: When baking very small choux buns the operator must inspect the oven regularly because the buns cook very quickly, e.g. 4 minutes approximately.

Various gâteaux

Gâteau St-Honoré   (yield 6 portions)

Ingredients: 350 g sweet short pastry, see page 332, 400 g choux paste, 300 ml crème St-Honoré or crème Chantilly and eggwash.

Sugar syrup for glazing: 200 g granulated sugar, 60 ml water and 50 g glucose.
Sugar syrup for spun sugar: 200 g sugar, 60 ml water and 15 g glucose.
Production details:
1   Roll out the pastry into a circle 175 mm in diameter and 3 mm in thickness then place onto a lightly greased baking sheet. Prick all over with a fork.
2   Eggwash around the outer edge of the pastry then pipe round a layer of choux paste using a 15 mm diameter plain tube. Carefully eggwash the top of the choux paste.
3   Using the remaining choux paste pipe out 12 choux buns (10 mm diameter plain tube) onto a lightly greased baking sheet. Carefully eggwash the tops of the buns.
4   Bake the pastry base and the buns at 220°C until crisp and golden brown, 25 minutes approximately, then place onto a cooling wire and allow to become cold.
5   Prepare a sugar syrup for dipping petits fours, see page 107, using quantities stated and boil to 154°C.
6   Dip the buns into the sugar syrup then neatly arrange around the top of the choux paste on the pastry base.
7   Fill the centre of the gâteau with the cream then place onto a round salver lined with a doily.
8   Using the remaining sugar and glucose with the addition of 60 ml water prepare a spun sugar veil, see page 107, and decorate over the top of the gâteau.

Gâteau Paris-Brest   (yield 6 portions)

Ingredients: 400 g choux paste, 300 ml praline-flavoured whipped cream, 30 g sliced almonds, icing sugar and eggwash.
Production details:
1   Pipe out a choux paste ring 175 mm diameter onto a lightly greased baking sheet; this should be done using a 15 mm diameter plain tube.
2   Increase the thickness of the choux paste ring by piping a further layer of choux paste onto and around the inner side of the ring; this should produce a thick ring of choux paste.
3   Eggwash the ring then sprinkle over the sliced almonds.
4   Bake at 210°C for 35 minutes approximately until very crisp and golden-brown then allow to cool.
5   Carefully slit around the gâteau under the sliced almond crust then fill with the praline-flavoured whipped cream.
6   Sprinkle over with a good layer of icing sugar then place onto a round salver lined with a dishpaper.

Croquembouche   (yield 12 portions)

Ingredients: 600 g choux paste, 1 litre of vanilla bavaroise, see page 396, 1 base of nougat Montélimar (175 mm diameter), see page 109.

ugar syrup for glazing: 400 g granulated sugar, 125 ml
water and 100 g glucose.
ugar syrup for spun sugar: 200 g granulated sugar, 60 ml
water and 15 g glucose.
Production details:

Prepare the vanilla-flavoured bavarois and allow to
set in a conical bombe mould.

Pipe the choux paste into round buns of various sizes:
one-quarter paste piped into buns using 15 mm
diameter tube; one-quarter using 10 mm diameter
tube; one-quarter using 7½ mm diameter tube and
one-quarter with a 5 mm diameter tube, all piped onto
lightly greased baking sheets.

Bake at 220°C for 30 minutes approximately until very
crisp and golden-brown then allow to cool.

Lightly oil a conical bombe mould which is the same
size as the one used to set the bavarois and place onto a
lightly oiled marble slab or board.

Prepare a boiled syrup for coating the buns with the
quantities stated and boil to 154°C, see page 107.

Dip the buns into the boiled syrup one by one and
place round the mould, allowing the buns to touch and
stick together; this should be done starting with the
largest buns at the base of the mould and proceeding to
the smaller buns as the mould is surrounded and
completely covered with dipped buns. Allow to cool
and set.

Turn out the bavaroise onto the nougat.

Detach the buns from the oiled mould then neatly
place over the bavaroise.

Prepare a spun sugar veil with the quantities stated and
colour to taste, see page 107, and decorate on the top of
the croquembouche.

Note: The croquembouche may be decorated with
rosettes of whipped cream, glacé cherries, diamonds of
angelica and crystallized violets if desired.

Section eight   Yeast goods

One means of aerating or leavening a whole range of foods
is to incorporate into the recipe a specially cultivated yeast
which produces carbon dioxide gas by means of
fermentation. This biological form of aeration is
extremely complex and it is important for the cook to have
some understanding of the main aspects of yeast
fermentation. This may be done by (a) looking at the main
ingredients used in yeast mixtures, and examining the
factors such as (b) temperature and (c) time during
fermentation.

(a)   *Main ingredients used in yeast goods*

Yeast: Yeast is a living micro-organism in the form of a
unicellular plant. When yeast is supplied with food,
moisture and warmth it multiplies and produces *carbon
dioxide gas*. The yeast feeds on the sugar of the recipe flour
by means of enzymes; these enzymes change cane sugar
and malt sugar into dextrose which can be absorbed by the
yeast as a food. During fermentation, the yeast's
production of carbon dioxide gas aerates the dough and
the other products produce flavour, texture and colour in
the finished article provided the fermentation and baking
have been carried out correctly.

Yeast for baking can be purchased in two forms: fresh
yeast, i.e. moist compressed yeast, and dried yeast.
Important: The recipes and fermentation times are
designed specifically for the *use of fresh yeast* (compressed)
and *not* dried yeast.

Flour: The type of flour that is required for yeast goods
is a *strong flour*, usually milled from a mixture of wheats in
which spring wheats predominate. This type of flour,
which may be called *strong flour*, *bread flour* or *spring flour* is
the most suitable for yeast work because it contains the
correct type of proteins both in quantity and quality to
impart strength into the flour. The main proteins are
glutenin and *gliadin*, which join together when the flour is
wetted to become an elastic network called *gluten*, and it is
this gluten which traps the gas produced by the yeast.
Gliadin imparts the elastic properties to the gluten and
glutenin provides stability and toughness to the protein. It
is important for the cook to note that a major contributing
factor to the production of good-quality yeast goods is the
use of flour which contains the correct quantity and
quality of gluten; much of the volume and bulkiness of
good bread and buns is directly related to the strength of
the gluten in the flour.

Water: To grow and multiply, yeast, like all other forms
of life, requires water or a water-containing liquid. Milk is
often added to yeast mixtures to produce a particular
texture and flavour, but because of the storage
requirements and the additional work in bringing the milk

to a suitable temperature to be added to the other ingredients, many bakers simply use milk powder and water; the use of milk powder also aids accuracy when a specific concentration of milk solids is required for a given yeast preparation.

Note: If fresh milk is not *scalded* it may affect dough consistency and loaf volume.

Salt: There are several reasons for adding salt to yeast preparations and the main reason, as one might suspect, is to promote flavour. However, there are several other important reasons for including salt in yeast recipes:

1 Salt added in the correct quantity to a yeast mixture has a strengthening and stabilizing effect on the gluten of the flour in turn assisting the production of well-aerated, bulky bread.
2 The bloom or appearance of yeast products is enhanced with the addition of salt to the yeast mixture.
3 Salt also has a controlling effect on the development and multiplication of yeast cells ensuring that a yeast mixture ferments at a desired pace.

The above ingredients are the *four essential ingredients* to the production of good bread.

(b) *Fermentation temperature*

The temperature at which a yeast mixture is allowed to ferment is extremely important because it is one of the major factors which determines yeast activity. The following table illustrates the relationship between temperature and yeast activity.

Table 9

Temperature (°C)	Yeast activity
0	Inactive or dormant.
5	Too slow for most fermented products.
15	Used for long, cool fermentation periods, see brioche.
18	Used for cool doughs, see croissants and Danish pastries.
25–29	Standard: best fermentation temperature range with an ideal temperature of 27 °C usually most acceptable.
30	Too high, producing a fast-moving activity and rapid skinning of the dough when left uncovered.
35–50	Far too high producing a very fast-moving activity which falls off or becomes inactive as the yeast is destroyed.

(c) *Fermentation time*

The duration of the fermentation period is another vital factor in the production of yeast goods. To understand the importance of ensuring that the correct period of fermentation is achieved we can take another look at some of the things that happen during fermentation. As stated earlier, the yeast during fermentation produces gas, alcohol and other products by feeding mainly on the sugar of the recipe flour. Now if the correct degree of fermentation is achieved the appearance or bloom of the baked goods will be as it should be, i.e. good crust colour. When the fermentation time is too short the sugar in the flour which has not been utilized by the yeast will produce a brick-red crust colour in the baked goods – termed *foxy* by bakers. On the other hand, when the fermentation time is too long, too much of the sugar will have been utilized by the yeast resulting in very little, if any, crust colour.

Another factor which is extremely important is that the *condition of the gluten changes* during fermentation. At the beginning of fermentation the gluten is inextensible but during fermentation the gluten becomes more extensible this allows the gluten to stretch, trapping as much gas as possible. Correct fermentation time produces goods which are high in volume and flavour with an even texture and soft eating crumb. Insufficient fermentation produces goods which tend to be lacking in flavour with a tough crust which very quickly become dry and unpalatable, whereas over-fermentation results in the gluten network being broken down and in turn losing its gas-holding properties; this results in the finished goods being low in volume and rather flat in shape with a poor texture.

Another important factor is that much of the flavour of good-quality yeast products is developed by correct fermentation. In addition to the yeast organisms which are multiplying and in turn contributing to flavour, other organisms are also present in the yeast mixture. Lactic and acetic bacteria are growing which produce acids in the mixture – these acids help to develop the gluten and contribute to the flavour and aroma of the yeast product when fermentation has been carried out correctly. However, when the mixture is over-fermented these acids predominate, producing an undesirable sour taste and smell.

Important: The above information indicates that the *production* of good yeast products *relies on correct fermentation* which necessitates the use of the *correct ingredients* in the *correct quantities*, fermented at the *correct temperature* for the *correct time*. When the yeast mixture has reached a point where optimum conditions have been brought about by fermentation the mixture or dough is said to be *ripe*.

Factors affecting the time required to produce a ripe dough

(a) Temperature of dough.
(b) The amount of salt, yeast and water present.

c) Quantity and quality of the gluten in the flour.
d) The use of yeast foods and bread improvers.
e) The amount of mechanical action or manipulation the dough receives.*

Ingredients which retard fermentation

Care must be taken to ensure that *salt and spices are weighed accurately* as these ingredients are *critical to recipe balance*. Too high a concentration of salt or spices seriously *retard yeast activity* and may even destroy the yeast cells.

Storage of yeast goods

Whenever possible yeast goods should be served freshly baked, although many types of bread, bread rolls and pizza pies etc., may be quick-frozen and stored for several weeks in a deep-freeze cabinet. Refrigerator storage is unsuitable for yeast goods because the dry atmosphere causes rapid staling (unless the goods are sealed in an airtight container).

The use of vigorous mechanical action and special chemicals can not only reduce the fermentation time but completely eliminate the bulk fermentation period – these doughs which do not require any bulk fermentation are called 'no time doughs'.

Table 10 *Recipe ingredients*

	Main items						Other items			
	Yeast	Flour	Water	Salt	Sugar	Fat	Milk powder	Eggs	Other ingredients
Bread and bread rolls	+	+	+	+	Some recipes	+	Some recipes	—	—
Currant bread	+	+	+	+	+	+	+	—	Currants
Various buns	+	+	+	+	+	+	+	Some recipes	Fruit, spices, icing and jam etc.
Pizza pies	+	Soft flour	+	+	+	+	+	+	Onions, garlic, tomatoes, cheese, oil and seasoning etc.
Crescents	+	+	+	+	+	+	+	+	Butter or pastry margarine.
Danish pastries	+	+	+	+	+	+	+	Some recipes	Butter or pastry margarine. *Also*: apricot glaze and icing etc.
Savarins	+	+	+	★	+	+ Butter	+	+	Soaking syrup, cream and fruit etc.
Babas	+	+	+	★	+	+ Butter	+	+	Currants, soaking syrup, cream and glacé cherries etc.
Brioche	+	+	+	★	+	+ Butter	+	+	Icing etc.

★ Salt is not usually present in these recipes because of the high butter and egg content which already contains salt in varying proportions.

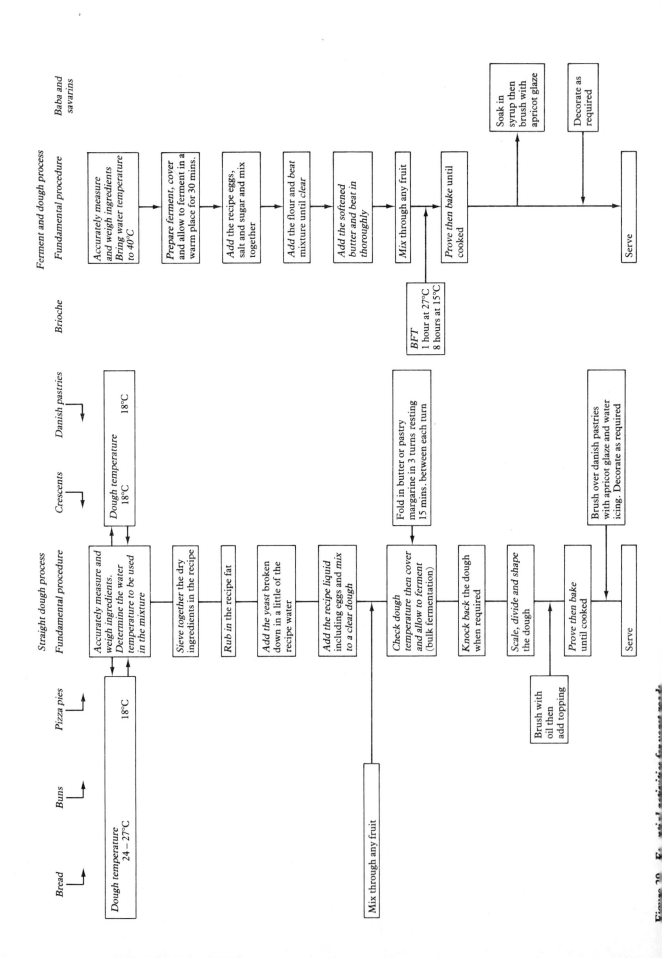

Ferment and dough process

Baba and savarins

Fundamental procedure

Accurately measure and weigh ingredients Bring water temperature to 40°C	
Prepare ferment, cover and allow to ferment in a warm place for 30 mins.	
Add the recipe eggs, salt and sugar and mix together	
Add the flour and beat mixture until clear	
Add the softened butter and beat in thoroughly	
Mix through any fruit	
Prove then bake until cooked	Soak in syrup then brush with apricot glaze
	Decorate as required
Serve	

Brioche

BFT
1 hour at 27°C
8 hours at 15°C

Straight dough process

Crescents   *Danish pastries*

Dough temperature   18°C
18°C

Fundamental procedure

Accurately measure and weigh ingredients. Determine the water temperature to be used in the mixture
Sieve together the dry ingredients in the recipe
Rub in the recipe fat
Add the yeast broken down in a little of the recipe water
Add the recipe liquid including eggs and mix to a clear dough
Check dough temperature then cover and allow to ferment (bulk fermentation)
Knock back the dough when required
Scale, divide and shape the dough
Prove then bake until cooked
Serve

Fold in butter or pastry margarine in 3 turns resting 15 mins. between each turn

Brush over danish pastries with apricot glaze and water icing. Decorate as required

Brush with oil then add topping

Bread   *Buns*   *Pizza pies*

Dough temperature
24–27°C   18°C

Mix through any fruit

Figure 20

ection eight part (A) Preparation of yeast goods using a straight dough process

ase method

tep 1	A Assemble ingredients.
	B Accurately measure and weigh the various ingredients.
	C Set oven thermostat to required temperature for baking the items.
	D Determine the water temperature for the dough concerned – see important points.
tep 2	Sieve together the dry ingredients stated in the individual recipe, i.e. flour, salt, sugar and milk powder etc., and place into a mixing bowl.
tep 3	Add the fat in small pieces and rub completely into the flour.
tep 4	Break down the yeast in some of the recipe liquid and add to the dry ingredients.
tep 5	Add any egg and almost all of the liquid, keeping back a small quantity to correct consistency and texture if necessary.
tep 6	Mix together (slow speed) to produce a *clear dough*, see important points.
tep 7	Add any fruit, e.g. sultanas, raisins, currants or mixed peel , and mix through the dough taking care not to burst the fruit.
tep 8	Cover the dough to prevent skinning and allow to ferment, see *bulk fermentation time*.
tep 9	*Knock back* the dough when required and continue the *bulk fermentation*.
tep 10	*Scale and divide* the dough into the quantities stated in the individual recipe.
tep 11	*Mould or shape* the dough as required and place onto prepared baking trays or into prepared baking tins etc.
tep 12	Allow to *prove* until ready for baking.
tep 13	*Bake* as stated in the individual recipe, i.e. at the correct temperature and for the correct period of time.
tep 14	When baked, remove from the oven and place onto cooling wires.
	Note: Carefully turn out any items which are baked in tins or moulds etc.

Important points

Straight dough process: This is the method of preparing the dough as stated in the base method. It is a popular method of preparing yeast goods because it is quick and simple and in turn suitable for most yeast products (with the exception of those goods which have a very high fat, sugar or spice content, see ferment and dough process on page 357).

Various recipe ingredients and their functions: This has been dealt with in detail on page 347.

Determining the water temperature to achieve a stated dough temperature: The fermentation temperature which should be used for a particular dough is achieved by adding the recipe liquid (usually water, see page 347) at a specific temperature. The temperature of the recipe liquid is calculated as follows:

1   Measure the flour temperature using a 'dough thermometer'.
2   Multiply by two the stated dough temperature then subtract the flour temperature.
3   The figure left is the required water temperature.

Example: Dough temperature required 25° C. Flour temperature 18° C.

Formula: (A) 25 × 2 = 50. (B) 50 − 18 = 32. Water temperature for particular dough is 32° C.

Note: This formula works extremely well in large-scale bakery conditions but when preparing very small quantities with equipment and materials which are cold or even chilled, the equipment and very cold ingredients such as eggs etc., should be slightly warmed.

Steps 4 and 5

Addition of recipe water: The amount of water required by a particular dough depends on the water-absorbing power of the flour used in the recipe. Some flours absorb less moisture than others, therefore it is good practice to keep back a little liquid when mixing the dough, then add at the last moment if required.

Step 6

Mixing to a clear dough: Mixing the yeast dough is a very important stage in the process. The dough must be mixed thoroughly to *develop the gluten*, see page 347. The dough should be mixed and worked until it becomes *silky smooth with a pliable elastic-like texture* and leaves the fingers cleanly without any feel of wet stickiness. A yeast dough which is mixed until it reaches the condition described above is called a *clear dough*.

Step 8

Bulk fermentation time: This is the period of time the whole dough lies fermenting, taking place between reaching a clear dough and scaling and dividing. It is important that the fermentation temperature be maintained during this period to reach the correct degree of *ripeness* in the dough when ready for baking, see page 348. As stated in the base method the dough must be covered or placed inside a plastic or polythene bag to avoid a skin forming on the surface of the dough.

Step 9

Knocking back the dough: During the fermentation period the dough is folded and pressed firmly down three or four times then covered and left to continue fermenting. The time at which this operation is carried out is stated in the individual recipe. The reasons for knocking back a dough are as follows:

(a)   Helps to even out temperature during fermentation
(b)   Aids the gluten distribution throughout the dough improving the texture of the finished item.
(c)   It is said to give the yeast a supply of free oxygen encouraging yeast development.

Step 10

Scaling and dividing a dough: This is dividing the dough into pieces by weight.

Step 11

Moulding or shaping the dough: This is the shaping of the pieces of dough prior to proving. The dough may be shaped or moulded (sometimes called 'chaffed') into individual units such as buns or rolls etc., or into larger items such as loaves. The moulding should produce *smooth-skinned* shapes which result in a texture which is free from holes or pockets in the finished items.

Step 12

Proving the dough: This is the final fermentation of the shaped items prior to baking. During proving the items are usually placed into a proving cabinet which provides warmth and moisture. Under these conditions the items ferment quite quickly without forming a skin. Care must be taken to ensure that the prover is at the correct temperature, which is approximately 28° C (temperature over 30° C should be avoided). During proving the dough should *double* in size approximately.

Step 13

Baking yeast goods: Fermented goods require *hot oven temperatures* when baking. Most items are baked at temperatures between 215–245° C with the general guideline that the larger, rich buns and breads are baked at lower temperatures than the smaller, less rich items. Another important factor in addition to temperature is the amount of steam present in the oven during baking; too dry an oven will form the crust before maximum volume of the goods is attained, therefore where possible fully-loaded ovens should be the rule. When small quantities or batches are being baked a pan of water placed in the oven is advantageous.

Yeast goods – straight dough process

Bread rolls (yield 15 rolls)
500 g strong flour, 10 g salt, 5 g white fat, 15 g yeast and 280 ml water.
Dough temperature: 27°C.
Bulk fermentation: 1 hour. Knock back after 45 mins. Scale at 50 g each.
Baking temperature: 235°C.

Cottage bread (yield 2 loaves)
Prepare as stated above but divide the dough into two pieces. Cut a small piece of dough from each of the two pieces of dough then mould into two cottage loaves. Use the same baking temperature but set in steam for the first 10 mins. of baking.

Milk bread (yield 2 loaves)
500 g strong flour, 10 g salt, 35 g milk powder, 10 g white fat, 15 g yeast and 300 ml water.
Dough temperature: 25°C.
Bulk fermentation: 2 hours. Knock back after 90 mins.
Divide the dough into two pieces. Mould as required.
Baking temperature: 230°C.
Approximate baking time: 30 mins.

Pan bread (yield 2 loaves)
500 g strong flour, 10 g salt, 5 g malt flour, 10 g milk powder, 10 g caster sugar, 25 g white fat, 20 g yeast, 300 ml water.
Dough temperature: 24°C.
Bulk fermentation: 90 mins. Knock back after 45 mins.
Divide the dough into two pieces. Mould and place into greased pan tins. Prove then bake at 230°C.

Vienna bread (yield 2 loaves)
500 g strong flour, 10 g salt, 15 g milk powder, 5 g caster sugar, 15 white fat, 15 g yeast, 300 ml water.
Dough temperature: 24°C.
Bulk fermentation: 2 hours. Knock back after 90 mins.
Divide the dough into two pieces. Mould and dry prove upside down in a cloth, then carefully invert onto a baking tray. Cut the loaves with a sharp knife prior to baking then bake at 235°C. Use steam for the first 10 mins.

Currant bread (yield 2 loaves)
500 g strong flour, 10 g salt, 15 g milk powder, 15 g caster sugar, 20 g white fat, 20 g yeast, 300 ml water and 140 g currants.
Dough temperature: 25°C.
Bulk fermentation: 2 hours. Knock back after 90 mins.
Divide the dough into two pieces. Mould and place into greased bread tins. Prove, then bake at 230°C for 30 mins. approximately.

Brown bread (yield 2 loaves)
200 g wholemeal flour, 250 g strong flour, 10 g salt, 15 g white fat, 20 g yeast and 280 ml water.
Dough temperature: 24°C.
Bulk fermentation: 45 mins. Knock back after 30 mins.
Divide the dough into two pieces. Mould and place into two greased bread tins. Prove, then bake at 230°C for 35 mins. approximately.

Fruited Easter bread (high-quality) (yield 2 loaves)
500 g strong flour, 10 g salt, 20 g caster sugar, 20 g milk powder, 40 g butter, 2½ g lemon zest, 20 g malt extract, 20 g honey, 50 ml egg (1 egg approximately), 10 ml egg yolk (1 yolk approximately), 50 g yeast, 200 ml water, 150 g sultanas, 35 g orange peel and 70 g pine kernels if available.
Prepare as stated in the base method, dissolving the honey, malt extract and lemon zest in some of the recipe water.
Dough temperature: 25°C.
Bulk fermentation: 90 mins. Knock back after 1 hour.
Divide the dough into two pieces and shape into two plaited loaves. Prove then brush with a mixture of 5 g ground hazelnuts, 5 g caster sugar, 10 ml egg white (½ egg white) and 30 g icing sugar. Dredge with icing sugar then bake at 210°C for 35 mins. approximately.

Christmas bread or stollen (yield 2 loaves)
500 g strong flour, 5 g salt, 25 g caster sugar, 25 g milk powder, 50 g white fat, 50 g butter, 50 ml egg (1 egg), 2½ g lemon zest, pinch nutmeg, 50 g yeast, 200 ml water, 300 g raisins and 50 g mixed peel.
Dough temperature: 25°C.
Bulk fermentation: 90 mins. Knock back after 1 hour.
Divide the dough into two pieces, then mould each piece into a cigar shaped bâton 250 mm in length approximately. Press a rolling pin into the centre of each bâton lengthwise, to slightly flatten the centre, then brush the hollow with melted butter. Fold over each end towards the centre then press together. Place the loaves on greased baking sheets, brush over with eggwash then prove with very little steam. Bake at 215°C for 35 mins. approximately and when ready, dredge heavily with icing sugar on withdrawing from the oven.

Cinnamon bread (yield 2 loaves)
400 g strong flour, 100 g plain flour, 10 g salt, 20 g milk powder, 50 g caster sugar, 50 g butter, 100 ml eggs (2 eggs), 70 g yeast, 150 ml water.
Filling: Melt 30 g butter and place aside. Mix together 30 g granulated sugar and 15 g cinnamon and place into a small bowl.
Dough temperature: 25°C.
Bulk fermentation: 1 hour. Knock back after 45 mins.
Divide the dough into two pieces then roll out into two

rectangles 20 mm in thickness approximately. Brush the surface of each rectangle with the melted butter, sprinkle with a coating of the cinnamon mixture then roll up tightly like a swiss roll and place into greased bread tins. Brush the tops with melted butter then allow to prove. Sprinkle with a good coating of the cinnamon mixture and bake at 220° C for 30 mins. approximately.

Various buns

Basic bun dough   (yield 16 buns)

500 g strong flour, 5 g salt, 75 g caster sugar, 75 g white fat, 25 g yeast, 250 ml water and any colouring or flavouring as desired.

Note: Eggs may be added to the above recipe as follows: Add 25–50 ml egg (½–1 egg) and correspondingly reduce the recipe water by the same quantity.

Dough temperature: 27°C.

Bulk fermentation: 1 hour. Knock back after 45 mins. Scale at 50 g each and shape as desired. Prove, then bake at 235°C.

Plain buns

Proceed as above moulding into small balls. Eggwash prior to proving if desired. When baked dredge with icing sugar or brush with bun wash immediately upon withdrawal from the oven.

Bun wash: Whisk together 50 ml egg (1 egg), 150 ml milk and 40 g sugar.

Cream buns

Prepare plain buns and allow to cool. Slit and pipe into the centre slighly sweetened whipped cream or crème Chantilly, see page 41.

Currant buns

Add 60 g currants into the basic bun dough and complete as plain buns.

Note: 10 g mixed peel may also be added to the recipe.

College buns

Prepare as plain buns but after shaping insert a small cork of stale bread which has been thoroughly dried into each bun. Prove and bake and when cold withdraw the cork. Coat with white fondant, see page 108, carefully passing a small palette knife over the top of the bun to remove the fondant from the open recess. Fill the recess with raspberry jam.

Swiss buns

Prepare the basic bun dough but scale at 40 g each. Mould into ball shapes then roll into finger shapes. Place side by side on the baking tray so that when proved* and baked the buns will touch together. When cold coat the buns with lemon-flavoured fondant.

* Ensure that the buns are not over-proved as this produces a wrinkled surface on the buns.

Chelsea buns

Prepare the basic bun dough and shape by rolling out 10 mm in thickness.

Filling: Melt 30 g butter and place aside. Mix together 50 g currants, 50 g sultanas, 10 g mixed peel, good pinch mixed spice and 30 g caster sugar and place into a bowl.

Brush the surface of the dough with the melted butter, then sprinkle on the fruit filling evenly over the surface of the dough. Roll up like a swiss roll then brush the dough with melted butter. Cut into 25 mm thick slices and place on a lightly greased baking tray close together. Prove and bake as stated but on withdrawing from the oven, brush with melted butter and sprinkle with caster sugar.

Note: Traditionally these buns are prepared square. This is done by placing the buns close together and in addition fitting a piece of oiled stick behind the last row of buns.

Doughnuts

Prepare the basic bun dough then proceed as stated on page 300.

Hot cross buns

500 g strong flour, 2½ g salt, 60 g demerara sugar, 20 g milk powder, 60 g white fat, 25 ml egg (½ egg approximately), 250 ml water, 30 g yeast, 50 sultanas, 50 g currants and 15 g mixed peel and good pinch mixed spice (1½ g).

Crossing mixture: 100 g plain flour, 25 g white fat, pinch baking powder (1 g B.P. per 100 g flour) and 90 ml water.

Preparation of crossing mixture: Thoroughly mix together the flour, baking powder and fat then add the water slowly while beating to produce a smooth paste.

Dough temperature: 25° C.

Bulk fermentation: 45 mins. Knock back after 30 mins. Scale at 50 g each and mould into balls. Allow to prove (25 mins approximately) then pipe on the crossing mixture. Bake at 238–240° C, approximate time 12 minutes, and glaze with bun wash immediately on removal from the oven.

Laminated yeast doughs (Straight dough process)

Some yeast doughs are prepared as cold doughs then completed in the same manner as *puff pastry* by folding through a quantity of butter or pastry margarine. The method of adding the butter or pastry margarine to the dough may be the French or English methods of preparing puff pastry although the *English method* is preferred in this text. The production of puff pastry is explained in detail on page 324.

Crescents (croissants)   (yield 24 croissants)

500 g strong flour, 5 g salt, 10 g sugar, 20 ml milk powder, 50 g butter, 50 ml egg (1 egg), 25 g yeast and 250 ml cold water.

Additional fat to be folded into the dough: 200 g butter or pastry margarine.

Dough temperature: 18°C (use cold water at 18°C).

Bulk fermentation: 1 hour, knocking back is not required.

Production details:

Prepare the basic dough above as stated then complete as English-style puff pastry using the additional fat and giving three half turns – allow to rest 15 minutes between each turn.

- Roll out the dough into a rectangle, 5 mm in thickness approximately then cut two strips 125 mm wide.
- Cut each strip into triangles with the base of each triangle measuring 125–130 mm.
- Roll up each triangle tightly starting at the base, bend to form a crescent then place on a greased baking tray.
- Brush with eggwash, prove, then bake at 240°C for 10–15 minutes.

Danish pastries   (yield 12–18 items depending on size)

500 g strong flour, 5 g salt, 90 g caster sugar, 40 g milk powder, 90 g butter, 30 g yeast and 280–300 ml cold water.

Additional fat: 300 g butter or pastry margarine.

Dough temperature: 18°C (use cold water at 18°C).

Bulk fermentation: 15 minutes, knocking back is not required.

Production details:

Prepare the basic dough above as stated then complete as English-style puff pastry using the additional fat and giving three half turns – allow to rest 15 minutes between each turn.

2 Roll out the dough and shape as desired.

3 Prove in very little steam for 20 mins. approximately then bake at 220°C.

Baking time: 25 minutes approximately.

4 When baked, brush over with hot apricot glaze and then water icing. Decorate as required.

Varieties: Many types of Danish pastry can be made by cutting the dough into different shapes and using a variety of fillings and garnishings. Examples of fillings and garnishings include pastry cream, almond butter, fruit pieces or purées and composite mixtures such as the strudel filling on page 383. Decoration of Danish pastries may be carried out by adding glacé cherries, angelica, currants or nuts etc.

Various shapes:

Lace or twist pastries: Strips of pastry (300 mm length × 10 mm width × 5 mm thick approximately) which are twisted and rolled into scrolls or figure-eights. Decorate to taste.

Windmills: Squares of pastry (120 mm sides and 5 mm thick) with each corner cut through with a knife to a point just short of the centre of the square, then each alternate divided corner folded to the centre to resemble a windmill. Decorate to taste.

Turnovers: Squares or circles of pastry (120 mm sides or diameter and 5 mm thick) with a filling placed in the centre. The edges of the pastry are lightly eggwashed, then the pastry folded over and sealed to enclose the filling. Decorate to taste.

Pizza pies (straight dough process)

The following recipe for the bread base is designed to produce pizza pies with the minimum of handling, fermentation time and equipment. It is important to note that plain (soft) flour (winter wheats) is used in the recipe and not bread flour. Alternatively the cottage bread, milk bread or brown bread doughs stated on page 353 may be used as a base.

Basic dough   (yield 5 pizzas (225 mm diameter) or 8 pizzas (150 mm diameter))

500 g plain (soft) flour, 5 g salt, 15 g milk powder, 75 g cake margarine, 30 ml egg (½ egg approximately), 25 g yeast and 280 ml cold water.

Dough temperature: 18°C (use cold water at 18°C).

Bulk fermentation: 15 minutes, knocking back is not required.

Production details:

1 Divide the dough to make 5 or 8 pizzas, i.e. 180 g or 100 g pieces.

2 Roll out round-shaped to the stated sizes and place on a greased baking tray.

3 Brush over the tops with oil then add the filling leaving a 10 mm clear border round the pie. Place over the cheese.

4 Dry prove at room temperature for 30–40 mins. approximately (depending on room temperature).

5 Bake at 225°C for 15–20 mins.

Basic filling: 100 g finely chopped onion, 5 g crushed garlic (1 clove), 50 ml oil, 750 g tinned tomatoes, 20 g tomato purée, 2 g oregano, 5 g salt and a pinch of white pepper.

Cheese topping: 200 g grated/sliced cheese (mozzarella).

Production details:

Sweat the onion and garlic in the oil for 2–3 mins. then add the oregano and continue sweating for a further 2 mins. Add the remaining ingredients and slowly simmer to a thick sauce consistency, i.e. 20 mins. approximately. Correct the seasoning. *Allow to become cold.*

Note: Cooking by 'sweating' is dealt with in Chapter 7.

Various pizzas

Napoletana

Basic tomato pizza.

Capricciosa

Basic tomato pizza adding slices of cooked ham, mushrooms, artichokes and olives.

Funghi

Basic tomato pizza adding plenty of sliced mushrooms cooked in oil. *Note:* The tomato filling can be reduced in quantity or omitted.

Calzone

This is a pizza which is filled with a garnish similar to a turnover then proved and baked.

Margherita

Basic tomato pizza adding chopped basil and pecorino cheese.

Prosciutto

Basic tomato pizza adding slices of cooked ham.

Romana

Basic tomato pizza adding chopped basil, anchovy fillets and a mixture of parmesan and mozzarella cheese.

Siciliana

Basic tomato pizza adding tuna fish and olives.

Würstel

Basic tomato pizza adding slices of German sausage.

Nan bread (Indian)   (yield 6 large nans)

500 g plain (soft) flour, 5 g salt, 10 g baking powder, 40 g caster sugar, 150 ml yoghurt, 70 ml oil, 20 ml egg (½ egg), 30 g yeast and 140 ml milk approximately.
Dough temperature: 18°C (use milk at 18°C).
Bulk fermentation: 15 mins., knocking back is not required.
Production details:
1   Divide the dough into six pieces then roll out thinly using flour and sesame seeds (traditionally the dough is shaped like a large teardrop). Place on to oiled plates.
2   Allow to dry prove at room temperature for 30–40 mins.
3   Carefully turn each nan out of the plate and into a hot, very lightly greased frying pan and cook until the base is brown (1 min. approximately).
4   Place under a very hot grill and brown.
Note: This is a suitable procedure when no tandoor oven is available.

Pitta bread   (yield 12 pittas)

250 g strong flour, 250 g plain flour, 10 g salt, 15 g yeast and 300 ml water.
Dough temperature: 27°C.
Bulk fermentation: 1 hour. Knock back after 45 mins.
Production details:
1   Prepare as stated then after the bulk fermentation divide the dough into 12 pieces (65 g each approximately).
2   Mould into balls then roll out into long ovals.
3   Place the shapes on a cloth towel then cover with a towel and prove (29°C approximately) for 15 mins. approximately.
4   Meanwhile lightly oil a tray and place in an oven to become hot (5–7 mins.)
5   Place the pittas on the hot tray then brush over the tops with water.
6   Bake in a very hot oven (230°C approximately) for 4 mins. approximately. The pittas will rise up but stay fairly white.
7   Allow to cool between dry cloths then very lightly flatten without bursting.
8   Store in sealed polythene bags.
Uses: Pittas may be reheated then stuffed with a variety of savoury fillings.

Section eight Part (B)   Ferment and dough process (suitable for rich goods)

Base method

Step 1	A Assemble ingredients.
	B Accurately measure and weigh the various ingredients.
	C Set the oven thermostat to the required temperature, i.e. 235–240° C at a suitable time for baking the items.
	D Bring the water temperature to 40° C for the ferment.

Step 2	*Preparation of ferment*: Ingredients (A)
	A Sieve together the flour and milk powder.
	B Break down the yeast in the water, add to the flour and mix to a smooth batter or dough.
	C Cover and leave to ferment in a warm place for 30 mins.

Step 3	*Adding ingredients (B)*:
	Add the eggs, any egg yolks, salt and caster sugar to the ferment and mix together.
	Add the flour and beat to a clear batter or dough, see page 352.

Step 4	Add the softened butter in three equal parts, beating thoroughly between each addition.

Step 5	Mix through any fruit, e.g. currants stated in the recipe.

Savarins and babas:

A   Grease the moulds then pipe in the mixture – add only enough mixture to reach a position slightly less than half way up the mould.

B   Fully prove and bake for 18–25 minutes depending on size, then remove from the moulds and place on cooling wires.

C   Allow to cool slightly then soak the items in the syrup for a few seconds until moist through to the centre. *Note*:   Rum flavoured syrup is often used for babas whereas any appropriate liqueur may be used for savarins, e.g. Grand Marnier, see page 107.

D   Glaze the items with apricot glaze, see page 103.

E   *Service*:   When cold place the sweet on a serving dish and decorate with whipped cream, glacé cherries and diamonds of angelica etc.
   Savarins: Fill the centre with fruit salad etc.
   Menu examples: Savarin aux fruits and babas au rhum.

Brioche:

A   Cover the mixture and continue with the bulk fermentation – see the time and temperature stated in the brioche recipe.

B   Beat the dough then scale off in 40 g pieces.

C   Roll the pieces into small balls, then roll one end of each ball down further until it resembles a small bulb which is still connected to the larger ball.

D   Place the large end of each ball into the greased tins, make a small hole on top with the finger then sit the small bulb into the hole – this resembles a cottage loaf.

E   Prove for 10 minutes (little steam), brush with eggwash then cut the top sides with scissors. Return to the prover and fully prove then bake for 10–15 mins.

F   When serving as a pastry, brush with icing and decorate to taste.

Savarin and babas   (yield 8 portions)

High-quality recipe
(A)   *Ferment*:
100 g strong flour, 5 g milk powder, 10 g yeast and 120 ml water.
(B)   *Ingredients*:
50 ml egg (1 egg), 20 ml egg yolks (2 yolks), 25 g caster sugar, 100 g strong flour, 50 g softened butter.
Babas: Add 50 g currants.
Soaking syrup: See page 107.

Good-quality recipe: As above but omit the egg yolks and increase the water in the ferment to 140 ml.

Brioche   (yield 28 small brioche approximately)

High-quality recipe
(A)   *Ferment*:
125 g strong flour, 10 g milk powder, 25 g yeast, 100 ml water.
(B)   *Ingredients*:
300 ml eggs (6 eggs), 20 g caster sugar, 5 g salt, 375 g spring flour, 250 g butter.
Bulk fermentation time and temperature: Allow to rest for 8 hours at 15° C.

Good quality recipe: As above but amend as follows:
1   Increase the yeast to 40 g.
2   Reduce the butter to 150 g.
3   *Bulk fermentation time and temperature:* 1 hour at 27° C.

Dishes

Marignans
Prepare a savarin mixture but cook in 'barquette moulds' instead of a savarin mould. When soaked in the syrup, allow to cool then slit along one side of each marignan and brush with apricot glaze. Fill each marignan with crème Chantilly and decorate to taste.

Brioche aux fruits
Slices of large brioche garnished with fruit salad and neatly coated with kirsch-flavoured apricot glaze. Pipe round crème Chantilly and decorate to taste.

Brioche au madère
As above, adding some sultanas, currants and raisins to the fruit salad and using Madeira-flavoured apricot glaze.

Brioche Victoria
Prepare as madère above, adding cherries and glazed chestnuts.

Savarin Joinville
Slices of savarin which have been soaked in a kirsch-flavoured syrup garnished with slices of pineapple. Coat with apricot glaze and decorate with chocolate pieces and whipped cream.

Muffins   (12 muffins)

The dough for these items is prepared in the same manner as a ferment adding the sugar and salt.
500 g strong flour, 5 g salt, 5 g sugar, 10 g yeast and 370 ml water at 40°C.

Beat the mixture until a tough and very soft dough has been achieved then cover and allow to ferment in a warm place for 2 hours. Knock back after 1 hour.
Moulding and cooking:
1   Turn out the very soft dough onto a well-floured board and cut off pieces with a palette knife and scale on a floured scale pan at 70 g each.
2   Mould between the hands into balls and place into hollows of rice flour set on a tray.
3   Cover to avoid forming a skin and prove until light and full.
4   Carefully lift the muffins with a broad palette knife and cook in greased hoops on a pre-heated griddle plate. Cook on side until a good colour has been developed then turn over and complete the cooking. Brush off any adhering rice flour before serving.
Important: These goods are difficult to make because the dough is very soft and sticks to almost everything it touches, *but, as is usual, practice improves performance.*

Frying batter (pâte à frire)

200 g strong flour, 5 g caster sugar, 10 g milk powder, pinch salt (2½ g approximately), 10 g yeast and 250 ml water at 40° C.
Prepare the batter in the same manner as a ferment adding the sugar and salt, then cover and allow to ferment in a warm place for 1 hour. See also page 321.

Section nine Powder-aerated goods

The oil emulsion process

This is one of the most simple methods of producing a range of powder-aerated goods such as scones, dropped scones, crumpets, sponge snowballs and doughnuts etc. Because of its simplicity this method is quick compared to other methods and produces goods with exceptional eating qualities.

Ingredients

Flour

The type of flour which should be used in most of the following recipes is medium-strength plain flour.

Baking powder

This is a mixture of cream of tartar or phosphoric acid derivative and bicarbonate of soda in the preparation of two parts acid to one part soda. This is not the exact ratio, which is 2.24 to 1, but is satisfactory for bakery purposes.
Important: Baking powder prepared with phosphoric acid derivative is slow-acting and allows the goods to have a resting period of 20 mins. approximately which is beneficial to the goods and in addition suits large-scale production in relation to time of baking and oven space. However, the acid may leave an aftertaste or bite in the goods. Baking powder made with cream of tartar produces goods with no bite or aftertaste but the goods must be baked when ready for the oven as the reaction and gas production commences on combining the ingredients.
Note: Commercial baking powder is usually made with phosphoric acid derivative.

Oil

Oil used in a recipe blends quickly and easily with the other ingredients. The function of fat in a cake-type mixture is explained on page 365.

Sugar

The type of sugar which should be used is fine grained caster sugar as it dissolves readily in the liquid. The function of the sugar is explained on page 365.

Eggs

Shell eggs or defrosted frozen eggs may be used. The function of the eggs is explained on page 365.

Milk

Fresh milk or reconstituted milk powder may be used. When using milk powder the reconstitution ratio is 100 g milk powder per litre of water. The function of the milk powder is explained on page 365.

Base method

Step 1	Mise en place
	A Assemble ingredients.
	B Accurately weigh and measure the ingredients.
Step 2	Sieve together the recipe flour and the baking powder, i.e. A ingredients, in the recipe then place aside.
Step 3	Place the B ingredients in the recipe into a mixing bowl, i.e. sugar, egg, oil and milk or treacle etc., see individual recipe.
Step 4	Whisk the ingredients together to form an emulsion.
Step 5	Add the flour and mix until smooth.
	Doughs: Mix to a smooth soft dough, *do not overmix*, see notes.
	Batters: Beat until smooth, see notes.
	Use as required, see individual recipe.

Important points

Step 2

Sieving together the dry ingredients: When sieving the flour and baking powder (and any spices), the ingredients should be sieved three times to ensure they are completely amalgamated.

Note: The flour and baking powder may be prepared in batches with small amounts taken and used as required: the name for this flour is scone flour (self-raising flour).

Step 5

Adding the flour: To form doughs – the flour is added and mixed with the emulsion only sufficiently to form a soft sticky dough. *Overmixing must be avoided or toughness in the goods will result.*

To form batters – when preparing thick batters, the flour is added and the mixture whisked until smooth. However, with *thin batters*, see crumpets, *only half the milk should be added to the emulsion and the remaining milk added to adjust the consistency* after a thick batter has been made – *this is to avoid lumps being formed.*

Important: When the flavour of butter etc., is desired, the oil may be replaced with fat which is rubbed into the flour.

Method – Oven scones

Step 1	Prepare the scone dough as stated in the base method.
	Set the oven to the correct baking temperature for scones – 240° C.
Step 2	Scrape out the mixture onto a board dusted with scone flour (self-raising flour).
	Important: The mixture will be soft and sticky and must be handled with care, avoiding additional flour being absorbed into the mixture.
Step 3	*Small individual scones* 1 Dust over the top of the mixture with scone flour then roll out to 25 mm thickness approximately. 2 Cut out the scones with a plain cutter and place onto a lightly greased tray. 3 Leave plain or brush over the tops with eggwash and stab lightly with a fork or docker. 4 Allow to rest 20 mins. (unless using cream of tartar baking powder, see notes) then bake for 12–15 mins. *Scone rounds* 1 Divide the mixture into two pieces then mould carefully into two balls with floured hands. 2 Roll out each ball into two rounds – 20 mm in thickness approximately then place onto a lightly greased baking tray. 3 Cut each round cross-wise into four wedge-shaped portions with an oiled scraper. 4 Brush over the tops with eggwash, allow to rest 15 mins. – see (4) above then bake for 12–15 minutes.

Scones   (yield 10 scones approximately)

Plain scones   (shape as desired)
Ingredients A:
200 g plain flour, 10 g baking powder.
Ingredients B:
25 ml oil, 30 g caster sugar, 50 ml egg (1 egg), 100 ml milk.

Fruit scones   (shape as desired)
Varieties: Sultana, raising and currant etc.
Prepare the same as plain scones adding 50 g selected fruit to the dough when mixing is almost completed.

Treacle scones   (shape as desired)
Ingredients A:
200 g plain flour, 10 g baking powder.
Ingredients B:
25 ml oil, 20 g caster sugar, 50 ml egg, 25 g treacle, 75 ml milk, pinch cinnamon.

Swiss scones   (scone rounds)
Ingredients A:
200 g plain flour, 10 g baking powder.
Ingredients B:

50 ml oil, 50 g caster sugar, 50 ml egg, 75 ml milk, 25 g mixed peel.
Prepare in scone rounds and sprinkle sugar nibs over the tops prior to baking.

Wheatmeal scones   (shape as desired)
Ingredients A:
50 g plain flour, 150 g wheatmeal flour, 10 g baking powder.
Ingredients B:
30 ml oil, 30 g caster sugar, 130 ml milk, pinch salt (1 g).

Method – hotplate scones

Step 1	Prepare the scone dough as stated in the base method.
Step 2	Roll out the scone dough and cut into individual scones or shape into scone rounds, see oven scones above. Allow to rest for 20 minutes.
Step 3	Place onto a lightly greased hotplate and cook for 3–4 mins.; until the first side is a good colour and cooked through.
Step 4	Carefully turn over and complete the cooking – a further 3–4 minutes.

Hotplate scones   (yield 12 small scones approximately)

Plain scones
Prepare as plain scones above but reduce the egg content by half, i.e. 25 ml egg.

Fruit scones
Prepare as plain hotplate scones adding 50 g selected fruit to the mixture.

Treacle scones
Prepare as treacle scones above but reduce the egg content by half, i.e. 25 ml egg.

Wheatmeal scones
Prepare as wheatmeal scones above but reduce the milk content by 30 ml, i.e. milk content 100 ml.

Method – dropped scones and crumpets

Prepare the batter as stated in the base method then cook on a lightly greased preheated hotplate as follows:
Dropped scones:
    Drop the mixture onto the hotplate using a ladle or piping bag.
    Turn over when the side being cooked has developed a good colour and complete the cooking.
Note: Some experience is required to know when to turn over the goods – one point is that the goods should still have a visible damp gloss on the point of turning.
Crumpets: Cook as dropped scones using a ladle to drop the thin batter onto the plate. Turn over when all the bubbles have burst on top of the uncooked side.

Dropped scones or **Scotch pancakes**   (yield 8–10 items)
Ingredients A:
200 g plain flour and 10 g baking powder.
Ingredients B:
25 g oil, 75 ml caster sugar, 50 ml egg (1 egg) and 130 ml milk.

Crumpets   (yield 6 items)
Ingredients A:
200 g plain flour and 10 g baking powder.
Ingredients B:
50 ml oil, 100 g caster sugar, 50 ml egg (1 egg) and 250 ml milk.

Method – doughnuts

1 Roll out the mixture to 10–12 mm thickness then cut with a doughnut cutter.
2 Fry the doughnuts in hot fat at 180°C until one side is a good brown colour, then turn over and complete the cooking – 5–7 mins.
3 Drain thoroughly then roll in caster sugar.
Note: See page 300, for further details.

Doughnuts   (yield 8 doughnuts)
Ingredients A:
150 g plain flour and 5 g baking powder.
Ingredients B:
20 ml oil, 70 g caster sugar, 25 ml egg (½ egg) and 50 ml milk.
Important: This type of doughnut is less suitable for jam doughnuts because of the difficulty in cooking through to the centre, see page 301.

Method – snowballs

1 Prepare the mixture as stated in the base method.
2 Pipe out into small round shapes (40 mm in diameter approximately) onto a lightly greased baking tray then bake at 215°C for 12–15 mins.
3 When cold, sandwich together with jam, coat with thin water icing then roll in coconut.

Coconut snowballs   (yield 8–10 items)
Ingredients A:
300 g plain flour and 10 g baking powder.
Ingredients B:
100 ml oil, 125 g caster sugar, 50 ml egg (1 egg) and 75 ml milk.

Miscellaneous items (non-derivative)

Method – Potato scones

1 Place the water, salt and fat in a pan and heat to 75°C approximately.
2 Add the potato powder and mix to a stiff mixture then allow to cool.
3 Sieve the flours together, add to the potato then dough up.
4 Divide the mixture in two, i.e. 170 g each piece then mould round. Roll out each round until quite thin – 3 mm approximately then cut into four.
5 Cook on a lightly greased hotplate the same as hotplate scones.

Potato scones   (yield 8 scones)
200 ml water, 20 g butter or margarine, good pinch of salt (2½g), 75 g potato powder, 25 g self-raising flour and 25 g plain flour.
Note: When using fresh mashed potatoes, replace the water content and potato powder with dry mashed potato, 275 g, then dough up in the same manner.

Method – sweetcorn pancakes

These are simply made by mixing the egg through the kernels then binding with the flour. Cook the same as dropped scones.

Sweetcorn pancakes   (non-derivative)
200 g cooked/tinned corn kernels, 50 ml egg (1 egg), 40 g self-raising flour and pinch of salt and pepper.

owder-aerated buns

ase method

Step 1	Mise en place
	A Assemble ingredients.
	B Accurately weigh and measure the ingredients.
	C Grease baking tray with white fat and ensure the oven is set at the correct temperature.

Step 2	Sieve together the recipe flour and the baking powder.

Step 3	Mix thoroughly through the flour any desiccated coconut or rice flour.

Step 4	Rub the fat into the flour to a sandy texture then mix through any fruit, e.g. sultanas, currants or peel etc. Make a bay in the flour.

Step 5	Place the sugar and eggs into the bay.

Step 6	Dissolve any essence or colouring in the recipe milk then add to the egg and sugar and mix to dissolve the sugar.

Step 7	Gradually bring in the flour and mix until combined – *do not overmix* as this will toughen the items.

Step 8	Complete as stated for each type of bun.

Recipes

Coconut buns

200 g plain flour, 10 g baking powder, 25 g desiccated coconut, 25 g butter or margarine, 25 g white fat (not lard), 50 g caster sugar, 50 ml egg (1 egg), 100 ml milk, 2–3 drops almond essence and 2–3 drops yellow colour.

Production details:

Turn out the mixture onto a floured dusted board then divide into small pieces – 40 g each.

Mould the pieces into balls with floured hands, wash over with milk then dip into desiccated coconut.

Place onto the greased baking tray then make several cuts across the top to form a lattice design.

Allow to rest 15 minutes then bake at 215°C for 15–20 minutes.

Coffee buns

200 g plain flour, 10 g baking powder, 85 g butter or margarine, 85 g soft brown sugar, 50 ml egg (1 egg), 25 ml milk and 25 g coffee essence.

Production details:

1   Mould the mixture into small balls as described above.
2   Shape the balls into oval shapes then brush with eggwash. Bake at 215°C for 15–20 minutes.
3   Mask the buns when cold with coffee fondant.

Raspberry buns

200 g plain flour, 10 g baking powder, 25 g butter or margarine, 25 g white fat (not lard), 50 g caster sugar, 50 ml egg (1 egg), 80 ml milk, 2–3 drops vanilla essence, 2–3 drops raspberry colour, 40 g raspberry jam.

Production details:

1   Shape the mixture into balls as above, brush over with milk then dip into caster sugar.
2   Make a small hole in the top of each bun then pipe a little raspberry jam into each hole.
3   Allow to rest for 15 minutes then bake at 215°C.

Rice buns

200 g plain flour, 10 g baking powder, 25 g rice flour, 25 g butter or margarine, 25 g white fat (not lard), 50 g caster sugar, 50 ml egg (1 egg), 80 ml milk, 2–3 drops vanilla essence and 2–3 drops yellow colour.

Production details:

1   Shape the mixture into balls as above, brush over with milk then dip into small sugar nibs.
2   Bake at 215°C for 15–20 minutes.

Rock buns/cakes

200 g plain flour, 10 g baking powder, 40 g butter or margarine, 25 g white fat (not lard), 75 g caster sugar, 50 ml egg (1 egg), 80 ml milk, 30 g each sultanas and currants, 15 g mixed peel, 2–3 drops each lemon essence and yellow colour.

Production details:

1   Place the mixture in rocky heaps onto a greased baking sheet and sprinkle with sugar.
2   Allow to rest for 15 mins. then bake at 215°C.

Section ten   Cakes: sugar batter process

The term 'cake' is used to describe many different mixtures and products but in this section it is used to define aerated mixtures which basically consist of flour, baking powder, eggs, sugar and fat.

Good cakes are not easy to make because there are many factors which must be taken into account during the production process. The reader should pay particular attention to the information concerning recipe components and method details.

Important points

Recipe components

Ingredient	Function		Possible faults
Plain (soft) flour See also Special cake flour	A	Essential to the formation of the cake structure.	*Insufficient flour in recipe*: Loss of cake volume or collapse. *Note*: This may also be caused by a weak flour, i.e. containing poor quality gluten.
	B	Imparts strength to the structure through the development of the gluten network, see page 347. *Note*: Cake flours may contain a fair content of protein but it is the quality of the gluten forming proteins which is important — the proteins in cake flour do not produce the *very* strong resistent gluten network like bread flours, see page 347.	*Excessive flour in recipe*: Dry, low volume cake which is lacking in flavour. *Too strong a flour*: Tough, textured, low volume cake – likely to have a 'peaked top'.
Baking powder See page 359.	A	Aerates the cake and increases cake volume.	*Insufficient baking powder*: Heavy, low volume cake with a close texture.
	B	Improves eating quality.	*Excessive baking powder*: Very crumbly open texture. Cake may also collapse because the excessive quantity of baking powder has stretched the structural ingredients in the cake beyond their elastic limit.
	C	Acts on proteins such as albumen and gluten making them more elastic – it therefore affects strength and structure of a cake. *Note*: Too much baking powder has the effect of softening the protein thus weakening the cake structure.	
Eggs	A	Adds structure to the cake by the coagulation of albumen.	*Excessive eggs in recipe*: May produce toughness in the cake and can even cause collapse.
	B	Aerates the cake via mechanical aeration.	*Insufficient egg in recipe*: Dry eating low volume cake.
	C	Adds richness and colour as well as flavour.	
Caster sugar	A	Sweetens the cake.	*Excessive sugar in recipe*: Open texture with possible collapse at the centre of the cake. The surface of the cake may exhibit many small crystals of sugar.
	B	Aids crust colour.	
	C	Breaks up the butter and enables the mixture to incorporate air when creaming the butter, sugar and eggs.	*Insufficient sugar in recipe*: Lack of sweetness with possible low volume and tight crumb structure.
	D	Has an opening effect on the crumb structure of the cake.	
	E	Aids keeping qualities of the cake.	
Fat (butter margarine or compound fat etc.	A	Adds flavour.	*Excessive fat in recipe*: Flat top with a greasy surface. Loose heavy greasy texture. In addition the cake may also collapse in the centre.
	B	Enriches and adds tenderness to the cake.	
	C	Has an opening effect on the cake structure. Aerates the cake when creaming with the sugar via mechanical aeration.	*Insufficient fat in recipe*: Low cake volume with the surface of the cake having a poor crust colour and showing cracks. Lack of tenderness and poor keeping quality are also likely.
	D	Enhances general appearance.	
	E	Improves keeping quality.	

Additional ingredients often used in a basic cake recipe

Milk

Milk is a *moistening agent* which is used in many cake recipes and may be used to replace some of the egg producing a cheaper or lower cost cake. However, milk restricts lightness and closes the grain of the cake, therefore the balance of the recipe is maintained by using additional baking powder.

Glycerine

This is often added to cake recipes to improve shelf life or keeping quality – the moisture absorbing properties of glycerine (hygroscopic) reduce the rate at which the cake dries out or stales.

Blackjack

This is caramel colour which is added to darken the crumb of the cake.

The above information indicates the basic ingredients of a cake and their function. This can be extended to include many other ingredients which are present in various cakes to produce the following recipe components diagram.

Method details

The important points regarding the method of preparing cakes are explained with the base method on page 368. However, one important factor which has not been covered is the *humidity of the oven* when baking cakes.

Table 11 *Recipe ingredients*

Small cup cakes	Victoria sandwich	Fruit cakes	Frangipane	Birthday/Xmas cake	Steamed sponges
Plain flour	Plain flour	Plain flour	Plain flour	Plain flour	Plain flour
Self-raising flour	Baking powder	Self-raising flour	—	—	Baking powder
Eggs	Eggs	Eggs	Eggs	Eggs	Eggs
Caster sugar	Caster sugar	Caster sugar	Caster sugar	Barbados/Trinidad sugar	Caster sugar
Butter or margarine and white fat	Butter or margarine and white fat	Butter or margarine and white fat	Butter or margarine	Butter or margarine and white fat	Butter or margarine
—	Milk in cheaper recipes	—	—	—	Milk
Angelica, glacé cherry, flaked almonds and currants etc.	Jam filling and icing sugar decoration	Sultanas, raisins, glacé cherries	Ground almonds	Treacle, blackjack, ground almonds, spices, currants, glacé cherries, mixed peel	Essence, fruit zest, currants, sultanas, cocoa powder or spices etc.

Steam present in the oven allows the cakes to expand to their maximum volume before the crust becomes firmly set. Too dry an oven results in the crust of a cake being formed very early, in turn restricting height and volume and also causing excessive moisture loss. A humid atmosphere in the oven can be produced by baking a batch of cakes at one time or by placing pans of water in the oven with the cakes.

There are several methods of preparing cakes but the most popular in catering establishments is *the sugar batter process* – this is the method used in the section. Two other important methods of preparing cakes are *the flour batter process* and *the blending process*.

Sugar batter process

See base method.

Flour batter process

This consists of the following steps:
A   Cream together the recipe fat and an equal weight of flour.
B   Whisk the eggs and sugar until thick and heavy then blend carefully through the creamed fat and flour.
C   Sieve together the remaining flour and baking powder then partially blend through the prepared mixture.
D   Add any milk then complete the mixing of the batter.

Blending process

This is used for high-ratio cakes and is explained on page 374.

Cake faults   (see also recipe components section)

Poor volume
1   Insufficient baking powder.
2   Insufficient sugar.
3   Batter not creamed sufficiently.
4   Curdled batter.
5   Finished batter temperature prior to baking too high or too low.

Peaked top
1   Flour too strong.
2   Overmixing the finished cake batter.
3   Too high an oven temperature and insufficient steam in the oven.

Sunken centre
1   Too much sugar or baking powder.
2   Overbeating the fat, sugar and eggs.
3   Removing the cake from the oven before fully set or cooked.
4   Knocking or banging the cake in the oven before it is cooked.
5   Too much liquid in the recipe – this will also cause the sides of the cake to fall inwards.

Sunken fruit in fruit cakes
1   Fruit not sufficiently dried before adding to the cake batter.
2   Too much baking powder or sugar in the recipe.
3   Overbeating the fat, sugar and egg.
4   Too weak a flour used in the recipe.
5   Insufficiently mixed batter, i.e. insufficient mixing when the flour is blended into the batter.
6   Too low a baking temperature.

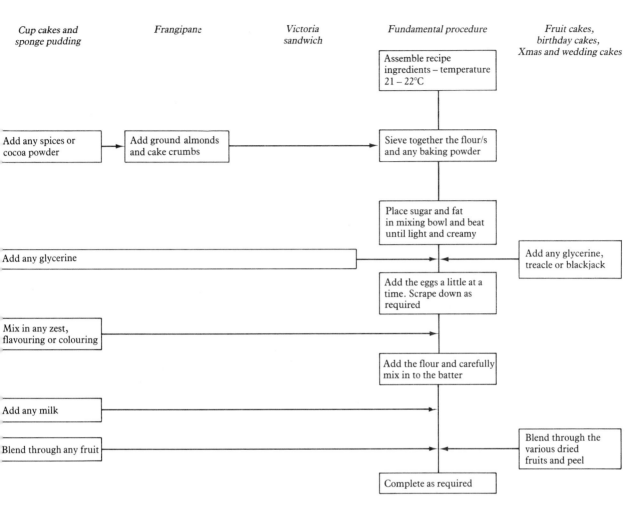

Cup cakes and sponge pudding	Frangipane	Victoria sandwich	Fundamental procedure	Fruit cakes, birthday cakes, Xmas and wedding cakes
			Assemble recipe ingredients – temperature 21 – 22°C	
Add any spices or cocoa powder	Add ground almonds and cake crumbs		Sieve together the flour/s and any baking powder	
			Place sugar and fat in mixing bowl and beat until light and creamy	
Add any glycerine				Add any glycerine, treacle or blackjack
			Add the eggs a little at a time. Scrape down as required	
Mix in any zest, flavouring or colouring				
			Add the flour and carefully mix in to the batter	
Add any milk				
Blend through any fruit				Blend through the various dried fruits and peel
			Complete as required	

Figure 30 *Essential activities for cakes – sugar batter process*

Sugar batter process

Base method

Step 1	Mise en place
	A Assemble ingredients – the *ingredients should be 21–22°C*, they *must not be chilled*, see notes.
	B Prepare the cake tins or hoops etc., e.g. lightly grease with white fat.
	C Accurately weigh and measure the ingredients.
	D Ensure that the cooking equipment is set at the correct temperature.
Step 2	Sieve together the flour/s and any baking powder, spices or cocoa powder stated in the recipe. Place aside until required.
Step 3	Place the sugar and fat into a mixing bowl and *beat together until light and creamy*, see notes. *Also add any glycerine.* Scrape down the bowl to ensure that the mixture is being evenly beaten.
Step 4	Add the eggs a little at a time while beating the mixture, see notes. Scrape down the mixing bowl as before and continue beating the mixture.
Step 5	When the last of the eggs has been incorporated, producing a light creamy mixture, lightly mix in any essences, colouring or fruit zest.
Step 6	Add the flour and carefully mix into the batter, see notes.
Step 7	Add any milk stated in the recipe and carefully mix into the batter, see notes.
Step 8	Carefully blend through any fruit.
Step 9	Place the mixture into the lightly greased tins or moulds and cook as stated, see individual recipe.

Important points

Step 1

Temperature of ingredients: The temperature of the ingredients is extremely important when creaming together the fat and sugar. When the ingredients are too cold the fat will be stiff, difficult to cream and *less likely to incorporate the recipe egg without curdling*. Alternatively, when the ingredients are too warm the fat runs to oil and loses its ability to trap and retain air.

Ideal temperature for ingredients: 22°C.

Measuring ingredients: The ingredients should be accurately measured and weighed to maintain recipe balance.

Greasing baking tins etc.   This should be done with white fat and not butter or margarine as these are likely to cause sticking.

Step 3

Creaming the ingredients: The fat and sugar should be thoroughly creamed together before adding any egg. This is an important point because it ensures proper aeration of the mixture while *reducing the risk of curdling*.

Curdled mixtures: There are several reasons why a cake mixture curdles, e.g. ingredients too cold, poor-quality fat, insufficient mixing and watery eggs. When a mixture begins to show signs of curdling one procedure which is often adopted is to add a little of the recipe flour with each further addition of egg to absorb surface liquid.

Important: One way to reduce the risk of curdling is to add a small quantity of recipe flour, i.e. 25% of the total weight of the recipe fat, to the fat and sugar when creaming together. This does not affect the quality of the cake.

Step 4

Adding the egg: When the fat and sugar have been properly aerated the eggs may be added in stages – thoroughly beating for a short period between each addition of egg.

Note: Provided the mixture is well aerated the eggs may be poured slowly into the mixture while beating at medium speed (machine mixing).

Step 6

Mixing in the flour: The flour should be carefully mixed in to avoid toughening the batter – *it must not be beaten into the mixture*.

Step 7

Adding milk to the batter: The flour is partially mixed into the batter then the milk added and mixing completed. When a recipe contains a high milk content, half the milk may be mixed into the batter, the flour added and partially mixed in, then the remaining milk added and mixing completed.

Important: *Avoid overmixing.*

Fairy cakes   (yield 16 cakes approximately)
90 g butter or margarine, 30 g white fat, 140 g caster sugar, 5 g glycerine, 150 ml egg (3 eggs), 150 g plain flour and 50 g self-raising flour. *Decoration*:   Diamonds of angelica and pieces of glacé cherry.
1   Grease and lightly flour a fairy cake tin.
2   Prepare the mixture as stated then neatly pipe into the greased and floured impressions.
3   Decorate the tops with the cherry and angelica then bake at 220°C for 15 mins. approximately.

Queen cakes   (yield 12 cakes approximately)
75 g butter or margarine, 25 g white fat, 100 g caster sugar, 5 g glycerine, 100 ml egg (2 eggs), 75 g plain flour and 25 g self-raising flour. *Decoration*:   Pieces of glacé cherry, currants and flaked almonds.
1   Prepare the mixture then neatly pipe into paper cases (or prepared tin – fill to within 15 mm of the tops of the paper cases).
2   Decorate the tops with the cherry, currants and flaked almonds.
3   Bake at 205°C for 20 mins. approximately.

Cup cakes   (yield 12 cakes approximately)
75 g butter or margarine, 25 g white fat, 100 g caster sugar, 5 g glycerine, 150 ml egg (3 eggs), 100 g plain flour and 50 g self-raising flour.
Prepare as queen cakes above.

Cherry cakes

Prepare as cup cakes above but add a little vanilla essence and 50 g glacé cherries cut into quarters.

Coconut cakes

Prepare cup cakes, and when cold, brush the tops with hot apricot purée, coat with white fondant and cover with desiccated coconut.

Victoria sandwich   (yield 1 × 6 portion cake)
100 g butter or margarine, 50 g white fat, 150 g caster sugar, 5 g glycerine, 150 ml egg (3 eggs), 100 g plain flour and 50 g self-raising flour.
Filling: 50 g red jam approximately.
Decoration: Caster sugar or icing sugar.
1   Prepare the mixture as stated then divide between two greased and floured sandwich tins (or place into one deep tin).
2   Bake at 185°C for 25 minutes approximately.
3   When cooked, allow to cool slightly then turn out onto a cooling wire and allow to become cold.
4   Sandwich the two halves together with the jam then dredge over the top with the caster or icing sugar. Serve on a round salver, lined with a doily.

Madeira cake   (yield 1 × 8 portion cake approximately).
100 g butter, 50 g white fat, 150 g caster sugar, 5 g glycerine, 190 ml egg (3 large eggs), 2½ g lemon zest (1 teaspoon approximately), 175 g plain flour and 50 g self-raising flour.
1   Line a suitable cake tin with paper – 150 mm cake hoop.
2   Place the mixture into the tin and lightly smooth down.
3   Bake at 180°C for 1 hour 15 mins. approximately.
Note: There should be sufficient steam in the oven for these cakes, therefore if a full ovenload of cakes is not being baked a small bowl of water should be placed in the oven.

Fruit cake (sultana and cherry etc.)   (yield 1 × 6 portion cake)
75 g butter or margarine, 25 g white fat, 100 g caster sugar, 5 g glycerine, 150 ml egg (3 eggs), 100 g plain flour, 50 g self-raising flour and 150 g sultanas or cherries etc.
Place into paper lined tins and bake as Madeira cake above. *Note*:   When preparing cherry cake the cherries should be washed and *allowed to dry thoroughly* before use.

Birthday cake (also Xmas cake)   (yield 2½ kg cake approximately)

These cakes may be made with a genoise, Madeira cake or heavy fruited mixture – the type of cake is usually dependent on the age of the person for whom it is being prepared, i.e. the younger the person the less fruited the cake. The following recipe is for a heavily fruited cake: 250 g butter or margarine, 50 g white fat, 300 g Barbados or Trinidad sugar, 10 g treacle, 25 g ground almonds, 10 g glycerine, 5 g blackjack, 375 ml eggs (7 eggs approximately), 400 g plain flour, good pinch of nutmeg (2½ g), 5 g mixed spice, 500 g currants, 400 g sultanas, 200 g glacé cherries and 150 g mixed peel.

1   Prepare the cake following the instructions in the base method adding the treacle, ground almonds, glycerine and blackjack to the fat and sugar prior to creaming together.
2   Place the mixture into a papered hoop – 250 mm diameter (or wooden frame) – then level the top with a moistened celluloid scraper.
3   Bake at 180°C for 1 hour then reduce the oven temperature to 165°C and continue baking for a further 2 hours approximately – total time 3–3½ hours.
4   Allow to cool then wrap the cake in greaseproof paper until ready for finishing and decorating, see wedding cakes below.

Wedding cake   (yield 13 kg cake approximately, this should produce a three-tier cake)

1.8 kg butter, 1½ kg Trinidad/Barbados sugar, 20 g blackjack, 2 kg eggs (40 eggs approximately), 20 g lemon zest, 1½ kg plain flour, good pinch nutmeg (2½ g), 10 g mixed spice, 200 g roasted nib almonds, 500 g diced lemon peel, 500 g mixed peel, 4 kg currants, 1¾ kg sultanas and 300 ml rum.

1   Place all the fruits in a bowl, pour over the rum* then cover with a cloth and leave overnight.
2   Prepare as stated in the base method adding the soaked fruit where indicated (general addition of fruit).
3   Place the mixture into hoops (or wooden frames) of approximately the following sizes which are well protected with paper and placed on top of cardboard and greaseproof paper: 300 mm, 220 mm and 170 mm diameter (or length).
4   Bake the same as birthday cake above ensuring that the largest gets sufficient cooking time, i.e. 3½–4 hours.
5   When cold, wrap the cakes in greaseproof paper and store for 6 weeks in an airtight tin to mature.

Covering cakes with marzipan or almond paste: The quantity of paste used varies but in best-quality cakes it is often equal to half the weight of the cake.

1   Take the amount of marzipan which is to cover the cake and divide it into two pieces. Mould the pieces into two smooth ball shapes.
2   Roll out one of the shapes to a size suitable to cover the cake using icing sugar for dusting.
3   Brush over the top of the cake with boiling apricot purée then invert the top neatly on to the rolled-out marzipan. Press the cake firmly on to the marzipan then rotate the cake and at the same time press the marzipan which is slightly overlapping up and on to the sides of the cake to achieve a neat finish.
4   Roll out the remaining paste to a long thick rope then flatten with a rolling pin to produce a strip of paste which will cover the sides of the cake.
5   Trim the strip to the correct width and length then brush over with boiling apricot purée.
6   Roll the cake along the strip until the sides/s are completely covered and trim if necessary. Smooth down with the palette knife and the cake is ready for coating with icing sugar.

Icing and decorating cakes: The preparation and use of royal icing is explained on page 408. The cake is mounted on a cake board then coated with 2–3 thin coatings of royal icing leaving 24 hours between each coating. After this the cakes are decorated to taste, e.g. piped royal icing, royal icing runouts and/or artificial decorations etc.

Important: When cakes are to be stored for prolonged periods, e.g. top tiers of wedding cakes etc. it is advisable to cover the marzipan with a thin layer of fondant prior to coating with royal icing. This prevents the almond oil in the marzipan forming grease stains in the icing.

Sponge puddings

Base recipe   (yield 4 portions)

60 g butter or margarine, 60 g caster sugar, 50 ml egg (1 egg), 100 g plain flour, 5 g baking powder and 20 ml milk. Prepare as stated in the base method.

Steamed sponge pudding

1   Place the basic mixture into a greased pudding basin or four individual greased pudding tins and cover with greased greaseproof paper.
2   Steam for 1½ hours, see page 146, then turn out on to a suitable dish and serve with an appropriate sauce.

Vanilla sponge pudding

Prepare as above adding a few drops of vanilla essence to the basic mixture and serve with a vanilla-flavoured sauce.

Lemon sponge pudding

Prepare the basic sponge pudding adding the finely grated zest of one large lemon and a few drops of lemon essence. Serve with a lemon sauce, see page 144.

---

* Instead of soaking the fruit in the spirit, the cakes can be made without the rum – the rum is later injected into the cakes at the maturing stage.

Orange sponge pudding

Prepare the basic sponge pudding adding the finely grated zest of one orange, a little grated lemon zest (¼ lemon), a few drops of orange essence and a little orange colour. Serve with an orange sauce, see page 144.

Currant sponge pudding, raisin sponge pudding, sultana sponge pudding

Prepare the basic sponge pudding adding 60 g selected fruit which has been washed and thoroughly dried. Serve with a sauceboat of custard sauce.

Cherry sponge pudding

Prepare the basic sponge pudding adding 60 g quartered glacé cherries. Serve with almond or custard sauce.

Chocolate sponge pudding

Prepare the basic sponge pudding but replace 20 g of the recipe flour with cocoa powder, i.e. 80 g plain flour and 20 g cocoa powder. Serve with chocolate sauce, see page 143.

Ginger sponge pudding

Prepare the basic sponge pudding adding ¼ tsp (1 g) of ground ginger to the recipe flour and 30 g of finely diced preserved ginger blended through after adding the milk. Serve with custard sauce.

Baked sponge pudding

Eve's pudding

Ingredients: Basic sponge pudding mixture, 400 g cooking apples, 50 g sugar and pinch of ground cloves.
1 Prepare the basic mixture as stated in the base method.
2 Wash, peel, core and slice the apples then mix with the sugar and ground cloves. Also add a little cold water (25 ml) and mix with the apples and sugar.
3 Place the apples into a suitable pie dish then spread the sponge pudding mixture neatly across the top.
4 Bake at 200° C for 20 mins. then reduce the temperature to 180° C and complete the cooking – a further 25 mins. approximately.
5 Clean round the sides of the dish, dust over the top of the sponge with icing sugar and serve with custard sauce.
Note: The apples may be replaced with another fruit, e.g. rhubarb for baked rhubarb sponge.

Heavy génoise

This cake mixture is used when preparing cakes and cake-type petits fours which are dipped in fondant. The mixture, although reasonably light, does not shed crumbs into the fondant as would be the case with the light génoise described on page 377.

Plain génoise

125 g butter or margarine, 25 g white fat, 10 g glycerine, 160 g caster sugar, 190 ml egg (4 medium eggs), 160 g plain flour (or high-ratio cake flour, see page 374) and 60 g self-raising flour.

Chocolate génoise

As above but using 140 g plain flour, 60 g self-raising flour and 30 g cocoa powder with the other ingredients.

Almond génoise

Prepare as plain heavy génoise but use 100 g plain flour, 60 g self-raising flour and 60 g ground almonds with the other ingredients.
Note: The ground almonds are added to the sugar and fat when creaming together.
1 Prepare the different flavoured cakes as stated in the base method.
2 The mixture is usually spread on to a suitably sized baking sheet which has been greased and lined with greaseproof paper (the mixture is usually spread to a thickness of 20 mm approximately).
3 Bake at 185° C for 30–35 minutes.
Note: A 750 mm × 450 mm baking sheet requires 3.65 kg of génoise mixture approximately, i.e. five times the stated recipe quantities.

Cakes and petits fours using heavy génoise

Many different types of fancy cake can be made and decorated as desired.
Preparation of génoise and production of cakes and petits fours glacés:
1 Allow the baked génoise to rest on papered boards, preferably in a cool moist store – this should be done with the bottom upwards and the lining paper still covering the cake. *Note:* The cake is often allowed to rest for 24 hours before use.
2 Remove the paper from a piece of sponge which is capable of being handled (e.g. 300 mm × 200 mm) then thinly trim off the top crust – the bottom crust may also have to be trimmed off if it is slightly crumbly.
3 Slice the génoise through the centre then sandwich together with a suitable filling, e.g. jam, lemon curd or buttercream. *Note:* Keep the smooth crumb-free surface uppermost.
4 Spread the top surface with hot apricot purée and if desired roll out a thin sheet of marzipan or almond paste to the same size and neatly invert the génoise on top – this will give a smooth, well-flavoured surface for the top of the génoise when reversed the correct way up.
5 Cut the génoise into neat squares, triangles or diamonds etc. then if desired pipe on the tops small shapes of buttercream, marshmallow or softened nougat paste etc. *Note:* Chill the shapes so that the

buttercream, etc. will retain its shape when dipped in fondant.

6 Dip the shapes in fondant then decorate to taste.
Note: The preparation of fondant for dipping pieces is described in detail on page 108.

The above cakes are sometimes called 'French cakes'.
Petits fours glacés: These are often prepared in the same manner as the cakes above but are cut very small, e.g. 20 mm in length.

Frangipane filling   (yield 200 g approximately)

Frangipane is a cake-type filling made with ground almonds used in the preparation of Bakewell tart, frangipane tarts and various small fancies.
50 g butter or margarine, 50 g caster sugar, 40 ml egg (1 egg), 40 g ground almonds and 20 g plain flour.
Note: Cheaper versions of this cake may be made by reducing the quantity of ground almonds and correspondingly increasing the recipe flour and adding almond essence.
Production details:
Prepare as stated in the base method, sieving together the flour and ground almonds.
Use as required, see Bakewell tart.

Section eleven   Biscuits: sugar batter process

Biscuits

Although the 'sugar batter method' usually refers to the production of cakes and sponge cakes, many biscuits are prepared by creaming together the fat and sugar, slowly adding any eggs then mixing in the flour.

Langues de chats

(Yield 100 biscuits 40 mm in length or 50 biscuits 80 mm in length)

100 g butter or margarine, 100 g caster sugar, 60 ml egg whites (3 small eggs), a few drops of vanilla essence and 105 g plain flour.

1 Prepare the mixture as stated in the base method.
2 Grease a baking tray ready for the biscuits.
3 Pipe out the mixture through a very small plain tube, 5 mm diameter into the desired lengths, see yield above.
4 Bake at 210° C until the edges of the biscuits turn brown.
5 Remove from the tray while warm. *Note:* While the biscuits are warm they may be shaped round a rolling pin or horn moulds.

Palets de dames

Prepare the same as langues de chats but pipe out into round shapes 10 mm diameter approximately. Decorate with chocolate when cold.

Biscuits marquis

Prepare langues de chats and when cold sandwich together with a mixture consisting of ganache, see page 377 (three parts), and praline, see page 107 (one part). Dip the ends of each biscuit in chocolate or write the word 'Marquis' on top.

Sablés à poche   (yield 20 biscuits approximately)

150 g butter or margarine, 100 g caster sugar, 2 egg yolks and 200 g plain flour.

1 Prepare the mixture as stated in the base method mixing in the flour to obtain a smooth paste.
2 Grease a tray ready for the biscuits.
3 Pipe out the mixture through a star tube into rosettes then decorate the top of each rosette with a half glacé cherry.
4 Bake at 190°C until the biscuits are light brown.

Sablés

These are sablés à poche, as above, piped very small: use as petits fours.

Viennese biscuits   (yield 12 biscuits)

200 g butter or margarine, 50 g caster sugar and 200 g plain flour.

1 Cream together the fat and sugar as stated in the base method.
2 Add half the flour and beat thoroughly into the fat and sugar.
3 Add the remaining flour and also beat thoroughly into the mixture.
4 Pipe the mixture through a star tube into the bottom of paper cases – this should be done in a whirl leaving a shallow depression in the centre.
5 Bake at 205° C until golden brown in colour.
6 Allow to cool, dust over the tops with icing sugar and pipe a bulb of raspberry jam into the centre of each biscuit.

Note: These biscuits may be piped out in various shapes, e.g. circles, hearts and fingers etc. In addition they may be sandwiched together with a suitable filling and the ends or sides dipped in chocolate.

Section twelve   High-ratio cakes

The term 'high-ratio' is used to describe a range of cakes where the recipe sugar and total recipe liquid are both in excess of flour weight. To attain balanced recipes containing these high ratios of sugar and liquid in relation to flour, special shortening and special cake flour must be used. These special ingredients, i.e. high-ratio flour and high-ratio shortening, make it possible to produce cakes and sponge cakes which are very light and tender, rich eating, economical and suit large-scale catering and baking.

Blending process

High-ratio sponge cake

Uses: Swiss roll, light génoise/gâteaux and steam puddings etc.

Base method

Step 1	Mise en place
	A Assemble ingredients – the ingredients' temperature should be 18–20°C.
	B Prepare the cake tins, trays or hoops etc.
Step 2	Sieve together the dry ingredients A and place into a mixing machine.
Step 3	Add ingredients B and mix together on slow speed for 30 seconds. Scrape down. Whisk for 3–4 minutes at fast speed. Scrape down.
Step 4	Mix together ingredients C then combine with the mixture on slow speed – finished batter temperature 18–20°C.

Base recipe: plain

Ingredients A:	250 g special cake flour, 10 g cream of tartar, 25 g milk powder, 2½ g salt and 260 g caster sugar.
Ingredients B:	75 g special shortening, 250 ml eggs, 100 ml water and 15 g glycerine.
Ingredients C:	25 ml water and 5 g baking soda.

Base recipe: chocolate

Ingredients A:	250 g special cake flour, 10 g cream of tartar, 35 g milk powder, 2½ g salt, 320 g caster sugar and 50 g cocoa powder.
Ingredients B:	90 g special shortening, 300 ml egg, 120 ml water and 20 g glycerine.
Ingredients C:	30 ml water and 5 g baking soda.

Production details:

Swiss rolls: Prepare the swiss rolls in the same way as on page 378, but spread the mixture quite thin as it will double on baking. Bake at 230°C for 6–8 mins.

Génoise: Bake at 200°C.

Steamed puddings: Place mixture in greased individual moulds and steam for 40 mins. approximately.

Fruit cakes

Base method

Step 1	Mise en place See mise en place above.
Step 2	Place ingredients A in mixing machine and mix to a paste for 1–3 minutes.
Step 3	Mix the B ingredients together then add at slow speed to the A ingredients – 1 min. approximately. Scrape down and mix at medium speed for 5 mins.
Step 4	Add the eggs at slow speed until combined – 1 minute. Scrape down then mix through fruit.
Step 5	Complete as for fruit cakes on page 369, baking temperature 190° C.

Base recipe

Ingredients A:	250 g special high protein cake flour. 5 g baking powder, 20 g milk powder, 35 g rice flour, 200 g special shortening.
Ingredients B:	275 g caster sugar, 2½ g salt and 125 ml milk.
Ingredients C:	250 ml egg, 450 g fruit and sultanas or raisins etc.

Section thirteen   Preparation of sponges and sponge goods

Sponges are aerated mixtures which chiefly consist of flour, eggs and sugar. The *aeration in traditional sponges is produced solely by mechanical aeration*, i.e. whisking together the eggs and sugar to incorporate air, and it is important for the student to note that no other means of aeration is used. However, sponge mixtures deteriorate quickly after the flour is added to the whisked egg and sugar, therefore *the recipes in this section contain very small quantities of baking powder to help counteract the loss of aeration which occurs when handling, dividing or shaping the mixture prior to baking. For traditional recipes use all plain flour.*

Note: Recipes for cheap sponges have been developed which have a lower egg content than good-quality sponges and may also include milk as an ingredient: these cheap recipes rely on chemical aeration (baking powder) as well as mechanical aeration to produce a light sponge. Another development is the high-ratio sponge, see page 374, which is of good quality and economical to prepare although it is not a true sponge by traditional definition because of the fat content in the recipe.

Base method

Step 1	Mise en place
	A Assemble ingredients.
	B Accurately weigh and measure the ingredients.
	C Scald the mixing bowl and whisk in boiling water then dry thoroughly, see notes.
	D Assemble any other equipment which is required prior to preparing the sponge, e.g. greased baking trays or tins.
	E Ensure that the cooking equipment is set at the correct temperature.
	↓
Step 2	Sieve together the dry ingredients in the recipe, ingredients B, and place aside until required.
	↓
Step 3	Place the eggs and sugar, ingredients A, into the mixing bowl then place over hot water and stir until warm, i.e. 32°C approximately, see notes.
	↓
Step 4	Whisk the eggs and sugar to *ribbon stage*, see notes.
	↓
Step 5	Add any colouring or essence stated in the recipe and carefully mix through the whisked mixture.
	↓
Step 6	Fold the dry ingredients, ingredients B, carefully through the whisked mixture until combined.
	Complete as stated in the individual recipe.

Important points

Step 1

Scalding the whisking equipment: The equipment should be rinsed with boiling water then dried to remove any presence of grease or oil as this will prevent the eggs and sugar whisking to a stiff mixture, see ribbon stage.

Warming the eggs prior to whisking: Warming the eggs and sugar ensures that they will whisk to a stiff mixture. However, it is important to ensure that the mixture is only warmed and not overheated as this will cook the eggs and reduce their aerating properties.

Step 4

Whisking the mixture: The mixture should be whisked at a

irly fast speed to incorporate as much air as possible; ery fast speeds should be avoided as some of the air which as been incorporated may be knocked out of the mixture. *Hand-whisking the mixture*: This is to be avoided and hould only be resorted to when there is no machine vailable to whisk the mixture. To achieve the correct egree of aeration by hand-whisking is difficult, requires xperience and is very time-consuming.

Procedure: Whisk the eggs and sugar over hot water – 0° C approximately, until the mixture doubles in volume nd is very light and fluffy, see ribbon stage.

Ribbon stage: This is when the whisked mixture ecomes very light and fluffy and shows the whisk marks ft by the whisk during whisking. The mixture, when eld on the whisk attachment, shows fairly stiff peaks hich slowly drop when held upright.

tep 6
Adding the flour and handling the mixture: The flour must e carefully folded through the whisked egg mixture by and and not machine to retain as much aeration as ossible. It is also important that the mixture be handled s lightly as possible when completed and baked nmediately.

Génoise sponge

his is a butter sponge or sponge cake which is raditionally used as a base for many types of cold sweets nd gâteaux.

Recipe (yield 2 × 200 mm diameter tins)
Ingredients A: 250 ml egg (5 medium eggs) and 200 g aster sugar.
Ingredients B: 175 g plain flour and 25 g self-raising lour.
Ingredients C: ★75 g butter or margarine.

Production details:
Follow the instructions in the base method for sponge goods but during the mise en place stage melt the butter. Continue with the steps stated in the base method then after folding through the flour very carefully blend through the melted butter.
Place the mixture into two greased and floured tins. Alternatively, place the mixture into a suitable sized baking sheet lined with lightly greased greaseproof paper, see heavy génoise, page 371.
Bake at 200° C for 25–30 minutes. *Note*: When cooked the centre of the cake should be firm to the touch.
Turn out on to a cooling wire and allow to cool. Store until required as for heavy génoise, page 371.

★ Butter must be used when naming the sponge a butter sponge.

Chocolate génoise/almond génoise
Replace 25 g of the plain flour in the recipe with cocoa powder for chocolate génoise or 30 g plain flour with ground almonds for almond génoise.

Various gâteaux

Chocolate gâteaux (gâteau au chocolat)
Ingredients: Two shapes of chocolate génoise, see above, 150 g chocolate butter cream, see page 42, 100 g melted chocolate, 50 g chocolate vermicelli and a little stock syrup or fruit juice, see page 107.
Production details:
1 Lightly dampen the sponge with the stock syrup or fruit juice – this will produce a gâteau with a moist eating texture.
2 Sandwich together the two pieces of génoise with the buttercream then apply a thin coat of buttercream around the sides.
3 Cover the sides with the vermicelli then neatly coat the top with the melted chocolate. When the chocolate is almost set, scroll over the surface with a serrated plastic scraper to produce an attractive finish.

Black Forest gâteau (gâteau fôret-noire)
Ingredients: Two shapes of chocolate génoise, 250 g ganache, 100 ml lightly sweetened whipped cream, 75 g black cherries, 200 g grated chocolate, a little melted chocolate for piping and the juice from the cherries flavoured with a measure of kirsch.

Ganache: Ganache is a mixture of chocolate and cream. It may be used as a cake coating (used warm then allowed to set), a filling for petits fours, flavoured chocolate pieces or beaten to a light mixture which is suitable for piping and spreading.

Recipe: 500 g chocolate and 250 ml cream (the quantity of cream may be increased or decreased to produce a softer or firmer mixture).

1 Melt the chocolate and bring the cream to the boil.
2 Thoroughly mix together.
3 Leave in a cool place for 24 hours.
4 Place into a bowl and beat like buttercream – if a light spreading mixture is required.

Note: Ganache may be flavoured with wine, spirit, liqueur or coffee extract etc.

Production details:
1 Dampen the sponge with the cherry juice and kirsch then spread a layer of ganache on the sponge which is to be the base of the gâteau.
2 Halve the cherries and place on top of the ganache then cover with the whipped cream.
3 Place the remaining sponge shape on top then coat the

sides and top of the gâteau with ganache — leave some ganache for piping and decoration.

4 Cover the sides with the grated chocolate then pipe around the top edge with ganache.

5 Pipe the words 'Fôret Noire' on top with the remaining ganache. *Note*: The words may be highlighted by piping plain chocolate on top.

Coffee gâteau (gâteau moka)

Ingredients: Two shapes génoise sponge (which may be coffee-flavoured), 250 g coffee buttercream, see page 42, 100 g roasted almond nibs and a little stock syrup.

Production details:

1 Dampen the sponge with the stock syrup then sandwich together with the buttercream.

2 Coat the sides and top with the buttercream then cover the sides with almonds.

3 Pipe around the top edge with buttercream then pipe the word 'Moka' on top.

Sponge goods

Sponge sandwich   (yield 2 × 200 mm diameter tins)

Ingredients A: 250 ml egg (5 medium eggs) and 200 g caster sugar.

Ingredients B: 175 g plain flour and 25 g self-raising flour.

Additional ingredients: 50 g jam and icing sugar.

Production details:

1 Prepare the mixture as stated then place into two greased and floured sandwich tins.

2 Bake at 200° C for 25–30 minutes then turn out onto a cooling wire and allow to cool.
   Note: When cooked the centre of the sponge should be firm to the touch.

3 Sandwich the sponges together with jam and/or cream and dust the top with icing sugar. Alternatively coat the top with water icing or fondant.

Chocolate sponge sandwich/almond sponge sandwich

Prepare as plain sponge sandwich above, replacing 25 g of the plain flour with cocoa powder for chocolate sponge sandwich or 30 g of the plain flour with ground almonds for almond sponge sandwich.

Swiss roll   (yield 10 portions approximately)

Ingredients A: 250 ml eggs (5 medium eggs) and 115 g caster sugar.

Ingredients B: 75 g plain flour and 40 g self-raising flour.

Additional ingredients: 150 g jam and caster sugar.

Production details:

1 Prepare the mixture as stated then spread on to a baking tray – 400 mm × 300 mm diameter approximately, lined with greased greaseproof paper.

2 Bake at 235°C for 4–5 mins. then invert on to a sheet of greaseproof paper sprinkled with caster sugar.

3 Remove the lining paper, spread lightly with jam and carefully roll up using the paper.

4 When cold remove the paper and use as required.

Chocolate roll   (yield 10 portions approximately)

Ingredients A: 250 ml egg (5 medium eggs) and 125 g caster sugar.

Ingredients B: 75 g plain flour, 15 g self-raising flour, 15 cocoa powder and chocolate colour.

Additional ingredients: 400 ml whipped cream and caste sugar.

Production details:

1 Prepare as ordinary swiss roll above to step 2.

2 Remove the lining paper then place a sheet of greaseproof paper on top of the sponge.

3 Roll up with the paper inside the sponge and allow to cool.

4 Unroll, remove the paper then spread with the whipped cream.

5 Re-roll and use as required.

Sponge biscuits (biscuits à la cuillère)   (yield 30 biscuits approximately)

Ingredients A: 200 ml egg (4 medium eggs) and 200 g caster sugar.

Ingredients B: 150 g plain flour, 50 g strong flour and 15 g self-raising flour.

Additional ingredients: Caster sugar.

Production details:

1 Prepare the mixture as stated in the base method.

2 Place the mixture into a piping bag fitted with a plain tube – 12 mm diameter approximately.

3 Pipe out the mixture into fingers or rounds on to a sheet of greaseproof paper.

4 Invert the biscuits on to a layer of caster sugar, press lightly with the finger then place on to a baking tray. Care and confidence is required for this operation.

5 Bake at 235° C for 4 mins. approximately.

6 Dampen the back of the paper to remove the biscuits and use as required.

Trifle   (yield 4 portions)

Ingredients:

16 sponge biscuits *or* 160 g génoise sponge, 30 g raspberry jam and stock syrup (page 107) *or* fruit juice to moisten. Thick custard using 250 ml milk, 15 g custard powder and 25 g sugar.

125 ml cream, blanched almonds, glacé cherries and angelica.

Production details:

1 *Using sponge biscuits*:   Sandwich the biscuits together with the jam then cut into pieces (25 mm approximately).
   Using génoise sponge: Split through the centre then

sandwich together with the jam. Cut into dice (15 mm approximately).

Place into the serving dish then lightly moisten with the stock syrup or fruit juice.

Prepare the custard sauce then pour over the sponge. Cool quickly and thoroughly chill.

Whip the cream. *Note*:   The cream may be lightly sweetened and flavoured, see crème Chantilly, page 41.

Decorate with the cream, almonds, cherries and angelica.

ruit trifle
repare as above adding a dice or small slices of selected pe or poached fruit to the sponge at step 2.

herry trifle
dd 25 ml sweet sherry when moistening the sponge.

Section fourteen   Soufflés and pudding soufflés

Base method

Step 1	Mise en place
	A Assemble ingredients.
	B Accurately measure and weigh the ingredients.
	C Separate the whites from the yolks and place into a clean scalded whisking bowl.
	D *Savoury soufflés*: Butter the soufflé case.
	Sweet soufflés and pudding soufflés: Butter the soufflé dish or dariole moulds then coat with sugar.

Step 2	Cream together the caster sugar, butter, flour and cornflour.

Step 3	Place the milk in a thick-bottomed pan and bring through the boil.

Step 4	Whisk the creamed butter, sugar and flour into the milk then stir with a spatula until the mixture thickens. Cook for 1 minute approximately.

Step 5	Add the ingredient/s which will flavour the soufflé, e.g. essence, fruit juice or zest, cheese or vegetable purée etc., see individual recipe. Mix thoroughly through the thickened mixture then allow to cool slightly.

Step 6	Transfer the mixture to a mixing bowl then beat in the egg yolks.

Step 7	Whisk the egg white to a stiff snow then carefully fold through the mixture.

Step 8	Place the mixture into the prepared soufflé case or dariole moulds then lightly smooth down with a palette knife.

Step 9	Clean the top 2 mm of the soufflé case (or each dariole mould).

Step 10	*Soufflés*	*Pudding soufflés*
	Place the filled soufflé cases on to a baking tray and bake at 200° C until fully risen and a good colour – 20 mins. approximately.	Place the dariole moulds in a tray with water, i.e. bain-marie, and cook in an oven at 200°C until fully risen and cooked through – 30 mins. approximately.

Step 11	Dredge the top of sweet soufflés with icing sugar. Place the soufflé case on a salver lined with a doily or napkin and serve immediately.	Carefully turn out the pudding soufflés on to a salver etc., and serve accompanied with a suitable sauce, see individual recipe.

Important points

soufflé: A very light-textured, sauce-type mixture which set firm and aerated with eggs. Soufflés may be sweet or savoury and are usually served in a soufflé case.

Pudding soufflé: These are similar to soufflés above but are cooked in dariole moulds (or any other suitable mould) and demoulded for service. They are a little heavier in texture than ordinary soufflés because they must be demoulded and in most instances are sweet.

Step 1

Preparing the eggs: When separating the egg yolks from the whites, it is of the utmost importance that no traces of yolk are present in the whites; to whisk egg whites to a stiff snow there must be a total absence of grease or fat in the whites or on any equipment, see the preparation of meringue, page 402.

Step 4

Whisking the fat and flour mixture into the hot milk: When whisking the creamed fat and flour into the milk, care should be taken to avoid hitting the whisk against the pan as this may cause discoloration of the mixture; especially when using an aluminium pan. When the mixture becomes a smooth thick paste it is desirable to replace the whisk with a spatula.

Step 5

Adding flavouring ingredients: Ingredients which impart a distinctive flavour to soufflés (with the exception of the base ingredients: butter and sugar etc.) are added after the base ingredients become a thick sauce, i.e. step 5.

Examples:
Essences: vanilla, almond, lemon or orange etc.
Fruits: juice, zest, pulp or purée etc.
Liqueurs: Cointreau, Grand Marnier or kirsch etc.
Cheese: grated parmesan and/or grated gruyère etc.
Vegetables: purées of spinach, aubergine or chicory etc.
Meat, game or poultry: purées of cooked ham or pheasant etc.
Fish and shellfish: purées of mackerel or lobster etc.

Step 7

Whisking the egg whites to a stiff snow: One of the most important factors to the production of a good soufflé is the condition of the whisked egg whites when folded through the sauce-type mixture. The egg whites should be whisked to a texture similar to a stiff snow which will hold firm on the whisk when it is removed from the mixing bowl. Under-whipped whites, which are soft in texture, and over-whipped whites which clump together and lose volume, will not supply the aeration necessary to produce an excellent soufflé. The whisking of egg whites is further explained on page 402.

The whites must also be very carefully folded through the sauce-type mixture to introduce as much aeration as possible.

Step 10

Cooking the soufflé or pudding soufflé: During baking the soufflé or pudding soufflé should not be moved, knocked or banged and when cooked should be served immediately.

Base recipe   (yield 3 × 115 mm soufflé cases)

Sweet soufflés

Ingredients: 60 g caster sugar, 60 g butter, 60 g plain flour, 10 g cornflour, 250 ml milk and 250 ml egg (5 eggs approximately).

Flavouring ingredients: See individual recipe.
Butter and caster sugar for greasing and coating soufflé cases.

Pudding soufflés (poudings soufflés)

Same recipe as above but reduce the egg content to 150 ml egg (3 eggs).

Sweet soufflés

Vanilla soufflé (soufflé à la vanille)
Prepare as stated in the base recipe and method adding 2–3 drops vanilla essence as indicated at step 5.

Lemon soufflé (soufflé au citron)
Prepare as stated adding the juice and grated zest of 1 lemon as indicated at step 5.

Orange soufflé (soufflé à l'orange)
Prepare as stated adding the juice and zest of 1 orange and the juice of a half lemon at step 5. Note: A little orange colour may also be added.

Chocolate soufflé (soufflé au chocolat)
Prepare as stated adding 100 g grated chocolate into the milk when heating, i.e. step 3. Note: An extra egg white may be required for these soufflés as chocolate tends to have a thickening effect on the mixture.

Harlequin soufflé (soufflé Arlequin)
This is a soufflé which consists of half a vanilla and half a chocolate soufflé mixture. The two mixtures are placed

side by side in the soufflé case; a plastic scraper may be used to act as a divider and aid an even distribution of the two mixtures.

Liqueur soufflé (e.g. Cointreau, Grand Marnier and kirsch etc.)
Prepare as stated adding 30 ml of the desired liqueur at step 5.

Fruit-based soufflés (e.g. apricot, peach, strawberry, raspberry and gooseberries)
When preparing these soufflés a special fruit base may be prepared in advance and added to the mixture as stated at step 5.
Fruit base: 1 kg fresh fruit pulp or puree, ½ kg glucose, 10 g citric acid or lemon juice and appropriate colouring.
Method:
1   Boil the fruit pulp and glucose to a sauce consistency.
2   Add the citric acid or lemon juice and allow to blend into the mixture.
3   Add colouring and use as required.
Production details:
Reduce the milk in the base recipe to 200 ml and add 100 g of the desired fruit base at step 5. *Note*:   A measure of appropriate liqueur will produce a more exotic flavour.

Pudding soufflés (poudings soufflés)

The various pudding soufflés may be prepared by:
A   Following the instructions given in the base recipe and method.
B   Adding the flavouring ingredients as instructed for soufflés above, e.g. lemon, orange or vanilla pudding soufflé etc.

Composite pudding soufflés

Pouding soufflé Montmorency
Add to the pudding soufflé mixture at step 5, 25 ml kirsch and a dice of cherries (30–50 g approximately). Serve with a sauceboat of apricot or cherry sauce.

Pouding soufflé Rothschild
Add to the basic mixture at step 5, 25 ml kirsch and 50 g candied fruits. Serve with a sauceboat of apricot sauce.

Pouding soufflé Régence
Prepare a vanilla mixture but place into dariole moulds which have been lined with caramel, see crème caramel, page 393. Serve caramel sauce separately.

Savoury soufflés

Follow the instructions in the base recipe and method *omitting the sugar*.

Base recipe

30 g butter or margarine, 30 g plain flour, 5 g cornflour, 200 ml milk, 2 egg yolks and 3 egg whites.

Parmesan soufflé (soufflé au parmesan)   (yield 3 soufflés, 80 mm diameter dishes)
Follow the instructions in the base method using the quantities of ingredients stated above with the addition of 40 g grated parmesan, see base method. Dust the buttered mould with parmesan prior to adding the soufflé mixture

Spinach soufflé (soufflé aux épinards)   (yield 4 soufflés, 80 mm diameter dishes)
Follow the instructions in the base method using the quantities of ingredients stated above with the addition of 150 g blanched chopped spinach, see base method.
Note: In some spinach soufflé recipes a small quantity of anchovy fillet is added, e.g. two fillets cut into a small dice

Endive soufflé (soufflé à la chicorée (frisée)   (yield 4 soufflés, 80 mm diameter dishes)
Follow the instructions in the base method using the quantities of ingredients stated in the basic savoury soufflé recipe with the addition of 150 g blanched chopped curly endives.

ction fifteen   Yorkshire pudding

se recipe   (yield 6–8 portions)

0 ml batter, see page 321 and 40 g dripping or oil proximately.

oduction details:

Prepare the batter as stated on page 321. Note the *resting time* of 1 hour approximately.

Place the Yorkshire pudding tins on a tray then add enough oil or dripping to cover the bottom of the tins i.e., 5 mm oil (1 teaspoon) per pudding tin.

Place the tins in a moderate oven (200° C) and allow to become very hot: 8–10 mins. in the oven.

Pour the batter into the hot oil and fill the moulds then replace into the oven.

Allow to cook for 30 mins. approximately (until risen and set).

Turn the puddings upside down to remove the fat from the centres and continue cooking until crisp – a further 10 mins. approximately.

ote: If the puddings are not crisp all over, place in a ol oven and allow to crisp.

ad in the hole   (yield 4 portions)

sausages, 30 g dripping or oil, 300 ml batter and 250 ml s lié (page 160).

eat the dripping or oil in a shallow roasting tray then add e sausages and *lightly* fry and colour. Neatly arrange the usages into portions then pour in the batter. Cook in the en at 200° C for 30–40 mins.

Section sixteen   Apple strudel (Apfel Strudel)

Recipe

Strudel dough:	See page 322.
Filling:	500 g tart eating apples, 50 g caster sugar, 75 g sultanas and a good pinch of cinnamon.
Lemon cream:	100 ml cream and the juice and zest of half a lemon.
Melted butter:	25 g butter.
Icing sugar:	Icing sugar to dust the top of the strudel.

Production details:

1   Prepare and shape the dough as explained on page 323. Trim off the ends to form a neat rectangle.
2   Peel and core the apples then cut into small pieces. Place into a bowl then add the sugar, sultanas and cinnamon.
3   Prepare the lemon cream: whip the cream until stiff then mix through the lemon zest and juice.
4   Mix the lemon cream through the apple mixture.
5   Spread the filling on the prepared dough leaving a short edge at the sides and top edge of 100 mm along the length of the dough.
6   Roll up the dough and filling, with the aid of the cloth, up to the top edge.
7   Brush over the surface with butter then roll over the top edge – this will be the surface of the strudel.
8   Lift the cloth and strudel and roll on to a greased and floured baking tray with the top surface upwards.
9   Brush over the surface of the strudel with butter.
10   Bake at 200° C until cooked and golden brown – 40 mins. approximately.
11   Remove from the oven and dredge over the surface with icing sugar.
12   Cut into slices and serve accompanied with crème Chantilly or sauce anglaise etc.

Assessment exercise

1 Explain the method of preparing fresh pasta paste.
2 What makes puff pastry rise?
3 What is the difference between a full puff pastry and a half puff pastry?
4 Explain how to make choux paste.
5 What is the meaning of the term 'short' when applied to pastry?
6 What is the difference between a sponge and a cake?
7 Describe the function of the following ingredients when preparing a cake: flour, eggs, sugar and fat.
8 What is meant by the term 'high-ratio cake'?
9 How does baking powder aerate a cake?
10 What is a strong or spring flour?
11 Explain how yeast goods are made by a 'straight dough process'.
12 What is the main reason for making some goods by a 'ferment and dough process'?
13 What is the difference between a soufflé and a pudding soufflé?
14 The term baking may be used to classify a range of processes. Give one example where the term baking refers to a simple process and another example where the term refers to a fairly complex process.

Chapter 15

Egg, egg yolk and egg white products

Eggs are often described as the most versatile of all foods, a statement which at first appears to make an exaggerated claim until one examines the incredible number of functions which eggs can fulfil. Eggs may be used in cookery to *add flavour, add colour or develop colour when cooking, to act as a binding agent, to act as a thickening agent, to act as an emulsifying agent, to act as an enriching agent,* to act as an aerating agent and of course to be *used as a food in their own right* served either boiled, poached or fried.

In this chapter the methods of preparing the egg mixtures which produce custards, sabayons, liaisons, meringues, egg white biscuits and royal icing are examined and explained.

Note: The preparation of fried eggs, omelettes and poached eggs etc., is explained in the various chapters dealing with shallow-frying and deep-poaching etc.

The methods of preparation for the egg mixtures and derivative dishes within the chapter are grouped or classified as follows:

a) *Thickened mixtures of egg yolk and liquid.*
   1 Mayonnaise sauce and derivatives.
   2 Sweet and savoury sabayons, sauce hollandaise and derivatives and bombe ices.
   3 Liaison and liaison-thickened soups.
   4 Fresh egg custard sauce, bavarian creams and ice-creams.
   5 Pastry cream and derivative sauces.
b) *Egg and liquid mixtures cooked until set or gelled.*
   Examples: sweet and savoury custards and derivative dishes.
c) *Egg white mixtures.*
   1 Meringue and meringue products.
   2 Egg-white based biscuits.
   3 Royal icing.

Important points

Sweet and savoury custards: Good-quality custards are basically a *mixture of milk and eggs* and contain sugar or seasoning depending on whether they are sweet or savoury, although the term is mostly used to refer to sweet mixtures. These custards which are cooked until *set and firm begin to coagulate at around 78–85°C*, depending on the amount of yolk, egg white and sugar used in relation to

liquid, and *curdle between 85–90°C*, approximately. The speed of cooking is extremely important; slow, even cooking will produce a smooth-textured custard with a good colour, whereas fast cooking will increase the likelihood of curdling, cause discoloration and produce bubbles in the finished product. *Cooking in a bain-marie is essential* when the mixture is to be cooked in a metal or porcelain container. When a custard mixture is to be cooked in a pastry case in the oven, the oven should be regulated to have a substantial amount of bottom heat to cook the pastry through and at the same time set the custard without overcooking; the baking sheets (trays) are also important – well cleaned, thin baking sheets should be used to pass the heat quickly to the pastry to offset the cooling effect of the custard.

Fresh egg custard sauce: This consists of egg yolks, sugar, milk and flavouring cooked to a stage where the egg yolks produce a thickening of consistency just prior to curdling point. This necessitates the *operator taking great care when cooking the mixture* to ascertain when maximum thickening has been reached without proceeding to a temperature which will curdle the mixture – the final temperature at which the custard is cooked and coats the back of a spoon is the same as stated above for set custards, i.e. 78–85°C depending on the amount of yolks present in the mixture and in addition the quantity of sugar present; this increases the temperature at which the mixture thickens.

Sabayons: These consist of a mixture of egg yolks and liquid (a small quantity of water, stock or wine etc.) whisked over hot water until very light and fluffy with a thick consistency. Like the egg mixtures above the operator must take care not to overcook or curdle the mixture by ensuring that the correct amount of liquid to egg yolk is present, that the mixture is whisked quickly and correctly, and, of course, not overheated.

Pastry cream (confectioner's custard) – crême pâtissière: Pastry cream is similar to fresh egg custard sauce but contains flour which increases the thickness considerably and allows the mixture to be boiled when cooking. Provided the mixture is stirred constantly, especially prior to reaching boiling point and during cooking to avoid burning on the base of the cooking utensil, there are no problems of curdling or separation as is the case with setting custards and fresh egg custard sauces.

Liaison: A liaison is simply a mixture of egg yolks and cream which is blended into a hot liquid. This thickens a mixture and produces a rich creamy flavour. To avoid curdling, mixtures to which liaisons have been added should never be reboiled after adding the liaison.

Meringue: Meringue consists of egg whites and sugar which are whisked to produce a very thick aerated mixture. Several types of meringue can be prepared but in all cases the operator must ensure that there is a *total absence of grease* in the whites, in the sugar and on any equipment used in the production of meringue.

Egg-white based biscuits: These consist of either a meringue mixture to which is added ground nuts, e.g. almonds, hazelnuts etc., or simply egg whites with the addition of sugar, ground nuts, ground rice or flour etc. When the mixture has been prepared, it is usually piped on to a prepared baking tray then cooked in the oven.

Royal icing: This is an icing prepared with egg whites and icing sugar. As is the case with all whisked egg white products, total absence of grease is essential to produce a good icing.

Section one   Mayonnaise sauce (sauce mayonnaise)

Base method

Step 1	Mise en place
	A Assemble ingredients.
	B Separate the yolks from the whites and place the yolks into a mixing bowl.
Step 2	Add the salt, pepper, mustard and three-quarters of the vinegar then whisk together until combined.
Step 3	Slowly add the oil in a thin stream while whisking continuously. If the sauce becomes too thick, adjust the consistency with the remaining vinegar.
Step 4	Add the lemon juice and check the seasoning.

Important points

Mayonnaise is a basic cold emulsion sauce which is used for a variety of purposes, e.g. salads, hors-d'oeuvre and fish sauces.

Consistency: The sauce should be thick enough to hold its shape when placed on a serving spoon.

Reasons for curdled mayonnaise:

  Ingredients at different temperatures, e.g. oil too cold, eggs too cold.

  Oil cloudy at room temperature.

  Oil added too quickly.

  Insufficient whisking when adding the oil.

  Stale egg yolks.

Storage: Store at 6–8°C for short periods.

Curdled mayonnaise may be corrected by whisking it slowly into an egg yolk or a little boiling water.

Mayonnaise sauce   (yield 275 ml)

250 ml salad oil, 20 ml vinegar, 2 small egg yolks, ½ g English mustard (one eighth of a teaspoon), squeeze lemon juice and pinch salt and white pepper.

Derivative sauces

Sauce andalouse

Add tomato ketchup to the mayonnaise to obtain a good pink colour (30 g approximately). Also add a garnish of sliced red peppers (50 g approximately).

Sauce Chantilly

Blend some stiffly whipped cream through the mayonnaise just prior to service – 50 ml approximately. *Note*:   The mayonnaise is usually placed in a sauceboat and a quenelle (egg shape) of whipped cream laid on top.

Sauce rémoulade

Flavour the mayonnaise with a little anchovy essence (5 ml – 1 teaspoon approximately) and French mustard. Add a garnish of chopped capers and gherkins (25 g each). Also add a little chopped chervil and tarragon.

Sauce Marie-Rose (shellfish cocktail sauce)

Combine with the mayonnaise, 2–3 drops of Worcester sauce, whipped cream (50 ml) and enough tomato ketchup or fresh tomato purée to produce a good pink colour (30 g approximately). Garnish with chopped parsley and finely chopped shallots (10 g approximately). *Note*:   This sauce is sometimes made without the mayonnaise.

Sauce tartare

Add a garnish of chopped gherkins (50 g), chopped capers (25 g) and chopped parsley to the basic mayonnaise.

Sauce tyrolienne

Prepare the same as sauce andalouse but garnish with chopped mixed herbs (chervil, parsley and tarragon) instead of pimento.

Sauce verte (green sauce)

Mix through the mayonnaise enough purée of herbs to obtain a good green colour. The herb purée is prepared as follows: take chervil, chives, spinach, tarragon and watercress and blanch until limp in boiling water. Refresh and squeeze dry. Pass through a fine sieve or place into a liquidizer with the mayonnaise and liquidize to a smooth green sauce.

Sauce Vincent

This sauce consists of half sauce tartare and half sauce verte mixed together.

Section two   Sabayon and sabayon sauces

Base method

Step 1	Mise en place
	Assemble ingredients.
Step 2	Separate the whites from the yolks and place the yolks into a sauteuse or whisking bowl.
Step 3	Add the water, stock, wine or lemon juice etc. stated in the recipe. Also add any sugar.
Step 4	Place the mixture in a bain-marie or over a pan of hot water and whisk continually until *ribbon stage* has been reached, i.e. very fluffy and light but stiff enough to leave peaks or whisk marks when the whisk is drawn out of the mixture (for a very short period only).
Step 5	Remove from the heat and continue whisking for a very short period to ensure that residual heat will not cause curdling. Use as required.

Important points

Sabayons are very light, smooth egg yolk mixtures which are produced by whisking egg yolks and liquid over hot water. Sabayons may be sweet or savoury.

Step 3

Liquid content of sabayons: The quantity of liquid added to the egg yolks is extremely important: too little liquid produces a heavy sabayon, likely to form lumps or curdle during cooking; too much liquid produces a light frothy sabayon with very little body which may easily break down, showing signs of free water. The amount of liquid required to produce a light, well-bodied sayabon is approximately equal quantities of egg yolk and liquid by volume, i.e. 1 egg yolk per 10–15 ml liquid (depending on the size of the yolk). Some cooks use a half egg shell as a measure – two-thirds of a half egg shell of liquid per egg yolk.

Step 4

Cooking the mixture: Although the mixture is cooked in a water bath there is still a risk of curdling. It may therefore be necessary to remove the sabayon from the hot water from time to time while whisking to avoid curdling. A mixture which is overcooked will be low in volume, heavy and may show signs of coagulated egg yolk. A mixture which is undercooked will be light but frothy, have little body and may break down easily showing signs of surface or free water. *Note*:   Some sabayons are meant to be very light bodied and frothy.

Base recipe

	Plain sabayon	Sabayon sauce (sweet)
Egg yolks:	2	2
Liquid:	20 ml water, stock or wine.	20 ml Madeira wine, squeeze of lemon juice.
Sugar:	—	40 g caster sugar.

Zabaglione

Prepare the same as sauce sabayon and serve in warmed glasses or special cups. Accompany with finger biscuits (page 378).

Sauce Arenberg/mousseline

Prepare a sauce sabayon using white wine in place of Madeira wine. Allow to become cold (occasionally whisking the mixture). Add 200 ml double cream then whisk until the desired consistency is achieved.

ection three   Hollandaise sauce

ase method

Step 1	Mise en place A Assemble ingredients. B Place the butter in a small pot and allow to melt slowly and become clear. C Crush the peppercorns.
tep 2	Place the vinegar and crushed peppercorns into a small sauteuse and reduce until almost completely evaporated. Allow to cool slightly.
tep 3	Add the cold water and egg yolks and prepare a sayabon as stated. When ribbon stage has been reached, remove the sabayon from the heat and slowly whisk in the melted butter. Do not use the water which has separated from the butter.
tep 4	Season the sauce and whisk through the lemon juice.
tep 5	Strain the sauce through a muslin into a clean bowl and keep *warm*.

Hollandaise sauce

This is the basic warm egg and butter emulsion from which many derivative sauces may be made.

Curdled hollandaise sauce may be corrected by slowly whisking it into a little Béchamel sauce.

Recipe

Vinegar reduction:	20 ml vinegar and 4 crushed peppercorns.
Sabayon:	2 egg yolks and 20 ml water.
Butter:	250 g butter.
Seasoning:	Pinch salt, pepper and a small pinch of cayenne pepper.
Lemon juice:	Squeeze lemon juice.

Béarnaise sauce (sauce béarnaise)

Prepare the same as hollandaise adding 20 g finely chopped shallot or onion and 10 g tarragon stalks to the peppercorns and vinegar prior to reducing, step 2. After straining the sauce, add a garnish of chopped tarragon and chopped chervil.

Note: Dried tarragon or tarragon vinegar may be used in place of fresh tarragon.

Sauce Choron

Prepare béarnaise sauce then add enough fresh tomato purée to colour and flavour (50 g approximately, page 273).

Note: Commercially prepared tomato purée may be used in place of fresh tomato purée (10 g approximately).

Sauce Foyot

Prepare sauce béarnaise then flavour with melted meat glaze.

Sauce maltaise

Prepare a sauce hollandaise but add the juice of two oranges (traditionally blood oranges) to the vinegar when preparing the reduction. Garnish the sauce with the grated zest of the oranges.

Sauce mousseline

Prepare a sauce hollandaise then fold through a little stiffly whipped cream (25 ml approximately) when ready for service. Alternatively place a quenelle of whipped cream on top of the sauce when serving – the waiter folds the cream through the sauce at the table.

Sauce paloise

Prepare the same as béarnaise but replace the tarragon with mint and add freshly chopped mint to the sauce.

Sauce noisette

Prepare hollandaise sauce but reduce the butter to 200 g. When the sauce is made prepare a nut-brown butter using 50 g butter then allow to cool slightly. Mix the nut-brown butter through the hollandaise.

Section four Liaison and liaison-type soups

Base method: *liaison*

Step 1	Mise en place Assemble ingredients.
Step 2	Separate the yolks from the whites and place the yolks into a small bowl.
Step 3	Add the cream and beat together with the yolks.
Step 4	Use the liaison as required, see important points.

Liaison-based soups

Step 1	Mise en place Assemble ingredients.
Step 2	Boil the stock then reduce the heat, allowing the mixture to leave the boil.
Step 3	Add the liaison to the stock, whisking thoroughly together, see important points.
Step 4	Cook for a short period but *do not reboil*, see important points.
Step 5	Check the seasoning, add any garnish then enrich with butter.
Step 6	Serve immediately in a tureen.

Important points

Liaison: This is an enriching and thickening agent consisting of cream and egg yolks. Liaisons are often used in soups, sauces and white stews, see page 182.

Use of the liaison: Care must be taken when adding a liaison to hot liquid as a liaison thickened mixture is quite unstable and may easily curdle.

Important points:
1 Remove the mixture to be thickened from the boil.
2 Blend the liaison into the hot liquid stirring continuously★.

3 The mixture must not reboil.
4 Add the liaison just prior to service.

Service: As stated in point 4 above, the liaison should be added when serving.

Note: Mixtures thickened with a liaison cannot be reheated.

★ Many cooks mix a little of the hot liquid into the liaison before adding the liaison to the hot mixture as an additional precaution against curdling.

ase recipe: liaison

arious stews and sauces ee notes)	1–2 egg yolks and 25–50 ml cream.
arious soups (4 portions):	4 egg yolks and 100 ml cream.
ecipe liquid:	1 litre stock. See individual recipe.
nriching butter:	20 g butter
ther ingredients:	See individual recipe.

iaison-thickened soups

otage Germiny

se a good strong white chicken or veal stock. Garnish ith 25 g of sorrel* leaves cut into fine shreds (chiffonnade) ad sweat in 20 g butter until tender. Enrich with a further) g butter. Serve cheese straws separately.

batis allemande (German giblet soup)

se a good strong white chicken stock prepared with ticken giblets. Garnish with 25 g barley (which can be ooked in the chicken stock prior to use) and a dice of ooked chicken livers and stomach. Enrich with 20 g utter.

izzo figatini

se a strong white chicken stock flavoured with celery. arnish with 100 g chicken livers cut into neat slices and weat in 20 g butter. Serve separately parmesan cheese.

Lettuce leaves may be used when sorrel is unobtainable.

Section five   Egg-custard mixtures

Base method

Step 1	Mise en place	
	A Assemble ingredients.	
	B Heat the milk.	
	C Break the eggs into a bowl.	

Step 2	*Savoury mixtures* Add the seasoning and beat through the eggs.	*Sweet mixtures* Add the sugar and vanilla essence then beat through the eggs.

Step 3	Whisk the hot milk through the eggs.	

Step 4	*Baked and moulded custards* Strain the mixture into the mould/s or pie dish.	*Mixtures cooked in a flan case* Strain the mixture into the flan case.

Step 5	Place the mould/s or pie dish in a tray half full of water and cook in a cool oven (150–160 °C)	Bake the flan in a moderate oven (190° C approximately).

Step 5	*Service* *Baked custard* Clean round the edges of the dish before serving. *Moulded custards* *Cold*: Allow to become thoroughly cold then carefully turn out on to the serving dish. *Hot* (cabinet pudding): Allow the mixture to cool slightly then carefully turn out on to the serving dish.	*Service* Allow to cool slightly before removing the flan ring and serving.

Important points

Step 5
Cooking custard mixtures: See important points on page 385.
Step 5
Cooking times: The following cooking times should only be used as a rough guide (all 4 portions).
Flans: 40 mins. approximately.
Small pastry cases: 20 mins. approximately.

Moulded custards (4 portion moulds):   1½–2 hours.
Moulded custards (individual moulds):   1–1½ hours.
Step 5
Test for cooking: The mixture should be set.
Physical test: A soft but consistent firmness should be felt when lightly pressing the top of the mixture with the fingers.
Internal temperature: 85° C approximately.

Base recipe (yield 4 portions)

	Sweet custards	Savoury custards
Eggs:	100 ml (2 eggs approximately).	100 ml (2 eggs approximately).
Milk:	300 ml.	300 ml.
Sugar:	30 g caster sugar.	—
Flavouring:	2–3 drops vanilla essence.	—
Seasoning:	—	Salt, pepper and a small pinch of cayenne pepper.

Sweet dishes

Baked egg custard
Prepare as stated for sweet mixtures baked in an earthenware pie dish. Sprinkle with a little grated nutmeg before baking.

Custard flans or tarts
Line a flan ring or tart tins with sweet short pastry (page 332) and prepare as stated for mixtures cooked in a flan case. Sprinkle with a little grated nutmeg prior to baking. When baking small tarts set the oven to a higher temperature than flans, i.e. 220° C.

Bread and butter pudding
Prepare as for sweet mixtures cooked in a pie dish but line the pie dish with two slices of buttered bread cut into triangles (crusts removed) and 25 g sultanas. Strain the mixture over the bread and sultanas and allow to stand until the bread absorbs the custard mixture. Dust over the top with icing sugar when serving.

Swedish pudding (pouding suédoise)
The same as bread and butter pudding adding a dice of candied fruits with the sultanas.

Queen of pudding
Prepare the same as sweet mixtures cooked in a pie dish but butter the dish and add 50 g cake crumbs then strain over the egg custard. Allow to stand prior to baking until the cake crumbs absorb the custard.
Prepare a meringue using 50 ml egg whites (page 402) and pipe lattice-style across the top of the custard when almost baked. Replace in the oven and continue cooking until it is an attractive brown colour. Pipe a little hot raspberry and apricot jam into the lattice design in alternate squares.

Savoury mixtures

Cheese and egg flan
Line a flan ring with savoury short pastry (page 332). Add 50 g grated cheese to the flan before straining in the savoury egg mixture.

Cheese and ham flan
Prepare as above adding 40 g diced cooked ham with the cheese.

Quiche lorraine
Line a flan ring with savoury short pastry (page 332). Add 50 g diced streaky bacon fried in a little butter and 30 g grated Gruyère cheese to the flan before straining in the savoury custard.
Note: A little crushed garlic may be added to the bacon when frying and some of the milk in the custard may be replaced with cream.

Quiche alsacienne
Prepare the same as above but increase the cheese to 50 g and replace the bacon with diced Alsatian ham sausage.

Royale garnish (soup garnish)
Prepare a savoury egg custard mixture using equal quantities of egg and milk (or strong white stock), e.g. 100 ml eggs and 100 ml milk. Cook as for the moulded custard. When cold, demould then cut the mixture into diamonds or small dice.

Various cream puddings

Crème renversée (demoulded cream) (cold)
This is the name for the basic sweet egg mixture cooked as stated in four dariole moulds or a charlotte mould. Decorate to taste.

Caramel cream (crème caramel) (cold)
Prepare the caramel as stated on page 107, and pour into four dariole moulds or a charlotte mould. Allow the caramel to firm then add the basic egg mixture. Cook as stated.

Crème Beau-Rivage (cold)
Butter a savarin mould then coat with praline, see page 107. Carefully add the basic egg mixture then cook as stated. Decorate the centre of the mixture when cold as follows: prepare twelve pastry coronets (see Langues de chats, page 373). Also prepare half a litre of lightly

sweetened whipped cream, see page 41. Fill the coronets with the cream and place the remaining cream into the centre of the mixture. Neatly arrange the coronets around the top of the cream with the points inwards then place a crystallized violet in the centre of the cream in each coronet.

Crème florentine (cold)
Prepare and cook a praline-flavoured cream mixture the same as Beau-Rivage above but use a charlotte mould or four dariole moulds. Decorate when unmoulded with kirsch-flavoured whipped cream sprinkled with chopped pistachios.

Crème Opéra (cold)
Prepare and cook a praline-flavoured cream mixture in the same manner as Beau-Rivage. Fill the centre of the mixture when unmoulded with crème Chantilly and sprinkle with crystallized violets. Neatly decorate around the top of the sweet with large strawberries macerated in a little kirsch flavoured syrup and cover with a veil of spun sugar when serving, see page 107.

Crème viennoise (cold)
Prepare the basic egg mixture as stated but reduce the quantity of sugar by half, i.e. 15 g, and the milk by one-third, i.e. 200 ml. Prepare a caramel the same as for crème caramel using 50 g granulated sugar and adding 50 ml hot water after cooking to caramel degree, see page 107. Allow the caramel to cool slightly then whisk into the basic egg mixture. Cook and serve as stated decorating to taste.

Crème renversée au café
Prepare the same as crème renversée but add enough coffee essence to the milk to produce a full coffee flavour.

Crème renversée au chocolat
Prepare the same as crème renversée but add 20 g cocoa powder (mixed until smooth with a little cold milk) or 40 g grated block chocolate into the hot milk.

Diplomat pudding (pouding diplomate) (cold)
Butter a charlotte mould or four dariole moulds then add the following garnish: 50 g diced sponge or four diced sponge biscuits, see page 378, 20 g diced glacé cherries, 25 g each sultanas and currants and 5 g diced angelica. Add the basic egg mixture and leave to stand for 2–3 minutes to allow the mixture to soak into the sponge. Cook as stated and decorate to taste for service. *Note*: This sweet may be prepared using a vanilla bavarois mixture, see page 396, in place of the basic egg mixture.

Cabinet pudding (pouding cabinet) (hot)
Prepare the same as pouding diplomate above but unmould and serve hot. Serve separately a sauceboat of apricot sauce or fresh egg custard sauce.

Pouding rizzio (cold)
Prepare the same as pouding diplomate above but replace the sponge or savoy biscuits with diced macaroon biscuits soaked in a little kirsch.

Crème brûlée (cold)
Note: Non-derivative recipe: This very rich sweet is made by replacing the whole eggs with four egg yolks, and using cream instead of milk; the recipe sugar and flavouring are included. Prepare as stated in the base method but use 1 × 4 portion soufflé case or four individual soufflé cases when cooking the mixture. When cooked sprinkle with soft brown sugar (40 g approximately) and glaze under a hot salamander. Serve in the soufflé case/s.

ection six   Fresh egg-custard sauce (sauce anglaise)

ase method

tep 1	Mise en place Assemble ingredients. ↓
tep 2	Place the yolks, sugar and essence into a small bowl and whisk together. ↓
tep 3	Place the milk into a saucepan, bring almost to the boil then whisk onto the egg yolks and sugar. ↓
tep 4	Return the mixture to a clean saucepan and place over a low heat. Stir constantly with a spatula until the mixture thickens then remove from the heat. *Do not boil* as the mixture will curdle.

mportant points

tep 4

ooking the sauce: See important points on page 385.

ase recipe   (yield 4 portions)

ngredients: 2 egg yolks, 25 g caster sugar, 250 ml
                        milk and 2–3 drops vanilla essence.

now eggs (oeufs à la neige)

Double the quantities of the ingredients for the egg custard sauce.

Prepare a meringue with the separated egg whites (100 ml egg whites) and 200 g caster sugar (see page 402).

Place the milk and essence into a wide pan and heat until very hot.

Shape the meringue between two tablespoons like eggs then poach in the hot milk – turn the eggs carefully when half cooked.

Drain the meringue eggs carefully on a napkin and place aside.

Prepare the sauce anglaise using the poaching milk then pour into a porcelain, silver or glass serving dish. Allow to cool.

Float the meringue eggs on top of the sauce and serve.

Section seven   Bavarian cream (bavarois)

Base method

Step 1	Mise en place
	A Assemble ingredients.
	B Place the leaf gelatine in a bowl, cover with cold water and allow to soak until pliable.
Step 2	Prepare a sauce anglaise as stated above with the egg yolks, sugar, milk and essence.
Step 3	Squeeze out the surplus water from the gelatine, add to the hot sauce and stir through until completely dissolved. Pass the mixture through a fine strainer into a clean bowl.
Step 4	Allow to cool then place the bowl on ice and stir to almost setting point.
Step 5	Meanwhile, lightly whip the cream then fold through the mixture.
Step 6	Pour the mixture into a charlotte mould, place in the refrigerator and allow to set.
Step 7	When set, dip the mould in tepid water and demould the bavarois onto the serving dish. Decorate to taste, e.g. rosettes of whipped cream, glacé cherries and diamonds of angelica.

Important points

Step 4

Cooling the mixture: The mixture must not only be stirred until cold but up to a stage just short of setting point, i.e. becoming thick and heavy. After this the cream must be folded through immediately as the mixture will set very quickly.

Base recipe   (yield 4 portions)

Ingredients: 2 egg yolks, 50 g sugar, 250 ml milk, 2–3 drops vanilla essence, 10 g leaf gelatine and 150 ml cream.

Vanilla bavarois (bavarois à la vanille)
This is the basic bavarois stated above.

Chocolate bavarois (bavarois au chocolat)
Blend together 20 g of cocoa powder and a little of the recipe milk (cold) until smooth. Stir into the hot milk (step 2) until combined. Complete as stated.

Coffee bavarois (bavarois au café)
Prepare as stated adding coffee essence to taste instead of vanilla.

Orange bavarois (bavarois à l'orange)
Add the grated zest of two oranges into the milk instead of vanilla essence*. A little orange colour may be added. Use the orange fillets when decorating.

Lemon bavarois
Add the grated zest of two lemons into the milk instead of vanilla essence*.

* Many flavoured bavarois may be prepared omitting the fresh fruit zest or purée and simply adding a commercially prepared essence.

Raspberry bavarois (bavarois aux framboises)
Reduce the milk in the custard to 150 ml. Add 200 g sieved or liquidized raspberries into the custard when cold. Use whole raspberries when decorating.

Strawberry bavarois (bavarois aux fraises)
Prepare as above using strawberries instead of raspberries.

Peach bavarois (bavarois aux pêches)
Prepare as raspberry bavarois replacing the raspberry purée with peach purée. A little orange colour may be added. Use peach slices when decorating.

Pineapple bavarois (bavarois à l'ananas)
Prepare as raspberry bavarois replacing the raspberry purée with a purée of poached or tinned pineapples.
Note: Fresh pineapple must be avoided (or heat treated) as the enzyme (bromylin) in the pineapple will break down the gelatine, resulting in the bavarois not setting.

Ribboned bavarois (bavarois rubané)
This bavarois consists of three layers of different mixtures set in the mould one after the other, i.e. raspberry, vanilla and chocolate.

Dishes incorporating bavarois mixture

Various charlottes

Charlotte russe
Line the bottom and sides of a charlotte mould with sponge finger biscuits, see page 378. The biscuits, which are cut heart-shape for the bottom of the mould and plain-finger for the sides of the mould, should be keyed in neatly together; to hold the upright biscuits neatly in place a very small rim of butter may be smeared round the inside of the mould before placing in the biscuits. Fill the lined mould with vanilla bavarois preparation and allow to set as stated. Demould and neatly decorate with crème Chantilly, glacé cherries and diamonds of angelica.
Note: Various flavoured bavarois preparations may be used and indicated in the dish title, e.g. charlotte russe aux framboises.
Important: Lining the bottom of the mould with finger biscuits, which is the traditional practice, is quite a difficult and time-consuming operation, therefore some chefs place the biscuits neatly on top after unmoulding the cream or alternatively set raspberry jelly on the bottom of the mould in place of the biscuit base.

Charlotte moscovite
Prepare the same as above setting raspberry jelly on the base of the mould in place of the biscuits.

Charlotte andalouse
Prepare as charlotte russe above using an orange-flavoured bavarois mixture. When set and unmoulded coat the top biscuits with orange fondant. Decorate with orange segments, blanched julienne of orange and whipped cream.

Charlotte Montreuil
Prepare the same as charlotte russe above using a peach bavarois mixture garnished with small slices of ripe peaches. Decorate with whipped cream and peach slices.

Charlotte royale
Prepare as charlotte russe above but line the mould with thin slices of small swiss roll, see page 378 instead of finger biscuits.

Sweet mousses
These may be made the same as a bavarois reducing the milk content in the base recipe by 100 ml and correspondingly increasing the cream content by the same amount. Whisk the egg whites removed from the yolks and fold through the bavarois immediately after the cream has been added.

Rice and bavarois preparations
These dishes consist of equal quantities of cooked rice milk pudding (créole), see page 142, and bavarois mixture.
Production details: Prepare the rice pudding mixture stated on page 142, but *use only half the recipe quantities* and allow to cool thoroughly. Prepare the bavarois mixture as stated but *increase the gelatine content*, i.e. 15 g. When the bavarois mixture is almost setting, fold together the rice, setting custard and whipped cream. Set and demould the same way as for a bavarois.
Note: The above procedure which is the traditional method of preparing cold set rice dishes may be simplified as follows:
1 Prepare the rice milk pudding stated on page 142, but increase the sugar content to 75 g and omit the recipe butter.
2 Add 20 g soaked leaf gelatine and stir until melted through the rice.
3 Allow to cool, stirring occasionally, and when almost set fold through 150 ml whipped cream.
4 Set and demould the same as bavarois.

Dishes

Riz impératrice
Prepare 100 ml red jelly and allow to set in the bottom of a charlotte mould – the jelly should be 10 mm in thickness approximately. Traditionally jelly made from redcurrants is used, see page 99. Prepare the basic rice and bavarois mixtures as stated above (or the simplified mixture) adding 30 g diced glacé cherries and 20 g diced angelica into the mixture. Pour into the mould with the jelly and

allow to set. Demould and decorate with whipped cream, glacé cherries and diamonds of angelica.

Note: A little apricot purée (25 g) and a small measure of kirsch is also sometimes added to the mixture.

Riz palermitaine

Prepare the same as impératrice above but use a savarin mould. When demoulded fill the centre with strawberries and decorate with whipped cream.

Riz sicilienne

Prepare the same as impératrice above but use a savarin mould. When demoulded fill the centre with strawberry ice-cream and decorate with whipped cream, glacé cherries and angelica.

Riz maltaise

Prepare the same as impératrice but use orange jelly in place of red jelly in the charlotte mould. In addition add the zest of one orange and a half lemon to the rice mixture on completion of cooking. Use crystallized orange peel instead of glacé cherries and angelica and correct the colour with a little orange colouring. *Note*: A little orange liqueur may also be added. Decorate with orange segments and whipped cream.

Section eight Pastry cream/confectioner's custard (crème pâtissière)

This is a very thick rich custard sauce which is used as a filling cream for various pastries and sweet dishes such as flans, éclairs, mille-feuilles and crêpes etc. It is made with the same ingredients as fresh egg custard sauce but includes flour. Unlike fresh egg custard sauce it is stirred continuously up to boiling point where it becomes very thick.

Base method

Step 1	Mise en place
	Assemble ingredients.
	↓
Step 2	Place the sugar and egg yolk into a bowl and cream together. Add the essence.
	↓
Step 3	Mix in the flour.
	↓
Step 4	Boil the milk in a saucepan then whisk onto the sugar, egg yolk and flour – ensure the ingredients are well mixed.
	↓
Step 5	Return to a clean saucepan and bring the mixture to the boil, stirring continuously.
	↓
Step 6	Pour the mixture into a small basin and cover with buttered greaseproof paper. Allow to cool and use as required.

Base recipe

Ingredients: 20 ml egg yolk (1 yolk approximately), 40 g caster sugar, 20 g plain flour, 200 ml milk and 2 drops of vanilla essence.

Various creams derived from crème pâtissière

Crème frangipane/crème frite (used for fritters)
Prepare as stated but increase the flour content to 25 g and add 5 g butter to the milk when heating. This cream is used to coat the fruit of some fruit fritters prior to passing through batter and deep-frying. The fruit is coated with the hot cream then placed onto an oiled tray. The cream is then allowed to cool and become firm before applying batter and deep-frying, see page 299. *Note*:   The cream may also be shaped when cold then passed through beaten egg and coated with a mixture of crushed macaroon biscuits and breadcrumbs. When the cream is prepared and deep-fried in this manner it is called 'crème frite'.

Crème St-Honoré/crème Chiboust
Prepare the crème pâtissière as stated, adding a stiff meringue prepared with two egg whites and 25 g caster sugar, see page 402, into the boiling sauce. The meringue is carefully folded into the boiling sauce then the mixture is cooled and stored ready for use in the same manner as crème pâtissière.

Section nine   Various ices and ice-creams

Iced confections may be divided into the following categories:

(A) *Cream ices*

These may be grouped as follows:

French ice-cream: This is the traditional kitchen-type ice-cream which consists of a rich thick sauce anglaise with the addition of cream and flavouring.

French ice-cream   (traditional kitchen ice-creams)
4 egg yolks, 125 g caster sugar, 500 ml milk, 250 ml cream and flavouring, e.g. vanilla essence (5 ml), fruit zest or fruit purée (400 g).
Production details:
1   Prepare a fresh egg custard sauce with the egg yolks, sugar and milk (page 395) then cool quickly.
2   Mix in the cream and flavouring.
3   Freeze in an ice-cream machine.

Italian ice-cream: This type of ice-cream is based on a custard thickened mixture with cornflour or potato starch.

Italian ice-cream   (traditional shop ice-creams)
400 ml milk, 10 g cornflour, 75 g sugar, 25 ml egg (½ egg), 25 g butter, 100 ml cream and flavouring, see above.
Production details:
1   Prepare a cornflour sauce using the milk, cornflour and sugar (page 143).
2   Pour the hot custard over the egg and butter and whisk thoroughly. Cool quickly.
3   Mix in the cream and flavouring.
4   Freeze in an ice-cream machine.

American ice-cream   This ice-cream was specially developed for mass-market consumption. The mixture, which contains emulsifying and stabilizing agents, is specifically developed for prolonged storage in a deep-freeze cabinet.

Bombe ices   These ices are frozen in bombe moulds which produce a conical-shaped ice similar to a shell from a gun. The ices usually consist of various flavours of mixture set in layers, see below for examples.
Note: Traditionally ordinary ice-cream, i.e. turbine frozen mixtures, is used to coat or clothe the interior of the bombe mould – thus forming the outer layer of the sweet.

Bombe ices (pâte à bombe)
4 egg yolks, 125 g caster sugar, 100 ml water (or wine etc.), 200 ml cream and flavouring, e.g. essence, grated fruit zest, nuts, crystallized fruits or colouring.
Production details:
1   Whisk the egg yolks, sugar and water in a pan over hot water until thick (ribbon stage).

2   Remove from the heat and cool quickly occasionally whisking.
3   Whisk the cream until light and fluffy then fold through the egg mixture together with any flavouring or colouring.
4   Mould and freeze, see below.

Iced biscuits (biscuits glacés)
These ices are frozen in 'brick-shaped moulds' which produce small ice-cream blocks. These blocks or ice-cream biscuits consist of layers of various flavours and colours of ice-cream and are decorated then sliced into portions for service.

Recipe
Prepare the same as bombe ices above but increase the cream to 400 ml. In addition, use the four egg whites (100 ml approximately) separated from the yolks, and whisk until stiff then fold through the mixture after the cream and flavouring.

Parfaits
These are iced biscuit mixtures of a single flavour, e.g. coffee, rum or chocolate.
Important: The freezing of ice-cream mixtures as indicated above falls into two distinct operations:
1   *Mixtures frozen in an ice-cream machine*:   Examples are French, Italian and American ice-cream.
    These are placed into a machine which freezes the mixture in a refrigerated turbine or drum. Fitted inside the turbine is a special paddle which revolves during the freezing operation, scraping the mixture away from the sides of the turbine and in addition incorporating air into the ice-cream. The air introduced into the mixture by the rotating or whipping action of the paddle is an important aspect of ice-cream production and is termed '*overrun*'; the overrun of this type of ice-cream is usually around 80–100% depending on the type of machine used. Sorbets are around 40% overrun, see page 107.
    Good-quality ice-cream should have a bright smooth sheen called 'bloom' and should be stored at −18–20° C. When serving ice-cream the temperature should be −10° C approximately, and portioning with scoops etc. should be carefully carried out with the minimum of pressure applied to ensure that the ice-cream is not compressed and portion yield reduced. Portion sizes vary considerably from 30–100 portions from a four-litre container depending on house policy.
2   *Moulded mixtures*:   Examples are bombes, iced biscuits and parfaits.
    These mixtures are placed into moulds then frozen. These sweets are cut into neat portions using a knife

dipped in warm water. The portioning is often carried out by the waiter at the service table in the dining room. When serving decorated bombes such as large baked alaskas or omelette soufflé milady etc., which are covered with meringue, the ice may be cut into portions in the kitchen before coating with the meringue for ease of service in the dining room.

B) *Water or syrup ices*

These are flavoured syrups frozen in an ice-cream machine. The various water ices or syrup ices are explained on page 107.

Note: Many aspects of the legislation regarding the production of ice-cream does not apply to sorbets.

Important: The production of ice-cream for consumption by members of the general public within the United Kingdom is governed by legislation, therefore it is advisable to consult the nearest local authority on production and service to the public.

Dishes

Vanilla ice-cream (glace à la vanille), raspberry ice-cream (glace aux framboises), strawberry ice-cream (glace aux fraises), coffee ice-cream (glace au café), chocolate ice-cream (glace au chocolat), mint ice-cream (glace à la menthe).

Service: Scoop the ice-cream into balls or rochers and place in a bowl or coupe. Serve on an underliner and doily accompanied with wafer biscuits.

Bombes

Aboukir   Pistachio-flavoured outer coating with praline-flavoured centre.

Africaine   Chocolate outer coating with rum and apricot centre.

Aïda   Strawberry outer coating with kirsch-flavoured centre.

Ceylan   Coffee outer coating with rum-flavoured centre.

Danicheff   Coffee outer coating with kirsch-flavoured centre.

Florentine   Raspberry outer coating with praline-flavoured centre.

Francillon   Coffee flavoured outer coating with brandy-flavoured centre.

Havanaise   Same as Ceylan above.

Orientale   Ginger-flavoured outer coating with pistachio-flavoured centre.

Royale   Kirsch-flavoured outer coating with chocolate- and praline-flavoured centre.

Vénitienne   Half strawberry- and half vanilla-flavoured outer coating with kirsch- and maraschino-flavoured centre.

Iced biscuits (*biscuits glacés*)

Bénédictine   Three layers consisting of one layer of strawberry, one layer of bénédictine and a layer of violet mixture.

Mont-blanc   Three layers consiting of one layer of rum, one layer of chestnut and one layer vanilla mixture.

Napolitaine   Three layers consisting of one layer vanilla, one layer of strawberry and one layer of pistachio mixture.

Tortoni   Two layers consisting of one layer of vanilla and one layer of pistachio mixture.

Section ten   Meringue mixtures

Base method for plain meringue

Step 1	Mise en place A Assemble ingredients. B Thoroughly clean and scald the pan, whisk, bowl and any spoons etc. then dry with a clean (grease-free) cloth.
Step 2	Place the egg whites into a whisking bowl and add the pinch of salt/cream of tartar or squeeze of lemon juice. Also add a small quantity of the caster sugar, i.e 20 g approximately when using the base recipe – see important points.
Step 3	Whisk the whites adding two-thirds of the sugar in small quantities at intervals of several seconds (20 seconds approximately) until a firm meringue is produced.
Step 4	Add the remaining sugar and gently fold through the meringue.

Important points

Cold meringue

The above method is for plain meringue which may be prepared heavy or light depending on the quantity of sugar used. The usual ratio of sugar to egg whites is 200 g sugar to 100 ml egg whites but the sugar content may be increased to produce a heavier meringue, e.g. 275 g sugar to 100 ml egg whites.

Type of sugar: Use a clean, hard-grained caster sugar.

Preparation of equipment: The equipment must be *scrupulously clean and free from grease*. To ensure that no traces of grease are present, the equipment should be cleaned in hot detergent water then rinsed or scalded with very hot clean water. This aspect of meringue production cannot be over-stressed as the slightest traces of grease or fat shortens the albumen strands causing collapse or curdling of the mixture.

Preparation of egg whites: The condition of the egg whites is a crucial factor to the preparation of good meringue, therefore the following points should be carefully noted:

1   Use fresh egg whites and never old egg whites.
2   Carefully separate the yolks from the whites *avoiding any* trace of yolk being left in the whites.
3   The concentration of the albumen in the whites is an important factor to the risk of curdling – the more watery the whites the greater the risk of curdling.

    The condition of the whites may be improved by allowing them to rest in a clean, cool, dry and draughty place for a few hours after shelling to evaporate off some of the water from the whites. The term used by confectioners for whites treated in this way is *stale whites*. It is important to note that this usage of the term does not refer to old, bad or deteriorated egg whites.

4   The strength of the albumen may be increased or toughened with the addition of *small quantities* of acid or salt.
5   A small quantity of sugar (10% approximately) may be added to the whites prior to whisking. This makes the liquid whites more dense which assists aeration. In addition this also reduces the likelihood of over whisking.

Dried powdered albumen or albumen crystals: Good quality albumen in powder or crystal form may be used in place of egg whites. The usual ratio is 10 g powder or crystals to 100 ml water.

Powder: Mix the powder and water together then proceed as stated.

Crystals: Pour the water which should be barely tepid over the crystals and allow to stand for 12 hours approximately. Proceed as stated.

Cooking meringue: Meringue shapes which are to be cooked through until very crisp and dry should be baked in a cool oven with temperatures *never exceeding 130°C*. Allow any steam produced by the meringue to escape from the oven by leaving the oven door slightly open (or opening the vents) at short intervals during baking.

Storage: Meringue shapes which have been thoroughly

cooked and dried may be stored on paper trays in an airtight container kept in a warm dry cupboard. The inner surface of the meringue should be pushed in to allow any internal moisture to escape if the meringue is to be stored for prolonged periods. Most meringue shapes are usually stored on their sides to reduce the risk of damage.

Base recipe

200 g caster sugar, 100 ml egg whites (4 eggs approximately) and a pinch of salt/or pinch of cream of tartar/or squeeze lemon juice.

Heavy hot meringue method

Proceed as above but place the sugar on a tray on a sheet of paper and warm in the oven – do not caramelize. Also add all the sugar at the whisking stage in small quantities.

Important points

Same as cold meringue.

Recipe

Same as cold meringue increasing the sugar to 275 g.

Method for Italian meringue

Step 1	Mise en place A Assemble ingredients. B Thoroughly clean and scald the scale pan, whisk, bowl and sugar boiling pot etc.
Step 2	Prepare a sugar solution with the granulated sugar, water and glucose and boil to 118° C (see page 105).
Step 3	Meanwhile place the egg whites into the whisking bowl, add the pinch of cream of tartar/salt/or squeeze of lemon juice and whisk to a stiff snow. *Important*: This should be done so that the whites come to a stiff snow at the same time the sugar reaches 118° C.
Step 4	Whisk the whites slowly and add the sugar solution in a steady stream. When all the sugar solution has been added continue whisking at medium speed until the mixture is cool and quite firm.

Recipe

Ingredients:	200 g granulated sugar, 60 ml water, 20 ml liquid glucose, 100 ml egg whites and a pinch of cream of tartar/salt/or squeeze of lemon juice.

Piping technique

Important: Although the following notes explaining piping technique are stated with reference to meringue it must be stressed that the information is also applicable to piping Duchesse potatoes, choux paste and sponge biscuits etc.

1 Place the appropriate tube into the piping bag.
2 Hold the bag in the right hand and fold the open end over the hand.
3 Spoon the mixture into the bag with a spatula using the fingers of the right hand behind the bag to lightly scoop the mixture cleanly from the spoon into the bag.
4 Close the bag lifting up the folded down ends and squeeze the mixture downwards. Squeeze the mixture to release any trapped air.
5 Hold the top of the bag with the left hand and lock the bag directly above the mixture with the thumb and forefinger of the right hand – this will stop the mixture moving upwards when pressure is applied, see Figure 31.

Move the remaining fingers of the right hand down

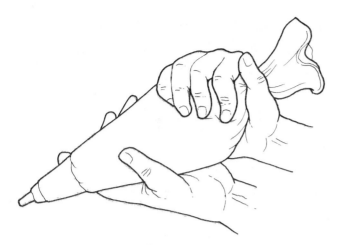

Figure 31 *Correct method of holding a piping bag*

and across the bag as far as possible to ensure an even pressure on a large area of the bag when piping.

6 Place the lower portion of the bag into the palm of the left hand. The two hands can now maintain an even steady pressure on all sides of the bag.

7 Various shapes may now be produced by pressing the bag and allowing the mixture to be piped at a controlled speed with the tube quite close to the baking tray. One common mistake often made by beginners is to lift the tube upwards and away from the tray during piping causing a badly shaped article to be produced. Correct pressure with controlled movement across and upwards when producing various shapes comes with constant practice.

   To avoid tube marks on the completed meringue shape move the back edge of the tube upwards as the pressure on the bag ceases.

Meringue shells
Pipe the meringue into oval or round shapes using a plain tube onto a tray lined with greaseproof paper. Dredge the piped meringues with caster sugar and bake as stated in the recipe notes.

Cream meringues
Prepare meringue shells as stated above and when cold sandwich together with crème Chantilly, see page 41. Decorate with glacé cherries, angelica, crystallized rose petals or violets.

Meringues with ice-cream (meringues glacées)
Place a ball of ice-cream between two meringue shells and serve in a coupe decorated with a rosette of whipped cream. Accompany with wafer biscuits.

Meringue glacée Chantilly
Prepare as meringue with ice-cream but decorate with a large rosette of crème Chantilly, see page 41.

Meringue mushrooms
Pipe out small flat bulbs of meringue on a sheet of greaseproof paper and lightly dust with cocoa powder. Also pipe blobs of meringue similar to mushroom stalks drawing upwards to a point. When the meringue shapes have been baked and cooled cut a small whole on the underside of the meringue tops, dip in melted chocolate and insert the meringue stalks and allow to set.

Individual vacherin shells
Pipe out the meringue into the shape of oval or round meringue cases and bake as stated in the recipe notes. When cold pipe a little fresh cream into each meringue, decorate with fruit and coat with a little fruit glaze.

Large vacherins and built meringue cases
Large meringue cases usually consist of several sections of dried meringue, placed one on top of the other to form a case of a given shape and size. One popular method of preparing these meringue cases is as follows:

1 Decide on the basic design, shape and dimensions of the meringue case and the number of sections to be prepared.

2 Trace the design of the various sections onto a sheet of greaseproof or silicone paper then place the paper onto a baking sheet – place the designed side of the paper downwards onto the tray to ensure that the meringue does not come in contact with the traced lines.

3 Prepare the meringue and pipe out neatly following the design on the paper. The meringue shapes required for the top and bottom sections are carefully filled in with lines of meringue, whereas the sides are left as open sections.

4 Dredge with caster sugar and bake until firm as stated in the recipe notes.

5 Allow the shapes to cool a little then carefully loosen them by running the tip of a small knife around the edges.

6 Place the base of the case on a clean tray and pipe on a line of meringue around the top surface of the outer edges. Neatly place one of the side sections on top and repeat the operation until all the side sections have been used – this should produce a height of between 60–80 mm approximately.
   Note: the sides of the case may also be neatly coated with meringue.

7 Place the case into a *very cool oven* (110°C) and allow to dry out.

8 Serve the meringue case filled with fruit and cream etc., and decorate to taste.

Buttercream (prepared with Italian meringue)
Cream 200 g fresh butter until very light then mix through the quantity of cold Italian meringue stated in the base recipe and method. Add colour and flavour as desired.

Marshmallow

Prepare the Italian meringue stated in the base recipe and method but increase the glucose content to 100 g. In addition whisk into the meringue when hot, 5 g leaf gelatine (soaked in cold water then squeezed out) melted with 10 ml water.

Marshmallow sweets

Pipe the marshmallow through a plain tube onto a tray coated with cornflour. The marshmallow, which is cut into small cylinders when piping, is dusted with cornflour and left to firm for 8–10 hours. When set and firm brush off the cornflour and roll in icing sugar.

Marshmallow snowballs

Pipe the marshmallow through a plain tube into round shapes onto a cornflour-dusted tray. Dust the shapes with cornflour and leave to firm for 4–6 hours approximately. When quite firm carefully brush off the cornflour, roll in melted chocolate then pass through desiccated coconut until completely coated.

High-quality buttercream prepared with marshmallow

This is prepared as follows:

1   Beat at medium speed in a mixing machine 300 g fresh butter until very light and creamy.
2   Add 300 g marshmallow and beat until combined, i.e. 2 minutes approximately, then scrape down and beat for a further 2 minutes.
3   Add 100 g of fondant (which should be softened by very slight warming) and beat into the above mixture until completely combined, i.e. 2 minutes approximately.
4   Add 50 g icing sugar and beat at medium speed for 2 minutes approximately.
5   Add 25 ml egg whites and beat until completely combined then scrape down and beat for a further three minutes at medium speed.

Note: Add any colour and flavour to taste prior to completing with the egg whites.

Nougat Montélimar

The preparation of this egg-white based confectionery is explained in detail on page 109.

Section eleven   Sweets incorporating ice-cream, meringue and sponge cake

Base method

Step 1	Mise en place
	A Assemble ingredients.
	B Commence preparation of the meringue, see pages 402–3.
Step 2	Cut a base for the sweet using the sponge and place onto the serving dish. *Note*: The thickness of the base is usually between 10–15 mm and may be round, oval or square in shape.
Step 3	Moisten the sponge base with the stock syrup, fruit juice or sherry etc.
Step 4	Garnish the sponge base with fruit if stated in the individual recipe.
Step 5	Place on the ice-cream. This is usually the moulded or bombe type of ice-cream which may be portioned into segments with a knife dipped into hot water.
	Note: The ice-cream may be neatly covered with thinly cut sheets of the sponge at this stage.
Step 6	Cover with a layer of meringue (traditionally Italian meringue is used) and smooth down with a palette knife. Pipe on a design of meringue using a piping bag and star tube with the remaining meringue.
Step 7	Decorate with the glacé cherries and pieces of angelica then sprinkle with the caster sugar, see individual recipe.
Step 8	Place in a very hot oven (230–245° C) and allow to develop a light brown colour then serve immediately.

Base recipe

Ice-cream:	1 small brick of ice-cream suitable for four portions – 300–400 g approximately.
Meringue:	Italian or plain meringue using 100 ml egg whites, see pages 402–3.
Sponge cake base:	1 small sheet of génoise sponge, see pages 376–7.
Liquor for moistening the sponge cake base:	25–40 ml stock syrup, fruit juice or sherry etc.
Decoration:	A Glacé cherries and shapes of angelica etc.
	B Caster sugar, i.e. plain or coloured.

Dishes

Baked Alaska (omelette soufflé en surprise)
Proceed as stated in the base recipe and method using vanilla ice-cream and decorate to taste.

Omelette norvégienne
This is prepared the same as baked Alaska above.
Note: The shape of the sweet is often oval when the term 'omelette' is used as a menu title.

Omelette en surprise Elisabeth
Proceed as baked Alaska but garnish and decorate with crystallized violets.

Omelette en surprise milady
Proceed as baked Alaska but use raspberry ice-cream and garnish the sponge with slices of ripe or poached peaches. A little maraschino is also sometimes used when moistening the sponge.

Omelette en surprise milord
Proceed as baked Alaska using vanilla ice-cream and garnishing the sponge with slices of ripe or poached pears.

Omelette en surprise Paquita
Proceed as baked Alaska using vanilla ice-cream and garnishing the sponge with fruit salad.

Section twelve   Egg-white based biscuits

Japonaise biscuits (biscuits japonaise)

This is a biscuit based on a meringue which contains ground almonds or hazelnuts.

1 Prepare a firm meringue with 200 ml egg whites, 160 g caster sugar and a pinch of cream of tartar.
2 Mix together 160 g caster sugar and 160 g ground almonds or hazelnuts (plain or roasted) and blend through the meringue.
3 Pipe the mixture onto trays which have been well-greased and lightly dusted with flour then bake at 180° C. Baking time: 25 mins. approximately.
4 Allow to cool slightly then trim or cut into shapes as required.

All-in mixtures

Many biscuits or fancies are simply prepared by mixing ground almonds, ground hazelnuts or coconut with unbeaten egg white, caster sugar and rice flour or flour.

Ratafia biscuits

Place the following ingredients into a mixing bowl: 100 g ground almonds, 30 g bitter almonds, 100 ml egg white, 250 g caster sugar and 20 g ground rice. Mix at slow speed with the cake beater for 3 minutes then scrape down and mix for a further 3 minutes at medium speed. Pipe out in small bulbs onto a baking sheet that has been greased and lightly floured then bake at 180° C until set and golden-brown. Store in an airtight container.
Note: To produce the small, fairly hard, type of ratafia biscuits reduce the egg white content to 80 ml.

Coconut macaroons

Place in a mixing bowl 60 ml egg white then stir in 200 g of warmed caster sugar. Mix together 40 g plain flour and 120 g desiccated coconut then add to the egg whites and sugar and blend thoroughly together. Place small neat spoonfuls of the mixture onto a greased and lightly floured baking sheet then bake at 180° C.

Parisian rout biscuits

Mix together in a mixing bowl the following ingredients: 150 g ground almonds, 150 g caster sugar and 70 ml egg whites. *Note:*   The desired consistency should be such that the mixture retains its shape when piped without being difficult to pass through the piping tube – to attain the exact consistency a little additional egg white is added when the mixture is too stiff.

Pipe out the mixture in small neat shapes using a star tube onto a greased and lightly floured baking sheet. Decorate to taste with small pieces of angelica, glacé cherries or nuts etc., then bake in a hot oven at 250° C. After baking brush over with stock syrup or gum-arabic solution.

Section thirteen   Royal icing

Base recipe

The basic recipe for royal icing is as follows: 100 ml egg whites★, 2–3 drops lemon juice or dilute acetic acid and 500–575 g icing sugar. A little edible blue colour may be added when preparing white icings but this should be omitted when any other colour is desired.

Production details:
1 Ensure that all equipment is scrupulously clean and free from grease.
2 Place the egg whites into a stainless steel† or china bowl and add the acid and any colouring.
3 Slowly add the icing sugar in small quantities, stirring constantly between each addition of sugar to aerate the icing sufficiently.§
4 Continue adding the icing sugar as stated until the following degrees of consistency have been achieved.
Coating consistency: Slowly draw the spoon out of the mixture to produce a long point – this point will slowly bend over when the consistency is just right for coating.
Piping consistency: Proceed to test the same as above but the mixture should be firmer with the long drawn point standing straight and erect.
Run out consistency: Royal icing for run out work should slowly run to a smooth surface when piped between the lines of a royal icing design.

Coating technique

1 Place the item/cake to be coated in the centre of the cake board etc., and place on a turntable.
2 Coat the sides of the item/cake using a palette knife. This is done by spreading the icing back and forwards with the palette knife held perpendicularly and using a slight paddling action. Continue this action and at the same time rotate the turntable until a good even coating of icing surrounds the sides of the cake.
3 To produce a fine finish on the sides of the item, hold the palette knife (or a plastic scraper) firmly and evenly against the sides of the item keeping the end of the knife a fraction above the cake board and turn the turntable one full revolution. When the revolution is almost complete begin to draw the knife or scraper away from the icing while still turning the turntable. This should produce good smooth sides with only a

---

★ Egg white substitutes are often used in place of egg whites.
† When preparing royal icing, equipment made from stainless steel, china or porcelain should be used to avoid discolouration.
§ When beating the mixture to achieve the correct degree of aeration it should be noted that care must be taken when using a machine as the mixture may be easily overbeaten producing a rough bubbly finish on the dried icing.

slight line showing where the knife/scraper finally left the icing. Carefully cut off the icing which protrudes over the top of the sides.

4   Add a quantity of icing to the top of the item/cake and smooth down with the same paddling action of the palette knife. This is done with the palette knife held horizontally and the end of the knife at the centre of the cake or item. The turntable is rotated while the paddling action helps to distribute a fairly smooth even layer of icing across the cake.

5   The final very smooth surface is now achieved by drawing a long straight edge across the top of the cake or item – a long clean metal ruler is often used.

6   When the sides and top have been completed, repeat once again the smoothing off of the sides (i.e. stage 3). If required, carefully and neatly trim the top edge.

7   Allow to dry in a warm, ventilated atmosphere.

8   The following day repeat the operation, attaining a fine smooth finish and allow time for the icing to dry out.

9   Decorate as required.

Piping royal icing

Fine neat piping is difficult to master and requires considerable practice to attain an acceptable end product. The following points are important when practising piping work:

1   Prepare a *small paper piping bag*, cut off the end and insert the piping tube. *Note*:   Confectioners do not usually use pumps or syringes with screw-on ends or tubes.

2   Fill the bag two-thirds full with icing then carefully fold down the end of the bag to produce a tight seal.

3   Pipe out the icing using a carefully controlled steady pressure.

4   Piped designs may be built up gradually but this should be done in stages. The operator should avoid going from a large tube to a small tube in one step as this often results in a poor appearance.

5   Allow time for the icing to harden when building up designs to avoid the design drooping or falling to one side.

6   Ensure that the design to be built is balanced with reference to *spacing*; plain spaces are every bit as important as piped areas.

Run out work

This is done by piping a lined design of royal icing on to silicone or wax paper and then allowing the design to set or harden. After this the spaces between the lines are filled in with icing of different colours, depending on the design required, then the whole model is allowed to completely dry out and harden. *Note*:   In most instances the operator places the original design under the paper and uses this as the guide to producing the model.

Storage of royal icing

Scrape down the mixing bowl and tightly cover with polythene to avoid contact with air; icing left in contact with air will form a hard skin, making it useless for piping and coating etc.

Preparing paper piping bags

1   Fold a sheet of greaseproof paper in half and cut neatly in two. Repeat this operation until small rectangles of paper suitable for preparing the bags have been produced; this may vary from 200–300 mm in length and 150–210 mm in breadth.

2   Halve each rectangle of paper lengthwise from corner to corner to form two triangles – each paper triangle will make one piping bag.

3   Hold the paper triangle at the point where the longest and shortest sides meet and roll round the opposite end to form a cone shape, see Figure 32.

4   Fold over the top edges to secure the bag firmly, see Figure 32.

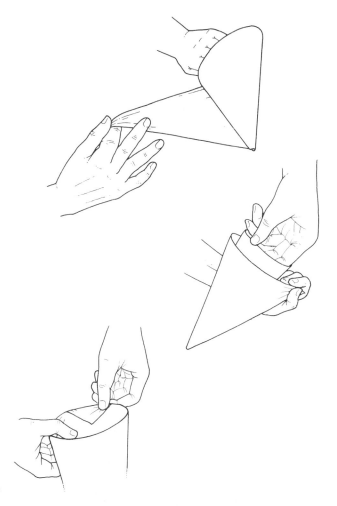

Figure 32   *Securing the bag firmly*

Section fourteen   Gum paste

Gum paste (pastillage)

This is used to produce decorative pastry models.

Soak 20 g leaf gelatine in 100 ml water until soft and pliable then heat the gelatine in the water until completely dissolved. Sieve together 475 g icing sugar and 25 g cornflour into a clean stainless steel or porcelain bowl then pour in the melted gelatine and water and mix to a smooth soft dough. Add icing sugar until a smooth pliable consistency suitable for moulding and rolling is obtained. Immediately cover the paste with a damp cloth or wrap in polythene to avoid skinning.

Note: Traditionally gum paste was made with gum tragacanth (now extremely expensive) which set very firm and hard, whereas pastillage was made with gelatine which sets less brittle than gum paste. Nowadays many confectioners use the terms interchangeably.

Procedure: The paste is rolled out on a fine smooth surface which is dusted with cornflour to avoid sticking, then cut into shapes as required – alternatively the rolled gum paste pieces may be pressed into cornflour dusted moulds or shells to attain a specific shape and effect. When shaped the pieces are allowed to dry for 24 hours approximately, on a smooth surface then turned over and left for a further period of 24 hours to dry out completely.

Note: To obtain a very smooth finish on the surface of the paste some confectioners rub the paste with fine smooth clean silk or the heel of the palm of the hand after rolling out.

The dried pastry pieces are stuck together with softened gum paste or thick royal icing to produce a wide range of decorative models or centre pieces.

Table 12   *Recipe ingredients*

	Custards (sweet and savoury)	Fresh egg custard sauce	Sabayons	Pastry cream	Mayonnaise	Meringue	Egg-white based biscuits	Royal icing
Main item (egg content)	Whole eggs	Egg yolks	Egg yolks	Egg yolks	Egg yolks	Egg whites	Egg whites	Egg whites
Liquid content	Milk/stock	Milk	Water, wine stock etc.	Milk	Vinegar, oil	—	—	—
Sweetening agent or	Caster sugar	Caster sugar	Caster sugar	Caster sugar	—	Caster sugar	Caster sugar	Icing sugar
Seasoning	Salt and pepper	—	Salt and pepper	—	Salt, pepper, mustard	—	—	—
Flavouring	Vanilla (basic)	Vanilla	Various	Vanilla	—	—	—	—
Additional ingredients	—	—	Butter, cream	Flour	Lemon	Acid	Ground nuts flour rice flour	Acid
Derivatives	Crème caramel, flans, quiches, cabinet pudding royale etc.	Various bavarois, charlottes, French ice-cream etc.	Sauce hollandaise, sauce Arenberg, bombe ices etc.	Crème, Crème frite etc.	Various sauces	Meringue sweets, vacherins, buttercream, marsh-mallow, etc.	Various petits fours, Various sweet dishes etc.	Various cakes etc.

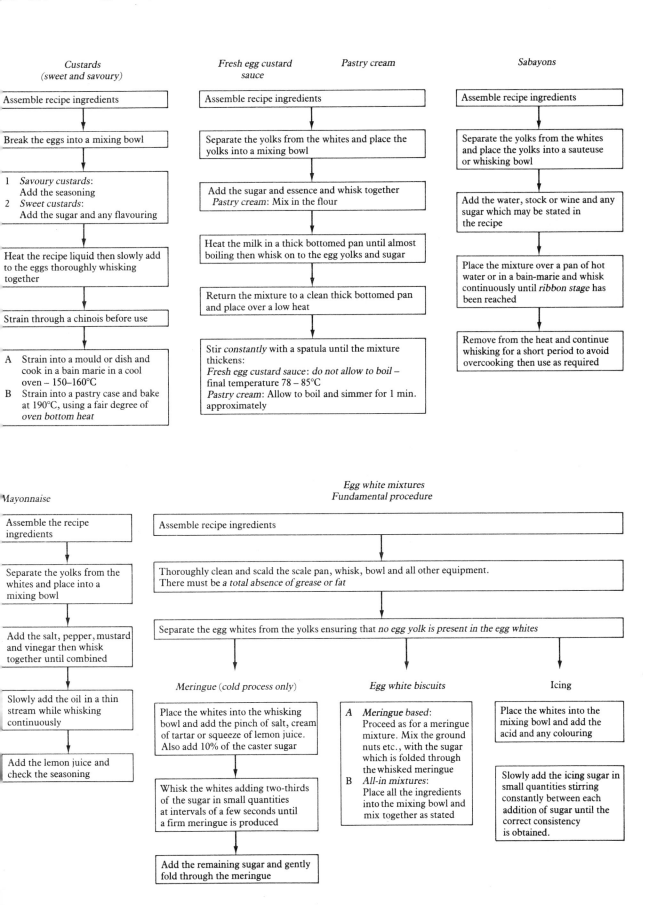

Custards
(sweet and savoury)

Assemble recipe ingredients

↓

Break the eggs into a mixing bowl

↓

1 *Savoury custards:*
   Add the seasoning
2 *Sweet custards:*
   Add the sugar and any flavouring

↓

Heat the recipe liquid then slowly add
to the eggs thoroughly whisking
together

↓

Strain through a chinois before use

↓

A Strain into a mould or dish and
   cook in a bain marie in a cool
   oven – 150–160°C
B Strain into a pastry case and bake
   at 190°C, using a fair degree of
   oven bottom heat

Fresh egg custard sauce   Pastry cream

Assemble recipe ingredients

↓

Separate the yolks from the whites and place the
yolks into a mixing bowl

↓

Add the sugar and essence and whisk together
   Pastry cream: Mix in the flour

↓

Heat the milk in a thick bottomed pan until almost
boiling then whisk on to the egg yolks and sugar

↓

Return the mixture to a clean thick bottomed pan
and place over a low heat

↓

Stir *constantly* with a spatula until the mixture
thickens:
Fresh egg custard sauce: do not allow to boil –
final temperature 78 – 85°C
Pastry cream: Allow to boil and simmer for 1 min.
approximately

Sabayons

Assemble recipe ingredients

↓

Separate the yolks from the whites
and place the yolks into a sauteuse
or whisking bowl

↓

Add the water, stock or wine and any
sugar which may be stated in
the recipe

↓

Place the mixture over a pan of hot
water or in a bain-marie and whisk
continuously until *ribbon stage* has
been reached

↓

Remove from the heat and continue
whisking for a short period to avoid
overcooking then use as required

Mayonnaise

Assemble the recipe
ingredients

↓

Separate the yolks from the
whites and place into a
mixing bowl

↓

Add the salt, pepper, mustard
and vinegar then whisk
together until combined

↓

Slowly add the oil in a thin
stream while whisking
continuously

↓

Add the lemon juice and
check the seasoning

Egg white mixtures
Fundamental procedure

Assemble recipe ingredients

↓

Thoroughly clean and scald the scale pan, whisk, bowl and all other equipment.
There must be *a total absence of grease or fat*

↓

Separate the egg whites from the yolks ensuring that *no egg yolk is present in the egg whites*

↓   ↓   ↓

Meringue (cold process only)   **Egg white biscuits**   **Icing**

Place the whites into the whisking
bowl and add the pinch of salt, cream
of tartar or squeeze of lemon juice.
Also add 10% of the caster sugar

↓

Whisk the whites adding two-thirds
of the sugar in small quantities
at intervals of a few seconds until
a firm meringue is produced

↓

Add the remaining sugar and gently
fold through the meringue

A *Meringue* based:
   Proceed as for a meringue
   mixture. Mix the ground
   nuts etc., with the sugar
   which is folded through
   the whisked meringue
B *All-in mixtures:*
   Place all the ingredients
   into the mixing bowl and
   mix together as stated

Place the whites into the
mixing bowl and add the
acid and any colouring

↓

Slowly add the icing sugar in
small quantities stirring
constantly between each
addition of sugar until the
correct consistency
is obtained.

Figure 33 *Essential activities for egg, egg yolks and egg white products*

Assessment exercise

1 Identify the important points to be taken into account when preparing mayonnaise.
2 Name six derivatives of mayonnaise.
3 Explain how to prepare baked egg custard.
4 What is quiche lorraine?
5 What is the temperature range which will curdle fresh egg custard sauce?
6 Describe how fresh egg custard sauce is extended to become Bavarian Cream (bavarois).
7 State four uses for pastry cream.
8 What is a liaison?
9 Identify the factors which are important to the production of meringue.
10 Describe how to make meringue using albumen crystals.
11 What is the difference between cold meringue, heavy hot meringue and Italian meringue?
12 What is a sabayon?
13 Name six derivatives of hollandaise sauce.
14 Describe the difference between omelette soufflé and omelette soufflé en surprise.
15 Explain how to make a paper piping bag.
16 What is royal icing?

Chapter 16

Microwave cooking

Microwaves are high-frequency electromagnetic waves which are similar to radio and television waves but operate at a much higher frequency and are much shorter – 2450 MHz and 122 mm length. Unlike other forms of heat transfer, microwaves can penetrate a considerable distance into the food – up to 35 mm.

Heat production by microwaves

This is based on the principle that food contains electrically charged particles. In terms of microwave cooking the most important of these charged particles are water molecules. When these are subjected to microwave radiation they try to line up with the electric field of the microwaves which is alternating at 2450 MHz. This means the molecules move backwards and forwards at the same rate, i.e. 2450 million times/second. However, the molecules are also subjected to restraining forces (viscous forces in liquid, fat and ice etc.) and as a consequence some of the microwave energy is converted to heat.

Features of a microwave oven

Microwave radiation within a cooker is produced by an energy generator called a 'magnetron'. When produced they are directed into the oven by wave guides and scattered by a stirrer/agitator and the reflective walls of the oven compartment; this allows the food to be penetrated by microwaves from various angles.

Microwave energy can be:

a) Absorbed – water-containing materials; food.
b) Transmitted – china, glass, plastic and paper; cooking containers.
c) Reflected – metal; the walls of the oven.

Microwave cooking is very fast and therefore demands careful control of the heating and cooking time to avoid overcooking. One important disadvantage is that *browning does not usually occur* unless some other form of heat transfer is also used, e.g. infra-red radiation or convection, see micro-aire oven (special browning dishes may also be used).

Factors which affect cooking and heating time

Density of food

The denser the food the longer it will take to cook, e.g. a hamburger which has a fairly open texture will cook more quickly than a steak.

Water content of food

The moisture content of the food and the way it is distributed within the food affect the speed and uniformity of heating.

Depth of food

Heat is generated within the food as stated up to a depth of 35 mm approximately. However the energy level diminishes the further the penetration – the molecules at the surface of the food are subjected to greater radiation than those deeper down. After 35 mm cooking may be *continued by thermal conduction*.

Volume of food

The larger the quantity of food the longer the cooking time, e.g. 1 beefburger may take 25 seconds; 4 beefburgers may take 75 seconds.

Shape of food

The more uniform the shape, the more likely it is to achieve consistent cooking. For example, when cooking a leg of lamb the thin knuckle will be cooked before the thick middle section.

Starting temperature of food

The lower the temperature of the food when commencing heating the longer the cooking.

Power output of oven

The higher the microwave power output the faster the heating, e.g. reheating an omelette may take 25 seconds in a 700 W oven but only 12 seconds in a 1.1 kW oven.

Cooking containers

Suitable containers may be made with glass, china, porcelain, polypropylene, high-density polythene or paper etc. Metal containers are unsuitable and should *not* be used as they reflect the waves, causing uneven heating, and may damage the magnetron.

Covering food

A cover is recommended when heating or cooking foods with the exception of flour products. The cover may be any of the materials listed above for cooking containers but is often heat-resistant film wrap.

Scope of operation

The microwave cooker adds a new dimension to kitchen equipment but like all types of equipment it may be excellent for some applications but not others (unfortunately there are manufacturers who make exaggerated claims of suitability to all types of cooking). The uses of a microwave cooker may be categorized as follows.

Regeneration

This is reheating pre-prepared dishes, snacks and sauces etc. Microwave cookers are very efficient for this purpose and reports indicate that this is the most popular application in commercial catering.

Defrosting

This is another very important function provided by the cookers. Items may be taken straight from the deep-freeze cabinet and rapidly defrosted using a defrost/pulsed power cycle; food should not be heated straight from the frozen state to service temperature.

Prime cooking

The microwave cooker is efficient at cooking many products where *development of colour is not essential*. For example, fish may be cooked in a comparable manner to *poaching* and *steaming*, e.g. it can be buttered then cooked or covered with a sauce when raw then cooked. Foods may be deep-poached or boiled in water, stock or sauce etc., but the time taken to cook the food will be similar to conventional cooking. This is also the case with casseroles and hotpots.

When browning is required, the food can often be browned first then cooking completed in the oven, e.g. chops, steaks and chicken etc. This results in products which are relatively comparable to *shallow-fried, grilled o* *oven roasted* items.

Foods which are cooked tender in a conventional oven like baked potatoes and apples, are also suitable (the quality of baked potatoes may vary with the type of potato used – age and variety etc.).

In general terms, the oven is less suitable for the baking of flour products. Cakes, scones and puff pastry items which rely on mechanical lift are less suitable for this typ of cooking; the cooking often tends to be too rapid to achieve full aeration and lift especially in high powered ovens – this is more successful in low powered with less rapid heating. Short pastry items cannot develop the crispness which is produced in a conventional oven.

General information on microwave cookery

1 Use small containers for heating food to reduce the heat being lost from the food to the container.
2 Compensate for the physical structure of the food in relation to heating time, e.g. spread out steak and kidney pie but do not add the crust until the last 15 seconds of cooking (or reheat separately), heap peas and dome-shape mashed potatoes etc.
3 When uncertain of an exact heating or cooking time use a shorter time, check the food then switch on again if necessary.
4 Sauces and soups should be stirred before being served as they usually reach a higher temperature at the edges of the bowl when reheating (or the power switched off and the mixture stirred then the power switched back on again).
5 Foods which should be served with a crisp finish are less suitable for microwave heating. Reheating deep fried items and crisp pastry items by microwaves is likely to soften the texture.
6 Devised heating and cooking times for the house menu should be posted and available so that staff apply the correct defrosting, heating and cooking times.
7 Keep the oven clean – the effectiveness of the oven reduced by spilt liquid or food particles left in the oven.
8 Keep the door rim and seal clean – *this is important a radiation leakage may occur* if this is not done.
9 It is advisable to leave a small bowl of water in the cooker when not in use to ensure that the cooker *cannot be switched on empty* – this may damage the magnetron.
10 Always follow the manufacturer's instructions on general usage and safety.

A microwave cooker is simple to operate but the time settings must be accurate to avoid over cooking.

Defrosting, reheating and cooking times are not given in this chapter because they vary considerably with different ovens – especially with energy outputs of ovens. Always follow the manufacturer's guidebook, tested recipe procedures or a catering establishment's own instructions concerning microwave products.

Operating procedure

1 Switch on the oven and allow for pre-heating time if required.
2 Open the door and place in the food to be defrosted, heated or cooked.
3 Close the door then set the cooker to defrost or cook as appropriate.
4 Set the timer to the required time period then press the start button.
5 When the cycle is completed, open the door and inspect the food for the correct degree of defrosting, heating or cooking.

Micro-aire ovens/cookers

This type of oven combines forced air convection and microwave cooking. Both methods of heat application can be used individually but it is simultaneous use which is the most important feature. The microwave output usually varies between 500 W–2.2 kW and the range of temperature with the forced air convection facility is from 100–300° C approximately. This produces a very versatile oven which can roast, bake, braise and poach etc. with the advantages of both systems. Another important feature is that metal cooking containers can be used, although metal lids should not be used with simultaneous or microwave application.

Assessment exercise

1 What are microwaves?
2 How is heat produced in a microwave oven?
3 What are the factors which affect heating and cooking times in a microwave oven?
4 How versatile is a microwave oven?
5 What products are less suitable for (a) heating and (b) cooking in a microwave oven?
6 List six points which are important when using a microwave oven.
7 Describe the important features of a micro-aire oven/cooker.

References

1 McCance, R. A. and Shipp, H. L., 'The chemistry of flesh foods and their losses on cooking', *Special Report Series*, no. 187, Medical Research Council 1933.

2 Cover, S., Dilsaver, E. M. and Hays, R. M., 'Retention of the B vitamins in beef and lamb after stewing. IV Niacin', *Journal of the American Dietetic Association*, no. 23 (1947), p. 769. Cover, S., Dilsaver, E. M. and Hays, R. M. 'Retention of the B vitamins in beef and lamb after stewing. VI Similarities and differences among the four vitamins', *Journal of the American Dietetic Association*, no. 23 (1947), p. 962.

3 Alexander, L. M. and Clark, N. G., 'Shrinkage and cooking time of rib roasts of beef of different grades as influenced by style of cutting and method of roasting', *Technical Bulletin*, no. 676, USDA 1939.

4 Cline, J. A., Trowbridge, E. A., Foster, M. T. and Fry, H. E., 'How certain methods of cooking affect the quality and palatability of beef', *Bulletin*, no. 293, Missouri Agricultural Experimentation Station 1930.

5 Ministry of Agriculture, Fisheries and Food, *Torry Advisory Note*, no. 6, rev. ed. (1970).

6 Hughes, O. and Bennion, M., *Introductory Foods*, 5th ed. Collier-Macmillan 1970, p. 78.

7 Hughes, O. and Bennion, M., *Introductory Foods*, 5th ed. Collier-Macmillan 1970, p. 80.

8 Hester, E. E., Briant, A. M. and Personius, C. J., 'The effect of sucrose on the properties of some starches and flours', *Cereal Chemistry*, no. 33, (1956), p. 91.

9 See Cline *et al.*

10 Vail, G. E. and O'Neill, L. 'Certain factors which affect the palatability and cost of roast beef served in institutions', *Journal of the American Dietetic Association*, no. 13 (1937), p. 34.

11 Harries, J. M., Jones, K. B., Houston, T. W. and Robertson, J., 'Studies in beef quality. I Development of a system for assessing palatability', *Journal of the Science of Food and Agriculture*, no. 14 (1963), p. 501.

12 Hughes, O. and Bennion, M., *Introductory Foods*, 5th ed. Collier-Macmillan 1970, pp. 148 and 149.

13 Campbell, A. M., Penfield, M. P. and Griswold, R. M., *The Experimental Study of Food*, 2nd ed., Houghton Misslin 1979, p. 129.

14 Hood, M. P., 'Effect of cooking method and grade of beef roasts', *Journal of the American Dietetic Association*, no. 37 (1960), p. 363.

15 Shaffer, T. A., Harrison, D. L. and Anderson, L. L., 'Effects of end point and oven temperatures of beef roasts cooked in oven film bags and open pans', *Journal of Food Science*, no. 38 (1973), p. 1205.

Index

Note: The index has been designed in four columns. Column one is a general reference column, which is further defined by appropriate individual references in column two. Two sets are included for most dish references, the first set of page numbers indicates the method element of a dish or group of dishes and the second set indicates the individual recipe and list of ingredients. Italics are used for all references which do not have recipes.

General	Examples	Method	Recipe
Chicken dishes, grilled	American, Casanova, devilled, katoff, plain, spatchcock, tandoori chicken	313	314
Chicken dishes, paper bag style	suprême de volaille en papillotte	230	230
Chicken dishes, pies, cooking of	chicken pie	331	331
Chicken dishes, pies, preparation of		77	
Chicken dishes, poached	English style, Métropole, Vichy, with braised rice and suprême sauce	114	115
Chicken dishes, poêler	poulet poêlé	248	250
Chicken dishes, reheated	creamed chicken, chicken à la king	196	196
Chicken dishes, roast	roast chicken with bread sauce	244	246
	roast stuffed chicken, with bacon	244	247
Chicken dishes, sauter	à la crème, aux champignons, bagatelle, cacciatori, chasseur, hongroise, romaine, Sarah-Claire	264	267
Chicken dishes, shallow fried	Kiev, Maryland	261	263
Chicken dishes, spiced stews	murgh kari	161	162
Chicory	preparation of	37	
Chocolate éclairs	various éclairs	344	345
Chocolate roll		378	378
Chocolates	liqueur and soft centre	108	108
Chops Champvallon style		220	220
Choux paste swans		344	345
Choux paste		344	345
Christmas pudding		341	343
Clam chowder		151	152
Clootie dumpling		341	343
Coconut snowballs (cake)		359	362
Cod, *see* fish			
Cold buffet	*see* menu classification	*25*	*26*
Commercially prepared sausages	service of	*49*	*49*
Commodity preparation	list of commodity preparation	*19*	*21*
Commodity preparation index		*19*	*19*
Compote of fruit		137	138
Corn on the cob with butter		130	131
Cornish pasties		338	338
Cottage pie		196	196
Coupés	Alexandra, andalouse, Edna-May, Jacques, Jamaïque, Vénus	139	139
Courgette dishes, boiled	boiled courgettes	130	131
Cougette dishes, deep fried	deep fried courgettes	295	295
Courgette dishes, sauté types	buttered courgettes, à la crème	270	271
	provençale	270	271
Courgettes	preparation for cooking	38	
Court-bouillon	plain/blanc, with vinegar, with wine	116	117
Crab	dressed	46	46
	preparation of	73	74
Cranberry purée		104	104
Crayfish	trussing of	73	73
Cream	brandy, Chantilly, curry, herb, liqueur, mustard, paprika, whisky	41	41
Cream buns		344	345
Cream horns		327	327

General	Examples	Method	Recipe
Sauce – *contd*	diable	176	177
	Dugléré	170	170
	egg	167	169
	espagnole	174	175
	Foyot	389	389
	gooseberry (jam type)	103	103
	gooseberry	104	104
	gribiche	41	41
	hollandaise	389	389
	hongroise	170	171
	horseradish	41	
	italienne	176	177
	ivoire	170	171
	jam	144	145
	jus lié	160	160
	lemon	144	145
	lobster	178	179
	lyonnaise, Madère (Madeira)	176	177
	maltaise	389	389
	Marie-Rose, mayonnaise	387	387
	melba (raspberry)	103	103
	mint	43	43
	Mornay	167	169
	mousseline	389	389
	mousseline (sweet)	388	388
	mustard	167	169
	noisette	389	389
	onion	167	169
	orange	144	145
	Oxford	103	103
	paloise	389	389
	parsley	167	169
	piquante	176	177
	poulette	170	171
	prawn	178	179
	ravigote	41	41
	Reform	176	177
	remoulade	387	387
	Robert	176	177
	sabayon	388	388
	scampi	178	179
	sherry	143	144
	smitaine	170	171
	Soubise	167	169
	strawberry (cold)	103	103
	suprême	170	171
	syrup	144	145
	tartare	387	387
	tomato	178	179
	tyrolienne, verte	387	387
	vin blanc	170	170
	Vincent	387	387
	whisky	143	144